THE PERSECUTION OF HUGUENOTS
AND
FRENCH ECONOMIC DEVELOPMENT
1680-1720

Publications of the
Bureau of Business and Economic Research
University of California

THE PERSECUTION OF HUGUENOTS AND FRENCH ECONOMIC DEVELOPMENT
1680-1720

BY

Warren C. Scoville

UNIVERSITY OF CALIFORNIA PRESS

BERKELEY AND LOS ANGELES

1960

UNIVERSITY OF CALIFORNIA PRESS
BERKELEY AND LOS ANGELES

✧

CAMBRIDGE UNIVERSITY PRESS
LONDON, ENGLAND

LIBRARY OF CONGRESS CATALOG CARD NO. 60–7083

PRINTED IN THE UNITED STATES OF AMERICA

TO
ARTHUR H. COLE

Preface

When I was a graduate student at the University of Chicago in 1934–1936, I seriously considered the revocation of the Edict of Nantes as the subject of my doctoral dissertation. As an undergraduate majoring in religion at Duke University, I had been struck by the fact that religious persecution seemed always to strengthen the spiritual fiber of those who were persecuted and to fall short of achieving the ends envisioned by the persecutors. Furthermore, I have never subscribed to the philosophy that holds that economic forces alone determine the course of human development. Spiritual and religious factors, I believe, have exercised an independent influence on the history of mankind, and in some instances they seem to have been more powerful than purely economic forces.

I have also long been intrigued by those hypotheses or presumably accurate interpretations of historical facts which suggest that the expulsion of religious minorities (like the Moors and the Moriscos from Spain, the Jews from Spain and Portugal, the Protestants from the Spanish Netherlands, or the Huguenots from France) has frequently had baneful repercussions upon economic activity and has slowed the rate of economic growth. In the first place, I suspect that many individuals, consciously or unconsciously, have assumed that an edict outlawing a particular religion or ordering a dissident group to leave the country accomplished its purpose. Passing a law and then enforcing that law are two different things. Even the Eighteenth Amendment to the Constitution of the United States did not stop the manufacture, sale, and transportation of intoxicating beverages in our interstate and foreign commerce. Yet law enforcement techniques and agencies in the United States of the twentieth century are superior to those which functioned in most countries in the fifteenth to nineteenth centuries. In the second place, the figures that have been offered for the number of refugees from a given country often seem too large and too conveniently well rounded to inspire my confidence in their accuracy. I have always believed that, if *one added up the number of Jews and Moors who were said to reside in various cities throughout Europe after having been driven from Catholic Spain, the total would be larger than the number who could conceivably have lived in that country. I have discovered that many people have quoted quite unrealistic figures for the number of Huguenots who fled France. The figures are often larger than the total number of Protestants ever living in France at any one time.*

My interest in the Huguenots also stemmed from another source. Persecution of an easily identifiable minority by the dominant majority has always seemed to me one of the most senseless and despicable forms of human cruelty. If historians and sociologists could demonstrate that such persecution usually has recoiled as a boomerang upon the persecutors, it might help improve human and social relationships. I have found myself in a peculiar quandary. On the one hand, I wanted to examine the economic consequences of the revocation of the Edict of Nantes in the hope that I could demonstrate even more conclusively than previous writers had done that the revocation and the persecution which preceded and accompanied it had been a major economic blunder for France. On the other hand, I was suspicious of the figures and the findings of those who had already studied the problem.

Professor John Ulric Nef, who was kind enough to take a personal interest in me while I was a student at Chicago, agreed wholeheartedly that a reëvaluation of the evidence concerning Louis XIV's action in outlawing Protestantism might prove enlightening. He strongly advised me, however, not to undertake such an ambitious program for my doctoral dissertation. Although I did not fully understand at that time why the topic was too ambitious for a neophyte in economic history, I bowed to his more mature judgment and decided, instead, to examine the factors that affected the spread of large-scale capitalistic production in French glassmaking before 1789. It was fortunate that I did. I had not realized that ten long years of continuous work would be required to complete the kind of study I had visualized. Nor had I known that I would have to rely so heavily upon intuition and inferences drawn from scanty contemporary accounts of the Huguenots.

A fellowship awarded by the John Simon Guggenheim Memorial Foundation, a sabbatical leave from the University of California, Los Angeles, for one semester, and a supplemental grant from the University's Bureau of Business and Economic Research for the second semester enabled me to spend fourteen months in Paris in 1948–1949 and work with the manuscripts in the Bibliothèque Nationale, the Archives Nationales, and the Archives du Ministère des Affaires Étrangères. I am indebted to staff members of these institutions for the help they rendered in locating much of the material. M. Paul de Félice, librarian of the Bibliothèque de la Société de l'Histoire du Protestantisme Français, deserves special mention. Not only did he offer encouragement by showing interest in my work, but he also allowed me to work in the library during the mornings even though the doors were not opened to the public before noon. He realized that I was under considerable time pressure; and, unlike many officials, he sought to accommodate me even though this meant suspending rules.

The Bureau of Business and Economic Research at the University of California, Los Angeles, has been most generous since 1949 in granting me funds for research assistance and for the preparation and the final typing of the manuscript. Its director, Professor Ralph Cassady, Jr., has been remarkably patient, as the time required to complete the study lengthened year by year; and the example of his own devotion to painstaking research bolstered my determination and spirit when they occasionally faltered. Professors Robert E. Baldwin, Paul T. Homan, Roland D. Hussey, Frank E. Norton, Dudley F. Pegrum, and Donald E. Stout, all of whom are colleagues at the University of California, have read all or at least significant portions of the manuscript, and have made many valuable suggestions for improving it. Misses Frances Frame, Martha Patterson, and Winifred Chinn likewise deserve my gratitude for their help as typists. In 1949–1950, Robert F. Filliou, a brilliant and resourceful graduate student from southern France who was then studying economics at UCLA, rendered me admirable service as a research assistant. Gysbert de Viet and Joseph J. Podoski helped me with difficult Dutch and German sources. Mrs. Grace H. Stimson, in editing the manuscript, has been far more coöperative and helpful with her suggestions than any author has the right to expect.

I have already paid tribute to Professor Earl J. Hamilton in the prefaces to my two earlier books, but what I owe him can never be repaid. It is like a large outstanding debt which one can never aspire to acquit but on which one tries to meet the interest pay-

ments and to acknowledge the principal at regular intervals. Professor Hamilton has always been much more to me than teacher, counselor, and helpful critic; he has been my godfather, my confidant, and the person after whom I have patterned my life as a teacher and a researcher in economic history. Not only has he critically read and appreciably improved several chapters in this study, but he has also provided me with many important references and information he has unearthed during his own research in England, Holland, and France.

I am also indebted to the editor of the Journal of Political Economy *and to the University of Chicago Press for permission to reproduce in revised form my long article on "The Huguenots and the Diffusion of Technology" (Vol. LX, August and October, 1952), and to the editor of the* Quarterly Journal of Economics *and to the Harvard University Press for permission to revise and reproduce "The Huguenots in the French Economy, 1650–1750" (Vol. LXVII, August, 1953).*

This volume could never have been completed had not my wife encouraged me to do so at every turn during the past ten years. She has suggested innumerable ways whereby I have improved my style; her interest and faith in my work have flared up whenever mine smoldered; and her continuous encouragement and her patience when progress was slowest have helped to keep alive my own interest.

Finally, I want to caution the reader that I alone am responsible for most of the French translations found in this study. I have tried to be accurate, yet I have been more interested in presenting readable passages which preserve the content and the spirit of the original than in giving a literal translation. In each instance I have informed the reader where he can find the original.

W. C. S.

Contents

I

Introduction

The Reformation, sweeping across western Europe in the sixteenth century, infected France. Lefèvre d'Étaples (1450?–1537) translated the Bible into French, and John Calvin soon emerged as the spiritual leader of the French Reformation. Calvin had been born in 1509 of a bourgeois family at Noyon in Île-de-France and had received his doctorate from the University of Orléans in June, 1533. Several years later he settled in Geneva, where he helped create a Protestant republic. This he headed until his death in 1564, except for the period from 1538 to 1541, when he was in exile at Strasbourg. While in Geneva he kept in constant contact with France, where nearly all Protestants, then as well as now, adopted his teachings. There were, it is true, significant groups of Lutherans and Anabaptists in Alsace and adjacent French territory, but it was the Calvinists who became known as Huguenots.[1]

---

[1] The exact origin of the term "Huguenot" is controversial. Some scholars seek its derivation from the German term "Eidgenosz," meaning "confederate," and believe that it was applied to French Protestants because they wished to follow the Swiss example and set up several city-states which would be joined in a confederacy (*Bulletin de la société de l'histoire du protestantisme français* [hereinafter cited as *BSHPF*], XXV [1876], 380; Helmut Erbe, *Die Hugenotten in Deutschland* [Essen, 1937], p. 14; F. Godet, *Histoire de la Réformation et du Réfuge dans le pays de Neuchâtel* [Neuchâtel, 1859], p. 234, n. 1; Abbé Rameau, "Les Huguenots dans le Mâconnais aux XVIe et XVIIe siècles," *Revue de la société littéraire, historique et archéologique du département de l'Ain*, VIII [1879], 270). Charles Benoist, *Condition juridique des protestants sous le régime de l'Édit de Nantes et après sa révocation* (Paris, 1900), pp. 6–7, suggests that the term was applied to them because they supported the Bourbons, who were descendants of Hugues Capet (10th century), and opposed the pretensions of the Guises who composed the Lorraine line. Charles de Grandmaison (*BSHPF*, LI [1902], 13) has found the terms "Huguenot" and "Huguenote" in writings dating from the fourteenth to the sixteenth centuries, but he has offered no suggestion as to why Frenchmen later applied the terms to Protestants.

Although the French monarchy vigorously opposed the Reformation, the movement rapidly gained strength. After the death of Henry II in 1559, a succession of unpopular and rival regents controlled the government; and disgruntled members of the nobility, thinking that Protestantism might prove a valuable ally in their fight against centralization in government, supported the Reformation. In 1562 friends of the Duke of Guise murdered some sixty Protestants at Wassy. This massacre initiated the first of eight religious wars, which strengthened Protestantism as fire strengthens steel. The massacres at Nîmes (1567) and on Saint Bartholomew's Day (1572), instead of emasculating the movement, only made Huguenots more steadfast in their faith and greatly enlarged their ranks. Henry IV, forced by political expediency to recant his own Protestant upbringing four years after becoming king in 1589, brought the religious wars to a close by signing his famous Edict of Nantes in 1598.

The edict itself consisted of two documents.[2] Henry signed the first, consisting of ninety-five general articles, on April 13; he signed the second, with fifty-six "secret" or "particular" provisions, on May 2. The Parliament at Paris refused to register these documents until February 25, 1599, and did so only upon the king's explicit command. In addition to the edict Henry signed two brevets on April 13 and 30,[3] pertaining to the rights and the responsibilities of Protestant pastors and allowing Huguenots to fortify certain cities in the realm. The king proclaimed the edict to be "irrevocable and perpetual"[4] and declared null and void all previous laws, edicts, truces, and judicial decisions that conflicted with it. The two documents constituting the edict, together with the two brevets, served as the Magna Charta of French Protestantism until Louis XIV issued the Edict of Revocation in October, 1685.

The Edict of Nantes guaranteed Protestants freedom of con-

---

[2] They have been reproduced in many places. I have utilized the copy found in *Recueil des Édits, Declarations et Arrests concernans la Religion Prétendue Réformée, 1662–1751, Précédés de l'Édit de Nantes*, ed. Léon Pilatte (Paris, 1885), pp. i–lxxxi.

[3] A brevet carried only the guarantee of the king's word of honor; it was not officially registered by any government agency.

[4] Some writers have contended that the term "irrevocable and perpetual" simply meant that the edict, in modern terminology, was analogous to a constitutional amendment rather than to a statutory law.

science and the right to conduct religious services wherever they had publicly done so in 1577 or in 1596–1597.[5] They could hold public office, they were eligible for public assistance, and they could attend any college or university. They could not work or sell goods on Catholic holidays, however, if they made enough noise to be heard by their neighbors or by anyone passing in the streets. Both Catholics and Protestants had to return to its original owner any property they may have seized during the religious wars; all persons convicted or imprisoned because of religion were pardoned forthwith; and those who had fled abroad, as well as their children born in foreign countries, could return to France and be repatriated before 1608. Protestants still had to pay the Catholic tithe, but the king agreed to appropriate 135,000 livres each year to support their church.[6] Henry also promised to establish special tribunals as courts of last appeal for all disputes that might arise between Catholic and Protestant. Finally, he urged his subjects to forget the past, to cease wrangling, to drop lawsuits growing out of previous religious differences, and to live together peaceably as blood brothers should.

Whether considered as a great piece of original statesmanship or as simply a mélange of earlier truces between religious factions,[7] the Edict of Nantes was the first religious truce that was seriously enforced by any French king. It inaugurated almost a century of internal peace. The most notable breach occurred in 1621–1629, after Louis XIII directly annexed Béarn. This little Protestant province had been ruled by Jeanne d'Albret, Queen of Navarre, and by her son, who later became Henry IV of France. Louis XIII, upon annexation, subjected Béarn to the Edict of Nantes and required its Protestants to surrender all the

---

[5] Henry, however, explicitly forbade public worship in Paris, in cities where a Catholic bishop or archbishop was stationed, wherever the royal court happened to be in residence, and on any property belonging to the king.

[6] As one scholar astutely observed, this particular provision was unfortunate. It meant that the Reformed Church was in the embarrassing position of having to ask the king for financial assistance, whereas the Catholic Church was able to provide him with funds through its "gratuitous gifts." (Claude-Carlomau de Rulhière, *Eclaircissements historiques sur les causes de la révocation de l'Édit de Nantes, et sur l'état des protestants en France, depuis le commencement du Règne de Louis XIV, jusqu'à nos jours* [new ed.; Geneva, 1788], I, 46–47.) To Louis XIV, who was constantly in need of money, this difference must have seemed very important (see also Jacques de Missècle, *L'Édit de Nantes et sa révocation* [2d ed.; Colmar, 1931], p. 23).

[7] See, e.g., Paul Beuzart, "L'Édit de Nantes: Création ou aboutissement," *BSHPF*, XCI (1942).

property they had confiscated from Catholics some seventy years earlier. Protestant nobles seized the opportunity to offer their last great resistance to royal authority and concentrated their forces in the cities that Henry IV had allowed Protestants to fortify. Cardinal Richelieu besieged and finally captured their stronghold at La Rochelle by cutting off foreign aid and supplies with a dam built across the harbor's entrance. The Treaty of Alais (1629) revoked the right of Huguenots to maintain fortified places, thereby removing all vestiges of a Protestant "state-within-a-state." After this French Protestantism shed its political character, and Huguenots began to support royal absolutism as the best way to maintain public order and as a symbol of social unity.[8]

In 1629, from Nîmes, Louis XIII reaffirmed the Edict of Nantes as "irrevocable and perpetual." So did the Regent Anne of Austria in 1643. Louis XIV, when he signed a similar document in May, 1652, acknowledged that "our subjects of the Reputedly Reformed Religion have given us incontrovertible proof of their affection and fidelity—notably during the recent disturbances [9]—which has pleased us very much." Therefore he would uphold all rights and privileges granted by the Edict of Nantes, regardless of previous orders or decisions issued by his courts or councils. Any persons who violated these rights or privileges were to be treated as disturbers of the common weal and punished accordingly.[10] Social, political, and economic discrimination against the Huguenots, nevertheless, mounted rapidly after Louis began to govern directly in 1661.

Colbert tried to shield Protestants from this underhanded persecution in order to keep them from emigrating. Although he was successful for a short time after 1669, persecution soon gathered new momentum. Police agents closed or demolished Protestant temples upon the flimsiest pretexts; various cities obtained permission to expel Huguenots on the basis of obscure laws that had once banned them from the locality; one gild after another denied them membership; Catholic priests began to harass their children and to torment their sick and dying; and

---

8 Missècle, *op, cit.*, p. 12.

9 Louis was here referring to the *Fronde*, when Catholic nobles tried to challenge his power.

10 Jean Bianquis, *La Révocation de l'édit de Nantes à Rouen, essai historique* (Rouen, 1885), pp. vii–viii.

the king himself signed orders excluding them from one public office after another.

Violence finally erupted in the province of Poitou, where the intendant Marillac began in 1681 to quarter royal dragoons in the homes of prominent Huguenots. Realizing that the king had become increasingly impatient with religious nonconformists, Marillac thought he saw a sure way to curry favor at court. He therefore instructed the soldiers to convert their hosts to Catholicism by any means short of death. Terror spread rapidly among the hapless Protestants, and many fled to other provinces or to foreign countries. The reverberations from all this grew so loud that Louis felt compelled to get rid of Marillac. Persecution, however, did not cease; it only became less open and less violent. Some months later the Catholic clergy and government officials inaugurated an extensive campaign to stamp out heresy. They convinced the king with long lists of supposed conversions that only a few thousand unregenerated Huguenots remained in his realm. On October 17, 1685, Louis signed the famous edict outlawing Protestantism in all provinces except Alsace.[11]

The terms of this edict will be analyzed in detail later; for the present it will suffice to indicate a few of its most salient provisions. On the one hand, the king ordered all Protestant temples and schools to close down immediately, all public worship to cease, and all pastors who refused to accept Catholicism to leave the realm; on the other hand, he forbade anyone to persecute Huguenots or to interfere with their private lives and economic activities so long as they did not attend religious gatherings or conduct public worship. This seemed to guarantee them liberty of conscience; yet neither Louis nor any other Frenchman respected the guarantee for one moment. All sorts of recrimination and violence flared up and became the sanctioned order of the day. For every 10,000 Huguenots who fled abroad, there were 100,000 who joined the Catholic Church. Most of the latter, known as "new converts," remained Protestant at heart, and they and their descendants were a source of trouble for both Church and state in the eighteenth century.

---

11 The revocation edict did not apply to Alsace, which was strongly Lutheran, because the Treaty of Westphalia (1648), which ceded the province to France, had guaranteed it religious freedom and because the king of Sweden had exacted from Louis in 1685 a promise to respect the terms of that treaty (Charles Weiss, *Histoire des réfugiés protestants de France depuis la révocation de l'Édit de Nantes jusqu'à nos jours* [Paris, 1853], II, 311).

The outbreak of the War of the League of Augsburg (1688–1697) diverted the government's attention from internal matters and led to a relaxation of religious persecution. Emigration consequently diminished. Then, in 1698, 1715, 1724, and 1746, the king promulgated new edicts which revealed that the government was still intent on suppressing Protestantism. Each of these four edicts was followed by a short period of unrest and renewed violence. Persecution then abated during the second half of the eighteenth century, and something like an informal truce developed between Catholics and Protestants. When speaking of nonconformists, contemporaries dropped the euphemistic term "new converts" and reverted to "Huguenots" or "Religionists." Protestants did not regain full civil and religious liberties, however, until the Revolutionary and Napoleonic era.

Throughout the entire period from 1562 to 1789, there were several distinct waves of Huguenot emigration. The first occurred when religious war broke out in 1562; another took place in 1568–1569 during the second war and after the massacre at Nîmes; a third followed the Massacre of Saint Bartholomew in 1572–1573; and a fourth accompanied the eighth religious war and the persecutions by the Holy League under the leadership of the Guises. While Richelieu and Louis XIII were besieging Protestant strongholds in the south of France in 1621–1626, emigration gained momentum. Many Huguenots escaped France in 1661–1666, after Louis XIV began to rule directly; and royal dragoons or "booted missionaries" in Poitou drove several hundred abroad in 1681–1682. By far the largest emigration occurred in the years immediately after the revocation of the Edict of Nantes. It subsided during the War of the League of Augsburg, flared up after the edict of 1698, and diminished once again during the War of the Spanish Succession (1701–1713). The edicts of 1715, 1724, and 1746, threatening renewed and harsh reprisals, led additional Huguenots to seek asylum in foreign countries.[12]

---

12 Archives Nationales, TT 435, *dossier* 10; 464, doc. 56; "Journal d'un marin protestant du XVIIᵉ siècle (Taré Chaillaud)," *BSHPF*, XV (1866), 320–322; *BSHPF*, XXIX (1880), 190–191; Charles Bost, *Récits d'histoire protestante régionale: Normandie* (Le Havre, 1926), p. 149; Géraud Dumons, *Les Réfugiés du pays Castrais* (Albi, 1924), p. i; L.-J. Nazelle, *Le Protestantisme en Saintonge sous le régime de la Révocation, 1685–1789* (Paris, 1907), pp. 22, 33–34, 190 ff.; Rulhière, *op. cit.*, II, 342–343.

THE NUMBER OF HUGUENOTS

It is difficult to say how many Frenchmen professed Protestantism during the first half of Louis XIV's long reign. Demographic figures and estimates for France during the seventeenth and eighteenth centuries are far from reliable. According to Émile Levasseur,[13] one of the ablest scholars in the field, the number of French subjects probably stood at 20,070,000 in 1700; and this figure may have reflected some decline from an earlier peak.[14] Most available evidence, though varying over a wide range, suggests that Protestants never accounted for more than 10 per cent of the total population. A census of all Protestants ordered by Henry IV in 1598 indicated that there were 274,000 Protestant families, 694 regular temples, and 257 places of worship on fiefs.[15] These figures have led one scholar to conclude that probably 1,250,000 Protestants lived in France at that time.[16] Their number increased thereafter and reached its peak sometime during the two decades preceding the revocation. A conservative estimate for 1680–1685 would most likely fall between 1.5 and 2 million.[17] In the 1750's, when many Frenchmen began

---

13 *La Population française,* I (Paris, 1889), 194–247, 284–288, especially. For a comparison of Levasseur's estimates with those of other writers, see Joseph J. Spengler, *France Faces Depopulation* (Durham, N.C.: Duke University Press, 1938), pp. 13–20.

14 Henry Martin estimated that the population fell from 22 or 23 million in the palmiest days of Colbert's ministry to about 19 million in 1700 (*Histoire de France depuis les temps les plus reculés jusqu'en 1789* [4th ed.; Paris, 1855–1860], XIV, 330–333).

15 *BSHPF,* I (1853), 123.

16 N. Weiss, in *BSHPF,* XXXVIII (1889), 551; L (1901), 305.

17 Rulhière, one of the first persons to study the revocation objectively, admitted that no one knew and probably would ever know the exact number of Protestants in France, and that many people had set the figure at 2 million, whereas some Catholic partisans and apologists had denied that there had ever been more than 600,000 (*op. cit.,* I, 125–126). The intendant Bâville in Languedoc, for example, stoutly maintained that in 1685 there had been only 650,000 Huguenots (Abbé J.-B. Rouquette, *Études sur la Révocation de l'Édit de Nantes en Languedoc* [Paris, 1908], III, 15–16, 20). Elie Benoît, in the Preface to his *Histoire de l'Edit de Nantes, contenant les choses les plus remarquables qui se sont passées en France avant et aprés sa publication . . . jusques à l'Edit de Révocation en Octobre, 1685* (Delft, 1693–1695), spoke of 2 million; Pierre Jurieu in 1682 gave the same figure (*Les Derniers efforts de l'innocence affligée* [4th ed.; 1682], pp. 25, 32, as quoted in *BSHPF,* LXIII–LXIV [1914–1915], 182); and a census conducted in 1679 by de la Mare, a commissioner of the Châtelet in Paris, revealed that there were 1.7 million Protestants (N. Weiss, "Le Nombre des prétendus Réformés six ans avant la Révocation, lettre de N. de la Mare," *BSHPF,* XXXVII [1888], 28–31). If Benoît and Jurieu might be suspected of exaggerating the number of fellow Protestants, so

to debate whether the government should reëstablish the Edict of Nantes or at least allow Religionists legally to marry outside the Catholic Church so as to legitimize children born of such unions, many persons estimated that from 1 to 3 million Frenchmen had never sincerely accepted Catholicism.[18]

Where did most of these Protestants live? If they concentrated in provinces and cities where trade and industry were important, this would be presumptive evidence that they were especially active in economic affairs. Also, to determine whether the revocation was a significant factor in the depression that beset France after 1683, it would be helpful to know whether the areas where Protestants lived suffered more than other sections of the country.

A southeastern crescent, extending from Dauphiné through Languedoc, Guyenne, Saintonge, Aunis, and Poitou, but excluding Provence,[19] contained a heavier density of Protestants than

---

might de la Mare be suspected of understating it. John Locke in 1676 thought that one-sixteenth of France's population was Protestant (*Life and Letters of John Locke* [2 vols.; London], as quoted in *BSHPF*, LVIII [1909], 421); and Abbé Novi de Caveirac, obviously intent upon justifying the revocation, estimated the number at only 1 million in *Apologie de Louis XIV et de son conseil, sur la révocation de l'Edit de Nantes, etc.* (n.p., 1758), pp. 72 ff., and accepted the usual estimate of 2 million in *Mémoire politico-critique, où l'on examine s'il est de l'intérêt de l'Eglise et de l'Etat d'établir pour les Calvinistes du Royaume une nouvelle forme de se marier* (n.p., 1756), p. 10. The Venetian ambassador at Paris reported in 1688 that France had 1.6 million Protestants in her total population of 15 million (Henry Austen Layard, "The Revocation of the Edict of Nantes. Illustrated from State Papers in the Archives of Venice," *Proceedings of the Huguenot Society of London* [hereinafter cited as *PHSL*], II [1887–1888], 149).

Among those writing in the nineteenth and twentieth centuries, David C. A. Agnew (*Protestant Exiles from France in the Reign of Louis XIV* [2d ed.; London, 1871–1874], I, 7), Léonce Anquez (*De l'État civil des réformés de France* [Paris, 1868], p. 65), Courtisigny (*BSHPF*, XXXVII, 537), Erbe (*op. cit.*, p. 15), Reginald Lane Poole (*A History of the Huguenots of the Dispersion at the Recall of the Edict of Nantes* [London, 1880], p. 25, n. 1), and Numa Recolin (*La Révocation de l'Édit de Nantes et ses conséquences* [Paris, 1885], p. 4) all accept from 1.5 to 2 million as the most likely number.

[18] Bibliothèque Nationale, *Fonds français*, MSS 7047, fols. 475–476, 555–556; 10628, fol. 31; Erman and Reclam, *Mémoires pour servir à l'histoire de réfugiés françois dans les états du Roi* (Berlin, 1782–1799), I, 177; Ripert Montclar and Abbé Quesnel, *Mémoire théoligique et politique au sujet des mariages clandestins des protestans de France* (2d ed.; n.p., 1756), p. 7; Chevalier de Beaumont, *L'Accord parfait de la nature, de la Raison, de la Révélation et de la politique* (Cologne, 1753), II, 134 ff. The number most likely was between 1 and 1.5 million. Caveirac grossly underestimated it at 400,000 (*Mémoire politico-critique*, pp. 5–19).

[19] Provence perhaps included only 6,000 or 7,000 Protestants (Eugène Arnaud, *Histoire des protestants de Provence, du comtat Venaissin et de la Principauté d'Orange* [Paris, 1884], I, 481–482; *BSHPF*, VII [1858], 23–26; J. Marchand, *Un Intendant sous Louis XIV: Étude sur l'administration de Le Bret en Provence (1687–1704)* [Paris, 1889], p. 289).

any other area of comparable size. The clergy and the government always considered Dauphiné a major center of heresy.
Several guesses made by the intendant there at about the time
of the revocation, though reflecting the inexactness of his information, nonetheless suggest that the province might have had
from 40,000 to 70,000 Huguenots in its estimated population of
543,585 in 1699.[20] The intendant complained that this minority
was so unevenly distributed throughout the province that conversion or assimilation was almost impossible. He said, for example, that there were no Catholics at all in the valley of Prajelas
near the Italian border, and that Protestants almost or actually
outnumbered Catholics in the valley of Queyras and in certain
rural areas close to Grenoble, Vienne, Romans, Valence, and
Gap.[21] The little Principality of Orange, lying between Dauphiné and Languedoc, was also a Protestant stronghold. As to
the remaining provinces in the crescent, the intendant Bâville and
other government officials in Languedoc expressed the opinion
that Languedoc included from 200,000 to 250,000 Huguenots in
its population of some 1,500,000.[22] Louvois wrote on July 31,
1685, that he believed the *généralité* of Montauban had as many
as 150,000, but other sources suggest that the actual number
there may have been only a third or a fifth that large.[23] Guyenne,
Saintonge, and the *généralité* of Bordeaux altogether probably
had between 150,000 and 200,000;[24] about a fifth of the inhabit-

20 Archives Nationales, G7 240; Bibliothèque Nationale, *Fonds français*, MSS
4288, fol. 122; 10621, fols. 15 ff.; 11419, pp. 97–98; Eugène Arnaud, *Histoire des
protestants du Dauphiné aux XVIe, XVIIe et XVIIIe siècles* (Paris, 1876), III, 17–18
and nn.; A. M. de Boislisle, *Correspondance des contrôleurs généraux des finances
avec les intendants des provinces*, I (Paris, 1874), 87; *BSHPF*, I, 239; XLVII (1898),
82.

21 Archives Nationales, G7 240; TT 243, *dossier 4*, doc. 37.

22 *Ibid.*, A1 795, doc. 62; 903, docs. 312, 328; 905, doc. 132; TT 247, doc. 186; 430,
doc. 126; Bibliothèque Nationale, *Fonds français*, MSS 4290, fols. 52, 127; 7044, fol.
166; 7045, fol. 97; 10621, fols. 15 ff.; *BSHPF*, XLVII, 85, and LI, 205; Émile Lesens,
*Le Protestantisme dans le pays de Caux (ancien colloque de Caux, Havre et Dieppe
excepté)*, ed. Victor Madelaine (Bolbec, [1906]), p. 169; Rulhière, *op. cit.*, I, 327;
C. Weiss, "Mémoire sur les protestants de France au XVIIe siècle," *Séances et travaux de l'Académie des sciences morales et politiques*, XX (1851), 114–117.

23 Archives Nationales, TT 255, *dossier 41*, docs. 125, 227; Boislisle, *op. cit.*, I,
309; Ch. Garrisson, "La Population protestante de la généralité de Montauban en
1685," *BSHPF*, XLVI (1897), 169–186; Rulhière, *op. cit.*, I, 299; R. L., "Statistique,"
BSHPF, LVII (1908), 82 (based on a list of new converts found in the Archives
Départementales de l'Hérault, C 279).

24 Bibliothèque Nationale, *Fonds français*, MSS 7044, fol. 134; 10621, fols. 15 ff.;
Boislisle, *op. cit.*, I, 309; *BSHPF*, XLVII, 82; Lesens, *op. cit.*, pp. 168–169; Rulhière,
op. cit., I, 299.

ants of the region around La Rochelle and Rochefort (Aunis and the islands of Ré and Oléron) were Protestant;[25] and Huguenots constituted about 10 per cent of Poitou's population shortly before 1681.[26]

Béarn, Normandy, Burgundy, and Alsace, among the provinces outside the crescent, also had substantial numbers of Protestants. Between a fifth and a half of Béarn's estimated population of 150,000 had been Protestant at one time or another before 1685.[27] Upper and Lower Normandy most likely could have counted between 60,000 and 100,000, although some estimates vary from 180,000 to 200,000.[28] Burgundy proper did not have very many. Its intendant wrote in July, 1682, that Catholics outnumbered Protestants by 200 to 1, and a report dated August 27, 1685, said that there were only 570 Protestant families, or about 2,561 individuals, in the province.[29] However, the little area of Gex, attached to Burgundy and lying due north of Geneva, had more than 6,000 Huguenots, or four times the number of Catholics. The intendant estimated the total population of Alsace at 235,000 in 1699, of which 66,500 were Lutheran, 8,700 Calvinist, 3,300 Jewish, and the rest Catholic.[30]

In order to assess the importance of Huguenots in the French economy, and to evaluate the consequences of the revocation of the Edict of Nantes, it may also prove helpful to know whether

---

25 Bibliothèque Nationale, *Fonds français*, MSS 4287, fol. 16; *Nouvelles acquisitions françaises*, MS 507, fol. 2; Archives Nationales, TT 263B, *dossier* 6, doc. 129; *BSHPF*, XLVII, 82.

26 Archives Nationales, G7 449; Boislisle, *op. cit.*, I, 2; François Baudry, *La Révocation de l'édit de Nantes et le protestantisme en Bas-Poitou au XVIIIe siècle* (Trévoux, 1922), pp. 11, 12, n. 1; Jean de la Monneraye, "La Révocation de l'Édit de Nantes et le protestantisme en Bas-Poitou au dix-huitième siècle," *Revue de Bas-Poitou*, 36th year (1923), 81–82; *BSHPF*, LXII (1913), 91.

27 Archives Nationales, TT 234, *dossier* 5, doc. 12; Bibliothèque Nationale, *Fonds français*, MS 8248, fols. 4–6; *BSHPF*, XLVII, 82; C. Weiss, "Mémoire sur les protestants," *op. cit.*, XX, 114–117.

28 Archives Nationales, TT 237, *dossier* 2, docs. 80, 108; Bibliothèque de la Société Protestante, MS 485[11], fols. 44 ff.; *BSHPF*, XLV (1896), 78 ff.; Philippe Le Gendre, *Histoire de la persécution faite à l'église de Rouen sur la fin du dernier siècle*, ed. Émile Lesens (Rouen, 1874), editor's preface, pp. xix–xx; J.-A. Galland, *Essai sur l'histoire du Protestantisme à Caen et en Basse-Normandie de l'édit de Nantes à la Révolution (1598–1791)* (Paris, 1898), pp. 65, 156–157; C. Weiss, "Mémoire sur les protestants," *op. cit.*, XX, 119, 120; Frank Puaux, "Ephémérides de l'année de la révocation de l'édit de Nantes," *BSHPF*, XXXIV (1885), 30; Émile-G. Léonard, *Problèmes et expériences du protestantisme français* (Paris, 1940), pp. 16–17.

29 Archives Nationales, TT 236, *dossier* II, docs. 4, 34.

30 Bibliothèque Nationale, *Fonds français*, MS 4285, fol. 7.

Protestants congregated in cities that served as nerve centers for commerce and industry. Two-thirds of Nîmes's population [31] and four-fifths of Strasbourg's [32] were Protestant. Both Montauban and La Rochelle were Protestant strongholds; Paris had only about 10,500 Huguenots among her half million inhabitants;[33] and Caen, Dieppe, and Rouen in Normandy still had important contingents in 1685, although losing a great many Protestants after 1650.[34] Half the families living in Pau (with 3,000 population)[35] and around Sedan (7,355 inhabitants)[36] were Protestant, as were a fourth of Aubusson's 4,000 inhabitants[37] and a fifth of the 20,000 people residing at Metz.[38] Of some 30,000 or 40,000 people living at Bordeaux, only about 2,000 were Huguenots.[39] Tours could count between 700 and 1,200,[40] Amiens

---

[31] Archives Nationales, TT 247, doc. 186; A¹ 795, doc. 62; Boislisle, *op. cit.*, I, 168–169; *BSHPF*, XXIX, 188–192.

[32] Rodolphe Reuss, *Louis XIV et l'église protestante de Strasbourg au moment de la révocation de l'édit de Nantes (1685–1686)* (Paris, 1887), p. 277, and *Notes pour servir à l'histoire de l'Église française de Strasbourg (1538–1794)* (Strasbourg, 1880), p. 67, n. 4.

[33] Bibliothèque Nationale, *Fonds français*, MSS 4282, fol. 335; 7051, fols. 364–365; Emmanuel-Orentin Douen, *La Révocation de l'Édit de Nantes à Paris d'après des documents inédits* (Paris, 1894), I, 158, 161; II, 478; G. Pagès, "Les Réfugiés à Berlin d'après la correspondance du comte de Rébenac (1681–1688)," *BSHPF*, LI (1902), 125.

[34] Caen's Protestant population seems to have declined from about 7,000 in 1608 to 4,000 in 1650 and to 2,749 in 1685; Dieppe's, from about 14,000 in 1650 to 4,167 in 1686; and Rouen's, from about 7,000 in 1646 to 4,000–5,000 in 1685 (Archives Nationales, TT 237, *dossier* 2, doc. 108; Bianquis, *op. cit.*, pp. vii, xlii–xliii; G. Dubois, "Les Protestants en Haute-Normandie à la fin du XVIIᵉ siècle. Statistiques et conditions sociales," *BSHPF*, LXXXIII [1934], 263–265; Galland, *op. cit.*, pp. 156–157; Léonard, *op. cit.*, pp. 16–17; Émile-G. Léonard, "Une Église protestante de notables (Caen) devant la persécution et la révolution" [unpublished manuscript]; Lesens, *op. cit.*, p. 175; C. Weiss, "Mémoire sur les protestants," *op. cit.*, XX, 120).

[35] *BSHPF*, XLVII, 323.

[36] J. Jailliot, "Le Protestantisme dans le Rethelois et dans l'Argonne jusqu'à la révocation de l'Édit de Nantes," *Revue d'Ardenne et d'Argonne*, XIII (1905–1906), 175.

[37] Cyprien Pérathon, "Le Protestantisme à Aubusson," *Mémoires de la société des sciences naturelles et archéologiques de la Creuse*, XIX (1915), 354.

[38] *BSHPF*, XLI (1892), 168; C. Weiss, "Mémoire sur les protestants," *op. cit.*, XX, 122; Orthon Cuvier, *Les Réformés de la Lorraine et du pays messin* (Nancy, 1884), p. 30.

[39] Bibliothèque Nationale, *Fonds français*, MS 4287, fol. 38; Paul Bert, *Histoire de la révocation de l'édit de Nantes à Bordeaux et dans le Bordelais (1653–1715)* (Bordeaux, 1908), p. 3.

[40] Archives Nationales, TT 272, *dossier* 22, docs. 128, 153; Abbé L. Bosseboeuf, "Histoire de la fabrique de soieries de Tours, des origines au XIXᵉ siècle," *Bulletin et mémoires de la société archéologique de Touraine*, XLI (1900), 277 ff.

about 2,000,[41] and Alençon about 3,000.[42] No more than 1,000
lived at Lyon, which had a total population of about 70,000.[43]
Rennes, Nantes, and Vitré—all in Brittany—each had approximately 100.[44]

OPINIONS ABOUT THE REVOCATION

It might be argued that a small minority of no more than 10
per cent of a country's population could not have exercised much
influence on that country's economic development, and hence
that persecution by the dominant majority could not have depressed industry and trade appreciably. Some individuals who
witnessed the persecution in the late seventeenth and the eighteenth centuries thought otherwise; others defended Louis XIV's
action and discounted the effects of the revocation. Although
opinions of contemporaries about historical events should never
be confused with the events themselves, such opinions may help
modern observers to understand the events, for ideas—whether
well or poorly founded—can, and frequently do, exercise an influence all their own upon historical change. Furthermore, the
views expressed by eyewitnesses tend to shape the opinions of
those who come along later. Contemporary opinions have been
marshaled by other writers either to support or to undermine
the hypothesis that the revocation was a significant factor in the
French depression. Before presenting and analyzing factual evidence, therefore, it seems appropriate to survey opinions expressed in the seventeenth and eighteenth centuries.

Maréchal de Vauban, author of *La Dîme royale* and the ingenious engineer who was responsible for many of Louis XIV's
impressive fortifications, was one of the few courtiers who dared
question the wisdom of the revocation. Although an ardent
Catholic, Vauban prepared in October, 1689, a memorandum
entitled "For the Recall of the Huguenots," which he hoped
the king would eventually see.[45] In 1691, and again in 1693, he
revised the original document and appended a supporting state-

41 L. Rossier, *Histoire des protestants de Picardie, particulièrement de ceux du
département de la Somme* (Amiens, 1861) , p. 246.

42 Archives Nationales, G 7 71; C. Weiss, "Mémoire sur les protestants," *op. cit.,*
XX, 121.

43 Archives Nationales, A1 756; Bibliothèque Nationale, *Fonds français*, MS 4288,
fols. 16, 18; Natalis Rondot, *Les Protestants à Lyon au dix-septième siècle* (Lyon,
1891) , pp. 45, 47–49 and nn.

44 Archives Nationales, TT 456, *dossier* 30, doc. 139; Bibliothèque Nationale, MS

ment prepared by a doctor at the Sorbonne.[46] Vauban compared the emigration of Huguenots with the expulsion of the Moors and the Moriscos from Spain, and argued that the re-establishment of the Edict of Nantes, by influencing most refugees to return, would strike a vital blow at France's archenemy, William of Orange. According to Vauban, between 80,000 and 100,000 Frenchmen had already fled abroad since 1685 and had taken out more than 30 million livres in specie; they were diffusing industries and techniques that had formerly been the backbone of France's export trade and the chief means of attracting silver from other European states; their departure not only had ruined domestic trade but had also provided enemy forces with 8,000 or 9,000 able seamen, 500 or 600 army officers, and 10,000 or 12,000 soldiers; and those who had been compulsorily converted were a constant source of trouble for the Church because of their insincerity and sacrilegious behavior.

Seignelay, son of Colbert and minister of the marine, also feared that persecution and emigration were hurting trade and industry. From 1685 until his death in 1690, he strove to lessen the impact upon the economy of the king's program to enforce religious conformity. For example, he upbraided one of his agents on June 6, 1687, for not taking emigration seriously:

In regard to those who are leaving the realm you are in error when you write that the consequences are not great and will have little effect on trade. You should be persuaded that the departure of a large number of subjects who transport their industry to foreign countries [and] enrich them at the expense of this kingdom [will occasion] the greatest harm to the state. This you must prevent with all your powers.[47]

Henri Daguesseau, who became the first president of the Council of Trade in 1700, wrote on one occasion that his father,

---

4283, fol. 83; B. Vaurigaud, *Essai sur l'histoire des églises réformées de Bretagne, 1535–1808* (Paris, 1870), III, 173–174.

45 He sent it first to Louvois, the minister of war, who wrote him on January 5, 1690: "I have read your memorandum which I found to contain some good things; but, between us, they are slightly exaggerated. I shall endeavor to read it to His Majesty." (*BSHPF*, XXXVIII, 243.)

46 Bibliothèque Nationale, *Fonds français*, MS 7044, fols. 298 ff.; Lesens, *op. cit.*, p. 219; Douen, *op. cit.*, I, 67. A copy of Vauban's original memorandum and his subsequent revisions may be found in the Bibliothèque Nationale, *Fonds français*, MS 7044, fols. 286 ff. *BSHPF* (XXXVIII, 194 ff.) has reproduced the original.

47 Archives Nationales, B2 *registre* 61, fols. 373–374.

while serving as intendant in Languedoc, had predicted that the revocation would drive out "those who cause the arts and manufactures to flourish."[48] He himself urged Chancellor Pontchartrain on May 14, 1708, to be lenient with Huguenots who still remained in France:

Experience has revealed only too well what great harm was done the realm by those Religionists who fled and took with them specie, arts and crafts, industry, and other sources of trade and wealth for the state. It is therefore essential at least to endeavor to retain those who still remain by leaving them a city where they can find some tolerance, and where they can live and die without being continually investigated and harassed over matters pertaining to their conscience, no matter how misguided they might be.[49]

He argued vigorously on October 26, 1713, against a proposal to require apprentices and masters in all gilds to secure a certificate of "good standing" with the Catholic Church. Such a measure, he predicted, would drive many craftsmen to England, where "they can earn more than in France because of the multitude of manufactories others have already established over there." The revocation already had caused "several thousand" to escape with "their personal property, their arts, their industry," and Daguesseau warned that "both Catholicism and the state will feel the consequences of this more keenly in the future than either has yet experienced."[50]

An important church official in Paris, probably the archbishop himself, had expressed similar views in 1698. If people had observed the last article of the revocation edict guaranteeing Huguenots freedom of conscience, if every city had tolerated them as Paris had done, or if people had not been suspicious of new converts and instead had treated them as sincere Catholics, he conjectured, "the realm would be more peopled, richer, and more powerful than it now is; commerce and industry would be better sustained; and there would be a larger number of sincere conversions."[51]

Most intendants were either too timid or too obsequious to question openly the wisdom of Louis XIV's action. Bouchu in

---

48 Quoted by Freddy Durrleman, *Éloge et condamnation de la Révocation de l'Édit de Nantes: Documents rassemblés* (Carrières-sous-Poissy, 1936), p. 24.
49 Bibliothèque Nationale, *Fonds français*, MS 7046, fol. 9.
50 *Ibid.*, MS 7046, fols. 28–29.
51 *Ibid.*, MS 7045, fol. 213.

Dauphiné, however, was one of the few exceptions. He asked the controller general on July 24, 1686, not to send any more booted missionaries into his province because "the area has already suffered a great deal from the change in religion."[52] A year later he drafted a long memorandum on the possible repercussions emigration might have on the economy and went so far as to suggest drastic modification of the king's program. As long as there had been reason to suppose that the campaign to convert all Huguenots would drive away only the most obstinate and troublesome, he argued, there had been some justification in seeking to unite all Frenchmen under one religion. When thousands of able-bodied workmen and farmers were choosing to flee rather than face forced conversion, however, it became apparent that the campaign was not achieving its purpose but was only driving away a large number of possible recruits for the Catholic Church and seriously threatening the stability of the French economy.[53]

Even Louis XIV at times became concerned over the effects of emigration. For example, when he sent Bonrepaus on a secret mission to England and Holland late in 1685, he asked the emissary to ascertain the number and the names of all refugees in the two countries, to persuade as many as he could to return home, to investigate the industries they had helped establish, and to scotch all rumors that the religious campaign in France employed coercion or violence. The king particularly wanted to know why the Dutch had recently cut down on their purchases of linen and hempen fabrics in France, and whether Huguenot refugees were helping them manufacture these goods.[54]

The deputies of trade who represented Bayonne, Lyon, Marseille, Nantes, and Rouen all admitted in reports to the Council of Trade in 1700–1701 that Huguenots had done France irreparable harm by transplanting some of her crafts to foreign soil and thereby creating an unfavorable balance of trade.[55] A

---

52 Archives Nationales, G7 240.

53 *Ibid.*, TT 243, *dossier* 4, doc. 37. Bouchu also wrote Louvois in 1689 that Protestant workmen in his district should be allowed as much freedom as possible lest they start another mass exodus (Germain Martin, *La Grande industrie sous le règne de Louis XIV* [Paris, 1898], pp. 218–219).

54 *PHSL*, II, 446 ff. The document containing Louis's instructions to Bonrepaus may also be found in the Archives du Ministère des Affaires Étrangères, *Ancien fonds*, "Angleterre," *registre* 157, fols. 1–12.

55 Bibliothèque Nationale, *Fonds français*, MS 8038, fols. 434–435, 506; Boislisle, *op. cit.*, II (1883), 477, 479–480, 489.

Frenchman writing in 1708 concurred in this view and denied that export duties on agricultural and industrial products had forced several industries to move abroad. "Everyone knows as well as I," he told the controller general, "that it was the Protestant emigrants who did this."[56] Jean Anisson, the deputy of trade from Lyon and one of the men sent to England in 1713 to negotiate a trade agreement, admitted in a report of June 17, 1713, that the balance of trade after 1689 had turned against France in favor of England, "especially after Englishmen had opened up manufactories of silk, paper, glassware, and other products similar to our own."[57] Michel le Vassor, anonymous author of *Les Soupirs de la France esclave* (1689), blamed the commercial depression upon "the despotic and sovereign power [in France] which prides itself on acting on every whim, on reordering everything, and reforming all things by an absolute power. . . . The persecution of the Huguenots, another effect of this despotic power, has completed the ruin of commerce."[58]

According to the economist Richard Cantillon, who died in 1734, France's political and economic power had begun to diminish after 1684, "when a number of Protestant Undertakers and artisans were driven out."[59] The anonymous author of the *Testament politique du Marquis de Louvois*[60] wrote in 1695 that Huguenot refugees had withdrawn huge amounts of specie, had transplanted important industries, had strengthened enemy naval and military forces, and had robbed France of essential man power. It was wrong, he said, to blame war for the deplorable conditions in France. If Louis had not first driven so many people abroad with his religious persecution, the country could easily have borne all the vicissitudes of war.

Protestant spokesmen, of course, underscored such opinions. The great theologian Pierre Jurieu wrote from exile that France had suffered no comparable misfortune in twelve centuries. Within the brief span of one or two years, he said, Louis had nullified all Colbert had done to strengthen the economy. Trade

---

56 Archives Nationales, G7 1692.

57 *Ibid.*, G7 1699. Anisson did not specifically allude to the Huguenots, yet he doubtless still held them responsible, as he had when he drafted his 1701 report as the deputy from Lyon.

58 As translated in Charles W. Cole, *French Mercantilism, 1683–1700* (New York, 1943) , p. 248.

59 *Essai sur la nature du commerce en générale*, ed. and trans. Henry Higgs (London, 1931) , p. 187.

60 (Cologne, 1695) , pp. 369–373.

had been destroyed; provinces had been desolated and royal revenues depleted; and Protestant fugitives had carried abroad their trade and their skills in making silk, woolens, linens, serges, hats, soap, and glass. He predicted that the country would suffer the baneful consequences of this just as Spain had suffered from the expulsion of her Moors.[61] According to Gaultier de Saint-Blancard, writing in 1688, Catholic propagandists who claimed that no violence or persecution had accompanied the revocation were either ignorant of the facts or were purposely trying to mislead the public. Persecution, he said, had forced some 200,000 persons to dispose of their property at sacrifice prices and to seek asylum abroad. These emigrants had been "of great utility to the realm and had contributed in no small way to making France prosperous."[62] A Swiss pastor who toured France in the early part of the eighteenth century remarked that, whenever he asked why there was so much misery and depression on every hand, he always received the same answer: "As soon as the Protestants left the country, poverty moved in and entrenched itself." [63] According to Antoine Court, perhaps the most influential spokesman of exiled Huguenots in the eighteenth century, the revocation had been the sole reason that France had grown weaker, her manufactures had decayed, and her trade had languished while her neighbors had prospered.[64]

Montesquieu also blamed Louis XIV for having revoked the Edict of Nantes. He doubtless had his own country in mind when, in his *Persian Letters,* he condemned a fictitious Persian prince for persecuting his Armenian subjects so unmercifully that they fled to India and thus deprived Persia of its most industrious and skilled workmen.[65] About fifty years later, on July 13, 1766, an official at Grenoble wrote the Duke of Choiseul:

---

61 *Lettres pastorales addressées aux fidèles de France, qui gemissent sous la captivité de Babylone* (4th ed.; Rotterdam, 1687–1688), I, 13; II, 9, 151–152.

62 *Histoire apologétique, ou Défense des libertéz des Églises réformées de France* (Mayence, 1687–1688), II, 551 ff.

63 J. B. Hollard, *Relation d'un voyage nouvellement fait en France* (London, 1717), p. 13, as quoted by Douen, *op. cit.*, I, 97.

64 *Lettre d'un patriote sur la tolérance civile des protestans de France* (n.p., 1756), p. 25.

65 *Lettres persanes* (1715), Usbek à Mirza (letter lxxxvi), as quoted by Durrleman, *op. cit.*, p. 35. Montesquieu later wrote the Baron de Stain from Amsterdam in 1729 that the king must have signed the revocation edict either through ignorance or because of intrigue at court. If Louis had foreseen that the edict would ruin French industry, he surely would never have signed it because he was in too great need of money and tax revenues. (Cited by Alfred Leroux, *Les Religionnaires de Bordeaux de 1685 à 1802* [Bordeaux, 1920], p. 20.)

"I shall not undertake, Sir, to recount to you the evils that have befallen France each time we have treated Calvinists too harshly; I shall only observe that the rigor with which they have been persecuted since the revocation of the Edict of Nantes has occasioned the ruin of our agriculture and trade and the depopulation of our state."[66] Several others—the Maréchal de Richelieu,[67] the eminent lawyer and royal councilor Gilbert de Voisins,[68] the Chevalier de Beaumont,[69] François Véron de Forbonnais,[70] and the Catholic priest Michel-Claude Gilbert,[71] to mention a few—expressed similar views at the same time.

These contemporary opinions were frequently reiterated in the nineteenth and twentieth centuries. Both David MacPherson[72] and Adam Anderson,[73] writing in England, concluded that Louis "had done much hurt to his country, by driving out of France so many industrious manufacturers, artisans, and merchants, whom necessity prompted to propagate their arts and skill in the countries to which they retired for shelter" and that "his persecution of his Protestant subjects nearly depopulated a considerable part of his country, and also greatly lessened the former vast consumption of French manufactures in foreign countries." "France, by its profitable commerce with England, etc., having acquired great riches in the times preceding this revocation," they said, "did not immediately feel the bad effects of driving out so many industrious merchants, manufacturers, and artificers; yet in process of time she found her manufactures and inland trade thereby greatly decayed." Saint-Simon declared that "the revocation of the Edict of Nantes, without the slightest pretext or need, and the divers proscriptions . . . that followed it were the fruit of this frightful conspiracy which depopulated a fourth of the realm, ruined its trade, weakened the country in all fields,

---

66 Archives Nationales, TT 463, doc. 44.

67 Bibliothèque Nationale, *Fonds français*, MS 7046, fol. 325.

68 *Ibid.*, MSS 7047, fols. 391–392, 418–419; 10621, fol. 9.

69 *Op. cit.*, II, 134 ff.

70 *Recherches et considérations sur les finances de France depuis 1595 jusqu'en 1721* (Liége, 1758), III, 305.

71 *Mémoires pour servir à l'histoire de Dieppe*, II, 228, as cited by Samuel Hardy, *Histoire de l'Église protestante de Dieppe* (Paris, 1896), p. 386.

72 *Annals of Commerce, Manufactures, Fisheries, and Navigation etc.* (London, 1805), II, 617; III, 43. This work apparently was a new edition of Anderson's volumes, which MacPherson edited and brought up to date without much rewriting.

73 *An Historical and Chronological Deduction of the Origin of Commerce, from the Earliest Accounts etc.* (London, 1801), II, 569; III, 63.

. . . led our manufactories to shift to foreign soil, caused foreign states to flourish and wax wealthy at our expense, [and] allowed them to build new cities. . . ."[74] The economist Sismondi, like Saint-Simon, thought that the foreign countries that welcomed the refugees acquired new industries and prospered while France stagnated or declined.[75] Friedrich List, the eminent German economist, referred to "the relapse of France" as a "consequence of the revocation of the Edict of Nantes."[76] Two French historians of the nineteenth century, Henri Martin[77] and Jules Michelet,[78] both ranked the revocation among the greatest mistakes any French government had ever committed. More recently, such economic historians as Émile Levasseur,[79] Germain Martin,[80] Henri Sée,[81] and Paul-M. Bondois[82] have concluded that it was a significant factor in the deterioration of French industrial and economic activity after Colbert's death.

Not everyone, of course, has agreed that the revocation was a political and economic blunder. Many contemporaries applauded Louis's action. Most government officials and courtiers at Versailles apparently thought that outlawing Protestantism would not harm the economy and would strengthen both Church and state. If they believed otherwise, they remained silent rather than risk incurring royal displeasure. When Huguenots began to flee in such numbers that they could no longer be ignored, apologists for the king referred to the emigration as a nuisance rather than as a misfortune, or as a definite victory for Catholicism

---

74 *Mémoires* (Hachette ed.; 1862), VIII, 143–144.

75 *Histoire des français* (Paris, 1821–1844), XXV, 520–521; see also XXVI, 112.

76 *The National System of Political Economy*, trans. Sampson S. Lloyd (new ed.; New York, 1904), p. 91. Professor Earl J. Hamilton called my attention to this reference.

77 *Op. cit.*, XIV, 37 ff., 335.

78 *Histoire de France* (3d ed.; Paris, 1863), XIII, *passim*. Michelet wrote that the Frenchmen who fled his country in the Reign of Terror (1793) differed primarily from those who had fled shortly after 1685 in that they were drawn from the idle rich and sought to save their lives, whereas the Huguenots had been among the most industrious and had fled abroad to save their consciences (*ibid.*, XIII, iv).

79 *Histoire des classes ouvrières en France depuis la conquête de Jules César jusqu'à la révolution* (Paris, 1859), II, 285–286; *Histoire des classes ouvrières et de l'industrie en France avant 1789* (2d ed.; Paris, 1901), II, 344; *Histoire du commerce de la France* (Paris, 1911), I, 350, 421.

80 *Op. cit.*, pp. 204 ff., 211, 352–353.

81 *Histoire économique de la France*, ed. Robert Schnerb (Paris, 1939), I, 272–273.

82 "Le Duc de Savoie Victor-Amédée II et la Révocation de l'Édit de Nantes," *Bulletin philologique et historique du Comité des travaux historiques et scientifiques*, years 1928–1929 (1930), 139–140.

rather than as a threat to economic stability: "The damage caused by those who fled was of little importance; the essential thing was the salvation of those who remained."[83] The Duke of Burgundy, Louis XIV's grandson and heir to the throne, argued in 1710 that emigration had not robbed his country of enough able-bodied men to threaten her industries and agriculture. He claimed that, by the most exaggerated estimates, only 67,732 men, women, and children had left. A single year of warfare, he continued, ordinarily occasioned a larger number of casualties.[84] Madame de Maintenon comforted the king in 1697 by suggesting that those who attributed France's current misfortunes to the flight of Protestants were overlooking vastly more important factors.[85] Even the deputies of trade in Paris, Lille, Dunkirk, La Rochelle, and Bordeaux carefully ignored the revocation when they prepared their 1701 reports on economic conditions;[86] and some of those who did mention it listed it as only one of a number of important factors. The intendant Bâville denied in his long memorandum of 1699 that "the change in religion" had had harmful effects upon trade in Languedoc. "Even if all the merchants here are poor Catholics," he wrote, "at least they have not ceased to be good businessmen."[87] According to a Catholic partisan writing in the latter half of the eighteenth century, "instead of the arts and industries having been ruined, they have never been more flourishing than since 1685, when the revocation brought peace and tranquillity to the realm." [88]

Abbé Novi de Caveirac expressed a similar view at about the

83 Ernest Lavisse and others, *Histoire de France illustrée depuis les origines jusqu'à la révolution* (Paris, 1911), Vol. VII, Part 1, p. 349.

84 Quoted by Charles Read, "L'Opinion du duc de Bourgogne sur la question protestante et le rappel des huguenots (1710) ," *BSHPF*, XLI, 347, and by A. Rébelliau in Lavisse, *op. cit.*, Vol. VIII, Part 1, p. 349.

85 Charles Read, "La Réponse de Madame de Maintenon consultée par Louis XIV, en 1697, sur un mémoire concernant les Huguenots, avec les Remarques de la Beaumelle (1755) ," *BSHPF*, XXXIX (1890) , 406.

86 Bibliothèque Nationale, *Fonds français*, MS 8038, *passim.*

87 *Ibid.*, MS 4290, fol. 323. A year earlier he had suggested that Huguenots habitually exaggerated the number who had fled and always predicted further mass flights in the hope of persuading the government to change its policies toward their religion (*ibid.*, MS 7045, fol. 109). Even Bâville, however, occasionally had qualms. He voiced the fear in 1701, for example, that the refugees might succeed so well in establishing their manufactories abroad that foreigners would eventually stop trading with France altogether (*ibid.*, MS 8038, fol. 467) .

88 *Ibid.*, *Nouvelles acquisitions françaises*, MS 944, fol. 97; see also *Fonds français*, MS 10628, fol. 40.

same time. He denied that the refugees, who he contended amounted to less than 0.25 per cent of France's population, had robbed her of valuable industrial secrets because many of them were unskilled and "vulgar" individuals. Though admitting, somewhat inconsistently, that Huguenots had diffused the manufacture of stockings, felt hats, coarse draperies, linens, and other fabrics, he denied that these industries had proven successful in foreign countries and that Frenchmen producing the same articles had experienced any shrinkage in their markets abroad. France would have lost her secrets anyway, he concluded, for no nation could keep its techniques to itself for very long.[89]

Ségur-Dupeyron and Abbé Rameau, in the second half of the nineteenth century, contended that the enterprises Huguenots had founded abroad had not hurt French industry. Ségur-Dupeyron maintained that the woolen industry, in particular, had not suffered and that France's economic troubles in the latter half of Louis XIV's reign stemmed from other and vastly more important causes than the revocation.[90] Abbé Rameau buttressed his argument by pointing to France's progress in the eighteenth century:

We forget too readily . . . that in less than twenty years after the revocation our industry had regained such a degree of prosperity by the end of the Spanish wars that the competition it offered was a subject of terror for England, and rendered fugitive Protestants powerless to establish large-scale industries on a permanent basis in either England or Holland.[91]

PURPOSE AND PLAN OF THE STUDY

It is obvious that reputable spokesmen have defended both sides of the issue as to whether or not the revocation penalized French economic development. By and large, few contemporaries

---

[89] *Apologie de Louis XIV*, pp. 98 ff., 155–156, 204–206; *Mémoire politico-critique*, pp. 108–109, 113, 115–116.

[90] *Histoire des négociations commerciales et maritimes de la France aux XVIIe et XVIIIe siècles, considérées dans leurs rapports avec la politique générale* (Paris, 1872–1873), II, 365 ff., 438 ff. Adolphe d'Avril, in his favorable review of Ségur-Dupeyron's work, voiced the opinion that the diffusion of French technology after 1683 could be almost completely explained in terms of the emigration to foreign countries of both Catholic and Protestant Frenchmen who could not find employment at home ("La Révocation de l'Édit de Nantes dans ses conséquences industrielles," *Revue des questions historiques*, 8th year, XV [1874], 591, 595).

[91] *Op. cit.*, IX, 134–135.

openly criticized Louis's religious policies; most of them, for one reason or another, either remained silent or defended his program. Later on, when someone else occupied the throne, and when French intellectual leaders became concerned with the common man and human liberties, the number of outspoken critics multiplied. During the nineteenth century the belief spread that the persecution and the emigration of Huguenots had been a primary reason for France's failure to keep pace with England in industrial development. Charles Weiss was the first person who attempted to substantiate this hypothesis by comprehensive study of the historical record. His two-volume work entitled *Histoire des réfugiés protestants de France depuis la révocation de l'Édit de Nantes jusqu'à nos jours* (1853) evoked considerable interest and stimulated research by other scholars. No one has since attempted to reëvaluate Weiss's factual evidence and analysis or to incorporate the findings of later researchers. The present study proposes to do this.

It is conceivable that the revocation might have hurt the French economy in many ways. It might have driven abroad so many resourceful entrepreneurs, skilled laborers, and ordinary workmen that industry declined because of a shortage of suitable leadership and man power. The emigrants might, by diffusing French technology, have lessened the dependence of other countries upon French exports. They might have carried with them productive capital in the form of raw materials, machinery, or consumer goods, or they might, by robbing their country of specie and purchasing power, have created a temporary scarcity of funds on the domestic market and a longer-run shift in the balance of trade with other nations. Any or all of these could adversely affect France's barter terms of trade and reduce the gains she realized from trading with other countries. The effects would be more pronounced if the emigrants were skimmed from the cream of her economy and if replacements of similar ability were not available. Whatever property and businesses the fugitives had to leave behind, therefore, might have fallen into hands less capable than theirs and might have been less fully utilized as productive resources. Even if emigration at first hurt only a limited number of industries or localities, the interdependence of markets and factor supplies might have caused repercussions throughout the economy. Unemployment and stagnation in one sector tend to spread to others.

The persecution of Protestants might also have interfered with the economic activities of Huguenots who remained at home. The latter were under continuous surveillance and were subjected to numerous acts of discrimination. They might not have been able freely to buy and sell property or to market their outputs; they might have found it difficult to find and hold jobs or to obtain credit; they might have been unduly taxed; or they might have been deprived of sufficient rewards to keep them attentive to business. If, because of discrimination, they produced less and hoarded rather than invested their savings, the French economy was bound to suffer. Unemployment would probably have mounted and the national income would have dwindled. The government would have had less to tax, and its expenditures would have climbed as it implemented its conversion campaign, policed its frontiers to prevent emigration, and took over charitable obligations formerly assumed by the Reformed Church.

Whether the revocation actually had such effects as these upon the French economy is a difficult question to resolve. Historical causation always involves many interdependent variables, and cause and effect are often interrelated. The historian confronts the formidable task of interpreting and explaining recorded events in terms of an almost endless array of interacting causes. The economic theorist also deals with a number of interdependent variables, and he fashions his tools and models for analyzing and understanding the real world by making whatever limiting assumptions he finds necessary. That is to say, he assumes that "all other things are equal" when he sets out to examine the impact of one or two variables upon a given problem. His models and theories are not reflections of reality but are tools for analyzing reality. To help him and others formulate desirable public policies, however, the tools must be practical and the theories must be applicable to real situations. The chisels, the screwdrivers, and the saws used by a Swiss watchmaker, for example, are among the finest tools made today; yet they would prove of little value to a carpenter engaged in building a house. This is one source of difficulty for economists. Even more troublesome is the frequent disagreement among economists as to the essential features of a real problem and the best method of solving the problem. This disagreement, often more apparent than real, stems primarily from the different weights economists assign to the variables involved, which may be either known or unknown, predictable or unpredictable, controllable or uncontrollable.

So it is with the study of history. The philosopher of history is, in many respects, like the economic theorist. He formulates hypotheses and deductively develops models of historical change. The historian, filling a role similar to that of the economist charged with guiding public policy, then attempts to explain and interpret particular historical events and relationships with frequent recourse to the ideas and the hypotheses suggested by philosophers of history. Although the task of the historian is never simply that of recording "facts," he can never afford to wander very far away from them. Not only does he have to cope with incomplete knowledge and to assign somewhat arbitrary weights to the facts and the forces that constitute his basic data; he also has no particular kit of analytical tools which philosophers of history have fashioned and which historians have accepted as the most useful. The economic historian at least has the essential tools of economic analysis with which to work, and he proposes to examine only the economic aspects of man's development rather than the whole picture. Even so, he has to exercise judgment as to which facts and factors are essential and which analytical tools are appropriate. Several seemingly different and conflicting interpretations of the same historical phenomena are hence possible, and all may be "true" in the sense that no one of them invalidates the others. This is why economic history needs to be rewritten and reinterpreted continuously as new materials come to light and as economic historians find it desirable to modify their orientation and to emphasize new and different relationships. It therefore seems appropriate to take another look at the period 1680–1720 in French history in order to reëxamine the hypothesis that the revocation of the Edict of Nantes seriously retarded the country's economic development.

If reliable quantitative data for this period were not so meager, one might construct time series for general prices, interest rates, foreign exchange quotations, tax yields, export and import volumes, gross national product, unemployment, and so on. Such series would certainly prove useful in limning the trend of economic activity and in identifying major recessions and revivals. It is not at all evident, however, that they would be useful in testing the particular hypothesis here under review. A complete and reliable series of foreign exchange quotations for the French livre, for example, would provide no basis for disassociating, on the one hand, the effects upon the exchange rates of unknown amounts of specie exported by fugitive Huguenots and, on the other hand, the effects of continuous revaluations of the French currency and of specie exported to meet shifting trade balances caused by war and a host of other factors. Or could one justifiably conclude that significant deviations in two complete price series —one for commodities in general and the other for goods produced mainly by Huguenots—reflected the impact of the Huguenot emigration? During a time of general shrinkage in purchasing power and employment it is conceivable that differences between the income-and-price elasticities of demand for the goods in the Huguenot index (especially if most of them were so-called "luxury" items) and the income-and-price elasticities of demand for those in the general series could have caused all the deviations. The sort of data required for testing the revocation hypothesis quantitatively would be output and employment figures for industries and geographic areas where Huguenots were especially prominent, as well as for industries and regions dominated by Catholics. Since such quantitative data are not now available (and most likely never will be), the historian must rely on such qualitative evidence as he can find. He must also use his intuitive judgment and rely upon inferences drawn from insufficient and oftentimes contradictory data. His conclusions, however cautiously and tentatively drawn, can be no more reliable than his original intuitive and inferential judgment.

These observations suggest that, in examining the hypothesis that the revocation was primarily responsible for much of the economic distress in France after 1685, it would be appropriate to determine whether segments of economic activity where Huguenots occupied key positions suffered relatively more than other segments, whether geographic areas with a significant Protestant population were more depressed than others, and whether the onset of economic decline coincided with the intensification of religious persecution and the upsurge of emigration. I shall attempt to show that much of the evidence adduced in support of the hypothesis has been either faulty or irrelevant, and also that the analysis employed has often been poor. For example, many industries used for illustrative purposes

do not bear close examination. Some began to decline long before
the revocation; others declined relatively less than the average.
Some industries were predominantly Catholic; and many Protestant firms did not fail, as has been alleged, when their key
workmen or entrepreneurs emigrated but, instead, continued
in operation and sometimes even expanded their activities. I
propose, therefore, to question the evidence and the analysis used
by others to support the hypothesis, and to present additional
information which suggests that other factors played a more
significant role than the revocation in retarding France's economic
development.

My over-all plan conforms to the following outline. The three
chapters that follow immediately describe and analyze the discriminations practiced against Protestants and newly converted Catholics both before and after Louis signed the edict
outlawing Protestantism, and examine why and how the government tried to prevent Huguenots from leaving the country and
whether its efforts met with success. Chapter v shows that French
Protestants were unusually successful in business before 1685,
and that in economic affairs they exercised an influence dispropor-
tionate to their numerical importance.

Shortly after Colbert died in 1683, France drifted into a long
period of economic stagnation and depression, lasting approximately from 1684 to 1717. Population decreased, the standard of
living deteriorated, most industries contracted and unemployment grew, agriculture became distressed, foreign and domestic
trade dwindled, and the government soon found itself on the
brink of bankruptcy. Because of these developments, which are
treated in chapter vi, it seems appropriate to inquire whether
the revocation and the emigration of Huguenots had significant
economic consequences. The next three chapters examine the
impact of religious persecution upon selected industries, trade
and shipping, finance, agriculture, and other segments of the
French economy. Chapter x considers whether Huguenot refugees robbed their country of many trade and industrial secrets
and whether they stimulated economic activity in the countries
that welcomed them. If they did, this may have worsened
France's barter terms of trade and have harmed her competitive
position in foreign markets.

The last two chapters attempt to rank the revocation as a factor in the depression alongside other causes which were simultaneously operating. Chapter xi, for example, examines the impact upon the economy of war, fiscal difficulties, increasing regimentation of economic life, restraints upon foreign and domestic trade, and depopulation and famine; and the final chapter summarizes all the evidence and suggests certain tentative conclusions.

II

Penalization of Huguenots before the Revocation

INTRODUCTION

Henry IV brought an end to open religious strife by signing the Edict of Nantes; he also reaffirmed most of the religious and civil liberties of his Protestant subjects. At the same time he exhorted both religious factions to forget past differences and to live and work together as members of one large family. The nobles and the professional men in both groups eventually heeded his exhortation and adopted more or less conciliatory attitudes after 1630. They continued to be at least superficially tolerant of religious differences until about 1660. On the other hand, the rank and file nursed their resentment, magnified their differences, and took delight in harassing members of the other faith. It is significant that the Catholic clergy never gracefully accepted Henry IV's truce. Priests fomented discontent among their parishioners and created social friction whenever they could. And Protestant pastors frequently did the same. Animosities were intensified wherever economic and social distinctions between groups coincided with religious differences. In the seventeenth century Catholics were guilty of discrimination in areas where they greatly outnumbered Protestants; and Protestants retaliated wherever they outnumbered or outranked Catholics in the social or the business world.[1]

Neither the central nor the provincial governments actively

---

1 See, e.g., Archives Nationales, TT 232, *dossier* 19, doc. 9; 235, *dossier* 4, doc. 50; Bibliothèque Nationale, *Fonds français*, MSS 7044, fol. 29; 17315, fol. 55; 21616, fol. 303; 21623, fol. 434; Paul Courpron, *Essai sur l'histoire du Protestantisme en Aunis et Saintonge depuis la Révocation de l'Édit de Nantes jusqu'à l'Édit de Tolérance (1685–1787)* (Cahors, 1902), pp. 26–27; Eugène Guitard, *Colbert et Seignelay contre la religion réformée* (2d ed.; Paris, 1912), p. 116.

discriminated against Huguenots before 1661.[2] In that year, however, when Louis XIV announced that he was going to rule directly, the government began to reshape its policy. The immediate excuse was a request by the Catholic Clerical Assembly that the king investigate the Reputedly Reformed Religion. In April, 1661, Louis appointed a Catholic and a Protestant commissioner in each province to see whether the affairs of the Reformed Church were "in good order" and whether the church meticulously conformed to the spirit and the letter of all royal decrees and regulations governing its activities.[3] The Catholic commissioner was usually the provincial intendant or another high-ranking dignitary; the Protestant commissioner was often an obscure individual of mediocre ability. The bias manifested in the choice of commissioners provides sufficient justification for questioning Louis's good faith. As constituted, these bipartisan commissions were hardly likely to present an impartial, accurate account of their findings. If the commissioners failed to agree on a particular point, they were to submit their differences to the king.

This nationwide investigation was the first overt indication that Louis was none too happy with Protestantism. Then, in January, 1669, he suppressed the bipartisan chambers of justice which Henry IV had established in Paris and Rouen for adjudicating all disputes between Catholics and Protestants. Because there had been no trouble for several decades, he pretended that religious animosity had subsided and that there was no longer any need for special tribunals.[4] Meanwhile, provincial and local authorities had begun to abridge the privileges of Huguenots whenever possible, and the central government took advantage of every opportunity to interpret and modify the law in their disfavor. Most Protestants, however, did not become alarmed until 1679, when Louis brought his campaign out into the open. He disbanded the bipartisan chambers of justice in Languedoc, Guyenne, and Dauphiné in July,[5] and multiplied the number of vexatious and discriminatory decrees directed against

---

[2] As a matter of fact, Louis XIV had solemnly reaffirmed the Edict of Nantes in May, 1652, as his mother Anne of Austria had done when she became regent in 1643, and as his father Louis XIII had done even earlier in his Edict of Nîmes.

[3] The king had first agreed to such an investigation on July 18, 1656, but apparently he had failed to appoint commissioners at that time (Jacques Lefèvre, *Nouveau recueil de tout ce qui s'est fait pour et contre les protestans* . . . [Paris, 1690], pp. 248–252) .

[4] Bibliothèque Nationale, *Fonds français*, MS 21616, fols. 278 ff.

[5] Archives Nationales, TT 239, *dossier* 1, doc. 99; Lefèvre, *op. cit.*, pp. 646–651.

Protestants. A perspicacious individual could no longer ignore
the trend of events or fail to realize the king's intention to crush
Protestantism.[6]

Why did Louis XIV begin in 1661 to undermine the privileges
and guarantees granted Huguenots by the Edict of Nantes? Why,
after 1679, did he openly work to destroy their religion? Ordinarily, motives must be inferred from facts, and individuals differ
in the inferences they draw from the same facts. Of the motives
suggested for Louis's actions, three deserve mention here. First,
Louis XIV was extremely egocentric. If he accepted Catholic
dogmas, why should any of his subjects dispute them? He seemed
to consider heresy a personal affront. Second, Protestant leaders
in the sixteenth century had opposed the centralization of political
power in France, and in the seventeenth century Protestantism
had become identified with republicanism in Holland, England,
and Switzerland. Louis doubtless considered the religion a threat
to national unity and absolute monarchy. Third, he himself
experienced a sort of spiritual conversion after 1678 and became
increasingly concerned with religious matters. On April 19 and
October 28, 1679, Madame de Maintenon joyously noted the
change in his attitude:

The king spent two hours today in my study. He is the most amiable
person in all his realm. Perhaps he is not as far from thinking about
his own salvation as the Court believes. He has good sentiments and
frequently turns toward God.

The king is full of good sentiments; he sometimes reads the Holy
Scripture and finds it the most beautiful of books. He confesses his
weaknesses. He recognizes his faults. . . . He is thinking seriously
about converting heretics and very shortly will work to bring this
about.[7]

Madame de Maintenon herself was a devout person. And she
was anxious to convert the king. She had considerable influence
over him as his friend and as the governess of his children.
When he secretly married her a little less than a year after
Queen Marie-Thérèse died on July 30, 1683, her influence
increased. The Earl of Stair, for example, wrote the English
Foreign Office from his Paris Embassy on March 8, 1715, that in

---

6 See, e.g., Charles Benoist, *Condition juridique des protestants sous le régime de
l'Édit de Nantes et après sa révocation* (Paris, 1900) , p. 71.

7 Ernest Lavisse and others, *Histoire de France illustrée depuis les origines
jusqu'à la révolution* (Paris, 1911) , Vol. VII, Part 2, p. 58.

state affairs she "has more to say than all the [royal] council put together." [8] Scholars have warmly debated whether she was directly or indirectly responsible for the persecution of Huguenots and the revocation of the Edict of Nantes.[9] She certainly wanted all Frenchmen to be members of the state religion, but it is doubtful that she actively encouraged Louis to go to the extremes he did in trying to destroy Protestantism. Recent research, for example, indicates that her letters warmly applauding his actions, heretofore regarded by historians as establishing her responsibility in the persecution of Huguenots, are not authentic.[10] She did, however, try to awaken and sustain Louis's interest in spiritual matters. After his own conversion the king convinced himself that it was his divine duty to bring all Protestants within the Catholic fold regardless of cost or methods. This religious factor lent a false aura of righteousness to a campaign that violated nearly all the recognized principles of humanitarianism and economic expediency.[11]

The responsibility of Madame de Maintenon appears to have been indirect rather than direct. It was primarily she who brought the king into closer contact with the clergy. Her confessor, Father La Chaise, was also the king's confessor. La Chaise apparently exercised a great deal of influence on both individuals through his persuasiveness and zeal for Catholicism. Bossuet was another cleric who used his position and prestige at court to encourage Louis to stamp out Protestantism.[12] In addition,

---

[8] Public Record Office, State Papers: *France*, 78/160, fol. 46. Professor Earl J. Hamilton was kind enough to supply this reference.

[9] She herself was from a Protestant family and may have been baptized in the faith when she was a girl. She had become a devout Catholic, however, long before she took up residence at Versailles.

[10] See, e.g., H. Gelin, "Madame de Maintenon convertisseuse," *Bulletin de la société de l'histoire du protestantisme français* (hereinafter cited as *BSHPF*), XLIX (1900), 169 ff., 250; Marcel Pin, *Madame de Maintenon et les protestants: Contribution à l'Étude de la Révocation de l'Édit de Nantes* (Uzès, 1944), pp. 74 ff.; Jean Orcibal, *Louis XIV et les protestants* (Paris, 1951), p. 92, n. 4.

[11] Although he was "unbelievably ignorant" in religious matters, according to Gilbert Burnet *(Mémoires pour servir à l'histoire de la Grande-Bretagne sous les règnes de Charles II et de Jacques II . . . ,* III [The Hague, 1725], 76) and Saint-Simon (Jacques de Missècle, *L'Édit de Nantes et sa révocation* [2d ed.; Colmar, 1931], p. 16), Louis on one occasion supposedly stated that even if the extirpation of heresy occasioned bloodshed, he would still have to do it for his own salvation, and, if success were to require the amputation of his own hand, he would gladly submit to the operation (Burnet, *op. cit.*, pp. 78–79).

[12] See his letters published in *BSHPF*, IV (1856), 113–119, 213–224; IX (1860), 62 ff., 350 ff.

whenever the Clerical Assembly voted the king a "gratuitous" sum of money, it usually emphasized the political and religious dangers of allowing heresy to fester in the realm and suggested that the conversion of all Huguenots would constitute the crowning achievement of Louis's glorious reign.[13] The only Protestant representative at court, the Marquis de Ruvigny, was powerless before so influential a group as the Catholic clergy.[14]

Colbert, so long as he could keep Louis's interest focused on economic development, and so long as he enjoyed his sovereign's complete confidence, had managed in one way or another to hold the clergy in check. He himself had tolerated Protestants and had even made use of them in his grandiose schemes to develop and diversify the economy despite his personal distaste for religious nonconformity.[15] He had invited foreign Protestants to come to France and establish new crafts and industries; he had granted exclusive privileges to French Protestants who evinced willingness and ability to undertake trade and manufacturing on a large scale; and he had appointed several Huguenots to high financial positions. He had also sought to check their emigration

---

[13] On July 1, 1682, for example, the assembly drafted a long request urging the reunion of the two churches (Bibliothèque Nationale, *Nouvelles acquisitions françaises,* MS 1555, fols. 37 ff.); and in July, 1685, it voted a gift of 3 million livres as a reward to the Crown for its aid in fighting heresy and urged Louis to crush Protestantism once and for all (August-François Lièvre, *Histoire des protestants et des églises réformées du Poitou* [Paris, 1856–1860], II, 149).

[14] Professor Émile-G. Léonard has advanced the interesting thesis that the Protestants themselves made the revocation of the Edict of Nantes easier because of their own desire for religious unity, their faith in and loyalty to the king, and their unqualified acceptance of the principle of the divine right of kings ("Le Protestantisme français au XVIIe siècle," *Revue historique,* CC [1948], 171 ff.).

[15] Benoist, *op. cit.,* p. 74; Pierre Bertrand, *Genève et la Révocation de l'Édit de Nantes* (Geneva, 1935), p. 15; Charles W. Cole, *Colbert and a Century of French Mercantilism* (New York, 1939), II, 147 ff.; Guitard, *op. cit.,* pp. 36, 39; Henry Lehr, *Les Protestants d'autrefois. Vie et institutions militaires,* II (Paris, 1907), 241; Émile Lesens, *Le Protestantisme dans le pays de Caux (ancien colloque de Caux, Havre et Dieppe excepté),* ed. Victor Madelaine (Bolbec, [1906]), pp. 141, 144; Germain Martin, *La Grande industrie sous le règne de Louis XIV* (Paris, 1898), pp. 64 ff.; Elie Benoît, *Histoire de l'Edit de Nantes, contenant les choses les plus remarquables qui se sont passées en France avant et après sa publication . . . jusques à l'Edit de Révocation en Octobre, 1685* (Delft, 1693–1695), IV, 26; James Westfall Thompson, "Some Economic Factors in the Revocation of the Edict of Nantes," *American Historical Review,* XIV (1909), 40, 42–43. Colbert, however, could never completely ignore the religious question and showed a preference for Catholics whenever he had a choice (Paul-M. Bondois, "Colbert et le développement économique de la Basse-Normandie," *Bulletin de la société des antiquaires de Normandie,* XLI [1934], 45). In 1669, for example, he wrote his sister that he intended to employ no Huguenots to manage his personal property and affairs (*BSHPF,* LI [1902], 51).

in the years immediately after 1661. But after 1679, when his personal influence appreciably decreased, the most he could do was urge government agents to proceed cautiously in implementing Louis's new religious policy so as not to embarrass business unduly or provoke further emigration.[16] People at court must have sensed the awkward position in which Colbert found himself, and some of them rejoiced in his discomfiture. Madame de Maintenon, for example, could not refrain from maliciously comparing him with Louvois on August 24, 1681:

The king is beginning seriously to think about his own salvation and that of his subjects. If God preserves him for us, there will no longer be but one religion in the realm. This is M. de Louvois's sentiment, and I believe he accepted the idea much more readily than M. Colbert, who thinks only about financial matters and rarely ever about religion.[17]

Louvois was doubtless aware of the trend of Louis's thinking. The conclusion of the Dutch War in 1678 had rendered Louvois, as minister of war, relatively inactive, and he began to search for ways to employ his talents and diplomatic skills so as to rise in favor at court. A campaign to convert all Huguenots, he concluded, offered the best opportunity. And he was not squeamish about the methods he might have to use. He condoned violence and even recommended coercion, if necessary, in his instructions to intendants and other missionaries. He of all courtiers probably had the heaviest and most effective hand in shaping events after 1679. He found his sovereign attentive when he offered obsequious advice on religion, and Louvois was careful to screen all information reaching him from the provinces before he passed it on to the king.[18]

---

16 Pierre Clément, *Lettres, instructions et mémoires de Colbert* (Paris, 1861–1884), VI, 138, 158 n. 2, 159; J. Garnier, "Tolérance de Colbert," *BSHPF*, XIV (1865), 371. For example, Colbert strove to protect the van Robais family at Abbeville from the importunities of priests and officials (Clément, *op. cit.*, II, 739, 743–744; L. Rossier, *Histoire des protestants de Picardie, particulièrement de ceux du département de la Somme* [Amiens, 1861], pp. 211–212; Maximilien Courtecuisse, *La Manufacture de draps fins Vanrobais aux XVIIᵉ et XVIIIᵉ siècles* [Paris, 1920], pp. 60–61).

17 Claude-Carlomau de Rulhière, *Eclaircissements historiques sur les causes de la révocation de l'Édit de Nantes, et sur l'état des protestants en France, depuis le commencement du Règne de Louis XIV, jusqu'à nos jours* (new ed.; Geneva, 1788), I, 206–207; Jean C. L. Simonde de Sismondi, *Histoire des français* (Paris, 1821–1844), XXV, 420–421. Orcibal, however, denies the authenticity of this letter (*op. cit.*, p. 92, n. 4).

18 Cf. Thompson, *op. cit.*, p. 45.

It is possible that Louis XIV never fully realized how his agents obtained the long lists of conversions he avidly and joyously scanned at Versailles. Occasionally, when he inadvertently learned that officials had resorted to violence in their missionary zeal, he upbraided or even punished them. He frequently admonished them to use only persuasion or other peaceful means. He attempted to explain and justify his own behavior in the *Mémoires* he addressed to the dauphin:

I believed, my son, that the best way to reduce the number of Huguenots in my realm bit by bit was, in the first instance, not to press them at all with new severity, to see that what they had obtained from my predecessors was observed, but not to accord them any additional privilege while I was administering their rights in the strictest manner consonant with justice and decency. Secondly, as to the favors which depended upon me alone, I resolved (and I have since punctiliously enough observed) not to grant them any new ones. I did this not through spite but as an act of kindness, in order to make them consider from time to time, of their own accord and not by coercion, whether their cause was sufficiently good to warrant their depriving themselves voluntarily of the advantages that could otherwise be theirs in common with all my other subjects.[19]

This rationale may have guided Louis's behavior before 1679, but his subsequent actions did not conform to it. Consciously or unconsciously, he must have modified his philosophy. How else can one explain the discriminations he sanctioned later and the revocation edict he signed in October, 1685? His courtiers and advisers, by misrepresenting facts, apparently led him to believe that only a few thousand Huguenots remained in the realm.[20] He may actually have believed—as he stated in the revocation edict—that the Edict of Nantes no longer served its purpose and that to recall it would merely tidy things up a bit and deliver a

19 Lavisse, *op. cit.*, Vol. VII, Part 2, p. 45. In behalf of the clergy, Gilbert de Choiseul, Bishop of Comminges, had addressed the youthful king in similar vein on April 11, 1651: "We do not ask that Your Majesty banish at once from the realm this unfortunate liberty of conscience which destroys the true liberty of God's children, because we do not presume that it will be an easy task; but we hope at least that this evil will not spread and that, if your authority does not crush it with one blow, at least you will cause it to languish and perish little by little by retrenching and diminishing its power" (Frank Puaux, "La Révocation à Marennes. Le temple et les écoles," *BSHPF*, XXXIII [1884], 4).

20 John Viénot (*Histoire de la Réforme française, de l'Édit de Nantes à sa révocation (1598–1685)* [Paris, 1934], p. 471 n. 1), among others, has not accepted this hypothesis.

merciful *coup de grâce* to the remaining handful of dissenters. If true, this helps to explain why the violence of the aftermath came as such a surprise to him and wounded his vanity so deeply.

Somewhat arbitrarily, I have grouped the decrees and declarations issued from 1661 to October, 1685, according to whether they primarily circumscribed religious, civil, or economic liberties of Protestants. The present chapter describes Louis's specific campaign after 1679 to win converts to Catholicism. The following chapter shows how Louis harassed those who refused to convert and how he tried forcibly to stamp out Protestantism after he had legally outlawed it in the revocation edict.

Religious Sanctions

Between 1661 and the recall of the Edict of Nantes the government issued more than 300 orders, declarations, and decrees that affected Huguenots. Many had to do with religious practices. Some laws set the conditions under which synods and consistories could meet; others determined where Protestants could or could not hold public worship; others established rules of conduct for ministers and specified the topics they could mention in prayers and sermons; still others prescribed how funds could be raised and spent. Some of the regulations had only a nuisance value; others definitely crippled the church by restricting its normal activities. All the laws were discriminatory; they stigmatized and penalized still further an already despised minority.

Protestants had experienced difficulty in obtaining permission to hold national synods long before 1661. Their first twenty-six synods had met rather regularly every two to five years; the twenty-seventh met after an interval of six years; the twenty-eighth, after seven years; and the twenty-ninth and last synod met at Loudon in 1659–1660 after a lapse of fifteen years.[21] The king thereafter refused permission for another. He declared on October 10, 1679, that, if he ever allowed another synod to convene, he would appoint a Catholic commissioner to attend its sessions and report to him just what transpired. He wanted to be sure that Protestants meticulously observed a declaration of 1623 which had limited their synodical discussions to religious matters; under no circumstances were they to consider political

---

[21] *BSHPF*, VIII (1859), 145–146.

issues.[22] He likewise ruled on August 21, 1684, that they could hold consistories, or regional business meetings, no more often than every fortnight, and then only if a royal judge was present to see that there was no discussion of prohibited topics.[23]

After 1661, upon one pretext or another the king reduced the number of Protestant temples from 813 to 243.[24] In August, 1662, and again in February, 1669, he declared that Huguenots could conduct public worship only in those localities where it had been permitted before 1598 and had never been discontinued.[25] This automatically banned organized Protestantism in all territories added to France since Henry IV had signed the Edict of Nantes, unless the inhabitants had been granted special religious concessions or guarantees at the time of annexation.[26] Louis also sought to prevent Huguenots living in areas where there were no temples from moving to places where public worship was still permissible. On August 6, 1661, for example, he ordered those who had established residence in La Rochelle since 1628 to leave the city; in 1662 he forbade Huguenots to migrate into Alsace; and on October 15, 1685, he expelled from Paris all those who had not lived there more than a year.[27] After 1679 he ordered Protestants to leave such places as Autun, Privas, Châlons-sur-Saône, Châlons-sur-Marne, and Dijon because they had never received explicit permission to reside in those towns.[28] In March, 1682, and again in July and August, 1685, he instructed

---

22 Bibliothèque Nationale, *Fonds français*, MS 21612, fols. 314–315; *Recueil des Édits, Declarations et Arrests concernans la Religion Prétendue Reformée, 1662–1751, Précédés de l'Édit de Nantes,* ed. Léon Pilatte (Paris, 1885), pp. 42–44.

23 Bibliothèque Nationale, *Nouvelles acquisitions françaises*, MS 1555, fols. 139–141.

24 Bibliothèque Nationale, *Fonds français*, MS 7057, fol. 2; *BSHPF*, XXXIV (1885), 449–450; Viénot, *op. cit.*, p. 471 n. 1; Lefèvre, *op. cit.*, pp. 663–672.

25 Bibliothèque Nationale, *Fonds français*, MS 21616, fol. 285; Gaultier de Saint-Blancard, *Histoire apologétique, ou Défense des libertéz des Églises réformées de France* (Mayence, 1687–1688), III, cxvi ff.

26 The areas that had received such guarantees were Metz; Béarn and Lower Navarre; the principality of Sedan; Bresse, Gex, Bugey, and Valromey; and Roussillon, Cerdagne, Franche-Comté, Alsace, and Lorraine (Bibliothèque de la Société Protestante, MS 6481, pp. 291 ff.). Alsace enjoyed a unique status. It was the only French province to which the revocation edict in 1685 did not apply. When Louis had annexed it in 1648, he had agreed by treaty to allow Alsatians who were already Protestants to retain their religious liberties in perpetuity. (Archives Nationales, A1 756; *Recueil des Édits,* pp. 1–7.)

27 Bibliothèque Nationale, *Fonds français*, MSS 7050, fols. 128–129; 21616, fol. 255; Archives Nationales, TT 232, *dossier* 19, docs. 16, 27; *Recueil des Édits*, p. 246.

28 Archives Nationales, TT 232, *dossier* 20; 240, *dossier* 5, doc. 25; 243, *dossier* 10, docs. 3, 4; Lefèvre, *op cit.*, pp. 672–673.

his intendants to conduct a secret census of Huguenots and of their temples in each province.[29] He did not give his reason for wanting the surveys, but in 1685 he probably wanted to know whether the appropriate time for revoking the Edict of Nantes had arrived; in 1682 he was searching for excuses to confine Protestantism to as small an area as possible and to restrict the number of places where worship was allowable.

It was not difficult for Louis to justify the destruction of 570 temples. Before 1679 he usually contended that the temples had been built or public worship instituted in particular localities after 1598; or that Protestants had discontinued their services at one time or another and hence had forfeited their right to hold public worship; or that it was illegal to have temples in cities his father had had to capture by force of arms during the internal religious troubles of 1621–1629. Later on he devised other excuses. In January, 1684, for example, he destroyed four temples in Languedoc because of recent religious disturbances in that province.[30] Several decrees issued in the early 1680's closed the doors of any church where (1) a Catholic had converted and received communion, (2) children under fourteen whose parents had abjured Protestantism had attended services, (3) a Protestant had married a Catholic, (4) a new convert had been allowed to worship, or (5) anyone had overheard "seditious" discourse.[31]

The Edict of Nantes had stipulated that there was to be no temple in Paris, Versailles, or other cities where the king maintained a residence or where a Catholic archbishop lived. Paris Protestants had therefore developed the habit of frequenting private services held at the Dutch, English, and Danish embassies. In July, 1684, the king commanded De la Reynie, lieutenant general of police at Paris, to clamp down on this practice and to ferret out and punish all Frenchmen who worshiped in foreign embassies or who served as elders or participated in religious activities sponsored by alien governments.[32] Protestant

29 Archives Nationales, O¹ *registres* 26, fol. 81; 29, fols. 351–352; A¹ 795, doc. 40; Bibliothèque de la Société Protestante, MS 485ᴵᴵ, fol. 2; Garnier, *op. cit.*, pp. 377–378.

30 Lefèvre, *op. cit.*, pp. 663–670, 672.

31 Bibliothèque Nationale, *Fonds français*, MSS 20966, fols. 220 ff.; 21617, fols. 14 ff., 113–115; *Recueil des Édits*, pp. 51–53, 196–198. The fervor of provincial persecutors sometimes led them to pay unprincipled converts to Catholicism to frequent Protestant services in order that the government might have an excuse for demolishing the temple (Lavisse, *op. cit.*, Vol. VII, Part 2, p. 69).

32 Archives Nationales, O¹ *registre* 28, fol. 202.

nobles also found that they could not take advantage of the right accorded them in 1598 to hold divine services on their estates unless they themselves actually stayed there, and only individuals who had lived on the estate for at least a year could attend. Finally, public worship was disallowed in any locality where fewer than ten Protestant families resided.[33]

Louis not only destroyed temples and restricted places of worship; he also harassed Protestant ministers. An edict of August, 1684, forbade a minister to remain at one church longer than three years because his parishioners might become personally attached to him. If this happened, the king thought it would be harder to persuade them to abjure their heresy and embrace Catholicism.[34] He also decreed that under no circumstances could ministers reside within six leagues of any locality where he had proscribed public worship.[35]

Protestant ministers also suffered financially. More and more of them lost their pastorates as the campaign to demolish temples gained momentum, and unemployment soon posed a serious problem. The royal council prevented their reallocation to areas where public worship was still allowed by ruling on November 4, 1681, that no church could take on additional pastors to serve its congregation. On January 8, 1685, Louis ordered his agents to include all ministers on the tax rolls and to assess their property for the taille despite the fact that in 1624 his father had extended them the same exemptions from property taxes as the Catholic clergy enjoyed, and although he himself had reaffirmed these exemptions in 1669. The king justified his action on the ground that the original exemptions had applied only to household furnishings, pensions, and salaries, and that administrative laxity alone had allowed acquired or inherited real property to escape taxation. In other words, he maintained that he was simply hewing to the letter of the law. It is significant, however, that he did not apply the same interpretation to property similarly acquired by priests.[36]

---

33 *Recueil des Édits*, pp. 117–118, 176–177, 189–190.

34 *Ibid.*, pp. 153–155; Bibliothèque Nationale, *Fonds français*, MS 21617, fols. 73 ff., 81–82. On July 13, 1685, the king also limited to three years the term of service of ministers employed on the private estates of Protestant nobles.

35 By *arrêts* dated July 13, 1682, and May 17, 1683, and by declaration dated August 6, 1685 (Bibliothèque Nationale, *Fonds français*, MS 21617, fols. 69, 83–84; *Recueil des Édits*, pp. 116–117).

36 Bibliothèque Nationale, *Fonds français*, MSS 21616, fol. 288; 21617, fols. 68, 76–77; *Recueil des Édits*, pp. 177–179; Lefèvre, *op. cit.*, pp. 540–541.

Another series of orders issued after 1679 held a minister personally responsible if any Catholic, relapser, or minor child of newly converted parents frequented his temple. The punishment for the minister involved was unusually severe: public confession of guilt, confiscation of property, and perpetual banishment from the realm.[37] On December 13, 1681, through his secretary of the marine, Louis ordered an agent at Rochefort to imprison six pastors who had provided parishioners planning to flee abroad with letters of introduction to foreign congregations.[38] The king was anxious to prevent lay Huguenots from leaving his realm, and he showered his wrath on anyone who directly or indirectly helped them escape. But he had no intention of restraining the ministers themselves from emigrating. Quite the contrary. He tried to goad them into leaving. Louvois, for example, wrote the Marquis de Boufflers that the king "has always believed that it would be easier to convert his subjects if their Protestant pastors fled abroad." Officials, he added, should not only readily issue passports to pastors upon request but should also prod them into leaving by stationing troops in their homes.[39] A little later the revocation edict ordered all clerics to quit France within fifteen days if they refused to embrace Catholicism, and allowed their wives and children under seven years of age to accompany them into exile.[40]

Some of the rules regulating ministerial behavior and the conduct of religious services seem exceedingly petty. According to orders of March 17, 1661, and February 1, 1669, ministers could not wear clerical garb outside temples, could not call themselves "ministers of the church" but simply "ministers," could not correspond with colleagues in other provinces, and could not greet visiting dignitaries as a group. They could comfort condemned criminals only in a low voice, might never preach or speak out against the Catholic Church or against the king and his policies, and could never censure parents for sending their children to Catholic schools. All their meetings had to be held in authorized temples.[41] Protestants could sing psalms only dur-

---

[37] Bibliothèque Nationale, *Fonds français*, MS 21617, fols. 70 ff., 78–80; *Nouvelles acquisitions françaises*, MS 1555, fols. 98–99; *Recueil des Édits*, pp. 133–134.

[38] Archives Nationales, B2 *registre* 44, fol. 493.

[39] Bibliothèque Nationale, *Fonds français*, MS 7044, fol. 142.

[40] The king even sent a special escort to see that the famous pastor Jean Claude, of the large temple at Charenton on the outskirts of Paris, crossed the boundaries within twenty-four hours (*ibid.*, MS 7050, fols. 126 ff.).

[41] *Recueil des Édits*, pp. 14–26; Lefèvre, *op. cit.*, pp. 550–551.

ing worship, and then only if the procession of the Holy Sacrament was not passing by in the street outside. They could not sing at all if a royal decree had set aside the day for firework displays. They had to bury their dead in Protestant cemeteries either at 6 A.M. or at 6 P.M. from April through September, and at 8 A.M. or at 4 P.M. in other months. The funeral cortege, specifically limited in size, could not stop along its route for any reason.

Many other royal pronouncements underscored these restrictions and further stigmatized the sect. Protestants could not assemble anywhere or anytime except in temples that had never been officially closed and except when their regular minister was present. By a declaration of June 26, 1684, individuals who violated this rule were to be banished for nine years from the district where the meeting was held, fined 3,000 livres, and corporally chastised.[42] Whenever an archbishop or bishop visited a town, all Protestant services there had to be suspended.[43] After May 22, 1683, each temple had to set aside certain pews for Catholics who might wish to attend its service in order to see that the minister uttered no "slanderous" remarks in sermon or prayer. Catholic visitors, furthermore, could always rise during the service to take issue with any statement made from the pulpit.[44] At the behest of the Catholic Clerical Assembly meeting on July 24, 1685, Louis forbade all ministers, publishers, or other persons professing the Reputedly Reformed Religion "to preach or write against the faith and dogma of the Catholic Church or to use slanderous or calumnious language in imputing to Catholics certain doctrines they disapprove or in speaking directly or indirectly about Catholicism."[45]

An order of April 19, 1681, denied pastors, under pain of corporal punishment, the right to visit members of their flock who lay sick and dying. This occasioned so great an outcry that Louis rescinded the order on June 16. At the same time, however, he forbade pastors and others to attempt to dissuade the sick from converting to Catholicism. Pastors might not interfere when priests attempted to convert individuals, nor could pastors use their prestige and persuasiveness to intimidate possible converts. When Louis heard rumors that Protestants had been raising

---

42 Bibliothèque Nationale, *Nouvelles acquisitions françaises*, MS 1555, fols. 84–85; *Recueil des Édits*, pp. 84–86, 120–122, 151–153.

43 *Recueil des Édits*, pp. 38–39.

44 *Ibid.*, pp. 137–139; Bibliothèque Nationale, *Fonds français*, MS 21617, fol. 13.

45 Bibliothèque Nationale, *Fonds français*, MS 21617, fols. 85–88; Lefèvre, *op. cit.*, pp. 220 ff., 269 ff.; *Recueil des Édits*, pp. 98–105, 234–235.

money ostensibly for their needy and sick, but actually to thwart his campaign against heresy, he reiterated in 1680 and 1684 earlier prohibitions against collecting funds without his consent. At the same time he ordered all Protestant churches to present before a royal judge, within thirty days, an exact accounting of every livre they had raised and spent over the past twenty-nine years. He also commanded them (on January 15, 1683, and again on August 21, 1684) to surrender to public hospitals and asylums all the money and properties they had accumulated and earmarked for the relief of their sick and needy.[46]

CIVIL SANCTIONS

Louis XIV signed a declaration of fifty-nine articles on April 2, 1666, regulating the civil conduct and privileges of those professing Protestantism. It evoked such loud protests from Catholics and Protestants alike that in the interest of "promoting peace" between the two groups he revised it by issuing another lengthy declaration on February 1, 1669.[47] These two documents, as modified by several later decrees, in a sense codified the civil and personal liberties of Huguenots and embodied most of the legal sanctions directed against them. A few examples will suffice to indicate the nature of the sanctions.

Over the years the king had become increasingly concerned about interfaith marriages, which he thought dangerously exposed the Catholic spouse to heretical beliefs. At first (in 1669) he ruled that ministers could not marry a Catholic and a Protestant if anyone raised an objection. Then, in November, 1680, he outlawed interfaith marriages in France under any circumstances and declared that the children of such unions would be illegitimate and incapable of inheriting property.[48] When he learned that young couples were evading the law by eloping to foreign countries and there being married before returning home, he issued another declaration on June 16, 1685, which proscribed this practice.[49]

He also tried to prevent Protestants from proselyting their

---

46 *Recueil des Édits*, pp. 86–88, 128–130, 171–172; Lefèvre, *op. cit.*, pp. 494–500; Bibliothèque Nationale, *Nouvelles acquisitions françaises*, MS 1555, fols. 90–93, 143–144.

47 Bibliothèque Nationale, *Fonds français*, MS 21616, fols. 284 ff.; *Recueil des Édits*, pp. 14–26.

48 Bibliothèque Nationale, *Fonds français*, MS 21617, fol. 114; *Recueil des Édits*, pp. 61–62, 143–144. He reaffirmed this in August, 1683.

49 *Recueil des Édits*, pp. 194–196.

employees. An order dated February 16, 1671, had forbidden Huguenots to persuade any of "their valets, servants, sharecroppers, and other domestic and paid employees" to renounce the Catholic faith. If a worker joined the Protestant Church while employed by a Huguenot or within six months after leaving his employ, or if a Huguenot hired a person within six months after the individual had renounced Catholicism, the employer faced a fine of 500 livres.[50] This law proved relatively ineffective, for enforcement was difficult and evasions were frequent. Each year many young Catholics working for Protestant merchants, for example, disappeared from their local communities after changing religion, and their friends at home later learned that they were serving as clerks and factors in their employers' foreign offices in England, Holland, and Geneva.[51] Such flaunting of the law naturally displeased Louis, and he doubtless would have taken more drastic action—such as denying Protestants the right to employ Catholics in any capacity—had he not been afraid of compromising industry and trade. However, on July 9, 1685, he did forbid Protestants to hire Catholics as domestic servants under any circumstances and established a fine of 1,000 livres for offenders.[52]

The king also wanted, insofar as possible, to protect the children of Protestant parents from heresy. This desire eventually led him to violate the sanctity of the home and to curb parental authority, though at the outset he moved with both caution and reluctance. His 1669 declaration, for example, had shown some respect for the family by forbidding priests and other missionaries to seek the conversion of sons and daughters under fourteen and twelve years of age, respectively. A special decree dated June 17, 1681, however, allowed children over six in Protestant families to be converted, and parents could not interfere. Once the children were converted, they could decide whether they wished to remain under the parental roof or to be reared elsewhere. If they chose the latter, no matter how much the converters had influenced the choice, the law required parents to provide subsistence and defray the expense of educating their children in a Catholic institution or private home. This decree

---

[50] Lefèvre, *op. cit.*, pp. 633–634.
[51] Archives Nationales, TT 430, doc. 90.
[52] *Ibid.*, B2 *registre* 55, fol. 416; Bibliothèque Nationale, *Fonds français*, MS 21617, fols. 116–117; *Recueil des Édits*, pp. 203–204, 268.

obviously threw the doors of Protestant homes wide open to priests and local authorities whose evangelical zeal often knew no limit. Catholic marksmen, in effect, had open season on Protestant children seven years of age and older. The king subsequently ordered (on January 31, 1682; June 17, 1683; July 12, 1685; and August 14, 1685) that all bastards had to be reared in the Catholic faith, all children under fourteen had to have Catholic tutors if their parents converted or if they were orphans, and they had to be reared in the mother's religion if she was Catholic and the father died a Protestant.[53]

The decree of June 17, 1681, had also ordered parents to bring home any child being educated abroad. Protestant merchants protested in vain that their sons should study in foreign countries so as to learn other languages, observe business practices, and develop commercial contacts which might later prove valuable. Louis was not impressed. He reiterated his sanction against sending abroad any child under sixteen. The danger of exposing young Frenchmen to heretical ideologies in England, Holland, Switzerland, and similar hotbeds of Protestantism seemed to him to outweigh by far the benefits that might conceivably accrue to the economy.[54]

The king also became interested in the education of young Protestants in France. The Edict of Nantes had allowed Huguenots to maintain their own schools for teaching reading, writing, and arithmetic. All had gone well until the king heard rumors that several of these schools had broadened their curricula to include the humanities and similar liberal subjects. On November 9, 1670, he ordered all headmasters to confine their instruction to the three essentials. Later on he acted more vigorously. On July 9, 1681, he closed the academy at Sedan because it was attracting Protestant ministers from Champagne and other neighboring provinces and because, he claimed, there were not enough Huguenots in the area to justify keeping it open. He also attacked the renowned Protestant university at Caen and circumscribed its activities. On January 11, 1683, he ruled that Protestants could not maintain schools in any locality where he

---

53 Bibliothèque Nationale, *Fonds français*, MS 21616, fols. 345–346; *Recueil des Édits*, pp. 88–90, 107–108, 141–143, 215–216, 231–232; Lefèvre, *op. cit.*, pp. 621–623.

54 Louis occasionally authorized exceptions to this rule if wealthy merchants posted a sufficient bond to guarantee their sons' return. See, for example, a letter written by Seignelay in the Archives Nationales, B² *registre* 55, fol. 120.

had forbidden public worship.[55] His purpose in all this, of course, was to bring education under the direct supervision and control of the Catholic Church.

Even the peace of the sick and dying did not remain inviolate. The declaration of 1669 had not allowed a Catholic priest or curate to invade a Protestant home unless the sick had sent for him and unless a "magistrate, alderman, or consul of the locality" accompanied him. But the stubborn reluctance of the sick to convert on their deathbeds eventually caused the king to lose patience and to change his policy in 1680–1681.[56] Thereafter, any ordinary judge or first consul could enter a sickroom and inquire whether its occupant wished to see a priest and abjure his heresy before dying. If the sick gave an affirmative answer, no member of the household nor any other Protestant could object or try to bolster the invalid in his original faith. Protestants had to shut their doors and deny succor to fellow Religionists who were indigent and sick. Instead, they were supposed to refer the suppliant to a public hospital. The king was anxious that no Protestant be available to a dying or starving patient who showed the slightest inclination to convert.[57]

Louis further discriminated against Huguenots by systematically removing them from public and quasi-public offices. This was in distinct violation of the Edict of Nantes, which had declared Protestants eligible for all offices and dignities whether elective or appointive, royal or seignorial, municipal or provincial. Protestants had taken full advantage of this eligibility in subsequent decades, and had become so firmly ensconced in officialdom that their power and influence, especially in areas where many other Protestants resided, made Louis uneasy. He decided at an early date to ease them out of office whenever he could devise a plausible excuse, and after 1679 he launched a comprehensive campaign directed toward that end.

His first move was to announce, on August 28, 1656, that all city consuls or aldermen in Montpellier had to be Catholic. The royal council later issued at least seventeen similar orders, mostly after 1669, for as many different cities.[58] These orders clearly

55 Lefèvre, *op. cit.*, p. 461; *Recueil des Édits*, pp. 96–97, 127–128.

56 By declarations dated November 19, 1680; April 7, 1681; and June 20, 1681; and by order of the king's council dated June 16, 1681 (*Recueil des Édits*, pp. 68–69, 75–77, 86–88, 91–92).

57 *Ibid.*, pp. 169–170; Bibliothèque Nationale, *Nouvelles acquisitions françaises*, MS 1555, fols. 123–124.

58 Lefèvre, *op. cit.*, pp. 449, 451, 453, 454–459; *Recueil des Édits*, pp. 71–73.

went against an earlier ruling of Louis XIII (October 19, 1631) providing that only the first consul in each city had to be Catholic and that no more than half the others could be Protestant. The 1669 declaration stated that only Catholics could serve as registrars of consular houses or as secretaries of municipal commonalties; it limited Protestants to such unimportant elective municipal posts as clockkeeper and porter. Seigneurs of "high justice," who had the right to pronounce capital punishment against people living on their lands, were forbidden to appoint Protestants as judges (after November 6, 1679) or as court recorders, notaries, attorneys, or constables (after December 2, 1680).[59] Colbert informed all intendants on October 18, 1680, that His Majesty, hoping to encourage many career officials to convert, had recently announced that he wanted to get rid of any Huguenot serving his royal person. Later on, in the summer of 1683, the king inquired of all intendants whether they had carried out his wish and removed from office anyone who refused to accept Catholicism. Most intendants replied that they had, and that Huguenots no longer held government offices in their jurisdictions.[60] A few apologized for having retained one or two nonconformists because they had been unable to find suitable replacements.

The number of offices from which Protestants were excluded continued to grow as new regulations appeared. According to orders dated June 28, 1681, and February 3, 1685, notaries had to vacate and sell their offices to Catholics; solicitors, bailiffs, and constables had to do the same after June 15, 1682; and an order of September 29, 1682, required Protestant members of the local police and the gendarmery to surrender their badges "within three months without delay."[61] On March 4, 1683, the royal council ordered that Protestant officials in royal households be relieved of their duties within two months. On January 19, 1684, and July 13, 1685, the council also ousted those who had become advisory secretaries to the king through purchase, re-

---

[59] Bibliothèque Nationale, *Fonds français*, MS 21616, fols. 332–333; *Recueil des Édits*, pp. 70–71. It is interesting to note that the Edict of Nantes had specifically allowed seigneurs of high justice to appoint Protestants as judges, and also that the royal council, in 1668 and 1673, had upheld this right by invalidating two attempts by the Parliament of Toulouse to abridge it (Bibliothèque Nationale, *Fonds français*, fols. 316–321).

[60] Clément, *op. cit.*, VI, 140–141; Archives Nationales, G7 101, 355, 449.

[61] Bibliothèque Nationale, *Nouvelles acquisitions françaises*, MS 1555, fols. 38, 154; *Recueil des Édits*, pp. 113–116, 124–125.

voked all the privileges and tax exemptions of those who had bought positions as "royal honorary secretaries," and canceled pensions to widows of such officials unless the women immediately joined the Catholic Church.[62]

Protestant nobles fared no better than others of their sect. They not only had to vacate whatever positions in government they had purchased and to surrender the prestige and social esteem they had thereby acquired, but sometimes they even had to prove that they belonged to the nobility. Louvois, for example, wrote the intendant Bâville on March 22, 1685, that the king heartily endorsed Bâville's suggestion as how best to persuade noble families in lower Poitou to convert:

I shall prepare immediately the necessary decree that will enable you to investigate the irregularities that emerged during the last general examination of nobility titles. This decree will be couched in general terms and will make no allusion to religion. His Majesty intends, nevertheless, that you employ it only against those of the Reputedly Reformed Religion. He does not think it appropriate that you investigate the titles of Catholic noblemen.[63]

Many Huguenots who were not of the nobility had managed over the years to entrench themselves in government finance at the local, provincial, or national level. They wielded considerable influence in their communities either because of the social prestige accorded to anyone in constant communication with intendants and other high royal officials, or because of the economic power exercised by those who collected and handled government funds.[64] Louis resented their influence. He felt that they were a potential threat to his conversion campaign, and he resolved to get rid of them. The "Regulation of the Tax Farms," signed on June 11, 1680, and reinforced by a formal order of council on August 17, forbade tax receivers to subcontract with Protestants or to employ them in any capacity whatsoever to collect direct and indirect taxes or to sell tobacco and salt.[65] Colbert instructed all intendants to see that the order was strictly observed.[66]

---

62 Bibliothèque Nationale, *Fonds français*, MSS 21616, fols. 368–369, 375–376; 21617, fols. 237–238; *Recueil des Édits*, pp. 135–136, 147–148, 219.

63 Bibliothèque Nationale, *Fonds français*, MS 7044, fol. 104.

64 Archives Nationales, G7 337; TT 232, *dossier* 20, doc. 18.

65 Bibliothèque Nationale, *Fonds français*, MS 21616, fols. 326–328; *Recueil des Édits*, pp. 54–55.

66 Archives Nationales, G7 1, 296, 390; Garnier, *op. cit.*, pp. 372 ff.; Rossier, *op. cit.*, pp. 213–214.

Enforcement was not simple or easy. Many Protestant tax farmers and collectors were so efficient and reliable that intendants could not replace them with local Catholics, whom they considered generally less trustworthy, without risking a reduction in the net revenues reaching the Crown.[67] While serving as intendant in Languedoc, Daguesseau, for example, admitted to the controller general in August, 1682, that Protestants were still farming taxes in his jurisdiction despite the king's orders. They managed to do this by employing Catholics to serve as their blinds. "Although everyone is aware of the deception," Daguesseau continued, "I have decided to do nothing about it unless I receive your explicit instructions to act; it will be difficult to correct the abuse without jeopardizing the king's fiscal interests."[68] At least once after 1680 Louis himself allowed a Protestant to continue as tax collector. He permitted the collector of the octroi at Grenoble, who still had three years remaining in the office he had purchased, to complete his term, but urged converters in the area to focus all their skills on the poor man.[69] That the 1680 regulations governing tax farming were not everywhere fully enforced may be inferred from a letter written by the intendant at Limoges on January 26, 1685, who suggested what he thought was a novel idea. If the king wanted to hasten conversions, he should seriously consider removing all Protestant tax collectors from office![70]

ECONOMIC SANCTIONS

As a penalized minority French Huguenots had concentrated their energies on economic activities with remarkable success. Catholics, envying their influence, distrusted and disliked them. Catholic laymen applauded their sovereign each time he curtailed the religious and civil liberties of Protestants, and especially when he sanctioned a new form of economic discrimination.[71] What occurred at Saint-Quentin in Picardy in 1664–1667

---

[67] Archives Nationales, G7 239.

[68] *Ibid.*, G7 1, 296.

[69] *Ibid.*, G7 1.

[70] Bibliothèque de la Société Protestante, MS 485[IV], fol. 40.

[71] Cf. *BSHPF*, XXV (1876); Benoist, *op. cit.*, p. 306; Paul Bert, *Histoire de la révocation de l'édit de Nantes à Bordeaux et dans le Bordelais (1653–1715)* (Bordeaux, 1908), pp. 29–32; Gaston-C.-A. Bonet-Maury, *Histoire de la liberté de conscience en France depuis l'Édit de Nantes jusqu'à juillet 1870* (1st ed.; Paris, 1900), p. 39; Guitard, *op. cit.*, p. 44; Émile-G. Léonard, "Une Église protestante de notables (Caen) devant la persécution et la révolution" (unpublished manuscript, 1940); Missècle, *op. cit.*, p. 25; Thompson, *op. cit.*, *passim*.

illustrates how Catholics felt about Protestants. The mayor, aldermen, and leading citizens complained bitterly to the controller
general at Paris that the local colony of Huguenots had increased
during the preceding fifty years from 2 to 130 households; that
the Protestants, arriving there as penniless artisans, had become
so wealthy that they rode around in carriages and bestowed excessively large dowries on their marriageable daughters; and that
they had come to dominate the linen industry after "having
ruined" manufacturers of other textiles. They then asked the
government to aid Catholics (1) by forcing all Protestants to
leave the area, (2) by helping other residents reëstablish the
textile industries that Protestants had destroyed by excessive
price-cutting, and (3) by prohibiting Protestants in the future
from making or dealing in any textiles so that they could never
again secure economic control.[72] Several embittered merchants
at Autun also complained (in 1669) that Protestants had invaded their town, impoverished Catholic tradesmen, and then
left with their ill-gotten riches.[73] It is therefore not surprising
that the Crown found economic sanctions meeting with popular
approval as a weapon against heresy.

Arbitrarily restricting the opportunities for profitable employment was one of the methods employed. Excluding Protestants
from public office, although primarily an infringement of civil
liberties, was also an economic sanction, for many offices—
whether elective, appointive, or venal—provided their incum-
bents with significant incomes. But the government did not stop
here; it systematically tried to ease Protestants out of the professions, various crafts, and trade.

Protestants, for example, found it increasingly difficult to practice medicine because the rules of admission were changed or
because, as in 1685, their licenses were revoked. The Parliament
in Normandy apparently led the way by drastically limiting
the number of Protestants who could practice medicine in the
province.[74] Louis supported this action by letters patent issued
in June, 1670, which stated that no Protestant could be admitted
to the deanery of the College of Medicine at Rouen and no
more than two might be enrolled in the college itself at any

---

72 Alfred Daullé, *La Réforme à Saint-Quentin et aux environs, du XVIe siècle
à la fin du XVIIIe siècle* (Le Cateau, 1901), pp. 133–134, 144.

73 Archives Nationales, TT 232, *dossier* 20, doc. 8.

74 Charles Bost, *Récits d'histoire protestante régionale: Normandie* (Le Havre.
1926). p. 81; Frank Puaux and A. Sabatier, *Études sur la révocation de l'Édit de
Nantes* (Paris, 1886), p. 191 n. 1.

one time.[75] With the passing years the king became increasingly concerned over reports that Protestants were dominating the medical profession. He feared they might fail to inform Catholic patients when death was imminent so as to prevent a priest from being called in to administer extreme unction. This possibility, he thought, justified excluding Protestant women from midwifery (February 20, 1680)[76] and forbidding any Religionist to enter the medical profession after August 6, 1685. A month later he ruled that only doctors, surgeons, and apothecaries who professed Catholicism could continue their practice no matter when or under what circumstances they had received their licenses.[77]

Protestants encountered similar difficulty when they sought to practice law. The Parliament of Normandy again took the initiative by arbitrarily ruling, on December 3, 1674, that only ten Religionists could be attached to its principal court and only two to its inferior court.[78] Later on the king ordered that Protestants could not fill subaltern judicial posts anywhere. Judges were forbidden in August, 1684, to appoint a Protestant as legal expert in any lawsuit because he might show prejudice against a Catholic involved in the suit. Finally, on July 10 and 11, 1685, Louis ordered judges, lawyers, and others of the judiciary to hire only Catholic clerks; he removed from the bench any judge married to a Protestant; and he barred all Religionists thenceforth from entering the legal profession.[79]

Although craftsmen usually wanted to exclude Huguenots from gilds, the Crown was reluctant to go that far. On June 28, 1665, for example, it explicitly reaffirmed the right of Protestants to join most gilds[80] and threatened any organization that violated this right with a fine of 3,000 livres.[81] According to the royal declaration of February 1, 1669, no gild could refuse to accept

---

[75] Lefèvre, *op. cit.*, pp. 444–446.

[76] *Recueil des Édits*, pp. 49–51. Louis also feared that Protestant midwives would allow the newborn to die without baptism and would rear in their own faith any illegitimate children whom they delivered, for custom placed such infants in the charge of the attending midwife.

[77] *Ibid.*, pp. 229–230, 237–238; Bibliothèque Nationale, *Fonds français*, MSS 10623, fols. 53–54; 21617, fols. 136–137.

[78] Lefèvre, *op. cit.*, pp. 437–438.

[79] *Recueil des Édits*, pp. 56–61, 162–163, 210–214; Lefèvre, *op. cit.*, pp. 441–442; Bibliothèque Nationale, *Fonds français*, MSS 21616, fols. 383–384; 21617, fols. 118–123.

[80] The king had declared on July 21, 1664, that only Catholics could join the gilds he had recently chartered to commemorate his marriage, the birth of his first son, and the end of the war with Spain (Archives Nationales, TT 231, *dossier* 2, doc. 28).

[81] Bibliothèque Nationale, *Fonds français*, MS 21616, fols. 272–273.

an individual who had satisfactorily completed its apprenticeship and masterpiece requirements simply because he was Protestant, nor could it oust him if he had already been accepted as a member without having met these requirements.[82] On at least two other occasions Louis appeared to be championing the economic liberties of Protestants: when the Norman Parliament ruled in 1665 that Protestants might constitute no more than one-fifteenth the membership of the goldsmiths' gild at Rouen, he invalidated the law;[83] and in 1670 he commanded a reluctant gild of Paris merchants to accept a Protestant applicant as an apprentice.[84] Colbert may well have been responsible for what the king did in these instances. He realized, if the king did not, that the economy as a whole would suffer if Catholics succeeded in barring Huguenots from craft and merchant gilds.

At no time, however, did Louis want to see Protestants dominate any gild. On April 24, 1667, upon hearing that they were practically monopolizing several crafts in Languedoc, he arbitrarily limited their number in any one gild there to one-third its total membership.[85] He reaffirmed this order on February 1, 1669, and at the same time stated that at least half the members of any guild in other provinces had to be Catholic.[86] These rulings failed to accomplish their purpose. Protestants still outnumbered Catholics in several gilds in Languedoc as late as 1684, and the king had to remind goldsmiths at Blois in 1680 that their gild included far too many Protestants.[87]

Huguenots found it increasingly difficult after 1669, and especially after 1679, to enter crafts either as apprentices or as master workmen. Both cities and gilds sought permission to exclude them.[88] Some officials suggested that the king incorporate each art or craft and issue it a charter explicitly restricting its

---

82 *Recueil des Édits*, pp. 14–26.

83 On September 18 and November 10, 1665 (Archives Nationales, TT 265, *dossier* 3, doc. 54; Bibliothèque Nationale, *Fonds français*, MS 21616, fols. 274–277).

84 Bibliothèque Nationale, *Fonds français*, MS 21616, fols. 292 ff.

85 *Ibid.*, fol. 287; Robert Garrisson, *Essai sur l'histoire du protestantisme dans la généralité de Montauban sous l'intendance de N.-J. Foucault (1674–1684)* (Musée du Désert en Cevennes, 1935), pp. 157–158.

86 *Recueil des Édits*, pp. 14–26.

87 Archives Nationales, TT 247, docs. 177, 180; 255, *dossier* 24, doc. 115; O1 *registre* 24, fol. 132.

88 *Ibid.*, TT 231, *dossier* 2; 232, *dossier* 20, doc. 8; 236, *dossier* 10, docs. 3, 4; G7 355; Bibliothèque Nationale, *Fonds français*, MS 21616, fol. 294; Bert, *op. cit.*, pp. 25–26, 28–29.

membership to Catholics.[89] Others recommended legislation limiting the proportion of Protestants in each craft whether it was organized as a gild or was free. The Parliament at Toulouse in 1682 followed both suggestions. It sought to establish an exclusively Catholic gild for silkworkers, and it also restricted to one-third the proportion of Protestants to Catholics in every other organized or unorganized craft in the province.[90] Several gilds in other places obtained legal permission to exclude Huguenots entirely: for example, seamstresses in Paris (August 21, 1665), hosiery dealers (May 13, 1681), barbers and wigmakers (June 13, 1684), printers and booksellers (May 14 and July 9, 1685), and grocers and apothecaries (January 22, 1685).[91] Because one Huguenot embroiderer presumably had persuaded a Catholic apprentice to convert, an order dated July 16, 1669, forbade all Protestant embroiderers to hire Catholics; and a Paris police ordonnance of May 13, 1681, went so far as to deny any craftsman of the Reputedly Reformed Religion the right to train apprentices of either sect.[92]

The king himself was reluctant to bar Protestants from gilds. He preferred more subtle and less overt forms of discrimination. He had earlier promised Protestants that they could freely undertake trade and industry, and he realized that open abrogation of this promise might create an unfavorable impression at home and abroad. He was also afraid it might encourage Protestants to leave the country. If at all possible he wanted to appear honorable in the eyes of the world and to avoid jeopardizing economic activity at home.[93] He recommended, therefore, that his representatives capitalize on the discriminatory practices of

89 Archives Nationales, TT 232, *dossier* 19, doc. 16; Bibliothèque Nationale, *Fonds français*, MS 7057, fol. 46; Daullé, *op. cit.*, p. 162.

90 Archives Nationales, F12 697; TT 247, doc. 69; Léon Dutil, "L'Industrie de la soie à Nîmes jusqu'en 1789," *Revue d'histoire moderne et contemporaine*, X (1908), 320–321; Paul Gachon, *Quelques préliminaires de la Révocation de l'Édit de Nantes en Languedoc (1661–1685)* (Toulouse, 1899), pp. 173–175.

91 Archives Nationales, TT 231, *dossier* 2, docs. 25, 27; Bibliothèque Nationale, *Fonds français*, MS 21617, fols. 235–236; *Nouvelles acquisitions françaises*, MS 1555, fols. 151–152; *Recueil des Édits*, pp. 182–183, 204–205; Puaux and Sabatier, *op. cit.*, p. 190 n. 1; Benoît, *op. cit.*, IV, 29; Lefèvre, *op. cit.*, pp. 433–434.

92 Bibliothèque Nationale, *Fonds français*, MS 21616, fols. 290–291, 341–342; *Recueil des Édits*, pp. 81–84; Lefèvre, *op. cit.*, pp. 431–433. The lieutenant general at Saintes in April, 1685, also forbade Huguenots to have Catholic or Protestant apprentices (Archives Nationales, TT 265, *dossier* 3, doc. 84).

93 See, especially, a letter written by Seignelay to the intendant at Rochefort on July 13, 1685 (Archives Nationales, B2 *registre* 52, fol. 233).

local Catholics rather than circumscribe Protestants' liberties directly through official action. Whenever aggrieved Protestants sought redress, government agents were to dissemble and procrastinate in rendering justice.[94] Seignelay explained this policy in a letter to a local official on December 20, 1679:

The king has learned that a cabinetmaker of the Reputedly Reformed Religion has settled at Clermont and is seeking to become a master craftsman. He has also heard that the provost of the said city has ruled that the man should be allowed to attempt his masterpiece. Although His Majesty wants to keep Religionists out of gilds as much as possible, he deems it inappropriate on this occasion to interpose his authority. I have been ordered, however, to write you that you should inform the provost of Clermont that he should devise so many difficulties that this cabinetmaker will be unable ever to gain admission to the gild.[95]

Louis was even more reluctant to exclude Protestants formally from trade and shipping than he was to bar them from gilds. Gild charters frequently contained technical provisions which he could use to justify exclusion, but he could scarcely expel Protestants from wholesale trade or restrict their maritime activities without letting everyone know that he was trying to herd them into the Catholic fold. He was also afraid of diminishing domestic and foreign commerce. Seignelay, for example, cautioned an agent at Rochefort on March 2, 1682, against handling Protestants in such a way that trade would suffer. Since the king "is not well enough informed about the present trouble at Rochefort," Seignelay continued, "he wishes me to state that his intention, in general, is to allow those of the Reputedly Reformed Religion freely to engage in commerce."[96] Louis repeatedly refused to push Huguenots out of the salt market around La Rochelle or to adopt any of the other drastic proposals suggested by the intendant at Rochefort, who claimed that Protestants were monopolizing the salt trade and discriminating against Catholic salters.[97] On another front, however, the king agreed to revoke certain privileges allowing Protestants to serve as public brokers

---

94 *Ibid.*, O¹ *registres* 24, fol. 132; 28, fol. 440; Guitard, *op. cit.*, p. 45.
95 Archives Nationales, O¹ *registre* 23, fol. 420.
96 *Ibid.*, B² *registre* 46, fol. 112; Guitard, *op. cit.*, pp. 35–36.
97 Archives Nationales, G⁷ 337; TT 232, *dossier* 19, doc. 9; B² *registres* 52, fol. 225; 55, fol. 416.

(*courtiers*). But he did not accomplish very much by doing so. The intendant at Bordeaux put his finger on the difficulty when he complained to the controller general on December 3, 1684, that three Protestants whom he had ousted from the brokerage business in 1680 still managed to dominate Bordeaux's trade with foreigners. The three men had simply employed subservient Catholics to serve as fronts.[98]

Although he hesitated to forbid others to carry on business with Protestant merchants and artisans, Louis saw no reason that he himself should patronize them. He accordingly rescinded the right formerly sold or given to some of them to follow his court as it moved from one royal residence to another, and ordered all of them, whether French or foreign, to sell their businesses to Catholics within a year's time.[99] In addition, Seignelay informed two of his agents in December, 1680, that the king had decided to hasten the conversion of his subjects in every conceivable way. The agents were to favor Catholic merchants over Protestants when they awarded contracts for provisioning the royal fleet, but they were to make sure that Catholics did not take advantage of this favoritism to raise their prices.[100] This particular scheme did not work out very well, at least around Rochefort, for Catholics there were reluctant to bid on government contracts. Five years later Seignelay was furious because no one of either faith was attending the auction. Apparently unmindful of the irony in the situation, he ordered the intendant on October 12 to command Protestant merchants who were sulking because of recent religious differences to submit their bids on naval contracts "as they have always done in the past."[101]

Protestant seamen posed a special problem. If they were unduly harassed because of religion, they might easily escape by jumping ship when their vessels reached foreign ports. This would deprive the French navy and merchant marine of badly needed personnel while strengthening the maritime resources of rival powers. Yet Louis was unwilling to abandon all hope of saving French seamen from eternal perdition. He moved cautiously but resolutely.

---

98 A. M. de Boislisle, *Correspondance des contrôleurs généraux des finances avec les intendants des provinces*, I (Paris, 1874), 34.

99 Archives Nationales, O1 *registre* 29, fols. 151–152; Benoît, *op. cit.*, V, 789.

100 Archives Nationales, B2 *registre* 42, fols. 430, 432.

101 *Ibid.*, B2 *registre* 55, fol. 461.

On December 10, 1680, without once specifically referring to religion, Louis forbade French pilots, calkers, gunners, sailors, and fishermen to serve under foreign flags, and changed the death penalty for offenders, established in August, 1669, to service in his galleys for life. In the same year he required all Protestant naval officers to attend a series of conferences on religion which he hoped would show them the errors of their faith. He also let it be known, through Seignelay, that he had decided gradually to dispense with the services of Protestant maritime officers and commissioners in the hope that mounting unemployment would force them to abjure.[102] As soon as word reached Paris that the dragoons or booted missionaries used in Poitou by the over-zealous Marillac were forcing scores of families to flee to England and Holland, the king on April 5, 1682, forbade Protestant captains to operate boats between La Rochelle and the islands off the coast. Such captains, he reasoned, might allow fugitive passengers to board foreign vessels at sea and thereby escape.[103] This was clearly an emergency measure designed to meet a particular threat. When the threat diminished and some semblance of calm reappeared in Poitou, Louis apparently suspended the order. Some officials along the Atlantic coast subsequently recommended that Protestants be permanently excluded from all maritime employment. Seignelay at once rejected their proposal on the ground that its adoption would inevitably drive the ablest seamen out of France.[104]

At that time he and the king were favoring less direct and less overt forms of penalization. Seignelay, for example, exhorted authorities at Dieppe on February 28, 1684, to see that all vessels armed or equipped in that port hired Catholic sailors in preference to Protestants or at least did not discriminate against Catholics. He had heard that Dieppe merchants always sought to consign their goods to ships commanded and manned by Protestants, and that it was almost impossible for Catholic sailors to find employment or to collect their wages after voyages if they did get berths on a ship.[105] Thirteen months later Seignelay voiced his indignation over what he considered an equally intolerable situation around La Rochelle and Rochefort, where

---

102 *Ibid.*, B2 *registres* 42, fols. 290, 439–440; 43, fols. 101, 195, 261, 278, 592–593.
103 *Ibid.*, B2 *registre* 46, fol. 172. See also *ibid.*, TT 251, *dossier* 15, doc. 123.
104 *Ibid.*, B2 *registres* 45, fol. 208; 51, fols. 353–354.
105 *Ibid.*, B2 *registre* 51, fol. 112.

one-third of all seafaring men and more than half of the 1,200 marine officers in the area were Huguenots. "There is nothing more prejudicial [to Catholicism]," he exclaimed, "than this preference for seamen of the Reputedly Reformed Religion." He recommended, therefore, that government agents reduce most Protestant marine officers to the rank of ordinary seaman.[106] On July 30, 1685, he also approved a plan for forcing Protestants to sell their barks and small sloops plying between La Rochelle and the island of Ré off the coast, provided the intendant could devise a sufficiently plausible explanation for doing so. Seignelay wanted, if possible, to avoid creating the impression that the government was gradually closing all shipping to Huguenots.[107] He became less sensitive on this score as the fatal date for the revocation of the Edict of Nantes approached. In August, for example, he supported a plan for hiring only Catholics on overseas vessels outfitted at La Rochelle, and on October 2 he had the intendant Arnoul inform all owners of small boats handling local wines that the king did not want them to employ Protestant captains or sailors.[108]

In addition to the foregoing restrictions on free choice of occupation, Huguenots suffered still another form of economic penalization: arbitrary and discriminatory taxation. As early as 1664 the city council of Saint-Quentin had tried to collect a special levy against wealthy Protestant merchants. The merchants immediately complained to Colbert, who reprimanded the city fathers and countermanded their action.[109] It is not known how many cities manifested their resentment against Protestants in the same way, or whether they were more successful than Saint-Quentin. After 1679, however, more and more royal officials endorsed discriminatory taxation as one of the best ways to convince Protestants that it would be in their economic interest to convert.[110]

A few persons—like Seignelay—urged caution and suggested

---

106 *Ibid.,* B2 *registre* 55, fol. 235.

107 *Ibid.,* B2 *registre* 52, fol. 243. A month earlier Seignelay had warned the intendant Arnoul that open discrimination against Protestant barks in unloading vessels bringing salt to the port would hurt trade (*ibid.,* B2 *registre* 52, fol. 226).

108 *Ibid.,* B2 *registre* 55, fols. 381–382, 434–435.

109 Daullé, *op. cit.,* pp. 138–141.

110 Archives Nationales, G7 345; Bibliothèque Nationale, *Fonds français,* MS 7044, fol. 28; Garrisson, *op. cit.,* p. 156; François Baudry, *La Révocation de l'édit de Nantes et le protestantisme en Bas-Poitou au XVIIIe siècle* (Trévoux, 1922), p. 23; Lièvre, *op. cit.,* II, 95.

that it would be better if local assessors and intendants dissimu-
lated rather than explicitly justified differential taxation on religious grounds. On November 18, 1681, for example, Seignelay
reluctantly approved a proposal of Arnoul at Rochefort to increase the taille for all Huguenots and to levy a special assessment against those who still held office. "I hope," he wrote,
"that you will be much more circumspect this time than you
have been in the past with most matters of this nature, and that
you will not allow yourself to be carried away by precipitate
zeal."[111] A month later he upbraided Arnoul for having foolishly
posted on the island of Oléron, a Protestant stronghold, placards
that promised all converts to Catholicism complete exemption
from the taille and threatened to double the assessment against
those who refused to convert.[112] Even Colbert, on January 21,
1682, approved Marillac's plan to reduce taxes in Poitou for
those who abjured their heresy and to collect special levies from
Huguenots in public office. Marillac, however, went too far. He
increased the taille from 12 livres to 150 livres for one Protestant,
from 40 to 300 for another, and from 300 to 950 for still another.
When called upon to justify his action, he claimed that he had
merely been trying to correct certain long-standing inequities in
the tax rolls which wealthy Protestants had established by intimidation or cajolery of Catholic assessors. Marillac caused so many
Protestants to flee abroad by "revising" taxes and using dragoons
to force conversions that the king felt compelled to recall him from
Poitou and send him to Rouen instead. Bâville, who replaced
Marillac in Poitou, admitted in a letter to the controller general
on June 29, 1682, that Protestants there "already have more taille
than they can bear."[113]

It is important to note that Arnoul at Rochefort and Marillac
in Poitou evoked reprimands from their superiors at Versailles,
not because they used taxes to penalize stubborn Protestants, but
primarily because they manipulated the tax rolls so ineptly that
they drove Protestants abroad or else caused them to remonstrate against discrimination. Louis was willing to reduce or for-
give taxes for those who converted and gradually to increase the
burdens on those who refused, but he did not want to give the
world cause for branding him a persecutor. He therefore en-

111 Archives Nationales, B2 *registre* 44, fol. 436.
112 *Ibid.*, B2 *registre* 44, fol. 511.
113 *Ibid.*, G7 449; Clément, *op. cit.*, II, 173; Boislisle, *op. cit.*, I, 36.

couraged his intendants to revise their tax rolls quietly and unostentatiously so that Protestants would eventually appreciate the economic advantage of joining the Catholic Church. To facilitate the process, he sometimes even reduced the sums to be collected in a particular province. He also seized opportunities to increase the financial burden on Protestants without openly discriminating against them. On July 9, 1685, for example, he found technical grounds for ruling that they had to contribute like everyone else to the repair and construction of Catholic churches through taxes on real property, even though they had been spared this expense since 1599.[114]

There was little that Protestants could do to stem the upsurge of economic sanctions directed against them. Their one representative at court, the Marquis de Ruvigny, actually had little influence upon government policy. About all he could do was to voice Protestant grievances to the king in the hope of striking a responsive chord. Once Louis made up his mind to exterminate Protestantism and to revoke the Edict of Nantes, Ruvigny was helpless. One of his last memoranda to his sovereign plaintively summarized the economic grievances of Protestants through January, 1685:

It is true that Protestants have not yet seen any order by Your Majesty which explicitly excludes them from the arts, crafts, professions, and commerce; nevertheless, Sire, it is indeed evident that the suppliants no longer enjoy full and complete liberty in these areas. Not to mention the fact that they may constitute only one-third the membership of arts and crafts in cities where they live in very large numbers, they have been excluded from all the trades connected with your household (which they were formerly privileged to exercise) on the ground that they are now unworthy. . . . Furthermore, the hurdles involved in becoming master craftsmen by completing a masterpiece are daily growing more and more insurmountable. Obstacles to their becoming apprenticed and later being accepted [into gilds] are being thrown in their path. . . . As far as commerce is concerned, they have already been forbidden and are daily being prohibited from engaging in trade in such places as Dijon, Autun, and particularly Amiens by orders of your council, which give no other reason for excluding them than their religion.[115]

114 Bibliothèque Nationale, *Fonds français*, MS 21617, fols. 233–234.

115 Puaux and Sabatier, *op. cit.*, pp. 189–192; Archives Nationales, TT 431, doc. 126 (see also docs. 52, 122).

OTHER CONVERSION EFFORTS

Most of the religious, civil, and economic sanctions against Protestants were designed to persuade them to convert. Louis never intended to drive them out of the country. As a matter of fact, he did a great deal to stop them. The possibility that they might escape, however, did not change his over-all plans. Intendants and other officials quickly sensed how their sovereign felt. Le Bret, intendant in Provence, reflected the general attitude of his colleagues when he acknowledged in a letter to Louvois on September 25, 1683, that "one can render no greater service to His Majesty than to convert a large number of Protestants to Catholicism."[116] Pamphleteers, priests, and government officials after 1679 bombarded the court with simple or elaborate schemes for speeding up the program. Their zealous fervor reached white heat in 1685. Intendants—especially in Béarn, Dauphiné, Languedoc, and Poitou—vied with one another to report the longest list of converts.[117] Louis advised his agents in every province to concentrate upon winning the masses rather than upon trying to bring particularly stubborn souls into the Catholic fold. Once the backbone of the sect had been broken, he said, there would be sufficient time to convert the stragglers.[118]

Enraptured and blinded by the progress reports from the provinces, Louis jubilantly wrote Cardinal d'Estrées at Rome, on January 17, 1686, that "of the more than 800,000 or 900,000 of my subjects who were infected with heresy, there remain today scarcely 1,200 or 1,500."[119] There was less reason for rejoicing than the king imagined. In the first place, the information in his possession underestimated the Protestant population before persecution started and exaggerated the number who were abjuring. Secondly, subsequent events were to reveal that most of the so-called conversions were insincere and in the long run did not greatly diminish France's Protestant population. The 1685–1686 reports of mass conversions, nevertheless, had some foundation in

---

116 Bibliothèque de la Société Protestante, MS 444, fol. 44.

117 Archives Nationales, A¹ 756; Bibliothèque Nationale, *Fonds français*, MS 7050, fol. 41; Boislisle, *op. cit.*, I, 48–49; A. Cadier, "Les Églises réformées du Béarn de 1664 à 1685," *BSHPF*, XXX (1881), 111–112; Lesens, *op. cit.*, pp. 168–169; N.-A.-François Puaux, *Histoire populaire du protestantisme français* (Paris, 1894), p. 230.

118 Archives Nationales, A¹ 756; Bibliothèque Nationale, *Fonds français*, MS 7044, fols. 134, 142, 153.

119 Quoted in Lavisse, *op. cit.*, Vol. VIII, Part 1, p. 350.

fact. How, then, were these conversions, sincere or insincere, brought about?

One writer has suggested that the moral and spiritual fiber of Huguenots had deteriorated during the long truce after 1598, when they had grown soft and worldly and had concentrated their energies on economic activities.[120] This would explain, if true, why they knuckled under so readily and in such large numbers when Louis intensified his campaign against them.

One of the most peaceful tactics specifically designed to step up the rate of conversion was to dangle financial benefits before those who appeared ready to renounce their religion. The king's council in 1666, 1668, and 1676 had granted new converts in Languedoc, Guyenne, Dauphiné, and Pignerol a three-year moratorium on the principal of private debts, and had restrained all creditors, especially other Protestants, from trying to recover through legal action the amounts owed them. This rule was extended to all provinces on November 18, 1680. On April 11, 1681, the king offered those who had converted since the first of the year, or who would do so in the future, a two-year exemption from the billeting of troops in their homes and from the cost of lodging soldiers elsewhere.[121] In Poitou, and perhaps elsewhere, Protestants after 1682 received temporary relief from property taxes when they abjured.[122]

The king tried to "buy" conversions in other ways. In 1676–1677 he established a "bank" or fund, with branch offices throughout the realm, to distribute monetary gifts to those who joined the Catholic Church, and placed a former Huguenot (Paul Pellisson) at its head. Its bribes ranged from 5 or 6 livres to 80 or 100 livres, depending upon the individual's social status or bargaining ability. Marillac, while still intendant in Poitou, was told that he could draw drafts on the royal treasury to reward those he converted and that all such drafts would be honored without question.[123] On March 5, 1685, Louvois wrote Marillac's successor the same thing:

---

120 Matthieu Lelièvre, *De la Révocation à la Révolution. Étude sur l'histoire morale et religieuse du protestantisme français pendant un siècle. Première période (1685–1715)* (Paris, 1911).

121 *Recueil des Édits*, pp. 33–35, 64–65, 79–80; Lefèvre, *op. cit.*, pp. 365–368; Bibliothèque Nationale, *Fonds français*, MS 21623, fols. 3, 37.

122 Archives Nationales, G⁷ 1, 449; Clément, *op. cit.*, II, 173.

123 Bibliothèque Nationale, *Fonds français*, MSS 7044, fol. 39; 7048, fols. 15–40; Guillaume-Adam de Félice, *Histoire des protestants de France* (8th ed.; Toulouse, 1895), p. 399; Emmanuel-Orentin Douen, *La Révocation de l'Édit de Nantes à Paris d'après des documents inédits* (Paris, 1894), I, 524; Orcibal, *op. cit.*, pp. 44–45.

His Majesty . . . wishes you to consider whether you could not persuade several individuals to convert if you offered them money to pay part of their debts. His Majesty will not complain if the sums are considerable. But it will be necessary to do all this secretly, for, if the gifts became known, it would defeat their purpose.[124]

Since bribery breeds corruption, graft naturally developed. Many persons abjured more than once just to receive additional gratuities; and at least one young Catholic student gained a scholarship and admission to a military academy by posing as a new convert.[125] Also, unscrupulous individuals began to counterfeit and sell certificates of abjuration to Protestants who found such documents useful in a variety of ways.

Several thoughtful individuals pointed out to the Crown that education and rational appeals constituted the best or the only means of winning sincere conversions. Louis recognized, however, that many local clerics were too ignorant, too corrupt, or too zealous to be entrusted with the task. He consequently urged his bishops and various religious organizations to do the work. To be effective, he thought, they must be ready and able to discuss disputed points of dogma intelligently and to render their sermons and discourses in French rather than in Latin. Foucault reported in 1685, while he was intendant in Béarn, that he had recently translated the ritual of Mass into French and had distributed the translation among Protestants in his jurisdiction. He claimed that this had been instrumental in winning 4,500 converts in three months.[126]

On the whole, however, such things as debt moratoria, tax exemptions, bribes, and appeals to reason either took too much time or affected too few people. And Louis grew impatient as the months and years rolled by. Whereas in 1682 he had roundly upbraided Marillac for wringing abjurations from Protestants in Poitou by force and had publicly shown his displeasure by

---

124 Frank Puaux, "Ephémérides de l'année de la révocation de l'édit de Nantes," *BSHPF*, XXXIV, 128–129.

125 Douen, *op. cit.*, I, 534–535. In an attempt to prevent such abuses an order dated October 10, 1679, required that all certificates of abjuration had to be filed with a royal attorney (Bibliothèque Nationale, *Fonds français*, MS 21616, fols. 312–313).

126 Archives Nationales, G7 113, 132; B2 *registres* 43, fol. 261; 44, fols. 406–407; 49, fol. 128; 55, fols. 381–382; Bibliothèque Nationale, *Fonds français*, MS 21622, fols. 77–106; Bert, *op. cit.*, p. 49.

transferring the intendant to Rouen, by October, 1685, the king had become much less finicky as to the methods used to complete his campaign. Violence and coercion meanwhile had increased in frequency.

Early in 1681 Marillac had turned loose several companies of royal dragoons upon Huguenots in his jurisdiction.[127] As soon as the troops were quartered in private homes they initiated a reign of terror. They emptied larders, destroyed furniture, tortured both men and women, ravished wives and daughters, and committed almost all other conceivable atrocities. Even with due allowance for exaggeration in contemporary accounts, one gets the impression of stark terrorism just as grim as the anti-Semitic nightmare in Nazi Germany.[128] Many thousand Huguenots rushed to abjure. At first the court at Versailles was delighted by the long lists of conversions; then it felt or feigned dismay when complaints and stories about the atrocities reached its ears. Louvois, who had originally encouraged Marillac to use dragoons, quickly dispatched a letter to the intendant on June 2, 1681, demanding to know whether the rumors were true. The minister went on to state that the king wished all troops stationed with Protestant families in Poitou and elsewhere to behave exactly as they did when quartered with Catholics, and that Marillac should refrain from threatening Protestants in any way if they did not renounce their religion.[129] The intendant hastily denounced the rumors of atrocities as untrue, and denied that large numbers of Huguenots had fled the realm and left their fields uncultivated and their shops and looms unattended. Meanwhile, Marillac continued his dragonnade until the king recalled him in February, 1682. Seignelay and other officials in Paris then warned their provincial agents to profit from Marillac's disgrace and to proceed cautiously in winning conversions.[130]

The disorders in Poitou proved to be a prelude to what followed elsewhere. Trouble next broke out in Dauphiné, Vivarais, and Cévennes during the summer of 1683, and troops invaded

---

127 Bibliothèque Nationale, *Fonds français*, MS 7044, fols. 38–40.

128 See, e.g., Benoît, *op. cit.*, IV, 472 ff.; *BSHPF*, XXVI (1877), 462; "Journal d'un marin protestant du XVIIᵉ siècle (Taré Chaillaud)," *BSHPF*, XV (1866), *passim*.

129 Bibliothèque Nationale, *Fonds français*, MS 7044, fols. 44–45.

130 Archives Nationales, G⁷ 449; B² *registres* 44, fols. 255, 377, 407, 417; 46, fol. 288; Bibliothèque Nationale, *Fonds français*, MS 7044, fols. 46, 47, 54; *Nouvelles acquisitions françaises*, MS 1555, fol. 60; Baudry, *op. cit.*, p. 21.

these areas to restore order.[131] Two years later, when nearly all officials were in a frenzy to convince the king that only a few thousand Huguenots remained in his realm, the dreaded dragoons marched again. They went from parish to parish, from city to city, and from house to house.[132] This time Versailles sanctioned the procedure. It is possible that the king was unaware of the horrors involved and merely intended to persuade Huguenots to abjure by threatening them with the inconvenience and financial expense of housing and feeding his soldiers. His instructions to the commanding officer at La Rochelle on September 8, 1685, would suggest this. The officer was to hang the first soldier "who demands anything whatever without paying for it, or who creates the least disorder in his host's household."[133]

Peaceful or violent, the dragoons proved effective missionaries. The intendant at Montauban complained on August 29, 1685, that Protestants in his jurisdiction were converting so rapidly whenever troops approached their town that it was difficult to find enough homes for lodging the soldiers overnight.[134] Marillac, believing himself and his methods in Poitou vindicated, wrote the controller general on October 26, 1685, from Rouen: "I experienced a great joy when I received the glorious edict revoking the Edict of Nantes and when I realized that I had not been so badly mistaken about the methods required to achieve such a great work as others had thought me to be. . . ."[135]

Getting Huguenots to sign abjuration slips did not destroy

131 Archives Nationales, G7 296; TT 276B, *dossier* 7, doc. 16; 452, *dossier* 10, *passim;* Bibliothèque Nationale, *Fonds français,* MS 7044, fols. 70 ff., 91; Bibliothèque de la Société Protestante, MS 444; N.-A.-François Puaux, *Histoire de la réformation française* (Paris and Geneva, 1857–1863), VI, 63 ff.

132 Archives Nationales, G7 450; A1 755, 756, 757; Bibliothèque Nationale, *Fonds français,* MS 7044, fols. 133–134; *BSHPF,* XXVIII (1879), 143; J. Jailliot, "Le Protestantisme dans le Rethelois et dans l'Argonne jusqu'à la révocation de l'Édit de Nantes," *Revue d'Ardenne et d'Argonne,* XIII (1905–1906), 203; Jean Bianquis, *La Révocation de l'édit de Nantes à Rouen, essai historique* (Rouen, 1885), p. lv; J.-A. Galland, *Essai sur l'histoire du Protestantisme à Caen et en Basse-Normandie de l'édit de Nantes à la Revolution (1598–1791)* (Paris, 1898), p. 214, n. 1. Seignelay, most of the time, and Louvois, occasionally, still cautioned their correspondents to treat all seamen, merchants, bankers, and heads of manufactories circumspectly, lest they flee to foreign countries (Archives Nationales, A1 756; B2 *registre* 55, fols. 368, 448, 453).

133 Archives Nationales, A1 756. Similar instructions were sent another person on July 31, 1685 (Bibliothèque Nationale, *Fonds français,* MS 7044, fols. 133–134).

134 Archives Nationales, G7 391.

135 Boislisle, *op. cit.,* I, 56.

Protestantism. They had to be kept from relapsing into their former beliefs and practices. As early as 1663–1666 the king had thrice declared that any new convert, Catholic priest, or person "engaged in the sacred orders" who accepted Protestantism was to be banished forever from his realm as a "relapser." The threat of perpetual banishment, however, was not sufficient to deter new converts from reverting to their former religion. They could retire to Savoy, Geneva, or similar neighboring places and still visit their relatives and friends in France clandestinely. On March 13, 1679, Louis accordingly stiffened the punishment to include confiscation of all property and amende honorable.[136] He also forbade (in July, 1667; June, 1680; and May, 1683) any Catholic to join the Protestant Church and any Calvinist pastor to receive such a person into the faith.[137] As the succeeding chapter will show, the laws against relapsing became much more severe after the revocation edict appeared.

Despite all the religious, civil, and economic discriminations he sanctioned or condoned, and despite his efforts to win conversions by bribery, persuasion, or force, Louis XIV was able only to subdue rather than to stamp out Protestantism before October, 1685. He made a great mistake when he concluded that his campaign had been highly successful. Most of his new converts had not sincerely abjured their faith and embraced Catholicism. As was clearly demonstrated later, they readily reverted to their former religious practices or awaited an opportunity to escape from France. After the first initial upsurge of panic among them subsided, persecution, like the religious wars of the preceding century, served mainly to strengthen their resolve and zeal. Louis's troubles with Protestants consequently multiplied, rather than diminished, after he outlawed their religion.

---

[136] *Recueil des Édits*, pp. 9–12, 36–38; Lefèvre, *op. cit.*, pp. 372–379.

[137] Bibliothèque Nationale, *Fonds français*, MSS 21616, fols. 303, 324–325; 21617, fols. 70 ff.; *Recueil des Édits*, pp. 51–53.

III

Penalization after the Revocation

From the Revocation through the Revolution

The "King's Edict Revoking the Edict of Nantes and Forbidding Any Public Exercise of the Reputedly Reformed Religion in His Realm" was duly sealed and proclaimed throughout France on October 18, 1685. The Council of Conscience, which dealt with religious matters, had drafted it in September; the royal council had then studied and revised it; and Louis had probably signed it on October 17.[1] The edict was not hastily conceived. As the evidence presented in chapter ii amply demonstrates, the king had long been fighting Protestantism, and he may have been planning to issue such an edict since 1679.

In the preamble Louis XIV attempted to justify revoking the Edict of Nantes. According to him, Henry IV had formulated and signed the religious truce in 1598 and Louis XIII had reaffirmed it in the Edict of Nîmes in 1629 only to give themselves sufficient time to convert all Protestants. War and other emergencies, however, had absorbed most of their energies, and they had not been able to do very much in the way of establishing religious unity. Louis XIV himself confessed that numerous national and international problems had prevented his working toward the same goal until the cessation of war in 1678. Since then he had diligently striven to rid his realm of heresy. He had been so successful, he said, that the Edict of Nantes and all subsequent decrees confirming it no longer served any useful

---

1 Bibliothèque Nationale, *Fonds français*, MS 21617, fols. 146–149; Frank Puaux, "Ephémérides de l'année de la révocation de l'édit de Nantes," *Bulletin de la société de l'histoire du protestantisme français*" (hereinafter cited as *BSHPF*), XXXIV (1885), 497.

purpose. Now was the time to efface from public memory all religious differences that had unhappily divided his subjects in the past. The best way to accomplish this, he concluded, was to revoke the Edict of Nantes.

The main body of the "perpetual and irrevocable" edict of October, 1685, included twelve articles. Article I formally revoked the Edict of Nantes—itself "perpetual and irrevocable" —and ordered the immediate destruction of all Protestant temples. Articles II and III forbade Protestants to assemble at any place or for any purpose and withdrew the right of seigneurs to hold Protestant services on their estates.

The next three articles concerned ministers. Those who refused to abjure had to leave the country within fifteen days and might not exhort or preach in the meantime, under pain of being sent to the galleys. Those who embraced Catholicism could continue to enjoy exemption from the billeting of troops and from property taxes (taille). The king also offered to pension them at a rate one-third higher than their former salaries and to give their widows half their pensions when they died. Any minister who wanted to enter the legal profession could do so by passing an examination and paying half the regular fees without having to study law for three years as was normally required.

Article VII prohibited any school from offering instruction in the Reputedly Reformed Religion; and, according to Article VIII, all Protestants, under pain of 500 livres fine, had to have their newly born infants baptized and reared in the Catholic Church.

The next two articles dealt with emigration. The king urged those who had already fled abroad to return to France within four months and recover their property; if they did not, they would permanently forfeit all their possessions to the state. Any man who tried to leave the country would face confinement in the galleys, and any woman would suffer "confiscation of body and property." The king reaffirmed in Article XI all his previous proscriptions against relapsing.

Finally, Article XII stated that "until such time as it may please God to enlighten them like the rest, those of the Reputedly Reformed Religion may live tranquilly in France, continue their business, and enjoy their possessions without let or hindrance, on condition that they perform no public exercise of their cult and do not assemble." [2] This curious article provoked considerable debate as to its meaning and intent. Taken at face value, it seemed to proclaim liberty of conscience and protection of Protestants from discriminatory and retaliatory violence.[3] Intendants and clerics at once voiced their misgivings to the king, predicting that the twelfth article would nullify all efforts to gain additional converts. They feared that Huguenots who had refused to abjure in the past would insult and taunt those who had been less steadfast, and that many would refrain from attending Mass and other Catholic services under the impression that the government no longer intended to enforce religious conformity.[4] As a matter of fact, many Protestants got this impression, and Louis felt compelled to clarify his intentions. Early in November he asked Louvois and Seignelay to prepare letters of instruction for all intendants and other important provincial officials.[5]

These letters were unambiguous. They flatly denied that the twelfth article in any way changed the king's attitude toward Protestantism. All officials were to work just as diligently at conversion as they had been instructed to do previously. They were to lodge additional troops in the homes of the most obstinate Huguenots "in order better to disillusion them of the false idea they may have gained from the edict." Protestants who insulted and upbraided others for having been too eager to abjure were to be severely punished with heavy fines and imprisonment. If a priest or a neighbor, however, accused a new convert of failing to attend Catholic services, officials were to investigate carefully before punishing the culprit because unreasonable fervor or passionate jealousy might have led the accuser to distort the facts. It was also suggested that persuasion,

---

2 *Recueil des Édits, Declarations et Arrests concernans la Religion Prétendue Réformée, 1662–1751, Précédés de l'Édit de Nantes,* ed. Léon Pilatte (Paris, 1885), pp. 239–245.

3 Charles Benoist, *Condition juridique des protestants sous le régime de l'Édit de Nantes et après sa révocation* (Paris, 1900), p. 278.

4 Bibliothèque Nationale, *Fonds français,* MS 7044, fol. 182; Bibliothèque de la Société Protestante, MS 444, fol. 136; Alfred Leroux, *Histoire de la réforme dans la Marche et le Limousin (Creuse, Haute-Vienne, Corrèze)* (Limoges, 1888), pp. 324–325; L. Rossier, *Histoire des protestants de Picardie, particulièrement de ceux du département de la Somme* (Amiens, 1861), p. 235.

5 Archives Nationales, A1 757; B2 *registre* 52, fols. 292–293; Bibliothèque Nationale, *Fonds français,* MS 7044, fols. 192–193; *Nouvelles acquisitions françaises,* MS 1206, fols. 8–9.

discussion, and education were more effective than and preferable to intimidation and force as methods of inducing new converts to perform their religious duties faithfully.

The king was most anxious to convert all Protestant nobles because of their influence over others of their faith. If peaceful means failed, the instructions stated, soldiers were to be stationed on their estates. At the outset, however, it would be preferable to single out and make examples of individuals whose nobility titles were least well established, whose children had rendered the state the least service, and who were currently embroiled in litigation with neighbors. "In a word," Louvois told his officials, "His Majesty desires you to persuade noblemen that they can expect neither peace nor consideration so long as they persist in a religion so displeasing to His Majesty; you must make them understand that those who seek the foolish glory of being the last to abjure will be treated much more grievously than they can presently imagine." The last instruction ordered that any Protestant receiving seditious letters or anti-Catholic literature had to turn the material over to a local judge at once or suffer a fine of 100 *écus*.

The future of Protestantism in France appeared bleak indeed at the close of 1685. Persecution was rampant everywhere. The outbreak of the War of the League of Augsburg in 1688–1689 provided some respite by diverting the king's attention from religious to military matters. Many Huguenots took hope that the crusade against them was over and that the powers in the Grand Alliance, if victorious over Louis, would insist that he reëstablish the Edict of Nantes as one of the conditions for peace.[6] Neither hope was realized. Because the allies did not want to create the impression that Louis's religious persecution was a cause of the war, they did not demand a reversal of his policy toward French Protestantism. They did, however, urge him to reëstablish liberty of conscience in his realm, release those he had sentenced to the galleys for religious reasons, and cease harassing his Protestant subjects.[7] This may have done more harm than good, for Louis was not one to receive kindly unsolicited advice from outsiders as to how he should govern his kingdom. Moreover, he was already perturbed by persistent rumors that Huguenots had begun to hold clandestine religious

---

[6] Bibliothèque de la Société Protestante, MS 617, *passim*.

[7] Bibliothèque Nationale, *Fonds français*, MS 7036, fols. 108–109.

services and that their ministers were secretly returning from
exile in defiance of his laws. Instead of following the allies'
advice, he decided to evaluate his whole anti-Protestant program
and, if possible, make it more effective.

In 1698 Louis asked several outstanding clergymen and statesmen to review events since the revocation and to suggest feasible
methods for accomplishing his original objective. No one went
so far as to recommend rescinding the revocation edict, but there
was disagreement as to whether peaceful or coercive tactics
were the better way to win sincere conversions. In general, those
from the northern part of France favored persuasion, education,
and kindness; those from the southern provinces advocated compelling Protestants to attend Mass and to send their children
to Catholic schools, and strictly enforcing all previous laws against
nonconformity and emigration. After Cardinal de Noailles had
collected and transmitted the advice of the group, Madame de
Maintenon informed him that she was disappointed in his report and warned him that it was likely to prove embarrassing to
the king. She thought it contained too many conflicting opinions
and suggestions, and that Noailles in his own comments appeared
to condemn what the king had sanctioned in the past.[8]

The report had as little effect in persuading Louis to change
his basic policy as the advice received earlier from the allied
powers. The king issued a new edict on December 13, 1698,
reaffirming the revocation, reiterating all regulations and penalties subsequently prescribed, and ordering rigorous enforcement
of all laws against Protestants and especially against Protestant
ministers. He did not mention the last article of the revocation
edict, which some had interpreted as guaranteeing liberty of
conscience, but concluded with the following statement: "We
wish, furthermore, that new converts enjoy their properties and

---

8 Jean Lemoine, *Les Évêques de France et les protestants, 1698* (Paris, 1900), p. 30.
Lemoine offers a useful summary and analysis of the reports submitted in 1698.
Some of the original reports may be found in the Bibliothèque Nationale (*Fonds
français*, MS 7045); and Lemoine states that all reports are in the *Archives de la
Guerre*. In addition, see A. M. de Boislisle, *Correspondance des contrôleurs généraux
des finances avec les intendants des provinces*, I (Paris, 1874), 496; Alfred Leroux,
Les Religionnaires de Bordeaux de 1685 à 1802 (Bordeaux, 1920), p. 16; Abbé Jean
Lestrade, *Les Huguenots dans le diocèse de Rieux, documents inédits* (Auch and
Paris, 1904), p. 160; Claude-Carlomau de Rulhière, *Eclaircissements historiques sur
les causes de la révocation de l'Édit de Nantes, et sur l'état des protestants en
France, depuis le commencement du Règne de Louis XIV, jusqu'à nos jours* (new
ed.; Geneva, 1788), II, 236–237.

exercise their trades as do all our other subjects, provided they continue to seek instruction and confirmation in the Roman Catholic Apostolic Religion."[9]

The king mitigated to some extent the severity of this new edict on January 9, 1699, by sending his intendants and bishops secret instructions about its interpretation and enforcement. Since all Frenchmen were "now happily united in the bosom of the Church," Louis wrote, "there should be uniform and common rules governing the conduct of new converts and other Catholics without drawing any distinction or difference between them." [10] Furthermore, he suggested, it might be unwise to conform to the precise letter of all his laws; they should be viewed as weapons with which to intimidate nonconformists rather than as inexorable rules for punishing offenders. In this connection he specifically mentioned his decrees against relapsing and intermarriage between new converts and Catholics. As a general rule, he continued, no enforcement agency was to resort to violence unless absolutely necessary.

Louis was understandably reluctant to publicize these instructions lest some people interpret them as indicating a tendency on his part to vacillate or recant, and lest new converts become less willing to perform their duties to the Church. Religious offenses had already become numerous, and new issues were constantly arising and absorbing too much of the royal council's time. Louis therefore decided, shortly after he had mailed the instructions, to create a special subcommittee of the council which would meet every two weeks to study religious problems and to make recommendations for handling them.[11]

The 1698 edict rudely disillusioned many Protestants who had foolishly construed the decline of persecution during the war years as reflecting a basic change in policy. Violence flared up once again as overzealous priests and low-ranking government officials, who had not received copies of the secret instructions, took the edict literally. They sought to force all converts to become and remain dutiful Catholics by punishing severely those who strayed from the straight and narrow path. A fresh wave of unrest spread through the provinces, leading many to emi-

---

9 Bibliothèque Nationale, *Fonds français*, MSS 20966, fol. 242; 21617, fols. 174 ff.; *Recueil des Édits*, pp. 371–379.

10 Bibliothèque Nationale, *Fonds français*, MS 20966, fol. 257 ff.

11 Archives Nationales, O1 *registre* 43, fols. 205–206.

grate. This is what happened in the Principality of Orange, a small area completely encircled by France.

The principality had recently endured rough treatment. It had been seized three times by France and twice restored to its rightful sovereign, William of Orange (William III of England). Louis, first seizing it in January, 1673, gave it to the Count of Auvergne; but the Treaty of Nimwegen (1678) returned it to William. Four years later French troops invaded the area under the pretext of preventing its citizens from rebuilding its walls, and remained there despite all William's efforts to reassert his sovereignty. Louis, for the second time, turned the principality over to the Count of Auvergne by brevet dated December 24, 1688, while reserving for himself all sovereign rights. Hence France had control during the critical years immediately preceding and following the revocation of the Edict of Nantes.

Whereas William had made Orange a haven of religious tolerance, Louis attempted to stamp out Protestantism. Dragoons were quartered in private homes and abjurations wrung from hapless victims just as in Poitou and Languedoc. Then, in 1697, the Treaty of Ryswick temporarily put an end to violence by returning the territory to William III. Protestants joyously rebuilt their temples, recalled their pastors, and received back into the church those who had nominally embraced Catholicism. Frenchmen from neighboring provinces began to flock there primarily to worship despite Louis's declarations of November 23, 1697, and January 13, 1698, prohibiting their moving to Orange or attending religious services while visiting there.[12]

Louis seized the principality once again in 1702, upon William III's death; temporarily placed it in the hands of the Prince of Conty, who had very tenuous claims as its heir; and then, on February 3, 1703, annexed and merged it with Provence after giving Conty other territories that would yield him equal revenues.[13] Louis again outlawed Protestantism and exiled all pastors. He also permitted persons who refused to abjure to escape to foreign countries although he later (on September 30, 1703), and somewhat treacherously, ordered the confiscation of their property. Regional historians have estimated that up to 3,000

---

12 Bibliothèque Nationale, *Fonds français*, MS 21623, fols. 16–17; *Recueil des Édits*, pp. 363–368.

13 The Utrecht Treaties formally recognized its annexation to France.

inhabitants sought asylum abroad in 1703 and shortly thereafter. Since he had outlawed Protestantism in the principality, and therefore thought his subjects visiting or settling there would no longer be exposed to contamination by heresy, the king on March 1, 1704, graciously rescinded his earlier orders forbidding Frenchmen to move to Orange.[14]

During the last few years of his long reign Louis seemed less and less willing to recognize or admit that his coercive tactics had not been very effective in destroying Protestantism. In 1711, for example, he initiated another campaign of violence by announcing his firm intention to convert every single person in Orange. At the same time he ordered a new inquiry as to why his Protestant subjects everywhere persisted in their heresy; he reiterated earlier prohibitions against emigration; and he reinvoked the most severe penalties against those who violated his decrees. On March 8, 1715, less than six months before his death, Louis declared that all Frenchmen who had formerly been Calvinists or had been born of Protestant parents would be considered to have joined the Catholic Church whether or not they had actually gone through the formality. They had remained in his realm long after he had outlawed their religion, he argued, and hence were to be treated and punished as relapsers if they failed to conform to all the usual practices of devout Catholics or died while refusing the Holy Sacrament.[15]

This was his last official thrust at Protestantism. It was as futile and as infantile as the action of King Canute, who tried to demonstrate his regal authority by commanding the incoming tide of the sea to halt. One week before Louis died a group of Protestant ministers and elders met in a quarry near Nîmes and held their first "Synod of the Desert." Had he learned of this on his deathbed, Louis might have realized that his harsh and persistent campaign to destroy Protestantism in France

---

14 Bibliothèque Nationale, *Fonds français,* MS 10623, fol. 140; *BSHPF,* XV (1866), 133 n. 1; Eugène Arnaud, "Les Derniers jours de l'église d'Orange, 1703–1731," *BSHPF,* XXXII (1883), 491–492, 497; *Histoire des protestants de Provence, du comtat Venaissin et de la Principauté d'Orange* (Paris, 1884), II, 362 and *passim;* Gaitte, "L'Émigration des protestants de la principauté d'Orange sous Louis XIV (1703)," *BSHPF,* XIX–XX (1870–1871), 337, 340; *Recueil des Édits,* pp. 421–423. Marion E. Grew, *The House of Orange* (London, 1947), pp. 140–185, was especially useful.

15 Bibliothèque Nationale, *Fonds français,* MS 21622, fol. 157; Ernest Lavisse and others, *Histoire de France illustrée depuis les origines jusqu'à la révolution* (Paris, 1911), Vol. VIII, Part 1, pp. 387–388.

had only driven it underground. Its leaders at that time were busily developing a new organization and a new *modus operandi* which were to sustain and revitalize its members spiritually until Napoleon proclaimed liberty of conscience and freedom of worship once again in France.

Religious persecution did not end in 1715. It waned and waxed in successive waves, but at no time was it so violent and so widespread as immediately before and after the revocation or after 1698–1699. The Duke of Orléans was relatively tolerant as regent during Louis XV's minority, and for a time it appeared that the government might again recognize liberty of conscience.[16] Violence diminished both in frequency and in intensity.[17] Emigrants started to drift back to their native land; individuals who still wanted to move to foreign countries encountered little difficulty in crossing the borders; and illegal religious assemblies grew more common and less clandestine.

The quiet interlude did not last long. On May 14, 1724, soon after the regent died, Louis XV issued a declaration approving and reaffirming all that his great-grandfather had done to destroy heresy.[18] He voiced regrets that the laws had been laxly enforced during his minority. The new declaration, by fortifying the zeal of a few local authorities and priests, revived religious unrest and caused some Protestants to emigrate; it did not, however, initiate another prolonged period of persecution.[19] From 1724 to 1745 not many more than twelve men were sent to the galleys; only a few Protestant ministers were hanged; and the police occasionally broke up illicit religious assemblies and imprisoned some of the participants. In this period both the government and the clergy centered their attention primarily upon forcing Protestants to marry and to baptize their children

---

16 Bibliothèque Nationale, *Fonds français*, MSS 7046, fol. 213; 7047, fol. 457; 20967, fol. 2; Jean de la Monneraye, "La Révocation de l'Édit de Nantes et le protestantisme en Bas-Poitou au dix-huitième siècle," *Revue du Bas-Poitou*, 36th year (1923), 79.

17 Only about 19 persons, for example, were condemned to the galleys for religious reasons in the Regency as compared with more than 1,100 in 1685–1715 (see Eugène and Émile Haag, *La France protestante, ou Vies des protestants français qui se sont fait un nom dans l'histoire* [Paris, 1846–1859], X, 407–428).

18 *Recueil des Édits*, pp. 534–550; Bibliothèque Nationale, *Fonds français*, MS 21617, fols. 200 ff.; Émile Lesens, *Le Protestantisme dans le pays de Caux (ancien colloque de Caux, Havre et Dieppe excepté)*, ed. Victor Madelaine (Bolbec, [1906]), p. 254.

19 Leroux, *Les Religionnaires de Bordeaux*, p. 15; B. Vaurigaud, *Essai sur l'histoire des églises réformées de Bretagne, 1535–1808* (Paris, 1870), III, 229.

in the Catholic Church. The last significant wave of violence, which saw 183 Huguenots sentenced to the galleys,[20] occurred between 1745 and 1754.

Most thoughtful Frenchmen had already begun to question the advisability of executing Protestants or of harshly punishing them in other ways. During the latter half of the eighteenth century, however, there were still partisans on both sides of the issue who expressed their views in writing. Some suggested that the king allow Huguenots to emigrate, and a few went so far as to plead openly for religious tolerance. On the other hand, some fanatics urged the completion of Louis XIV's "glorious project" to rid the realm of all religious nonconformity, and others strongly advocated as a minimal program the rigorous enforcement of all extant marriage and baptismal laws. Assailed and bewildered by such conflicting counsel, Louis XV decided in the latter part of his reign to take little or no action.[21] Although their cause became stronger with each passing year, Protestants had to wait until November 17, 1787, for the restoration of many of their civil liberties. In an edict presented to Parliament at that time Louis XVI allowed them to remain in France and follow any profession or trade of their own choosing, to marry before civil justices, to register their children's birth in local courts, and to bury their dead without Catholic ritual.[22] In 1790 the National Assembly went even further and restored all civil and political liberties to Protestants, and Napoleon finally legitimized Protestant worship in 1803.

RELIGIOUS SANCTIONS

The preceding section has done little more than sketch in bold outline the history of penalization from the revocation to the end of the eighteenth century. Innumerable orders and declarations dealing with specific problems and implementing the king's general policy must be examined, for they, more than the

---

20 Haag, *op. cit.*, X, 407 ff.

21 For a fuller discussion of persecution after 1715, see Shelby T. McCloy, "Persecution of the Huguenots in the 18th Century," *Church History*, XX (1951).

22 Bibliothèque Nationale, *Fonds français*, MS 21622, fols. 18–19; François Baudry, *La Révocation de l'édit de Nantes et le protestantisme en Bas-Poitou au XVIII* *siècle* (Trévoux, 1922), p. 225; G. Hérelle, *Documents inédits sur le protestantisme à Vitry-le-François . . . depuis la fin des Guerres de Religion jusqu'à la Révolution française* (Paris, 1903–1908), II, 273. This edict was enrolled by Parliament on January 29, 1788.

major edicts, reveal the intensity and thoroughness of the campaign against Protestantism. Persecution had begun a good many years before October, 1685, and it certainly did not end then. Several hundred thousand Huguenots had not yet converted, and those who had converted rarely behaved as the king and the clergy thought good Catholics should. The revocation edict in some respects was only the first step toward the outlawing of Protestantism; it was little more than a statement of ultimate objectives.

Louis treated Protestant ministers very harshly, for he believed them to be an important potential obstacle to the success of his conversion campaign. In the revocation edict he offered liberal pensions and other concessions to those who abjured, and ordered permanent banishment for those who would not. Louis instructed officials to seize and execute any minister who remained in France or returned from exile without converting. He also offered a reward of 5,500 livres for information leading to the capture of a minister, and threatened to confine to the galleys for life any man, and to imprison for life any woman, who gave shelter or succor to a minister. The pressure became so great that many ministers knuckled under and abjured;[23] others went into hiding among friends; some fled abroad.

It was not very long, however, before a few of the ministers who had emigrated began to return secretly. Both Seignelay and Louis became aware of this infiltration in September and October, 1687. When war broke out about a year later, more and more returned. William III apparently sent several ministers back to France to foment rebellion or at least to stir up trouble in areas with a significant Protestant population.[24] Fear of espionage and internal uprisings led French officials to redouble their vigilance. Between 1685 and 1762 they caught and executed at least forty-six fully ordained or neophyte ministers, and hanged sixteen others in effigy.[25]

The revocation edict outlawed all Protestant assemblies and public worship on French soil, and a special interpretive decree

---

23 Bibliothèque Nationale, *Fonds français,* MSS 10623, fols. 69–70; 21617, fols. 160–163; *Recueil des Édits,* pp. 291–294; Benoist, *op. cit.,* p. 295. Forty-five abjured in Languedoc in 1685 and 1686 and received annual pensions ranging from 350 to 1,200 livres (*BSHPF,* XXXII, 408–412).

24 Archives Nationales, A1 *registre* 903, "Introduction"; B2 *registre* 62, *passim;* Bibliothèque Nationale, *Fonds français,* MSS 7045, fol. 27; 7055, fols. 193–206; 21617, fols. 286–302.

25 Haag, *op. cit.,* X, 406–407.

a week later extended the coverage to French warships and merchant vessels at sea. Participation in such services was punishable by death, according to a declaration of July 1, 1686.[26] The need for galley slaves in the Mediterranean, however, led the minister of war to write Bâville in Languedoc on January 22, 1688, that the king was perfectly willing for him to execute about one of every six men captured at religious meetings provided he sentenced the others to the galleys.[27] Despite Draconian measures like these, Protestant assemblies multiplied in 1689, specially in Dauphiné and Vivarais. A special *ordonnance* of March 21, 1689, reaffirmed the death penalty for worshipers taken during raids and ordered officials to sentence to the galleys for life all others who escaped and were later convicted of having participated.[28] The law was strictly enforced in the provinces during the next few years as fear of internal rebellion and enemy invasion mounted. Troops ruthlessly slaughtered men, women, and children whenever they came upon a Protestant assembly in the open hills and hidden valleys.[29] Terrorism checked the growth of "assemblies in the desert," at least temporarily, but they rapidly increased in number during the eighteenth century.

The diplomatic immunity accorded representatives of foreign governments created a special problem. From July 1, 1686, Louis allowed Protestant countries to send clergymen to France on business or to conduct religious services in their Paris embassies, provided they meticulously confined themselves to official business or to serving the spiritual needs of their compatriots. Frenchmen, however, continued to slip into these religious services as they had done before the revocation. Louis angrily blamed the foreign representatives for admitting his subjects and threatened severe reprisals against them and their countrymen residing in France if they did not conform to his orders.[30] Perhaps his threats had some effect, for apparently he never violated diplomatic immunity. He was unwilling, however, to allow citizens of foreign countries to hold Protestant services while they were in France on private business. When some English

---

[26] *Recueil des Édits*, pp. 247, 291–294.

[27] Archives Nationales, A1 835.

[28] Bibliothèque Nationale, *Fonds français*, MS 10623, fols. 93–94; *Recueil des Édits*, pp. 325–326.

[29] Archives Nationales, A1 *registres* 797, 903, 904, 907, *passim.*

[30] *Ibid.,* O1 *registres* 30, fol. 34; 31, fol. 13; 43, *passim; Recueil des Édits*, pp. 256–257.

merchants, for example, inquired in February, 1686, whether they could worship if they came over to trade, Seignelay informed them that they could pray in private without fear of molestation but could not hold services.[31]

Louis hoped to break the backbone of Protestantism through spiritual starvation. That was why he exiled its ministers and forbade public worship everywhere except in foreign embassies. But he did not stop with this. Once he had outlawed the religion, he felt that he could justifiably use force to get its members to join the Catholic Church. The Venetian ambassador at Paris, writing home on November 14, 1685, made the following comment about Louis's zeal: "At the present moment the only thought of the king is how utterly to exterminate heresy. He does not, however, act with the same dignity he has been accustomed to show in putting down those who offer resistance to him, or who have sought in times past to question his greatness."[32]

After the revocation edict appeared, companies of dragoons again marched from one town to another—this time with full royal sanction—and won over thousands of converts by physical violence or economic spoliation. As troops approached a town, or as rumors spread that they were on their way, thousands of Huguenots converted or fled across the frontier.[33] The instructions Louvois gave his subordinates at Dieppe on November 19, 1685, show why the booted missionaries created such terror:

Spare the obstinate Protestants none of the inflictions that have been prescribed. You cannot make the billeting of troops in their homes too hard on them or too onerous. For example, you should increase as

---

31 Archives du Ministère des Affaires Étrangères, *Ancien fonds*, "Angleterre," *registre* 160, fol. 79.

32 Henry Austen Layard, "The Revocation of the Edict of Nantes. Illustrated from State Papers in the Archives of Venice," *Proceedings of the Huguenot Society of London*, II (1887–1888), 131.

33 Archives Nationales, G7 492; O1 *registre* 29, fols. 545–546, 565; TT 273, *dossier* 2, docs. 3–4; 450, *dossier* 17, doc. 79; A1 757; 906, doc. 116; Bibliothèque Nationale, *Nouvelles acquisitions françaises*, MS 1206, fol. 8; *Fonds français*, MS 7044, fol. 188; Bibliothèque de la Société Protestante, MSS 485II, fol. 111; 648I, pp. 69 ff.; Boislisle, *op. cit.*, I, 54, 58, 309; *BSHPF*, XIII (1864), 232; Rossier, *op. cit.*, p. 235; Paul Courpron, *Essai sur l'histoire du Protestantisme en Aunis et Saintonge depuis la Révocation de l'Édit de Nantes jusqu'à l'Édit de Tolérance (1685–1787)* (Cahors, 1902), p. 27; Jacques Lefèvre, *Nouveau recueil de tout ce qui s'est fait pour et contre les protestans, particulièrement en France où l'on voit l'establissement, le progrez, la Décadence et l'Extinction de la R.P.R. dans ce Royaume* (Paris, 1690), Appendix, p. ii.

much as possible the number of soldiers lodged with each family . . . and instead of the usual twenty sous a day for lodging and food you should allow each soldier to exact ten times this amount. You should allow the dragoons to create all the disorder necessary to bring about a change in their hosts' attitude. This will set a good example for the province as a whole and may serve to intimidate other Protestants to convert.[34]

A month later Louvois wrote an intendant that he was to treat Protestant nobles just as roughly. If the nobles refused to abjure after the troops quartered in their homes had eaten or destroyed all available subsistence, then the intendant should clap the nobles in prison and leave the soldiers in their homes to complete the spoliation; moreover, he should burn to the ground the dwelling of any gentleman who had sought refuge elsewhere.[35]

Bâville, in Languedoc, reported to the controller general on November 18, 1686, that he had recently ordered the winter quartering of troops in the troublesome Cévennes area in order "to cause there a great desolation." By January the soldiers had won so many abjurations and had pillaged the region so completely that the intendant requested permission to distribute among the new converts most of the 100,000 livres given him to reward those who had joined the Church in Languedoc. The controller general, however, denied his request on February 26, 1687. The king was unwilling, he wrote Bâville, to have any of the money distributed in Cévennes, no matter how great the suffering, because the Cevenoles would probably interpret the gesture as a sign of royal repentance or weakness. Hence the beneficence would most likely serve only to counteract whatever success had already been achieved in subduing Protestantism.[36]

The dragoons did not spare important merchants and financiers. Although the rich Parisian banker Samuel Bernard had abjured on December 17, 1685, soldiers entered his home by mistake eighteen days later. Their thefts, property damage, and board amounted to 10,016 livres.[37] Not many Protestants were wealthy enough to withstand such plundering for very

---

34 Bibliothèque Nationale, *Fonds français*, MS 7044, fol. 200.

35 *Ibid.*, fol. 221.

36 Archives Nationales, G7 297; Boislisle, *op. cit.*, I, 88, 97. Boislisle himself estimated that the winter quartering in Cévennes cost the area 310,000 livres.

37 Th. Muret, "Le Banquier protestant Samuel Bernard, dragonné nonobstant conversion en règle, épisode de la révocation de l'Édit de Nantes (1685)," *BSHPF*, V (1857), 49–53.

long. In December, 1685, the attorney general at Paris requested permission to close the shops of the most obstinate merchants and to station archers in their homes. He and the lieutenant general of police both received word on December 11 that "His Majesty approves the proposition and wants you to execute it in the most effective manner consistent with your usual prudence." Ten days later, when they wanted to bring in troops from the outside, Seignelay informed them that the king deemed this unwise. They had royal permission only to use the city's archers and police force; they could, however, threaten to send for dragoons if they felt this might frighten Huguenots into abjuring.[38]

Louis was so carried away by the apparent success of his dragonnades in the provinces that he sent soldiers to help win conversions in Savoy during the first six months of 1686. He had earlier persuaded, or intimidated, the Duke of Savoy into publishing a decree against Protestantism similar to the revocation edict. Fearing that the duke might not seriously attempt to enforce his decree, Louis, without awaiting a request for aid, dispatched troops into the neighboring valleys of Piedmont and Savoy under the pretext of hunting down Frenchmen who had fled across the frontier. According to one French official, "this campaign succeeded so well that, after several clashes, the Savoyard Protestants were all killed or captured or constrained to implore the clemency of their sovereign within less than two months."[39]

The dragonnade was not the only coercive tactic employed against those who refused to renounce their beliefs and shift their religious affiliation; authorities frequently resorted to imprisonment as well. Women were confined to convents, and men were sent to the galleys or were locked up in prison. The Bastille was a favorite place for incarcerating obdurate Huguenots of noble lineage. Although it is impossible to estimate how many Frenchmen served prison terms because of religion, extant records suggest that thousands caught trying to cross the frontier went to prison, at least for a short time, before they were released and returned to their homes.[40] The intendant in Dauphiné bitterly complained in 1686 that the cost of holding

---

38 Archives Nationales, O1 *registre* 29, fols. 545, 546, 559–560.
39 See especially the "Introduction" and other documents in *ibid.*, A1 776.
40 See especially *ibid.*, TT 243, *dossier* 4, doc. 37.

so many Protestants in prison was burdening the province unduly. All the jails in his jurisdiction were so overcrowded, he said, that he had to use stables and similar buildings to house the fugitives his guards were capturing each day at mountain passes.[41]

At least 704 Huguenots were chained to the galleys in 1685–1690; 428, in 1691–1715;[42] 19, during the Regency; and 211, after 1725.[43] The punishment was particularly unjust and harsh because authorities frequently failed to release those condemned to serve only a specified time when their sentences expired. A large percentage died in their shackles.[44] The plight of these galley slaves outraged Protestants throughout the world. The Earl of Stair, while serving as the English ambassador at Paris, for example, wrote home to Secretary Stanhope on March 2, 1715, that he had recently spoken to the French statesman M. de Torcy "about the Galerians as a thing of little consequence to France and for which the King my Master interested himselfe out of pity to these poor people that suffered so much for their religion." De Torcy replied that he could do little to alleviate their suffering for "that was the [one] point in [all] the world that the [French] king was the most delicate upon and [the] hardest to be managed."[45]

Once his booted or frocked missionaries had secured, by fair means or foul, the signatures of Protestants on abjuration slips, Louis hoped the new converts would eventually become good Catholics in spirit as well as in action and would faithfully attend Mass and partake of Communion. In this matter he never sanctioned compulsion so long as they did not attend illegal Protestant assemblies and did not try to escape to foreign countries. He much preferred education and persuasion as a means of getting converts to perform their duties to the Church.

---

41 *Ibid.*, G7 240; Bibliothèque de la Société Protestante, MS 444, fol. 199.

42 About 215 others were similarly punished before 1705, but the exact date of confinement is not known.

43 Haag, *op. cit.*, X, 407–428. See also Bibliothèque de la Société Protestante, MS 628, pp. 620 ff., 702 ff.; [Antoine Court], *Le Patriote françois et impartial ou réponse à la lettre de Mr l'evêque d'Agen à Mr le controleur genéral contre la Tolerance des Huguenots, en datte du 1 mai 1751* (new ed.; Villefranche, 1753), II, 558–559 n., and pp. 107 ff. of the "mémoire historique" at the end of the volume.

44 Ernest Moret, "Fragment d'histoire sur les dernières persécutions sous Louis XIV (1711–1715)," *Séances et travaux de l'Académie des sciences morales et politiques*, XLIII (1858), 83–85.

45 Public Records Office, State Papers: *France*, 78/160, fols. 36–37. Professor Earl J. Hamilton graciously provided this interesting reference.

There were many high-ranking officials and clergymen, however, who argued that the king should punish by fines, imprisonment, economic discrimination, or heavy billeting of troops all converts whose religious practices fell short of the standard set by other Catholics.[46] But Louis followed the advice of others who contended, with equal fervor, that coercion would only cause converts to commit acts of sacrilege, to despise the Church rather than respect it, and to swell the tide of emigration.[47]

Louvois attempted to explain his master's policy on this score in a letter addressed to several officials on November 8, 1685. In persuading converts to attend Mass and perform other religious duties, he said, the king wanted "to rely upon gentleness rather than constraint." Only those who made a public spectacle of their obstinacy or who chided and taunted others for conforming to the king's wishes were to be severely punished.[48] When Seignelay heard that certain priests were threatening to send for royal dragoons unless new converts in their parishes attended church, he asked one of his agents on October 28, 1686, to identify the priests so he could personally reprimand them for doing what was so contrary to established policy.[49] Even Bâville, who could never be accused of coddling Protestants, spoke out in 1669 against coercing converts: "I have always believed that the worst procedure was to exert too great pressure on new converts to approach the Sacrament. . . . This produces only sacrilege. One must assault their hearts, for that is where religion resides."[50]

---

46 Archives Nationales, TT 243, *dossier* 4, doc. 37; 435, *dossier* 1; Bibliothèque Nationale, *Fonds français*, MS 7044, fol. 201; Boislisle, *op. cit.*, II (1883), 29; III (1897), 451, 464; Paul Gachon, *Le Conseil royal et les protestants en 1698. L'Enquête, la question de la Messe et le Rôle de Bâville* (Nogent-le-Rotrou, 1904), p. 9.

47 Archives Nationales, G7 339; TT 431, doc. 155; 251, *dossier* 15, doc. 151; B2 *registre* 65, fol. 326; Archives du Ministère des Affaires Étrangères, *Ancien fonds*, "Hollande," *registre* 150, fol. 65; Bibliothèque Nationale, *Fonds français*, MSS 7044, fol. 249; 7045, fols. 75–76, 77–78, 79–83, 140, 141, 145, 149; 20966, fols. 272–281; Bibliothèque de la Société Protestante, MS 444, fol. 199; Boislisle, *op. cit.*, II, 23, 31, 44, 189; Emanuel-Orentin Douen, *La Révocation de l'Édit de Nantes à Paris d'après des documents inédits* (Paris, 1894), I, 66–67; Lemoine, *op. cit.*, pp. 7, 15.

48 Archives Nationales, A1 757; Bibliothèque Nationale, *Nouvelles acquisitions françaises*, MS 1206, fol. 8. See also Louvois's letter to Seignelay, October 21, 1686 (Bibliothèque Nationale, *Fonds français*, MS 7044, fol. 248).

49 Archives Nationales, B2 *registre* 58, fols. 769–770.

50 Bibliothèque Nationale, *Fonds français*, MS 4290, fol. 143. Bâville's advice was not always consistent. In a memorandum of May 11, 1698, entitled "On the Present State of Religious Affairs and How One Should Act toward New Converts," for example, he advocated pressing older converts to attend Mass in every way short of

Louis actually spent about 537,000 livres on religious books and tracts which he distributed gratuitously to former Protestants.[51] Fénelon, who later became the preceptor of the youthful Duke of Burgundy, and still later (1695) was disgraced because of his quietist sympathies and banished from court to Cambrai as its new archbishop, visited several areas badly infected with heresy in 1685–1686. He recommended that the king rely upon appeals to reason and enlightened missionaries rather than upon force to persuade converts sincerely to accept Catholicism.[52] Cardinal Le Camus at Grenoble was another churchman who looked askance at violence. He instructed his own clerics to treat new converts as friends of the Church rather than as enemies, not to menace them if they did not always behave properly, and not to meddle in the affairs of royal agents sent into their parishes to implement the law.[53]

Officials at Versailles often found it necessary to constrain the zeal of provincial and local officials. Seignelay and Louvois counseled their subordinates to handle new converts astutely and circumspectly. Seignelay wanted to calm economic unrest as much as possible and to dull the desire to emigrate.[54] On October 19, 1687, for example, he wrote that "His Majesty does not wish to imprison anyone in the future for religious causes."[55] Louvois suggested on November 1, 1685, that the intendant at Rouen should not station troops in the homes of important merchants and manufacturers unless they caused trouble or openly comforted fellow Protestants and converts. The same statesman advised local officials not to look for occasions requiring a display of violence, but merely to intimidate Huguenots by threatening

---

outright coercion, and claimed that this would not cause many to flee abroad. Past experience had already revealed, he said, that most Protestants were more bound to France by property ties than to their faith by religious scruples. (*Ibid.*, MS 7045, fols. 84–86; Archives Nationales, TT 430, doc. 126.)

[51] Bibliothèque Nationale, *Fonds français*, MS 7054, *passim*. According to Jean Orcibal (*Louis XIV et les protestants* [Paris, 1951], pp. 118–119, 134–135 and n. 44), about a million tracts, costing about 800,000 livres, were distributed.

[52] Bibliothèque Nationale, *Nouvelles acquisitions françaises*, MS 507, fols. 2 ff., 31–33.

[53] *Ibid.*, *Fonds français*, MS 21623, fols. 145 ff.

[54] See, for example, certain letters in the Archives Nationales, G7 133; TT 232, *dossier* 19, doc. 9; B2 *registres* 57, fol. 445; 58, fols. 513, 531–532, 651, 895; 61, fol. 382; Bibliothèque Nationale, *Fonds français*, MS 7044, fols. 177, 194; *Nouvelles acquisitions françaises*, MS 1206, fols. 18, 57; Eugène Guitard, *Colbert et Seignelay contre la religion réformée* (2d ed.; Paris, 1912), pp. 112–113.

[55] Archives Nationales, B2 *registre* 62, fol. 335.

to employ force.[56] Pontchartrain, as head of the Breton Parliament, observed to Colbert de Croissy on July 13, 1686, that "the severity with which this parliament deals with such matters surpasses what is desirable for national welfare and what is necessary to execute the king's orders."[57] At that time he was seeking a pardon for two young men who had been captured at Saint-Malo when trying to escape abroad and had been sentenced to the galleys for life.

Louis was especially reluctant to use force in Paris, probably because his sense of delicacy abhorred the possibility that he and his intimates at court might witness the victims' anguish. His ambassador in Holland wrote him on October 23, 1687, that if "all new converts throughout the realm had received the same treatment as those in Paris, Rouen, and elsewhere within eyesight of Your Majesty, more than half who have fled France would never have left."[58] To share in this relative immunity, hundreds and perhaps thousands of refugees flocked to Paris from the provinces. An ordonnance of October 15, 1685, expelling all Protestants who had not resided there for a year or longer, and a threat the following December to deport to the provinces any Parisian who failed to abjure, were both ineffective.[59] The lieutenant general of police tried by threats, cajolery, and pleas to get artisans, merchants, and nobles to forsake their old faith and then to behave like good Catholics. He deployed his archers and policemen to terrify them, and threatened to call in dragoons. It looked for a time as though his efforts might prove successful. Paris, nevertheless, continued to provide excellent hiding places. Even after rumors reached the king that Protestants there were holding secret assemblies and were collecting funds to send to England, he refused to sanction a dragonnade for the capital.[60]

---

56 *Ibid.*, A¹ 757, 797, 798. The *Testament politique du Marquis de Louvois* (Cologne, 1695), especially pp. 384, 387, expresses regret that the government used coercion and suggests that persuasion and other peaceful tactics would have eventually succeeded in converting all Protestants. One should not conclude, however, that these were the opinions of Louvois, for scholars now believe that he had nothing whatever to do with the book.

57 Archives Nationales, TT 448, *dossier* 18, doc. 39.

58 Archives du Ministère des Affaires Étrangères, *Ancien fonds*, "Hollande," *registre* 152, fols. 107–109.

59 Archives Nationales, O¹ *registre* 29, fols. 561, 563–564; *Recueil des Édits*, p. 246.

60 Archives Nationales, O¹ *registres* 30, fols. 2–3, 34; 36, fol. 182; G. Pagès, "Les Réfugiés à Berlin d'après la correspondance du comte de Rébenac (1681–1688)," *BSHPF*, LI (1902), 125.

Louis's "tender" solicitude for new converts and his unwillingness to use violence in Paris did not apply to relapsers—those who reverted to Protestantism or refused the Holy Sacrament on their deathbeds. At the outset he felt that the crime called for the most severe and degrading punishment. According to one of his declarations (April 29, 1686), any relapser who died professing heresy forfeited all his property to the state and had his naked body dragged through the streets and tossed on a public dump. The punishment for a living male relapser included confiscation of property, amende honorable, and confinement for life in the galleys; for a female, confiscation of property and imprisonment for life in a religious or penal institution. Louis reaffirmed these penalties on December 13, 1698, March 8, 1712, and March 8, 1715.[61] The declaration of 1712 also saddled doctors with the responsibility of informing patients who were likely to die that they must call in a priest. The doctor could not pay a second call unless his patient had a certificate showing that a priest either had been there or had been officially summoned.[62] Louis ruled in 1715 that any Protestant, whether or not he had ever formally embraced Catholicism, was to be considered a Catholic, and hence a relapser if he died professing the doctrines of Calvinism.

Strict enforcement of the laws against relapsers did the king's cause more harm than good. The practice of dragging naked bodies through the streets and leaving them exposed on the city dump where rats and dogs got at them and where lewd individuals arranged them in shocking positions revolted even the most ardent Catholics, outraged the public's sense of decency, transformed the dead into martyrs, and alienated thousands who might otherwise have accepted Catholicism.[63] It was not long before Louis realized his mistake, but he was unwilling to repeal the laws lest Protestants get the erroneous impression that he was

---

[61] Bibliothèque Nationale, *Fonds français*, MSS 10623, fols. 165–166; 21623, fols. 10–19; *Recueil des Édits*, pp. 282–284, 459–462, 482–484; Lemoine, *op. cit.*, pp. 31–32. According to a seventeenth-century map of Paris, one of the public dumps where the bodies of relapsers were thrown, and later furtively retrieved by friends for a Christian burial, was located just north of the "Grands Boulevards" near the Porte Saint-Martin.

[62] *Recueil des Édits*, pp. 459–462. If his patient did not obtain such a certificate, the doctor faced a fine of 300 livres if he administered treatment anyway and permanent revocation of his medical license if he returned still another time.

[63] Archives Nationales, F12 *registre* 115, fol. 36; G7 136; Boislisle, *op. cit.*, I, 475; II, 58.

relaxing his stringency. Instead, he secretly informed officials that they should not adhere to rigid enforcement except in unusual circumstances. Seignelay told the Bishop of Saintes on December 16, 1686, for example, that he should not dispose of corpses as provided by law unless the relapser before his death had openly defied the king or unless fellow Protestants made a scandalous incident of the event.[64] Government agents and priests were advised to ignore violations insofar as possible, and not to summon local judges to witness a relapser's death; otherwise they would have to go through with the punishment. In 1699 Louis explicitly told intendants in secret instructions interpreting his edict of December 13, 1698, not to treat offenders as harshly as the law allowed.[65] Thus, except for a few months in 1686, relapsers were largely spared the indignities decreed as their punishment.[66]

Considering all the religious sanctions as a whole, it appears that Louis endorsed or at least condoned violence much more readily in 1685–1690 than he or his successors did thereafter. Although he continued his severity toward Protestant ministers, after 1690 he noticeably relaxed his efforts to force all Huguenots to convert. He began to urge local officials to handle converts circumspectly, and he suggested punishing relapsers and other religious offenders less rigorously than his laws stipulated. The outbreak of war with the Grand Alliance probably had a great deal to do with Louis's shift toward moderation; also, the king's and the public's enthusiasm for harsh treatment may have waned after the great majority of Protestants had been officially inscribed on the rolls of the Catholic Church. Terrorism did not disappear overnight. The change was more a matter of emphasis than an outright repudiation of earlier tactics. Neither the campaign of violence in 1685–1690 nor the subsequent shift toward moderation, however, succeeded in crushing Protestantism. As an organized religion, it simply went underground; and in the long run Louis's "baptism by fire" tempered rather than broke the spiritual fiber of Huguenots.

---

64 Archives Nationales, B2 *registre* 58, fol. 895; Baudry, *op. cit.*, pp. 70–71. See also Auguste-François Lièvre, *Histoire des protestants et des églises réformées du Poitou* (Paris, 1856–1860), II, 179–180.

65 Archives Nationales, O1 *registre* 31, fol. 30; A1 798; Bibliothèque Nationale, *Fonds français*, MSS 7044, fol. 261; 7045, fol. 241; Lemoine, *op. cit.*, pp. 31–32.

66 The king apparently discontinued the practice of dragging cadavers through the streets in Paris somewhat earlier than in other places (Bibliothèque Nationale, *Fonds français*, MS 7046, fol. 10).

CIVIL SANCTIONS

It might be presumed that most civil and economic sanctions against Protestants disappeared after the Crown had outlawed their religion and after most of them had joined the Catholic Church. This did not happen. It might have been otherwise had the Catholic majority completely assimilated the Protestant minority. Like the Moriscos in Spain, new converts in France remained a class apart, enveloped in a cloud of suspicion and distrust. Most of them actually did little to dispel the cloud. They never completely and sincerely repudiated Calvinist doctrines, and they sought solace and strength by consorting with one another rather than with their oppressors. Apparently with more vigor than ever before, they channeled their activities along economic lines and achieved enviable success in the business world. In July, 1759, an astute observer wrote that "the penchant of Protestants directs them much more toward manufacturing and trade than toward making conquests by force of arms."[67] Small wonder, then, that less successful members of the Catholic majority were resentful and often accused converts of illegal practices and of violations of the laws proscribing their religion. Ingrained discriminatory practices against an easily identifiable minority die slowly. This is particularly true if there are legal sanctions which condone discrimination. Also, persistent differentiation of a social group by some distinctive name serves to freshen the remembrance of old frictions.

There were two revealing shifts in the terms contemporaries employed to refer to nonconformists in the seventeenth and eighteenth centuries. Prior to the revocation and until about 1690 most persons called them "Huguenots," "Religionists," "Calvinists," or simply "Protestants"; thereafter the usual term was "new converts." This first shift probably occurred because the large majority of Protestants formally abjured their heresy, voluntarily or involuntarily, and also because the king and his officials elected to encourage the myth that Protestantism no longer existed in France. In the mid-eighteenth century, however, people began once again to refer to nonconformists as "Protestants" or "Huguenots." This second shift, more realistic than the first, recognized that the group and its descendants

---

[67] *Ibid.*, MS 10628, fol. 27.

had never lost their identity during the five or six decades they had been known as "new converts." The remark of the intendant at Montauban, in a letter to the controller general on October 29, 1702, that "there is no longer any appreciable distinction drawn in this *généralité* between regular Catholics and new converts,"[68] should be construed more as an attempt to please his superior than as a realistic statement of conditions in his jurisdiction, or in any other section of the country. It is true that progressive nonenforcement over the years dulled the keen edge of many legal sanctions aimed at Protestants, but there were other sanctions that were kept alive by heated controversy and special circumstances. Whether Protestants or new converts should be allowed to marry without first confessing their sins, receiving Communion, and seeking priestly instructions, for example, was still a lively issue at the middle of the eighteenth century.[69]

Interfaith marriages, first outlawed in November, 1680, continued to be illegal; and in January, 1686, Louis deprived any Protestant wife or widow who refused to abjure after her husband had accepted Catholicism of the right to will or sell her property.[70] After the revocation only the Catholic Church could wed individuals; hence unconverted Protestants could not legally marry. The Church, furthermore, insisted upon certain matrimonial formalities and rituals which many converts found repugnant and refused to perform. This meant that they, too, could not marry legally. Louis became increasingly concerned as concubinage spread. He was unwilling to sanction civil marriages, and he also thought it unwise to dictate to the Church and its clerics what their attitude should be. Marriage, to him, was a religious matter. He did appeal to the clergy, however, to relax their requirements for the sake of public morals and economic welfare. Seignelay informed the bishops at Saintes and La Rochelle on February 28, 1687, for example, that the king considered their priests injudicious in refusing to marry new converts unless the couples first confessed their sins, received absolution, and partook of Communion. Unless the priests relented, Seignelay predicted, many able-bodied seamen would desert their native land.[71]

---

68 Boislisle, *op. cit.*, II, 127.

69 See especially Archives Nationales, TT 446, and Bibliothèque Nationale, *Fonds français*, MS 7047, fols. 326 ff.

70 *Recueil des Édits*, pp. 259–260.

71 Archives Nationales, B2 *registre* 61, fol. 161.

Whereas Louis had forbidden Catholics to wed Protestants before the revocation, he now felt that Catholics might be instrumental in confirming and educating converts if they intermarried. He accordingly stated in his secret instructions to intendants and bishops in 1699 that they should encourage, rather than discourage, such marriages. Here again, however, the attitude of many local priests proved to be a stumbling block.

It is interesting to note how Protestants and new converts reacted to the matrimonial sanctions imposed by the Church and the state. In the first place, a large number seeking to be married chose to emigrate and settle down in foreign countries rather than remain at home and suffer the social and legal stigmas of "living together scandalously" and of bearing illegitimate children. Second, many living near the frontier defied the law of June 16, 1685, slipped across the border to be wed by a Protestant minister, and then returned home. Third, some waited until an itinerant underground minister could perform the ceremony. Having thereby made peace with their own consciences, they could settle down, like those in the second group, and live in legal concubinage. Fourth, according to government officials who based national welfare in large measure upon an increase in population, too many Huguenots chose to remain bachelors or spinsters rather than compromise their consciences or bring illegitimate children into the world. Fifth, a good many went through only the civil part of the ceremony; or, if they were wealthy enough, bribed priests to perform the religious rites while omitting the confessional and Communion. And, lastly, probably the largest number met the requirements of the Church until they were married and then had nothing more to do with it.[72]

The king was most anxious that children of Protestant parentage be reared and educated in the Catholic religion; his zealous determination led him to endorse snatching young children from their parents. Even before he revoked the Edict of Nantes, he had severely circumscribed the freedom and the activities of Protestant schools, had forbidden parents to send

---

[72] Archives Nationales, F12 1356; TT 435, *dossier* 10; Bibliothèque Nationale, *Fonds français,* MSS 7045, fols. 35–37, 43–45; 11419, pp. 98–99; 20967, fols. 214–215; Maurice Mousseau, "Protestants sedanais au XVIIIe siècle," *BSHPF,* LXXXIII (1934), 486–487, 494–495; L.-J. Nazelle, *Le Protestantisme en Saintonge sous le régime de la Révocation, 1685–1789* (Paris, 1907), pp. 49 and n. 1, 86–87.

their sons and daughters abroad to study, and had allowed anyone to work at converting minors seven years of age or older. In January, 1686, he signed a new edict permitting officials to take children between five and sixteen years of age out of their homes and to place them in the care of their nearest Catholic kin or with an outside Catholic family, a public hospital, or an orphanage. The anguished parents, of course, were powerless to interfere and yet had to pay the full cost of their children's subsistence and education away from home.[73] Although most of the clergy and many intendants and other government agents vociferously approved the king's action, there were some sensitive individuals who recoiled from the idea of abducting children of such tender age and who predicted that this practice, more than any other, would drive numerous Protestant families abroad.[74] In 1687 the intendant Bouchu in Dauphiné reported that there were so many children in his jurisdiction who did not attend Catholic schools that he would not know where to begin if he tried to enforce the edict. He felt so keenly on the matter that he was willing to jeopardize his future career in government by observing that "the advice reaching the king about conditions in other provinces (perhaps intended more to please than to instruct) may give His Majesty an impression entirely different from that . . . warranted by actual circumstances, at least in Dauphiné."[75] The practice of kidnaping children ceased in most provinces before 1693. It persisted in some regions much longer, and there were occasional child abductions through most of the eighteenth century.[76]

In 1687 Louis reiterated the proscription he had formulated in 1681 against sending children abroad ostensibly to learn foreign languages. In exceptional instances he was willing to allow merchants to educate their sons in foreign countries for a short time provided permission was first obtained from the intendant and a sufficient bond was posted to assure the students' return. He also established schools specializing in foreign lan-

---

[73] *Recueil des Édits*, pp. 261–263.

[74] Archives Nationales, G⁷ 71; TT 464, doc. 53; Bibliothèque Nationale, *Fonds français*, MSS 4286, fol. 19; 7044, fol. 249; 7045, fols. 84–86; Boislisle, *op. cit.*, II, 44.

[75] Archives Nationales, TT 243, *dossier* 4, doc. 37.

[76] *Ibid.*, TT 463; Lavisse, *op. cit.*, Vol. VIII, Part 1, p. 368; Ernest Moret, "Les Dernières persécutions contre les protestants, sous Louis XIV (1711–1715)," *BSHPF*, VII (1858), 500 n. 1.

guages at a few major seaports so that merchants would have less excuse for seeking special permission.[77] Protestants and new converts, nevertheless, continued to send their children abroad whenever they could; and many youths, once they had left France, never came back. The Bishop at Nantes, among others, was perturbed over the procedure followed. He complained in 1723 that intendants frequently granted merchants permission to send their children out of the country without requiring the posting of cash bonds. Since many failed to return, he said, this practice not only robbed the Church of an opportunity to save "an infinity of souls," but also deprived the state of many "subjects whose talents and trade would have enriched the realm."[78]

The king continued to discriminate against Protestants by restricting their liberty to hire whomever they pleased as servants. Fearing that they might subvert employees, he had ruled on July 9, 1685, that they could not engage Catholics to work in their homes. On this particular point he reversed himself after the revocation. According to an ordonnance dated January 11, 1686, neither Protestants nor converts could hire anyone except Catholics. Louis now thought it wise to have Catholics stationed in Protestant homes as servants so that they might undermine the faith of their employers and spy upon their activities. The penalties for violating the ordonnance were surprisingly severe. A Protestant manservant found working for another Protestant or a new convert was to be sent to the galleys; a maidservant in the same circumstances was to be publicly whipped and branded with the fleur-de-lis; and the employer was to be fined 1,000 livres.[79]

Protestants were still excluded from public office.[80] A formal renouncement of heresy, furthermore, would not always gain them admittance; they usually had to have a certificate of good

---

[77] Archives Nationales, G7 133; B2 *registre* 60, fols. 43–44; TT 451, *dossier* 54, doc. 181; Henry Lehr, *Les Protestants d'autrefois. Vie et institutions militaires,* II (Paris, 1907), 48 n. 1.

[78] Archives Nationales, TT 436.

[79] Bibliothèque Nationale, *Fonds français,* MS 21623, fols. 8–9; *Recueil des Édits,* pp. 268–270.

[80] Archives Nationales, G7 339; O1 *registre* 29, fol. 563; Bibliothèque Nationale, *Fonds français,* MS 7044, fol. 181; *Recueil des Édits,* pp. 255–256; Benoist, *op. cit.,* p. 286.

standing in the Church as well. In 1685–1686, and again in 1692, the king instructed several intendants not to allow new converts to hold civic posts unless they furnished such certificates,[81] and he also suggested that it would be unwise to appoint former Huguenots to judicial positions since their religious prejudices might influence their legal opinions and lead them to render judgments unfavorable to Catholic litigants.[82] This sort of discrimination persisted much longer in some regions than in others. Well into the eighteenth century new converts around Bordeaux and La Rochelle, for example, found it difficult to hold public office;[83] and as late as 1765 and 1767 the Parliament at Toulouse was still seeking to require candidates to furnish papers certifying that they were Catholics in good standing.[84]

As previously noted, the state had been unable to dispense with the services of some Protestants in regional and local governments before October, 1685. It likewise experienced difficulty in excluding converts from office thereafter. Since Protestants and converts usually had an enviable reputation for probity and industriousness, it was not always financially expedient to oust them from positions of trust. In 1699–1700, for example, there were at least ninety-eight new converts employed in collecting taxes throughout the realm and seven Lutheran or Calvinist collectors in Alsace.[85] Bâville, for once, took a realistically dim view of orders from Paris to remove converted Huguenots from civic posts in Languedoc. He pointed out to the controller general on December 28, 1692, that to appoint a few as mayors of certain towns where no Catholics resided would help mollify the Protestant population in the province and at the same time would add about 100,000 *écus* to the royal treasury.[86] Much later, on December 2, 1767, an official at Nîmes remonstrated against the stand recently taken by the Parliament at Toulouse to require church certificates of all officeholders. To comply with this, he said, would prove highly embarrassing to the city of

---

81 Archives Nationales, G⁷ 2; O¹ *registres* 29, fol. 568; 36, fol. 182; Bibliothèque Nationale, *Fonds français*, MS 7045, fol. 28; Bibliothèque de la Société Protestante, MS 444, fol. 174.

82 Bibliothèque Nationale, *Fonds français*, MS 4287, fol. 12.

83 Leroux, *Les Religionnaires de Bordeaux*, pp. 8–9.

84 Archives Nationales, TT 463, doc. 70.

85 Boislisle, *op. cit.*, II, 9. Alsace was the one major province in France where the revocation edict did not apply.

86 *Ibid.*, I, 308.

Nîmes because it was "absolutely impossible" to elect a city council without including several Protestants, "as has always been done in the past."[87]

The civil sanctions limiting the rights of Protestants to marry freely, to rear and educate their offspring, to hire servants, and to hold public office represented extensions or modifications of similar restrictions adopted before the revocation. The outbreak of the War of the League of Augsburg provided an excuse for additional discrimination. On October 16, 1688, the king forbade most Protestants and converts who had accepted Catholicism within the past five years to keep any weapons in their homes.[88] This was clearly a security measure designed to prevent insurrection during the national emergency. The common people had to surrender all their arms immediately, and new converts of noble birth could keep only two swords, two guns, two pairs of pistols, six pounds of lead, and six pounds of powder. Royal authorities eventually had to make exceptions to this rule, for some converts were gunsmiths or powder makers by trade and some were traveling merchants who had to protect themselves and their property from highwaymen.[89] Although the original ordonnance was to remain in force for only two years, successive renewals prolonged its life until May 18, 1734.[90] Another discriminatory order (July 30, 1689) compelled any Protestant or new convert to leave France and turn over his property to the government if a parent, a child, or a close relative of his was serving with enemy forces and refused to return home within a month.[91]

Rumors of an impending English landing at La Rochelle in 1689 and of possible invasions by Protestant troops poised on the Swiss border alarmed the government.[92] It was said that William

---

[87] Archives Nationales, TT 463, doc. 70.

[88] Bibliothèque Nationale, *Fonds français*, MS 10623, fols. 81–82; *Recueil des Édits*, pp. 313–315.

[89] Archives Nationales, O¹ *registre* 43, fol. 87; TT 450, *dossier* 28, doc. 138; A¹ 837, doc. 89.

[90] Bibliothèque Nationale, *Fonds français*, MSS 7046, fol. 208; 10623, fols. 99–100; *Nouvelles acquisitions françaises*, MS 1206, fols. 137, 147; *Recueil des Édits*, pp. 342–344.

[91] Lefèvre, *op. cit.*, Appendix II, pp. 24–25; *Recueil des Édits*, pp. 329–330. This particular ordonnance apparently applied only to inhabitants of provinces recently added to France (the *pays de conquête*) and not to those residing in older sections of the country (Boislisle, *op. cit.*, I, 192).

[92] Archives Nationales, A¹ 902, 903, 906; Bibliothèque Nationale, *Fonds français*, MS 7053, fol. 242.

III, recently enthroned in England, was sending Huguenot ministers back to France as firebrands to stir up trouble; and French refugees in Switzerland supposedly stood ready to aid fellow Protestants who had remained at home. It was feared in government circles that new converts in Dauphiné and Languedoc might heed the exhortations of the English to arm themselves and assist their "liberators" at the moment of invasion. Louis therefore attempted in 1689 to police the trouble spots in order to suppress immediately any outward sign of unrest.[93] When the enemy failed to appear, there was a momentary relaxation of tension. A new wave of apprehension, however, developed in 1691–1692. Had the Crown not interposed its authority on at least one occasion, Catholics at Caen probably would have taken matters into their own hands and have punished new converts whom they suspected (without reliable evidence) of having provided the English with treasonable information which presumably had led to the capture or destruction of several ships from that port.[94] This incident gives some indication as to how high popular feeling was running. Throughout the war Huguenots and their sympathizers lived continuously under a cloud of suspicion. Both officials and Catholic neighbors were warily and constantly on guard as though they expected at any moment to detect signs of treason or to uncover stealthy plots of insurrection.

Revolt, in fact, did break out in midsummer of 1702 in the barren, mountainous section in the south known as Cévennes. A zealous priest named François de Langlade du Chayla had been persecuting Huguenot peasants in his region so persistently that some of them finally decided to flee. Chayla, after capturing a goodly number of these fugitives, locked them up in his house for the night until he could arrange their transfer to prison. A band of irate peasants then liberated their friends and in the process burned down the house and killed the priest. This was the spark that kindled the fire. Other Protestant sympathizers spontaneously rallied in armed groups, preventing new converts from attending Mass and burning churches and presbyteries. For two years these Protestant bands (known as Cam-

---

93 Archives Nationales, G⁷ 241; A¹ 903, 904, 907; Boislisle, *op. cit.,* I, 182.
94 Bibliothèque Nationale, *Fonds français,* MS 7045, fol. 27; Boislisle, *op. cit.,* I, 245–246, 288.

isards) and royal troops sent to suppress them tried to outdo each other in brutality.[95] Things quieted down a bit after 1705, only to flare up once more in the same area in 1709–1710.

The Camisard insurrection was an outburst of pent-up resentment against the relentless fanatical zeal of Languedocian priests. Its participants did not think of themselves as traitors to their country but rather as protectors of their fellow countrymen from merciless harassment and persecution. And they acted accordingly. They did not rush to aid the enemy, for example, when a contingent of English troops temporarily landed at Sète in July, 1710.[96] Despite their denials, it now appears certain that foreign governments and refugees abroad aided and abetted the Camisards, but so did many French Catholics who disapproved of the harsh treatment of Protestants in southern France.[97] This internal unrest unquestionably embarrassed the government while it was at war in 1688–1697 and 1702–1713. Louis had to divert troops from the battle front to police his own kingdom, but there is little evidence that converts supplied the enemy with military information or engaged in other treasonable activities. On the whole, they remained stanch royalists and thoroughgoing Frenchmen as they had always been.

ECONOMIC SANCTIONS

Huguenots continued to be subjected to various forms of economic discrimination after October, 1685, even though they might have formally renounced their heresy. Catholic laymen distrusted and resented their economic power and affluence. One of the most effective arguments a plaintiff or a defendant could use in a lawsuit involving the sale of property or the execution of a contract was to allege that the other party was, or had been, a Protestant.[98] On the sole basis of a personal grudge or of animosity engendered by competition in business, local priests or businessmen often accused new converts of participating in illicit cults, of failing to perform their obligations to the Church,

---

95 McCloy, *op. cit.*, pp. 68 ff.; Lavisse, *op. cit.*, Vol. VIII, Part 1, pp. 378 ff.; Jean Germain, *Sauve, antique et curieuse cité* (Montpellier: Imprimerie de la presse Montpellier, 1952), pp. 247 ff.

96 Boislisle, *op. cit.*, III, 291, 303, 325.

97 Bibliothèque Nationale, *Fonds français*, MSS 7046, fols. 212–213; 20967, fols. 1 ff.; McCloy, *op. cit.*, pp. 70–72.

98 Moret, "Fragment d'histoire," p. 73.

or of discriminating against Catholic employees and tradesmen.[99] There were frequent complaints around La Rochelle and in other areas where Protestants clustered in significant numbers that they monopolized certain trades, hired only fellow Religionists who refused to attend Mass, tried to run sincere converts out of business, dominated markets, and controlled local politics.[100]

Louis apparently had foreseen the possibility of irresponsible accusations against economically successful converts, for he had had Louvois and Seignelay instruct their agents in November, 1685, to investigate each charge thoroughly before punishing the accused. This did not prevent innocent persons from being victimized during the early years when anti-Protestantism was especially strong. And some nonconformists were undoubtedly guilty of the practices imputed to them. After 1700, however, the controller general rarely took action on the basis of charges in anonymous communications.

New converts, as a rule, continued to pay more than a fair share of taxes except in places where they controlled assessments and hence could protect themselves while penalizing others.[101] They also were singled out for excessive billeting of soldiers and for special militia levies (*taxes de milice*) which sometimes doubled or tripled their property taxes. The intendant at Bordeaux, for example, wrote on August 11, 1691, that he had raised four new regiments as Louvois had ordered and had paid them from taxes collected entirely from new converts.[102]

It has already been pointed out that Protestants were excluded from elective and appointive offices in government, and that a Huguenot who had abjured could not hold public positions without a document from the Church certifying the sincerity of his conversion. Very much the same applied to the professions. Louis had excluded Huguenots from medicine, surgery, and pharmacy in September, 1685, and had drastically limited

99 See, for example, Archives Nationales, F12 1353; G7 72; Bibliothèque Nationale, *Fonds français*, MS 7046, fol. 36; Lehr, *op. cit.*, II, 110.

100 Archives Nationales, TT 247, doc. 94; 255, *dossier* 45, doc. 240; 431, doc. 155; 435, *dossiers* 1, 13; 448, doc. 295; Bibliothèque Nationale, *Fonds français*, MS 7045, fols. 40–42; Courpron, *op. cit.*, pp. 26–27; Lehr, *op. cit.*, II, 40–41.

101 Archives Nationales, O1 *registre* 41, fols. 134–135; TT 435, *dossier* 13; Paul Bert, *Histoire de la révocation de l'édit de Nantes à Bordeaux et dans le Bordelais (1653–1715)* (Bordeaux, 1908), p. 85.

102 Archives Nationales, G7 135; Bert, *op. cit.*, p. 85; Boislisle, *op. cit.*, I, 309. Louvois had ordered the intendant at Montauban to do the same.

their activities in the field of law. On November 5 his council categorically denied them the right to appear as lawyers before any court or parliament; and twelve days later the king forbade them to practice law anywhere in his realm under pain of 1,500 livres fine.[103] If they had formally accepted Catholicism, they could enter or remain in law or medicine only if they first convinced local authorities that their conversion had been real and that they were faithfully performing all their duties as good Catholics. There were many breaches of the regulations covering the professions. Protestant doctors and lawyers continued to practice wherever their religion had been dominant, and new converts did not always bother to obtain the certificates required by law. They never knew from one day to the next, however, when a priest or a disgruntled or envious Catholic would make trouble for them with the authorities.[104]

Artisans who refused to renounce their faith found employment opportunities greatly restricted even though Article XII of the revocation edict stated that they could pursue their crafts "without let or hindrance." The royal council on November 15, 1685, for example, forbade gilds in Paris to admit any applicant who was not a member of the Catholic Church.[105] Even more significant was the growing conviction among Catholic craftsmen and consumers that they could harass and discriminate against Protestant tradesmen with impunity. The latter, of course, had no court or authority to which they could turn for legal protection or redress.

In order to hasten the process of conversion the king utilized gilds as he did every other institution. He urged them to open their doors to new converts and to reduce the admission fee for them by three-fourths.[106] Catholic artisans did not view such favoritism kindly. They were not anxious to have former Protestants as competitors. Many Catholics urged the king to require religious tests of converts engaged in trade and manufacturing as he had already done for those holding public office or practicing law or medicine. Louis refused, however, to heed their pleas. Michel Amelot—state councilor, director of com-

---

103 Bibliothèque Nationale, *Fonds français*, MS 21617, fols. 243–244; *Recueil des Édits*, pp. 249, 252–253; Lefèvre, *op. cit.*, Appendix, pp. 18–22.
104 Courpron, *op. cit.*, pp. 51–52.
105 Lefèvre, *op. cit.*, Appendix, p. 36.
106 Archives Nationales, O¹ *registre* 29, fols. 513, 515–516, 523, 526–527.

mercial affairs, and influential member of the Council of Trade —stated on February 5, 1701, that "up to the present time the king has issued no edict or declaration that closes the doors of gilds to insincere Catholics."[107] Henri Daguesseau, president of the Council of Trade, agreed with the king that it would be unwise to require religious certification of artisans and merchants. In his 1713 "Memorandum on the Ways to Procure the Conversion of Those of the Reputedly Reformed Religion," Daguesseau argued that "a very large number" of artisans would flee to England and other countries if they had "no other property or ties to bind them to the realm except their skills and trades." He also pointed out that they knew they could earn a great deal more elsewhere than in France.[108]

Catholic laymen and priests continued to pester the government with proposals to require converts to submit proof that they were in good standing with the Church. In reply to such a suggestion from a group of priests at Montauban in 1731, an intendant pointed out that the king had never required religious certification of English, Dutch, or Jewish merchants trading on French markets; why, then, should he require it of his own subjects?[109] Although the government never acted to exclude former Huguenots from commerce and industry, it sometimes tried to prevent their occupying positions of authority. The controller general, for example, informed the inspector of manufactures at Sedan in 1724 that no Protestant or new convert was to be elected as juryman in the gild of cloth and serge manufacturers, even though forty-one of the ninety manufacturers in that city were Huguenots.[110]

Economic sanctions were employed against Protestants, first, to convince them that they should abjure and, second, to prod them into performing their duties as good Catholics. They could not hold public office or practice law or medicine unless the Church was willing to certify that they were in good standing as Catholics. Although Louis refused to deprive merchants and artisans of an opportunity to earn a livelihood in business unless they showed by action as well as by word that their conver-

---

107 *Ibid.*, F12 *registre* 115, fols. 16–17.
108 Bibliothèque Nationale, *Fonds français*, MS 7046, fols. 28–29; Rulhière, *op. cit.*, II, 154–155.
109 Archives Nationales, TT 255, *dossier* 45, doc. 240.
110 *Ibid.*, F12 1356.

sion had not been sincere, private individuals and especially their economic competitors sniped at them whenever a favorable opportunity presented itself. Protestants who had never converted were barred from public office, law, medicine, and other occupations; they also stood defenseless against other forms of economic discrimination. In short, economic sanctions—whether supported by law or simply stemming from prejudices of the majority—persistently buttressed the religious and civil sanctions directed against both converted and unconverted Protestants. Their over-all effect was to stigmatize and penalize a minority of industrious Frenchmen whom the revocation of the Edict of Nantes presumably had wiped out or, at least, had merged with the majority. All these sanctions help explain why emigration continued to plague the French economy despite heroic efforts on the part of the government to prevent it and to repatriate those who had left before and immediately after the revocation. It is the purpose of the following chapter to ascertain, if possible, how many Huguenots sought refuge abroad and how successful were Louis's attempts to prevent their flight or to lure refugees back to France.

IV

The Huguenot Dispersion

The religious, civil, and economic sanctions directed against Protestants both before and after the revocation of the Edict of Nantes drove multitudes of them to seek asylum abroad. This was far from what the king had intended. He was almost as anxious to prevent emigration as he was to bring all Frenchmen into the Catholic fold and keep them there. Some individuals attempted to reassure him that there was little likelihood of a mass emigration. They insisted that only Protestants who were in difficulty with creditors or who possessed no property or unusual economic skills would try to escape. Their departure hence would occasion no great loss to the state.[1] According to these optimists, important businessmen were merely talking about leaving the country in order to frighten the government into a more conciliatory attitude toward them and their religion. Other spokesmen and royal advisers were more realistic. Both Seignelay and Louvois, Louis's two most influential ministers, were concerned lest emigration rob France of many of her ablest seamen and marine officers.[2] They and other responsible officials also feared that Protestant merchants, financiers, manufacturers, artisans, and peasants would escape and thereby deprive the country of valuable man power, specialized skills and knowledge, industrial secrets, material wealth, and specie. Several foreign countries, they pointed out, were too anxious to cripple the French economy not to take advantage of her internal troubles and to welcome cordially all refugees who sought a haven with them. The Catholic clergy were afraid that large numbers of potential converts would elude their grasp and be forever lost to the Church.

---

[1] Archives Nationales, B3 *registre* 48, fol. 272; Bibliothèque Nationale, *Fonds français*, MS 10621, fol. 9; *Nouvelles acquisitions françaises*, MS 507, fol. 47.

[2] Archives Nationales, A1 756; B2 *registre* 55, *passim;* Eugène Guitard, *Colbert et Seignelay contre la Religion réformée* (2d ed.; Paris, 1912), p. 111.

Mass emigration, in fact, did develop, and Louis did everything in his power—short of restoring religious freedom—to combat it. At one time or another he decreed death, lifetime imprisonment, confinement in the galleys, transportation to New World colonies, heavy fines, and confiscation of property for those caught trying to escape the country or for those helping to spirit them out. He had the coast patrolled and the frontier passes blocked. He tried to enlist the aid of peasants by offering rewards to individuals who would turn fugitives over to the authorities. At one time he even threw the doors of his kingdom wide open in the hope that nonconformists would give up all idea of leaving if they realized the government was not trying to compel them to stay.

Louis exerted almost as much effort to lure refugees back to France as he did to block their departure in the first place. He enlisted the services of his entire diplomatic corps and even sent special emissaries to persuade fugitives in England and Holland to return. He employed private spies and paid individual informants. He tempted Huguenots with bounties and other privileges if they would abjure and come back, or offered to restore their confiscated property.

Neither his efforts to check their flight nor his attempts to repatriate refugees prevented emigration. Religious persecution before and after the revocation drove upward of 200,000 men, women, and children from France. It is probable, however, that the number might have been even larger had Louis allowed Protestants to leave freely. The present chapter analyzes most of the laws and regulations designed to keep them in the country or to bring them back, and attempts to estimate how many left and where they settled.

RESTRICTIONS ON EMIGRATION

Louis signed an edict in August, 1669, restraining all his subjects—but particularly those engaged in shipbuilding, fishing, and similar maritime occupations—from moving to foreign countries without permission from the appropriate authorities. The penalty for disobedience was "confiscation of property and body" (i.e., death) and loss of citizenship.[3] Although there was no

---

3 *Recueil des Édits, Declarations et Arrests concernans la Religion Prétendue Réformée, 1662–1751, Précédés de l'Édit de Nantes*, ed. Léon Pilatte (Paris, 1885), pp. 26–29; Claude-Carlomau de Rulhière, *Eclaircissements historiques sur les*

reference in the edict to Protestants as such, Louis probably had them in mind, for earlier that year he had abolished the bipartisan chambers of justice in Paris and Rouen which adjudicated disputes between Protestants and Catholics. On December 10, 1680, he again forbade pilots, calkers, gunners, sailors, and fishermen to serve under foreign flags and changed the punishment from death to confinement in the galleys for life.[4]

On the basis of these two antiemigration laws of 1669 and 1680, the authorities arrested hundreds of Huguenots who sought to flee in 1680–1682 after the king had openly initiated a campaign to stamp out Protestantism and especially after Marillac had started the first dragonnade in Poitou (1681).[5] The first offenders were not severely punished, possibly because most authorities were ignorant of the law; even Seignelay, minister of the marine, was apparently unaware of the penalties. When a subordinate suggested that fugitives should be chained to the galleys when captured, Seignelay immediately replied that this was out of the question, for existing legislation did not approve such severity! He wrote his men at La Rochelle on November 18 and December 31, 1681, and again on January 5, 1682, that they should merely imprison the individuals taken while trying to escape to England and Holland, as well as their friends who had extended them aid, and after a short time should release them and send them back to their homes.[6]

The first antiemigration orders specifically directed against Protestants appeared on May 18 and July 14, 1682. According to these orders Protestant seamen, artisans, and others could not leave the country; and any disposition or sale of property they might have made during the year preceding their flight was to be null and void.[7] The king implemented these orders in 1685 by

causes de la révocation de l'Edit de Nantes, et sur l'état des protestants en France, depuis le commencement du Règne de Louis XIV, jusqu'à nos jours (new ed.; Geneva, 1788), I, 75–76.

4 Archives Nationales, B2 *registre* 42, fols. 439–440.

5 Bibliothèque Nationale, *Fonds français*, MS 21618, *passim;* Pierre Clément, *Lettres, instructions et mémoires de Colbert* (Paris, 1861–1884), VI, 158 n. 2; J. Gaberel, "Les Suisses romands et les réfugiés de l'édit de Nantes," *Séances et travaux de l'Académie des sciences morales et politiques,* LIV (1860), 98; J. Garnier, "Tolérance de Colbert," *Bulletin de la société de l'histoire du protestantisme français* (hereinafter cited as *BSHPF*), XIV (1865), 376–377; Guitard, *op. cit.*, p. 39; Rulhière, *op. cit.*, I, 221.

6 Archives Nationales, B2 *registres* 44, fols. 436–437; 45, fol. 493; 46, fol. 16; Bibliothèque Nationale, *Nouvelles acquisitions françaises*, MS 1555, fols. 21–22.

7 Archives Nationales, O1 *registre* 26, fol. 212; Bibliothèque Nationale, *Fonds*

(1) reaffirming the commutation of the death penalty to confinement for life in the galleys for men captured while trying to escape (May 31), (2) having an armed corvette stop and search each vessel sailing from Aunis and Saintonge for hidden fugitives (September 10), and (3) forbidding merchant ships owned by Protestants to leave France unless two-thirds of the crew were Catholic (October 2).[8] At the same time he and his ministers exhorted all law-enforcement agents in the provinces and especially at seaports to exert every effort to intercept refugees quitting the country.[9]

A few persons boldly warned the government that such forthright action might provoke many Protestants to emigrate who otherwise would have stayed at home. Protestants, they said, were already so on edge and so fearful of the future that coercive retention would only drive them away. It was further pointed out that the law confiscating the property of refugees was already harming normal business activity because everyone was afraid to deal with Huguenots. Those who had no intention of fleeing abroad could not readily buy on credit or market their goods through regular channels. The uncertainty about the future was causing others to sacrifice their possessions at distress prices and to neglect planting or harvesting crops. On the other hand, it was suggested, Protestants could easily circumvent the law if they were really planning to escape. For example, they could sign contracts turning their property over to relatives or trusted friends to settle simulated debts or as fictitious gifts or sales. In such circumstances it was next to impossible to prove intent to evade the law or to defraud. Huguenot creditors, in their turn, took their revenge by foreclosing on mortgages held against Catholics and by insisting upon the prompt payment of all indebtedness.[10] According to this point of view, the prerevoca-

---

français, MSS 21616, fols. 354–355, 360 ff.; 21617, fol. 143; *Recueil des Édits*, pp. 112–113, 119–120; Jacques Lefèvre, *Nouveau recueil de tout ce qui s'est fait pour et contre les protestans, particulièrement en France où l'on voit l'establissement, le progrez, la Décadence et l'Extinction de la R.P.R. dans ce Royaume* (Paris, 1690), pp. 504–505.

8 Archives Nationales, B2 *registre* 52, fols. 256–257, 267; Bibliothèque Nationale, *Fonds français*, MS 21617, fols. 109 ff.; *Recueil des Édits*, pp. 192–194.

9 See, e.g., Archives Nationales, O1 *registre* 29, fols. 435, 438; A1 795, doc. 45; B2 *registres* 44, *passim;* 45, fol. 349; 47, fols. 169, 179; 49, fol. 258; 55, fol. 130; 67, fols. 233, 247.

10 *Ibid.*, TT 430, doc. 97; 431, docs. 42, 157; Bibliothèque de la Société Protestante, MS 485^VI, fol. 93.

tion laws restraining Protestants from leaving France unsettled the economy far more than they checked emigration. The argument, however, did not sway Louis. If anything, it convinced him that he must redouble his efforts.

The revocation edict expelled Protestant ministers who refused to accept Catholicism, but expressly forbade anyone else to leave the country.[11] Louis set to work systematically to implement the law and to plug up all its holes he could.[12] On seven different occasions from 1686 to 1713 he issued declarations, special edicts, or orders of council reaffirming earlier prohibitions against leaving the realm, and extending the coverage to new converts as well as to Protestants who had never abjured.[13] Prior to the revocation he had refrained from specifically forbidding converts to cross the border, for he was afraid this would give the impression that the government did not accept their conversion to Catholicism as sincere;[14] after he had outlawed their religion, however, he showed little leniency toward new converts captured while trying to escape to foreign countries. In the last two months of 1685 and throughout 1686, for example, Seignelay instructed officials to release any Huguenot taken at the border if he consented to abjure his heresy, but rigorously to punish any convert attempting to flee.[15] This

---

11 Louis allowed his able general the Duke of Schomberg, his incomparable admiral Abraham Duquesne, and the Marquis de Ruvigny, the official Protestant representative at court, to leave the country; he also gave similar permission to a few others of the Protestant aristocracy—e.g., the Princess of Tarente, the Countess de Roye, the Marquise de Gouvernet, Mme Herwarth, M. and Mme d'Olbreuse, the Marquis and Marquise de la Roche-Giffard, the Countess de Ducé, and the Dutchman Le Laët (Emmanuel-Orentin Douen, *La Révocation de l'Édit de Nantes à Paris d'après des documents inédits* [Paris, 1894], II, 414).

12 See, e.g., Archives Nationales, O1 *registre* 29, fol. 435; A1 755–757, *passim;* B2 *registre* 55, fol. 480; Bibliothèque Nationale, *Fonds français,* MSS 7044, fol. 93; 21616, fols. 150–151; A. M. de Boislisle, *Correspondance des contrôleurs généraux des finances avec les intendants des provinces,* I (Paris, 1874), 78; Gaultier de Saint-Blancard, *Histoire apologétique, ou Défense des libertéz des Églises réformées de France* (Mayence, 1687–1688), I, 376–377.

13 Bibliothèque Nationale, *Fonds français,* MSS 7057, fol. 267; 10623, fols. 68, 117–119, 157–158; 21617, fols. 180–181, 186–189; 21623, fols. 14–15, 18–21; *Recueil des Édits,* pp. 286–287, 384–387, 391–395, 465–469; Charles Benoist, *Condition juridique des protestants sous le régime de l'Édit de Nantes et après sa révocation* (Paris, 1900), pp. 288–289.

14 See, especially, one of Louvois's letters dated October 6, 1685 (Bibliothèque de la Société Protestante, MS 485II, fol. 71), and Ernest Lavisse and others, *Histoire de France illustrée depuis les origines jusqu'à la révolution* (Paris, 1911), Vol. VIII, Part 1, p. 341.

15 Archives Nationales, O1 *registre* 29, fol. 516; B2 *registre* 58, fol. 580; Bibliothèque de la Société Protestante, MS 485II, fol. 324.

meant that they were to send male converts to the galleys, confine females for life in religious institutions after having their heads shaved, and confiscate all property belonging to persons of either sex.

What might surprise and amuse many twentieth-century Americans was an experiment in 1687 and 1688 with a new form of punishment which the French government hoped would frighten stubborn Protestants into joining the Church. The government publicized its intention to deport captured fugitives to French colonies in Mississippi, Canada, Martinique, and other West Indian islands. Several ships laden with religious prisoners were actually sent to the New World, and one or two of them foundered in storms off the American coast. So great were the fear and ignorance about conditions in the colonies and so reluctant was the typical Frenchman to move far from his native land that the threat of transportation across the Atlantic appalled Huguenots and converts much more than the possibility of being chained to the galleys for life![16]

Simply passing laws forbidding emigration and decreeing severe penalties against offenders was not in itself sufficient to stem the tide. The laws had to be effectively enforced, and enforcement created an embarrassing dilemma. If the government seriously attempted to apprehend persons seeking to escape, the cost of policing the frontiers would mount rapidly, prisons would soon overflow, and the expense of feeding the inmates would drain local treasuries. Furthermore, the government would run the risk of arousing Catholic sympathies for the men, women, and children herded together in custody. On the other hand, if the government pardoned and released its captives, they would only bide their time until another opportunity to escape arose.[17] Several individuals therefore advised the king in 1686 to withdraw his guards quietly from the frontier and allow Huguenots to escape if they wanted to. They suggested

[16] Archives Nationales, G⁷ 298; A¹ 775; Charles W. Baird, *History of the Huguenot Emigration to America* (New York, 1885), I, 221; Elie Benoît, *Histoire de l'Edit de Nantes, contenant les choses les plus remarquables qui se sont passées en France avant et après sa publication . . . jusques à l'Edit de Révocation en Octobre, 1685* (Delft, 1693–1695), V, 976–978; [Pierre Jurieu], *Lettres pastorales adressées aux fidèles de France, qui gemissent sous la captivité de Babylone* (4th ed.; Rotterdam, 1687–1688), II, 31; Francis Waddington, "Les Assemblées du Désert," *BSHPF*, IV (1856), 138; Eugène and Émile Haag, *La France protestante, ou Vies des Protestants français qui se sont fait un nom dans l'histoire* (Paris, 1846–1859), X, 431–432.

[17] Archives Nationales, TT 243, *dossier 4, doc. 37*.

that only a few would leave if all restraints were removed and that France would be better off without them.[18] Louis finally decided to try this proposal. He secretly recalled his guards in December, 1686, and instructed provincial and civic officials not to arrest anyone crossing the border.[19]

The plan, operating through most of 1687, was a dismal failure. Instead of diminishing, emigration increased. The frontiers were again closed and were not reopened, except for a brief period in 1688 through misinterpretation of orders from Versailles. In February Louis had decided to exile all Protestant prisoners who steadfastly refused to abjure and had instructed his intendants to escort them from his realm and to see that they took no property with them.[20] A few officials, misconstruing the directive, allowed any convert or Huguenot—whether inside or outside prison—to leave the country. Seignelay and Louvois set matters straight as soon as they heard of the mistake, explaining that the king had intended only to get rid of recalcitrant prisoners whose detention added to the government's financial burden.[21]

Effective policing of France's extensive water and land frontiers was both costly and difficult. Seignelay as secretary of the marine had first begun to patrol the Atlantic and Mediterranean coasts in October, 1685.[22] From then until the start of the Augsburg war[23] armed frigates sailed along the coast, guarded river mouths, and policed the lanes to offshore islands. Coast guard units and naval officers on land attempted to intercept refugees boarding ship at all important seaports.[24] In the spring of 1686

---

18 *Ibid.*, A1 775; Bibliothèque Nationale, *Nouvelles acquisitions françaises,* MS 507, fol. 39; Benoît, *op. cit.,* V, 979; Douen, *op. cit.,* I, 66–67; Guillaume-Adam de Félice, *Histoire des protestants de France* (8th ed.; Toulouse, 1895), p. 438; Lavisse, *op. cit.,* Vol. VIII, Part 1, pp. 341–342.

19 Archives Nationales, G7 240; O1 *registre* 30, fol. 43; TT 243, *dossier* 4, doc. 37; B2 *registres* 58, fols. 927 ff.; 61, fol. 204; 62, fols. 198, 335; Douen, *op. cit.,* II, 552–553.

20 Archives Nationales, O1 *registre* 32, fols. 62–63; B2 *registres* 64, fol. 94; 65, fols. 178–179 and *passim;* Bibliothèque de la Société Protestante, MS 485III, fols. 93, 202; Lavisse, *op. cit.,* Vol. VIII, Part 1, p. 355; L. Rossier, *Histoire des protestants de Picardie, particulièrement de ceux du département de la Somme* (Amiens, 1861), pp. 258–259.

21 Archives Nationales, A1 835; 906, doc. 7; B2 *registres* 65, fol. 360; 69, fol. 58.

22 *Ibid.,* B2 *registre* 55, *passim.*

23 Except for the months in 1687 when the king lifted all bans on emigration.

24 Archives Nationales, B2 *registres* 52, fols. 270–273, 275–276, 280–281, 282, 295, 299; 53, fols. 116–117; 57, fol. 251; 58, fols. 548, 552–553, 569, 820; 61, fols. 154, 161 ff.; 62, fols. 108, 187; 65, fol. 364; 86, fols. 102 ff., 179, 186; Bibliothèque

Seignelay told the Marquis de Lavardin, Louis's lieutenant general in Brittany, to station coast guards at every significant port in Brittany to search each vessel before it sailed and to seize it and imprison its captain if a Protestant was found on board. He was also to post one or two men at each river port to watch the loading of small coastwise boats. City officials were to report any stranger who might be a Religionist. Seignelay further advised Lavardin to reassure all alien merchants that they could freely enter and leave France; but he was not to grant permission to unnaturalized foreign residents to leave the country nor issue passports to converted Frenchmen engaged in foreign trade unless they left their families and property behind. Seignelay sent similar instructions to subordinates in Upper Normandy and in Saintonge.[25]

Louis also had units of militia stationed at the major mountain passes to Switzerland and Germany and along the chief routes to the Low Countries. He empowered excise collectors to search all persons crossing the frontier and to arrest any Huguenots they discovered. He constantly reminded intendants that one of their chief responsibilities was to prevent emigration.[26] Because of difficulties in policing land routes and in identifying refugees, the state solicited the help of local peasants and of anyone else who would turn informer for the sake of pecuniary reward. Louvois told peasants that they could despoil refugees with impunity and in addition would be paid three gold coins for each individual they captured and turned over to the authorities. The intendant in Béarn wrote the controller general on August 8, 1686, that he had recently posted a reward of 20 *écus* payable to any Frenchman or Spaniard who seized a Huguenot trying to cross the Pyrenees. He claimed that his action brought good results.[27] A royal ordonnance of April 26, 1686, allowed frontier guards to divide among themselves all the possessions taken from captives and assured private citizens that they

Nationale, *Fonds français*, MS 7044, fol. 182; Boislisle, *op. cit.*, I, 97; B. Vaurigaud, *Essai sur l'histoire des églises réformées de Bretagne, 1535–1808* (Paris, 1870), III, 159.

25 Archives Nationales, B2 *registre* 56, fols. 45 ff., 53 ff., 70 ff., 79 ff.

26 *Ibid.*, G7 133, 134; O1 *registre* 29, fol. 296; A1 774, 775; B2 *registres* 55, fol. 479; 57, fol. 115; 58, fol. 794; B3 *registre* 51, fol. 79; TT 243, *dossier* 4, doc. 37; Bibliothèque Nationale, *Nouvelles acquisitions françaises*, MS 1206, fols. 75, 78; Boislisle, *op. cit.*, I, 82–83, 120.

27 Archives Nationales, A1 758; G7 113; Boislisle, *op. cit.*, I, 104–105.

could retain one-third the spoils if they apprehended fugitives themselves or supplied the guards with information leading to arrests. Another ordonnance of the same year (July 7) offered a reward of 1,000 livres for each Huguenot taken while hiding aboard any ship, no matter under what flag it was sailing.[28]

While the government was attempting to enlist the support of guards and informants, it also imposed severe penalties on those who helped Protestants escape. An ordonnance dated November 5, 1685, for example, forbade anyone to extend them direct or indirect aid under pain of 3,000 livres fine and corporal punishment, and specifically warned merchants, shipmasters, pilots, and other seamen not to violate the law. In May, 1686, the king changed the punishment to lifetime confinement in the galleys for men, to permanent imprisonment in religious institutions for women, and to confiscation of all property for both. Still later, on October 12, 1687, he decreed death for anyone helping new converts to flee abroad.[29]

Despite rewards for informants and penalties for assisting fugitives, a veritable "underground railway" of escape sprang up and functioned effectively for several years. There were several specifically outlined routes to the frontier, a recommended list of guides and counselors, and a number of hotels, taverns, and private homes where refugees could stop over or hide while traveling. Catholic peasants, when they surprised individuals or groups headed for the border, frequently robbed the travelers and then sent them on their way without informing the authorities. Many Frenchmen and foreigners served as professional guides for a fee and often succeeded in bribing guards to let them complete their mission if they were stopped at the frontier. The corruptibility of customs collectors and border patrols made strict enforcement of the Crown's antiemigration laws impossible. There also appeared a lively black market in counterfeited passports and certificates of abjuration. Several important officials engaged in these illicit operations, and aliens who obtained passports for themselves and their families frequently sold them to Frenchmen desirous of leaving. Foreign diplomatic representatives

---

28 *Recueil des Édits,* pp. 281–282; Archives Nationales, B2 *registre* 56, fols. 128–129.

29 Bibliothèque Nationale, *Fonds français,* MSS 10623, fols. 73–74; 21617, fol. 151; 21623, fols. 14–15; *Recueil des Édits,* pp. 248, 286–287, 300–301; Benoist, *op. cit.,* pp. 288–289.

spirited many Huguenots out of the country under the guise of domestic servants or as household members. The state severely punished the few guides and other offenders who fell into its clutches, but it was unable to disrupt the underground railway or to put an end to bribery and the black market.[30]

Cities along the Atlantic coast were favorite ports of escape. Many sympathizers, for example, stood ready at Bordeaux and La Rochelle to befriend and hide refugees, and Protestant merchants there were continually sending their ships to England, Holland, and the New World. Furthermore, ships from Protestant nations frequently called at the major Atlantic ports. Authorities at Bordeaux and similar cities found it impossible to distinguish Protestant from Catholic and bona fide merchant from refugee, especially when the great annual or seasonal fairs drew throngs of people from the surrounding countryside. Thus it was comparatively easy for Huguenots to escape. Many of them of either sex and of various ages shipped out on French and foreign vessels disguised as seamen. French sea captains often complained that a number of their crew jumped ship as soon as they dropped anchor in a foreign port. Huguenots and new converts stowed away on shipboard between barrels of wine and dry cargo; a few crouched in empty or partially filled packing cases and casks; some found safety and greater comfort in secret compartments especially designed by foreign shipbuilders for that purpose; and others lay hidden beneath the deck's planking. Refugees could also smuggle out their gold, silver, jewelry, furniture, and clothing with comparative ease. All they had to do was hide their possessions in barrels of salt, grain, and ashes, or package and consign them as exports destined for foreign buyers.[31]

---

30 Archives Nationales, G7 3, 85, 492; O1 *registres* 29, fols. 293, 311; 30, *passim;* 32, fol. 291; A1 775, 907; B2 *registres* 44, fols. 436–437; 57, fols. 300, 328 ff.; 58, fol. 572; 62, fols. 324–326; 65, fol. 38; 66, fol. 100; 67, fol. 233; B3 *registres* 51, fols. 261, 283; 57, fol. 35; Archives du Ministère des Affaires Étrangères, *Ancien fonds,* "Angleterre," *registre* 157, fols. 20–21; "Hollande," *registres* 143, fols. 137–138; 145, fols. 42, 74–75, 115–116; 147, fol. 200; 148, fol. 233; 152, fols. 18–19, 31; Bibliothèque Nationale, *Fonds français,* MSS 7044, fol. 108; 7050–7055, *passim;* 21619, *passim;* 21622, fol. 3; Bibliothèque de la Société Protestante, MSS 444, fols. 137, 225; 485I, fol. 283; 485II, fol. 320; 816I; François Baudry, *La Révocation de l'édit de Nantes et le protestantisme en Bas-Poitou au XVIIIe siècle* (Trévoux, 1922), p. 268; Boislisle, *op. cit.,* I, 51; Douen, *op. cit.,* II, 435–436, 450; Alfred Leroux, *Les Religionnaires de Bordeaux de 1685 à 1802* (Bordeaux, 1920), p. 8; Vaurigaud, *op. cit.,* III, 90, 109.

31 Archives Nationales, G7 133; B2 *registres* 47, fol. 169; 55, fols. 130, 180, 624; 56,

The government could hardly prevent goods and persons from leaving the country without seriously embarrassing legitimate trade. The measures it adopted were not extensive and vigorous enough to stop fleeing refugees, but they were onerous enough to compromise commercial freedom. An ordonnance of 1685, for example, fined Protestant coastal pilots 500 livres if they escorted ships into or out of French ports. The excuse for this was that such pilots might help other Huguenots board outbound vessels. Another ordonnance the same year (November 20) forbade any French ship to leave port unless two-thirds its crew were Catholics. Seignelay explained that the king meant only "regular" Catholics because he did not yet consider it wise "to place full and complete confidence in new converts." A ship could sail if its captain had formerly been a Protestant, provided he left his family behind and, upon his return, reported on everything that had happened to his crew during the voyage. Whereas Seignelay had advised the intendant at La Rochelle in December, 1685, not to imprison the master of a foreign vessel caught aiding refugees to escape but rather to delay its departure long enough to destroy all chance of profits from the voyage, the king sanctioned more drastic action on June 24, 1686, when he ordered the confiscation of all foreign ships coming into French waters and taking on board any refugee without royal permission. The declaration of December 5, 1699, once again forbade captains of any nationality to accept as passengers new converts who did not have official passports.[32]

Several officials realized that all such measures threatened trade. Seignelay, in particular, was fearful of the consequences. Again and again he reprimanded overzealous agents for adopt-

---

fols. 39–40; 57, fols. 49–50, 121, 139, 141, 428; 58, *passim;* 61, fol. 224; 62, fol. 7; 66, fol. 112; B³ *registres* 48, fols. 314–317; 55, fols. 500–506; A¹ 775; Archives du Ministère des Affaires Étrangères, *Ancien fonds,* "Hollande," *registre* 146, fol. 106; Bibliothèque Nationale, *Nouvelles acquisitions françaises,* MS 1206, fol. 17; Boislisle, *op. cit.,* I, 82–83, 97; Paul Courpron, *Essai sur l'histoire du Protestantisme en Aunis et Saintonge depuis la Révocation de l'Édit de Nantes jusqu'à l'Édit de Tolérance (1685–1787)* (Cahors, 1902), p. 17; Pierre Dez, *Histoire des protestants et de l'Église Réformée de l'île de Ré* (La Rochelle, 1926), p. 67; Guitard, *op. cit.,* p. 116; L.-J. Nazelle, *Le Protestantisme en Saintonge sous le régime de la Révocation, 1685–1789* (Paris, 1907), p. 186; Vaurigaud, *op. cit.,* II, 63.

32 Archives Nationales, B² *registres* 52, fols. 277, 295–296; 55, fols. 545, 573, 604–605; 56, fols. 118–119; *Recueil des Édits,* pp. 254, 395–397; Bibliothèque Nationale, *Fonds français,* MS 10623, fol. 126.

ing tactics that could conceivably harm commerce more than they might help the Catholic cause. For example, on June 15, 1686, he roundly upbraided the intendant at La Rochelle for having prevented ships from leaving that port: "[Your suggestion] is so extraordinary that I have nothing whatever to say in its favor; it would be the greatest mistake one could make, for it would completely ruin trade which is already quite badly interrupted."[33] He also vetoed proposals to forbid French sailors from seeking berths on foreign merchantmen, to prevent Protestant captains from sailing from Nantes, to refuse Dutch vessels permission to call at French ports, and to prohibit all ships from putting to sea at night when the tide was high.[34] On February 28, 1686, when he heard that inspectors and guards who searched departing vessels were soliciting bribes and gratuities, Seignelay persuaded the king that in order "to avoid the consequences of such an abuse which can only prejudice trade," he must explicitly outlaw the exaction of fees by searchers.

How could officials—however conscientious and well intentioned—distinguish Protestants and converts whose legitimate business took them to foreign countries or from one French province to another in coastwise boats, from those who used their business as an excuse to board vessels and escape to countries where they could find religious freedom? The intendant at Bordeaux in 1688 admitted that it was well-nigh impossible, for there was no way to prevent merchants from loading their own ships at out-of-the-way places up the two rivers from Bordeaux and then hiding themselves on board. Short of unloading the entire cargo when the ships passed through the city on their way to the open sea, the intendant would be unable to detect fugitives.[35] Merchants planning to escape ordinarily liquidated their assets as quickly as possible, smuggled their cash out of France, bought letters of exchange payable in foreign countries, and gradually shipped their unsold possessions abroad disguised as legitimate exports. The intendant at Lyon explained that there was no effective remedy for these evils unless one could ascertain beforehand the intentions of financiers and merchants trading on the open market. He warned against procedures that

---

33 Archives Nationales, B2 *registre* 57, fol. 453.

34 *Ibid.*, B2 *registres* 55, fols. 542, 582; 58, fols. 770, 931; 66, fols. 151–152.

35 *Ibid.*, G7 134. See also Boislisle, *op. cit.*, I, 167–168.

might drive all specie into hiding or disrupt the sale of real property.[36] Officials elsewhere agreed with the intendants at Lyon and Bordeaux.[37] Once a merchant had transferred most of his wealth out of the country, and especially if he had already sent his family abroad, there was practically no way to prevent his escape.

About all the government could afford to do to implement its laws against emigration was to require a converted merchant to obtain a passport from his intendant if he wished to visit a foreign fair or to leave France temporarily for business reasons. Before issuing a passport the intendant was to ascertain whether the merchant had recently sold property or had transferred its title to relatives, whether any members of his family had deserted, and whether he himself had been faithfully performing his religious obligations as a Catholic. Frequently the applicant had to post a sufficient bond to guarantee his return.[38] New converts seeking to travel by boat from one French province to another for business or personal reasons also had to secure passports; and laborers who lived close to the frontier in order to find seasonal employment in Spain, Italy, Switzerland, and Germany temporarily had to get permission to cross the border, but this bothersome requirement was soon dropped.[39]

At different times Louis tried every conceivable expedient to keep nonconformists at home except the obvious one of reëstablishing religious freedom. His ambassador in Holland, for example, employed informants who enjoyed the confidence of refugees to find out which persons in France were getting ready to escape, where the vessels sent to pick them up were to land and when they were to sail, how much specie was to be smuggled out and where it was hidden, and who was operating the underground railway. Most of the spies' reports—nearly al-

---

36 Bibliothèque de la Société Protestante, MS 444, fol. 222.

37 Archives Nationales, G⁷ 133; TT 243, *dossier* 4, doc. 37; Bibliothèque Nationale, *Fonds français*, MS 20966, fol. 287; Vaurigaud, *op. cit.*, III, 61–62, 90.

38 Archives Nationales, TT 454, *dossier* 37, doc. 170; B² *registres* 56, fols. 45 ff., 53 ff., 70 ff., 79 ff.; 57, fol. 77; 58, fol. 552; Bibliothèque Nationale, *Nouvelles acquisitions françaises*, MS 1206, fol. 51; Paul Bert, *Histoire de la révocation de l'édit de Nantes à Bordeaux et dans le Bordelais (1653–1715)* (Bordeaux, 1908), p. 99; *Recueil des Édits*, pp. 465–469; Vaurigaud, *op. cit.*, III, 110.

39 Bibliothèque Nationale, *Fonds français*, MS 7057, fols. 267–268; Bibliothèque de la Société Protestante, MS 485ᴵᴵ, fol. 82; Boislisle, *op. cit.*, I, 81, 302; Germain Martin, *La Grande industrie sous le règne de Louis XIV* (Paris, 1898), p. 248; Ernest Moret, "Fragment d'histoire sur les dernières persécutions sous Louis XIV (1711–1715)," *Séances et travaux de l'Académie des sciences morales et politiques,* XLIII (1858), 75–76.

ways in code—make fascinating reading.[40] The state encouraged intendants to develop their own espionage rings, and individuals seeking to recoup family fortunes or adventurers hoping to win royal favors offered to turn informer.[41] The government also tried to suppress the circulation of notices from foreign governments which offered the persecuted in France political and religious sanctuary, and to intercept exhortatory communications from refugees and exiled pastors addressed to persons at home. On the other hand, intercepted letters or communications that dwelt upon the misery and hardships of refugees in a strange environment were given wide publicity.[42] Although it was suggested that the government censor all mail coming from abroad in order to suppress undesirable information and to discover letters suitable for its propaganda machine, Seignelay did not approve and convinced the king that tampering with the mails would undermine what little confidence foreigners had in his government and would strike a harsh blow at commercial freedom.[43]

Still another tactic to keep Religionists at home was the confiscation of all their property if they left. They naturally tried to evade the law by liquidating their assets and transferring the funds abroad. Their panicky sale of property frequently disrupted local markets and depressed real estate prices. Many people sought to improve their personal fortunes by buying up as much as they could at these distress sales. The state was not the least sympathetic. A royal declaration of July 14, 1682, had voided any sale of property concluded within one year before the seller fled abroad. This remained the basic law until 1699, when Louis forbade converts to sell or dispose of their possessions in the next three years without first getting the approval of authorities. Successive extensions continued the prohibition until 1778.[44]

---

40 Archives Nationales, B2 *registre* 55, *passim;* Archives du Ministère des Affaires Étrangères, *Ancien fonds,* "Hollande," *registres* 143, *passim;* 145–146, *passim;* 148, fols. 111 ff.; 149, *passim;* 150, fols. 257–258; 164, fols. 110–111.

41 Archives Nationales, G7 3; B2 *registre* 55, fol. 604; Bibliothèque Nationale, *Fonds français,* MSS 7052, fols. 367 ff.; 7053, fol. 187; 21621, fols. 351–352.

42 Archives Nationales, A1 773; B2 *registres* 47, fol. 179; 61, fol. 343; Bibliothèque Nationale, *Fonds français,* MS 21619, fol. 265; Charles Weiss, *Histoire des réfugiés protestants de France depuis la révocation de l'Édit de Nantes jusqu'à nos jours* (Paris, 1853), I, 129.

43 Archives Nationales, B2 *registre* 57, fols. 69, 103; A1 757; Bibliothèque Nationale, *Fonds français,* MS 7044, fols. 211, 229.

44 Archives Nationales, G7 240, 492; O1 *registre* 29, fols. 512, 526–527; TT 436,

It is impossible at the present time to estimate even roughly the amount of property nonconformists disposed of before they tried to leave or the amount they lost to the Crown through confiscation. There are no data on distress sales, and those pertaining to confiscations are fragmentary and often confusing.[45] A few figures, however, will suggest the magnitude of the sums involved.

The intendant in Languedoc reported that up to March 9, 1687, property valued at 4,224,700 livres had been seized in his jurisdiction, of which "more than" 200,000 *écus* had since been returned to repatriates and a third was still tied up with outstanding debts. According to official statements for Saintonge and Aunis, refugees had lost property worth 250,000 livres by September 10, 1687, and by November 12, 1689, the total amounted to almost 2,000,000 livres, of which some 1,159,000 livres was clear of debt.[46] Confiscations in the jurisdiction of Rouen in 1686 involved properties yielding about 198,000 livres in annual income;[47] in the little area of Sedan, such revenues totaled almost 26,000 livres by July 31, 1687; and in 1688 and 1689 the king's receiver-general in Dauphiné collected revenues amounting to a little more than 116,000 livres. In 1688 the state seized properties in Champagne valued at approximately 500,000 livres, and a single wealthy Protestant who escaped from another province left possessions valued at 1,051,500 livres.[48] The historian Douen has estimated the value of property confiscated in Paris through 1724 at 6,500,000 livres;[49] another historian wrote in 1844 that "the registers for 1685 and 1686 carry the property added to the king's domain at 17,000,000 livres."[50] Together

"A Memorandum from the Bishop of Nantes"; B2 *registre* 55, fols. 135, 505, 539, 591; Boislisle, *op. cit.*, I, 56, 90–91, 535; II (1883), 58; Samuel Hardy, *Histoire de l'Église protestante de Dieppe* (Paris, 1896), p. 386; Lefèvre, *op. cit.*, pp. 504–505; Bibliothèque Nationale, *Fonds français*, MSS 7045, fols. 99, 272; 21617, fols. 192 ff.; Benoist, *op. cit.*, p. 292; Moret, *op. cit.*, pp. 69–70; *Recueil des Édits*, pp. 119–120, 407–410, 428–430, 445–448, 457–459, 474–477, 493–495, 496, 594–596.

45 Most of these data have been classified in Series TT, Archives Nationales, Paris.

46 Archives Nationales, TT 232, *dossier* 19, doc. 5; 247, doc. 183; B2 *registre* 62, fol. 201.

47 Jean Bianquis, *La Révocation de l'édit de Nantes à Rouen, essai historique* (Rouen, 1885), p. ciii; Francis Waddington, *Le Protestantisme en Normandie depuis la révocation de l'édit de Nantes jusqu'à la fin du dix-huitième siècle (1685–1797)* (Paris, 1862), p. 21.

48 Archives Nationales, TT 240, *dossier* 9, doc. 2; 243, *dossier* 4, doc. 20; 266, *dossier* 28, doc. 182; Bibliothèque Nationale, *Fonds français*, MS 21621, fol. 413.

49 *Op. cit.*, II, 499.

50 Jean-B.-H.-R. Capefigue, *Louis XIV, son gouvernement et ses relations diplomatiques avec l'Europe* (new ed.; Paris, 1844), I, 260.

these figures create the impression that material wealth worth many million livres passed from private into government hands.

What happened to all this property, and how was it managed? The law of 1682 had stipulated that it should be managed by the intendant in whose jurisdiction it lay. A little later (August 20, 1685) the king, hoping to spur neighbors to denounce refugees and reveal their holdings, offered to give half the property to any informant who helped the government locate it.[51] According to an edict of January, 1688, the confiscated property would be added to the king's domain unless Catholic heirs successfully filed claim to it within a year after their relative had fled.[52] Another edict signed in December, 1689, reaffirmed the right of Catholic kinsmen in good standing with the Church to claim the property provided they agreed not to sell or alienate it within five years after gaining possession; all the assets formerly owned by ministers and by organizations of the Reputedly Reformed Religion were to belong to the Crown.[53] Louis modified the law once again on September 13, 1699, when he established a special administrative agency to receive and manage confiscated property and refused to recognize the future claims of any heir.[54]

The last modification was apparently designed to correct a rather curious legal anomaly. Before 1699, if a nonconformist failed in his attempt to escape, he and his family lost everything to the state; if he succeeded, his family or his relatives could regain possession of his property provided they were Catholics in good standing. Frenchmen have always had strong family ties. Hence the relatives commonly considered themselves as trustees of property acquired in this way, managed it as though it still belonged to its original owner, and regularly remitted to him any revenues they collected and could smuggle out.[55]

The Protestant protagonist Charles Ancillon, writing in 1690, charged Louis with profiting personally from the confiscations.[56] There is little evidence, however, to support his accusation.

51 Archives Nationales, O¹ *registre* 29, fols. 525–526; Bibliothèque Nationale, *Fonds français*, MS 21617, fols. 142–143; *Recueil des Édits*, pp. 232–234; Benoist, *op. cit.*, p. 290.

52 *Recueil des Édits*, pp. 302–306.

53 *Ibid.*, pp. 330–336; Bibliothèque Nationale, *Fonds français*, MS 7050, fols. 226–227.

54 Archives Nationales, O¹ *registre* 42, fols. 68–69; TT 430, doc. 130; 436, "A Memorandum from the Bishop of Nantes"; 461, doc. 67.

55 Bibliothèque de la Société Protestante, MS 485ᴵᴵ, fol. 400.

56 *La France intéressée à rétablir l'Édit de Nantes* (Amsterdam, 1690), p. 141.

Aside from awarding some property seized in the Principality of Orange to the Prince of Conty in compensation for territories surrendered to the King of Prussia in 1707,[57] Louis apparently conformed to an order of council issued on March 31, 1688, which expressed his intention "to consecrate the said property entirely to the service of God and uniquely to employ it in what he considered the most useful way to advance the true religion and to instruct his subjects who have recently converted and to take care of children whose parents have left the realm." [58] There is ample evidence that a good portion of the revenues went to provide pensions and gratuities for those who abjured their heresy, to maintain Catholic charitable institutions which supposedly educated and cared for children of deserters, and to defray the cost of winning additional converts.

At first the Crown, regarding the confiscations as tentative, had planned to lure refugees back to France by offering to return their property if they joined the Church. Seignelay informed his subordinates on November 26, 1685, that the king was happy to return the possessions to any fugitive Huguenot who had been arrested at the frontier and who consented to repudiate his religion.[59] According to a royal declaration of January 10, 1686, anyone who had planned to escape and had hastily sold his property at distress prices could regain possession of it if he later decided to remain in France and become a Catholic. The king also promised in July of that year to surrender confiscated property if the owners returned from abroad before March 1, 1687, and abjured.[60] He held this offer open long after the original time limit had expired. He again invited refugees to return home and join the Church on February 10, 1698, and on December 29 promised that they would regain possession of their wealth, including any that had already gone to relatives, provided they took advantage of his offer within six months. The sons and daughters of refugees received the same promise if they returned within two years.[61]

---

57 Eugène Arnaud, "Les Derniers jours de l'église d'Orange, 1703–1731," *BSHPF*, XXXII (1883), 491–492.

58 Bibliothèque Nationale, *Fonds français*, MS 21617, fol. 222.

59 Archives Nationales, G7 297; B2 *registres* 55, fols. 337, 602; 61, fol. 289; O1 *registre* 29, fol. 523.

60 Bibliothèque Nationale, *Fonds français*, MSS 10623, fols. 69–70; 21623, fols. 56–57; *Recueil des Édits*, pp. 266–268, 291–294; Lefèvre, *op. cit.*, Appendix, pp. 28–29.

61 Bibliothèque Nationale, *Fonds français*, MSS 20966, fols. 251 ff.; 21617, fols. 172–173; *Recueil des Édits*, pp. 368–370, 379–384.

After the turn of the century the government became much less lenient in its treatment of repatriates. An ordonnance of 1713 required all refugees to obtain official permission to reënter the country; and at least two former Protestants were flatly denied their claims to property after they had belatedly returned. Louis XV, on October 27, 1725, retreated a bit from the stand taken by his great-grandfather. He permitted religious refugees and their descendants to return and regain French citizenship without any expense, but he barred them from recovering their property or from disturbing those who had taken it over.[62]

EFFORTS TO LURE REFUGEES BACK

Restoration of confiscated property was only one of several tactics Louis XIV employed to encourage refugees to repatriate. Immediately before and after the revocation edict appeared he ordered his entire diplomatic corps in foreign countries to work unceasingly at persuading nationals to return home. On April 13, 1685, Seignelay commanded consuls to send back any French sailor who had jumped ship in a foreign port; and on May 31 he wrote Barrillon, the French ambassador at London, to exert every effort to induce Huguenots arriving there to retrace their steps.[63] Late in December the same minister sent François d'Usson de Bonrepaus, intendant-general of the marine, to England as the king's special agent with secret instructions to repatriate as many refugees as he could. He was authorized to pay their passage home and even offer them additional gratuities if necessary. He was also to keep his ears open for expressions of public opinion and to deny at any and all times that his king was forcing Protestants to convert or was physically mistreating them in any way. Bonrepaus was then to visit The Hague and other Dutch cities, where he was to investigate Holland's general economic condition and commercial prospects in addition to serving as a recruiter of refugees and as royal propagandist.[64] Two special agents named Forant and Robert had gone to England several weeks before

---

62 Bibliothèque Nationale, *Fonds français*, MSS 7057, fol. 267; 10623, fols. 157–158, 181–182, 187–190, 217–218; 21617, fols. 204–205; 21623, fols. 18–21; *Receuil des Édits*, pp. 465–469.

63 Archives Nationales, B2 *registre* 55, fols. 153, 270.

64 Archives du Ministère des Affaires Étrangères, *Ancien fonds*, "Angleterre," *registres* 157, fol. 6; 160, fol. 270; Archives Nationales, B2 *registres* 52, fols. 307, 330 ff.; 57, fols. 189–190, 395. Bonrepaus's letters and reports during this, his first, mission are in *registres* 157 and 160 of the series for England in the Archives du Ministère des Affaires Étrangères.

Bonrepaus to work exclusively with Huguenots there, and an agent named Le Danois had been sent to the Netherlands to aid Louis's ambassador d'Avaux at The Hague and the French consul general Chabert in similar work.[65]

The correspondence between these special agents and their superiors at Versailles reveals how intensely Louis desired to repatriate all seamen and skilled craftsmen who might conceivably bolster the naval and economic strength of foreign powers.[66] During his first mission to England Bonrepaus persuaded about 507 refugees, or a little more than 10 per cent of those he found there, to return home. During his second mission to England, from May through December, 1687, he tried to repatriate some more.[67] Seignelay, however was not very sanguine of success. He wrote Bonrepaus on July 31:

You should continue your efforts to send fugitives back to France if you think you can persuade a considerable number. This would be a very useful way to serve His Majesty and would render him a great deal of pleasure. But if you find that your troubles are not crowned with enough success, you may abandon your efforts. I leave the decision entirely up to you.[68]

James II of England was quite willing to coöperate with Louis and Seignelay. He was already in the pay of the French king and considered the refugees in his realm to be his enemies. He would gladly have deported them had his own subjects felt otherwise than they did toward Huguenots. He secretly promised Louis that he would delay as long as possible before sanctioning a

---

[65] Archives Nationales, B² *registres* 52, fols. 322, 325 ff.; 55, fol. 603; 57, fols. 57–58; Archives du Ministère des Affaires Étrangères, *Ancien fonds,* "Angleterre," *registre* 157, fols. 13 ff.

[66] See, for example, Archives Nationales, A¹ 795, doc. 134; B² *registres* 47, fol. 441; 52, fol. 307; 55, fols. 205, 603; 57, fols. 140, 189–190, 212, 395; 58, fols. 654, 709, 857; 62, fols. 94–95, 98; 65, fols. 43–44; 66, fol. 191; Archives du Ministère des Affaires Étrangères, *Ancien fonds,* "Angleterre," *registres* 157, fols. 20, 82; 160, fols. 140, 270; "Hollande," *registres* 145, fol. 79; 146, fols. 71–72, 158; Bibliothèque Nationale, *Fonds français,* MS 7044, fol. 239; Prosper Boissonnade, "La Marine marchande, le port et les armateurs de la Rochelle à l'époque de Colbert (1662–1682)," in *Bulletin de la section de géographie: Comité des travaux historiques et scientifiques* (Paris, 1922), p. 36.

[67] Archives du Ministère des Affaires Étrangères, *Ancien fonds,* "Angleterre," *registres* 157, fols. 134, 139; 164, fols. 45, 109; Archives Nationales, B² *registre* 61, fol. 381; René Durand, "Louis XIV et Jacques II à la veille de la Révolution de 1689: les trois missions de Bonrepaus en Angleterre (1686–1687–1688)," *Revue d'histoire moderne et contemporaine,* X (1908), 115.

[68] Archives Nationales, B² *registre* 62, fol. 97.

public drive to collect funds for refugee aid, and he punished at least one English captain for having brought a group of fugitives to England on his ship.[69] Most Englishmen were unsympathetic with Louis's religious campaign. While in England Bonrepaus reported to Seignelay on May 5, 1686, that there had been "several plots" against his life, supposedly incited by refugees and supported by the Bishop of London.[70] Neither the government nor the people in Holland sympathized with the French agents working at repatriation. The burgomasters of Amsterdam and Rotterdam in 1687 even went so far as to compel French ship-masters to pay the wages due Protestant sailors who had deserted their ships upon arrival in Dutch ports, and they also menaced the French consul Chabert for having persuaded a few refugees to return home. Louis, livid with rage, immediately ordered his ambassador d'Avaux to inform the Dutch government that France would not tolerate such action. Louis threatened in reprisal to seize any Dutch ship dropping anchor in French waters and to prevent any Dutch merchant found in France from ever leaving the country.[71]

Louis encountered similar trouble from the Elector of Brandenburg. Early in 1688 the elector published a notice that French refugees could not leave Prussia without a passport issued by his authorities. Louis immediately had his Prussian envoy inform the elector that such action was intolerable and that France was prepared to retaliate in ways that would not be "agreeable" to the elector.[72] Louis had had little difficulty in bringing Geneva to heel in October, 1685. When that city ignored his demands to close its gates to all Huguenots seeking a haven, to turn out those already admitted, and to banish its most troublesome preachers to areas farther away from the frontier, he refused to allow its people to harvest and import the grain they had grown in the little adjacent French territory known as Gex. Geneva, fearing a shortage of food, acquiesced the second time Louis made his demands and on October 17 ordered all Frenchmen who had arrived during the past year to leave. Louis

---

69 *Ibid.*, B2 *registres* 57, fols. 57, 285–286; 61, fol. 382.

70 Archives du Ministère des Affaires Étrangères, *Ancien fonds,* "Angleterre," *registre* 157, fol. 135.

71 *Ibid.*, "Hollande," *registre* 150, fols. 231–233; Archives Nationales, B2 *registres* 61, fols. 258–259, 418; 62, fols. 67–68.

72 Archives du Ministère des Affaires Étrangères, *Ancien fonds,* "Prusse," *registres* 30, fol. 54; 33, fol. 18.

adopted a more conciliatory attitude toward the little republic after his enemies had formed the League of Augsburg and the threat of war loomed ever closer. By 1692 he was no longer making a major issue of the Huguenots befriended by Geneva.[73]

In addition to diplomatic representatives, still working as late as 1699–1700 to repatriate refugees in England, Holland, Germany, and Switzerland,[74] Louis enlisted the aid of French shipmasters. He urged them to bring home any emigrants they could persuade to come aboard and promised not only to pay the passengers' fares but also to reward the masters handsomely. After elaborate preparations and amid great secrecy he dispatched several vessels to England and Ireland in 1685 and 1686 for the sole purpose of bringing former subjects back into his realm. To those who agreed to return and to abjure he offered full pardon for the crime of escaping, complete recovery of possessions, freedom to work without fear of molestation, and even special financial aid in some instances.[75] Perhaps no one knows, or has ever known, how many refugees reëntered France because of such inducements, or because they could not endure the difficulties of earning a livelihood in an alien environment among hostile or resentful strangers. The most that can be said now is that there is little or no evidence that Louis succeeded in luring back a very large number.

THE NUMBER WHO EMIGRATED

I have already suggested that France might have had from 1.5 to 2 million Protestants among her citizens in 1680–1685, or roughly 10 per cent of her total population. How many of these fled to foreign countries before the zealous wrath of converters and the dogged determination of the king to stamp out their religion is a vital question, but an extremely difficult one to

---

[73] Bibliothèque de la Société Protestante, MS 628, pp. 243–245; Pierre Bertrand, *Genève et la Révocation de l'Édit de Nantes* (Geneva, 1935), pp. 55, 89.

[74] Archives Nationales, O1 *registre* 43, fol. 80; TT 464, doc. 53; Bibliothèque Nationale, *Fonds français*, MSS 7045, fol. 103; 20966, fols. 286–288; Guillaume-B. Depping, *Correspondance administrative sous le règne de Louis XIV* (Paris, 1850–1855), IV, 497.

[75] Archives Nationales, A1 757; 795, doc. 183; B2 *registres* 52, fols. 297–298, 300–301, 307; 55, fols. 249, 497, 540; 57, fols. 21–22, 189–190, 238; 58, fol. 596; 61, fol. 219; 62, fols. 87, 94–95, 98, 131, 144; 66, fol. 205; 73, fol. 182; B3 *registre* 51, fol. 314; Archives du Ministère des Affaires Étrangères, *Ancien fonds*, "Angleterre," *registre* 157, fol. 42; Vaurigaud, *op. cit.*, III, 162.

answer. The pertinent data so far uncovered are inadequate and far from reliable.[76]

Any attempt to estimate the number who emigrated must therefore rest primarily upon guesswork.[77] Scarcely any two authors in the past have agreed on the same figure. In 1753 Antoine Court, one of the most famous French Protestants in exile, stated that "more than 800,000" had left, and three years later he revised the figure to "more than 2,000,000."[78] Several others, writing at various times from the seventeenth century to the present, have given what they considered to be firm estimates; the higher estimates vary from 500,000 to 1,500,000. At the other extreme, the Duke of Burgundy confidently reported in 1710 that official statistics revealed an emigration of only 67,732 persons,[79] and Novi de Caveirac asserted in 1758 that not more than 50,000 Protestants had fled.[80] None of the estimates at either extreme is acceptable. A conservative statement, based upon calculations made by more than a hundred authors,[81] as

---

[76] Perhaps the chief sources for comprehensive data are the memoranda prepared by intendants at the turn of the century. For various reasons one should not place too much faith in their accuracy, (J.-A. Galland, *Essai sur l'histoire du Protestantisme à Caen et en Basse-Normandie de l'édit de Nantes à la Revolution (1598–1791)* [Paris, 1898], p. 253; Ph. Sagnac, "L'Industrie et le commerce de la draperie en France à la fin du XVIIᵉ siècle et au commencement du XVIIIᵉ," *Revue d'histoire moderne et contemporaine*, IX [1907–1908], 31, n. 1; Charles Weiss, "Mémoire sur les protestants de France au XVIIᵉ siècle," *Séances et travaux de l'Académie des sciences morales et politiques*, XX [1851], 114.)

[77] The documents compiled by officials charged with administering emigrants' property are abundant, but they are so fragmentary and inadequate in coverage that they afford little help. Perhaps most Huguenots left no property to be confiscated. Some owned little tangible wealth that could not be taken with them, and many others succeeded in liquidating their possessions or in deeding them to relatives before they fled. Hence their names do not appear in the records kept by administrators. (*BSHPF*, XLVIII [1899], 372.) Nevertheless, Eugène and Émile Haag thought that after 1689 the government confiscated property belonging to some 100,000 refugees (*op. cit.*, I, lxxxii).

[78] *Lettre d'un patriote sur la tolérance civile des protestans de France et sur les avantages qui en resulteroient pour le royaume* (n.p., 1756), p. 12; *Le Patriote françois et impartial ou response à la lettre de Mᵣ l'evêque d'Agen à Mᵣ le controleur genéral contre la Tolerance des Huguenots, en datte du 1 mai 1751* (new ed.; Villefranche, 1753), I, 379.

[79] Charles Read, "L'Opinion du duc de Bourgogne sur la question protestante et le rappel des huguenots (1710)," *BSHPF*, XLI (1892), 347; Lavisse, *op. cit.*, Vol. VIII, Part 1, p. 349.

[80] *Apologie de Louis XIV et de son conseil, sur la révocation de l'Édit de Nantes, etc.* (n.p., 1758), pp. 72 ff.

[81] Some representative "guesses" will illustrate how greatly opinions have varied. A spy for the French ambassador at The Hague reported on May 24, 1686, that a

well as upon inferences drawn from scattered statistics in contemporary manuscripts, would be that approximately 200,000
Frenchmen sought a haven in foreign countries in the period
1681–1720 because of the revocation of the Edict of Nantes. In

---

list of 75,000 refugees had already been turned over to William of Orange (Archives
du Ministère des Affaires Étrangères, *Ancien fonds,* "Hollande," *registre* 149, fols.
180–181). The famous Protestant theologian Pierre Jurieu thought that 200,000
had already left France by February, 1688, and predicted that half a million would
eventually flee (*op. cit.,* II, 91, 151, 152). Gaultier de Saint-Blancard agreed that
200,000 had left (*op. cit.,* II, 50–51, 551 ff.), and the exiled theologian Jacques
Basnage estimated the number in 1686 at 150,000, and somewhat later at 300,000–
400,000 (Reginald Lane Poole, *A History of the Huguenots of the Dispersion at
the Recall of the Edict of Nantes* [London, 1880], p. 167). Some have said that
184,000 persons left Normandy alone (Henri Amphoux, *Essai sur l'histoire du
Protestantisme au Havre et dans ses environs* [Le Havre, 1894], p. 236, and Henry
M. Baird, *The Huguenots and the Revocation of the Edict of Nantes* [New York,
1895], II, 100). Although Émile-G. Léonard appears to have accepted the figure of
200,000 for all France in his article "Le Protestantisme français au XVIIe siècle"
(*Revue historique,* CC [1948], 176), in his Sorbonne lectures which I attended in
1949 he stated that 200,000 was too small an estimate and 600,000 too large. N.
Weiss also thought 200,000 was too small (*BSHPF,* LXIII–LXIV [1914–1915], 183);
and Charles Weiss settled upon 250,000 or 300,000 ("Mémoire sur les protestants,"
op. cit., XX, 101, 113). Capefigue, writing in 1844, tried to determine the number
as accurately as possible and came up with an estimate of 225,000 or 230,000
(*op. cit.,* I, 260). Beaumelle in 1759 suggested about 300,000 (Bibliothèque Nationale,
Fonds français, MS 7047, fol. 476). Poole thought 300,000 or 350,000 would be a
reasonable estimate (*op. cit.,* p. 169); Léonce Anquez suggested 300,000 (*De
l'État civil des réformés de France* [Paris, 1868], p. 65); and Sismondi gave 300,000
or 400,000 (*Histoire des français* [Paris, 1821–1844], XXV, 552).

Jean Claude, in *Les Plaintes des Protestants . . .* (Cologne, 1713), p. xx, estimated
the number of fugitives at 400,000 or 500,000, as did Félice (*op. cit.,* p. 440). A half
million or "more than 500,000" has been a popular guess (Novi de Caveirac,
*Mémoire politico-critique, où l'on examine s'il est de l'intérêt de l'Eglise et de
l'Etat d'établir pour les Calvinistes du Royaume une nouvelle forme de se marier*
[n.p., 1756], pp. 5–19; Herbert W. Ellinger, *Les Réfugiés Huguenots en Saxe-
Weimar; leurs manufactures de bonneterie* [Gap, 1933], pp. 6, 131; Urbain de
Robert-Labarthe, *Histoire du protestantisme dans le Haut-Languedoc, le Bas-
Quercy et le comté de Foix de 1685 à 1789* [Paris, 1892–1896], I, 94 n. 1; James Mac-
Pherson, *The History of Great Britain from the Restoration to the Accession of
the House of Hanover* [London, 1775], I, 462; Frank Puaux and A. Sabatier, *Études
sur la révocation de l'Édit de Nantes* [Paris, 1886], p. 4 n. 2; Voltaire as quoted in
Poole, *op. cit.,* p. 166; N. Weiss as quoted in H. M. Baird, *op. cit.,* II, 100). Erman
and Reclam (*Mémoires pour servir à l'histoire des réfugiés françois dans les
états du Roi* [Berlin, 1782–1799], I, 177) suggested that about one-third of the 2 or
3 million Protestants in France left; Charles Ancillon (*Histoire de l'établissement
des françois réfugiés dans les états de son altesse electorale de Brandebourg*
[Berlin, 1690], p. 62) put the figure at 1 million; more than two centuries later
Rébelliau did the same (in Lavisse, *op. cit.,* Vol. VIII, Part 1, p. 343); a German
correspondent of the Abbé Raynal near the end of the eighteenth century voiced
the opinion that 600,000 Huguenots fled, and another person at about the same
time thought that 1.5 million would be nearer the truth (*BSHPF,* VIII [1859], 328;

other words, from 10 to 13 per cent of the Protestants—or roughly 1 per cent of the country's total population—left France.

If correct, this estimate means that in the four critical decades an average of 5,000 Frenchmen left their homes each year. In view of the inadequate travel facilities of the time and the government's efforts to police all frontiers, even this number may appear to be too large. As a matter of fact, the exodus did not take place uniformly over the four decades but was concentrated in a relatively brief period (1685–1688) when perhaps 40,000 individuals crossed the frontier each year.

Between 1661, when Louis XIV began to govern directly and first showed hostility to Protestantism, and 1681, when Marillac employed royal dragoons in Poitou for the first time, a few families had hearkened to the beckoning calls of other countries and had left.[82] Then, in 1681–1683, large numbers fled from Poitou and La Rochelle, and wealthy Protestants in Paris and other commercial centers also grew alarmed and embarked for England or Holland.[83] A 1683 report on passenger boats between Calais and England stated that their traffic and passenger revenues had increased markedly during the past two years because so many Huguenots were seeking asylum in England.[84] Emigration next assumed alarming proportions when the king signed the revocation edict and published it throughout his realm in October, 1685. Except during the winter months, when snow closed the mountain passes leading into Switzerland and Germany and when travel by boat was difficult, the mass exodus continued

Lettres à M. l'abbé Raynal sur l'histoire de la Révocation de l'Édit de Nantes qu'il se propose de publier [1782]; Bibliothèque Nationale, *Fonds français*, MS 7047, fols. 555–556). Ripert Montclar and Abbé Quesnel (*Mémoire théologique et politique au sujet des mariages clandestins des protestans de France* [2d ed.; n.p., 1756], p. 7) claimed that "historians" accepted 1.5 million as the best estimate, and about 1780 Bertrand stated in his manuscript memorandum on Protestants that about 1 million left France (Bibliothèque Nationale, *Fonds français*, MS 6432, pp. 187, 191). The Marquis de la Fare (*Mémoires et Réflexions sur les principaux événements du règne de Louis XIV* [Amsterdam, 1775], p. 223) claimed that the king's cruelty drove 800,000 individuals from his realm (as quoted by Sophronyme Beaujour, *Essai sur l'histoire de l'Église Réformée de Caen* [Caen, 1877], pp. 346–348).

[82] Albert Carré, *L'Influence des Huguenots français en Irlande aux XVIIᵉ et XVIIIᵉ siècles* (Paris, 1937), pp. 3–5; C. Weiss, *Histoire des réfugiés*, II, 4.

[83] Archives Nationales, TT 267, *dossier* 17, doc. 69; Bibliothèque Nationale, *Fonds français*, MS 21618, *passim;* Baudry, *op. cit.*, pp. 231–232; Benoît, *op. cit.*, IV, 493; Nazelle, *op. cit.*, pp. 22, 33–34; "Journal d'un marin protestant du XVIIᵉ siècle (Taré Chaillaud)," *BSHPF*, XV (1866), 320–322.

[84] Archives Nationales, G⁷ 84.

until the activities of the League of Augsburg and the Bloodless Revolution in England frightened the Crown into shifting its major attention from religious to political and military matters. During the long war that erupted in 1688–1689 emigration slackened and remained at a relatively low level. Many Protestants who had been on the verge of leaving took heart from the lull in persecution and decided to stay at home. Some even thought that peace might bring a reversal in the government's policy, but they were rudely disillusioned when Louis reiterated his un-compromising stand against their religion in his 1698 decree. Mass emigration then revived,[85] though on a much smaller scale than in 1685–1688. Perhaps 3,000 Huguenots fled their homes in the Principality of Orange as soon as Louis reannexed the territory in 1703 and banned their religion. The War of the Spanish Succession, like the preceding war, brought a temporary halt to persecution, and relatively few Huguenots sought to escape. Peace, however, permitted the king once again to give his attention to Protestants, and in 1715 he proclaimed that all of them would thereafter be treated as though they had at one time or another abjured their faith and joined the Catholic Church. The mild revival of coercive tactics during the last two years of his reign led to another small wave of emi-gration.

Where did most of the fugitives settle? There is a real danger of double counting, for many fugitives who figured in the official records of Swiss cities, for example, were transients who finally settled in Germany, where they again appeared on the rolls. Conclusions drawn from the data now available for each country must therefore be tentative.

In England, a group seeking financial aid from King William in 1694 stated that there were already 33,000 Huguenots in his realm and that more were arriving daily from Germany and Switzerland.[86] Gilbert Burnet, Bishop of Salisbury, after traveling in France after the revocation and seeing the misery there, wrote

---

85 *Ibid.*, O1 *registre* 42, *passim;* Bibliothèque Nationale, *Fonds français*, MS 7045, fols. 256–257.

86 George B. Beeman, "Notes on the City of London Records Dealing with the French Protestant Refugees, Especially with Reference to the Collections Made under Various Briefs," *Proceedings of the Huguenot Society of London* (herein-after cited as *PHSL*), VII (1901–1904), 139 n. 1; César Pascal, "Les Collectes nationales anglaises en faveur des réfugiés protestants (1681–1699)," *BSHPF*, XLI, 323.

that from 40,000 to 50,000 refugees had settled in England.[87] Anisson and Fénellon, in their "Mémoire sur la négotiation faite à Londres pour la traitté de commerce en années 1713 et 1714," bewailing the fact that a very large number of their countrymen had settled in England, estimated that "the French who are in and around London, together with their children born since their retreat, amount to 90,000 souls."[88] Both James MacPherson and Adam Anderson believed that approximately 50,000 had settled in England proper.[89] It has been definitely established that there were about thirty Huguenot churches in and around London at the turn of the century;[90] and the available information indicates that the number of refugees receiving financial aid each year varied from approximately 9,000 in 1687 to about 2,500 in 1693 and 1696, and to about 7,000 in 1721.[91] From 20,000 to 50,000 would be a cautious estimate of the number who settled throughout England, and an actual count would most likely have placed the figure somewhere between 40,000 and 50,000.[92]

After 1661 the Lord Deputy and the Parliament of Ireland tried to attract French emigrants to that island. The data as to how many responded to their appeals, especially after 1685, are even scarcer than those for England. Most of the Huguenots did

[87] *Mémoires pour servir à l'histoire de la Grande-Bretagne sous les règnes de Charles II et de Jacques II avec une Introduction, depuis le Commencement du Règne de Jacques I, jusqu'au Rétablissement de la Famille Royale*, III (The Hague, 1725), 93.

[88] Archives Nationales, G7 1704.

[89] Adam Anderson, *An Historical and Chronological Deduction of the Origin of Commerce, from the Earliest Accounts etc.* (London, 1801), II, 569; MacPherson, *op. cit.*, I, 462.

[90] Fernand de Schickler, *Les Églises du Réfuge* (Paris, 1882), p. 102; Émile Lesens, *Le Protestantisme dans le pays de Caux (ancien colloque de Caux, Havre et Dieppe excepté)*, ed. Victor Madelaine (Bolbec, [1906]), p. 210; C. Weiss, *Histoire des réfugiés*, I, 274–276; Henry J. Cowell, *The Edict of Nantes and Afterwards. The Story of the Huguenots, 1685–1935* (3d ed.; London, [1936]), p. 12. Weiss thinks that only about a third of the refugees settled in the immediate vicinity of London.

[91] Beeman, *op. cit.*, pp. 139–140. In the single month of November, 1687, there may have been as many as 15,500 in London receiving charity (Puaux and Sabatier, *op. cit.*, p. 4 n. 2).

[92] Bonrepaus, Louis XIV's special emissary, wrote from London on March 11, 1686, that "about 4,500" had arrived in England since 1682 (Archives du Ministère des Affaires Étrangères, *Ancien fonds*, "Angleterre," *registre* 157, fol. 90). His figure, based on the number seen attending churches where services were conducted in French, appears wholly unreliable. Like most other agents of his king, Bonrepaus had important reasons for underestimating the effects of the revocation.

not come directly from France but from Switzerland, Germany, Holland, and England, where they had first sought refuge. One authority has concluded that the number could scarcely have been above 10,000.[93] A minimal figure would perhaps be 5,000.[94] In all, there were ten Huguenot churches established in Ireland; five colonies of refugees had ministers but no church buildings; six towns possessed too few Huguenots to maintain a minister; and there may have been, in addition, seven other places where a mere handful settled.[95]

Holland, or more accurately the seven United Provinces, also welcomed French refugees. Between 1681 and March, 1684, some 1,500 arrived at Amsterdam with about 226 looms. At least 428 of these were registered as citizens before the end of 1684, and Amsterdam added more than 1,700 others to its citizenship roll in 1685–1691.[96] A Huguenot spy in the employ of the French ambassador wrote on January 28, 1687, that in the past six months, according to church records, more than 1,800 Protestants had arrived in various Dutch cities. The same individual had reported on April 15, 1686, that there were about 16,000 refugees in the country. A member of the French Embassy wrote Paris toward the end of 1685 that there were already "more than" 5,000 in Rotterdam and an even larger number in Amsterdam.[97] Protestant crews of French vessels putting into Dutch ports deserted ship en masse;[98] pastors exiled from Normandy reported that they were ministering to the spirtual needs of up to two-thirds of their old congregations;[99] each ship arriving in Holland unloaded scores of refugees;[100] and entire sections of The Hague,

---

93 Carré, *op. cit.*, p. 14.

94 One refugee in Ireland was so amazed to see only 200 immigrants arrive during some five or six weeks after the dragoons had begun to march in Poitou in 1681, that he set about to enlighten his fellow countrymen as to the opportunities offered by Ireland. With this purpose in mind he published a little book entitled *De l'État présent d'Irlande et des Avantages qu'y peuvent trouver les Protestants français* (Carré, *op. cit.*, pp. 6–7).

95 Grace Lawless Lee, *The Huguenot Settlements in Ireland* (London, 1936), pp. 23–24. See also Carré, *op. cit.*, p. 12; Cowell, *op. cit.*, p. 12.

96 Leonie van Nierop, "Stukken Betreffende de Nijverheid der Refugiés te Amsterdam," *Economische-Historisch Jaarboek*, VII (1921), 180–195; IX (1923), 210.

97 Archives du Ministère des Affaires Étrangères, *Ancien fonds*, "Hollande," *registres* 143, fol. 167; 149, fol. 139; 153, fols. 15–16.

98 Thomas Miller Maguire, "Frenchmen on the Seas," *PHSL*, VIII (1905–1908), 168.

99 Bianquis, *op. cit.*, p. xciv.

100 Archives du Ministère des Affaires Étrangères, *Ancien fonds*, "Hollande," *registres* 150, fol. 236; 152, fol. 174.

Rotterdam, and Amsterdam were peopled by Frenchmen.[101] By 1715 the total number of Huguenots in Holland was probably larger than the number permanently settled in any other country. Fragmentary data like the above and inferences drawn from contemporary records leave the impression that the number may have fallen between 50,000 and 75,000.[102]

What about Germany? Because of censuses taken in the eighteenth century and because of careful research by German historical scholars, opinions as to the number of Huguenots who settled there are less uncertain and divergent than for any other area. Of the approximately 30,000 who migrated to all German provinces, about two-thirds found a haven in Brandenburg, which had a total population of about 1.5 million. Almost 6,000 of these founded the "new city" outside old Berlin or settled within the walled area itself. They constituted about one-fifth or one-sixth of the capital's population. Perhaps 2,000 to 3,000 settled in Hesse-Cassel; approximately 2,000 in Lüneburg; 1,000 or 2,000 in Bavaria; and the rest in other provinces. About 40 per cent passed from France via Switzerland and up the Rhine, and the remainder came through Holland.[103]

Geneva and the Swiss cantons have been called the arch under which some 60,000 refugees surged between 1682 and 1720.[104]

---

101 Charles Weiss, "Mémoire sur l'influence littéraire des réfugiés protestants de France en Hollande," *Séances et travaux de l'Académie des sciences morales et politiques*, XXV (1853), 309.

102 According to both Weiss (*ibid.*, XXV, 309) and Rébelliau (in Lavisse, *op. cit.*, Vol. VIII, Part 1, p. 343), the French ambassador at The Hague reported 75,000 refugees already in Holland in 1686. I was unable to find any such figure in the official correspondence, but did discover an estimate of 16,000 made by d'Avaux's spy in 1686. Poole (*op. cit.*, p. 169) estimates 100,000; Cowell (*op. cit.*, p. 11) accepts 75,000; and Novi de Caveirac, whom one would not suspect of exaggeration because of his strong Catholic sympathies, is said by Weiss to have suggested 55,000.

103 Archives du Ministère des Affaires Étrangères, *Ancien fonds*, "Prusse," *registres* 25, fol. 450; 26, fol. 76; 28, fol. 348; 30, fol. 94; "Suisse," *registre* 81, fol. 384; Bibliothèque Nationale, *Fonds français*, MS 6432, pp. 122, 139; Anderson, *op. cit.*, II, 568; C. Couderc, "L'Abbé Raynal et son projet d'histoire de la Révocation de l'Édit de Nantes, documents sur le Réfuge," *BSHPF*, XXXVIII (1889), 592 ff.; Helmut Erbe, *Die Hugenotten in Deutschland* (Essen, 1937), pp. 34, 39, 255-256, 262-265; Erman and Reclam, *op. cit.*, II, 35-38; VI, 134; P. Sagnac, in Lavisse, *op. cit.*, Vol. VIII, Part 1, p. 207; Novi de Caveirac, *Apologie de Louis XIV*, pp. 86-87; *PHSL*, XVI (1938-1941), 266-268; C. Weiss, *Histoire des réfugiés*, I, 138. Louis XIV's representative at Berlin, of course, always attempted to minimize the number of refugees.

104 Gaberel, *op. cit.*, pp. 98-99; Johann-Caspar Moerikofer, *Histoire des Réfugiés de la Réforme en Suisse*, trans. G. Roux (Paris, 1878), p. 199; Edmond Chevrier, *Le Protestantisme dans le Mâconnais et la Bresse aux XVIe et XVIIe siècles* (Mâcon,

Of this number perhaps 25,000 remained in Switzerland, and the rest moved on to Germany, Holland, and elsewhere.[105] The influx, beginning in 1682, reached its peak in 1686–1687. In each of several weeks in the last half of 1687 from 700 to more than 1,000 emigrants filed through Geneva,[106] and by the end of that year upward of 28,000 refugees probably had passed that way.[107] The inhabitants of Gex and neighboring valleys in Dauphiné fled almost as a body in 1685–1686. The migration dwindled in the 1690's only to be followed by the mass exodus of some 3,000 individuals from Orange in 1703.

The Swiss cantons were unable to absorb all the arrivals. Geneva had opened the French Exchange (*Bourse*) and Bern the Chamber of Refugees to aid the most necessitous newcomers and to find ways to resettle them in other Swiss areas or in Germany.[108] According to Tambonneau, Louis XIV's envoy to Switzerland, representatives of four cantons had already met before October 20, 1685, to consider the best way to handle the mounting tide.[109] An official delegation, appointed in 1688, visited various German states and other countries in northern Europe to enlist their aid.[110] The Elector of Brandenburg, the Landgrave of Hesse-Cassel, and the Prince of Bayreuth, among others, rallied to the plea.[111] The Chamber of Refugees on

---

1868), p. 66. Bertrand, in his memorandum written shortly before the French Revolution, stated that some 140,000 passed into or through Switzerland (Bibliothèque Nationale, *Fonds français*, MS 6432, p. 187), and Couderc ("L'Abbé Raynal," *BSHPF*, XXXIX [1890], 48) apparently accepted this figure. Novi de Caveirac's estimate of 12,000 (*Apologie de Louis XIV*, pp. 86–87) falls far short of any reasonable figure.

105 Poole (*op. cit.*, p. 169) arrived at the same conclusion.

106 Bertrand, *op. cit.*, p. 68.

107 Solomiac, "Le Réfuge dans le pays de Vaud (1685–1860)," *BSHPF*, IX (1860), 143.

108 The records kept by these two agencies provide the most important data available as to the number and the financial condition of refugees. The Bibliothèque de la Société Protestante at Paris has a list of those assisted by the French Exchange at Geneva (MS 151[1]).

109 Archives du Ministère des Affaires Étrangères, *Ancien fonds*, "Suisse," *registre* 80, fol. 370. The French ambassador at The Hague wrote Louis on November 21, 1686, that the states of Zurich and Bern had recently asked the Estates-General of Holland whether the Dutch provinces could help relieve the pressure of immigrants by providing permanent homes for some of them (*ibid.*, "Hollande," *registre* 148, fol. 179).

110 Bibliothèque de la Société Protestante, MS 6171, *passim*; Mme Alexandre de Chambrier, "Projet de Colonisation en Irlande, par les réfugiés français, 1692–1699," *PHSL*, VI (1898–1901), 374.

111 Archives du Ministère des Affaires Étrangères, *Ancien fonds*, "Suisse," *registre* 81, fol. 384; Bibliothèque Nationale, *Fonds français*, MS 6432, p. 184.

July 3, 1698, published a statement recommending that as many Protestants as possible should pass on to Germany, where they were assured of a permanent home and the right to engage in business.[112]

Of the 25,000 who may have remained in Switzerland, between 3,000 and 4,000 settled in Geneva and comprised about one-fourth its population.[113] By 1698 the present canton of Vaud (in the seventeenth and eighteenth centuries part of the State of Bern) provided a refuge for more than 6,000 Frenchmen, and the populations of Vevey and Lausanne were from one-half to one-fourth immigrant.[114] Bern itself contained about 2,000 refugees, or one-fifth its population.[115] From December 3, 1683, to January 1, 1689, according to an official list, 23,345 Huguenots sought assistance from Zurich, but most of them soon moved on to Germany. Perhaps from 4,000 to 8,000 remained permanently in the area.[116] The cantons of Neuchâtel and Saint-Gall also harbored some Frenchmen.[117]

The minimum figures given for the number of Huguenots settling in England, Ireland, Holland, Germany, and Switzerland total 150,000 and the maximum figures add up to 190,000. As controls, these suggest that the original estimate of 200,000 for those leaving France may not be unreasonable. Relatively small groups settled in other areas—such as the New England and South Atlantic American colonies, the Channel Islands, South Africa, Constantinople, Denmark, and Sweden—but their number was not large enough to justify a revision of the total

---

112 Moerikofer, *op. cit.*, pp. 248–249.

113 Bertrand, *op. cit.*, pp. 106, 118; Émile Piguet, "Les Dénombrements généraux de Réfugiés au Pays de Vaud et à Berne, à la fin du XVIIe siècle," *BSHPF*, LXXXII (1933), 37–38. The censuses taken in 1693 and 1698 have proven most helpful.

114 Solomiac, *op. cit.*, pp. 143–144; Piguet, *op. cit.*, pp. 37–38; Mme Alexandre de Chambrier, *Henri de Mirmant et les réfugiés de la Révocation de l'Édit de Nantes, 1650–1721* (Neuchâtel, 1910), p. 64; Jules Chavannes, *Les Réfugiés français dans le pays de Vaud et particulièrement à Vevey* (Lausanne, 1874), pp. 25–26 n., 137–138.

115 Bibliothèque Nationale, *Fonds français*, MS 6432, pp. 181, 184; Piguet, *op. cit.*, pp. 37–38; Chavannes, *op. cit.*, pp. 25–26 n.; Mme Alexandre de Chambrier, "Les Réfugiés français en Suisse de 1593 à 1699 et la convention entre Berne et les cantons évangéliques," *BSHPF*, LVIII (1909), 108.

116 Archives du Ministère des Affaires Étrangères, *Ancien fonds*, "Suisse," *registres* 80, fol. 399; 83, fols. 471–472; Moerikofer, *op. cit.*, pp. 215, 230–231; Solomiac, *op. cit.*, p. 143; Ernest Combe, *Les Réfugiés de la Révocation en Suisse* (Lausanne, 1885), p. 67; G. Desdevises de Dézert, *L'Église et l'état en France depuis l'Édit de Nantes jusqu'au Concordat (1598–1801)* (Paris, 1907), p. 157.

117 See, especially, Mme Alexandre de Chambrier, "Naturalisation des Réfugiés français à Neuchâtel," *Musée neuchâtelois*, 37th year (1900); and Théodore Rivier, *L'Église réformée française de Saint-Gall (1685 à nos jours)* (Paris, 1909).

estimate. There is no way of ascertaining how many unconverted refugees returned home surreptitiously or, after renouncing
their faith, sought to regain title to their possessions. Bonrepaus
persuaded 507 to return from England; many who had hysteri-
cally deserted their homes in Gex and the valleys lying close to
the Swiss or Savoy frontiers gradually drifted back;[118] Ambassador
d'Avaux wrote Louis that many in Holland were trying to return;[119] Rébenac from Berlin assured His Majesty in 1687
that several in Germany were repatriating;[120] and some who
had fled Poitou eventually went back.[121] There is little reason
to believe, however, that repatriation reduced the number of emigrants appreciably even though Louis XIV tried his best to effect
their return, and even though life in a foreign environment was
hard on many during their first years.

A loss of 200,000 individuals, or no more than 1 per cent of
the entire population, may seem an inconsequential matter.
Perhaps this is one reason that several writers, convinced that
emigration caused significant economic damage, have consciously
or unconsciously exaggerated the number who fled. But emigration does not necessarily involve extremely large numbers of
people in order to wreak havoc upon a country's social and economic relationships. Most economists now recognize that incremental variations in magnitudes can create disproportionately
difficult problems. As far as inflation and deflation and their
effect upon the redistribution of real wealth and income among
social classes are concerned, for example, increases or decreases
in the government debt are much more significant than its
absolute size. Reductions or additions to the volume of savings
and investments, regardless of the total amounts saved and in-

---

118 Archives Nationales, G7 241.

119 Archives du Ministère des Affaires Étrangères, *Ancien fonds,* "Hollande,"
registre 150, fols. 232–233.

120 G. Pagès, "Les Réfugiés à Berlin d'après la correspondance du comte de
Rébenac (1681–1688)," *BSHPF,* LI (1902), 135.

121 Baudry, *op. cit.,* pp. 269 ff. The intendant in Dauphiné reported that, of 2,434
who had left since 1685, 156 returned in the single year 1699 (Archives Nationales,
TT 243, *dossier* 4, doc. 36; 435, *dossier* 1). Bâville claimed on October 16, 1699, that
of 4,000 who had deserted Languedoc, 1,300 had come back (Bibliothèque Nationale,
Fonds français, MS 7045, fol. 270); but only about 1 per cent of those fleeing
Vitry-le-François ever returned (G. Hérelle, *Documents inédits sur le protestantisme
à Vitry-le-François . . . depuis la fin des Guerres de Religion jusqu'à la Révolution
française* [Paris, 1903–1908], III, 484).

vested each year, usually act as powerful depressants or stimulants to the entire economy. Even relatively small variations in the volume of foreign trade may have significant repercussions upon every segment of economic life, although—as is true of the United States—foreign trade may account for less than 10 per cent of the national income. Small increments in total output in certain sectors, such as agriculture, may so depress prices as to create real distress among producers and occasion embarrassing problems of surpluses; small decrements in output or in the market demand for products—for example, in industries specializing in heavy capital goods—may snowball into an alarming degree of unemployment throughout the economy and into a shrinkage in national income. In the past several decades economists have become concerned about incremental variations and have devised such concepts as "leakages," "the multiplier effect," and "the acceleration of derived demand" to help them analyze and explain developments which appear on the surface to be disproportionately large vis-à-vis the initiating causes. It is conceivable, therefore, that an appreciable increase or decrease in a country's adult population might touch off a series of chain reactions which eventually would seriously disturb the country's volume of employment and the level of its national income.

The Huguenot dispersion, therefore, might well have been the most important single factor responsible for the long depression that plagued the last three decades of Louis XIV's protracted reign. Many historians have long thought that it was. If the refugees were drawn from the most industrious, the most enterprising, and the wealthiest classes, their departure must have struck more directly at the nerve center of the country's economy than if they had played an unimportant role in its economic life. Among the 281 individuals listed in one document as having fled from Nîmes were 40 nobles, 34 ministers or theological students, 7 lawyers, 5 doctors or surgeons, 32 merchants, 1 bookseller, 1 schoolmaster, several military officers, 45 artisans, and 72 children.[122] Refugees from Vitry-le-François in Champagne included 8 persons who later became members of the Royal

---

[122] A. M. de Boislisle, "Liste des protestants de Nîmes émigrés à la suite de la révocation d'édit de Nantes," *Revue des sociétés savantes des départements,* 6th series, VIII (1878), 256–257. The remaining forty-four persons presumably were wives. See also Charles Sagnier, "Une Liste de réfugiés Nîmois en 1686," *BSHPF,* XXVIII (1879), 261.

Society of London or of the Academy of Berlin, 3 who became diplomatic agents or plenipotentiaries for their adopted countries, 26 churchmen, 8 judges, 37 army officers, 10 doctors, 19 surgeons, 11 apothecaries, 1 architect, 1 expert in fortifications, 1 painter, 2 master engravers, 7 schoolmasters, 1 director of public information, 4 bankers, 62 merchants, 28 peasants, and 286 tradespeople and artisans.[123] Paris lost 21 or more goldsmiths and at least 1 lapidary, 10 clockmakers, 1 dyer, 7 stocking knitters, 5 embroiderers, 3 rug weavers, 10 skilled workers in passementerie, 6 button coverers, 4 weavers of gold and silver cloth, 8 silkworkers, 2 wigmakers, 14 or more bankers, 6 merchants specializing in gold and silver lace, and 20 or more other merchants.[124] Some 140 families had fled Dieppe by 1686. They included 8 drapers, 4 mercers, 5 ivory workers, 3 lacemakers, 1 rug weaver, 2 bakers, 1 goldsmith, 2 tailors, 2 chandlers, 3 combmakers, 1 fishmonger, 1 hatter, 1 brewer, 1 tool sharpener, 16 sailors, 1 lawyer, 1 apothecary, 1 interpreter, 1 engineer, 19 merchants, 22 widows, and 38 others whose occupations were not given.[125] These are all incomplete lists. Yet they leave the impression that scarcely any occupation was unaffected by the Huguenot emigration. The remainder of this study will be primarily concerned with the following questions: Did the departure of 200,000 Huguenots hurt certain industries in which they were especially active, and did it depress foreign and domestic trade, finance, and agriculture? May religious persecution be ranked as a major cause of the economic stagnation that developed after 1683?

---

123 Hérelle, *op. cit.*, III, 484–486. The tradespeople and artisans may be grouped as follows: (1) 8 bakers and confectioners, 4 brewers, 3 butchers, 3 cooks, 5 domestic servants, 1 grocer, and 3 mercers; (2) 5 operators of restaurants and cabarets, 1 chair porter, and 1 barber; (3) 10 bookkeepers and 1 printer; (4) 5 carpenters, 4 hod carriers, 5 masons, and 1 stonecutter; (5) 2 carters, 5 cutlers and tool sharpeners, 1 cooper, 7 clockmakers, 1 founder, 2 furbishers, 7 glaziers and glassmakers, 3 makers of hardware, 4 locksmiths, 4 millers, 1 maker of sieves, 1 tin potter, and 1 wheelwright; (6) 14 jewelers and goldsmiths and 4 lapidaries; (7) 13 dressmakers and tailors, 6 hatters, 20 glovers, 7 leather dressers and tanners, 18 shoemakers and cobblers, and 12 wigmakers; and (8) 20 knitters of stockings and 6 more who knitted other things, 6 workers in passementerie, 2 workers in silk and 3 others in velvet, 1 rug weaver, and 44 woolworkers (shearers, carders, combers, weavers, dyers, drapers, and makers of serge and camelet).

124 Douen, *op. cit.*, II, 481–482.

125 Hardy, *op. cit.*, p. 371.

V

The Economic Status
of Huguenots

At the outset, Protestantism appealed to Frenchmen in all social and economic classes: the intelligentsia and professional circles, the peasantry, the artisan and commercial groups in cities, and the nobility.[1] There had been no indication that one group or another would eventually dominate the movement. In the latter half of the sixteenth century and until 1629 the nobility exerted a strong influence. From a third to a half of the nobles turned from Catholicism to Protestantism. They sought to align the new religion on their side in the fight against the centralization of governmental authority and the power of the Guises, or they hoped to use it to further their own private interests. With the end of the Religious Wars in 1598, and after the fall of La Rochelle and the promulgation of the Edict of Alais in 1629,[2] the most powerful nobles abjured their new faith and reëntered the Catholic Church; the lesser nobility remained Protestant but sank into political oblivion. As a result of the persecution immediately preceding and following the revocation, most of the latter group also abjured. The more faithful participated in the underground resistance movement during the next hundred years, and only a few emigrated.[3] Several hundred gentlemen glassmakers

---

1 Émile-G. Léonard, *Problèmes et expériences du protestantisme français* (Paris, 1940), p. 27; Henri Hauser, *La Réforme et les classes populaires en France au XVIe siècle* (Paris, 1899), *passim;* Johann-Caspar Moerikofer, *Histoire des Réfugiés de la Réforme en Suisse,* trans. G. Roux (Paris, 1878), p. 11.

2 After Louis XIII and Richelieu successfully besieged the Protestant stronghold of La Rochelle, Protestants lost their right to maintain fortified places and thus ended the so-called Protestant state-within-the-state.

3 Charles Benoist, *Condition juridique des protestants sous le régime de l'Édit de Nantes et après sa révocation* (Paris, 1900), p. 74; J.-A. Galland, *Essai sur l'histoire du Protestantisme à Caen et en Basse-Normandie de l'édit de Nantes à la Revolu-*

(*gentilshommes verriers*) in the south and southwest of France were predominantly Protestant, and they continued to engage in intrigue and to cause the authorities considerable concern.[4] Their social and economic status, however, set them apart from other nobles.[5] On the whole, the regular nobility ceased to dominate the Protestant movement after 1629 and had practically nothing to do with it after 1685.

As the nobles withdrew, Protestantism shed its political nature, and its followers became stanch supporters of royal absolutism. They refused, for example, to aid the Prince of Condé when he and other nobles opposed the throne in Louis XIV's minority,[6] and even in the darkest hours of persecution they remained royalist and were prone to blame ministers and government advisers rather than the king himself for their plight.[7] Those who went into exile experienced difficulty in adjusting to the constitutional monarchy of England or to the republican forms of government in Holland and Switzerland. They continued to hope that the revocation edict would be rescinded and that they could return to their homeland as loyal subjects of their king. They even tried to persuade France's enemies to insist upon the reëstablishment of the Edict of Nantes as one of the terms in the peace treaties of Ryswick (1697) and Utrecht (1713).[8]

---

tion (1598–1791) (Paris, 1898), pp. 92–93; J. Jailliot, "Le Protestantisme dans le Rethelois et dans l'Argonne jusqu'à la révocation de l'Édit de Nantes," *Revue d'Ardenne et d'Argonne*, XIII (1905–1906), 214–215; Jean de la Monneraye, "La Révocation de l'Édit de Nantes et le protestantisme en Bas-Poitou au dix-huitième siècle," *Revue du Bas-Poitou*, 36th year (1923), 12; L. Rossier, *Histoire des protestants de Picardie, particulièrement de ceux du département de la Somme* (Amiens, 1861), p. 247; C. Weiss, "De la Conversion de la noblesse protestante au XVIIᵉ siècle," *Bulletin de la société de l'histoire du protestantisme français* (hereinafter cited as *BSHPF*), I (1853), 47–50.

[4] The intendant in Languedoc, for example, wrote Louvois on January 4, 1689, that he feared Protestant glassmakers in his province and in Foix would lead a revolt if they were not disarmed (Archives Nationales, A¹ 902, doc. 15).

[5] Warren C. Scoville, *Capitalism and French Glassmaking, 1640–1789* (Berkeley and Los Angeles, 1950), pp. 84–87.

[6] *Testament politique du Marquis de Louvois, premier ministre d'Etat sous le Règne de Louis XIV, Roy de France, où l'on voit ce qui s'est passé de plus remarquable en France jusqu'à sa mort* (Cologne, 1695), p. 374; A. Crottet, "Les Préludes de la révocation de l'édit de Nantes dans le pays de Gex," *BSHPF*, I, 293.

[7] Jacques de Missècle, *L'Édit de Nantes et sa révocation* (2d ed.; Colmar, 1931), pp. 14–15; Émile-G. Léonard, "Le Protestantisme français au XVIIᵉ siècle," *Revue historique*, CC (1948), 159–161, 166 ff.

[8] Frank Puaux, "Essai sur les négociations des réfugiés pour obtenir le rétablissement de la Religion réformée au traité de Ryswick (octobre 1697)," *BSHPF*, XVI (1867), *passim*.

Although, as Professor Hauser has suggested,[9] one reason that Protestantism never supplanted Catholicism as the dominant religion in France may have been its failure to sink its roots deep enough into the peasantry in the sixteenth century, its adherents in the southern provinces were more or less normally proportioned among all social classes.[10] The area was heavily agricultural, and there was a clear numerical preponderance of peasants. The same was true in Dauphiné and the little area of Gex. In addition, there were widely separated rural clusters of Protestants in Normandy and other northern and central provinces. A Catholic missionary, nevertheless, could write of Protestantism in about 1681 that "nearly all those of this sect are nobles, merchants, or workers; there are very few from the lowest classes among them."[11] It is noteworthy that Huguenot peasants, though constituting a small minority of all peasants, were considered to be among the best cultivators in France. It was said in 1759, for example, that the "cantons peopled by Religionists in Languedoc, Cévennes, and Vivarais are the best cultivated and the most productive despite the difficult terrain." [12] And the intendant at La Rochelle somewhat begrudgingly admitted in 1699 that there was no place in all his province of Saintonge where the soil was better tilled than on the island of Oléron, with its heavy Protestant population.[13]

THE PROTESTANT BOURGEOISIE

Special interest centers on the Protestants who were members of the *bourgeoisie*. Most scholars have agreed that they dominated and typified seventeenth-century Protestantism. Girolano Venier, the Venetian ambassador at Paris, stated in his summary report in 1688 that "the Protestants, having no hope of advancement at court or in the army, had chosen to reside in the provinces best adapted to trade and had added greatly to the wealth of the kingdom by their industry, their financial operations, and their

---

9 *Op. cit.*, pp. 33, 37.

10 Émile-G. Léonard, *Histoire ecclésiastique des réformés français au XVIII* *siècle* (Paris, 1940), p. xii.

11 Bibliothèque Nationale, *Fonds français*, MS 21622, fol. 97. Professor Léonard made the same point in regard to Normandy in his lectures at the Sorbonne in 1949, which I was privileged to attend.

12 Bibliothèque Nationale, *Fonds français*, MS 7047, fols. 440 ff. M. le Comte de Saxe, Maréchal of France, attested the same fact in 1746 (Bibliothèque de la Société Protestante, MS 339, fol. 28). See also Roger Lacoste, "Notes sur la bourgeoisie du Bergeracois à la veille de la Révolution," *BSHPF*, LXXXIII (1934), 447–483.

13 Bibliothèque Nationale, *Fonds français*, MS 4287, fol. 37.

shipping. . . . It is believed that two-thirds of the business of the country was in their hands."[14] A Huguenot magistrate at Toulouse in 1664 affirmed that "nearly all trade of this country is in the hands of those of the Reputedly Reformed Religion."[15] The statesman Daguesseau likewise wrote that "by an unhappy fate the Protestants were the most skillful artisans and the richest merchants in nearly all branches of the arts." [16] And Seignelay, as minister of the marine, deplored the fact that the directors of the great commercial companies were for the most part Protestant and ordinarily employed only members of their sect on their ships.[17] If an astute observer had visited the great ports and cities throughout France at the time of the revocation, he probably would have arrived at a similar conclusion.

The Protestant merchants at Bordeaux and in some of the smaller communities in Guyenne were very influential. Bezons, as intendant in that area, reported on December 12, 1688, that several of them were apparently planning to flee:

It would be very unfortunate for trade, considering its present state, if several of these merchants were to leave because it is they who have the most money and who are responsible for the greatest part of Bordeaux's commerce. I would have arrested one of them for having sold his household possessions had I not feared that such action would have destroyed trade entirely. Trade is very badly disrupted at present. New converts are practically the only individuals who undertake it, and their habits and background give them an advantage in carrying it on over all other merchants.[18]

Bezons's predecessor had complained four years earlier that Protestant brokers who had been ousted by royal order after 1680 still managed to control foreign trade at Bordeaux by using sub-

14 Barozzi and Berchet, *Le Relazioni degli Stati Europei lette al Senato dagli Ambasciatori Veneti nel secolo decimosettimo*, Series II, "Francia," Vol. III (Venice, 1857–1863), as quoted by Henry Austen Layard, "The Revocation of the Edict of Nantes. Illustrated from State Papers in the Archives of Venice," *Proceedings of the Huguenot Society of London* (hereinafter cited as *PHSL*), II (1887–1888), 150.

15 *BSHPF*, XXXIII (1884), 135.

16 Camille Rabaud, *Histoire du protestantisme dans l'Albigeois et le Lauragais depuis la révocation de l'édit de Nantes (1685) jusqu'à nos jours* (Paris, 1898), p. 104.

17 Eugène Guitard, *Colbert et Seignelay contre la religion réformée* (2d ed.; Paris, 1912), p. 116. See also Charles W. Cole, *Colbert and a Century of French Mercantilism* (New York, 1939), II, 91, 101.

18 Archives Nationales, G7 134.

servient Catholic middlemen as dummies and by capitalizing on their religion to obtain commissions from foreign buyers who were also Protestant.[19] Seignelay was distressed to learn on September 18, 1685, that Huguenots owned and operated nearly all vessels plying between Bordeaux and the American isles.[20] The same religious group practically monopolized the wine trade; occupied important positions in the markets for tobacco, oils, cheese, white lead, starch, and salt fish; figured prominently in the legal and other professions; more than held its own in various craft gilds, although outnumbered; and punished Catholics and new converts by black-listing and refusing to employ them.[21]

La Rochelle, another important commercial center, was one of the greatest Protestant strongholds. The Huguenots there owned and operated most of the boats engaged in coastwise trade, armed and supplied French warships based at neighboring Rochefort, and accounted for a third of all sailors and half of the 1,200 marine officers in the area.[22] Bonrepaus, while intendant-general at the Rochefort arsenal, further confirmed the hegemony of Protestants in a letter to Seignelay on May 19, 1685:

You know, Monseigneur, better than I that the trade of this country is in the hands of Religionists, and that we cannot take it from them at the present without causing it great harm because Catholics are not enterprising enough to take it over. The same may be said of shipping. The chief shipmasters are members of the Reputedly Reformed Religion and own most of the merchant vessels. These men do all in their power to keep Catholics from earning a living. . . . I do

---

19 A. M. de Boislisle, *Correspondance des contrôleurs généraux des finances avec les intendants des provinces*, I (Paris, 1874), 34; see also p. 91.

20 Archives Nationales, B³ *registre* 48, fol. 331. See also Frederic C. Lane, "Colbert et le commerce de Bordeaux," *Revue historique de Bordeaux et du département de la Gironde*, XVII (1924), 188–189.

21 Archives Nationales, G⁷ 134; TT 431, doc. 155; Bibliothèque Nationale, *Fonds français*, MSS 4287, fols. 49, 50; 7047, fols. 440 ff.; Paul Bert, *Histoire de la révocation de l'édit de Nantes à Bordeaux et dans le Bordelais (1653–1715)* (Bordeaux, 1908), pp. 3, 4, 41, 50; C. Weiss, "Mémoire sur les protestants de France au XVIIᵉ siècle," *Séances et travaux de l'Académie des sciences morales et politiques*, XX (1851), 103–105.

22 Archives Nationales, TT 232, *dossier* 19, doc. 9; 435, doc. 10; 448, doc. 295; B² *registre* 55, fol. 235; B³ *registre* 48, fol. 271; Bibliothèque Nationale, *Fonds français*, MSS 4287, fol. 34; 7044, fol. 28; Prosper Boissonnade, "La Marine marchande, le port et les armateurs de la Rochelle à l'époque de Colbert (1662–1682)," in *Bulletin de la section de géographie: Comité des travaux historiques et scientifiques* (Paris, 1922), pp. 21, 36; Guitard, *op. cit.*, p. 44; Henry Lehr, *Les Protestants d'autrefois. Vie et institutions militaires*, II (Paris, 1907), 38 ff.

not have to dissemble with you. These Religionists occupy the top rank in all places hereabout, and they view Catholics, and especially new converts, as miserable creatures whose standard of living makes them despicable.[23]

There were also frequent complaints that a dozen or more wealthy Huguenots monopolized the wine and salt trade around La Rochelle. According to contemporary documents, it was they to whom most foreign buyers addressed their orders; it was they who received, weighed, and handled all the salt produced by peasants in the region; it was they who offered employment to vast numbers; and it was they who rigged the prices, bribed the judges, and changed their buying policies so as to punish Catholics and reward Protestants. Bonrepaus joyfully reported to Seignelay on September 14, 1685, that he had recently converted three Rochelais merchants who owned several sailing vessels as well as a sugar refinery, and who provided a livelihood for some 700 or 800 families in La Rochelle. The Abbé de Cordemoy at La Tremblade, a little community near Rochefort, admitted in a letter dated January 1, 1695, that Protestants in Saintonge and Aunis and on the islands off the coast were so affluent that they even controlled the judiciary. Most of the local judges were poor Catholics, he said, who often had bought their seats on the bench with borrowed funds. They hence found themselves financially embarrassed and often sold justice to the highest bidder. Huguenot litigants, who were among the wealthier individuals in the region, showered the judges with costly gifts and thus nearly always obtained favorable decisions from the court at the expense of poorer Catholics.[24]

The majority of the hundred or more Protestants in the Breton port of Nantes served as agents for important commercial houses in England and Holland and were counted among the city's richest inhabitants.[25] Nicolas Dumoustier, lieutenant general at Caen, had represented to Colbert as early as February 27, 1665, that "the larger portion of the merchants of this

---

[23] Archives Nationales, B³ *registre* 48, fols. 289 ff. See also *ibid.*, fols. 314–317; Boissonnade, *op. cit.*, pp. 21–22.

[24] Archives Nationales, G⁷ 338; TT 232 *dossier* 19, doc. 9; B³ *registre* 48, fol. 302; Bibliothèque Nationale, *Fonds français*, MS 7045, fols. 33, 38–39, 40–42.

[25] Archives Nationales, TT 258, *dossier* 1, doc. 3; Émile Gabory, "La Marine et le commerce de Nantes au XVIIᵉ siècle et au commencement du XVIIIᵉ (1661–1715)," *Annales de Bretagne*, XVII (1901–1902), 369, 371–372.

city profess the Reputedly Reformed Religion; and, since they have better access to English and Dutch markets and more experience in dealing with merchants from England and Holland because their religion is the same, they handle all the trade in cloth and other merchandise which originates in this region."[26] When Dumoustier proposed that certain Catholics establish a royal manufactory of fine woolens in the Dutch tradition, as the Huguenots Massieu and Jemblin had recently done, they were "very distant" to his suggestion and doubtful of their success, "not having the entrepreneurial spirit or the facilities of these two Protestants."

In the three chief ports in Upper Normandy—Rouen, Le Havre, and Dieppe—a good many Protestants were wealthy merchants. According to one zealous Catholic, Norman ports shortly before the revocation were "filled with Huguenots who, in sharp contrast with Catholic merchants, always receive the most valued and best commissions from businessmen in England, Holland, Germany, Denmark, and Sweden."[27] The intendant accused several Protestant merchants at Rouen and Caen on January 26, 1685, of being responsible for a shortage of money in the area. According to him, they had recently become incensed over legal sanctions directed against their religion and had tightly closed their purses. These were the same individuals who a short time earlier had imported supplies from neighboring regions when a local shortage of grain threatened famine. The intendant, however, reassured the controller general that the money shortage would not endure very long because the men, after all, were "merchants by profession who could not abstain from trade for very long."[28]

So many wealthy employers in Rouen were Protestant that religious disputes there often resembled an economic class struggle between a Catholic proletariat and a Protestant *bourgeoisie*.[29]

---

26 Dumoustier's letter has been reproduced in Paul-M. Bondois, "Colbert et le développement économique de la Basse-Normandie," *Bulletin de la société des antiquaires de Normandie,* XLI (1934), 43–45.

27 Archives Nationales, TT 260, *dossier* 13, doc. 169.

28 Boislisle, *op. cit.,* I, 42.

29 Léonard, *Problèmes et expériences du protestantisme français,* pp. 27–28; Émile-G. Léonard, "Une Église protestante de notables (Caen) devant la persécution et la révolution" (unpublished manuscript, 1940); Hauser, *op. cit., passim;* Jean Bianquis, *La Révocation de l'Édit de Nantes à Rouen, essai historique* (Rouen, 1885), p. vii; Philippe Le Gendre, *Histoire de la persécution faite à l'église de Rouen sur la fin du dernier siècle,* ed. Émile Lesens (Rouen, 1874), p. xxi.

In a memorandum of February 15, 1683, an inhabitant of Rouen noted that only about a fifth of the population of Dieppe was Protestant. Yet this minority—"richer than the others and . . . [with] nearly all trade within their hands"—dominated civic affairs by faithfully attending all public meetings and by skillfully using their wealth and economic power.[30] New converts and regular Catholics sometimes had to sue Protestant employers in order to collect back wages.[31] And as late as 1742 a frustrated Catholic merchant who had recently purchased a captaincy in the Norman militia to gain social and economic distinction complained bitterly that he had been cheated. All the colonels and other officers in his unit, he said, were of Huguenot extraction and steadfastly refused to recognize his rank or to consort with him.[32]

Protestants and new converts constituted the most influential group of citizens in Nîmes, an important center in silk and woolen manufacturing. The intendant Bâville, who ordinarily was more prone to belittle than to exaggerate the importance of Huguenots, reported in 1699 that they "have a higher standard of living and are more active and more industrious than regular Catholics," and that Huguenot merchants, "skillful in trade and daring in enterprise, apply themselves well to commerce and have all the genius that is needed to succeed in their profession. . . . Even if all of them are still not devout Catholics, at least they have not ceased to be very good businessmen."[33] Several years before 1685 a Catholic had protested that Protestants dominated the gilds and municipal posts in Nîmes so completely that Catholics could not find employment.[34] Apparently the revocation did not alter matters significantly, for the Abbé de Saint-Maximin, who could boast of a doctorate from the Sorbonne, voiced the same complaint in 1737. "Catholics," he said, "being in the small minority and very poor, are gradually being alienated from the Church by self-interest or complaisance. . . . Since trade and manufacturing are entirely in the hands of Religionists, workers and artisans have to conform to the standards set

---

30 Archives Nationales, TT 264, *dossier* 19, doc. 83.

31 Guitard, *op. cit.,* p. 44.

32 Léonard, "Une Église protestante de notables"; Galland, *op. cit.,* pp. 372–373.

33 Bibliothèque Nationale, *Fonds français,* MSS 1490, fol. 138; 4290, fol. 323.

34 Archives Départementales de l'Hérault, C. 1656, as reproduced in Paul Gachon, *Quelques préliminaires de la Révocation de l'Édit de Nantes en Languedoc (1661–1685)* (Toulouse, 1899), Appendix, pp. vii–viii; see also pp. 146–147.

by those upon whom they depend for good standing, protection, and employment."[35]

Reports from other cities had a similar tone. Huguenot manufacturers at Sedan operated almost half of the looms in that city and offered employment to hundreds of workers;[36] those who were fleeing Saint-Quentin in September, 1685, had carried on most of the trade of the city and had precipitated its economic ruin with their departure;[37] and the intendant at Alençon complained on January 27, 1687, that new converts, "the richest inhabitants of this city," were deserting and would greatly decrease tax revenues from his province.[38] Protestants in Metz were among the city's wealthiest merchants and most successful industrialists and, according to the intendant, monopolized wholesale trade.[39] In 1668, the Catholic half of Montauban's population had paid in the aggregate only one-sixth as much in property taxes as the other half.[40] The few hundred Calvinists in Lyon were either Swiss and other foreigners who engaged in trade as representatives of foreign firms or Frenchmen who had made a name for themselves in banking, commerce, and publishing.[41] The intendant at Lyon, after asserting in 1699 that the revocation had not caused a very great exodus from that city, commented that those who had fled "were rich and cut a good figure in trade and carried away with them a considerable amount of wealth."[42] As to be expected of a city the size of Paris, its colony of some 10,000 Huguenots did not dominate its economic life. Significantly enough, however, when an acute shortage of

35 Archives Nationales, TT 247, doc. 94.

36 *Ibid.*, TT 435, *dossier* 5; Boislisle, *op. cit.*, II (1883), 37–38; Stephen Leroy, "Les Protestants de Sedan au XVIIIe siècle," *BSHPF*, XLV (1896), 339–340.

37 Archives Nationales, G7 85. See also Boislisle, *op. cit.*, I, 56; Alfred Daullé, *La Réforme à Saint-Quentin et aux environs, du XVIe siècle à la fin du XVIIIe siècle* (Le Cateau, 1901), p. 183.

38 Archives Nationales, G7 71.

39 Maurice Thirion, *Étude sur l'histoire du protestantisme à Metz et dans le pays messin* (Nancy, 1884), pp. 394–398; Orthon Cuvier, *Les Réformés de la Lorraine et du pays messin* (Nancy, 1884), pp. 26, 44–45; Reginald Lane Poole, *A History of the Huguenots of the Dispersion at the Recall of the Edict of Nantes* (London, 1880), pp. 170–171 n.

40 Ch. Garrisson, "La Population protestante . . . de Montauban," *BSHPF*, XLVI (1897), 120–121.

41 John Viénot, *Histoire de la Réforme française, de l'Édit de Nantes à sa révocation (1598–1685)* (Paris, 1934), pp. 414–415; Natalis Rondot, *Les Protestants à Lyon au dix-septième siècle* (Lyon, 1891), p. 52.

42 Bibliothèque Nationale, *Fonds français*, MS 4288, fol. 66.

bread and grain threatened Paris in November, 1698, the lieutenant general of police turned first to a Protestant merchant as the person most capable of providing relief.[43]

It is also important for our purposes to know whether Protestants occupied key positions in particular industries. Most of the reports and letters of intendants and other government officials indicate that the Huguenot *bourgeoisie* not only was wealthy and inclined to trade but also provided employment for large numbers of Frenchmen in manufacturing. One writer has claimed that Protestants lent more support than Catholics to Colbert's efforts to encourage large-scale capitalistic forms of production and also helped to diffuse foreign technology at home by copying English and Dutch industrial methods observed during their frequent travels abroad.[44] The Dutch family van Robais, which established in 1665 the famous fine woolen works at Abbeville and kept sixty-five or more looms constantly at work, was Calvinist;[45] so were Massieu, Jemblin, and their descendants, who acquired the Dutch secret of making fine cloth from Spanish wool and long operated a famous factory at Caen.[46] Two Huguenot entrepreneurs founded a manufactory at Elbeuf which specialized in strong white cloth and found great favor in Colbert's eyes;[47] other Protestants did the same at Louviers;[48] and a large number of clothiers and woolen manufacturers at Sedan and in various cities in Languedoc were of the same religion.[49] In July, 1684, a little more than a year before he outlawed their religion, Louis granted four Protestants exclusive letters patent to make heavy crepe in the Zurich fashion throughout Champagne and Brie for twenty years. They succeeded in launching their enterprise and in establishing it on a firm footing before persecution forced them to flee. In Lower Poitou, a region not given to large-scale industry, Huguenots made up most of the population in centers where woolens were manufactured

---

43 Boislisle, *op. cit.*, I, 502.

44 Weiss, "Mémoire sur les protestants," *op. cit.*, XX, 106.

45 Archives Nationales, F12 822A.

46 Bondois, *op. cit.*, pp. 43–46; Léonard, "Une Église protestante de notables."

47 Cole, *op. cit.*, II, 150–151.

48 Weiss, "Mémoire sur les protestants," *op. cit.*, XX, 106–107.

49 Leroy, *op. cit.*, pp. 339–340; Émile-G. Léonard, "Économie et religion, les protestants français au XVIIIe siècle," *Annales d'histoire sociale*, II (1940), 16–17; Boislisle, *op. cit.*, II, 37–38.

under the putting-out system rather than by gilds or in households.[50]

At Nîmes and to a lesser extent at Tours the silk industry was in the hands of Protestant throwsters, dyers, weavers, and entrepreneurs.[51] Some even found employment in the silk mills at Lyon, a predominantly Catholic city, and acquired the secrets of making the damasks, taffetas, and velvets for which that city was famous. In Picardy—and even in Brittany at Nantes, Rennes, and Vitré—Huguenots maintained important works which turned out fine linen fabrics or heavy sailcloth.[52] They operated several paper mills in Auvergne and Angoumois, a large number of tanyards in Touraine and other provinces, so many glass factories that some writers have erroneously concluded that they controlled the industry, several sugar refineries along the Atlantic coast, many forges and metallurgical works producing all kinds of articles ranging from kitchenware to armaments, hat manufactories in Normandy, clock and watch works, and several printing establishments in the largest cities.[53] In 1685 three very wealthy Protestant families at Villière-le-Bel near Versailles were said to employ all members of their sect who lived in the same community to produce lace and silverware under the putting-out system.[54]

The position occupied by Huguenots in the realm of finance has already been mentioned. At Lyon those of Swiss nationality vied with Italian bankers for top rank. Throughout the eighteenth century they enjoyed comparative peace and quiet there,[55]

50 François Baudry, *La Révocation de l'édit de Nantes et le protestantisme en Bas-Poitou au XVIIIe siècle* (Trévoux, 1922), pp. 305–307.

51 Bibliothèque Nationale, *Fonds français*, MSS 7047, fols. 440 ff.; 17315, fol. 55; Weiss, "Mémoire sur les protestants," *op. cit.*, XX, 111; Armand Dupin de Saint-André, *Un Coup d'oeil sur l'histoire du protestantisme en Touraine* (Paris, 1901), p. 66; Gachon, *op. cit.*, pp. 146–147.

52 Weiss, "Mémoire sur les protestants," *op. cit.*, XX, 109–110. According to a manuscript dated 1759, Huguenots ran seventeen houses in Picardy which produced "a prodigious quantity of linens which experience has shown they alone can do with success" (Bibliothèque Nationale, *Fonds français*, MS 7047, fols 440 ff.).

53 Archives Nationales, A¹ 902, doc. 15; Bibliothèque Nationale, *Fonds français*, MS 7047, fols. 440 ff.; David C. A. Agnew, *Protestant Exiles from France in the Reign of Louis XIV* (2d ed.; London, 1871–1874), II, 136; Bianquis, *op. cit.*, p. xl; Galland, *op. cit.*, p. 105; Poole, *op. cit.*, pp. 8–9; Weiss, "Mémoire sur les protestants," *op. cit.*, XX, 107 ff.

54 Bibliothèque Nationale, *Fonds français*, MS 7052, fols. 314–315.

55 Rondot, *op. cit.*, pp. 32–33, 51–52.

whereas native-born financiers of the Protestant faith in most cities other than Lyon, Rouen, and Paris suffered sporadic harassment. Many Huguenots throughout the realm engaged in banking and lending operations, either as their main interest or, more frequently, as a side line. Catholics were often their debtors, and as such loudly complained upon occasion that Protestant creditors wreaked revenge on them for acts of persecution directed against their religion.[56]

The participation of Protestants and new converts in government finance further reveals their political and social status. Douen, one of the most meticulous and cautious students of French Protestantism, has counted forty-eight Protestants who filled important government financial posts under Sully, Louis XIII, and Mazarin from 1596 to 1650, and thirty-one others who were employed under Herwarth and Colbert from 1650 to 1680.[57] Herwarth, intendant of finance and later controller general, was himself a Calvinist and introduced many of his coreligionists into public office;[58] Samuel Bernard, perhaps the most important banker in Paris and the one who saved the government from bankruptcy at a critical moment, was of the same faith before his conversion; and John Law, of course, was Protestant until near the end of 1719 when he abjured.[59] The eighteenth-century scholar Claude-Carlomau de Rulhière noted that a list of some 100 Huguenots who lived in Paris in 1686 included "the names of the principal persons who today [i.e., about 1785] engage in banking at Paris and who are still known as Protestants."[60]

Many Huguenots, especially where they constituted a significant minority, had also worked their way into public office as tax farmers, measurers of salt, notaries, law clerks, members of provincial parliaments, mayors, city councilmen, and officers of local militia. The explanation frequently given was that in many districts they were the only ones financially able to buy the charges or to post adequate bonds.[61]

---

56 See, e.g., Archives Nationales, TT 431, doc. 157.

57 *La Révocation de l'Édit de Nantes à Paris d'après des documents inédits* (Paris, 1894), III, 395–401.

58 Guillaume-Adam de Félice, *Histoire des protestants de France* (8th ed.; Toulouse, 1895), pp. 385–386; Guillaume-B. Depping, "Un Banquier protestant en France au XVIIe siècle: Barthélemy Herwarth, contrôleur général des finances (1607–1676)," *Revue historique*, X–XI (1879), 286–287.

59 *BSHPF*, XII (1863), 456.

60 Bibliothèque Nationale, *Fonds français*, MS 7044, fol. 257.

61 Archives Nationales, G7 239, 337, 390; TT 232, *dossier* 19, doc. 9.

PROTESTANTISM, CAPITALISM, AND PENALIZATION

It is difficult to evaluate the economic position of Huguenots in French society. A few contemporaries and later writers have argued that Protestants were not wealthier, more industrious and enterprising, or more successful in agriculture, finance, trade, or industry than the average Frenchman. Most spokesmen, like the nineteenth-century economist Sismondi, have taken the opposite viewpoint. Sismondi wrote: "Since the best part of trade and industry of France was in the hands of Protestants, their houses in provincial cities were furnished with expensive items, and their stores were stocked with merchandise; all these riches, placed at the mercy of dragoons, were destroyed, and nothing contributed so much to the impoverishment of France."[62]

The impartial historian of the twentieth century must recognize that Protestants who were well off financially, even though they may have constituted only a small percentage of the total, probably attracted the most attention from contemporary observers and government officials; their names were most often mentioned, and their economic position was most often noted, in the documents that have come down to the present day. Since the historian's knowledge of Huguenots largely depends upon extant records, and since the selective process determining which records would be preserved was itself biased, the possibility remains that government documents do not represent a reliable sample of relevant data. I believe, nevertheless, that the evidence as a whole strongly supports the view that the Huguenots exercised a greater influence on the French economy than their numbers would suggest.[63]

A direct correlation, no matter how marked, does not in itself establish a causal connection between two phenomena. The mere fact that Huguenots made a favorable showing in economic activity does not prove that Protestant ideology reinforced their economic drives or that Protestantism as a way of life conflicted with such drives less than Catholicism; but the high correlation of Protestantism and economic success has been taken by some scholars as presumptive evidence that some such causal connection existed. Many philosophers, sociologists, economists, and his-

---

[62] *Histoire des français* (Paris, 1821–1844), XXV, 510.

[63] The fragmentary data pertaining to the property confiscated from those who fled France and the size of the estates left by new converts upon their death confirm this belief.

torians in the past decades have developed hypotheses as to the relationship between Protestantism and capitalism. Some writers have stressed the impact of the doctrines of predestination and man's calling upon economic behavior; others have found it significant that both Protestantism and free-enterprise capitalism rest upon individualism; others have pointed out that Protestant teachings were compatible with the rationalization of economic life whereas Catholicism was not; and some have thought that the Reformation, by multiplying religious sects and evoking heated debates over church dogma, weakened the influence of organized Christian religion over the everyday activities of individuals. Still others, while contending that Protestant countries had a higher rate of saving and investment than predominantly Catholic areas, have sought an explanation for this in the attitudes of the two religions toward interest. Other writers have suggested that in some places—England, for example— the Reformation shifted the ownership of certain natural resources from ecclesiastical to lay hands and that the allocation of these resources among alternative uses thereafter conformed more closely to rational economic principles than formerly. And some have stressed the impact upon capitalism of religious wars which dislocated production, destroyed property and life, and diffused technology through the migration of religious minorities skilled in economic processes and techniques.

There is little reason here to attempt a detailed critical evaluation of these various hypotheses—especially of those that pertain to the generalized relationship of Protestantism to capitalism and rest upon philosophical, sociological, and psychological premises. It should be pointed out, however, that even if a philosopher found that nothing in Calvinist dogma provided a more rational basis for intense capitalistic activity than did contemporary Catholic dogma, it is still possible that interpreters and followers of Calvin may have construed his teachings as exhorting or condoning the rational pursuit of profits.[64] If evidence of this exists, the economic historian cannot afford to neglect it.

---

64 Amintore Fanfani, R. H. Tawney, and Max Weber have all agreed that the effects of Protestantism upon capitalism were really unintentional and unconscious. According to Weber, its consequences were in large measure those "that the Reformers did not foresee, and indeed definitely did not desire, and which often differed from or conflicted with all that they hoped to obtain by their ideals" (see Fanfani, *Catholicism, Protestantism, and Capitalism* [New York, 1935], pp. 190–191).

One of the chief problems for the present study is to explain why the Huguenots in France were so successful in economic matters, and whether the direct correlation between their religion and their success in business was mainly fortuitous or, instead, had a reasonable causal basis. The hypotheses mentioned above may provide some clues, although a case study of the Huguenots, based upon historical facts, can in itself neither refute nor substantiate such broad generalizations abstracted from the world of ideas. One cannot conclude, for example, that the impact of Protestantism upon capitalism in France was identical with or necessarily similar to the results observed elsewhere. If for no other reason, this would be true simply because the position of the Huguenots in the seventeenth and eighteenth centuries was nowhere exactly duplicated. It is significant that Huguenots remained a small and in many respects a "penalized" minority, and as such were forced into a role similar to that played by other penalized minorities, whether the basis for penalization was racial, social, religious, political, or economic. Unlike some other Protestant groups, the Huguenots were part of a society that was determined to keep Catholicism as its official religion, a society whose ruler strongly opposed heresy for reasons that did not always stem from personal religious piety. The mere fact that Calvinism differed in many ideological and practical ways from Anglicanism and Lutheranism, for example, would preclude identifying its effects on group and individual behavior with the effects of Protestantism in the abstract.

Max Weber, in *The Protestant Ethic and the Spirit of Capitalism*,[65] seized upon the twin doctrines of predestination and of man's calling as the crucial and unique core of Calvin's teaching. According to the first of these doctrines, God bestowed his grace and eternal salvation upon some and denied them to others, and nothing that the saved or the condemned could do could possibly alter God's plan. Hence "the relation between earthly and eternal recompense" was denied.[66] How, then, could such a doctrine, instead of inculcating a fatalistic attitude, encourage its adherents to enter into all forms of economic activity with a zeal approaching religious fervor? Weber thought he had found the answer in Calvin's concept of man's calling. Calvin taught that the world existed solely to glorify God and that the

---

[65] Trans. Talcott Parsons (New York, 1930).
[66] Fanfani, *op. cit.*, p. 205.

Christian elected to eternal life by God's grace was in duty bound to contribute to this glory, among other ways, through social achievement. Thus all social and economic activity that served the life of the community became an obligation of the elect, although it never could be a means of gaining grace. No matter into what station in life a person was born, no matter with what skills and capabilities he was endowed, he was obligated—like the three servants in the parable of the talents[67] —to make the most of what his Master had given him. He could not fulfill this obligation by building up a store of good deeds sufficient, on net balance, to compensate for his sins and occasional backslidings. Rather, the elect had to face up to his obligation continually. Good works, furthermore, were "indispensable as a sign of election" to the rest of the community, and constituted one way "of getting rid of the fear of damnation."[68] Thus Calvinism, as interpreted by Weber, taught that the chosen, who would ultimately have citizenship in the City of God, could find fulfillment for their lives in the city of man and at the same time best glorify God by devoting themselves to those callings for which they had been specifically endowed by divine ordinance. A spiritual monastic life was inherently no better or more godly than one devoted largely to mundane trucking and bartering.[69] It was easy, therefore, for the rank and file to distort the Calvinist dogmas of predestination and man's calling into the belief that success in one's profession could reveal the action of grace.[70] Viewed in this light, these dogmas may have acted as a powerful stimulus to economic activity.

Although Calvin held that no man should seek his own gain at the expense of others and that each Christian was "his brother's keeper," Protestantism in France embraced certain practices that tended to support individualism. The relationship of man to God was an individual relationship which did not

---

[67] Matt. 25:14–30.

[68] Weber, *op. cit.,* p. 115.

[69] Henri Hauser believed that the central idea of Protestant morality was the secularization of sainthood. "Men of all classes and of all trades are predestined to salvation or to damnation; the only means, then, of collaborating with the work of God is to do the best you can in the profession in which God has placed you." ("L'Économie calvinienne," a paper presented at the "Exposition Jean Calvin et la Réforme français" held in 1935 by the Société de l'Histoire du Protestantisme français, and published in *BSHPF,* LXXXIV [1935]).

[70] See the extract from a circular published by the Crédit industriel d'Alsace et de Lorraine in July, 1932, in *BSHPF,* LXXXI (1932), 325.

require the intercession of priest or saint. The good Huguenot read the Bible himself,[71] conducted individual and family prayers, and believed that God through his omnipotence and omniscience was continually aware of his actions in the market place as well as in the church.

As Fanfani has pointed out,[72] in some respects the doctrine of predestination had the effect of separating life on this earth and life in eternity into watertight compartments. Whereas Catholicism was concerned with the subsistence of the whole of society and considered all temporal means and goals as subservient to the ultimate attainment of immortality, Protestantism represented "the stage at which religion perceives that business morality has legitimate foundations in the earth. If an action is to have no reward but its results, the rationalizing principle of action will remain that of the maximum result."[73] The compartmentalization of eternal goals and temporal goals hence weakened both traditionalism[74] and the subordination of economic to moral problems. In sanctioning the maximization of output over input, it placed a premium on technical improvements, savings, and the satisfaction of material (as contrasted with spiritual) human wants with the least expenditure of time and effort.

Calvinism's attitude toward interest, like the support it gave individualism and the rationalization of economic activities, may have had causal influence on the economic success achieved by

---

[71] The Calvinist was just as familiar with the Old Testament as with the New; the Catholic Church emphasized the New Testament almost (but not quite) to the exclusion of the Old. Since the New Testament is fundamentally spiritual and primarily concerned with immortality, and since the Old Testament mainly concerns temporal matters and life on this earth, it may well be that Huguenots were led through their reading of the Bible and their church attendance to accept a more balanced view of temporal and spiritual matters than Catholics. This suggestion, if it has any merit at all, relates to the effect that the Bible may have had upon the rank and file of members rather than upon an exceptional minority of either sect. The historian, however, simply cannot ignore the fact that capitalism made great strides in many Catholic areas, especially before the Reformation.

[72] *Op. cit.*, pp. 29, 120 ff.

[73] *Ibid.*, pp. 207–208. Fanfani elsewhere (p. 198) noted that "once the idea was admitted that salvation was independent of works, with the idea of free enquiry, a Protestant was only acting in a logical manner if he accepted the rational order of the world as it resulted from the free operation of man. While the Protestant who still envisaged a 'should be' state was illogical. The fundamental principles of Protestantism lead inevitably to the sanctification of the real; the obstinate attempt to prescribe other worldly limits to the world is a remnant of doctrines that Protestantism seeks to overthrow."

[74] See Weber, *op. cit.*, pp. 58 ff.

French Huguenots as a group. John Calvin, born into a bourgeois world, lived most of his life in such commercial centers as Strasbourg and Geneva, where lending money at interest was a daily practice. Unlike the monkish Luther, he was brought up in a rather rapidly changing economic order, and was aware that the economic environment of his time was quite different from that of the Greeks or Romans or from that which had existed in the earlier days of Western civilization.[75] He saw the necessity of buying and selling, of lending and borrowing, and of taking interest. He admitted he could find no prohibition against interest in the Scriptures; he refuted Aquinas' contention that money was sterile by pointing out that money could buy things which in turn could yield a surplus; he even refused to forbid his pastors to lend at interest, but advised them not to do so lest their actions be misunderstood by their parishioners; and he explicitly justified interest on loans made to merchants for business purposes or to landlords for the acquisition of more property. On the other hand, there is ample evidence that Calvin's approval of interest-taking was qualified: "I would not wish at all, in justifying it, to favor usury [i.e., interest-taking], and I would like to see even the phrase disappear from the earth."[76] Calvin urged his followers to lend sums to necessitous consumers, from whom no interest should be exacted, and to small businessmen, who could pay no interest and even showed little prospect of repaying the principal, in preference to merchants and manufacturers who offered adequate guarantees for high rates of return. In other words, while recognizing the validity of lending and interest, Calvin urged his disciples to temper their capitalist spirit with the Christian principle of charity. According to Hauser's apt summary, "Calvin made use of interest as an apothecary mixes poisons—a necessary remedy, perhaps indispensable, but oh! so dangerous."[77]

Even though Catholicism had long recognized unusual circumstances under which the collection of interest was permissible, and even though numerous subterfuges had been devised for circumventing the Church's proscription under usual circumstances, Calvin's views to some extent liberalized the Christian's attitude toward lending. But to assess the effect of his views on

---

[75] See Hauser, "L'Économie calvinienne."
[76] Quoted in *ibid.*
[77] *Ibid.*

Huguenot behavior is an entirely different and far more difficult problem. Some writers have maintained that French Protestants showed less restraint than Catholics in lending at whatever rates of interest they could get,[78] and contemporary documents provide abundant evidence that in some areas of the country they were, on net balance, creditors of their Catholic brethren. Some may argue, of course, that the approval of interest-taking itself led to the rise of a *rentier* class which was reluctant to engage in risky ventures conducted for profit, and hence discouraged the development of the capitalist spirit. This does not seem to have been true. Calvinism, like Puritanism, became the gospel of hard work, thrift, and temperance. In 1723 an exiled pastor, after advising the Huguenots who had remained behind in Languedoc to learn to live "in temperance, justice, and piety," urged them to give attention

. . . to the bad effects of intemperance, which weakens one's discernment, destroys health, [and] ruins families. Idleness is its mother. Be industrious and you will have neither the time nor the fancy to flatter your discernment with superfluities. Remember that you live in the presence of God, that virtues are your true glory, and you will not at all give yourselves over to all these vanities of which men of the world make their merit consist by reason of not having anything better.[79]

Despite the plausibility of postulating a causal relationship, either direct or indirect, between Calvinist doctrine (as interpreted by Calvin's disciples) and the highly successful economic activities of his followers in France, the fact remains that French Protestants constituted a "penalized minority" throughout most of the seventeenth and eighteenth centuries and were conscious of the social and legal discriminations directed against them. This was a significant factor in their behavior, perhaps more significant than the impact of Calvin's doctrines of predestination and man's calling, or than the support his teachings gave to individualism and the rationalization of economic activity, or even than his qualified approval of interest-taking. According to Arnold J. Toynbee, penalization may act as a very powerful stimulus to individual and group behavior:

---

[78] See, e.g., Benoist, *op. cit.*, p. 305.
[79] Archives Nationales, TT 247, doc. 54.

The dominant race [or, here, the dominant majority] is apt to re-serve certain avocations as its own exclusive preserves, and to impose upon the penalized race [here, the minority] the necessity of cul-tivating other fields of social activity if it is to find a living at all. The "reserved" occupations usually include all those which have high social prestige—the priesthood, the business of government, the owner-ship of land, the bearing of arms, and the civilian "liberal pro-fessions"—as well as the fundamental economic activity of Society, which has usually been agriculture in the social economies of societies in process of civilization down to recent times. By a process of ex-haustion the penalized race [minority] is apt to find itself virtually confined to the field of trade and handicraft; and, just because the field is narrow, the penalized race [minority] is stimulated to make this field all its own and to conjure out of it, by a *tour de force* which fills the dominant race [majority] with astonishment and resentment, a harvest of wealth and power which this Naboth's vineyard would hardly have yielded to hands not debarred from other handiwork.[80]

This idea did not originate with Toynbee. An old Spanish proverb declared that "heresy promotes business spirit";[81] and Sir William Petty, in his *Political Arithmetic* (London, 1691), claimed that "trade is more vigorously carried on, in every state and government, by the heterodox part of the same; and such as profess opinions different from what are publicly established . . . and even in France itself, the Huguenots are, proportion-ately, far the greatest traders."[82] More recently, Émile-G. Léonard has expressed a similar belief: "Each minority, each dissident group—because it tempers the character of its mem-bers, because it exalts their individual capacities, because it pro-tects them from improvidence and expensive vices—in normal circumstances sets them on the road of economic and social achievement."[83]

If, as seems to be true, there is a general psychological and sociological principle that individuals or groups are led to tap little-used and unsuspected sources of power within themselves and to "respond" vigorously when confronted with challenges like penalization, then it appears likely that those with strong

---

80 *The Study of History* (London: Oxford University Press, 1934), II, 217.

81 Quoted by F. L. Nussbaum, *A History of the Economic Institutions of Modern Europe* (New York: Crofts, 1937), p. 138.

82 Reprinted in Edward Arber, *An English Garner* (London, 1883), pp. 343–344.

83 "Économie et religion, les protestants français au XVIIIᵉ siècle," p. 7. See also his "Le Protestantisme français au XVIIᵉ siècle," pp. 161, 177–178.

spiritual beliefs, like the Huguenots, will have a better-than-average chance of attaining great success. The Huguenots who responded to the challenge of penalization by fleeing France found another stimulus in the strangeness of a new environment, but their assimilation into the society of their adopted countries became more or less complete after several generations. By the nineteenth and twentieth centuries they no longer stood out from the rest of the population as captains of trade and industry. The Huguenots and their descendants who refused to flee continued to constitute an easily identifiable minority in France, and this helps to explain why French Protestants in the twentieth century still maintain an importance in the economy which is more than proportionate to their numbers. The degree of their "penalization," however, has been greatly reduced since the eighteenth century, and concomitantly their relative superiority in finance, trade, and industry has diminished.[84]

The forms this penalization assumed in the seventeenth century have already been described. The Edict of Nantes in 1598 had promised all Protestants equality of opportunity in the professions, in public office, and in economic jobs; yet entry into judicial, top military, and administrative positions became less and less accessible to them after 1661. In various ways Louis XIV also narrowed, particularly after 1679, the range of economic opportunities open to Huguenots. By 1685 they were eligible for very few positions outside private industry, trade, and finance; and even several gilds had shut them out. If penalization had consisted solely of such legal restrictions as these, it would be difficult indeed to argue that Huguenots gained conspicuous success in business before the revocation mainly because this field remained the only major area where they could freely deploy their energies. Several years of exclusion from other occupations appears too short a period to have exercised a pronounced effect on the economic activities of an entire minority. Yet several contemporaries have explained the economic success of Huguenots in terms of such penalization.[85] Such views would have been

---

[84] Cf. Toynbee, *op. cit.*, II, 250. As Professor Jacob Viner has pointed out to me in private correspondence, the test as to whether penalization effectively motivates people should not be absolute success in business but, rather, success relative to economic opportunities. Even if Huguenots had been poorer than their Catholic neighbors, this would not in itself have invalidated the penalization argument.

[85] For example, the deputy of trade at Bayonne (Bibliothèque Nationale, *Fonds français*, MS 8038, fol. 434); the author of the "Mémoire sur le commerce de

more appropriate for the eighteenth century, when legal sanctions were a potent factor. The explanation for the seventeenth century must be sought rather in the fact that much of the penalization never crystallized into formal law and explicit government pronouncement, but was more in the nature of spontaneous, unorganized economic and social discrimination by the Catholic majority.

As often happens with penalized minorities, the Huguenots who gained a foothold in public office or achieved positions of favor and prominence used their influence, insofar as possible, to place their brethren in similar ranks. Sully and Herwarth as finance ministers, for example, appointed a large number of fellow Protestants to important financial posts in government;[86] and Mazarin, Fouquet, and Colbert readily employed Protestants in important positions because of their honesty and zeal, and these appointees in turn favored others of their religion whenever occasion permitted.[87]

Another factor in the success of Huguenots appears to have been their willingness to remain in trade and industry even after they had made their fortunes. An individual who has remained anonymous prepared a long memorandum in 1787 in which he wrote: "One has not been able to exclude them from trade which, according to natural law, is a free profession; and that has been a very good thing for commerce and manufactures, which since 1685 have flourished in several cities precisely because Protestant families, enriched by this means, have not been able to leave their vocations in order to pass into the order of the nobility as have Catholic families."[88] The intendant at La Rochelle had complained to Colbert as early as 1664 that Catholic merchants engaged in outfitting naval vessels ordinarily

France" (*ibid.*, fols. 14–15); Pierre Jurieu (*Réflexions sur la cruelle persécution que souffre l'église réformée de France* . . . [2d ed.; n.p., 1685], p. 44); the author of *Testament politique du Marquis de Louvois* . . . (pp. 369–370); and the Venetian ambassador at Paris at the time of the revocation.

86 Léonard believes that this, more than Weber's thesis of man's calling, was largely responsible for the success of Huguenots in the financial world ("Le Protestantisme français au XVIIe siècle," p. 169).

87 Archives Nationales, TT 287, *dossier* 6, doc. 32; Bibliothèque Nationale, *Fonds français*, MS 7047, fol. 727; Boissonnade, *op. cit.*, p. 18; Erman and Reclam, *Mémoires pour servir à l'histoire de réfugiés françois dans les états du Roi* (Berlin, 1782–1799), I, 81; Depping, *op. cit.*, p. 286; Émile Lesens, *Le Protestantisme dans le pays de Caux (ancien colloque de Caux, Havre et Dieppe excepté)*, ed. Victor Madelaine (Bolbec, [1906]), p. 144.

88 Bibliothèque Nationale, *Fonds français*, MS 7047, fol. 727.

deserted their trade for public office as soon as they had amassed a fortune.[89] The deputy of trade at Bayonne in 1701 listed the revocation of the Edict of Nantes with its Huguenot dispersion as an important factor in the deterioration of economic conditions. He claimed that Protestants, excluded "from the dignities and employs of the robe and sword," had been uniquely occupied with trade:

In a manner of speaking, they made commerce the sole subject of their meditations. It was their custom to marry their daughters to other merchants, and in this way they did not dissipate their capital. In all justice one has to admit that there were a large number of individuals among them who were powerful and very intelligent in business affairs.[90]

Huguenot merchants enjoyed a distinct advantage over Catholics in trade with such Protestant countries as England, Holland, Switzerland, and certain German states. Foreign Protestants preferred to transact their business with Protestant Frenchmen; and Catholics in Bordeaux, La Rochelle, Nantes, and Rouen often complained of being practically excluded from foreign trade. Huguenot merchants usually sent their sons to Geneva, England, or Holland at an early age to develop contacts, to observe the practices of foreign traders and manufacturers, and to attend school. In this way they became familiar with new technical processes and commercial procedures.[91] Members of Huguenot families who fled France in the sixteenth or seventeenth century remained in close commercial contact with relatives who elected to remain at home, and served as their foreign brokers. In the eighteenth century several Huguenots had family connections in the major commercial centers of Protestant Europe which allowed them to build up small empires in international trade.

Calvinism, by recognizing fewer religious holidays than Catholicism, lengthened the work year for its followers by about 15 or 20 per cent. Through its emphasis upon religious education and individual study of the Bible, its intensive training of pastors, and its organizational and administrative structure, it helped to

---

89 Boissonnade, *op. cit.*, p. 18.

90 Bibliothèque Nationale, *Fonds français*, MS 8038, fol. 434.

91 C. Weiss, *Histoire des réfugiés protestants de France depuis la révocation de l'Édit de Nantes jusqu'à nos jours* (Paris, 1853), I, 31; Weiss, "Mémoire sur les protestants," *op. cit.*, XX, 104–105; *BSHPF*, XXXIII, 135–136.

make Huguenots, on the average, more enlightened than their neighbors.[92] In a memorandum of uncertain date entitled "Design for the Reunion of the Church in France by a Conference Which Has Been Proposed by Cardinal Richelieu," the author confessed that one reason that Huguenots remained in their heresy was because few priests were capable of instructing them and of refuting their erroneous beliefs. "There are only a few Catholic clerics," he wrote, "who know anything about these matters, whereas there is not a single [Protestant] minister who knows not something to sustain them in their error."[93] On October 20, 1699, another writer expressed the belief that Protestants in Cévennes had developed traits that made them "sober, industrious, and active in trade for which they have the real spirit," and that all were determined to acquire an education so they could read, write, and master arithmetic.[94]

One perspicacious Frenchman named Beaumelle, about the middle of the eighteenth century, summarized and explained the position occupied by Huguenots in his country:[95] "Although Protestants comprise only one-tenth of the nation by numerical count, it is nevertheless certain that, measured by their riches and industry, they constitute at least one-eighth of the whole; these two million subjects are worth perhaps three million Catholics." They are "more active than Catholics because they can become their equals only through activity." "The severity of the laws directed against them leads to perpetual self-examination." They are "aided and abetted by the principles of their religion" which render them "more enlightened" and "capable of grasping all new ideas" and borrowing new technical processes from abroad which will help them gain success. "Their zeal for work," "their frugality" and "old-time thrift," their opposition to "luxury and idleness," and their "great fear of the judgment of God" lead them to focus their energies and to justify their faith and nonconformity by unusual achievements in the economic realm.

---

92 Weiss, "Mémoire sur les protestants," *op. cit.*, XX, 105, 106.

93 Bibliothèque Nationale, *Fonds français*, MS 20967, fol. 40.

94 *Ibid.*, MS 20966, fols. 272–281.

95 Beaumelle turned his memorandum over to Claude-Carlomau de Rulhière, who was busily engaged in writing his *Eclaircissements historiques sur les causes de la révocation de l'Édit de Nantes, et sur l'état des protestants en France, depuis le commencement du Règne de Louis XIV, jusqu'à nos jours* (new ed.; Geneva, 1788); and the memorandum in manuscript form may be found in the Bibliothèque Nationale, *Fonds français*, MS 7047, fols. 440 ff.

Although Beaumelle did not explicitly label Huguenots a "penalized minority," it is quite clear that his interpretation of their behavior is not at variance with the interpretation presented in this chapter. No matter on what level an easily identifiable minority is penalized, the penalization itself may provide a challenge of sufficient impact to call forth remarkable achievements by the minority in certain areas of human endeavor. This appears to have been true of the French Huguenots. Excluded from many public offices after 1661 and discriminated against in the professions, in military and political assignments, and even in many arts and crafts, they focused their energies on commerce, industry, and finance. Like many other penalized minorities in history, they took refuge in the free-price market where automatic impersonal forces either bestow rewards upon the more efficient or weed out the inefficient irrespective of their religious or social status. Although this interpretation of why Huguenots turned to business stresses their reaction to various sanctions, it is quite clear that their religious beliefs and practices influenced the outcome in two ways: (1) it was their religion that made Huguenots a penalized minority, and (2) the theological doctrines of Calvinism predisposed their response and allowed them to seek "compensation" for their penalization in economic activity.

The expulsion of an appreciable portion of an economically active minority might very well have had a pronounced effect upon any economy. Whether the emigration of some 200,000 Huguenots seriously crippled economic life in France during the last three decades of Louis's reign is, in fact, the central problem of the present inquiry. Before examining the evidence on this score, it seems advisable first to survey economic conditions from 1683 to 1717 and to indicate where and when signs of economic stagnation and deterioration appeared.

VI

Economic Stagnation, 1684–1717

THE FRENCH ECONOMY IN 1683

When Colbert died on September 6, 1683, France was perhaps the richest, most populous, and strongest nation in western Europe. She had experienced no important internal disturbances after the suppression of the *Fronde* in 1653. The Treaty of Westphalia (1648) had ended the Thirty Years' War; the Treaty of the Pyrenees (1659) had brought peace after the war with Spain; France had quickly overrun Flanders (1667–1668); and she had fought the Dutch and the Spanish (1672–1678). Both internally and externally the authority of her king was greater than ever before. When Cardinal Mazarin died in 1661, Louis XIV decided not to replace him but, instead, to govern the realm directly. From then until 1683 he had the able and devoted assistance of Jean-Baptiste Colbert, whom he made intendant of finances in 1661 and controller general in 1665. Colbert also served as secretary of the navy, as superintendent of construction, and as what today would be called minister of the interior.

Both Louis and Colbert took their responsibilities seriously and worked hard at making France a great country, envied and respected by all. Colbert in particular realized the necessity of creating a well-balanced, vigorous economy and of introducing and maintaining order in government finance. He strove tirelessly to strengthen existing industries, to introduce new manufactures, to attract foreign artisans with special skills, to encourage both foreign and domestic trade, to create a powerful navy and merchant marine, to improve agriculture, and to balance the state's budget. His efforts were surprisingly successful. Trade and industry prospered, especially from 1664 until the Dutch war broke out in 1672. Colbert had helped to provoke this conflict by relentlessly attacking the Dutch economy with tariffs and other economic weapons, and he seems to have welcomed the war as an opportunity for France to crush her chief economic rival. But the war lasted much longer than Colbert had anticipated, and France's victory was not nearly so decisive as he had hoped. Before the war ended it had seriously impeded the economic expansion he had so carefully nurtured and nullified many of the gains he had painfully won. It also lessened his influence at Versailles and boosted the prestige of his rival Louvois. As the king's primary interests shifted from internal improvements to military and diplomatic matters, Louis turned to Louvois for counsel more often than to Colbert.[1]

How effective were Colbert's policies in promoting prosperity, and in what condition did he leave the economy upon his death? Although these questions are difficult to answer, it is essential at least to raise them and to consider them briefly in order to place the troubles that subsequently emerged in proper perspective.

In 1683 France, with its 20 or 21 million inhabitants, had a density of population of about 100 persons per square mile. This was roughly the same as in the late fourteenth century. Between a tenth and a fifth of these people lived in towns of 2,000 or more inhabitants. Paris was the largest city, and London was the only other metropolis in western Europe which rivaled Paris in size. Many French cities boasted of more than 10,000 residents, and a few like Marseille, Lille, Rouen, and Lyon had upward of 50,000. Most of these cities, however, had not grown very much since the time of Henry IV.[2] Not only was France predominantly rural in 1683, but there was also no significant urban trend.

Agriculture accounted for a larger share of the national income than any other segment of the French economy. The amount of land owned by the nobility varied from province to province and ranged from 11 per cent in Upper Auvergne to 35 per cent in Burgundy. The Church probably held about 6 per cent. The peasants, sharecroppers, and quasi-independent farmers, who cultivated the remainder, rarely had clear title to the land and worked under seignorial authority. There was little

[1] Germain Martin, *La Grande industrie sous le règne de Louis XIV* (Paris, 1898), p. 352.

[2] It is interesting to note that a survey in 1787 listed seventy-nine cities, including Paris, which had more than 10,000 inhabitants and which together accounted for about 10 per cent of the total population of France (Émile Levasseur, *La Population française* [Paris, 1889], I, 227).

agricultural wage labor. Individual holdings often were so small that the occupants would have found it difficult to eke out an existence had they been suddenly deprived of their traditional rights to common pasture, forest, and wastelands, or had they been unable to supplement their income with part-time employment in household crafts.[3]

Although brandy, flax, hemp, olive oil, wool, silk, and animal products were marketed at home and abroad, the chief commercial staples were wine and grain. Wheat, a luxury crop, was much less important in French agriculture than rye and other inferior grains. The specter of regional or national food shortages always hovered in the background. A large part of France—mountains, swampy areas alongside rivers, common pastures, and forests—had not yet been brought under cultivation, and peasants still allowed a sizable portion of their arable land to lie fallow each year as they blindly followed traditional methods of crop rotation. Agricultural techniques were so backward that grain harvests provided only four- or fivefold yields. Whenever and wherever nature was inclement, famine threatened. Crops were poor in 1621, 1626, 1630, and 1648–1652; and just as Colbert was coming into power, a succession of poor harvests commencing in 1660 created a severe famine in the winter of 1663–64. This helps to explain why agricultural unrest and peasant revolts remained common throughout the seventeenth century, and why Colbert meticulously regulated the internal and external trade in grain. Although he paid less attention to agriculture than to industry and trade, he sought to ease the tax burden of peasants by reducing the taille and increasing indirect taxes on commodities which all consumers would have to pay; he drained swamps and reclaimed other lands; he established stud farms for improving the breed of horses; and he bettered transportation facilities in the hope of widening farm markets. Nevertheless, agriculture apparently showed less improvement during Colbert's ministry than either trade or industry.

According to Professor Henri Sée,[4] commerce still "dominated" French industry in the seventeenth century in the sense that the most striking changes in industry stemmed from developments in commerce. It is not possible to estimate, even roughly,

---

[3] Henri Sée, *Histoire économique de la France,* I, ed. Robert Schnerb (Paris, 1939), 173 ff.

[4] *Ibid.,* I, 221.

how many people engaged in wholesale and retail trade or how much commerce as a whole contributed to the national income. Wholesale trade—especially the part that concerned foreign markets—apparently developed more rapidly in 1661–1683 than did retail trade. Only those who bought and sold at wholesale were able to call themselves "merchants"; retailers, classed as "tradesmen," were considered no less menial than ordinary craftsmen. Many wholesalers amassed fortunes and frequently supplied significant capital and entrepreneurship to the great monopolistic companies sponsored by the government in the foreign trade field. Most of these men managed in one way or another to escape from the corporative restrictions of gilds, and some bought their way into the nobility. It was in wholesale trade that the sleeping partnership (*société en commandite*) and the joint-stock company (*société anonyme*) first became really important in the French economy.

The seasonal fairs and weekly markets still played significant roles. Toward the end of the seventeenth century the *généralité* of Paris had no less than 194 fairs, and all other provinces together had at least 301. Permanent financial and commodity markets, however, had been developing rapidly as transportation and communication facilities improved and as middlemen and brokers increased in number. Several rivers were made more navigable, and a few canals were dug. During the reign of Henry IV, Sully had spent up to 1 million livres a year in building roads; thereafter, the annual expenditure had fallen to 40,000 livres. Colbert increased it to more than 600,000 livres, reconstituted the administration of roads and bridges, and tried to persuade provincial officials and peasants to spend more time on repairing local roads. Like Sully before him, he did not succeed in fulfilling his dream of leaving his country with a network of roads suitable for commercial travel; still, in 1683, French roads were better than English roads and probably were as good as those in any European country.

Despite persistent and Herculean efforts, Colbert was able to abolish or reform only a few tolls and excises which hampered the movement of goods, and local tradition thwarted his attempt to simplify France's heterogeneous system of weights and measures. His famous tariff of 1664 reformed the customs collected in the northwest-central portion of the country known as the Five Great Farms, and came close to making this region a great free-trade area. Colbert also tried, with his Ordonnance of Trade (1673), to assure the good faith of merchants by regulating bankruptcies and punishing fraud and by expediting litigation arising from commercial transactions.

Foreign trade expanded more spectacularly than domestic trade during Colbert's ministry. Colbert believed that at least 15,000 of the approximately 20,000 merchant vessels engaged in Europe's trade in 1660 were Dutch, whereas only 500 or 600 were French.[5] He therefore determined to build up his country's merchant marine. The number of French sailors increased from 36,000 in 1670 to almost 78,000 in 1683, and the marine's tonnage grew almost proportionately.[6] Whereas the French East India Company had had to buy its first ships from Dutch builders, French shipyards constructed at least 70 vessels for various companies in 1671. At the same time the French navy was also rapidly increasing in size and power. Between 1661 and 1677 it grew from 6 or 8 worm-eaten galleys and between 20 and 30 sailing vessels, which for the most part were small and aged, to 199 ships, more than half of which carried from 24 to 120 guns each. In 1677 the navy was manned by 1,089 officers, 8,227 sub-officers, and 20,861 sailors, and boasted of almost seven times more cannons than it had had in 1661.[7]

By 1683, although French merchants still relied upon English and Dutch carriers in their overseas trade, they had recaptured a good part of it for themselves. They were once more developing their contacts with the Levant, and were handling about a fourth of Europe's trade with Spain and her colonies. William Petty guessed that French exports in 1690 totaled between 100 million and 130 million livres. Colbert had founded several overseas companies and had given them important privileges to encourage their activities. He had also sought to develop marine insurance at Paris, had remolded Marseille into a free port, and had built or rebuilt important naval bases at Toulon, Brest, and Rochefort. The Dutch war interfered with the expansion of France's foreign trade and helped ruin several large companies,

---

[5] Charles W. Cole, *Colbert and a Century of French Mercantilism* (New York, 1939), I, 344.

[6] Émile Levasseur, *Histoire des classes ouvrières et de l'industrie en France avant 1789* (2d ed.; Paris, 1901), II, 283.

[7] Ernest Lavisse and others, *Histoire de France illustrée depuis les origines jusqu'à la révolution* (Paris, 1911), Vol. VII, Part 1, pp. 235, 253; Cole, *op. cit.*, I, 451 ff.

but at the time of Colbert's death France boasted of the most powerful navy and largest merchant marine she had ever had. Many of her industrial products were being marketed in all parts of the world.

France was foremost among all nations in total industrial activity. Her craftsmanship had long enjoyed world-wide esteem, and Colbert worked tirelessly to bring additional trade secrets, new industries, and skilled workmen in from other countries. Most French manufactures were still wrought in the homes of workers and peasants on either a household, gild, or putting-out basis. Colbert strongly supported the gild system in order to make regulation of production easier, to maintain the quality of output, and to provide revenue for the royal treasury. Yet he also encouraged the growth of large-scale enterprise by giving individuals and groups of entrepreneurs special privileges and financial assistance. A survey of all industries in 1683 probably would have revealed that there were several hundred large manufactories and quasi factories at work, each of which may have employed anywhere from a score to a few hundred individuals. Not all these plants used expensive or complicated machinery, nor were all of them strictly private enterprises. Some were owned and operated by the government, and others depended upon royal patronage and subsidies for survival. Still, some of the largest and most truly capitalistic enterprises in Europe at that time were in France. Since modern production units capture the eye and stimulate the imagination of economic historians, one must be careful not to exaggerate their over-all importance. It is unlikely that more than 3 or 5 per cent of all individuals engaged in manufacturing worked together in either large or small manufactories.

Colbert created several new industries, and was directly or indirectly responsible for the expansion of a great many more. At one time or another he attempted to stimulate or to regulate almost all branches of the textile industry, ranging from cloths of gold and silver and the finest woolens and silks to serges and fabrics containing admixtures of wool, cotton, linen, and other fibers. He promoted the knitting of silk and woolen stockings; the making of French and foreign-style laces; the weaving of rugs and tapestries; the manufacture of plate glass, mirrors, crystal, and fine earthenware; and the production of tin plate, ironware, brass, and copper. He showed special interest in the production of all kinds of naval supplies and munitions, and he was solicitous about the techniques employed and the expansion of output in the soap, sugar, paper, tobacco, hat, and leather-goods industries. He issued about 113 letters patent for privileged or royal manufactories[8] and drew up several detailed regulations to govern the activities of individual craftsmen and major companies alike. In 1672 French industry was more prosperous than it had ever been before, though it is debatable whether the advancement was due entirely to Colbert's efforts.

By fair means or foul, Colbert had also managed to reduce the public debt, to increase tax revenues reaching the treasury, and to institute a semblance of order in government finance. He reduced the *rentes* the government had to pay its creditors from more than 20 million livres in 1660 to about 7 million in 1670; and he succeeded for a few years in balancing the budget. As a result of his administration as controller general, the government improved its credit rating among lenders.

On the whole, the French economy was still relatively prosperous in 1683, although there was a slackening in growth after 1672. The national income was certainly larger than that of any other European nation, and most Frenchmen probably were as well off as the subjects of other states. Almost immediately after Colbert's death, however, difficulties began to arise, and France plunged into one of the most acute and prolonged periods of economic distress in her history.

The precise date when the trend turned downward is difficult to determine. Harvests were poor in 1684, and unemployment threatened. The next year the number of pessimistic reports reaching the controller general from the provinces multiplied. According to a report in the autumn of 1685, peasants throughout Limousin were so poor that they had only chestnuts and turnips to eat, and were feeding their livestock brake instead of hay.[9] Nicolas Desmaretz, Colbert's nephew and controller general from 1708 to 1715, admitted in a memorandum in 1686 that such jeremiads were warranted:

---

8 Levasseur, *Histoire des classes ouvrières et de l'industrie*, II, 239.

9 *Ibid.*, II, 333; Shelby T. McCloy, *Government Assistance in Eighteenth-Century France* (Durham, N.C., 1946), p. 21; Jules Michelet, *Histoire de France* (3d ed.; Paris, 1863), XIII, 287; A. M. de Boislisle, *Correspondance des contrôleurs généraux des finances avec les intendants des provinces*, I (Paris, 1874), 37, 41, 44, 50, 54; Bibliothèque Nationale, *Fonds français*, MS 21773, fol. 142; Archives Nationales, G7 492.

Most sensible men [in government] gradually become inured to all such talk about poverty because they always hear the same thing on every hand. But it can be said that never before has anyone spoken of the people's misery with so much justification. All one has to do to become convinced of this assertion is to observe existing conditions in several provinces.[10]

Another individual reported in January, 1686, that people were everywhere abandoning their farms, nobles were facing financial ruin, merchants were in bankruptcy, peasants were lost in despair, artisans were migrating to foreign countries because of unemployment, incomes from land had fallen by 40 per cent, population in provincial towns had dropped to one-tenth, and all public hospitals and charitable institutions were crowded beyond capacity. More people were dying in one day than ordinarily died in a week; and the number of monks, beggars, vagabonds, and pickpockets was increasing rapidly. Credit was no longer available, and money was so scarce throughout Flanders, he continued, that the largest coin seen in circulation was the six-sou piece. The scarcity of money struck him forcefully because the king had recently spent millions of livres in the area building and repairing the port and fortifications of Dunkirk.[11]

The writer, in attempting to interest the Crown in a pet reform project, probably exaggerated conditions. It is certain, nonetheless, that times were becoming hard. Two contemporary economists and another writing in the first half of the nineteenth century were all convinced of the fact. Le Pesant de Boisguillebert thought that the national income had declined greatly;[12] Richard Cantillon wrote that "the power of France has been on the increase only from 1646 (when Manufactures of Cloths were set up there, which were until then imported) to 1684, when a number of Protestant Undertakers and Artisans were driven out of it, and that kingdom has done nothing but

---

10 Boislisle, *op. cit.*, I, 545. See also Dom H. Leclercq, *Histoire de la Régence pendant la minorité de Louis XIV* (Paris, 1921–1922), I, xlix.

11 Archives Nationales, A¹ 795, doc. 51.

12 *Factum de la France* (1707), in *Collection des principaux économistes*, Vol. I: *Économistes financiers du XVIIIᵉ siècle*, ed. E. Daire (2d ed.; Paris, 1851), p. 253 and *passim*; *Le Détail de la France* (1697), in the same *Collection*, pp. 163, 165, 169. Voltaire, in his attack on Boisguillebert, was at fault when he said that the good times after the death of Mazarin lasted until 1689 (*Age of Louis XIV*, Vol. XXIII of *Works of Voltaire* [La Vérité ed.; New York and Paris, 1901], pp. 261–262).

recede since this last date";[13] and Sismondi stated that "general misery was making frightful progress."[14]

Until after the death of Louis XIV in 1715 and, in fact, until the shock treatment administered by John Law during the Regency took effect, signs of stagnation were visible on every hand.[15] The pervading grimness was accentuated periodically by crises and panics; the two worst occurred in 1692–1694, when general crop failures brought widespread famine, and in 1708–09, when one of the severest winters on record caused unbelievable suffering. The present chapter describes economic conditions during the last decades of Louis XIV's reign; subsequent chapters evaluate the role of the revocation of the Edict of Nantes and of various other factors in the depression.

DEPOPULATION

It is generally recognized by economic historians and demographers alike that a decline in population usually accompanies prolonged depression and that an increase ordinarily occurs when economic conditions permanently improve. Population trends therefore often indicate the direction of important shifts in economic development.

Nearly all contemporary observers—as well as most modern historians—agree that French population declined drastically in the last half of Louis's reign. Émile Levasseur has suggested that France had about 20,000,000 inhabitants in 1590, 21,136,000 in 1700, and about 18,000,000 in 1715–1720 in the territories enclosed by her borders of 1889. He thought that her population increased under Louis XIII and Louis XIV until Colbert's death in 1683, when the decline set in. Hence he suggested that his figure of 21,136,000 for 1700 was not the highest point reached during the seventeenth century.[16] If he was right in thinking

---

13 *Essai sur la nature du commerce en générale,* ed. and trans. Henry Higgs (London, 1931), p. 187.

14 *Histoire des français* (Paris, 1821–1844), XXV, 532–533.

15 [Claude Brousson], *Lettres et opuscules de feu Monsr. Brousson, ministre et martyr du St. Evangile; avec un abrégé de sa vie* . . . (Utrecht, 1701), pp. 322–323; Emmanuel-Orentin Douen, *La Révocation de l'Édit de Nantes à Paris d'après des documents inédits* (Paris, 1894), I, 97; Charles Ferrare Dutot, *Réflexions politiques sur les finances et le commerce* (1738), in *Collection des principaux économistes,* ed. E. Daire, p. 804; Levasseur, *Histoire des classes ouvrières et de l'industrie,* II, 352; Émile Levasseur, *Histoire du commerce de la France* (Paris, 1911), I, 350, 422; Martin, *op. cit.,* pp. 284, 304–305; Sée, *op. cit.,* I, 272, 274.

16 *La Population française,* I, 286–287. He further suggested (pp. 213, 286) that

that total population declined by about 3 million between 1700 and 1720, surely it must have fallen by at least another million between 1683 and 1700 because of the emigration of Protestants after 1685 and the mortality accompanying the famine of 1692–1694. The Venetian ambassador at Paris wrote home in 1695 that France had lost 2 million inhabitants since 1689,[17] and Henri Martin concluded that the decline from the most prosperous years of Colbert's ministry to 1700 amounted to 3 or 4 million.[18] Martin's figure is probably too large, and Professor Sagnac was probably too conservative when he estimated a decrease of "at least" 1 million for the entire period from 1685 to 1715.[19]

The memoranda prepared by intendants in 1698–1700 at the king's request contain the best demographic data for the seventeenth century, but they are not always reliable. Many intendants did not take their instructions seriously and frequently accepted uncritically the informed or uninformed guesses and observations of their subordinates. Others were more anxious to write what they thought would please their sovereign than to render him a faithful report on conditions in their jurisdictions. Nevertheless, most of them admitted that population had declined in the preceding two or three decades and that some cities and towns had been hit especially hard. The intendant at Alençon, for example, said that the number of people subject to the general property tax in his province had fallen greatly; Picardy had lost one-twelfth of its inhabitants; Touraine was less populous by 25 per cent than it had been thirty years earlier; rural and urban areas in the *généralité* of Orléans had suffered a decrease of one-fifth; since 1632, population in the Three Bishoprics had fallen by two-thirds; the *généralités* of Lyon and La Rochelle had one-sixth and one-third less people, respectively; Dauphiné, Béarn, and Lower Normandy had also experienced an appreciable decline; Guyenne and Bourbonnais had lost a fifth or a third of their

France had only approximately 14,000,000 subjects within her boundaries in 1581, 20,070,000 in 1700, and between 16,000,000 and 17,000,000 in 1715. Vauban estimated the 1700 figure at 19,094,146 (*La Dîme royale* [1708], in *Collection des principaux économistes*, ed. E. Daire, p. 118); and Arnould, at 20,094,000 (*De la Balance du commerce . . .* [Paris, 1791], I, 185, 188).

17 Henry Austen Layard, "The Revocation of the Edict of Nantes. Illustrated from State Papers in the Archives of Venice," *Proceedings of the Huguenot Society of London* (hereinafter cited as *PHSL*), II (1887–1888), 151–152.

18 *Histoire de France depuis les temps les plus reculés jusqu'en 1789* (4th ed.; Paris, 1874), XIV, 330–333.

19 Lavisse, *op. cit.*, Vol. VIII, Part 1, p. 273.

inhabitants; and in the *généralité* of Paris, the districts of Mantes and Étampes had lost one-half their residents while several other districts had lost one-third or one-fourth. Although many intendants failed to comment on population in their reports, the only one who claimed that his area was as populous as ever was the official in Artois.[20]

The same reports give the impression that many cities shrank in size after 1683. This is especially significant, for much of the country's industry and trade was centered in the cities. Rouen (Normandy) supposedly had lost 20,000 of her 80,000 inhabitants[21] and Troyes (Champagne) about half of her population; Thiers (Auvergne) had shrunk greatly; Châtillon-sur-Seine (Burgundy) no longer resembled her former self; Villefranche, Saint-Chamond, and Saint-Étienne (all in Lyonnais) had decreased, and Lyon itself had fallen from 90,000 to 70,000; Cambray (Flanders) was only one-half its former size; Châlons (Champagne) was "greatly diminished" in population and wealth; Saumur (Anjou) and Alençon (Maine) were, respectively, only one-half and two-thirds as large as formerly; Riom (Auvergne) was so depopulated that it appeared deserted; and Mâcon (Burgundy) had shrunk by one-fourth.[22]

Other sources support the belief that France's population was decreasing. Dieppe and its surrounding territory, with about 40,000 inhabitants in 1650, had only about a fifth as many in 1720. This severe decline was partially attributable to the bombardment by the English in July, 1694.[23] The intendant Bégon wrote the controller general on May 8, 1695, that the number of persons in the diocese of Saintes had fallen from 400,000 to 300,000,[24] and in the same year the intendant in Auvergne

---

20 Bibliothèque Nationale, *Fonds français*, MSS 4282, fols. 333–334; 4283, fols. 20, 36; 4284, fols. 22, 29; 4285, fol. 117; 4286, fols. 28, 30, 31, 32, 76, 102, 169, 172; 4287, fols. 7, 18, 47, 50; 4288, fols. 18, 30. See also Eugène Bersier, *Quelques pages de l'histoire des Huguenots* (Paris, 1891), p. 184.

21 Bibliothèque Nationale, *Fonds français*, MS 4286, fol. 13. See also Henry M. Baird, *The Huguenots and the Revocation of the Edict of Nantes* (New York, 1895), II, 100; Jean Bianquis, *La Révocation de l'édit de Nantes à Rouen, essai historique* (Rouen, 1885), p. ci; Lavisse, *op. cit.*, Vol. VIII, Part 1, p. 234; Leclercq, *op. cit.*, I, lv; Charles Weiss, "Mémoire sur les protestants de France au XVIIe siècle," *Séances et travaux de l'Académie des sciences morales et politiques*, XX (1851), 119.

22 Bibliothèque Nationale, *Fonds français*, MSS 4283, fol. 43; 4284, fol. 101; 4285, fols. 123–124, 139; 4286, fol. 121; 4288, fols. 10, 16, 17, 18; 4289, fols. 178, 218.

23 Samuel Hardy, *Histoire de l'Église protestante de Dieppe* (Paris, 1896), pp. 389, 391–392, 396; Émile-G. Léonard, *Problèmes et expériences du protestantisme français* (Paris, 1940), pp. 16–17.

24 Bibliothèque Nationale, *Fonds français*, MS 7045, fols. 43–45; Victor Bujeaud,

complained that his province had lost one-third its inhabitants.[25] According to a census conducted by its city council, Montpellier had declined appreciably by 1689;[26] the number of hearths in Vitry-le-François (Champagne) had dwindled from 3,600 to scarcely 2,600 by 1688;[27] and a traveler who toured Argonne near the close of the seventeenth century reported that Charleville and Mézières each had lost a significant portion of its population.[28] Metz was said to have been only one-third as large in 1700 as in 1552;[29] Tours lost many citizens after 1685;[30] and Le Havre also declined.[31] Various historians writing in the nineteenth and twentieth centuries have concluded that depopulation also beset the provinces of Anjou,[32] Languedoc,[33] Normandy,[34] and Poitou.[35] The controller general in 1714 replied to Pontchartrain, who had suggested the desirability of peopling French colonies, that population in France had declined to such an extent in the past decades that it would be foolhardy to favor

Chronique protestante de l'Angoumois, XVIe, XVIIe, XVIIIe siècles (Paris and Angoulême, 1860), p. 311; L.-J. Nazelle, *Le Protestantisme en Saintonge sous le régime de la Révocation, 1685–1789* (Paris, 1907), pp. 38–39; Claude-Carlomau de Rulhière, *Eclaircissements historiques sur les causes de la révocation de l'Édit de Nantes, et sur l'état des protestants en France, depuis le commencement du Règne de Louis XIV, jusqu'à nos jours* (new ed.; Geneva, 1788), I, 327.

25 Boislisle, *op. cit.*, I, 405.

26 Philippe Corbière, *Histoire de l'Église Réformée de Montpellier depuis son origine jusqu'à nos jours* (Montpellier, 1861), pp. 275–276.

27 G. Hérelle, *Documents inédits sur le protestantisme à Vitry-le-François . . . depuis la fin des Guerres de Religion jusqu'à la Révolution française* (Paris, 1903–1908), I, 326–327.

28 J. Jailliot, "Le Protestantisme dans le Rethelois et dans l'Argonne jusqu'à la révocation de l'Édit de Nantes," *Revue d'Ardenne et d'Argonne*, XIII (1905–1906), 173.

29 Maurice Thirion, *Étude sur l'histoire du protestantisme à Metz et dans le pays Messin* (Nancy, 1884), p. 394 n. 1.

30 Bersier, *op. cit.*, p. 184; Abbé L. Bosseboeuf, "Histoire de la fabrique de soieries de Tours, des origines au XIXe siècle," *Bulletin et mémoires de la société archéologique de Touraine*, XLI (1900), 227 ff.

31 Henri Amphoux, *Essai sur l'histoire du Protestantisme au Havre et dans ses environs* (Le Havre, 1894), pp. 235, 236.

32 Bersier, *op. cit.*, p. 184.

33 *Bulletin de la Société de l'histoire du protestantisme français* (hereinafter cited as *BSHPF*), XXIX (1880), 188–192.

34 Baird, *op. cit.*, II, 100; Émile Levasseur, *Histoire des classes ouvrières en France depuis la conquête de Jules César jusqu'à la révolution* (Paris, 1859), II, 286.

35 François Baudry, *La Révocation de l'édit de Nantes et le protestantisme en Bas-Poitou au XVIIIe siècle* (Trévoux, 1922), p. 282; Comte Louis de La Boutetière, "Note sur l'émigration protestante du Poitou à la suite de la révocation de l'Édit de Nantes," *Bulletins de la société des antiquaires de l'Ouest*, XIV (1877), 352–353; August-François Lièvre, *Histoire des protestants et des églises réformées du Poitou* (Paris, 1856–1860), II, 225, 250; N. Weiss, "Aperçu de la Révocation de l'Édit de Nantes en Poitou (1660–1686)," *BSHPF*, LIV (1905), 355–356.

emigration to the New World.[36] Recurrent reference to depopulation in the correspondence received by the controller general and his predecessors from intendants in 1684–1717 had made a deep impression on this official.[37]

One reason for depopulation was the excessive mortality accompanying famines. Regional food shortages had always plagued the country, and the government had tried to cope with the problem by regulating the transportation of grain between provinces and its sale on domestic foreign markets. The famine of 1692–1694, however, was probably the worst general famine of the century.[38] The price of wheat in 1694 was more than four times as high as its average in 1686–1690.[39] The intendant at Bordeaux first complained of grain shortages in his jurisdiction in 1691; by the end of the following year other officials had become concerned. Starvation was widespread after the summer of 1693, and the national emergency did not diminish until the harvests of 1694 began to reach the market.[40] Several hundred thousand individuals may have perished. The intendant at Bordeaux wrote on April 19, 1692, that "every day such a great number of people die that some parishes will not retain a third of their population."[41] Another official on June 6, 1693, used these same words to describe conditions in the *généralité* of Limoges.[42] Vauban had predicted in November, 1692, that sickness and hunger would cause three-fourths of the people in Dauphiné to perish if help was not immediately forthcoming.[43] The Bishop of Montauban wrote on April 16, 1694, that "we find nearly every day at the city's gate seven or eight dead persons, and in my diocese, which includes 750 parishes, at least 450 individuals die each day from lack of food."[44] Other reports channeled to Paris and Versailles contained such statements as "an infinity of people are here dying of hunger"; certain "parishes have to hold ten or twelve funerals daily"; "a prodigious number are dying"; "only one-fourth of the population

---

[36] Boislisle, *op. cit.*, III (1897), 557.

[37] See *ibid.*, I, II (1883), III, *passim*.

[38] Charles W. Cole, *French Mercantilism, 1683–1700* (New York, 1943), p. 195; McCloy, *op. cit.*, p. 195; Leclercq, *op. cit.*, I, lii ff.; Levasseur, *Histoire du commerce*, I, 422.

[39] Levasseur, *Histoire des classes ouvrières et de l'industrie*, II, 350 n. 4.

[40] Archives Nationales, G7 135, 136; Boislisle, *op. cit.*, I, 244, 298, 371 ff.

[41] Levasseur, *Histoire des classes ouvrières et de l'industrie*, II, 351.

[42] Boislisle, *op. cit.*, I, 319.

[43] Leclercq, *op. cit.*, I, lii.

[44] *Ibid.*, I, liv; Levasseur, *Histoire des classes ouvrières et de l'industrie*, II, 351.

[of a town] remain alive"; "within the past three years, more than three-fourths of the people of Lower Armagnac have died"; and "of the twenty-eight who perished in one day last week, only two died of sickness and the rest from hunger."[45] Most intendants who mentioned the famine in their 1698–1700 memoranda listed it as one of the most important causes, if not the chief cause, for the decrease in population.[46]

Although harvests were short once again in 1699–1700, mortality was not excessive. The severe winter of 1708–09, however, rivaled the famine of 1692–1694 in creating hardship and misery. Grapevines and olive and fruit trees froze, all crops already planted were lost and harvested grains rotted after the thaw, livestock died on farms, all kinds of wildlife perished, and thousands of persons succumbed to the intense cold and lack of food. Trudaine, intendant at Lyon, wrote that "everyone here says that the misery is infinitely greater at present than it ever was in 1693 and 1694";[47] and Saint-Simon exclaimed that France's plight was so piteous that no Frenchman capable of reflective observation could keep from worrying and any foreigner who had formerly been jealous of the country could now feel only commiseration.[48] Sismondi painted the picture in vivid colors and concluded that misery was frightful.[49] Both Leclercq and Levasseur described the months following February, 1709, as the time when the country plumbed the darkest and deepest abyss of the seventeenth and eighteenth centuries.[50]

About ten years later a severe epidemic of the bubonic plague ravaged Marseille and southeastern France.[51] No one knows how many Frenchmen perished as a result of the 1708–09 winter and the 1720–1722 plague.[52] In September and October of 1720, it has been estimated, about a thousand persons were dying daily,

---

45 Leclercq, *op. cit.*, I, liii, liv; Boislisle, *op. cit.*, I, 319, 352, 360, 419.

46 Bibliothèque Nationale, *Fonds français*, MSS 4284, fol. 22; 4285, fol. 137; 4286, fols. 12, 76, 94; 4287, fols. 7, 47; 4288, fols. 16, 18; 4290, fol. 310.

47 Boislisle, *op. cit.*, I, 491 ff.; III, 115.

48 "Projects de restablissement du royaume," in *Écrits inédits de Saint-Simon* (Paris, 1882), IV, 193 (as quoted by Leclercq, *op. cit.*, I, lxii–lxiii).

49 *Op. cit.*, XXVII, 71–72.

50 Leclercq, *op. cit.*, I, lix–lx, lxv; Levasseur, *Histoire des classes ouvrières et de l'industrie*, II, 352. Germain Martin also speaks of the period as one of "heavy misfortune" (*op. cit.*, p. 306).

51 McCloy, *op. cit.*, pp. 135 ff.

52 Abbé Novi de Caveirac spoke of 400,000, but there is no reason to believe he had access to reliable vital statistics (*Mémoire politico-critique, où l'on examine s'il est de l'intérêt de l'Église et de l'État d'établir pour les Calvinistes du Royaume une nouvelle forme de se marier* [n.p., 1756], p. 64).

and the intendant at Marseille (Le Bret) reported that Provence alone lost 93,290 victims before the plague subsided.[53]

One cannot be too cautious in judging the reliability of the official reports reaching the king or his controller general, especially if they buttressed appeals for local tax relief or government assistance. The unanimity of cries about distress and mortality, however, makes it difficult to dismiss the reports altogether. The conclusion is inescapable that the famine of 1692–1694, the severe winter of 1708–09, and the plague of 1720–1722 were important factors making for depopulation.

War was yet another. The last two major wars of Louis XIV drained France's man power much more than his earlier wars with the Dutch. They lasted longer; the French armies were much less decisive in victory and faced defeat more often than previously, when Turenne and Condé had planned their strategy and guided their maneuvers; and fatalities on the battlefield and mortality in camps and hospitals may have been greater. Here again, it is impossible to estimate accurately the number who perished. It is significant, however, that government officials usually listed the War of the League of Augsburg and the War of the Spanish Succession as prime causes for the decline in population in their jurisdictions.

In the latter half of Louis's reign large numbers of Frenchmen also emigrated. Approximately 200,000 fled to foreign countries for religious reasons. Others left because of famine, contagious diseases, high taxes, obligatory military service, unemployment, regimentation of economic life restricting freedom of entry into gilds and industry, and general economic depression.[54] Louis's special emissary, Bonrepaus, wrote Seignelay from London on February 11, 1686, that many French Catholics were working in newly established industries and manufactories throughout England; and the French ambassador in Holland (d'Avaux) stated on January 10 that "more than" 800 French or Walloon Catholics were employed in the woolen enterprises at Leiden.[55] Colbert had tried to enrich his country by enticing skilled craftsmen from abroad; other countries retaliated by luring away French artisans when the pall of depression began to envelop France. Silkworkers left Lyon after 1693 because of unemploy-

---

53 McCloy, *op. cit.*, pp. 137, 138.
54 Lavisse, *op. cit.*, Vol. VIII, Part 1, p. 273.
55 Archives du Ministère des Affaires Étrangères, *Ancien fonds,* "Angleterre," *registre* 157, fol. 60; "Hollande," *registre* 145, fol. 27.

ment;[56] many laborers fled Lille when the Treaty of Utrecht ceded that city to France;[57] ironworkers and others from Alsace, Lorraine, and Franche-Comté moved to Germany and Switzerland, thereby endangering France's metallurgical and armament industries;[58] poverty drove "a great many" Catholic rug and tapestry workers from Aubusson after 200 Huguenots had fled;[59] and other cities and provinces cried that their inhabitants were seeking employment abroad because there were so few opportunities at home.[60] In a memorandum to the lieutenant general of police at Paris on March 31, 1684, an anonymous author wrote that "more than" 30,000 laborers had left the capital since 1681.[61] Another individual sponsoring a reform project told the government that for every French Catholic employed in a foreign country twenty years earlier there were 3,000 similarly employed in January, 1686.[62] Although these estimates are wholly unreliable, the statements themselves support the conclusion that hard times at home were forcing workers to seek employment elsewhere.

Whether France's population fell by 4 million or more between 1683 and 1720, or by only 1 million, the foregoing evidence indicates that many officials were concerned over the trend and attributed the decline to (1) the heavy mortality accompanying famines and hardships, (2) the toll of war, (3) the expulsion of Huguenots, and (4) the emigration of others seeking jobs abroad or fleeing to escape creditors.

DETERIORATION IN LIVING CONDITIONS

That France was not prosperous after 1683 is further attested by other evidence. Even when times were good, the masses lived precariously. Human misery and poverty appeared to be increasing everywhere. In his financial brief for 1681 Colbert had called

---

56 E. Pariset, *Histoire de la fabrique lyonnaise. Étude sur le Régime social et économique de l'Industrie de la Soie à Lyon, depuis le XVIᵉ siècle* (Lyon, 1901), p. 120; Henri Sée, *L'Évolution commerciale et industrielle de la France sous l'ancien régime* (Paris, 1925), p. 152.

57 Archives Nationales, G7 *registre* 1700A, p. 127; G. Martin, *op. cit.*, p. 247.

58 Boislisle, *op. cit.*, I, 352; II, 210; G. Martin, *op. cit.*, p. 247.

59 Bibliothèque Nationale, *Fonds français*, MS 4287, fol. 19.

60 *Ibid.*, MSS 4283, fol. 23; 4284, fol. 101; Charles Ancillon, *Histoire de l'établissement des françois réfugiés dans les états de son altesse electorale de Brandebourg* (Berlin, 1690), p. 249; Boislisle, *op. cit.*, I, 32; II, 23; Douen, *op. cit.*, I, 97; Lièvre, *op. cit.*, II, 251; G. Martin, *op. cit.*, pp. 245, 247; Sée, *Évolution commerciale et industrielle*, pp. 152, 153; Sée, *Histoire économique de la France*, I, 274.

61 Bibliothèque Nationale, *Fonds français*, MS 21773, fol. 143.

62 Archives Nationales, A1 795, doc. 51.

the king's attention to the necessity of reducing peacetime expenditures so as to be ready if "some glorious occasion arises for declaring war. . . . But an even more important and deserving reason [for retrenching] is the very great poverty of your people."[63] After the minister's death, reports from the provinces assumed a more and more doleful tone. The intendant at Poitiers wrote on March 26, 1684, that workers were so poor that they had to knock on the poorhouse door the moment they lost their jobs in order to keep from starving.[64] Local grain shortages caused high prices and suffering in certain provinces in 1684–1685;[65] and workers could not find employment in Rouen even though they were willing to work at half their regular wages.[66] Cévennes was always poverty-ridden, but misery increased there, and also in Poitou and Saintonge, in 1686; peasants were reportedly eating nothing but acorns and boiled grass and "an unbelievable number of families" lacked bread.[67]

An official investigation of conditions in Maine and Orléanais in 1687 uncovered a dismal picture. Exclusive of those who had left because of religion, population had everywhere greatly diminished because people roaming the countryside seeking alms were perishing along the roadsides and in homes for the poor; houses were falling into ruin in both cities and villages; many dwellings were abandoned; and miserable sharecroppers tilled the soil instead of well-to-do farmers. Bereft of furniture, peasants slept on piles of straw and ate only black bread; or, lacking this, they boiled fern roots mixed with barley or oat flour.[68] The intendant in Auvergne stated two years later that "three-fourths" of the people in his area ate roots and grasses "three or four months out of the year"; they could always be seen browsing in the fields like cattle or eating carrion. So many destitute persons

---

63 Pierre Clément, *Lettres, instructions et mémoires de Colbert* (Paris, 1861–1884), II, 141. In his letters to intendants, however, Colbert discounted heavily all their claims that the masses were unable to pay taxes because of poverty (see, e.g., *ibid.*, II, 137, 219, 714–715; IV, 141–142).

64 Archives Nationales, G7 450; Boislisle, *op. cit.*, I, 16–17.

65 Boislisle, *op. cit.*, I, 23, 27, 28–29, 35, 50, 54; Baudry, *op. cit.*, pp. 62 ff.

66 Archives Nationales, G7 492; Boislisle, *op. cit.*, I, 43, 44, 49. One writer also reported considerable unemployment among silk merchants and artisans in Paris in 1684 (Bibliothèque Nationale, *Fonds français*, MS 21773, fol. 142).

67 Archives Nationales, G7 297, 450; B2 *registre* 57, fol. 121; Bibliothèque Nationale, *Nouvelles acquisitions françaises*, MS 507, fol. 2; Boislisle, *op. cit.*, I, 64, 65. Yet crops were good in France as a whole in 1686 and 1687 (Boislisle, *op. cit.*, I, 70, 73, 106, 107, 108).

68 Lavisse, *op. cit.*, Vol. VII, Part 1, p. 341; Vol. VIII, Part 1, p. 272; Levasseur, *Histoire du commerce*, I, 422; *Histoire des classes ouvrières et de l'industrie*, II, 351.

from the surrounding countryside descended upon towns that contagious fevers developed and carried off thousands.[69] The Prince of Condé wrote Pontchartrain in August, 1691, that he had discovered more misery during a recent trip through Burgundy than he thought could possibly exist and that he had never encountered a single villager who had not begged alms.[70]

Conditions worsened during the black years of 1692–1694.[71] Reports reaching Paris painted an appalling picture. Almost half of Reims's 25,000 or 26,000 people were reduced to beggary, and trade had ceased entirely; more than 3,000 families, or about 15,000 persons, in three cantons of Béarn were without any resources whatever; the shortage of grain in Lyon made it difficult to restrain workers from violence; all of Blois was on the threshold of death from hunger; "according to an investigation made with all the exactitude imaginable, more than 70,000 individuals of all ages and of both sexes" around Limoges were fast being reduced to beggary; there were 26,000 beggars and 5,000 wretchedly poor in the Moulins area; and those in Bordeaux who were better off made bread from bran whereas others had no bread of any kind.[72] The Bishop of Noyon in desperation asked the controller general to forbid the poor to assemble in crowds; he said the wretches were already menacing curés, priests, and leading citizens and were demanding far more relief than could be provided.[73]

For four years after 1694 conditions improved. Then they deteriorated again. From Auvergne the intendant wrote in November, 1698, that "misery is incomparably greater than in 1693 and 1694."[74] There were complaints of increasing beggary, of the tide of vagrants and vagabonds who roamed the countryside, of fields lying uncultivated, and of mounting unemployment in Tours, Laval, Orléans, and similar places.[75] Intendants in their

---

69 Archives Nationales, G7 103.

70 Leclercq, *op. cit.*, I, lii; Boislisle, *op. cit.*, I, 248. See also the letters written the controller general by the intendants of Bordeaux and Limoges in May and June, 1691 (Boislisle, *op. cit.*, I, 245–246, 248).

71 Boislisle, *op. cit.*, I, 297, 299, 313, 364; Guillaume-B. Depping, *Correspondance administrative sous le règne de Louis XIV* (Paris, 1850–1855), I, 900; Lavisse, *op. cit.*, Vol. VIII, Part 1, p. 272; Levasseur, *Histoire des classes ouvrières et de l'industrie*, II, 351; G. Martin, *op. cit.*, p. 244; Sée, *Histoire économique de la France*, I, 274.

72 Boislisle, *op. cit.*, I, 274, 313, 321, 343, 349; Leclercq, *op. cit.*, I, lii–liii.

73 Levasseur, *Histoire des classes ouvrières et de l'industrie*, II, 351–352 n.

74 Boislisle, *op. cit.*, I, 501.

75 Bibliothèque Nationale, *Fonds français*, MS 4283, fols. 31 ff.; Boislisle, *op. cit.*, I, 524, 533–534, 536; II, 4, 12, 41–42; Leclercq, *op. cit.*, I, lvii.

1698–1700 memoranda were not at all cheerful.[76] In the *généra-lité* of Alençon, poverty was so great that owners could not repair the roofs on their houses, and "frightful gloom and surprising ferocity" were spreading everywhere. Neither masters nor artisans in Bourbonnais could buy bread for want of money even though wheat was then selling at low prices. Even nobles in Brittany had no way to meet their expenses when they attended Parliament.[77]

The War of the Spanish Succession, beginning in 1701, brought additional hardships. Peasants in certain areas resorted again to boiling and eating ashes, roots, and grasses; workers in many trades again faced unemployment.[78] Boisguillebert reminded the controller general in 1704 that the number of tennis courts in Paris had fallen from 160 (in 1660) to 60, and in Rouen from 25 to 3, and that about 10,000 cabarets in Normandy alone had gone out of business. Such changes indicated a decrease in the standard of living, he said, because tennis courts and cabarets were "signs of opulence."[79]

When the terrible winter of 1708–09 struck, France was already reeling from the austerities of war. Industries ground to a stop, unemployment mounted, money ceased to circulate, mobs sought help from government and church officials, tax collections declined, soldiers and officers went unpaid and desertions mounted, hungry peasants again took to the fields like cattle, cities and churches combatted unrest by opening relief stations and workhouses, and desperate beggars and vagabonds made traveling unsafe.[80] Conditions improved somewhat after 1710, but until 1717 or 1718 poverty and depression remained manifest on every hand.

No one has yet denied that human well-being in France was much greater before 1683 than in the three and a half decades that followed. Vauban wrote in *La Dîme royale* (1707) that one-tenth of the population was reduced to beggary, five-tenths

---

[76] See, e.g., Bibliothèque Nationale, *Fonds français*, MSS 4284, fol. 22; 4285, fol. 137; 4286, fols. 12, 76; 4287, fols. 7, 47; 4288, fols. 15, 16, 18; 4290, fol. 310; Comte de Boulainvilliers, *Etat de France . . . extrait des Mémoires dressés par les Intendans du Royaume* (London, 1737), I–VI, *passim*.

[77] Leclercq, *op. cit.*, I, lv–lvii.

[78] Boislisle, *op. cit.*, II, 102, 166, 172, 185, 207, 281, 331–332, 358, 444, 450; III, 40, 57, 65, 492.

[79] *Ibid.*, II, 538.

[80] *Ibid.*, III, 102, 115–116, 125, 180, 200, 231, 239–240, 249, 308, 603; Leclercq, *op. cit.*, I, lxii; G. Martin, *op. cit.*, pp. 306 ff.; Sismondi, *op. cit.*, XXVII, 90.

could not proffer alms because they themselves were barely sub-
sisting, three-tenths were harassed by debt and litigation, and
no more than 100,000 persons of the wealthiest 10 per cent were
in a position to render aid to others. In fact, he said, only about
10,000 persons in all France lived "on easy street."[81] The economist Dutot stated in 1738 that even nobles and clerics had experienced financial hardship in the years immediately preceding
John Law's ascent to power.[82] Fénelon had been so moved by
what he had observed on every hand that he had the temerity to
blame Louis for much of the suffering:

The cultivation of land is almost abandoned; depopulation is hitting
cities and countryside alike; crafts are languishing and no longer
nourish their workers. All trade has vanished. You have destroyed
half the real strength inside your realm in order to make vain conquests outside. Instead of taking money from your poor people, you
should be giving them alms and nourishment. All France is nothing
more than one large poorhouse [*hôpital*], desolate and provisionless.[83]

Fénelon wrote others in 1710 that "it is a miracle that anyone
is alive" and that "France appears to be an old dilapidated
machine . . . which will fall to pieces at the first jolt."[84]

INDUSTRIAL STAGNATION

It is difficult to assess the extent and amount of unemployment
or to generalize about industrial conditions. Some industries—
particularly those contributing to the war effort—apparently
prospered while others declined or actually disappeared in certain provinces. It is not true that France's industrial structure,
which Colbert had buttressed so well, collapsed after his death.
If it had, the sudden revival of economic life after 1717 and
France's vigorous prosperity during most of the eighteenth century would become incomprehensible. This is not to deny, however, that war and depression severely shook the structure in the
closing decades of Louis's reign.[85]

---

[81] *Op. cit.*, p. 36.

[82] *Op. cit.*, p. 804.

[83] Quoted by Leclercq, *op. cit.*, I, xxii, and Levasseur, *La Population française*,
I, 211.

[84] Émile Lesens, *Le Protestantisme dans le pays de Caux (ancien colloque de
Caux, Havre et Dieppe excepté)*, ed. Victor Madelaine (Bolbec, [1906]), p. 194;
Sée, *Histoire économique de la France*, I, 274–275.

[85] Bibliothèque Nationale, *Fonds français*, MS 21785, fol. 103; Cantillon, *op. cit.*,

One of France's most important industries was the manufacture of wool and part-wool fabrics. Some branches of the industry were composed of more or less independent workers spinning and weaving in their own households; others were dominated by wealthy merchants who employed people under the so-called domestic or putting-out system; and still others were in the hands of capitalist employers who headed manufactories which, protected and subsidized by the government, produced on a large scale. The industry supplied both foreign and domestic markets and produced a great variety of cloth ranging from the extra fine fabrics made by the van Robais family at Abbeville to the coarsest woolens for peasants and troops.

The years from 1683, and especially from 1690,[86] to 1717 were not prosperous ones for the woolen industry as a whole. In Lower Poitou, for example, the number of master workmen at Moncoutant had fallen from 40 to 17 by 1714; the number of pieces of cloth made in the same town declined from 2,500 in 1692 to 1,500 in 1704 and output in a nearby community dropped from 1,000 pieces to 300 in the same period.[87] The intendant in Maine stated in 1699 that the manufacture of serge and etamine had sharply declined everywhere in the province except at Le Mans;[88] Colbert's serge factory at Seignelay near Paris closed its doors soon after 1683 because of inadequate markets; [89] the intendants at Alençon and in Burgundy and Bourbonnais reported in 1698–1699 that the industry was "greatly diminished" at various places in their districts;[90] the official at Tours at the same time stated that the number of looms in that town had

---

p. 159; Lavisse, *op. cit.,* Vol. VIII, Part 1, pp. 202–203, 247; Leclercq, *op. cit.,* III, 333; Levasseur, *Histoire des classes ouvrières et de l'industrie,* II, 287–288. The king's instructions to intendants in 1698, when he asked them to prepare detailed memoranda about conditions in their provinces, are significant: "His Majesty desires to be especially . . . informed of changes that may have occurred during the past forty or fifty years in trade and manufactures . . . and . . . whether foreign countries during this time or even earlier did not start some branches of trade which have since disappeared [in France], in which event he wants to know the reasons for their discontinuance and the appropriate means for reëstablishing them." (Bibliothèque Nationale, *Fonds français,* MS 4282, fol. 18.)

86 Sée, *Évolution commerciale et industrielle,* pp. 152–153.

87 Baudry, *op. cit.,* p. 309. See also Bibliothèque Nationale, *Fonds français,* MS 4287, fol. 54.

88 Bibliothèque Nationale, *Fonds français,* MS 4283, fols. 22, 23; Levasseur, *Histoire des classes ouvrières et de l'industrie,* II, 349.

89 Bibliothèque Nationale, *Fonds français,* MS 4282, fol. 693.

90 *Ibid.,* MSS 4286, fol. 123; 4287, fol. 18; 4289, fol. 168.

fallen from "more than" 250 to a mere 15 and that, except at Ambroise, only one-fourth the people formerly engaged in the industry throughout the province remained at work;[91] in Auvergne the manufacture of etamines and *burats* had disappeared by 1689;[92] in Upper Normandy, the looms at Fécamp, which Colbert had encouraged to make cloth in the Dutch manner, had become idle by 1700, and there were only 357 looms working at Rouen in 1709 out of the "several thousand" that had hummed there previously;[93] and in Lower Normandy, the town of Valognes had lost all but four of its weavers.[94]

The woolen industry in Flanders, Champagne, and Picardy was especially depressed. The number of looms at Lille making a particular kind of cloth declined from 1,161 in 1684 to 397 in 1697; in Valenciennes, the decrease was 80 per cent; and in Menin, the industry had completely disappeared.[95] In Champagne, Reims by 1699 had lost 862 of the 1,812 looms she had possessed in 1686; Mézières had only 8 instead of 100 looms; Sedan, the chief center for woolen drapery in the province, was hit hard; Vitry-le-François had only 10 men making woolens in 1688 (and only 7 in February, 1732) instead of the "more than 100" similarly engaged at an earlier date; and Troyes, Chaumont, Châlons, Bar-sur-Aube, Rethel, Sézanne, Joinville, and several other communities had fewer woolworkers than formerly. In only one or two places in Champagne were weavers well off, and they made special kinds of wool fabrics.[96] According to the intendant

---

91 *Ibid.*, MS 4283, fol. 25; Levasseur, *Histoire des classes ouvrières et de l'industrie,* II, 349.

92 Archives Nationales, G7 103; G. Martin, *op. cit.*, pp. 242–243.

93 Boislisle, *op. cit.*, II, 23; G. Martin, *op. cit.*, p. 308; Sée, *Évolution commerciale et industrielle*, p. 153.

94 Bibliothèque Nationale, *Fonds français*, MS 4286, fol. 51; Leclercq, *op. cit.*, I, lvi.

95 Bibliothèque Nationale, *Fonds français*, MS 4284, fols. 26, 59, 81; Levasseur, *Histoire des classes ouvrières et de l'industrie*, II, 314, 348.

96 Archives Nationales, F12 1359; Bibliothèque Nationale, *Fonds français*, MSS 4285, fols. 126–127, 137, 142–144, 145, 147, 150, 151; 8037, fol. 297; Boislisle, *op cit.*, I, 410; Hérelle, *op. cit.*, I, 326–327; Levasseur, *Histoire des classes ouvrières et de l'industrie*, II, 348–349; Lavisse, *op. cit.*, Vol. VIII, Part 1, p. 234; Sée, *Évolution commerciale et industrielle*, p. 154; Sée, *Histoire économique de la France*, I, 275; Ph. Sagnac, "L'Industrie et le commerce de la draperie en France à la fin du XVIIe siècle et au commencement du XVIIIe," *Revue d'histoire moderne et contemporaine*, IX (1907–1908), 32; C. Weiss, "Mémoire sur les protestants," *op. cit.*, XX, 121. By stating that the number of fine-cloth looms in Sedan increased from about 12 in 1666 to 62 in 1670, to 70 about 1683, and to 111 in 1693, Professor Charles W. Cole leaves the impression that the woolen industry there

in Picardy, about one-fourth the looms turning out heavy serges for furniture and linings were idle in 1699 because of high prices for raw wool.[97] Even the fine van Robais enterprise at Abbeville was not so prosperous at the end of the century as it had once been or as it was later to become.[98] At Romorantin the number of fulling mills fell from 20 in 1704 to 9 in 1714, and its looms weaving cloth for the king's troops lay idle in 1709 although the war still raged.[99] The intendant leaves the impression that weavers were not very busy anywhere in Picardy.

The woolen industry fared somewhat better in the center of France, in the western provinces, and in Languedoc. This was probably because these areas produced cloth mainly for French troops or for the Levantine trade.[100] War decreased imports of cloth and raw wool from England and Holland and forced Frenchmen to clothe themselves in domestic fabrics woven from local or Spanish wool. When imports began to enter more freely and when royal purchases for the army declined, these manufacturers found it increasingly difficult to market their output and to maintain the level of employment.

The drapery industry in Normandy normally kept thousands of looms and about 40,000 workers busy. Elbeuf, famous for its fine cloth since Colbert's early days, still had 300 looms operating and more than 2,000 persons working at the close of the century, but it was less prosperous than it had been before 1684. The intendant wrote in May, 1709, that woolen manufacturers throughout Normandy were finding it hard to keep all their employees at work after the king withdrew his orders for clothing for troops.[101] The intendants at Bourges and Bordeaux stated in 1699

did not suffer very much after 1685 (*Colbert*, II, 154). If one can believe the cries of despair which emanated from manufacturers and workers alike, however, the woolen industry in and around Sedan could not have been very prosperous during the last half of Louis's reign.

[97] Bibliothèque Nationale, *Fonds français*, MS 4284, fols. 24–25; Boislisle, *op. cit.*, II, 8; Leclercq, *op. cit.*, I, liv–lv; Levasseur, *Histoire des classes ouvrières et de l'industrie*, II, 348.

[98] It was keeping 80 looms active in 1698 instead of 100 as formerly (Archives Nationale, F12 822A; Bibliothèque Nationale, *Fonds français*, MS 4284, fols. 23–24, 25; Levasseur, *Histoire des classes ouvrières et de l'industrie*, II, 316 n. 3, 421–423).

[99] Boislisle, *op. cit.*, III, 534; G. Martin, *op. cit.*, p. 308.

[100] Bibliothèque Nationale, *Fonds français*, MS 4290, fol. 296; Lavisse, *op. cit.*, Vol. VIII, Part 1, p. 234.

[101] Bibliothèque Nationale, *Fonds français*, MS 4286, fols. 27–28; Baird, *op. cit.*, II, 100; Boislisle, *op. cit.*, III, 141–142, 180; Cole, *Colbert*, II, 150; Lavisse, *op. cit.*, Vol. VIII, Part 1, p. 234.

and 1701 that the industry was expanding in their districts.[102] Artisans in Languedoc working for themselves or for merchant capitalists experienced hard times until 1713, whereas such important manufactories as Saptes, Clermont, and Carcassonne in the same province managed more or less to hold their own. These enterprises benefited from subsidies from the provincial parliament and specialized in fine and common fabrics for the Levant. Between 1713 and 1723 small producers in Languedoc almost tripled their output in 1703–1713, but the subsidized manufactories had to cut back production. The small producers and factories lumped together made about 60 per cent more cloth in the decade beginning in 1713 than in the preceding ten years.[103]

Another branch of the textile industry scattered widely over the country produced all kinds of hempen and linen cloth (*toile*), ranging from the coarsest burlap used in sacking wheat and packaging parcels to sailcloth for the king's navy and to fine batistes. Brittany was the most important production center; Normandy, Picardy, Maine, and Champagne came second. Wherever hemp and flax could be raised, however, there were always some people engaged in spinning and weaving the fibers and, more rarely, in bleaching the cloth for local markets. A good deal of the output from Brittany, Normandy, Picardy, and Maine found its way to markets in England, Holland, Spain, and the New World.[104]

By the late 1680's the linen and hemp industry was declining.[105] England and Holland had successfully begun domestic manufacturing, and high tariff walls protected their producers from French competition. The outbreak of the War of the League of Augsburg disrupted foreign trade channels, and French consumers themselves by that time had come to prefer cotton textiles to linens in spite of sumptuary laws designed to reduce the

102 Bibliothèque Nationale, *Fonds français*, MSS 4289, fols. 20, 23, 26; 8038, fol. 411; Boislisle, *op. cit.*, I, 196.
103 Archives Nationales, F12 1349; Bibliothèque Nationale, *Fonds français*, MSS 4290, fols. 290, 294–296; 8037, fol. 72; Boislisle, *op. cit.*, I, 256; III, 19, 239; Cole, *Colbert*, II, 170; Lavisse, *op. cit.*, Vol. VIII, Part 1, p. 235; Levasseur, *Histoire des classes ouvrières et de l'industrie*, II, 349; G. Martin, *op. cit.*, pp. 285, 286, 305; Sée, *Histoire économique de la France*, I, 276.
104 Bibliothèque Nationale, *Fonds français*, MSS 4283, fols. 11, 22, 41; 4284, fols. 25–26; 4285, fols. 114, 147; 4287, fol. 23; 4290, fols. 23–24, 26; Boislisle, *op. cit.*, II, 333; Bujeaud, *op. cit.*, p. 311.
105 Sée, *Histoire économique de la France*, I, 275.

demand for cottons.[106] At the end of the century the intendant in Champagne wrote that "the manufacture of [hempen and linen] cloth continues as well as it can"; the official at Lyon stated that the output of fustians there was only about one-tenth its former volume; the industry in the *généralité* of Alençon had declined to half its size before the last war;[107] and weavers at Saint-Georges near Rouen contended (while official measurers of cloth denied) that they were marketing only half as much linen as they had sold each year before 1683.[108] According to the intendant in Brittany in 1699, the sailcloth works around Rennes, whose annual exports some twenty years earlier had been worth 300,000 or 400,000 livres, had had to cut back production sharply; the industry in the Bishopric of Léon had first declined by two-thirds and then had ceased entirely after the war was over; and at Morlaix, whose trade in linens and hemp had amounted to 4,500,000 livres a year in the decade preceding the war, workers were idled by the "complete disruption" of the industry.[109]

France's silk industry, centered primarily at Lyon, Tours, and Nîmes, drew most of its raw materials from abroad and marketed its output in foreign countries or sold to members of the French upper classes. Thus it was particularly vulnerable to disturbances in foreign trade and, as a luxury item, to decreases in national and individual incomes. After 1683 the industry experienced grave difficulties. Its craftsmen were beginning to migrate to foreign countries and to diffuse some of France's most cherished trade secrets; foreign countries then erected protective tariffs against silks which they had long been accustomed to import from France; austerities of war and depression shrank domestic markets; and government regimentation hastened the decline of the industry at Tours and Nîmes by giving Lyon distinct advantages, which, however, failed to sustain production there.

---

106 Boislisle, *op. cit.*, III, 142; Levasseur, *Histoire des classes ouvrières et de l'industrie,* II, 350; G. Martin, *op. cit.,* p. 288.

107 Bibliothèque Nationale, *Fonds français,* MSS 4285, fol. 125; 4286, fols. 93–94; 4288, fols. 123–124.

108 Archives Nationales, F12 1423.

109 Bibliothèque Nationale, *Fonds français,* MS 4283, fols. 39, 40, 62, 67, 68; Levasseur, *Histoire des classes ouvrières et de l'industrie,* II, 328, 350. Shortages of sailcloth during the war had forced the king to establish his own factory for outfitting his fleet (Bibliothèque Nationale, *Fonds français,* MS 4283, fol. 65).

Officials in Lyon complained in 1693 that they could not cope with the horde of unemployed silkworkers, who were clamoring for relief, and at the same time take care of the dependents of men drafted into the army.[110] The intendant reported at the close of the century that, instead of the 18,000 looms in operation in more prosperous times, there were now only 6,000, and that the neighboring town of Saint-Chamond with its considerable trade in silk ribbon had declined greatly in population and prosperity.[111] The Chamber of Commerce wrote in 1702 that the number of workers making all kinds of silk had fallen from 12,000 to 3,000;[112] and the intendant informed the controller general on August 27, 1709, that the province was "in a frightful state" and that the manufacture of silk and ribbons around Saint-Étienne was at its lowest level.[113] Manufacturers themselves complained on February 6, 1715, that the industry was rapidly deteriorating and would surely disappear if government aid was not forthcoming. Other countries, they said, had recently established silkworks and were currently "troubling our own trade."[114]

The intendant at Tours in 1699 attested that the industry there was in a deplorable state. "More than 3,000 men and women," all unemployed silkworkers, were forming threatening mobs and demanding public relief. Their employers could render no help, for they themselves were loaded with huge stocks of unsold goods.[115] Instead of the 8,000-odd looms, 700 mills, and 40,000 workers engaged in making silk during Richelieu's time, there were no more than 1,200 looms, 70 mills, and 4,000 employees at the end of the century. In addition, there were only 60 ribbon looms in Tours and neighboring communities, whereas formerly there had been 3,000.[116] Other sources indicate that from 1672 through 1685 an average of 100 journeymen had been

---

110 G. Martin, *op. cit.*, p. 244; Pariset, *op. cit.*, p. 120.

111 Bibliothèque Nationale, *Fonds français*, MS 4288, fols. 18, 120; Levasseur, *Histoire des classes ouvrières et de l'industrie*, II, 349; Pariset, *op. cit.*, p. 116.

112 Lavisse, *op. cit.*, Vol. VIII, Part 1, p. 237; Sée, *Évolution commerciale et industrielle*, p. 154.

113 Boislisle, *op. cit.*, III, 115–116.

114 Archives Nationales, G7 *registre* 1702, fols. 70 ff. See also Boislisle, *op. cit.*, II, 335, 444; G. Martin, *op. cit.*, p. 306.

115 Boislisle, *op. cit.*, II, 12; Leclercq, *op. cit.*, I, lvii.

116 Bibliothèque Nationale, *Fonds français*, MS 4283, fol. 23; Levasseur, *Histoire des classes ouvrières et de l'industrie*, II, 349.

admitted to the silkworkers' gild at Tours each year; in 1686–1700 the average fell to 52. In 1689 and 1690 only 18 and 22 individuals, respectively, were admitted.[117] Despite some hopeful signs in 1700 that recovery was on its way, unemployment and surplus inventories continued to plague silk production in Touraine until after 1713.[118]

Bâville at Nîmes, in his 1699 memorandum, refused to acknowledge that the industry was depressed in his jurisdiction. He stated that manufacturers there turned out silk fabrics worth 1,800,000 livres and sold all but one-sixth of the output in other provinces or abroad.[119] Some historians, however, have concluded that silk production in Languedoc declined drastically after 1684 and that Bâville was simply refusing to admit that the revocation of the Edict of Nantes had had baneful effects.[120]

Laces and embroideries, which were luxury items, encountered shrinking markets both at home and abroad, not only because of war and depression but also because of unfavorable changes in style. In Auvergne the manufacture of laces had been very important during the ministry of Colbert and had maintained a payroll estimated at 600,000 or 700,000 livres; the industry had practically disappeared by 1700 or soon thereafter, and its payroll had dwindled to "30,000 livres or less."[121] Lacemaking at Sedan and Alençon likewise had declined, and the intendant in Languedoc reported on April 12, 1708, that the lace trade in his district had "almost perished."[122]

The rug and tapestry industry shared the same fate. The intendant in Bourbonnais wrote in 1699 that depressed conditions at the famous Aubusson works had driven "a great many workers" out of the country;[123] and according to Pontchartrain himself,

117 Bosseboeuf, *op. cit.*, pp. 277 ff.

118 Bibliothèque Nationale, *Fonds français*, MS 8038, fols. 444, 449; Boislisle, *op. cit.*, II, 41; G. Martin, *op. cit.*, pp. 245, 291.

119 Bibliothèque Nationale, *Fonds français*, MS 4290, fols. 296 ff., 342 ff., 348 ff.

120 Levasseur, *Histoire des classes ouvrières et de l'industrie*, II, 349; Sée, *Évolution commerciale et industrielle*, p. 154; Sée, *Histoire économique de la France*, I, 275; Louis-Henri Monin, *Essai sur l'histoire administrative du Languedoc pendant l'intendance de Basville (1685–1719)* (Paris, 1884), p. 19.

121 Archives Nationales, G7 103; Bibliothèque Nationale, *Fonds français*, MS 4288, fols. 82, 83; Boislisle, *op. cit.*, I, 405; II, 190; G. Martin, *op. cit.*, pp. 242–243, 296.

122 Bibliothèque Nationale, *Fonds français*, MSS 4285, fol. 151; 4286, fols. 94–95; Boislisle, *op. cit.*, III, 18; Levasseur, *Histoire des classes ouvrières et de l'industrie*, II, 348; Sée, *Histoire économique de la France*, I, 275.

123 Bibliothèque Nationale, *Fonds français*, MS 4287, fol. 19.

the equally famous enterprise at Beauvais had suffered excessively during the war and was employing only eighty workers in 1700.[124] The state factory of Gobelins in Paris had had to close its doors in 1694 and managed to reopen them only after the war ended.[125]

The spread of knitting machines had already thrown the manufacture of such goods as stockings and underwear into turmoil by 1685 and was threatening to wipe out the meager incomes of hand knitters.[126] But knitwear was one of the few items in textiles and wearing apparel which apparently did not suffer greatly from the general stagnation. Most of the unrest and unemployment among its workers stemmed from technological change and from government regulations limiting the number of new looms.[127]

On the whole, metallurgy remained vigorous. In the second half of the seventeenth century there were foundries and forges in every region where forests offered plentiful fuel; but except in Béarn and Foix near the Pyrenees, in Anjou and Maine, and in the northeastern provinces stretching like a large thick crescent from Hainaut through Saint-Étienne near Lyon and into Auvergne, the industry was not significant to any region's economy. It is difficult to form an opinion as to how important metallurgy was in the nation's economy as a whole. In 1699 Hainaut had 10 or 14 smelteries, 22 or 28 forges, and 4 foundries which together occupied some 2,000 workmen; Franche-Comté had almost 30 forges and smelteries;[128] and Alsace, Lorraine, and Burgundy each had a substantial number. A report on the industry throughout France, prepared in 1693 but not comprehensive in its coverage, listed more than 211 iron forges, 20 or more battery works, 101 iron smelteries, more than 12 foundries, and 7 plating mills.[129] Most of these establishments worked on a relatively small scale and, especially in the war years, sold their output to the government or to private purchasers on the domestic market. Some tin plate factories and steelworks in various places had to

124 *Ibid.,* MS 21785, fol. 91.
125 Cole, *French Mercantilism,* p. 128.
126 Sée, *Évolution commerciale et industrielle,* pp. 139–140.
127 Bibliothèque Nationale, *Fonds français,* MS 4283, fol. 31; Boislisle, *op. cit.,* II, 30–31; III, 102.
128 Bibliothèque Nationale, *Fonds français,* MSS 4284, fols. 64, 65, 70; 4285, fol. 72.
129 Cole, *French Mercantilism,* p. 142.

shut down during 1684–1715, or at least failed to achieve financial success; the number of master craftsmen at the brass pin factory at Limoges dwindled from 20 to 3 or 4; shops making scissors, razors, and similar articles at Thiers in Auvergne saw their export trade decline as a result of war; and it was reported that competent founders were leaving Lorraine in order to cast bells and cannons in foreign countries. The intendant at Lyon feared in 1694 that the factory at Saint-Étienne making the best arms in the realm would soon have to close its doors if workers continued to desert that city, and in 1709 all metallurgical works there were said to be in danger of suspending operations because of the business crisis.[130] Such evidence, scattered and fragmentary though it is, suggests that depressed conditions in the economy as a whole did retard metallurgy to some extent; yet the industry apparently expanded somewhat in spite of these conditions and seemed relatively prosperous to contemporaries. The last wars of Louis XIV greatly increased the demand for cannons, bullets, swords, anchors, and other armaments, and most of the industry diverted its efforts to meeting wartime needs. Only the production of household hardware such as pots and pans, cutlery, pins, and wrought iron decorations for buildings faced a continuously shrinking market.[131]

Mining was not very important in France. The country possessed few deposits of copper, silver, and gold, and the expense of exploiting them left little margin for returns to entrepreneurs. In the last decades of Louis's reign coal was just beginning to replace wood as a fuel in a few industries such as glassmaking and lime-burning, and Frenchmen were locating and exploiting a few coal seams. By the end of the seventeenth century coal miners were at work around Saint-Étienne, Brassac in Auvergne, Boulogne, Décize and other places in Nivernais, and a few scattered localities in other provinces. The outlook was not good. It was generally admitted that English coal was of superior quality and that buyers of French coal would likely turn to foreign fuel as soon as international trade became freer after the war.

---

130 Bibliothèque Nationale, *Fonds français*, MSS 4287, fols. 75–76; 4288, fols. 10, 11, 83; 4289, fol. 25; Boislisle, *op. cit.*, I, 352; III, 115–116; G. Martin, *op. cit.*, pp. 247, 298–299.

131 Bibliothèque Nationale, *Fonds français*, MSS 4283, fol. 77; 4285, fols. 114–115; 4286, fol. 47; 4287, fols. 6, 23, 64; 4289, fols. 26, 168; 4290, fols. 42, 308; Boislisle, *op. cit.*, I, 196; Lavisse, *op. cit.*, Vol. VIII, Part 1, pp. 202–203, 244; Sée, *Évolution commerciale et industrielle,* p. 155.

Mines in Hainaut, ceded to France in 1659, were producing less than they did when the area was under Spanish rule. France did not provide a large enough market, and former customers in the Low Countries had already turned to English coal after they found they had to pay import duties on the Hainaut product.[132] Frenchmen mined iron in rather small quantities, largely because of the shortage of wood for smelting iron. The increased demand for armaments, however, probably supported iron mining in the same way that it bolstered metallurgy.[133]

The slowing down in economic development after 1684 also affected other industries adversely. The manufacture of fine felt hats in Normandy, especially at the village of Caudebec, practically disappeared, and exports shrank after foreign countries learned to imitate the French product. On the other hand, Frenchmen continued to make ordinary hats of wool, rabbit's fur, and admixtures of beaver, rabbit, or wool.[134]

Papermaking, especially of the finer grades, was also hit hard. In Auvergne and Angoumois the number of mills declined drastically, and their workers sought employment abroad or in other domestic industries. The number of mills around Angoulême, for example, fell from sixty at the outbreak of the Dutch war to sixteen at the close of the century.[135] Exports of fine paper from Auvergne, formerly amounting to an estimated 240,000 livres annually, "declined a great deal" and resulted in regional unemployment.[136] Mills in Provence had decreased in number from fifty-five to forty-five by 1700, and these were said to be operating with difficulty.[137] A government official, after completing a na-

---

132 Bibliothèque Nationale, *Fonds français*, MSS 4284, fols. 17, 63–64; 4285, fol. 6; 4287, fols. 6, 28, 64; 4288, fol. 85; 4290, fols. 26, 42. The intendant at Lyon wrote the controller general on July 16, 1709, that mines in his area were filled with water and that the demand for coal was so slight that their proprietors were doing nothing to put them back into use (Boislisle, *op. cit.*, III, 188).

133 Bibliothèque Nationale, *Fonds français*, MSS 4284, fol. 18; 4286, fol. 32; 4287, fols. 16–17, 64.

134 Bibliothèque Nationale, *Fonds français*, MSS 4285, fol. 114; 4286, fol. 29; 4288, fols. 23–25; 4289, fol. 26; Boislisle, *op. cit.*, II, 330–331; III, 180; Boisguillebert, *Détail de la France*, p. 196; G. Martin, *op. cit.*, p. 296.

135 Bibliothèque Nationale, *Fonds français*, MS 4287, fols. 28–29; Levasseur, *Histoire des classes ouvrières et de l'industrie*, II, 349. In 1703 the intendant reported that the export of paper had "absolutely ceased because of the war" (Boislisle, *op. cit.*, II, 164–165).

136 Bibliothèque Nationale, *Fonds français*, MS 4288, fols. 11, 83; Leclercq, *op. cit.*, I, lvi.

137 Levasseur, *Histoire des classes ouvrières et de l'industrie*, II, 349.

tional survey of the industry in 1701, concluded that papermaking had lost much of its former importance.[138]

Sugar refining, as a relatively new industry, enjoyed government protection against New World and European competition.[139] The depression apparently hurt it somewhat less than most industries. Hostilities, however, sometimes interrupted the flow of raw sugar from the French West Indies. Entrepreneurs at Rouen, for example, complained in January, 1709, that ten of their thirteen refineries had had to cease operations for this reason.[140]

Tanning and leatherworking were depressed in several provinces. The number of families directly concerned with this work in Touraine dropped from 400 to 54; during the war years the output of leather at Argentan declined by one-third; activity at tanneries in Auvergne was lessening in 1699; most men who operated leatherworks at Troyes in Champagne had gone to Paris and only 9 shops remained open at the end of the century; what had formerly been an important trade for Maine had almost disappeared; and in several other places tanning had declined either absolutely or relatively.[141]

Saltmaking in the vicinity of La Rochelle was chronically depressed after 1684, if one can believe all the jeremiads emanating from that area. Prices were extremely low, exports had fallen off, and its poor, small-scale producers were always at loggerheads with the wealthier middlemen.[142] Book printing at Lyon lost many customers in both foreign and domestic markets.[143]

Glassmaking, on the whole, was also languishing. Military battles in the seventeenth century destroyed practically all the numerous shops making windowpanes, ordinary bottles, green glassware of all kinds, and white glass tableware in the forests of northeastern France; after 1700, however, entrepreneurs began slowly

---

[138] G. Martin, *op. cit.*, p. 299. The intendant at Caen, a few months earlier, had affirmed that fifteen mills in the district of Vire had previously been quite active but that war had disrupted their export trade with England and other countries (Bibliothèque Nationale, *Fond français*, MS 4286, fol. 168).

[139] Lavisse, *op. cit.*, Vol. VIII, Part 1, pp. 246–247; Sée, *Évolution commerciale et industrielle*, p. 155.

[140] Archives Nationales, F12 662–670.

[141] Bibliothèque Nationale, *Fonds français*, MSS 4283, fol. 26; 4285, fols. 126–127, 145; 4286, fols. 47, 97, 124; 4288, fol. 10; Levasseur, *Histoire des classes ouvrières et de l'industrie*, II, 330, 349.

[142] Archives Nationales, TT 232, *dossier* 19, doc. 21; Bibliothèque Nationale, *Fonds français*, MS 4289, fols. 14–15; Boislisle, *op. cit.*, I, 37.

[143] Bibliothèque Nationale, *Fonds français*, MS 4288, fols. 126–127.

to relight their furnaces. In all France there were only five shops in 1714 producing Italian crystal, which suggests a considerable decline in this branch of glassmaking. The production of heavy bottles copied after the English had not yet made a successful beginning by 1700; ten years later there was only one such factory in France and in 1720 there were only four. Thereafter production expanded rapidly. The common-glass branch of the industry in Provence, Languedoc, Normandy, and several other provinces, and the window-glass branch in Normandy, did not contract very much from 1684 to 1717, but there is no evidence that manufacturers in these areas were prosperous. Even the Royal Plate Glass Company experienced difficult times. It had first been organized in 1665 and received a new twenty-year charter in 1683. Then a group of entrepreneurs formed a separate organization in 1688 for casting large plates. The king merged the two companies in 1695, but the enterprise was hopelessly bankrupt by 1702. It had closed down operations in its branch factory at Lessigne in 1695 and in its crystal shop at Rougefossé in 1702; its important plate-glass works at Tourlaville remained idle from 1702 to 1714. The company gradually regained its footing in the years after its reorganization and eventually became one of the largest and most profitable enterprises of its kind in the world. The independent plate-glass factory established at Beauregard in Dombes in 1699 soon failed and ceased operations entirely in 1708.[144]

This hasty survey of selected industries leaves the impression that French industry lost much of the vitality it had acquired under Colbert, and fell upon evil days after 1683. Some branches, supplying munitions to the army and navy and equipping troops with arms and clothing, suffered less than others and may even have prospered at times. It is also possible that such industries as soapmaking, shipbuilding, and private construction, which have not been mentioned, may have shown relatively little change. The historian must be cautious in generalizing on the basis of the little evidence now available. After 1683 entrepreneurs continued to advance plans for establishing factories in various industries, and the government continued to issue charters for new enterprises. But both the number of projects

---

[144] For the glass industry as a whole, see Warren C. Scoville, *Capitalism and French Glassmaking, 1640–1789* (Berkeley and Los Angeles, 1950).

formulated and the number of charters granted each year were smaller than before 1683 or after 1720. Many projects came to naught, and many authorized ventures failed to materialize. Pessimism and gloom characterized the intendants' reports on industry. When depression hit industries so important as those making woolens, linen and hempen fabrics, silk, tapestries and rugs, minerals, hats, paper, and glass, it is reasonable to assume that economic activity in general was adversely affected. It would be a mistake, however, to conclude that industrial output suddenly dipped and then remained at the same low level for three and a half decades. Activity increased, for example, after the Ryswick and Utrecht treaties were signed, especially for several months in 1701. The available evidence, however, strongly suggests that the industrial norm for 1684–1717 was appreciably lower than it had been during Colbert's ministry or than it became after John Law's scheme for priming the pump initiated an accelerating upward trend.

AGRICULTURAL DISTRESS

In at least two respects, farming is more vulnerable than most industries. It is subject to vagaries in weather, and the demand for its products is often relatively inelastic over significant price ranges. In other words, purchasers of farm products may not be very price-conscious when they get ready to buy.

Weather conditions cause crop yields to vary greatly from year to year, and this in turn causes prices to fluctuate widely because of the nature of the demand for farm products. Professor C. E. Labrousse has suggested, and attempted empirically to verify, the interesting hypothesis that industrial crises in France in the latter half of the eighteenth century and the first half of the nineteenth were intricately related to agricultural yields.[145] The money incomes of most farmers, according to Labrousse, declined when agricultural output fell, thereby decreasing their demand

---

[145] *Esquisse du mouvement des prix et des revenus en France au XVIIIᵉ siècle* (Paris; Dalloz, 1932), and *La Crise de l'économie française à la fin de l'Ancien Régime et au début de la Révolution* (Paris: Presses universitaires de France, 1944). See also A. Chabert, *Essai sur les mouvements des prix et des revenus en France de 1798 à 1820* (Paris: Médicis, 1945), and *Essai sur les mouvements des revenus et de l'activité économique en France de 1798 à 1820* (Paris: Médicis, 1949). David S. Landes has critically examined these works in his article, "The Statistical Study of French Crises," *Journal of Economic History*, X (1950), 195–211, and more recently he and André Danière have debated the merits of Labrousse's hypothesis and empirical tests in the same journal (XVIII [1958], 317–344).

for manufactured products and causing unemployment and distress in the industrial sector to mount. Two aspects of this hypothesis are of interest here: (1) Did market conditions for farm products help or injure French farmers in unusually good years, as contrasted with "normal" years? (2) Did farmers suffer from reduced incomes in years of extremely poor harvests?

The great majority of French peasants could market only that part of their crops which they did not need for seed, family consumption, and fixed payments in kind to landlords. Hence the marketable surplus varied over time much more than the annual output. It was small comfort to peasants to see farm prices rise rapidly in years of poor harvest if they had no marketable surpluses above their own requirements. Also, since there was considerable regional specialization in farming, a great many peasants had to buy grain, wine, or other foodstuffs on the open market; thus they suffered along with urban consumers from high agricultural prices. Speculators and large-scale farmers might have benefited from years of very poor harvests, but most peasants raising one or two crops on a small scale must have suffered from having less of their own output to consume and also from having little or none to sell.

What happened when there were bumper crops? This depended to a great extent upon the price elasticity of demand. The market demand for inferior grains probably was less elastic over a wider price range than was the demand for wheat. In other words, people were less price-conscious in buying inferior grains than they were in buying wheat. When all grain prices were relatively low, people could indulge by substituting wheat for bran, barley, rye, and beans; but when grain prices were high, there were no cheaper foods to substitute for inferior grains. Furthermore, one would expect the demand for all grains to be relatively inelastic, at least in the lower price ranges. These two assumptions, if true, would mean that bumper yields would exert considerable downward pressure upon farm prices (more so for inferior grains than for wheat), and would perhaps reduce the total market value of the year's crop below what it would have been had nature not been so generous. Of course, as compared with years of very poor harvests, peasants were better off when crop yields allowed them to consume more of their own output and also left them with a marketable surplus. But extremely abundant yields might have caused prices to fall so low that the total money income received by farmers was less than in normal years, and it might then have been difficult for peasants to pay their taxes and purchase goods from manufactories.

What does all this mean? When there was a general crop failure, the entire French population suffered a decline in real income, and the barter terms of trade between the agricultural and the industrial sectors shifted in favor of farm products. Landlords and farmers who had surpluses to market gained, relative to other groups; the vast majority of peasants who had no marketable surplus could not share in this gain. When there were unusually large crops, the entire population was absolutely better off than in years of crop failure, but as compared with normal years the barter terms of trade probably shifted in favor of the industrial sector. Also, most farmers found themselves with less money income with which to buy manufactured goods than in years when farm and industrial outputs were in better balance. Whether or not one attempts to explain industrial crises during the *ancien régime* entirely, or mainly, in terms of agricultural yields, it is reasonable to assume that farm output exerted an appreciable influence upon economic conditions in other sectors.

Until the French Revolution regional or local crop failures recurred frequently and occasioned much distress. When failures were widespread, famine conditions usually developed. Crops were poor in 1684 in several provinces; the intendant in Soissons wrote on September 1 that wheat had more than doubled in price in the past twelve months and was currently selling at a higher figure than "ever existed before in this area in harvest time."[146] The crop failure in 1684 was insignificant by comparison with the disaster that struck the entire country in 1692–1694. In some areas, severe freezes killed grapevines; in other sections, peasants were unable to sow and till their fields because they lacked seed and because disease and death had created a shortage of man power. Everywhere yields fell far short of normal.[147]

Harvests were again short in many provinces in 1700. Then followed several years when abundant yields of grapes, fruits, and grains pushed farm prices down to unusually low levels. Since domestic demand was relatively inelastic in the lower price

---

146 Boislisle, *op. cit.*, I, 28; see also pp. 17, 19–20, 22, 29–30.

147 Archives Nationales, G7 137; Boislisle, *op. cit.*, I, 299; Levasseur, *Histoire des classes ouvrières et de l'industrie,* II, 350; Sismondi, *op. cit.*, XXVI, 112.

range, and consumers did not increase their purchases commensurately with the decline in prices, peasant incomes were much less than normal. War and tariffs made foreign markets inaccessible, and years of partial employment reduced the purchasing power of domestic consumers. The taille collector at Bordeaux on March 15, 1704, described the plight of peasants in his district:

This district subsists entirely on wine. . . . Trade is quite dead around here; one cannot sell any wine at all. Peasants, ordinarily well off because of this product, are dying of hunger in spite of what they have to sell; their vineyards remain uncultivated. The poor cultivator, who normally lives from day to day, formerly paid his taxes with whatever advances he could get on his work from members of the middle class. He no longer has this resource to fall back on because members of the middle class are in such financial straits themselves that they can scarcely find the wherewithal to buy their own subsistence.[148]

In 1705 and 1707 other intendants attributed agricultural distress in their areas to low prices and lack of sales.[149]

Suddenly, when the severe winter of 1708–09 struck, this embarrassing abundance gave way to acute scarcity.[150] Six years later a terrible epizoötic attacked French livestock. By March 20, 1715, in the *généralité* of Metz, 32,747 cattle, 24,929 sheep, and 18,033 horses had died; in sixteen districts (*bailliages*) of Burgundy, 72,475 cattle perished; of 6,788 cattle in the Paris area, 1,371 were lost.[151] The plague was widespread and had devastating effects in many provinces.

Scant harvests and epizoötics were natural misfortunes which peasants could not escape. They found it almost as difficult to avoid the crushing burden of France's highly regressive tax structure. The property tax was especially onerous and tended to penalize anyone who improved his farm properties; and forced military service hit agricultural workers harder than any other group.[152] Both Vauban and Boisguillebert valiantly but unsuccessfully pleaded that a general tax reform not only would provide more revenue to the government but would also alleviate

---

148 Boislisle, *op. cit.*, II, 172.

149 See, e.g., *ibid.*, II, 258, 418, 446.

150 *Ibid.*, III, 115–116, 239–240, 249.

151 McCloy, *op. cit.*, p. 115; Lavisse, *op. cit.*, Vol. VIII, Part 1, p. 225; Levasseur, *Histoire du commerce*, I, 422.

152 The Venetian ambassador at Paris mentioned these facts in his report of 1695 (Layard, *op. cit.*, pp. 151–152).

the peasant's lot. According to Vauban, rural property was yielding its owners one-third less income than thirty or forty years earlier;[153] according to Boisguillebert, net farm yields had fallen by one-half since 1661, 100,000 arpents of vineyards had been pulled out, and much other usable land was either untended or poorly tilled.[154] In his *Détail de la France* Boisguillebert stated that more than half of the land in France was uncultivated, though much of it was arable.[155] The intendant in Languedoc reported in August, 1699, that peasants in the diocese of Albi had ceased to till 41,000 arpents of the 148,000 or more they had formerly worked.[156] Other officials frequently complained that land once used was lying fallow because of a shortage of man power, the extreme poverty of farmers, or inadequate markets.[157] Even when harvests were good, as in 1715, the shortage of agricultural labor resulting from war and depressed conditions in farming drove wages so high that peasants farming on a relatively large scale could scarcely garner their crops.[158]

Most of the evidence, it seems, points to agricultural distress. It would be unwarranted, of course, to conclude that agriculture suffered acutely in all years from 1684 to 1717, or that all French peasants faced insupportable hardships and, like the least fortunate, lived precariously on the edge of famine. But it can scarcely be denied that agriculture, like industry, was sick during the latter half of Louis's reign.[159]

FOREIGN AND DOMESTIC TRADE

The lack of reliable quantitative data makes it very difficult to ascertain the trends of foreign and domestic trade after Colbert's death. Foreign trade is always sensitive to war, and France was fighting formidable powers two-thirds of the time from 1684

---

153 *Op. cit.*, p. 51.

154 Boislisle, *op. cit.*, II, 533. Boisguillebert also stated that in the district around Mantes in Normandy half the vineyards had been uprooted and a third of the remainder suffered from poor cultivation and insufficient fertilization (*ibid.*, II, 550).

155 P. 236.

156 Boislisle, *op. cit.*, I, 536.

157 Bibliothèque Nationale, *Fonds français*, MSS 4286, fol. 12; 4287, fol. 47; Leclercq, *op. cit.*, I, lvi; Lavisse, *op. cit.*, Vol. VIII, Part 1, p. 273; Sismondi, *op. cit.*, XXVII, 220.

158 Boislisle, *op. cit.*, III, 596.

159 Cf. Lavisse, *op. cit.*, Vol. VIII, Part 1, p. 228.

to 1717. Nevertheless, her Levantine trade remained vigorous and may even have expanded; she gained a foothold in the China and Far Eastern markets; and in the brief intervals of peace she traded actively with her colonies in the New World. Her commerce with England, Holland, and other European countries, on the other hand, deteriorated.

Better diplomatic relations with the Barbary States and less piracy in the Mediterranean allowed French merchants to gain an edge over Dutchmen in Levantine trade and to push close behind Englishmen. Whereas France had imported from the Levant products valued at almost 6 million livres in 1683, her annual imports in 1688–1701 averaged 7.7 million livres and at one time even reached 10 or 11 million. Levantine imports passing through Marseille amounted to 11 million livres in 1713 and to 13 million in 1717.[160] French exports to that area were considerably less than imports, and the resultant drain of specie constantly irritated French mercantilists. Trade with Italy remained good and accounted for about 23 million livres of exports and 11 million livres of imports in 1715.[161] The Barbary States offered French merchants only mediocre opportunities. Their purchases and sales there declined from 800,000 livres in 1700 to 139,000 in 1714.[162]

France maintained her precarious foothold in India and the East Indies. What was more important, she gained access to China and the Pacific area and after 1705 rapidly developed this branch of trade. Each year about ten ships bound for the Far East left her ports, and in 1714 fourteen made the voyage.[163]

In the New World Frenchmen traded with Canada for furs and with the Antilles for sugar. Privateers, pirates, and enemy warships played havoc with this trade during war years, but Nantes began to grow wealthy from it during the interval of peace between the Augsburg and Spanish Succession wars and after the Treaties of Utrecht. It is worth noting that the asiento—the exclusive privilege of providing Spanish possessions in the New World with slaves—did not prove very lucrative in the short time France possessed it (1701–1713).

---

160 *Ibid.*, pp. 256–257; Sée, *Évolution commerciale et industrielle*, p. 116. See also Boislisle, *op. cit.*, II, 607; III, 19, 239; Depping, *op. cit.*, III, 634, 650, 661.
161 Sée, *Histoire économique de la France*, I, 241.
162 Lavisse, *op. cit.*, Vol. VIII, Part 1, p. 256.
163 *Ibid.*, p. 264.

In rather sharp contrast to these developments, France's Atlantic trade with Europe languished. To a great extent it was in the hands of English and Dutch nationals who operated through agents stationed in France's leading Atlantic ports. After 1685 the intendant at Bordeaux dolefully reported, year after year, that the number of Dutch and English vessels calling at that port was declining markedly, that "this region is absolutely ruined by the complete discontinuance of trade," and that unsold casks of wines were cluttering warehouses.[164] At the same time La Rochelle was experiencing difficulty in selling her salt;[165] Carentan in Lower Normandy was losing population because her maritime trade was dropping off;[166] Le Havre suffered damage from bombardment in 1694, and the port of Dieppe was virtually destroyed;[167] and Alsace was no longer sending large quantities of brandy and vinegar to Holland and Germany.[168] Toward the end of Louis's reign French exports to the Dutch were less than half of their volume in 1658.[169] France's trade with Spain declined in the war years although it was never seriously interrupted. In 1715 it included exports valued at about 20 million livres and imports amounting to approximately 17 million livres.[170]

The last two wars of Louis XIV hurt Atlantic trade badly. Privateering increased on all sides, and the French may have lost more merchantmen to her combined enemies than she herself captured.[171] Also, the man power needed for constructing and operating warships left few shipyards and sailors available for the merchant marine.[172] Even when peace prevailed, tariff barriers persisted. A tariff war preceded the War of the League

---

[164] Archives Nationales, G⁷ 133, 136; Boislisle, *op. cit.*, I, 347; II, 50.

[165] Nazelle, *op. cit.*, p. 187.

[166] Bibliothèque Nationale, *Fonds français*, MS 4286, fol. 31.

[167] Levasseur, *Histoire du commerce*, I, 338.

[168] Bibliothèque Nationale, *Fonds français*, MS 4285, fol. 6.

[169] Arnould, *op. cit.*, I, 185–194.

[170] Lavisse, *op. cit.*, Vol. VIII, Part 1, p. 253. See also Boislisle, *op. cit.*, III, 395.

[171] French privateers probably were more successful than either the English or the Dutch, but they were no match for the combined enemy (Cole, *French Mercantilism*, pp. 13–14; Adam Anderson, *An Historical and Chronological Deduction of the Origin of Commerce, from the Earliest Accounts* . . . [London, 1801], II, 596–597; David MacPherson, *Annals of Commerce, Manufactures, Fisheries, and Navigation* . . . [London, 1805], II, 650, 654; see also chap. xi, below, pp. 371–372).

[172] Bibliothèque Nationale, *Fonds français*, MS 4286, fols. 20–21; Boislisle, *op. cit.*, III, 561; Cole, *French Mercantilism*, p. 6; Lavisse, *op. cit.*, Vol. VIII, Part 1, p. 203; Levasseur, *Histoire du commerce*, I, 423.

of Augsburg; and French statesmen, without the imagination that had been one of Colbert's great virtues, blindly followed his protectionist policies. After the Treaty of Ryswick, France and Holland reduced tariffs on a few goods bought from each other and maintained these reductions in their reciprocal trade agreement of 1713. The English Parliament, on the other hand, refused to ratify the section of the Treaty of Utrecht which would have liberalized trade with France.[173]

In addition to war and tariffs, another development hurt France's trade with Holland and England. For some time these two countries had been trying to duplicate many French industries, and they finally succeeded in producing certain goods they had formerly imported from France. It is worth noting also that several French ports along the Atlantic, such as Nantes and La Rochelle, had gradually been sanding up and could no longer receive as large ships as they had accommodated earlier.

The big monopolistic trading companies, chartered and encouraged by the state, were far from prosperous in 1684–1715. Colbert had thought that such organizations could develop and maintain overseas commerce much more easily than individuals trading on their own. His companies had not been financially successful for their owners, nor were the companies that replaced them. The new Levantine Company, formed in 1685, failed and another succeeded it in 1689. It, too, failed within five years. The Sénégal Company received its charter in 1685, underwent reorganization in 1693 or 1694, and had failed by 1706; the Guinea, the Cap Nègre, and the African companies lasted only a short time. The East India Company, started by Colbert, was bankrupt before 1715 and was finally absorbed by John Law's Company of the Indies. Neither the Arcadia nor the Canada Company was a success, and the China and the South Seas companies underwent numerous reorganizations in a fruitless effort to stave off failure.[174] The fate of such ventures as these, although not incontestable proof, strongly suggests that foreign trade was languishing.

An archival document entitled "A General Table Containing the Annual Growth in the Intrinsic Value of All Exports and

---

[173] Cole, *French Mercantilism*, pp. 12 ff.; Lavisse, *op. cit.*, Vol. VIII, Part 1, pp. 260–262. See also chap. xi, below, pp. 401–402.

[174] Consult Cole, *French Mercantilism*, chaps. i, ii, and Lavisse, *op. cit.*, Vol. VIII, Part 1, pp. 252 ff.

Imports" placed total exports to all countries other than the American islands, Guinea, and the East Indies at about 47,000,000 livres in 1716, and total imports at about 33,400,000 livres.[175] Arnould, however, estimated in his *Balance du commerce* that France's European trade for the same year included 71,000,000 livres of imports and 105,000,000 livres of exports, and that her trade with Asia, Africa, and the New World amounted to 25,268,000 livres for imports and 12,502,000 livres for exports.[176] MacPherson thought that French exports to all the world amounted to £215,566,633 in 1683 and had dropped 35 per cent, to only £140,278,473, by 1733.[177] The truth probably is that no one yet knows the volume of France's foreign trade in the few decades preceding 1715. Most of the evidence suggests that it was appreciably less than it was during Colbert's ministry. Despite wars and economic stagnation at home, France managed to maintain nearly all her commercial contacts with foreign countries; she also made a few new connections. She was thus more or less ready for the remarkable expansion in her overseas markets in the eighteenth century and, in fact, may have been enjoying the initial upsurge in 1716–1720.

The paucity of quantitative data renders the course of domestic trade even more obscure than that of foreign trade. Transportation facilities remained unimproved or actually worsened. National, regional, and local governments after 1683 were too embarrassed financially to do very much. Harbor facilities deteriorated, existing roads and bridges were inadequately maintained, there was no new construction of important canals or roads, and some rivers became less navigable.[178] Tolls and excises continued to impede the flow of traffic by land as well as by water. The government did little after 1683 to expedite domestic trade or to counteract the general decline in purchasing power.

Marillac, while intendant at Rouen, wrote in January, 1686, that wine and cider merchants were suffering from extreme

---

175 Archives Nationales, F12 1834A.

176 I, 262, 276, 299–300, 326.

177 *Op. cit.*, II, 609.

178 See Lavisse, *op. cit.*, Vol. VIII, Part 1, pp. 249 ff. Traffic on the Languedoc canal, completed in 1681, apparently increased. Its gross receipts quadrupled between 1686 and 1698. (Théophile Malvezin, *Histoire du commerce de Bordeaux depuis les origines jusqu'à nos jours* [Bordeaux, 1892], II, 329.)

poverty because of a sharp decline in the demand for their products;[179] and the intendant at Bordeaux complained almost continuously for several years after 1687 that a "complete cessation of trade" in wines and brandies was afflicting his region more than any other.[180] Lyon was also suffering. It seems that Geneva was stealing her trade, that the flow of spices had been diverted to Atlantic ports, and that drapers could not halt a marked decline in their business.[181] Depression plagued Auvergne near the turn of the century, and the inspector of manufactures there reported in 1704 that "commerce is diminishing every day."[182] According to a memorandum written in 1708, "a drop of more than 50 per cent in trade" had hit merchants so hard in the *généralité* of Limoges over the preceding five or six years that many had failed or had shifted their activities to other fields.[183] Countless other reports of similar tone arrived in Paris from nearly all provinces. More than a century later Sismondi wrote that trade had been destroyed by 1715, and he placed much of the blame upon frequent revaluations of currency which had transformed business into a mere "game of chance."[184]

Most contemporaries agreed that money and credit were extremely scarce. As usually happens when depression strikes, and especially when government tinkers with the value of money, private hoarding increased sharply and specie fled abroad.[185] Complaints about the shortage of money were chronic. In April, 1688, white money—as contrasted with black or debased coins —commanded a premium in Lyon, and all persons who possessed any were trying to smuggle it out of the country.[186] Officials everywhere were saying that the money shortage was responsible for the failure of merchants and manufacturers to

---

179 Boislisle, *op. cit.*, I, 60.

180 Archives Nationales, G⁷ 133, 134, 135; Boislisle, *op. cit.*, I, 244, 245.

181 Archives Nationales, F¹² 673; Bibliothèque Nationale, *Fonds français*, MS 4288, fols. 124–126.

182 Bibliothèque Nationale, *Fonds français*, MS 4288, fol. 9; Boislisle, *op. cit.*, I, 419; II, 208.

183 Bibliothèque Nationale, *Fonds français*, MS 8037, fol. 148.

184 *Op. cit.*, XXVII, 6–7, 220.

185 Arnould estimated in 1791 that France's stock of specie fell from 18.5 million marks of silver in 1683 (or 500 million livres, with the mark tariffed at 27 livres) to 13.5 million in 1715 (or 474 million livres, with the mark tariffed at 35 livres) (*op. cit.*, II, 205).

186 Boislisle, *op. cit.*, I, 144. Gold and silver exports from Lyon and other cities increased rather than diminished after this date (*ibid.*, II, 64, 73–74, 84–85, 184).

carry on their usual affairs, of creditors to meet their obligations, and of taxpayers to acquit their obligations to the government.[187] The Parisian banker Samuel Bernard complained to the controller general on August 6, 1709, that "business is becoming inexpressibly bad; one cannot collect a sou from the best payers; one cannot find a penny at any price nor can one obtain any credit."[188] Religious institutions discovered that they could not borrow funds even though they offered to pay higher rates of interest than lenders could get from business.[189] Dutot, a treasurer of John Law's India Company, characterized the money market in the closing years of Louis XIV's reign in the following terms:

The most moderate lenders commonly put their money out at 12 or 15 per cent. Nothing had any value. There was absolutely no confidence, no hope at all of resolving the chaos. A common and reciprocal distrust caused those who had money to hide it. They dared not put it to any use. Farmers paid badly because money was rare and consequently dear and because their produce was selling at very low prices.[190]

Only usury was flourishing, Dutot added, and the best letters of exchange were being discounted at 20, 25, and 30 per cent.[191]

It was only natural that bankruptcies increased in number. The intendant at Bordeaux began his complaints on this subject in 1684 and 1685. Sometimes as many as three or four merchants, he said, failed each day, and in less than two months in 1715 twenty-two bankruptcies occurred in that port.[192] Fénelon thought that the desertion of Protestants around La Rochelle in 1686 stemmed more from a desire to escape creditors than from an unwillingness to accept Catholicism. Bâville in Languedoc shared his opinion.[193] Fraudulent bankruptcies appeared on

---

[187] Archives Nationales, G7 85, 1689; Boislisle, *op. cit.*, I, 217, 234, 387, 533–534; II, 9–10, 77–78, 91, 144, 164–165, 267, 268, 444; Paul Bert, *Histoire de la révocation de l'édit de Nantes à Bordeaux et dans le Bordelais (1653–1715)* (Bordeaux, 1908), p. 100.

[188] Boislisle, *op. cit.*, II, 511; G. Martin, *op. cit.*, pp. 322–323.

[189] According to the intendant at Amiens in 1710 (Boislisle, *op. cit.*, III, 293).

[190] *Op. cit.*, p. 804.

[191] *Ibid.*, pp. 807–808.

[192] Archives Nationales, G7 133; Boislisle, *op. cit.*, I, 41; III, 582; Alfred Leroux, *Les Religionnaires de Bordeaux de 1685 à 1802* (Bordeaux, 1920), pp. 8–9.

[193] Bibliothèque Nationale, *Nouvelles acquisitions françaises*, MS 507, fol. 47; *Fonds français*, MS 7045, fols. 84–86.

every hand in 1701–1715, and the government sought desperately to cope with them.[194] Legitimate failures occurred in such major cities as Paris, Bordeaux, Marseille, Lyon, and Nantes.[195] Some merchants at Nantes in July, 1715, described how bleak were local conditions:

The richest persons find their credit altered. Merchandise is without sale. No one dares buy anything from fear of embarrassment when the time comes to pay, and no person dares sell anything on credit because he would be unable to collect. Each merchant's assets are tied up in goods which do not sell or in letters of exchange on Paris which are not honored. No one any longer acquits his obligations. When letters of exchange go to protest, this hurts the provinces. To top it all, government treasurers and tax collectors drain the provinces of funds and specie which they collect and then transfer to Paris.[196]

From all indications trade on the domestic market—like foreign commerce, agriculture, and industry—was depressed. Not enough is known at present about the great annual or seasonal fairs to conclude whether they declined in relative or absolute importance in the same period.[197] Lyon remained one of the great trading centers and also served as an important clearing-house for financial transactions. Geneva, however, was making significant inroads into its business. The fairs at Paris, Nantes, Bordeaux, and Beaucaire continued to handle large quantities of merchandise; and, according to Jacques Savary,[198] wholesale trade improved its organization. Some merchants doubtlessly waxed wealthy while their competitors went out of business or barely managed to remain solvent; but the decrease in general purchasing power, the disruptions occasioned by incessant warfare, and the economic uncertainties stemming from the government's desperate fiscal situation appear to have stunted commercial activity.

PUBLIC FINANCE

The financial difficulties of France's government multiplied at an alarming rate after Colbert's death. Although fiscal troubles

---

194 See especially Archives Nationales, F12 854B.

195 Bibliothèque Nationale, *Fonds français,* MSS 8037, fol. 141; 21773, fols. 146–147; Boislisle, *op. cit.,* III, 587, 589.

196 Lavisse, *op. cit.,* Vol. VIII, Part 1, pp. 211–212.

197 See, e.g., Sée, *Histoire économique de la France,* I, 229 ff.

198 *Le Parfait négociant* (new ed.; Paris, 1736).

do not occur only when an economy is stagnant or depressed, a period of prolonged depression nearly always results in financial embarrassment. This embarrassment, in turn, may cause government to resort to expedients that further intensify the depression. It is appropriate, therefore, to examine at this point what transpired in the field of public finance after 1683.

Except for about nine years (1662–1671) Colbert had never succeeded in balancing the budget.[199] On June 13, 1683, he informed his sovereign that the annual deficit up to that date amounted to 3.6 million livres.[200] The actual situation (in millions of livres) for the entire fiscal year 1683 and for the first eight months of 1715 appears to have been somewhat as follows:[201]

	1683	1715 (Jan. 1–Sept. 1)
Gross revenue	117.0	165.5
Deductions and charges	23.4	96.5
Net revenue	93.6	69.0
Expenditures	109.0	147.0
Deficit	15.4	78.0

The deficit for the first eight months of 1715 was more than net revenue, and the net revenue of the state then was appreciably less than it had been at Colbert's death. In no intervening year had the budget been balanced.

Louis XIV had never had any real desire nor made any real effort to limit expenditures. His personal expenses, pensions to favorites, construction and maintenance costs at Versailles and other palaces, and army and navy expenditures made all his direct aid to industry and commerce seem insignificant. During his lifetime Colbert had exercised some small constraining influence on the king; his successors exercised none. In each of the five years of relative peace from 1684 through 1688, payments

---

199 Germain Martin and Marcel Bezançon, *L'Histoire du crédit en France sous le règne de Louis XIV* (Paris, 1913), I, i–ii.

200 Clément, *op. cit.*, II, 221.

201 Louis XIV died on September 1, 1715. These figures are no more than "informed guesses," to be used only for rough comparisons. Nearly everyone who has written on the subject has come up with slightly different estimates. The figures for 1715 come from Marion and Leclercq; the figures for 1683 are based on Lavisse, Dutot, and Boislisle (Boislisle, *op. cit.*, I, 583; III, "Mémoire de M. Desmaretz au roi, 1715," pp. 612, 615; Dutot, *op. cit.*, pp. 885–886; Lavisse, *op. cit.*, Vol. VIII, Part 1, pp. 166–167; Leclercq, *op. cit.*, I, 182; Marcel Marion, *Histoire financière de la France depuis 1715*, I [Paris, 1927], 64).

from the state treasury averaged about 109 million livres; in the years of the Augsburg war (1689–1697) they averaged approximately 153 million. From 146 million livres in 1701 and 160 million in 1702, the annual average jumped to 218.7 million livres in 1703–1713.[202] War was the major cause for the increase. The budget item called "extraordinaries of war" (which, by the way, did not include usual expenditures on fortifications, galleys, the marine, the artillery, and the army)[203] averaged 38 million livres yearly in 1684–1688, 68.5 million in 1689–1697, 44.1 million in 1698–1700, and 91.3 million in 1701–1713. It totaled 2,189.5 million livres from 1684 through 1714.

The ordinary revenues of government were wholly inadequate to cope with such expenditures. Not only was the tax structure highly regressive in effect; it was also inflexible as to yield and costly to administer. The figures in table 1 clearly demonstrate

TABLE 1

ORDINARY GOVERNMENT REVENUES FOR SELECTED YEARS [a]

(In millions of livres)

Year	Gross	Charges and hypothecations	Net
1685	124.3	35.3	89.0
1690	141.1	34.5	106.6
1695	135.3	44.2	91.1
1700	119.2	50.2	69.0
1708	119.7	73.7	46.0
1710	96.2	58.8	36.4
1714	118.4	86.2	32.2

SOURCE: François Véron Duverger de Forbonnais, *Recherches et considérations sur les finances de France depuis 1595 jusqu'en 1721* (6 vols.; Liége, 1758), III, 307; IV, 64, 115, 167, 327, 397; V, 57.

[a] These figures differ considerably from those in A. M. de Boislisle, *Correspondance des contrôleurs généraux des finances avec les intendants des provinces* (3 vols.; Paris, 1874, 1883, 1897), I, 583–597. Jean C. L. Simonde de Sismondi, *Histoire des français* (30 vols.; Paris, 1821–1844), XXVI, 221–222, n. 1, uses Forbonnais's data. Revenues from the capitation and the *dixième* are not included.

202 These figures are derived from data in François Véron Duverger de Forbonnais, *Recherches et considérations sur les finances de France depuis 1595 jusqu'en 1761* (Liége, 1758), IV, 38, 145, 291, 328, 351, 397; V, 57. They include interest payments and reimbursement of various short-term and long-term advances.

203 In 1706, for example, the *extraordinaires de guerres* amounted to 106 million livres; the total spent on all military matters was about 142 million livres (*ibid.*, IV, 291).

the point. The taille rested primarily upon the lower classes, and especially upon peasants. From about 38 million livres in 1683 its yield fell to 33.8 million in 1686, rose to almost 37 million in 1693, fell again to 30 million in 1699, and rose successively thereafter to 41 million in 1715.[204] Revenues from all excises and indirect taxes included in the Five Great Farms climbed from almost 66 million livres in 1683 to 69.9 million in 1690; then they fell to 63 million in 1692, 58 million in 1700, and 47 million in 1715.[205] These figures are more significant for present purposes than the taille yields because collections from excises reflected the downward trend in the volume of trade and consumption. The gabelle or salt tax, probably the most hated and the least fair of all indirect duties, yielded about half the total collected by the Five Great Farms in 1705 and 1715. The government paid producers about 40 livres for a muid of salt and then sold it for 2,900 livres to unwilling buyers who had to purchase a certain amount each year regardless of their need.[206]

The yield from the ordinary tax structure was so inflexible that the controller general had to resort to other measures as royal expenditures mounted. By declaration of January 18, 1695, Louis introduced the capitation, a sort of progressive income tax. All Frenchmen were divided into twenty-two categories according to their arbitrarily presumed incomes, and the tax ranged from 2,000 livres on princes of royal blood to 1 livre on the poorest peasants. The clergy bought exemption from the new duty with an extra large "gratuitous gift." The capitation was very unpopular, especially with the rich and privileged classes who previously had paid little or no taxes. It yielded, on the average, about 22.5 or 23 million livres annually in 1695–1697. It was then suppressed for a few years only to be revived by another royal declaration dated March 12, 1701. Although it brought in 7 million livres more each year than formerly, it no longer retained its distinctive features. Several provinces, for example, bought freedom from the tax, and many organizations and wealthy individuals succeeded in having their levies reduced. Those individuals who had to pay the taille found that the

---

204 Lavisse, *op. cit.,* Vol. VIII, Part 1, p. 168. Professor Sagnac, who wrote this section in Lavisse, apparently drew his data from reports of the controller general.
205 *Ibid.,* pp. 171–172; Sée, *Histoire économique de la France,* I, 160.
206 Marion, *op. cit.,* I, 17.

capitation was nothing more than a surtax on their regular property assessment.[207]

The *dixième*, which was levied in 1710 and removed in January, 1718, underwent a similar evolution. At the outset it was a 10 per cent tax on the gross revenue of each Frenchman, regardless of his station in life. Its proportional rates, however, soon became regressive. The clergy, various cities, and five provinces either bought themselves free of the *dixième* or agreed to pay a lump sum each year in return for the privilege of raising the amount in any way they saw fit. Thus, the third estate in Languedoc paid 780,000 livres, whereas the nobility which owned about a third of the wealth in that province paid only 115,482.[208] The tax yielded about 22 or 23 million livres a year.

Louis and his financial ministers also created and sold new offices in the judiciary and in the civil and financial branches of government. They multiplied municipal officeholders and greatly augmented the number of inspectors and controllers for crafts and trade. One historian has estimated that the king raised about 900 million livres in this way.[209] Judged in terms of its effect on the economy, the creation and sale of offices was very ill advised. It burdened industry and trade with useless red tape and excessive charges; it reduced the base for most taxes, for officeholders were usually tax exempt; it enticed capital funds and individual initiative away from business into relatively useless make-work positions; and it spread the evils usually associated with tax farming to new segments of the economy.[210]

Desperately trying to find additional revenues, the government devalued the circulating medium at least five times (in 1689, 1693, 1701, 1704, and 1709), either by increasing the livre equivalent of its hard currency or by actually recoining it. The silver *écu*, for example, was tariffed at 3 livres before 1689, at 3 l. 6 s. in 1689, at 3 l. 12 s. in 1693, at 3 l. 16 s. in 1701, at 4 livres in 1704, and at 5 livres in 1709. Meanwhile, the livre equivalent

---

207 See Lavisse, *op. cit.*, Vol. VIII, Part 1, pp. 190–194. In Brittany the nobility contributed only 100,000 or 125,000 livres a year, whereas the third estate paid 1,400,000 livres (Sée, *Histoire économique de France*, I, 164).

208 Lavisse, *op. cit.*, Vol. VIII, Part 1, p. 197.

209 John B. Wolf, *The Emergence of the Great Powers, 1685–1715* (New York, 1951), p. 186. Apparently the creation and sale of public offices was a more important source of wartime revenue than either voluntary or forced loans.

210 Levasseur, *Histoire des classes ouvrières et de l'industrie*, II, 367–368; Boislisle, *op. cit.*, II, 234; Lavisse, *op. cit.*, Vol. VIII, Part 1, pp. 181–185; Leclercq, *op. cit.*, I, l–li; Marion, *op. cit.*, I, 44.

of specie was further adjusted (usually downward) about forty other times.[211] The king made a "paper" profit of about 146 or 164 million livres from devaluing the currency.[212] Against this must be set the increased prices the Crown had to pay for things it bought on the domestic market, the sharp increase in the cost of maintaining armies abroad because of the immediate depreciation of the livre in foreign exchange, the decline in general tax revenues as monetary tinkering depressed trade and consumption, and the "paper" losses on specie in the royal treasuries when currency was revalued upward several times after each major recoinage.

The government also resorted to issuing paper money (*billets de monnaie*). The first issue appeared in 1701, when the mints exchanged promissory notes for specie turned in for recoinage. The 6.7 million livres issued at that time was probably retired by 1704. The financial exigencies brought on by the War of the Spanish Succession, however, led the government to issue short-term interest-bearing notes. These rapidly depreciated by about 54 per cent until the end of 1706, when approximately 180 million livres were in circulation.[213] The government then realized that it had to take drastic action. It converted 101 million of the 173 million livres outstanding in 1707 into five-year notes and rents on the Hôtel de Ville (equivalent approximately to municipal bonds); the remainder it exchanged for 72 million livres of new paper money which it made legal tender for two-thirds of all payments above 400 livres. By taking advantage of the general recoinage of all specie in 1709, the treasury was able to suppress 43 million livres of this new paper money. The 29 million livres that remained (after having depreciated by 60 or 65 per cent) and the five-year notes of 1707 were then converted into claims against the gabelle and other specific sources of government revenue.[214]

One may perhaps debate whether or not the treasury in the long run benefited from such monetary manipulations, but one

---

211 Lavisse, *op. cit.*, Vol. VIII, Part 1, pp. 186–187; Marion, *op. cit.*, I, 46.

212 Forbonnais's data lead to the larger estimate (*op. cit.*, IV, 98, 136, 195, 220, 393); Sagnac gives the smaller figure (Lavisse, *op. cit.*, Vol. VIII, Part 1, p. 187). See also Boislisle, *op. cit.*, I, 583–597.

213 Boislisle, *op. cit.*, III, 620; Lavisse, *op. cit.*, Vol. VIII, Part 1, pp. 180–181.

214 This manipulation actually only replaced most of the *billets de monnaie* by other short-term notes of various kinds (including the *billets d'État*). There were more than 600 million livres of depreciated *billets d'États* outstanding and circulating as money in 1715.

cannot seriously question that the government's policies failed to check the outflow of specie and further depressed trade. Uncertainty about the value of the livre increased at home and abroad; consequently, people hoarded specie or smuggled it out of the country whenever they could. Money became scarcer on the domestic market rather than more abundant; exchange rates shifted against France, since few people wanted to build up their livre balances; and both public and private credit became available only if borrowers were willing to pay high rates of interest. Intendants and other officials rightly blamed irredeemable paper money, recoinages, and crying the currency up or down for aggravating the economy's problems after 1689.[215]

As expenditures skyrocketed during the War of the Spanish Succession, by far the costliest war Louis XIV ever waged, ordinary tax receipts, the new capitation and *dixième,* the creation and sale of government offices, the sale of nobility titles, currency revaluation, and paper money issues all proved insufficient. The government therefore had to rely upon forced loans at high rates of interest. The public debt, which had been approximately 157 million livres in 1683 and entailed service charges amounting to about 8 million livres (or one-fifteenth of the public revenue), stood at about 3,000 million livres in 1715—an almost twentyfold increase.[216] The funded debt (variously estimated at 1,200 or 2,000 million livres, depending on the interest rate used in capitalizing the interest payments) cost the government about 86 million livres in interest each year, or an amount almost equal to its annual net revenue. When Louis died, interest payments were two years in arrears, the income for 1716 and 1717 was almost entirely hypothecated, and short-term promissory notes and paper money with a nominal value of more than half a billion livres were circulating at heavy discounts.

On September 1, 1715, the royal treasury held only 700,000

---

215 See, e.g., Boislisle, *op. cit.,* I, 470; II, 9–10, 64, 73–74, 77–78, 84–85, 473–474; III, 544, 567, 582, 597.

216 The estimates for 1715 range from 2,746 million to 3,460 million livres, with the difference arising mainly from the interest at which the *rentes* (annual payments made to the creditors) were capitalized. The chief sources for information on the French debt are: Forbonnais, *op. cit.,* IV–V, *passim;* Earl J. Hamilton, "Origin and Growth of the National Debt in Western Europe," *American Economic Review, Proceedings,* XXXVII (May, 1947), 118–130; Leclercq, *op. cit.,* I, 181–182; Levasseur, *Histoire du commerce,* I, 422, 428; Lavisse, *op. cit.,* Vol. VIII, Part 2, p. 9; Marion, *op. cit.,* I, 42; Ph. Sagnac, "Le Crédit de l'État et les banquiers à la fin du XVIIe et au commencement du XVIIIe siècle," *Revue d'histoire moderne et contemporaine,* X (1908), 259; Sée, *Histoire économique de la France,* I, 161.

or 800,000 livres in cash and expected to receive no more than 4 or 5 million livres from taxes during the remainder of the year. The government was actually bankrupt. Indeed, Desmaretz as controller general recommended bankruptcy to extricate the government from its fiscal morass. In many earlier years Louis's credit had fallen so low that he had had to pay 5.55 per cent, 7.14 per cent, or 8.33 per cent interest to obtain funds. In 1702 he borrowed at 10 per cent by selling life incomes; and when he was in desperate need of cash just before his death, he obtained 8 million livres in return for notes totaling 32 million livres.[217]

The Regency, in effect, admitted bankruptcy. The Duke of Noailles, acting for the regent, converted about 600 million livres of the unfunded debt and bills of credit into 250 million livres of 4 per cent treasury notes (*billets d'État*), which immediately depreciated by about 40 per cent; suppressed many public offices and failed to reimburse their occupants fully for the sums they had advanced to secure appointment; opened the Chamber of Justice which condemned 4,410 individuals to restitutions and fines totaling 219.5 million livres, of which the government probably received less than half; devalued and recoined the money once more to obtain about 90 million livres in seigniorage; and arbitrarily reduced the interest on the funded debt from 8.33 per cent to 4 per cent[218] and scaled down its principal by denying some creditors their claims.[219] Noailles managed in these drastic ways to cut the funded debt to about 1,700 million livres and to reduce the amount of depreciated short-term notes roughly from 600 to 250 million livres.

The government's fiscal problems were both a symptom and a cause of the nation's economic difficulties. The present chapter, however, has been mainly devoted to fiscal matters as a symptom of general depression; in a later one I shall attempt to evaluate their causal influence. Intendants after 1684 were everywhere crying about the difficulty of collecting taxes.[220] The collector of the taille at Fontenay-le-Comte wrote the controller general on May 15, 1707, that "misery is so great that most taxpayers,

---

217 Dutot, *op. cit.*, p. 805.

218 Desmaretz had already done this in 1713 for certain bonds.

219 See especially Earl J. Hamilton, "Prices and Wages at Paris under John Law's System," *Quarterly Journal of Economics*, LI (1936), 44; Levasseur, *Histoire du commerce*, I, 428–429.

220 See the numerous letters in Boislisle, *op. cit.*, II–III, *passim*.

reduced to the last extremity and having nothing to lose, rebel against collectors and daily mistreat them with scythes, pitchforks, and other iron instruments."[221] Chamillart as controller general warned tax farmers on August 25, 1701, that all his dealings with them in the future would probably be unpleasant, for "times are becoming so difficult that it will not be possible to survive without extraordinary help."[222] The intendant at Rouen had written a few years earlier that his jurisdiction included about 700,000 people. But, he added,

. . . population decreases every day. The years of famine have carried away a great many; war, forced military service, and depression cause others to leave the province continually. Hence there is a shortage of man power for ordinary work, and several fields lie uncultivated. . . . Everywhere trade appears ruined because of the war and because people are dejected and consume [practically] nothing. . . . The capitation, the tax on tools, levies to maintain troops, water and fountain assessments, duties on brandy, diverse charges collected by provinces, and an infinity of other taxes have all reduced the people to such a miserable state that one is filled with compassion for them. Of 700,000 souls there are not 50,000 who freely eat bread and who sleep on anything but straw.[223]

More than a century later Sismondi declared that the government had long taken all it could from its people, but they had managed somehow or other to keep pace with the growing exactions and to repair whatever damage taxes caused the economy. After about 1684, however, poverty spread so rapidly that "although the royal treasury still stood ready to expropriate mercilessly whatever it could find, it no longer knew where to turn."[224] Davenant, the English economist and inspector general of the customs, correctly evaluated the situation when he wrote in a memorandum comparing the public debts of England and France in 1698 that England would probably be able to reëstablish its trade and industry after the war more easily and rapidly than France. He pointed out that the French government had revenues almost twice those of his own government, yet the French public debt was five times larger and its annual expenditures considerably more than those of the English.[225]

221 Leclercq, *op. cit.*, I, lviii.
222 Depping, *op. cit.*, III, 322.
223 Leclercq, *op. cit.*, I, lv.
224 *Op. cit.*, XXV, 532–533.
225 Forbonnais, *op. cit.*, V, 85 ff., reproduced this memorandum in full.

Although subsequent research in primary sources may invalidate or substantially modify a few of the statements presented in this chapter, it is not likely that historians in the future will ever disprove that 1684–1717 was a period of economic stagnation for France. So many different contemporaries making similar observations about economic activities could scarcely all be in error. It is noteworthy that no informed observer in the latter part of Louis's reign nor any modern historian has maintained that prosperity blessed the realm during these years as it did during Colbert's ministry and at a later date under Louis XV and Louis XVI. The decline in population and the deterioration of living standards after 1684 would be incomprehensible if economic development had followed an upward trend. Certain industries clearly languished, others disappeared in one province or another, and only a few closely associated with war may have prospered. Both agriculture and trade were less healthy than they had been or were destined to become. And the government itself was on the brink of financial disaster.

What is surprising is the rapid recovery after 1717. The "underemployment" therapy administered by John Law, on net balance, probably did more good than harm. Professor Earl J. Hamilton has concluded that one reason that prices in Paris, Bordeaux, Toulouse, and Marseilles failed to rise proportionately with Law's expansion of the circulating media was the increased employment of idle resources and the concomitant growth in commodity output.[226] The Council of Trade addressed letters to merchant groups in various cities in July and August, 1717, congratulating them upon the favorable turn that trade had recently taken.[227] Germain Martin even concluded that the revival may have begun as early as 1713 and certainly by 1715.[228] Many large-scale enterprises had weathered the depression, and foreign trade showed signs of expanding after the Treaties of Utrecht. Commerce with the New World acquired new vigor and rapidly equaled France's trade with the Levant. Nevertheless, Martin may have antedated the recovery. A drastic and ill-timed monetary deflation occurred in 1715 and 1716.[229]

---

226 "Prices and Wages at Paris under John Law's System," pp. 60, 62; "Prices and Wages in Southern France under John Law's System," *Economic History (Supplement)* (1937), 454. Sismondi shared this view (*op. cit.,* XXVII, 407–408).

227 Archives Nationales, F12 662–670.

228 *Op. cit.,* pp. 285, 353.

229 See Hamilton's two articles on Law's System.

Since economic activity rarely ever expands when price levels fall rapidly, a more reasonable approximate date for the start of recovery would be 1717. A sharp but remarkably short period of deflation and business uncertainty ensued after Law's disgrace in 1720. Ten years later the economy was unmistakably well launched on one of its greatest and most prolonged periods of expansion.

Why did stagnation develop in the first place, and why was it so acute and protracted? Earlier chapters have described how Louis XIV and most of his subjects penalized and persecuted Huguenots both before and after the revocation of the Edict of Nantes, and how the Protestant minority reacted to the pressure. It is almost a commonplace in history to blame the revocation for the economic distress of 1684–1717. Some have called the revocation the worst economic, political, and religious blunder Louis XIV ever committed. In the following chapters I propose to examine whether there was any causal relationship between religious persecution and the decline in economic activity, and, in a still later chapter, whether war, government regulations, fiscal policies, and other developments might not have contributed significantly to the decline. In the final chapter I shall attempt to assess the relative importance of the revocation of the Edict of Nantes as a positive depressant during the period of economic stagnation.

VII

Effects of the Revocation on Selected Industries

Partisan bias ran strong in the decades immediately after the revocation. Protestants at home and abroad maintained that religious persecution had plunged the French economy into its most severe depression, and that other nations were reaping large gains from the Huguenot artisans, traders, and bankers to whom they had given asylum. By appealing to Louis XIV's material self-interests and by marshaling public opinion abroad on spiritual and humanitarian grounds, Protestants hoped to persuade their ruler either to reinstitute religious freedom or at least to relax persecution. They waged a veritable war of propaganda. Merchants and manufacturers who entertained no serious intention of emigrating circulated rumors that they were getting ready to leave or harped upon the economic consequences persumably occasioned by the flight of others. Protestant churchmen in exile approved all this. Some government agents, however, were alert enough to realize what was afoot and, like Bâville in Languedoc, counseled the king and the controller general to discount most of such talk as propaganda. They pointed out that economic self-interest bound most successful, wealthy Protestants to France, and that it was unlikely they would ever leave. Yet about 200,000 men, women, and children actually did leave France because they were unwilling to renounce their faith. Did this exodus seriously injure any particular industry? Was the revocation responsible to any significant degree for the secular stagnation that beset French industry in general after 1683? Attention will be primarily focused on industries and geographic areas heretofore cited as evidence that the revocation was indeed an important factor.

THE SILK INDUSTRY

Many contemporaries and later writers have thought that the emigration of Huguenots hit the manufacture of silk especially hard. The broadcloths, lustrous taffetas, brocades, and figured fabrics produced at Tours, Lyon, or Nîmes readily found buyers among the wealthy all over Europe. Most countries, anxious to acquire industrial secrets that would permit them to meet French competition, welcomed all artisans and entrepreneurs who were skilled in working silk. In the latter half of Louis's reign England and Holland, and Germany and Switzerland to a lesser extent, began successfully to imitate French fabrics and patterns. French immigrants provided the skilled labor and knowledge, and prohibitory tariffs, war, and government subsidies protected the infant firms from competition.[1] Many (but not all) Frenchmen employed in foreign silkworks were Protestant. The revocation of the Edict of Nantes hence contributed to the rise of the industry abroad, and this in turn shrank French export markets. Whether enough Huguenots fled Tours, Lyon, and Nîmes to deprive producers of necessary man power and skill is not an easy question to answer.

The silk industry at Tours seems to have been much less prosperous at the beginning of the eighteenth century than it had been during the time of Richelieu, Mazarin, and Colbert. Charles Weiss, accepting the figures given by the intendant in 1699, concluded that the number of looms around Tours had fallen from 8,000 to 1,200; the number of throwing and reeling

---

[1] Archives Nationales, G⁷ 1687, 1692, 1699, 1701 (fol. 136 of the *registre*); Bibliothèque Nationale, *Fonds français*, MS 4288, fol. 117; Adam Anderson, *An Historical and Chronological Deduction of the Origin of Commerce, from the Earliest Accounts etc.* (London, 1801), II, 597; A. M. de Boislisle, *Correspondance des contrôleurs généraux des finances avec les intendants des provinces*, II (Paris, 1883), 489; Justin Godart, *L'Ouvrier en soie* (Lyon, 1899), p. 218; W. H. Manchée, "Memories of Spitalfields," *Proceedings of the Huguenot Society of London* (hereinafter cited as *PHSL*), X (1912–1914), 318–319; David MacPherson, *Annals of Commerce, Manufactures, Fisheries, and Navigation etc.* (London, 1805), II, 651; W. J. C. Moens, "The Walloon Settlement and the French Church at Southampton," *PHSL*, III (1888–1891), 71; Natalis Rondot, *Les Protestants à Lyon au dix-septième siècle* (Lyon, 1891), pp. 63–64; Ph. Sagnac in Ernest Lavisse and others, *Histoire de France illustrée depuis les origines jusqu'à la révolution* (Paris, 1911), Vol. VIII, Part 1, pp. 237–238; Samuel Smiles, *The Huguenots, Their Settlements, Churches, and Industries in England and Ireland* (6th ed.; London, 1889), p. 136; Charles Weiss, *Histoire des réfugiés protestants de France depuis la révocation de l'Édit de Nantes jusqu'à nos jours* (Paris, 1853), I, 322–325.

mills, from 700 to 70; the number of silkworkers, from 40,000 to 4,000; the number of ribbon looms, from 3,000 to 60; and the consumption of raw silk, from 2,401 bales to somewhat "more than" 700 or 800.[2] A deputy of trade, while pleading that raw silk should be allowed to enter the realm via Nantes instead of exclusively through Lyon, claimed on June 1, 1701, that the number of looms at Tours had declined from 12,000 to 1,200 after manufacturers were forced to buy silk at Lyon and to pay high overland shipping charges as well as customs duties collected there. Formerly, he said, Tours had been able to export a large part of its output, but now was not producing enough to satisfy the domestic market.[3] Other contemporary records also attest a substantial decline in activity, but the figures vary considerably.[4] Most of the estimates are in such convenient round numbers as to make their accuracy questionable,[5] and no one estimate seems more reliable than the others. Taken together, however, they create the conviction that the industry was not prosperous.

What evidence is there that the emigration of Huguenots was responsible for the decline? In a total population of 30,000 to 40,000, Tours had about 2,500 Protestants in 1670, from 1,200 to 1,500 in 1685, and only about 400 (or 100 families) in 1699.[6]

---

2 *Op. cit.*, I, 328; Charles Weiss, "Mémoire sur les protestants de France au XVIIᵉ siècle," *Séances et travaux de l'Académie des sciences morales et politiques,* XX (1851), 111, 118. Germain Martin (*La Grande industrie sous le règne de Louis XIV* [Paris, 1898], pp. 206–207) and the Abbé Bosseboeuf ("Histoire de la fabrique de soieries de Tours, des origines au XIXᵉ siècle," *Bulletin et mémoires de la société archéologique de Touraine,* XLI [1900], 255, 275) give these same figures, which came originally from the intendant's 1699 report on Touraine (Bibliothèque Nationale, *Fonds français,* MS 4283).

3 Archives Nationales, G7 1686. See also the statement of several merchants at Nantes in the same year (Bibliothèque Nationale, *Fonds français,* MS 8038, fol. 197).

4 Most of the estimates for the industry at its peak vary from 16,000 to 7,000 looms, and, at its nadir, from 3,000 to 500 (Archives Nationales, F12 641; G7 519, 520, 1686; [Pierre Jurieu], *Lettres pastorales addressées aux fidèles de France, qui gemissent sous la captivité de Babylone* [4th ed.; Rotterdam, 1687–1688], II, 151–152). One document prepared about 1687 states that the number fell from only 900 to "less than" 50, and that there were scarcely any workers in the surrounding countryside engaged in reeling silk, whereas formerly there had been from 18,000 to 20,000 so employed (Archives Nationales, G7 1685). The deputies of trade asserted on February 18, 1755, that there were then only 1,000 looms in operation at Tours and that 7,000 had been busy before 1667 (*ibid.*, F12 709).

5 The figure 40,000 for the number of workers is particularly suspicious because the entire population of Tours was not much larger than this and because in its heyday the industry at Lyon supposedly employed only about 12,000 individuals.

6 Bosseboeuf, *op. cit.*, pp. 277 ff.; Lavisse, *op. cit.*, Vol. VIII, Part 1, p. 237;

Although conversions to Catholicism accounted for part of the decline, government officials and other contemporaries asserted that many Protestants deserted the city. Those who found refuge in England and Holland were mainly merchant employers or skilled workmen. Even though they constituted a small percentage of Tours's total population, it is conceivable that their departure hurt silk production, for a good number of them had been closely associated with the industry in one way or another. The evidence on this point, however, is not at all conclusive.

At exactly what period the industry was most prosperous and had the 8,000 looms, 700 reeling mills, 3,000 ribbon looms, and 40,000 workers mentioned earlier is not clear. The intendant who gave these figures in 1699 did not specify any date. He could have had in mind a vaguely defined period in Richelieu's ministry, or a year shortly before 1667. He might have even meant 1683.[7] A royal decree dated November 10, 1685, stated that a 1667 law favoring Lyon over Tours had caused the number of looms to fall from 7,000 to 1,000.[8] After a subsequent decree allowed weavers at Tours to use a more narrow loom than the industry's regulations prescribed, according to some sources the number increased to 3,000 in 1691 and then fell to 1,000 or 1,200 when manufacturers at Lyon gained the same concession.[9] All this suggests that the departure of Huguenots did not initiate the industry's troubles. It is possible, on the other hand, that the manufacture of silk may not have been so depressed as contemporaries tried to make people believe. Colbert, for example, was not convinced. He wrote the intendant at Tours on December 16, 1682, that he found it hard to believe that the industry there was suffering as much as reports claimed.[10]

Armand Dupin de Saint-André, *Un Coup d'oeil sur l'histoire du protestantisme en Touraine* (Paris, 1901), pp. 66, 74; Bibliothèque Nationale, *Fonds français*, MS 4283, fol. 33. Two other sources state that in 1688 there were only 450 or 711 Protestants in Tours (Archives Nationales, TT 272, *dossier* XXII, docs. 128, 153).

[7] Bosseboeuf, Martin, and Weiss, for example, have each inferred a different date.

[8] Charles W. Cole, *Colbert and a Century of French Mercantilism* (New York, 1939), II, 400; Archives Nationales, F12 641. Nointel, the intendant, wrote in 1688 that the decline was from 7,000 in 1668 to 1,600 in 1686 (Dupin de Saint-André, *op. cit.*, p. 74).

[9] Archives Nationales, F12 641; G7 520.

[10] Pierre Clément, *Lettres, instructions et mémoires de Colbert* (Paris, 1861–1884), II, 742. Perhaps this is one reason that Cole erroneously concluded that the "period of actual decadence did not come until after his [Colbert's] death" (*op. cit.*, II, 192).

The revocation may have been partially responsible for deepening the depression after 1683. Miroménil, intendant at Tours, wrote the controller general in 1689 that all trade in that city "has declined and continues to decline at an alarming rate."[11] The same official stated in his memorandum of 1699 that silk production had been in dire straits throughout the last part of the seventeenth century, and that the blame rested in part upon Protestant employers and skilled workmen who had emigrated and in part upon Catholic workers who had moved away when they could no longer find employment.[12] Gild records for silk merchants and workmen, furthermore, reveal that the number of journeymen taken into the gild declined markedly after 1688. The yearly average was as follows:[13]

1669–1670	271	1696–1700	39
1671–1675	127	1701–1705	22
1676–1680	95	1706–1710	16
1681–1685	90	1711–1715	22
1686–1688	121	1716–1720	25
1689–1690	22	1721–1725	19
1691–1695	42	1726–1730	18

The industry at Lyon scarcely fared better than that at Tours, although the Crown accorded it preferential treatment. The number of silk looms, for example, dropped from 18,000 in 1650 to 10,000 in 1675 and to 4,000 at the end of the century. There were also fewer looms making ribbons and passementerie.[14] Customs receipts on raw silk entering Lyon in 1695 were almost half what they had formerly been, and the Chamber of Commerce complained in 1702 that the industry was currently employing only 3,000 workmen instead of the 12,000 formerly em-

11 Archives Nationales, G7 519.

12 Bibliothèque Nationale, *Fonds français*, MS 4283, fol. 23. See also his letter of November 16, 1699, to the controller general (Boislisle, *op. cit.*, II, 12).

13 Archives Départementales d'Indre-et-Loire, E. 468, as given in Bosseboeuf, *op. cit.*, pp. 517–518.

14 Bibliothèque Nationale, *Fonds français*, MS 4288, fol. 120; Archives Nationales, G7 1685; Edmond Chevrier, *Le Protestantisme dans le Mâconnais et la Bresse aux XVIe et XVIIe siècles* (Mâcon, 1868), p. 141; E. Pariset, *Histoire de la fabrique lyonnais. Étude sur le Régime social et économique de l'Industrie de la Soie à Lyon, depuis le XVIe siècle* (Lyon, 1901), p. 116; Natalis Rondot, *L'Industrie de la soie en France* (Lyon, 1894), p. 65; Weiss, *Histoire des réfugiés*, I, 328; Weiss, "Mémoire sur les protestants," *op. cit.*, XX, 112–113, 118.

ployed.[15] Conditions continued bad for several years. During the summer after the unusually severe winter of 1708–09, according to an official representative of Lyon merchants, 3,000 silkworkers were unemployed and reduced to beggary.[16]

It is difficult to ascertain to what extent the revocation contributed to the decline at Lyon. Of the total population of some 70,000, Protestants numbered no more than 1,000. Many were resident foreigners engaged in wholesale trade and financial activities, and others were native-born or naturalized Frenchmen in the same fields; some, however, were directly connected with the silk industry either as merchants or as workers. There is no way of knowing how many in this last group converted or how many left the country. Godart has inferred from certain gild records that 267 master craftsmen fled between 1685 and 1687.[17] It seems that the gild had had to relocate or dismiss 267 apprentices because their masters, who were allowed only one apprentice each, had taken refuge in England and Holland. There is additional evidence in contemporary documents that fugitives from Lyon started silkworks in England and Holland and thus reduced the volume of French silks exported to these markets.[18] Manufacturers at Lyon, for example, contended in a memorandum they prepared in 1695 that refugees were making taffetas in London under the protection of William III and were threatening to capture the English market permanently.[19] The intendant confirmed this in his 1699 report to the king;[20] the Chamber of Commerce asserted in 1702 that many silkworkers had gone to England, Holland, and neighboring states;[21] and Anisson, the Lyon deputy on the Council of Trade, wrote on December 6, 1704, that the silk industry was "altogether ruined as a result of the flight of our Religionists, who have carried their skills into Holland, England, and Germany,

---

15 Lavisse, *op. cit.*, Vol. VIII, Part 1, p. 237.

16 Boislisle, *op. cit.*, III (1883), 169. See also *ibid.*, II, 335; III, 227; Archives Nationales, F12 641. Recovery apparently began some time after the death of Louis XIV. By 1739 the number of active looms had increased to 8,380 (Rondot, *L'Industrie de la soie*, p. 65).

17 *Op. cit.*, p. 103.

18 Rondot was in error in writing that extant records relating to silkmaking at Lyon made no allusion to the revocation of the Edict of Nantes (*Les Protestants à Lyon*, p. 62).

19 Archives Nationales, G7 1685.

20 Bibliothèque Nationale, *Fonds français*, MS 4288, fols. 118–119.

21 Lavisse, *op. cit.*, Vol. VIII, Part 1, p. 237.

where they have initiated this manufacture and have built such strong establishments that more than half the workers who remain at Lyon have been reduced to utter beggary."[22]

Nîmes, the third most important center for silk, was a citadel of Protestantism. One-half or two-thirds its total population was Protestant, and Protestants dominated the industry.[23] In 1682, nevertheless, Catholic craftsmen succeeded in establishing a *maîtrise*, which meant that only Catholics could become masters and all had to attend Mass. The position and credit of Protestants in the industry at once deteriorated, and several of them left the country. Daguesseau quickly used his authority as intendant to suspend the *maîtrise* on the ground that Catholics did not possess the means to maintain the industry on its old footing. He suggested, instead, that the government might use the *maîtrise* as a threat to persuade Protestants to accept Catholicism.[24]

By 1685 there were only 200 taffeta looms, 300 ribbon looms, and 80 silk mills at work in the vicinity of Nîmes, as compared with 1,100 taffeta and ribbon looms and 130 silk mills in 1681. The revocation drove many skilled workmen and wealthy employers abroad, and the industry declined still further. According to a report prepared by the artisans' corps in 1691, there were 11 master dyers, 42 spinners and throwsters, 19 taffeta weavers, and 100 ribbon and passementerie workers. Only 15 master silkmen were present at a meeting in 1696 to nominate magistrates, and they supposedly constituted a majority of all masters. Despite some recovery in the industry after 1717 or 1720, there were still only 503 looms making all kinds of silk fabrics in 1735, or roughly half as many as before 1682. The branch devoted to knitting silk (and woolen) stockings had not shrunk nearly as much as weaving. Approximately 807 stocking frames were in operation in 1706, and, according to the city consuls, 1,000 or 1,100 in 1711; a memorandum drafted about 1738 asserted that 4,500 frames were then knitting stockings throughout the district.[25]

---

22 Archives Nationales, G7 1688.

23 Léon Dutil, "L'Industrie de la soie à Nîmes jusqu'en 1789," *Revue d'histoire moderne et contemporaine*, X (1908), p. 320; Louis-Henri Monin, *Essai sur l'histoire administrative du Languedoc pendant l'intendance de Basville (1685–1719)* (Paris, 1884), p. 364; Lavisse, *op. cit.*, Vol. VIII, Part 1, p. 237.

24 Dutil, *op. cit.*, p. 321.

25 *Ibid.*, pp. 321 ff. See also Cole, *op. cit.*, II, 192. Dutil's article is the best study of the silk industry at Nîmes I have come across.

Bâville, intendant in Languedoc from 1685 to 1719, tried to minimize the industry's depression in his 1699 report; he belittled particularly the effect of Protestant emigration upon the regional economy. This memorandum was somewhat inconsistent with the concern he had voiced in an earlier report and in letters he had written Louvois and the controller general in 1686 and 1687. At that time he had admitted that "religious troubles" and the preferential treatment accorded producers at Lyon had been responsible for a two-thirds decline in output around Nîmes, and he had urged the government to use every legitimate means to encourage silkmaking in Languedoc.[26]

It would be unwise to place most of the blame for the depression in silk at Tours, Lyon, and Nîmes upon the flight of Huguenot entrepreneurs and craftsmen. The industry at Tours apparently had begun to decline soon after the royal decree in 1667 favored producers at Lyon and well before religious persecution became intense. It had also lost much of its earlier prosperity at Lyon before 1682–1685.

Since the entire economy was depressed in the latter part of Louis's reign, the significant questions are whether silk suffered more than most industries, and whether it suffered more than those industries in which Protestants did not occupy key positions. Most writers have inferred that silkmaking did suffer more than other industries. And well it might have. A large part of its output had customarily found markets abroad, and the domestic and foreign demand for a luxury item like silk probably had both a high income elasticity and a high price elasticity. The industry must therefore have been particularly sensitive to international politics, to national income, and to tariffs and other excises which raised its prices relative to other goods. Changes in all three spheres were unfavorable in 1685–1715. Furthermore, silk was everywhere facing new competition in the form of Indian-style cottons. These and others exogenous developments could have accounted for the drop in French production.

Protestants dominated the industry only in Nîmes; in Tours and Lyon they supplied no more than a significant minority of its work force. The fact that the industry in Tours and Lyon suffered as much as it did in Nîmes, therefore, suggests that the revocation was not the only factor at work. It is unlikely that emigration prevented the industry as a whole from maintaining

---

[26] Archives Nationales, G7 297; A1 774; Boislisle, *op. cit.,* I (1874), 67.

a high level of activity by robbing it of adequate man power and industrial skills. After 1685 government and trade reports usually showed more concern about unemployment than about a shortage of skilled labor. When the industry began to revive in the first half of the eighteenth century and eventually prospered, there was never any hint that an insufficient supply of talent and skill at any level hampered its growth. In an interesting document which it sent to the government on February 24, 1753, the Lyon Chamber of Commerce said:

The epoch of 1685 was fatal for our industry not so much because it deprived us of man power as because it occasioned new establishments to arise in England and Holland. Despite this competition, what progress our industry has made since then! In 1685 one could count only 2,000 looms which occupied scarcely 10,000 persons. According to a survey conducted in 1739, there were then 7,500 looms and 48,500 individuals dependent upon them. Finally, the last survey which has just been completed shows that we possess 10,000 looms which keep 60,000 persons busy.[27]

Two additional observations on the other side of the story are pertinent. In the first place, some of the wealthiest silk merchants and manufacturers in all three cities had been Huguenots. Insofar as any of them fled for religious reasons, they must have disrupted production at least temporarily and have contributed to the industry's decline. There is ample evidence, for example, that Catholic as well as Protestant workers sought employment abroad when they could not find jobs after their employers had departed and especially after the depression lengthened beyond 1700.[28] In the second place, to the extent that religious refugees aided foreign countries in establishing their own silkworks, the revocation was partially responsible for the ground eventually lost by producers at Tours, Lyon, and Nîmes in foreign markets.

All these considerations suggest that those who have blamed the industry's decline in all three cities entirely or mainly on religious persecution may have fallen victim of the common *post hoc, ergo propter hoc* fallacy. On the other hand, the same considerations clearly indicate that the revocation did not help

---

[27] Reproduced in E. Pariset, *La Chambre de commerce de Lyon. Étude faite sur les registres de ses délibérations, 1702–1791* (Lyon, 1886–1889), I, 46–47.

[28] Rondot, in particular, has emphasized this point (*Les Protestants à Lyon,* pp. 61–62, 66–67n).

matters; on the contrary, it worsened conditions at Tours, Lyon, and Nîmes. To go much beyond such broad but cautious generalizations would be hazardous in the light of present knowledge.

THE LINEN AND HEMP INDUSTRY

It has already been pointed out that the manufacture of linen and hempen fabrics suffered alongside other industries during the long stagnation after 1683. Like many industries, it felt the damaging impact of war, high tariffs, decreases in national income, excessive taxes, extensive government regulation, and nascent competition from new sources of production in foreign countries. Many persons have also identified it as one of the industries hurt most by Protestant emigration, especially in the sections of Brittany, Normandy, Picardy, and Maine where manufacturers customarily produced for a wide domestic or foreign market and where a significant portion of the wealthier merchants and the artisans were Protestant. Just what evidence can be adduced to support this view?

In the first place, Huguenot refugees were instrumental in developing the Irish linen industry, in opening new sailcloth and fine-linen works in England, in strengthening existing enterprises in Holland, and in initiating important undertakings in Hamburg which later threatened to send their products not only into foreign markets formerly served by French merchants but also into France itself.[29] French exports consequently declined, although it is not possible to ascertain to what extent expanding production abroad or war and trade barriers were responsible. Not all those who helped diffuse French industries and processes abroad after 1683 were religious dissenters. Many Catholic linen weavers and bleachers, hoping to find employment elsewhere at better pay, left their native land. On March 28, 1686, while serving as special envoy to England, Bonrepaus wrote home that

---

[29] Archives Nationales, G7 1692; B7 *registre* 495, fol. 39; Bibliothèque Nationale, *Fonds français*, MSS 4283, fol. 40; 8038, fol. 136; Anderson, *op. cit.*, II, 597; Eugène Bersier, *Quelques pages de l'histoire des Huguenots* (Paris, 1891), p. 178; Boislisle, *op. cit.*, II, 489; Edouard Fleury, "Notice sur l'histoire du protestantisme dans le département de l'Aisne," *Bulletin de la société académique de Laon*, XI (1861), 257; J.-A. Galland, "Le Protestantisme à Condé-sur-Noireau (Calvados) et dans le Bocage normand de la Révocation à Napoléon Ier (1685–1812)," *Bulletin de la société de l'histoire du protestantisme français* (hereinafter cited as *BSHPF*) LXI (1912), 102. See also chap. x, *passim*.

most of the Frenchmen at the two sailcloth works recently opened in that country were Catholic rather than Protestant.[30] Most contemporaries, however, agreed that it was the Huguenots who were primarily responsible for diffusing the art of making certain kinds of linens and who supplied most of the entrepreneurship and skills needed by new foreign enterprises during their early years.

In the second place, the domestic industry in a few communities declined in importance after influential Protestants sought freedom of conscience abroad. Alençon, where Protestants comprised a third or a fourth of the population before 1685, specialized in fine linens and laces. According to the intendant in 1698, its population had fallen "by more than a third," and its linen output had "greatly diminished" after Huguenot merchants and artisans emigrated.[31] The industry, nevertheless, somehow managed to maintain the enviable reputation of its output, for the deputies of trade asserted on December 29, 1717, that "the linens of Alençon are the best that can be fabricated."[32] On September 28, 1685, an official in Picardy wrote his superiors in Paris that one linen merchant had already fled Saint-Quentin to join his son in London, two batiste weavers had also left their looms, two others were trying to sell their furnishings before they departed, and thirteen additional "merchants and linen finishers" were suspected of getting ready to leave.[33] Before the revocation, exports from Breton sailcloth works at Rennes, Nantes, and Vitré had been valued each year at 300,000 or 400,000 livres; in 1699 the intendant reported that the industry in those places had dwindled to almost nothing because the English and the Dutch had started their own works and because Louis had recently subsidized the production of sailcloth at Brest and Rochefort.[34]

---

30 Archives du Ministère des Affaires Étrangères, *Ancien fonds,* "Angleterre," *registre* 157, fol. 99; see also fol. 82.

31 Bibliothèque Nationale, *Fonds français,* MS 4286, fols. 93–94, 121, 122.

32 Archives Nationales, F12 694.

33 *Ibid.,* TT 271, *dossier* 21, doc. 157. See also Lavisse, *op. cit.,* Vol. VIII, Part 1, p. 343. When Catholics at Saint-Quentin sought in 1681 to incorporate the industry into a gild and thereby to exclude Protestant manufacturers, the latter at once protested to Colbert. They said that their Protestant forefathers had learned to imitate Dutch linens and had so perfected their skill that France had ceased to import linens from Holland. (Alfred Daullé, *La Réforme à Saint-Quentin et aux environs, du XVIe siècle à la fin du XVIIIe siècle* [Le Cateau, 1901], p. 162.)

34 Bibliothèque Nationale, *Fonds français,* MS 4283, fol. 40.

Most of the Protestants in Brittany before the revocation had resided at Rennes, Nantes, and Vitré, and those who had not been active in wholesale trade had been connected with the sailcloth industry. The number of linenworkers in the province of Maine was said to have fallen from 20,000 in the past to scarcely 6,000 by 1698.[35] It is impossible to say whether religious persecution was mainly or only partially responsible for this decline.

Protestant sympathizers have been too eager to attribute an industry's decline to the dispersion of Huguenots. Charles Weiss, for example, hastily inferred that the disappearance of linen looms from Coutances in Normandy, mentioned by the intendant in his 1698 report, came after the town's "entire Protestant population" had fled. Weiss overlooked, or possibly did not accept, the intendant's explanation that the industry had languished after 1663, when a Protestant noble nearby had established a linen market on his Céresy estate and had stolen all business from Coutances by handling fabrics of inferior quality and selling them at lower prices.[36] Victor Bujeaud said that Lower Poitou lost its linen and woolen manufactures because of the revocation.[37] According to François Baudry's recent and more careful study, however, both industries remained in rather good condition for several years after 1685 and began to show signs of decay only at the end of the seventeenth century and early in the eighteenth. Baudry, finding that few artisans left Lower Poitou immediately after 1685, concluded that religious troubles were not primarily responsible for the decline in its output of linen and woolen textiles.[38]

Except for Alençon, Saint-Quentin, Rennes, Nantes, Vitré, and possibly some places in Normandy, there is little indication that the output of linen declined drastically because the emigation of Protestants depleted the supply of skilled labor, en-

---

35 Weiss, "Mémoire sur les protestants," *op. cit.,* XX, 110, 123. The intendant did not specify when 20,000 workers had been employed. The roundness of his numbers makes them suspect.

36 *Ibid.,* XX, 120; J.-A. Galland, *Essai sur l'histoire du Protestantisme à Caen et en Basse-Normandie de l'édit de Nantes à la Revolution (1598–1791)* (Paris, 1898), p. 109 and n. 7.

37 *Chronique protestante de l'Angoumois, XVIᵉ, XVIIᵉ, XVIIIᵉ siècles* (Paris and Angoulême, 1860), p. 311.

38 *La Révocation de l'édit de Nantes et le protestantisme en Bas-Poitou au XVIIIᵉ siècle* (Trévoux, 1922), pp. 305 n. 2, 308 ff., 314. See also Jean de la Monneraye, "La Révocation de l'Édit de Nantes et le protestantisme en Bas-Poitou au dix-huitième siècle," *Revue du Bas-Poitou,* 36th year (1923), 84.

trepreneurial talent, or available capital. There can be little doubt that the industry as a whole declined, but the slump cannot very well be blamed on religious persecution in places where there were no Huguenots. The over-all retrenchment therefore justifies the presumption that the revocation was not the most important factor at work in the few places where Protestants made linens. The causes for the decline were complex and varied.

THE MANUFACTURE OF WOOLENS

Woolens constituted by far the most important branch of the French textile industry. A memorandum apparently drafted near the end of the seventeenth century claimed that the French woolen industry was in a deplorable state: "The English and the Dutch have gradually seized control of the production and sale of drapery by applying themselves to perfecting the product and to procuring a market for it." Consequently, the author continued, they have caused manufacturers to fail in France. The government should do everything in its power to restore production "because foreigners, having capitalized upon France's religious troubles by acquiring a great many of her workers, are now in a position to compete with her in fine woolens by employing workmen just as capable and just as skilled as those who formerly gave France a comparative advantage."[39] Other similar appraisals were formulated at the same time. How valid were they? One way to assess the impact of religious developments upon the manufacture of woolens is to examine the history of the industry in localities where Protestants constituted a significant proportion of its employers and employees.

The manufacture of fine draperies was a keystone in the regional economy around Sedan in Champagne. About half the population, including the wealthiest merchants and manufacturers, were Protestants. When Louvois wrote the Archbishop of Reims on October 15, 1685, that he was sending troops into Sedan to win conversions, he urged the prelate to get there before the troops did and see to it that bankers and leading manufacturers were not handled too roughly.[40] Despite this precaution, many Sedanese fled. A Protestant minister in Holland reported in 1687 that most of the 550 refugees in his congregation at Maastricht were

---

[39] Bibliothèque Nationale, *Fonds français*, MS 21785, fol. 223.
[40] Archives Nationales, A1 756.

from Sedan,[41] and Germany was sheltering more than 500 of them in 1700.[42] It has been said that altogether about 2,000 fled or perished, thereby reducing the area's total population by approximately one-fourth.[43] On December 26, 1695, the intendant in Champagne recommended to the controller general that the inhabitants of Sedan be exempted from certain import duties because the emigration of many employers had caused acute suffering.[44] Workers went so far in 1700 as to petition authorities to release manufacturers imprisoned for religious reasons so that people without jobs might again find work.[45] Unemployment was said to have reached 2,000 at one time.[46] City officials even suggested that the government be lenient with the Protestant manufacturers who remained, for this would reassure everyone, would persuade many exiles to return, and would revive economic life in the region.[47] Their suggestion went unheeded.

It would be easy to infer from such evidence that the woolen industry around Sedan declined a great deal more than it actually did. It certainly was not prosperous, but perhaps the depression was less acute than the evidence thus far presented would lead one to believe. In a total population of about 8,000, there must have been many individuals too old or too young to work at any trade, and surely a significant portion of the potential labor supply normally must have found employment in other occupations. How then could the revocation have caused 2,000 employers and woolen workers to flee and also have caused, a short time later, unemployment of another 2,000 individuals in the industry? The figures are too well rounded and much too large to inspire confidence. Professor Charles W. Cole has found evidence that the number of looms specializing in fine woolens

41 Archives du Ministère des Affaires Étrangères, *Ancien fonds,* "Hollande," *registre* 153, fol. 25.

42 Helmut Erbe, *Die Hugenotten in Deutschland* (Essen, 1937), pp. 255-256.

43 *BSHPF,* L (1901), 249; LXV–LXVI (1916–1917), 118; Weiss, "Mémoire sur les protestants," *op. cit.,* XX, 121; J. Peyran, *Histoire de l'ancienne principauté de Sedan jusqu'à la fin du dix-huitième siècle* (Paris, 1826), II, 228.

44 Boislisle, *op. cit.,* I, 410.

45 Archives Nationales, O1 *registre* 44, fol. 615; TT 435, *dossier* 5.

46 Weiss, "Mémoire sur les protestants," *op. cit.,* XX, 121; Lavisse, *op. cit.,* Vol. VIII, Part 1, p. 234; Ph. Sagnac, "L'Industrie et le commerce de la draperie en France à la fin du XVIIe siècle et au commencement du XVIIIe," *Revue d'histoire moderne et contemporaine,* IX (1907–1908), 32.

47 Archives Nationales, F12 1356; *BSHPF,* LXXXIV (1935), 40–41.

(as contrasted with ordinary grades) increased at Sedan from 70 to 111 in the decade ending in 1693.[48]

Finally, it should be pointed out that not all Protestant manufacturers in the community left France after 1685. Nineteen of them still had 114 looms at work in 1700, and 40 of the 88 manufacturers active in 1724 were new converts who did not fulfill their duties to the Church and 3 others were sincerely converted.[49] These men, it is true, could not devote themselves as wholeheartedly to business as before 1685 or exercise the same influence in gild affairs because representatives of Church and government continued to harass and discriminate against them.[50] The inspector of manufactures, for example, took it upon himself in 1724 to report that almost half of the manufacturers at Sedan were insincere converts and did not regularly attend Mass. The deputies of trade, who had themselves been practical and successful businessmen, looked askance at such evidence of discrimination and advised the Council of Trade on August 21 that the inspector had been meddling in matters that did not concern him:

It appears to the deputies that M. Trignart oversteps his functions as inspector when he informs the Council of Trade about the number of manufacturers who are new converts and who he pretends do not perform their religious duties faithfully. Since such matters do not concern this council, the deputies think that he should be told to limit his functions and remarks to whatever can prove useful and advantageous to the manufactures in his department.[51]

A few days earlier the deputies had affirmed that "the manufacture of draperies at Sedan is certainly one of the most considerable in all the realm."

The woolen industry at Lille and Douai declined after many workers fled into Austrian Flanders to escape military service and religious persecution.[52] The intendant at Limoges reported on June 10 and July 22, 1687, that the departure of Protestants

---

48 *Op. cit.*, II, 154.

49 Archives Nationales, F12 *registre* 43, fol. 22; *liasses* 695, 1356; Boislisle, *op. cit.*, II, 37–38; Stephen Leroy, "Les Protestants de Sedan au XVIIIe siècle," *BSHPF*, XLV (1896), 339–340.

50 Archives Nationales, F12 1356. An ordonnance of 1706 had required half the gild officials to be new converts and half to be regular Catholics. The Council of Trade ruled on April 27, 1724, that Protestants and insincere converts should not be appointed, but only those who were really converted. (*Ibid.*, F12 *registre* 44, fol. 105.)

51 *Ibid.*, F12 695.

52 Sagnac, *op. cit.*, p. 30; Lavisse, *op. cit.*, Vol. VIII, Part 1, p. 233.

had caused the manufacture of coarse woolens at Saint-Jean-d'Angély practically to cease.[53] The industry in Poitou did not suffer immediately after 1685, but by the end of the century it, too, was depressed. The intendant there reported in 1699 that the number of idle looms had increased in several towns, and that the withdrawal of Huguenots had been partly responsible.[54] Baudry, on the other hand, has concluded that the woolen industry in Poitou was already suffering, and that emigration merely intensified the depression.[55] The collector who farmed the tax on raw wool sold at Metz complained in 1688 that his receipts had fallen by 25 per cent; although few master drapers had fled because of religion, nevertheless they were making much less cloth than formerly.[56]

It is doubtful that the industry in Normandy and Languedoc, which was carried on by workers in their own homes for themselves or for merchant-capitalists, felt the loss of Protestants very keenly. Reliable data on this point are lacking. The controller general was informed on November 4, 1691, that weavers in the vicinity of Rouergue in Languedoc were having difficulty in buying raw wool as a result of the departure of many Huguenot merchants and workers.[57] In view of the depressed state of affairs throughout the economy, however, both Normandy and Languedoc maintained their output of woolens rather well.[58]

---

53 Boislisle, *op. cit.*, I, 106; Charles W. Cole, *French Mercantilism, 1683–1700* (New York, 1943), p. 114.

54 Bibliothèque Nationale, *Fonds français*, MS 4287, fols. 54–55, 56.

55 *Op. cit.*, pp. 308 ff. See also [Antoine Court], *Le Patriote françois et impartial ou reponse à la lettre de Mr l'evêque d'Agen à Mr le controleur genéral contre la tolerance des Huguenots, en datte du 1 mai 1751* (new ed.; Villefranche, 1753), I, 386–387; Bujeaud, *op. cit.*, p. 311; Auguste-François Lièvre, *Histoire des protestants et des églises réformées du Poitou* (Paris, 1856–1860), II, 224–225.

56 Maurice Thirion, *Étude sur l'histoire du protestantisme à Metz et dans le pays messin* (Nancy, 1884), pp. 395–396.

57 Archives Nationales, F[12] 662–670.

58 Cole, *Colbert*, II, 170; Lavisse, *op. cit.*, Vol. VIII, Part 1, p. 234; Martin, *op. cit.*, p. 204; Sagnac, *op. cit.*, p. 33. Some writers, however, have disagreed with this conclusion. See, e.g., Charles Bost, *Récits d'histoire protestante régionale: Normandie* (Le Havre, 1926), p. 155; Galland, *Essai sur l'histoire du Protestantisme à Caen et en Basse-Normandie*, p. 257; Jurieu, *op. cit.*, II, 152; Monin, *op. cit.*, pp. 305–306; Urbain de Robert-Labarthe, *Histoire du protestantisme dans le Haut-Languedoc, le Bas-Quercy et le comté de Foix de 1685 à 1789* (Paris, 1892–1896), I, 126–127; R. Le Clerc, "Le Protestantisme à Saint-Lô," *Notices, mémoires et documents publiés par la société d'agriculture, d'archéologie et d'histoire naturelle du département de la Manche*, XXXVIII (1926), 1, 9–10. Le Clerc, however, said that although the revocation caused the industry at Saint-Lô a temporary setback, woolens continued to be a source of wealth and prosperity for the community until after 1725, when competition from a new kind of drugget spelled its doom.

The drapery industry at Langres in Champagne also remained stable after 1685.[59]

Contrary to what has frequently been alleged, not a single one of all the woolen manufactories that operated on a relatively large scale anywhere in France seems to have folded up because of the revocation. Two continued production under Catholic management, and the Protestants who headed two others remained in control and managed to run their businesses prosperously. Instead of strengthening the argument that religious persecution severely limited industrial activity, these instances evoke two relevant points: first, that Protestant entrepreneurship was not always indispensable or irreplaceable, and, second, that many Protestant entrepreneurs never left France but remained in control of their enterprises.

Four Protestants received exclusive letters patent in July, 1684, for making fine English and Dutch draperies and other wool fabrics copied after Brussels and Zurich styles at Montmirel in Brie. After building a plant and putting several looms into operation, the owners fled early in 1686 because of religion. A Catholic named Gilbert Paignon then acquired the property and managed to maintain production. Louis XIV visited the establishment in 1687 and reportedly found everything in good order. The enterprise was still producing quality goods in 1694, but by 1707 it was encumbered with debts and appeared to be on the brink of bankruptcy. Somehow or other its difficulties were resolved, and the Paignon family prospered. The deputies of trade recommended on December 19, 1727, that the government renew for twenty years the special privileges accorded the manufactory.[60]

At Elbeuf, near Rouen, a Protestant family by the name of Mousnier (or Meusnier) had succeeded in making fine cloth from Castilian wool in the English and Dutch fashion and had enlisted the interest of Colbert. Early in 1686 two members of the family fled to Holland, accompanied by several of their best workmen, and the manufactory at Elbeuf rapidly declined.[61]

---

59 Louis Marcel, "La Révocation de l'édit de Nantes à Langres," *Nouvelle revue de Champagne et de Brie*, III (1925), 168 and n. 2.

60 Archives Nationales, E *registre* 776B, fols. 132 ff.; F12 697, 1359.

61 *Ibid.*, B7 *registre* 58, fols. 23–24. An informant in Holland wrote on December 11, 1686, that he had recently seen a letter from the owners of the enterprise which asserted that "of the twenty households adhering to our religion which made up the work force at the Elbeuf manufactory there are only twelve individuals who now remain there" (Archives du Ministère des Affaires Étrangères, *Ancien fonds*, "Hollande," *registre* 149, fols. 368–370).

Two Catholic merchants from Paris then took it over and managed to keep it going. In the last decade of the seventeenth century, according to the intendant, they and other entrepreneurs in and around Elbeuf had 300 looms humming and, with the aid of some 8,000 workers, made from 9,000 to 10,000 pieces of drapery a year which were valued at 2 million livres.[62] Even so, the intendant added, the industry was much less extensive than formerly. It participated in the general economic revival after 1717 and expanded greatly in the middle decades of the century.[63]

Two large-scale enterprises which produced some of the finest draperies in France—Massieu's factory at Caen and van Robais's at Abbeville—continued to operate successfully after 1685 even though their owners, many of their supervisors, and some of their key workmen were Protestants. Colbert had protected and subsidized both enterprises, and their owners continued to enjoy special privileges long after the minister died. The inspector of manufactures at Caen wrote in 1701 that Massieu employed more than 500 persons, all but 6 of whom were Catholic. The skill and secret knowledge of the 6 Protestant workers, he said, made them indispensable. Also, Massieu and his son were men of great industry and integrity and conducted themselves quietly in matters of religion.[64]

Van Robais supposedly employed about 1,500 workers in the latter part of the seventeenth century, and had 80 looms at work in 1698 and 90 in 1708.[65] The king was anxious to protect this enterprise. He even ordered his booted missionaries to stay away from the factory and not to molest the owner or any of its personnel. When Louvois heard that eight cavalrymen had been lodged in the company's fulling mill, he ordered them to withdraw at once and to return any money and goods they

---

62 Cole, *Colbert*, II, 150; Lavisse, *op. cit.*, Vol. VIII, Part 1, pp. 233–234; Sagnac, *op. cit.*, p. 31.

63 Novi de Caveirac, *Mémoire politico-critique, où l'on examine s'il est de l'intérêt de l'Eglise et de l'Etat d'établir pour les Calvinistes du Royaume une nouvelle forme de se marier* (n.p., 1756), p. 114; Noël de la Morinière, *Second essai sur le département de la Seine-Inférieure* (Rouen, 1795), pp. 188–189.

64 Galland, *Essai sur l'histoire du Protestantisme à Caen et en Basse-Normandie*, pp. 106–107, 256–257, 295; Émile-G. Léonard, "Une Église protestante de notables (Caen) devant la persécution et la révolution" (unpublished manuscript, 1940). Direct descendants of the original founder got their letters patent renewed on August 1, 1730 (Archives Nationales, F12 *registre* 77, pp. 255–256, 417–418).

65 Bibliothèque Nationale, *Fonds français*, MS 8037, fol. 270; Sagnac, *op. cit.*, p. 28; Émile Levasseur, *Histoire des classes ouvrières et de l'industrie en France avant 1789* (2d ed.; Paris, 1901), II, 316 n. 3, 421–423.

had requisitioned.[66] Some of the peasants and artisans around Abbeville who prepared and wove wool under the handicraft and putting-out systems may very well have fled to foreign countries, since the king's protection covered only van Robais's factory. Consequently, the output of coarser draperies may have fallen. But there is no basis for concluding, as one author has done,[67] that "the skilled Dutch cloth-workers, whom Colbert had induced to settle at Abbeville, emigrated in a body, and their manufacture was extinguished."

The revocation does not appear to have dealt the French woolen industry as a whole a crushing blow. Sedan probably suffered the most; Elbeuf was shaken but managed to survive; the Protestant founders of the important enterprise at Montmirel in Brie left the country soon after they got production under way, but a Catholic family took over and achieved great success; some Flemish towns lost a good many weavers, but they may have left more because of war and a shift in national boundaries than because of religious persecution; numerous Huguenots in a few small towns like Saint-Jean-d'Angély abandoned their looms; and the industry in Poitou may have suffered some bad effects. On the other hand, production in Languedoc and Normandy did not seriously decline. The Protestant factories at Caen and Abbeville not only continued to produce fine draperies, but also enjoyed royal protection. This does not mean that the industry throughout France maintained its earlier output level. Far from it. Along with the rest of the economy, it suffered from the prolonged stagnation after 1683. But there is little evidence that the religious policies of Louis XIV were primarily responsible for the drop in woolen output.

THE HAT INDUSTRY

The manufacture of fine felt hats at Rouen, Caudebec, and other places in Normandy lost many skilled workmen to England and Holland. The intendant there reported on June 9, 1685, that two Protestant master hatters and their families had already left Rouen for Rotterdam and that seven other masters or journeymen had also recently fled. Five had deserted Caudebec.[68] It is not known how many more sought refuge abroad after

66 Archives Nationales, A1 773; Bibliothèque de la Société Protestante, MS 6481, pp. 69 ff.

67 Smiles, *op. cit.*, p. 176.

68 Archives Nationales, TT 264, *dossier* 11, doc. 51.

October, 1685. The deputy of trade from Marseille stated in 1701 that "more than 3,000" hatters left France;[69] and, according to Maréchal Vauban, who supposedly obtained his information from people in the industry, 10,000 fled Normandy alone.[70] Vauban's estimate is incredible, and even the figure of 3,000 is suspect. Other contemporary statements that Protestants dominated the industry in Normandy, that many deserted because of religion, and that output consequently declined drastically and disappeared in a few places, appear more reasonable.[71] The French ambassador at The Hague reported on May 9, 1686, that a Rouen refugee in Holland was already exporting his hats to La Rochelle,[72] and in 1701 hats made in England arrived in French ports.[73] These were disturbing developments because France formerly had exported large quantities to both countries.

The little town of Caudebec, for example, is said to have had 1,000 or 1,100 people engaged in making hats in the mid-seventeenth century, and its output enjoyed a good reputation both at home and abroad. Many of its master hatters fled to escape religious persecution, and about 500 workers were consequently without jobs in 1691–1692. According to the intendant, the town had lost its foreign market entirely by 1699; still its hats yielded 3,200 livres in taxes (*droits de visite et de marque*) in 1701. Hatmaking practically ceased at Caudebec sometime before 1758.[74] According to a tax roll, it had only eight hatters on the eve of the Revolution.[75]

---

69 Bibliothèque Nationale, *Fonds français,* MS 8038, fols. 506–507.

70 Lavisse, *op. cit.,* Vol. VIII, Part 1, pp. 239–240n.

71 Archives Nationales, G7 1687, 1692; Bibliothèque Nationale, *Fonds français,* MS 4286, fol. 29; Anderson, *op. cit.,* II, 597; Le Pesant de Boisguillebert, *Le Détail de la France* (1697), in *Collection des principaux économistes,* Vol. I: *Économistes financiers du XVIIIᵉ siècle,* ed. E. Daire (2d ed.; Paris, 1851), p. 196; Paul-M. Bondois, "Colbert et le développement économique de la Basse-Normandie (draperie, bonneterie et dentelles à Caen et Alençon, etc.)," *Bulletin de la société des antiquaires de Normandie,* XLI (1934), 133–134; Bost, *op. cit.,* p. 155; Court, *op. cit.,* I, 384–385; Levasseur, *op. cit.,* II, 411; Martin, *op. cit.,* p. 296; Noël de la Morinière, *op. cit.,* pp. 134–135; Novi de Caveirac, *Apologie de Louis XIV et de son conseil, sur la révocation de l'Édit de Nantes, etc.* (n.p., 1758), pp. 110–113; Weiss, "Mémoire sur les protestants," *op. cit.,* XX, 108; XXI, 78; Gustave Valmont, *Esquisse de l'histoire de Caudebec-en-Caux et de sa région* (Caen, 1913), pp. 31–33.

72 J. Arnal, "De l'Influence des réfugiés français aux Pays-Bas," *Bulletin de la commission pour l'histoire des églises wallonnes,* 4th series, 2d issue (1929), 14.

73 François Véron Duverger de Forbonnais, *Recherches et considérations sur les finances de France depuis 1595 jusqu'en 1721* (Liége, 1758), IV, 62–63.

74 Valmont, *op. cit.,* pp. 22, 31–33.

75 Ch. Leroy, "À Caudebec-en-Caux à la fin du XVIIIᵉ siècle," *Annuaire des cinq départements de la Normandie,* 105th year (1938), 129.

Caudebec hats had a wide market primarily because manufacturers had discovered how to mix fine vicuna wool with rabbit fur so that the felt was soft and at the same time impermeable to moisture. Emigrants took this trade secret with them and revealed it to assistants in foreign countries, and England and Holland then began to make their own "Caudebec" hats. But unless all those acquainted with the secret process left France —and it appears improbable that they did—emigration alone cannot be held responsible for the disappearance of the industry. Other factors played a part. The increasing popularity of beaver hats reduced the demand for fine felt hats. At the same time, import duties on raw materials and export duties on the finished product increased; the king tightened his regulations and raised manufacturing costs by levying new charges for inspecting and marking output;[76] and the quality of the product apparently diminished as hatters began to mix domestic wool with inferior rabbit fur or to use cheap grades of wool exclusively.

The manufacture of all kinds of hats throughout France did not suffer after 1685 as much as the manufacture of fine felt hats did in Normandy. Output around Marseille remained large and supplied the Levantine market;[77] in many provinces hatters continued to make coarse wool caps for the lower classes;[78] manufacturers in Paris and in a few other places still produced beaver hats and, after a decree of August 10, 1700, legalized the practice, hats of beaver fur and vicuna wool.[79] One author with strong mercantilist and pro-Catholic sentiments even claimed that the disappearance of the industry around Caudebec, whether caused by the emigration of Protestants or not, had been a blessing in disguise. Felt manufacturers, he reasoned, had had to import their vicuna wool from Spain, whereas France could get all the beaver it needed for fur hats from its own colonies.[80]

PAPERMAKING

Primarily because its spring water was excellent for the purpose, the province of Angoumois specialized in papermaking. Its

---

[76] Archives Nationales, G7 1692; Boisguillebert, *op. cit.*, p. 196; Forbonnais, *op. cit.*, IV, 62–63.

[77] Boislisle, *op. cit.*, II, 330–331; Lavisse, *op. cit.*, Vol. VIII, Part 1, pp. 239–240n.

[78] See, for example, Bibliothèque Nationale, *Fonds français*, MSS 4285, fol. 114; 4288, fols. 23–25; 4289, fol. 26; *BSHPF*, L, 249–250.

[79] Cole, *French Mercantilism*, pp. 66 ff., 151, 178.

[80] Novi de Caveirac, *Apologie de Louis XIV*, pp. 112–113.

annual output, supposedly worth approximately 600,000 livres, consisted mainly of white paper suitable for books and engravings. Much of it had always found a market in England, Holland, and Paris. In Louis XIV's time, the industry first expanded and then declined drastically. Its history is reflected in the number of mills actually at work in different years. In 1635 there had been approximately 30 mills in operation. After the government removed all excises and regulatory duties on paper in 1640, the number rapidly expanded until 1656, when it stood at 90 for Angoulême and vicinity and at 110 for a somewhat larger territory embracing neighboring Périgord. The reapplication of the old taxes at increased rates in that year caused about half the mills to disappear, leaving approximately 50 at work in 1688. According to the intendant, 12 mills were making paper in 1697 and 16 in 1699. Shortly thereafter, enough new mills were built and old ones reactivated to bring the number up to 35 in 1701. Twelve years later there were only 10; and in 1717, according to a special survey by the intendant, there were about 24 in operation.[81]

Auvergne also was famous for its paper. Its specialty was rag paper made in Ambert, Thiers, and a few other communities. According to one student of the industry, the imposition of new duties in 1680 inaugurated a long period of idleness. As late as 1717, he concluded, workers were operating only half the mills in the area.[82] Masters and journeymen complained to the Council of Trade in June, 1703, that merchants at Thiers were trying to corner the market on rags and were adding to the

---

[81] Archives Nationales, F^{12} 1475; G^7 3, 345, 1685, 1691; Bibliothèque Nationale, *Fonds français*, MS 4287, fols. 28, 29; Boislisle, *op. cit.*, I, 106; II, 164–165; Prosper Boissonnade, *L'Industrie du papier en Charente et son histoire* (Ligugé, 1899), pp. 4–5, 8–9; Bujeaud, *op. cit.*, pp. 302–303, 305; Henri Lacombe, "Le Moulin à papier du Verger de Puymoyen," in Henri Alibaux and others, *Contribution à l'histoire de la papeterie en France*, I (Grenoble, 1933), 58; Auguste Lacroix, *Historique de la papeterie d'Angoulême suivi d'observations sur le commerce des chiffons en France* (Paris, 1863), pp. 8–9; Lavisse, *op. cit.*, Vol. VIII, Part 1, p. 239n; Francisque Michel, *Histoire du commerce et de la navigation à Bordeaux principalement sous l'administration anglaise*, II (Bordeaux, 1870), 245; G. Maneaud, "Histoire de l'Angoumois des origines à nos jours," *Études locales: Bulletin de la Charente*, IV (1923), 162 and n. 3, 164; Daniel Touzaud, "Histoire de la Réforme en Angoumois," *Bulletins et mémoires de la société archéologique et historique de la Charente*, 8th series, VII (1917), 238–239; Weiss, "Mémoire sur les protestants," *op. cit.*, XX, 108–109, 118.

[82] Henri Gazel, *Les Anciens ouvriers papetiers d'Auvergne* (Clermont-Ferrand, 1910), pp. 18 and n. 5, 19, 106.

industry's troubles. Output had declined so much, the paper-makers said, that the tax on paper made in Auvergne yielded only 9,453 livres in 1702 as compared with 30,000 in 1695.[83] There were several other indications that the industry had declined after 1680 or 1685 and did not prosper again until well into the eighteenth century.[84]

The intendant at Rouen reported on April 1, 1701, that paper-making in his jurisdiction "had formerly been very extensive" and that merchants had carried its output to "England, Holland, Germany, Switzerland, Spain, and even the Indies." Although about 40 mills were still in operation, "trade has almost ceased, paper has become dear, and [the industry] is headed for total ruin unless matters are remedied." The controller general learned in 1713 that the output of playing cards, "formerly one of the most important industries" at Rouen, had greatly diminished; and in 1717 the intendant affirmed that the paper industry was still quite depressed and that only 56 mills were active. In the 1680's manufacturers in the *généralité* of Caen had turned out about 500,000 pounds of good-quality paper each year, which yielded "more than 60,000 livres" in taxes; in 1701, according to the intendant, "the manufacture of paper is not as considerable . . . as it has been," and of the 68 or 70 mills still in existence 5 or 6 were lying idle.[85]

All evidence points to the conclusion that papermaking in Angoumois, Auvergne, and Upper and Lower Normandy decreased in importance in the last decades of the seventeenth century and did not permanently revive until the reign of Louis XV. Although these four provinces were not the only ones that produced paper,[86] contemporary and subsequent authorities have affirmed that they manufactured the best grades and were the

---

83 Archives Nationales, F12 *registre* 51, fols. 191–192.

84 *Ibid.*, F12 696, 1475; Bibliothèque Nationale, *Fonds français*, MS 4288, fols. 11, 83; Michel Cohendy, *Note sur la papeterie d'Auvergne antérieurement à 1790* (Clermont, 1862), p. 7; Weiss, "Mémoire sur les protestants," *op. cit.*, XX, 108–109, 117–118. But Sagnac concluded that papermaking suffered far less in Auvergne than in Angoumois (Lavisse, *op. cit.*, Vol. VIII, Part 1, p. 239n); and a government official reported on August 22, 1687, that "we are assured that the paper mills of Auvergne are not at all cutting back their output of paper we use" and that "trade in paper along the Loire River does not diminish in the least" (Archives Nationales, B7 *registre* 58, part 3, fol. 73).

85 Archives Nationales, F12 1475; Boislisle, *op. cit.*, I, 51; III, 511.

86 Archives Nationales, F12 1475; Bibliothèque Nationale, *Fonds français*, MSS 4285, fol. 114; 4287, fols. 58–59.

only areas that supplied other than local markets. Since most French industries were suffering from a contraction of demand after 1683, the question naturally arises whether paper manufacturers were relatively harder hit than others. Extant documents give the impression that they were. Assuming this impression to be trustworthy, how can the absolute and relative decline in papermaking be explained?

The emigration of paperworkers and entrepreneurs, driven abroad by the revocation of the Edict of Nantes, has been one of the most common explanations. And one can easily find a basis for this explanation in documentary references. Many government officials who had direct or indirect contact with papermakers named the emigration of Huguenots as one reason for the industry's troubles. In 1685–1686, Louvois himself, for example, several times exhorted the intendant in Angoumois to do his utmost to prevent Protestant paper manufacturers from leaving the country and to repair quickly whatever damage might have been caused by those who had slipped out.[87] The intendant apparently was unable to fulfill these wishes, for three of his successors complained, in 1687, 1701, and 1717, that the foreign mills built and staffed by refugees recruited from the Angoulême area were threatening to ruin domestic producers.[88] The intendant at Rouen, on October 22, 1713, wrote that the output of playing cards had declined "after most workers had escaped to foreign countries."[89] The deputies of trade advised the Council of Trade to turn down the request of a Dutch merchant in 1708 that he be allowed to send desperately needed alum to French paper mills. The deputies justified their position by pointing out that it did not seem reasonable for a Dutchman to be concerned about the needs of French papermakers, especially since his own country had helped ruin the industry "after the flight of our Religionists" by building competitive mills. Many other officials, after surveying the industry in their jurisdictions in 1701 and again in 1717, reported that the quality of the paper produced there had deteriorated and that managers and workers were not so adept as they had been before the Protestants departed.[90]

---

[87] Bibliothèque de la Société Protestante, MS 485[II], fols. 86, 156, 220, 244.
[88] Archives Nationales, F[12] 1475; G[7] 3; Boislisle, *op. cit.*, I, 106.
[89] Boislisle, *op. cit.*, III, 511.
[90] Archives Nationales, G[7] 1691; F[12] 1475.

One may infer that the Huguenot dispersion severely affected the industry because the state tried to repatriate paperworkers just as hard as or harder than it tried to lure back refugees engaged in weaving silk and linen. The controller general advised his chief agent at Limoges on July 17, 1687, that "it is important to support papermaking and if possible to prevent the migration of its workmen to England." He specifically suggested that the intendant extend financial aid to a Protestant manufacturer named Juliart (or Juillard), who was purportedly in debt and likely to leave the realm.[91] Juliart, as a matter of fact, did flee and appeared a short time later as the director of a paper mill near Southampton. Barrillon, the French ambassador at London, finally succeeded in bribing him to return to France despite the efforts of the millowners to keep him at Southampton. Bonrepaus, while on his three special missions to England, worked diligently with Barrillon to induce other papermakers to return.[92] Five were enticed away from a mill at Colbrook and thereby caused its failure. At least one other returned to France, but he soon wound up in prison. He was not repatriating, it seems, but was recruiting additional workers at Angoulême to take back to England.[93]

The French ambassador in Holland, like Barrillon in England, grew concerned when he realized that a number of Frenchmen were helping the Dutch make the finer grades of printing paper which Holland had formerly imported from Auvergne and Angoumois.[94] He was especially interested in a manufacturer from Angoulême named Vincent. This man was of Protestant faith and also of Dutch nationality, so when Louis signed the revocation edict, Vincent sought and received a passport allowing him to leave Angoulême and go to Holland. Since he had been employing some 500 persons in his mill at Angoulême, the ambassador in Holland and the intendant at Limoges both feared that his departure might leave many paperworkers unemployed and might even cause them to follow him to Holland. Some did emigrate, but there is no basis for concluding, as some writers

91 *Ibid.*, G7 3.

92 Archives du Ministère des Affaires Étrangères, *Ancien fonds*, "Angleterre," *registres* 157, fol. 75; 159, fol. 272; 162, fols. 65–66, 319–320; Archives Nationales, G7 345; A1 795, docs. 134, 169.

93 Boislisle, *op. cit.*, I, 51.

94 Archives du Ministère des Affaires Étrangères, *Ancien fonds*, "Hollande," *registre* 143, fol. 183; Arnal, *op. cit.*, p. 19.

have done, that Vincent took all or even the major part of his 500 employees with him.[95]

Most of the evidence confirms the impression that Huguenot fugitives helped to diffuse trade secrets and processes employed in papermaking and thereby harmed the industry at home. Papermaking, like the production of silk fabrics, was one of France's export industries. No matter how hard they tried, Louis's officials were able to repatriate only a few refugee workers and entrepreneurs. England and Holland enriched their store of technological knowledge and skilled man power and ultimately capitalized upon those gains.[96]

An important question still remains unanswered. How much of the decline in France's industry can be attributed to her internal religious troubles? Surely not all of it. Adam Anderson, writing in 1801, mentioned England's high wartime import duties on foreign paper as one of the reasons that she finally overcame her dependence upon French mills.[97] The Dutch War and the War of the League of Augsburg interrupted French exports and gave effective protection to foreign manufactures.[98] In addition, the increased charges and regulations heaped upon papermaking at home proved both costly and irksome. In 1655 and 1656 the king reëstablished marking and control, raised the excise on paste and rags, and levied a new tax on paper destined for judicial and commercial use. By an *arrêt* of July 21, 1671, his council placed the entire industry under government supervision, and consequently the amount of red tape increased and the number of complicated regulations multiplied. In order to raise revenue, export duties were increased and a special tax was levied on playing cards.[99] It is significant that the number of mills

95 See, e.g., Boissonnade, *op. cit.*, pp. 8–9; Lacombe, *op. cit.*, p. 58; Weiss, *Histoire des réfugiés*, II, 145. Touzaud (*op. cit.*, pp. 238–239) agrees with me.

96 Archives Nationales, F12 1475; G7 1692 (M. David's memorandum of 1708 to the controller general); Bibliothèque Nationale, *Fonds français*, MS 8038, fol. 136; Boislisle, *op. cit.*, II, 489; W. E. J. Berg, *De Réfugiés in de Nederlanden, na de Herroeping van het Edict van Nantes* (Amsterdam, 1845), p. 172; Boissonnade, *op. cit.*, p. 5; Bujeaud, *op. cit.*, pp. 305–306; Cohendy, *op. cit.*, p. 7; Weiss, "Mémoire sur les protestants," *op. cit.*, XX, 108–109, 117–118. See also chap. x, below, pp. 327–329, 346.

97 *Op. cit.*, II, 594.

98 Archives Nationales, F12 1475; Bibliothèque Nationale, *Fonds français*, MS 4287, fol. 28; Boislisle, *op. cit.*, II, 164–165; Bujeaud, *op. cit.*, p. 304; Lacroix, *op. cit.*, pp. 8–9.

99 Archives Nationales, F12 1475; G7 1685, 1692; Bibliothèque Nationale, *Fonds français*, MS 4287, fols. 28, 29; Bujeaud, *op. cit.*, pp. 310–311; Gazel, *op. cit.*,

in Angoumois began to diminish after 1656 and well before 1685, even though the decline did not reach its nadir until the end of the century. The industry in Auvergne also began to contract soon after 1680, when the king levied new duties on its output. As every economist and most businessmen know, excises tend to restrict output, and it is not likely that taxes on paper were an exception.

It should be remembered, too, that the Dutch War and the War of the League of Augsburg coincided roughly with the period when the number of mills in operation around Angoulême dropped most sharply. The brief but unmistakable revival of papermaking in the same area after the Treaty of Ryswick (1697) and before the War of the Spanish Succession broke out (1701) also suggests that prosperity in the industry depended to a large extent upon easy access to foreign markets and hence upon international political relations.

A final word of caution may prove desirable. Not all paper-workers who fled abroad shortly before or sometime after 1685 were Protestant. The entire province of Auvergne, where the industry suffered less than in Angoumois and in Upper and Lower Normandy, never had many more than 1,000 Huguenots, and the original demographic data offer no basis for concluding that they clustered particularly around Ambert and Thiers, where the best paper mills were located.[100] It is possible, however, that Charles Weiss was correct when he stated that some of the wealthiest manufacturers at Ambert were Protestants and that their flight to escape persecution forced many of their workers to seek employment in foreign mills.[101] This might explain the special order issued on January 24, 1687, forbidding paperworkers in Auvergne, whether Protestant or Catholic, to leave the country under pain of perpetual confinement in the galleys.[102]

After all the evidence is weighed, it still appears reasonable to conclude that the revocation appreciably depressed the French

---

pp. 18 and n. 5, 28, 30, 31, 38, 106; Lacroix, *op. cit.*, pp. 8–9. The compulsory fee for inspection and marking was 6 s. per ream for the better grades and 4 s. per ream for ordinary grades.

100 Archives Nationales, G7 105; Henri Hauser, "La Réforme en Auvergne, notes et documents (1535–1671 [1568–1685])," *BSHPF*, XLVII (1898), 449 n. 1; Adolphe Michel, *Louvois et les protestants* (Paris, 1870), p. 221.

101 "Mémoire sur les protestants," *op. cit.*, XX, 117–118.

102 Gazel, *op. cit.*, p. 105. The king justified his action on the ground that emigration would create an embarrassing shortage of skilled man power.

paper industry. Papermaking recovered and even prospered later on in the eighteenth century, but it never entirely regained its west European markets nor did it completely recapture its former advantage over foreign mills in quality of output. Important manufacturers who sought a religious haven abroad built new mills on foreign soil and attracted many former employees to operate them. As employment opportunities at home declined, many Catholics also sought work abroad. Finally, it is appropriate to observe that the industry seems to have suffered less in Auvergne, where Protestants were less numerous, than in Angoumois and in Upper and Lower Normandy, where Protestants were quite influential in papermaking.

THE MANUFACTURE OF RUGS AND TAPESTRIES

In addition to Gobelins and Savonnerie, which the king owned and operated, and the factory at Beauvais, which belonged to private individuals who enjoyed many special privileges and could use the title of "royal manufactory," several manufacturers at Aubusson specialized in rich tapestries and luxurious rugs and employed some 1,500 or 1,600 persons. About 1,000 Protestants lived at Aubusson, and many of them were tapestry weavers. Near the end of 1685 Louvois learned with obvious pleasure that most of the heretics there had been converted, but he recognized the need "to spread a little money about the town in order to compensate for the departure of several manufacturers who have retired to Paris." [103] Not all these manufacturers remained at the capital permanently; several appeared later in Germany and other countries where, under government protection or subsidy, they opened rug and tapestry shops. The intendant at Moulins stated in 1698 that about 200 inhabitants had fled Aubusson for religious reasons.[104] The actual number who left may well have been larger since government officials were prone to understate figures that might cause the king displeasure. Be this as it may, the tapestry industry at Aubusson experienced difficult times after 1685.[105]

---

[103] Boislisle, *op. cit.*, I, 57, 58.

[104] See, e.g., Alfred Leroux, *Histoire de la réforme dans la Marche et le Limousin (Creuse, Haute-Vienne, Corrèze)* (Limoges, 1888), pp. 331, 332–333, 342.

[105] See especially Cyprien Pérathon, *Histoire d'Aubusson: la vicomté, la ville, les tapisseries, la maison d'Aubusson* (Limoges, 1886), pp. 68–70, 320–322; "Le Protestantisme à Aubusson," *Mémoires de la société des sciences naturelles et archéologiques de la Creuse,* XIX (1915), 354–355.

Although the emigration of some Protestant manufacturers and artistic workers may have contributed to the troubles of the tapestry industry, it was probably not the whole cause or even the primary one. Gobelins, Savonnerie, and Beauvais—where Protestants did not occupy key positions—were all depressed after 1685.[106] The decrease in market demand provides the most satisfactory explanation. Tapestries and fine rugs were luxury items even for the very rich, and producers had long come to rely upon royal purchases as their mainstay. When continuous warfare began to deplete his treasury and ruin his credit, Louis XIV had to cut down on his patronage and to delay paying his bills. The shrinkage in the national income caused private individuals also to curtail their purchases. The inability of producers to market their output at profitable prices was probably a much more significant factor in the decline of tapestry weaving and rugmaking than were the persecution and the emigration of Huguenots.

LACEMAKING

Because France had been sending Italy sizable sums of money each year to pay for Venetian lace worn by fashion-conscious courtiers, Colbert had gone to considerable trouble and expense to import workmen and to initiate domestic production of this particular pattern. He had also encouraged the women at Alençon, Chantilly, Sedan, Charleville, and Aurillac to increase or at least to maintain production of their special styles of lace. Aurillac and other towns in Auvergne had reputedly employed thousands of women to make an annual output valued at approximately 600,000 livres.[107] By the end of the century, however, lacemaking was everywhere depressed. The intendant at Alençon reported in 1698 that the city population had declined "by more than a third following the revocation and that its output of lace, like its output of linen, had dropped off considerably."[108] The intendant at Paris likewise stated that the quantity of gold and silver lace made in the Paris area had decreased.[109]

---

106 See Cole, *French Mercantilism,* pp. 126–133; Martin, *op. cit.,* pp. 294–295; Lavisse, *op. cit.,* Vol. VIII, Part 1, p. 239 n. 1.

107 Martin, *op. cit.,* pp. 180–190.

108 Bibliothèque Nationale, *Fonds français,* MS 4286, fols. 121, 122.

109 Weiss, "Mémoire sur les protestants," *op. cit.,* XX, 119. The ambassador to Holland informed His Majesty on October 3, 1686, that an important lace merchant and his wife from Paris had recently arrived at The Hague and had

Several letters from Auvergne in 1688 informed the controller general that spinners of thread for laces and embroideries were suffering at Aurillac because so many Protestants in Guyenne and Languedoc, who had been among their best customers, had emigrated; and he was advised on July 2, 1704, that lacemaking in Auvergne "has perished."[110]

As with all industries catering to the wealthy and supplying a product for which the demand had a high income elasticity, lacemaking confronted a rapidly shrinking market after 1683. A change in fashion at about the same time also caused consumers either to wear less lace than formerly or to shift to foreign styles.[111] When unemployed lacemakers in Auvergne asked the controller general in 1699 to order all courtiers to wear only French lace, he would not even seriously consider their proposal.

Many Protestant lacemakers left France and plied their craft in foreign cities. Their departure may have curtailed the industry in a few communities, but it was probably not primarily responsible for the troubles everywhere besetting the manufacture of lace. Only at Alençon, Sedan, and perhaps some of the towns near Paris, like Villière-le-Bel, were Protestants numerous enough to have created a labor shortage by leaving.

THE KNITTING INDUSTRY

In the mid-seventeenth century Frenchmen began to make silk stockings on knitting frames. Colbert had encouraged the practice, for silk stockings made on machines were cheaper than those made by hand, and may also have been of superior quality. But when manufacturers began to use machines to make caps, stockings, underwear, and other knit goods from wool and linen, as they did before 1684, the government grew alarmed lest hand knitting disappear and leave unemployed many peasant women and children whose hands might otherwise be kept busy during winter months. Those who had a vested interest in knitting woolens also resisted the introduction of machinery. The king accordingly ruled in 1684 that manufacturers could employ frames for knitting woolens and linens provided they devoted at least

---

opened a store (Archives du Ministère des Affaires Étrangères, *Ancien fonds,* "Hollande," *registre* 148, fol. 20).

[110] Boislisle, *op. cit.,* I, 151; II, 190; Cole, *French Mercantilism,* p. 126; Martin, *op. cit.,* p. 296.

[111] Lavisse, *op. cit.,* Vol. VIII, Part 1, p. 239; Martin, *op. cit.,* p. 243.

half their machines exclusively to silks and used fine yarn for
all their output so as not to compete with the coarser wear
knitted by hand. Something akin to a mild revolution in technology resulted, for consumers preferred machine-made goods.
Hand knitting declined, and unemployment became common.
In 1700 Louis revised his 1684 policy and restricted knitting
frames to seventeen cities (Paris, Dourdan, Rouen, Caen, Nantes,
Oléron, Aix-en-Provence, Nîmes, Toulouse, Uzès, Romans, Lyon,
Metz, Bourges, Poitiers, Amiens, and Reims).[112]

Normally an industry that supplies basic and relatively inex-
pensive items like underwear and stockings does not decline so
much during a prolonged depression as industries that confront
a sensitive and highly elastic demand. Nor does an industry that
benefits from cost-reducing innovations suffer so much as those
that have no such advantage. It is not surprising, therefore, that
the knitwear industry did not decline in relative importance, but
may actually have improved its position. Necessary adjustments
to the new technology were probably responsible for the cries
of distress after 1684. Although many Huguenot knitters carried
their manual dexterity or their looms to foreign countries, there
is little evidence that they seriously curtailed domestic production. The inspector of manufactures at Nîmes, for example,
told the controller general on March 8, 1700, that Nîmes had
"a considerable number of all kinds of manufacturers, both in
wool and in silk but especially in stockings," and that the industry not only had sustained itself well but had also greatly
expanded its activities. There were almost 800 knitting frames
actually at work in and around the city, and they employed "more
than 3,000 persons." Most of the entrepreneurs and workers,
the inspector added, were new converts.[113] Two local historians
of the Reformation at Metz, however, have concluded that the
industry there suffered after many artisans sought refuge abroad,
but they offer no documentary support.[114]

SUGAR REFINING

Colbert had assiduously encouraged sugar refining at home in
order to provide a steady and sure market for raw sugar drawn

112 Bibliothèque Nationale, *Fonds français*, MS 4289, fol. 20; Cole, *French
Mercantilism*, pp. 179–180; Martin, *op. cit.*, pp. 169–174, 292–294.

113 Boislisle, *op. cit.*, II, 30. See also Gouron, "L'Industrie nîmoise aux XVIIᵉ et
XVIIIᵉ siècles," *Ecole antique de Nîmes*, 17th session (1936), 173 ff., 180.

114 Orthon Cuvier, *Les Réformés de la Lorraine et du pays messin* (Nancy, 1884),
p. 47; Thirion, *op. cit.*, p. 396.

from the French West Indies and to avoid sending specie to Holland to pay for the refined product. At first he had allowed colonists to operate refineries, but he decided to protect home refineries in 1682 by doubling the duties on colonial sugar imported into France. Soon after his death the government forbade the construction of new plants on the islands. Colbert's efforts met with substantial success. Whereas in 1661 the industry had been practically nonexistent in the home market, by 1683 there were approximately twenty-nine refineries in various French cities.[115] The number stood at thirty in 1697 and at thirty-six in the first years of the eighteenth century.[116] If measured by the refineries at work, the industry did not decline at all in the critical years 1684–1717. Its rate of expansion, however, dropped markedly after Colbert's death, and it did not pick up again until after the Regency. These facts are significant because several Protestants occupied key positions in the industry.

The revocation caused unrest among refiners, and some of them emigrated. Seignelay wrote the French ambassador at The Hague on April 18, 1687, that a sugar manufacturer had recently fled from Saumur to Holland. The government had then confiscated his refinery, but Seignelay said the king was willing to return it if the man abjured Calvinism and returned home. Otherwise, the government would dispose of the property by public sale. This would not be difficult, Seignelay predicted, because many Catholics were anxious to acquire so profitable a business.[117] When rumors of impending dragonnades reached Rouen early in October, 1685, many wealthy citizens immediately began to dispose of their possessions so they could flee. The intendant wrote the controller general on October 5 that one entrepreneur had already closed his refinery and that others were threatening to do the same. The official had called the manufacturers together and had tried to reassure them, but the more he had talked, the more convinced they had become that the rumors were true. He closed his report by assuring the controller general that as a precautionary measure he had already persuaded several Catholic entrepreneurs and at least two wealthy new con-

---

115 Cole, *Colbert,* II, 360–361.

116 Cole, *French Mercantilism,* pp. 87–88. The deputy of trade from La Rochelle said in 1701 that there were twenty-five or thirty refineries in France (Bibliothèque Nationale, *Fonds français,* MS 8038, fol. 324).

117 Archives Nationales, B2 *registre* 61, fol. 289.

verts to stand by with enough capital to take over and operate any refineries that might close down.[118]

The revocation did not greatly disturb the industry because many wealthy Catholics and new converts were willing to replace Huguenots who left so lucrative a business. Furthermore, the government protected refiners so they would have less cause to flee from dragoons and overzealous authorities. Seignelay wrote the intendant at Rouen on November 20, 1685, for example, that His Majesty wished the Dutch and German Protestants at the Dieppe refinery to be spared all forms of persecution, insofar as possible. A month later he told the lieutenant general of police, as well as the intendant, to give the owner of the Dieppe refinery (Allard) every kind of protection and not to station troops on his premises. The owner eventually accepted Catholicism and continued in charge of his prosperous and expanding business.[119] Seignelay similarly evinced interest in reports that the proprietors and the workers in several Bordeaux refineries were preparing to flee. He commissioned the intendant there to investigate the situation carefully because it was "extremely important to prevent this from happening."[120] In 1700 the six sugar plants at La Rochelle still employed a good many foreign Protestants, and the intendant excused the practice because the men were well behaved and held no religious services.[121]

TANNING AND LEATHERWORKING

Frenchmen tanned leather in many cities and provinces.[122] Activity in the industry slowed down appreciably after 1683 although it is not clear whether tanning declined relative to other lines of work. Two local historians have concluded that the number of tanners in the vicinity of Metz dropped after 1685. By

---

118 *Ibid.*, G7 492; Boislisle, *op. cit.*, I, 54–55. I have found no evidence to support Émile Lesens's conclusion in *Le Protestantisme dans le pays de Caux (ancien colloque de Caux, Havre et Dieppe excepté)*, ed. Victor Madelaine (Bolbec, [1906]), p. 175, that the flight of Protestants robbed Rouen of its sugar refineries.

119 Archives Nationales, B2 *registres* 55, fols. 546–547; 61, fols. 259–260; O1 *registre* 29, fol. 557. The government continued to protect Allard. On August 1, 1694, for example, it ordered local officials to extend him every aid and to protect him from false and defamatory rumors being circulated by envious Catholics who questioned the sincerity of his conversion. (Bibliothèque Nationale, *Nouvelles acquisitions françaises*, MS 1206, fol. 124.)

120 Archives Nationales, B2 *registre* 58, fol. 701.

121 *Ibid.*, G7 339. See also Bibliothèque Nationale, *Fonds français*, MS 4287, fol. 11.

122 See, e.g., Martin, *op. cit.*, pp. 191–192.

1749 the area was producing only enough leather to meet local needs, they said, whereas in its heyday it had exported appreciable quantities to other French provinces and to foreign countries.[123] The intendant in Touraine reported in 1699 that the number of tanneries in his jurisdiction had fallen from "more than 400" at some unspecified date to 54.[124] The famous kid glove and tanning industries in and around Caudebec in Normandy, which dated from the thirteenth century, shrank drastically in the last decades of Louis XIV's reign, and most artisans sought work abroad.[125] Whereas 60 master tanners were said to have been preparing cow leather for shoe tops in the Norman town of Saint-Lô at some time before 1684, only 2 remained there in 1708.[126] One author has affirmed that Rochefoucauld near Angoulême lost its renowned tanneries after 1685.[127] According to the intendant in Champagne, of the 12 large tanneries formerly located at Vitry-le-François, only 3 were operating in 1732.[128] Finally, the controller general learned in 1687 from his agent at Limoges that the departure of Protestants had "almost entirely stopped" the preparation of leather in the district of Saint-Jean-d'Angély.[129]

The original documents providing these data on the leather industry do not always ascribe its decline to religious troubles. The temptation to attribute the industry's plight to the emigration of Protestants is understandably strong if the historian abhors minority persecution and especially if he is himself a member of the persecuted minority. Charles Weiss, for example, apparently assuming that Protestants had founded and operated the "more than 400" tanneries in Touraine, had some basis for implying that religious persecution had been responsible for re-

---

[123] Cuvier, *op. cit.*, p. 47; Thirion, *op. cit.*, p. 396.

[124] Bibliothèque Nationale, *Fonds français*, MS 4283; Martin, *op. cit.*, p. 206; Weiss, "Mémoire sur les protestants," *op. cit.*, XX, 111, 118.

[125] Noël de la Morinière, *op. cit.*, pp. 134–135.

[126] Bost, *op. cit.*, p. 155; Galland, *Essai sur l'histoire du Protestantisme à Caen et en Basse-Normandie*, pp. 105, 257.

[127] Bujeaud, *op. cit.*, p. 311. Bujeaud refers to a memorandum prepared in 1725 by someone named Gervais, who stated that the little town had been much more prosperous before the revocation than it currently was and that many well-to-do Protestants had fled abroad and left relatives behind to manage their properties.

[128] G. Hérelle, *Documents inédits sur le protestantisme à Vitry-le-François . . . depuis la fin des Guerres de Religion jusqu'à la Révolution française* (Paris, 1903–1908), I, 327 n. 1.

[129] Boislisle, *op. cit.*, I, 106; Cole, *French Mercantilism*, p. 114; Émile Levasseur, *Histoire du commerce de la France* (Paris, 1911), I, 421.

ducing the number to 54. Since Touraine was never heavily Protestant, it is unlikely that Huguenots dominated the industry there. There is no specific information on the point. It is, however, likely that tanning in the vicinity of Metz, Caudebec, Saint-Lô, and Vitry-le-François suffered from the revocation, for many inhabitants of these communities were Protestant. Even so, the conclusion must rest primarily on inference rather than upon known fact. Contemporaries explicitly attributed the decline in leatherworking to Protestant emigration only at Saint-Jean-d'Angély and Rochefoucauld.

METALLURGY

It has been suggested that the manufacture of iron suffered less than most industries after 1683 because military needs expanded rather than contracted the market for its output. It is possible, and perhaps probable, that all metallurgy declined absolutely after Colbert's death and yet improved its relative position in the economy as a whole. Even so, metallurgy was never so important in the French economy as most textiles and many industries making luxury items for people all over Europe. France has always been relatively poor in mineral resources, and she did not seriously exploit her potential underground wealth until the latter part of the eighteenth century. Consequently, despite Colbert's efforts to encourage metallurgy, particularly armament foundries, tin plate plants, and steel mills, France continued to import raw metals and certain metal goods. Her own mines, furnaces, foundries, and forges could not supply the whole domestic market. Smelting, refining, and metalworking required ample and cheap supplies of wood. Frenchmen had not yet learned how to burn coal or coke. Wherever forests were still abundant—as in Dauphiné, Franche-Comté, Alsace, Lorraine, Auvergne, Foix, Béarn, Anjou, and Maine—anybody rambling around the countryside could come upon a small group of workers clustered around a furnace or a forge.

It is uncertain whether the revocation adversely affected the industry. Voltaire stated that "Calvinists, who held the secret of making tin plates and steel, took it away with them in 1686 and imparted their knowledge . . . to foreign nations."[130] This is not exactly true. A Frenchman, aided by Bohemian workers,

---

[130] *Age of Louis XIV*, Vol. XXIII of *Works of Voltaire* (La Vérité ed.; New York and Paris, 1901), p. 237.

had made tin plates at Beaumont-la-Ferrière in Nivernais as early as 1665; and after several reorganizations the same factory was still operating in 1716. Sometime after 1684 a Huguenot named Robelin and two associates built a tin plate factory at Chenissy (or Chenecey) in Franche-Comté, and ran it with the help of native or German Lutherans and Calvinists. Robelin, described as a distinguished engineer and a director of fortifications in Franche-Comté, was still operating the plant in 1700. The intendant of the area praised Robelin to the controller general, even though the entrepreneur and many of his workmen had never accepted Catholicism. Exactly when the works at Beaumont-la-Ferrière and Chenissy closed down is not known. The proprietors of the former were wrangling among themselves over financial difficulties in 1713–1714, and in 1718 one of them was seeking permission to start another enterprise. A group of men who took over the Chenissy plant in 1713 and moved it to another location requested special privileges and tax exemptions in 1718. Both enterprises must have ceased operations shortly thereafter, for a report to the government in 1720 affirmed that France was no longer producing tin plate.[131]

Voltaire's implication that the industry disappeared shortly after 1686 is surely wrong; yet he may have been correct in saying that Protestant refugees were instrumental in diffusing the industry's secrets to foreign countries. The king went back on his original promise of religious freedom to foreign Protestants brought in to staff the plant at Beaumont-la-Ferrière. His missionaries harassed them after the revocation when they refused to abjure. Perhaps workers at Robelin's plant at Chenissy also eventually lost heart and left. This is mere conjecture. Since both factories continued to produce until well after 1710, it is likely that their later disappearance was due to declining economic conditions in France.

Voltaire's statement is no more accurate for steel than for tin

131 Archives Nationales, F12 *registres* 51, fols. 221, 358–359; 54, fols. 31–32, 34–35, 37, 40, 46, 61, 229–300; 55, fol. 59; 58, fols. 141, 275–276; 114, fols. 43, 67; *liasses* 693, 694; Boislisle, *op. cit.,* I, 467; II, 33; Cole, *French Mercantilism,* pp. 121–122; Martin, *op. cit.,* pp. 185, 190–191, 298; Levasseur, *Histoire des classes ouvrières et de l'industrie,* II, 267, 323; Gaston Gauthier, "Le Protestantisme et la révocation de l'Édit de Nantes dans la paroisse de Beaumont-la-Ferrière (Nièvre)," *Bulletin de la société nivernaise des lettres, sciences et arts,* XVIII (1900), 227–228. Some of the documents place Chenissy in Franche-Comté and others place it in Burgundy.

plate. An intendant stated in 1699 that Dauphiné alone had nine steelworks and six forges for fashioning sword blades.[132] Early in the eighteenth century workers were also making steel at Metz and at Orléans and in the little region of Bugey (Ain); one entrepreneur in Berry kept "more than 400" workmen occupied.[133] Daguesseau agreed on December 10, 1691, to issue letters patent to one of the king's engineers named Richebourg, who claimed to have discovered a new process for making steel and had already demonstrated it to government experts.[134]

Many Protestants, especially foreigners, employed their special skills in this branch of metallurgy. Several may have left Dauphiné and northeastern France after 1685. It is problematical that the intendant in Dauphiné specifically had metallurgy in mind when he wrote in 1691 that his region had suffered acutely from the emigration of Protestants. Consequently, he did not agree with Louvois that the government should appoint an inspector for industry; instead, it should try to revive economic activity by leaving workers with a free hand rather than by burdening them with exacting regulations.[135]

The revocation may have affected the output of metal goods other than tin plate and steel in a few places. In Lower Normandy the little town of Villedieu-les-Poëles, as its name suggests, had acquired fame and modest fortune from its copper stoves and frying pans. Before 1685 the industry provided employment for several hundred persons. Production dropped after some of the best artisans deserted to England and Holland, but it never ceased entirely.[136] Copper deposits at Najac in Rouergue (Aveyron) had been exploited at one time by Protestants who supposedly fled and allowed the mines to fill with water. Craftsmen in neighboring Aurillac and Saint-Flour therefore found it more difficult to get all the copper they needed for stove vessels.[137] One final bit of evidence, pertaining to the Principality of Sedan, is worth noting. Within less than a month sixty artisans making

---

132 Bibliothèque Nationale, *Fonds français,* MS 4288, fols. 23–25; Martin, *op. cit.,* p. 186; Levasseur, *Histoire des classes ouvrières et de l'industrie,* II, 327.

133 Martin, *op. cit.,* p. 299; Lavisse, *op. cit.,* Vol. VIII, Part 1, p. 243.

134 Archives Nationales, F12 662–670.

135 Cole, *French Mercantilism,* pp. 153–154.

136 Bondois, *op. cit.,* p. 88; Galland, *Essai sur l'histoire du Protestantisme à Caen et en Basse-Normandie,* p. 258.

137 Léon Brother, *Histoire de la terre* (3d ed.), p. 177, as quoted in *BSHPF,* XVII (1868), 304.

stoves, kitchenware, scythes, sickles, and similar objects of iron deserted the little villages of Givonne and Daigny and seriously crippled what had once been the inhabitants' occupational mainstay.[138]

All the evidence thus far uncovered does not justify the conclusion that a mere handful of metalworkers left France, or that they neither diffused technology nor reduced the domestic output of metal goods in certain areas.[139] On the other hand, nor does it warrant the conclusion that the revocation of the Edict of Nantes seriously retarded the growth of metallurgy in the country as a whole.

OTHER INDUSTRIES

A few other industries may have suffered from the Huguenot dispersion. To make the survey as complete as possible, they should receive at least brief mention.

Several Protestant publishers and printers, located mainly at Paris and Lyon, competed along with Catholics for the domestic and foreign market in books. Quite a few of these Protestants sought religious haven in either Switzerland or Holland, and the publishing business at Lyon in particular found its external market shrinking.[140] Excessive duties on paper may have been of equal importance in this decline, and publishers at Lyon also blamed their competitors at Paris for paying authors more handsomely than they and thereby attracting more and more of the book trade to the capital.[141]

Several goldsmiths and silversmiths also fled France. It is diffi-

---

[138] Peyran, *op. cit.*, II, 228; Weiss, "Mémoire sur les protestants," *op. cit.*, XX, 121. Stephen Leroy published a document taken from the municipal archives of Sedan (HH 15) in the April, 1901, issue of the *Revue d'Ardenne et d'Argonne* (reproduced again in *BSHPF*, L, 249–250). A petition addressed to the police authorities about 1696 stated that of the "7,000 Religionists, who were the richest and principal merchants [in the Sedan area], scarcely 1,400 remain," and that ten years earlier the village of Givonne had had an output of ironware valued at almost 100,000 *écus* a year. Since the petitioners were seeking special privileges and financial aid, they may have exaggerated their ills.

[139] David MacPherson has claimed that whereas England had been importing large quantities of knives and similar items from Auvergne before 1683, she herself was making better ware at lower costs in 1805 and was selling it throughout Europe (*op. cit.*, II, 609–610).

[140] Apparently some presses in Dauphiné and Orange also had to close down (Pierre Bertrand, *Genève et la Révocation de l'Édit de Nantes* [Geneva, 1935], p. 151).

[141] Bibliothèque Nationale, *Fonds français*, MS 4288, fols. 126–127.

cult to determine whether religion drove them abroad or whether legislation to conserve the country's stock of precious metals for coinage was responsible.[142] Many Protestants took their skill in making clocks abroad.[143] At Blois, for example, the deliberations of the gild prior to 1685 were usually signed by thirty-eight master craftsmen; in 1686, only seventeen signed.[144] And ten left their trade in Paris and found refuge in Saxony.[145]

No less an authority than the economist Boisguillebert has asserted that the New World fishing fleet stationed at Fécamp in Normandy had at one time numbered fifty vessels and that before the outbreak of the War of the League of Augsburg it included only three. Although he thought that excessive taxes, especially the taille, had been primarily responsible for this decline, Boisguillebert wrote that some of the fishermen "had entirely left their trade; others had moved elsewhere; and the greatest part, being of the new religion, have gone to Holland where they have since acquired immense wealth."[146] According to a memorandum on trade dated December 20, 1687, three of the five shops for bleaching wax at Rouen had recently shut down, and some of their staff had escaped to England and Holland, where they set up similar enterprises.[147]

Such evidence is hard to evaluate properly. Even if the "facts" are presumed to be true, it does not necessarily follow that workers who remained at home were unable to produce enough to supply the market. Glassmaking is a good case in point.

Most of the gentlemen glass blowers in southern France were Protestant, as were many of their colleagues in Normandy and Picardy.[148] Several of them joined their fellow Religionists in

---

142 Joan Evans, "Huguenot Goldsmiths in England and Ireland," *PHSL*, XIV (1930–1933), 508–509; David C. A. Agnew, *Protestant Exiles from France in the Reign of Louis XIV; or, The Huguenot Refugees and Their Descendants in Great Britain and Ireland* (2d ed.; London, 1871–1874), II, 134–136. According to Emmanuel-Orentin Douen, fifteen or more goldsmiths left Paris for England (*La Révocation de l'Édit de Nantes à Paris d'après des documents inédits* [Paris, 1894], II, 481–482).

143 J. Gaberel, "Les Suisses romands et les réfugiés de l'édit de Nantes," *Séances et travaux de l'Académie des sciences morales et politiques*, LIV (1860), 109; Lièvre, *op. cit.*, II, 225; Robert-Labarthe, *op. cit.*, I, 127.

144 Louis Belton, "Notes sur l'histoire des protestants dans le Blésois," *Mémoires de la société des sciences et lettres de Loire-et-Cher*, XI (1886–1887), 134–135n.

145 Douen, *op cit.*, II, 481–483.

146 *Op. cit.*, p. 176.

147 Archives Nationales, G^7 1685.

148 *Ibid.*, A^1 902, doc. 15; Bersier, *op. cit.*, p. 178.

emigrating. Some from Normandy carried their special skill of blowing fine crown window glass to England and Holland, which were then able substantially to reduce their annual imports from France.[149] Adam Anderson wrote in 1801 that before the Augsburg war "not only very near all the plate-glass of our coaches and chairs, and of our fine looking-glasses, came from France, but likewise our finest window-glass, which was usually called Normandy-glass and French crown-glass: both which we have since made entirely our own manufacture in the highest perfection."[150] He went on to explain that Huguenot refugees had helped establish these industries but that "the improvement of them . . . could not have been so speedily nor so effectually accomplished, had it not been for the strict prohibition of intercourse between the two nations by this war." The Protestant spy Tellières reported to the French ambassador in Holland on August 13, 1687, that a sizable group of glassmakers from Saint-Menehould in Argonne had recently arrived at The Hague with expectations that many others would soon join them.[151] Nonetheless, glassmaking in Normandy and northeastern France did not suffer greatly from emigration; and almost no glass blowers in Languedoc and Foix deserted their furnaces.[152] It would be incorrect to infer from the departure of several Protestant glass manufacturers and workers that the industry disappeared in certain places or seriously declined in any province.[153]

The Huguenot dispersion that resulted from Louis XIV's efforts to establish religious conformity certainly did not contribute to industrial prosperity. In fact, insofar as it had any influence, it deepened the economic stagnation beginning after 1683 and delayed recovery. Few countries in the past have ever grown so lustily that a sudden 1 per cent loss in population did not retard progress. The 200,000 Huguenots who fled France shortly before and after 1685 were drawn from its most industrious, most enterprising, and most economically active citizens. As a penalized

---

[149] Archives Nationales, G7 493; B2 *registre* 62, fols. 126–127.

[150] *Op. cit.,* II, 597.

[151] Archives du Ministère des Affaires Étrangères, *Ancien fonds,* "Hollande," *registre* 153, fol. 197.

[152] See, e.g., Warren C. Scoville, *Capitalism and French Glassmaking, 1640–1789* (Berkeley and Los Angeles, 1950). There is no evidence whatever that Huguenots were responsible for diffusing the secret of blowing or casting plate glass abroad.

[153] Lesens was guilty of such an error (*op. cit.,* p. 175).

minority they had thrown themselves into economic life with fervor and had gained responsible positions in a number of industries either as entrepreneurs and merchant-capitalists or as skilled artisans. Penalization often tempers the spirit and hardens resolve, and migration itself may serve as a selective process. Ordinarily, only the more venturesome and courageous, the more independent and resourceful, or the more wealthy and skilled who think they can readily put their assets to work abroad, accept the challenge offered by emigration. Others may take the "easier" course and remain at home, although they must then compromise their consciences or suffer indignities and discrimination.

As a subsequent chapter attempts to demonstrate, Huguenots who accepted the challenge of emigration fortified and diversified the economy of countries that received them and thereby diffused many of France's industrial secrets and processes. They were responsible for narrowing the technological gap that separated France from other European countries and for causing the barter terms of trade to shift against France. Throughout the eighteenth century France was never able to restore her exports of certain high-quality products to the relative importance they had enjoyed during most of the seventeenth century. Her rapid expansion in foreign trade after 1717 came primarily from the opening up and development of new trade channels and from the commercial growth of Europe as a whole.

Historians in the past have usually inferred a great deal more than this from the revocation. More often than not, they have accepted the view that the Huguenot expulsion robbed France of essential know-how, capital, and man power, and left her with empty plants and workshops, idle equipment, market shortages, and countless unemployed who could not find work after key entrepreneurs and capitalists had deserted industry and trade. It now seems that such a view needs revision. If the revocation had been the only damper and if the depression had been equally severe and prolonged, one might be justified in concluding that Louis XIV committed a serious economic blunder when he unintentionally forced so many Protestants to flee. But monistic causation is extremely rare in history. There were enough other deterrents spreading their baneful influence throughout the economy to "explain" the stagnation. Yet such an explanation would be neither accurate nor adequate. No historical analysis that neglects any contributory cause, no matter how minor its significance, can be completely adequate. Historians cannot afford to disregard the "fact" that Louis XIV revoked the Edict of Nantes and the "fact" that some 200,000 of his subjects fled abroad. The presumption should be that the refugees reduced the country's economic potential to some extent, but the crucial question—and the one at issue in the present inquiry—is exactly to what extent.

Attention has been focused in this chapter on industries cited by others as supporting the hypothesis that the revocation was primarily responsible for the decline in industrial activity after 1683. And all the evidence usually adduced has been surveyed. On the negative side, some of it was irrelevant because it pertained to firms or industries in which Protestants had little or no part; some of it did not meet the simplest tests of reliability; and very little of it was conclusive. Several Protestant firms that supposedly went out of business after the revocation actually continued to operate successfully either under Catholic ownership or under their old management; certain industries (like woolens and linens) in different parts of the country suffered as much from the depression whether Catholics or Protestants were in control; and at least three (knit stockings, sugar refining, and metallurgy) improved their relative position, and one of them (sugar refining) actually did not decline absolutely. Others—like silk at Tours and Lyon (and possibly even at Nîmes), papermaking in Angoumois and Auvergne, and possibly tanning in Touraine— were already declining a good many years before the revocation. Several industries produced luxury and export products that were particularly vulnerable to decreases in national income, to style changes, and to wars and tariffs which cut off foreign markets. Others had to cope with increased taxes on raw materials and output and with additional restrictive regulation by the government. On the positive side, some of the evidence suggests that the emigration of Protestant entrepreneurs and key workmen injured a few industries in certain areas—for example, the manufacture of linens in parts of Normandy and Picardy, the production of fine felt hats in the vicinity of Caudebec, the woolen industry in Sedan, tapestry weaving at Aubusson, and lacemaking at Alençon. Also, industrial activity in general seems to have suffered more in regions where Protestants concentrated than in others. Sedan, Picardy, Normandy, and Dauphiné were hard hit; Languedoc, Poitou, Angoumois, Touraine, Maine, and Lyonnais felt the impact of the revocation, but to a lesser extent; and production in other provinces apparently suffered only minor damage.

Even if one concludes, despite the evidence presented in this chapter, that religious persecution was a primary depressant of the French economy in the period immediately after 1683, it would not necessarily follow that the revocation seriously retarded economic development throughout the eighteenth century. Modern society, time and again, has shown a remarkable ability to recover from temporary setbacks and to rebuild its capital and replace its entrepreneurs and skills after the ravages of wars, military occupations, and natural disasters. French industry as a whole made great progress after 1717 and especially after 1730. Economic growth proceeded at a rapid pace in the eighteenth century. It is conceivable, of course, that the expansion might well have been more striking had Louis XIV not driven 200,000 Protestants from his realm. On the other hand, if emigration had really drained the country of irreplaceable entrepreneurs, capital, and skilled labor, the economic recovery and rapid growth after 1717 would be inexplicable. One must remember that between 1 and 1.5 million Protestants stayed in France. Most of them, it was true, wore the thin disguise of "new converts," and as such continued to be the target for all kinds of discriminatory practices. Instead of weakening and reducing their energies, religious persecution seems to have strengthened their resolve and to have tempered and purified their spirit. Throughout the eighteenth century they threw themselves into economic activities with greater zest than before; they not only retained their superior position on the economic ladder, but climbed higher.

A subsequent chapter examines other causal forces that help to account for the period of secular stagnation. The most that can be said at this stage of the inquiry is that the revocation, coming when it did, reënforced these other depressants and intensified the difficulties besetting French industry. But the revocation and the emigration that accompanied it, taken by themselves, cannot adequately explain why France eventually fell behind Great Britain, Belgium, Germany, and the United States in industrialization and economic growth.

VIII

Effects of the Revocation
on Trade and Shipping

In a manuscript entitled "Mémoire sur le commerce de France,"[1] drafted in 1701, the deputies of trade claimed that France's trade had begun to decline soon after the edict outlawing Protestantism appeared. According to them, the edict had been "highly prejudicial to commerce." The religious truce signed by Henry IV at Nantes in 1598 had allowed Protestants to worship as they pleased and to lead more or less normal lives. Then, when Louis XIV abrogated some of their privileges and initiated his policy of gradually but systematically excluding them from military, judicial, and administrative posts, they had turned to trade as the surest road to financial and social success. Their religion had given them an advantage over French Catholics in developing favorable commercial contacts with merchants in such Protestant countries as England, Holland, and several German states; they had been able to establish themselves securely and prominently in both foreign and domestic markets. The revocation of the Edict of Nantes had caused so many of them to flee abroad or to neglect their businesses at home that trade had languished. Consequently, the deputies concluded, Louis had found it necessary to bolster commerce by revising tariff duties and modifying excises on commodities.[2]

Several contemporary observers would have agreed with these deputies. The Venetian ambassador at Versailles, for example, wrote home on October 26, 1686, that so many Huguenots had fled or had gone into hiding or had been converted that trade

---

[1] Bibliothèque Nationale, *Fonds français*, MS 8038, fols. 14–15.

[2] On this particular point see Camille Rabaud, *Histoire du protestantisme dans l'Albigeois et le Lauragais depuis la révocation de l'édit de Nantes (1685) jusqu'à nos jours* (Paris, 1898), p. 104.

was stagnating everywhere.[3] Prominent citizens of Vitry-le-François testified in 1686 that their community could not bear the added expense of a new hospital which the government wanted them to build for the poor because all their business had dwindled after some 150 merchants and wealthy home owners of the Reformed Religion had departed. A priest, who was one of those who offered testimony, stated that the refugees had been "rich and opulent" and had "carried away with them nearly all the money in circulation and had stopped all trading." A nobleman also declared that they had withdrawn immense sums and thereby "caused all commerce to cease." "They were the ones," he said, "who lent their funds to several merchants and tradespeople who are now reduced to beggary."[4]

A Protestant minister from Switzerland also noted in an account of his travels through France, published in 1717, that the revocation had caused merchants "to drop their contacts with foreign countries." Consequently, "trade has been ruined, workers are no longer employed, . . . the roads are filled with poor beggars, . . . [and] many people who would never have left France have been forced to seek employment elsewhere."[5] The English economist Davenant at the end of the seventeenth century apparently attributed much of the commercial decline in France to the departure of her merchants. He predicted that England would be able to rebuild her postwar trade sooner than France.[6] Both Maréchal de Richelieu and the councilor of state Gilbert, in the mid-eighteenth century, expressed the opinion that the revocation had had a baneful effect upon trade and shipping.[7] They advised the government not to allow, and certainly not to request, all Huguenots left in the realm to get out. This would complete the ruin of manufactures and trade, they said, and

3 Henry Austen Layard, "The Revocation of the Edict of Nantes. Illustrated from State Papers in the Archives of Venice," *Proceedings of the Huguenot Society of London* (hereinafter cited as *PHSL*), II (1887–1888), 149.

4 G. Hérelle, *Documents inédits sur le protestantisme à Vitry-le-François . . . depuis la fin des Guerres de Religion jusqu'à la Révolution française* (Paris, 1903–1908), I, 319 ff. Hérelle obtained his information from documents in the municipal hospital archives at Vitry-le-François.

5 J. B. Hollard, *Relation d'un voyage nouvellement fait en France* (London, 1717), p. 13, as cited by Emmanuel-Orentin Douen, *La Révocation de l'Édit de Nantes à Paris d'après des documents inédits* (Paris, 1894), I, 97.

6 François Véron Duverger de Forbonnais, *Recherches et considérations sur les finances de France depuis 1595 jusqu'en 1721* (Liége, 1758), V, 131.

7 Bibliothèque Nationale, *Fonds français*, MSS 7046, fol. 325; 7047, fols. 418–419.

would constitute the "culmination of the political misfortunes which followed the revocation of the Edict of Nantes."

The fact that persons living at the time or shortly thereafter attributed the decline in commercial activity to the revocation does not in itself prove that this was so. On-the-scene observers frequently lack the necessary acumen for distinguishing cause and effect, and rarely are able to appraise objectively a situation of which they are a part. Rather than accept their statements as trustworthy summaries of the facts, one should consider them as suggestive hypotheses requiring further verification. Nineteenth- and twentieth-century historians have not always done this. I believe that they have been too prone to accept uncritically the observations of contemporaries or of earlier historians. Down to the present time most of them have agreed with the deputies writing in 1701 that the revocation of the Edict of Nantes was "highly prejudicial to commerce." It is the purpose of the present chapter to determine whether they were right.

THE DECLINE OF TRADE IN SELECTED AREAS

Bordeaux, a major seaport, exported large quantities of wines and brandies to northern Europe. Her most important merchants were native-born Frenchmen of the Protestant faith or naturalized or unnaturalized foreigners. All of them frequently served as brokers and factors for foreign houses.[8] Dragonnades in neighboring Poitou had already made Bordeaux's Protestants apprehensive before 1685; and the publication of the revocation edict caused many of her wealthiest merchants to convert their assets into cash and flee abroad. Bezons, intendant in the province, became thoroughly alarmed because he thought religious unrest was causing trade to decline and money and credit to disappear from the market.[9] He suggested to the controller general on March 11, 1687, that the current low wine prices at Bordeaux may have resulted from the rumors spread maliciously by refugees in Holland that Bordeaux merchants had unusually large quantities of wine on hand that season. Business became so depressed around Bordeaux that Bezons hastily advised his supe-

---

8 *Ibid.*, MS 4287, fol. 36.

9 See, e.g., the letters Bezons addressed to the controller general on September 7, 17, 26, October 24, December 17, 1686; January 4, February 18, March 1, 11, 22, 1687; December 12, 21, 1688 (Archives Nationales, G⁷ 133; A. M. de Boislisle, *Correspondance des contrôleurs généraux des finances avec les intendants des provinces*, I [Paris, 1874], 91, 97, 167–168).

rior in May, 1688, that it would be a grave mistake to expel all
Jews from the port as the king had recently proposed:

It seems to me that trade has already diminished so much (because
of the departure of new converts which occurs every day) that the
government should not consider expelling the Portuguese from the
realm at this time. They supply most of the money for bills of
exchange here. I have long believed that nothing should be done
about the Jews until new converts get over their desire to flee.[10]

The flight of Protestant merchants both alarmed and frustrated
Bezons because he could do little to prevent it. He tried through
greater vigilance and secret investigation to ascertain the names
of those who were planning to flee; and he and his agents frequented the port and docks at Bordeaux during its great seasonal fairs in the hope of picking up useful information and of
recognizing refugees when they sold their goods or went aboard
ship. He explained his predicament in a letter written at Bayonne
on December 12, 1688. Most wealthy merchants, he said, were
trying to liquidate their possessions and escape to Protestant countries. Their departure would deal Bordeaux a crippling blow,
for they dominated its trade. Yet, if he arrested those whom he
suspected of preparing to leave, others would become panicky
and try to leave also.

Thus the only feasible course is to let each individual know that I
suspect him and that he is being carefully watched. At the same time
I shall do everything possible to discover when he plans to embark.
But this will be very difficult. Merchants visit rural areas ostensibly
to buy wine; then they hide themselves aboard vessels which they own.
Unless each ship is completely unloaded [when it passes through the
port on its way to the open sea], they will never be discovered. . . . All
new converts have their eyes fastened on the present international
situation. . . . We shall have to watch them carefully during the coming
year. We must not permit them to do anything that is openly scandalous, but there are many little things we should overlook and appear
not to notice. . . .[11]

There can be little doubt that trade in the Bordeaux area
languished after 1684. Ris, Bezons's predecessor in the inten-
dancy, twice wrote the controller general in January, 1685, that

---

[10] Boislisle, *op. cit.*, I, 148, 149; Archives Nationales, G7 134.
[11] Archives Nationales, G7 134.

bankruptcies had recently shown a marked increase and had caused creditors to withdraw funds from the market.[12] Another intendant wrote on October 9, 1703, that the money market had never been so tight as it was then. And at least twenty-two business failures occurred at Bordeaux between March 8, 1715, when Louis issued his last proclamation against Protestantism, and May of that year.[13] According to figures found in the National Archives,[14] exports fell from an annual average of 133,380 tons for 1679–1683 to 103,149 tons in 1689, and then plummeted to 47,063 tons in 1690. Professor Frederic C. Lane discovered from admiralty records in the departmental archives at Bordeaux that 88 ships (with a combined capacity of 7,539 tons) left that port for the American isles in 1684–1685, and that in the next two years only 61 ships (totaling 5,515 tons) sailed for the same destination.[15] Since the names of many shippers who traded with the New World were on the rolls of the Protestant church at Bordeaux, Lane concluded that about half of the trade was in Protestant hands and implied that the revocation had had something to do with its decline. Perhaps it did, but until more complete data on the tonnage of all goods passing through Bordeaux become available, it will be difficult to assess accurately the part the revocation played in the reduction of Bordeaux's maritime trade.

The sharp drop in Bordeaux's total exports in 1690 can readily be attributed to the War of the League of Augsburg, which kept Dutch and English vessels away from the port. Before then the Dutch had handled more of Bordeaux's freight than the French, and the English had carried almost as much as the French. The National Archives at Paris have yielded a few scattered monthly figures on the goods shipped from Bordeaux in the years immediately preceding and following the revocation; they are presented in table 2 as monthly averages. Although their reliability may be questioned because the data for so many months are lacking, they create the impression that exports from Bordeaux did not decline appreciably after Louis brought an end to religious tolerance. As a matter of fact, Bezons, when transmitting

---

12 *Ibid.*, G7 133.

13 Paul Bert, *Histoire de la révocation de l'édit de Nantes à Bordeaux et dans le Bordelais (1653–1715)* (Bordeaux, 1908), pp. 77, 100; Boislisle, *op. cit.*, II (1883), 154.

14 Archives Nationales, G7 132–139.

15 "Colbert et le commerce de Bordeaux," *Revue historique de Bordeaux et du département de la Gironde,* XVII (1924), 188–189.

TABLE 2

AVERAGE MONTHLY TONNAGE EXPORTED FROM BORDEAUX, 1682–1688

Month	1682–1684	1685–1688[a]
January	14,080[b]	14,963[c]
February	11,713[b]	16,427[d]
March	21,023[d]	24,222[b]
April	12,819[b]	12,891[d]
May	7,340[b]	7,971[e]
June	5,791[d]	5,419[b]
July	2,854[d]	3,931[c]
August	2,445[d]	2,260[b]
September	3,014[d]	3,051[c]
October	13,037[d]	13,907[c]
November	28,933[d]	21,123[c]
December	15,116[b]	15,308[d]

[a] The year 1685 was included in the postrevocation period because emigration had already begun; 1689 was not included because the outbreak of war would have vitiated the results for the last few months.

[b] The average was computed from figures for three years. The figure for February, 1682–1684, was low because a very small number of Dutch ships called at Bordeaux in 1682 and 1684.

[c] The average was computed from figures for four years.

[d] The average was computed from figures for two years.

[e] The figure for only one year was available.

some of the figures to Versailles, pointed out that exports for September, 1686, exceeded those for September, 1685, by 1,060 tons. He suggested that "this increase may very well reflect the fact that new converts are changing their assets into merchandise and are shipping them out of the realm."[16] Although there is no way of verifying the statement, Huguenots leaving the area might very well have been able to salvage enough of their property in this way to have sustained the level of commodity exports for a few years after 1685.

It is unlikely that the departure of Protestants caused all the bankruptcies at Bordeaux after 1684, or that it was primarily responsible each time the money and credit market tightened. It is worth noting that the intendant who wrote about the shortage of loanable funds in 1703 did not think that the export of specie by emigrant Huguenots had been the cause, for "few such individuals have left in the immediate past." Instead, he attributed the shortage to the transfer of tax revenues out of the province

---

16 Archives Nationales, G⁷ 133.

in the form of specie. By no means did all wealthy Huguenots desert the area. They were said still to control the wine trade as late as 1705.[17] The flight of many of them after the revocation, however, must have aggravated the commercial crisis in Bordeaux to some extent.[18]

La Rochelle, another important port and commercial center, almost tripled the tonnage of its merchant marine between 1664 and 1682.[19] Most of its vessels, owned and operated by Huguenots or newly converted Catholics,[20] carried cargoes of wine and salt for merchants of the same religious background. The intendant for the area frequently complained that Protestants practically monopolized the salt trade and so discriminated against Catholic salters and boatmen—and especially against new converts—that he was unable to make much headway in converting the inhabitants to Catholicism. At various times he suggested that the government (1) fix the price of salt, (2) show favoritism to Catholics who acquired lighters for loading salt on foreign ships, (3) allow only Catholics to weigh salt brought into the town by peasant salters, (4) encourage Catholics to become middlemen in the salt trade in order to break the monopoly presumably held by Protestant brokers, and (5) protect all Catholics and new converts who were indebted to Huguenots from being squeezed into bankruptcy by their creditors.[21] At other times the intendant and subordinate officials proposed that the Crown try to supplant Protestants with Catholics as owners and operators of the port's merchant marine. Despite such suggestions, the government limited its activities mainly to harassing Protestant salt merchants and shipmasters, but it never was able to drive them from these fields or greatly to diminish their predominance.[22]

---

17 Boislisle, *op. cit.*, II, 235.

18 Archives Nationales, TT 235, dossier 4, doc. 103; Bert, *op. cit.*, pp. 93, 94; Théophile Malvezin, *Histoire du commerce de Bordeaux depuis les origines jusqu'à nos jours* (Bordeaux, 1892), II, 291. Yet it is interesting to note that Francisque Michel, *Histoire du commerce et de la navigation à Bordeaux principalement sous l'administration anglaise* (2 vols.; Bordeaux, 1870), never mentions the revocation; and Abbé Novi de Caveirac belittles its effect (*Apologie de Louis XIV et de son conseil, sur la révocation de l'Edit de Nantes, etc.* [n.p., 1758], p. 114).

19 Prosper Boissonnade, "La Marine marchande, le port et les armateurs de la Rochelle à l'époque de Colbert (1662–1682)," in *Bulletin de la section de géographie: Comité des travaux historiques et scientifiques* (1922), pp. 2, 14–15, 17.

20 Archives Nationales, B3 *registre* 48, fols. 289 ff.

21 *Ibid.*, TT 232, dossier 19, docs. 9, 21; 430, doc. 97; Bibliothèque Nationale, *Fonds français*, MS 7045, fols. 33, 38–39.

22 Bibliothèque Nationale, *Fonds français*, MS 4287, fols. 27, 34, 37; L.-J. Nazelle,

Is there any evidence that the discrimination against Protestants hurt trade around La Rochelle? As early as 1682 a local Protestant seaman noted in his diary that commerce had begun to decline and that most merchants in the area were thinking of nothing else except how to escape.[23] In February, 1686, Seignelay received a memorandum from his agent at La Rochelle which emphasized the depression in the region's wine and salt trade; seventeen months later, he received a more optimistic report and immediately replied that he was "pleased to note that La Rochelle's trade has not declined" but that local officials should continue their efforts to check emigration. A tax farmer in October, 1699, reported that the revival of persecution after the lull imposed by the War of the League of Augsburg was again causing many merchants to flee abroad and that this "will ruin the commerce of this port entirely."[24] Although Émile Garnault concluded in his five-volume study of trade at La Rochelle that the revocation dealt it a cruel blow, he pointed out in a subsequent article that, according to admiralty records, Rochelle merchants, who were almost all Protestant, sent to the American colonies 82 vessels in 1685, 65 in 1686, 75 in 1687, and 70 in 1688. After the outbreak of war they outfitted 53 vessels in 1690, 37 in 1691, and 62 in 1692. These figures led Garnault to remark that navigation at La Rochelle "maintained itself at a respectable level" despite the revocation and demonstrated its force and vitality.[25] Another regional historian has concluded from notarial records in a small outlying community that the commercial crisis evoked by emigration began to wane about 1690.[26] Some have thought that it lasted much longer.[27]

The evidence is neither conclusive nor very convincing. Some of it is hearsay; some is inferential. Perhaps historians will never know exactly to what extent maritime trade decreased at La

---

Le Protestantisme en Saintonge sous le régime de la Révocation, 1685–1789 (Paris, 1907), pp. 186–187.

[23] "Journal d'un marin protestant du XVIIe siècle (Taré Chaillaud)," *Bulletin de la société de l'histoire du protestantisme français* (hereinafter cited as *BSHPF*), XV (1866), 321.

[24] Archives Nationales, B2 *registres* 57, fols. 95 ff.; 62, fol. 7; G7 338.

[25] *Le Commerce rochelais au XVIIIe siècle* (La Rochelle, 1886–1898), II, 13; *Les Bourgeois rochelais des temps passés et les causes de la décadence du commerce rochelais* (Rogent-le-Rotrou, 1899), pp. 8, 9.

[26] Charles Dangibeaud, "Contribution à l'histoire du protestantisme à Cozes (1675–1699)," *Revue de Saintonge et d'Aunis*, XLI (1924), 209–210.

[27] See, e.g., Boissonnade, *op. cit.*, p. 44; Nazelle, *op. cit.*, p. 187. Boissonnade said that shipping declined in the area after 1682 because so many of the ablest seamen and merchants forsook La Rochelle for religious reasons.

Rochelle, or when the decline actually set in. Until they do, it is difficult to establish conclusively any high degree of correlation between religious troubles and commercial depression. Still, since the port was a Protestant stronghold and since Huguenots apparently dominated its economic life, one may reasonably conclude that the persecution and emigration of Protestants both before and after the revocation must have dampened its trade.

Nantes was another important port on the Atlantic. According to statistics compiled for 1704, she accounted for a larger portion of France's merchant marine than any other city.[28] English and Dutch traders who resided there handled most of her export-import business. It also seems that her wealthiest merchants, whether French or alien, were Protestant. Several of them fled immediately after the revocation. Much later, a resident of Nantes wrote that Louis XV's declaration of May 14, 1724, reaffirming all previous anti-Protestant legislation, would likely not affect his city:

There are scarcely five or six well-to-do merchants or individuals still at Nantes who have ever professed Protestantism themselves or were born of parents who did, and I do not believe that they are disposed to leave the realm. . . . About thirty-five or forty years back some rich traders, who had previously arrived from foreign countries and established themselves in business mainly around the city's bridges, left because of the restrictions imposed on Religionists by the 1685 edict. Since they have never come back, I do not foresee at the present time that the latest declaration of the king will have any pernicious effects in this area.[29]

Various persons complained early in the eighteenth century that English ships were calling at Nantes less frequently than in the past, but they attributed this more to discriminatory tolls levied on goods coming down the Loire River and to high import duties on English draperies than to religious troubles.[30] There is no

---

[28] Archive Nationales, F12 1641, as reproduced by Émile Gabory, "La Marine et le commerce de Nantes au XVIIe siècle et au commencement du XVIIIe (1661–1715)," *Annales de Bretagne*, XVII (1901–1902), 397. The merchants at Nantes told the Council of Trade in 1701 that they and others together owned 213 boats based at the port and part interest in 50 others sailing from Sables d'Olonne (Bibliothèque Nationale, *Fonds français*, MS 8038, fols. 210–211).

[29] Reproduced in B. Vaurigaud, *Essai sur l'histoire des églises réformées de Bretagne, 1535–1808* (Paris, 1870), III, 229.

[30] Archives Nationales, G7 1686; B7 *registre* 495, fol. 39. The deputies of trade also adopted this explanation.

evidence that Nantes suffered as much as Bordeaux or La Rochelle from the revocation.[31]

Upper Normandy and Lower Normandy, with much larger proportions of Protestants than Brittany, were more vulnerable.[32] The intendant at Caen, writing on September 15, 1686, that "one of the most important merchants of this city" (named Vaumichel) had fled to Holland, expressed the fear that others would soon do likewise.[33] Still later, near the turn of the century, he commented that trade in linens "as well as in other commodities has declined considerably since 1685, when most merchants or traders who were Religionists fled to foreign countries and abandoned their businesses; those who remained have been unable to reëstablish commerce."[34] Officials at Rouen also showed concern. According to them, Protestant merchants and financiers began early in 1685 to withdraw funds from the market; later in the year, when the conversion campaign really got under way, a number of them badly disrupted trade by selling their possessions at sacrifice prices in order to flee the country.[35] One partisan historian has asserted that 250 merchants, many of them quite wealthy, left Rouen in 1687–1688;[36] and the intendant admitted in 1699 that "a great many foreigners, especially Dutchmen, formerly called at Rouen and several settled down in the region, where their industry and consumption greatly benefited trade . . .; but when they found themselves deprived of the right to practice their religion, most of them left."[37] Seignelay urged Marillac on November 23, 1685, to encourage newly converted persons at Dieppe to step into the breach whenever Protestant merchants departed "so that we may bring to an end as quickly as possible the prejudice that has resulted from the almost complete suspension of trade."[38] Commercial activity at

---

[31] Gabory, *op. cit.*, pp. 371–372.

[32] J.-A. Galland, *Essai sur l'histoire du Protestantisme à Caen et en Basse-Normandie de l'édit de Nantes à la Revolution (1598–1791)* (Paris, 1898), pp. 110–111, 257; "Le Protestantisme à Condé-sur-Noireau (Calvados) et dans le Bocage normand de la Révocation à Napoléon Ier (1685–1812)," *BSHPF*, LXI (1912), 102; Charles Weiss, "Mémoire sur les protestants de France au XVIIe siècle," *Séances et travaux de l'Académie des sciences morales et politiques*, XX (1851), 120.

[33] Bibliothèque de la Société Protestante, MS 485[V], fols. 146–147.

[34] Bibliothèque Nationale, *Fonds français*, MS 4286, fol. 12.

[35] See, e.g., the intendant's letters to the controller general dated October 5 and November 5 and 28 (Boislisle, *op. cit.*, I, 54–55, 56).

[36] Émile Lesens in his Preface to Philippe Le Gendre, *Histoire de la persécution faite à l'église de Rouen sur la fin du dernier siècle* (Rouen, 1874), p. xxi.

[37] Bibliothèque Nationale, *Fonds français*, MS 4286, fol. 29.

[38] Archives Nationales, B2 *registre* 55, fol. 551.

Le Havre likewise dwindled after several Protestants emigrated, but most of the decline resulted from mounting fiscal burdens and from wartime interruption of shipping.[39]

Cities along or near the Atlantic coast were not the only places where the revocation and religious persecution supposedly hurt trade. The town of Gien in Orléanais, for example, was said to have suffered severely after its Religionists "withdrew to Paris or left the realm." They had been its "richest and most prosperous citizens" and had controlled the wood and grain trade.[40] Contemporary records reveal that most of the important merchants in Alençon fled to England and Holland;[41] the little town of Guînes near Calais was impoverished;[42] a citizen of Saint-Quentin in Picardy predicted in September, 1685, that if many others followed the example set by three wealthy Huguenot merchants who had recently escaped abroad, the city would face certain ruin because Protestants controlled its trade;[43] and Blois, a resort center approximately midway between Tours and Orléans, was depressed because "Huguenots and an infinity of foreigners" had stopped coming there to enjoy its salubrious climate or to learn the language.[44] Metz, which was heavily Protestant and lay fairly close to the border, lost many inhabitants.

Commerce has suffered [the intendant admitted] from their departure. The damage would have been even greater if the flight had occurred suddenly. Since it did not, Catholics were able to take over the businesses vacated by fugitives. But this procedure has not been entirely successful. Catholics have not easily acquired the standing and credit [their predecessors enjoyed] in the foreign cities with which Metz does all its trading.[45]

---

39 Henri Amphoux, *Essai sur l'histoire du Protestantisme au Havre et dans ses environs* (Le Havre, 1894), pp. 256–257.

40 Bibliothèque Nationale, *Fonds français*, MS 4283, fol. 31. See also the intendant's letter dated March 23, 1689 (Boislisle, *op. cit.*, I, 177).

41 Bibliothèque Nationale, *Fonds français*, MS 4286, fol. 102.

42 William Minet, "Isaac Minet's Narrative," *PHSL*, II, 430. Minet drew upon a five-volume manuscript history of Calais (in the Calais public library), written in the eighteenth century by Pigault de l'Epinoy.

43 Archives Nationales, G⁷ 85; Boislisle, *op. cit.*, I, 56; Alfred Daullé, *La Réforme à Saint-Quentin et aux environs, du XVIᵉ siècle à la fin du XVIIIᵉ siècle* (Le Cateau, 1901), p. 183; L. Rossier, *Histoire des protestants de Picardie, particulièrement de ceux du département de la Somme* (Amiens, 1861), pp. 253–254.

44 Boislisle, *op. cit.*, I, 209, 343. The intendant wrote in this vein on December 10, 1689, and again on October 26, 1693.

45 Maurice Thirion, *Étude sur l'histoire du protestantisme à Metz et dans le pays messin* (Nancy, 1884), p. 400. See also *ibid.*, pp. 396, 397; Weiss, "Mémoire

Lyon, at the confluence of the Rhône and Saône rivers, was an important center of finance and trade. "The spirit of business reigns here," the intendant wrote in 1699, and the inhabitants "are industrious, inventive, adaptable, motivated by [economic] interests, orderly, and devoted to business."[46] Before the revocation many Swiss and French Protestants had occupied prominent positions there in commerce and banking. Since the Swiss were not molested very much after 1685, most of them remained in the city. About twenty French families converted, and the rest withdrew to Geneva and later settled in Holland, England, and Germany. The fugitives "were rich and had cut a pretty figure in trade, and they carried away with them considerable wealth."[47] This was as far as the intendant went in his report. He did not say, for example, that the revocation had curtailed commercial activity nor even that trade was depressed. Four years earlier, however, an official or businessman at Lyon had written that "everyone is aware that the city's trade has diminished considerably, whereas Geneva is infinitely more prosperous now than thirty years ago."[48] Although the revocation probably damaged Lyon's economy, at least temporarily, by driving away some French merchants, there is little evidence to support the conclusion of one historian that it "destroyed the Reformed Church at Lyon and at the same time the commercial prosperity of the city."[49]

Trade declined in the parish of Job (Auvergne) after several Protestants left; the intendant in Dauphiné affirmed in 1687 and again in 1691 that economic activity in his jurisdiction had declined because Huguenots "had carried on most of its trade";[50] and when a group of citizens at Sedan became disturbed over conditions in 1716, they begged the government to be more

---

sur les protestants," *op. cit.*, XX, 122; Orthon Cuvier, *Les Réformés de la Lorraine et du pays messin* (Nancy, 1884), pp. 44, 46.

[46] Bibliothèque Nationale, *Fonds français*, MS 4288, fol. 15.

[47] *Ibid.*, MS 4288, fol. 66.

[48] Archives Nationales, F12 673.

[49] Edmond Chevrier, *Notice historique sur le protestantisme dans le département de l'Ain (Bresse, Bugey, Pays de Gex) et lieux circonvoisins (Savoie, Lyon, Mâcon)* (Paris, 1883), p. 141. A Catholic partisan has concluded that neither the population nor the commerce of the region around Mâcon (just north of Lyon) suffered very much (Abbé Rameau, "Les Huguenots dans le Mâconnais aux XVIᵉ et XVIIᵉ siècles," *Revue de la société littéraire, historique et archéologique du département de l'Ain*, IX [1880–1881], 135).

[50] Boislisle, *op. cit.*, I, 120, 256, 419.

lenient with newly converted merchants so that those who had stayed in the area would become more active in business and those who had escaped would return home.[51] The lieutenant general in Provence informed the controller general on July 22, 1703, that many Huguenots had recently fled Orange after Louis XIV annexed the principality, and that "this small country will need a little time to repair the damage the exodus has caused, especially in the field of commerce."[52]

Bâville was one of the few intendants who stanchly denied that the revocation had adversely affected economic life. According to his 1698 memorandum, only about 4,000 Protestants had left Languedoc, and of these no more than "forty had had any standing in the province and are still remembered. . . . Their departure has not occasioned the least loss so far as trade in this province is concerned, for it has never been more flourishing than at present."[53] This was too optimistic a statement. In other documents, when he was seeking tax relief or other financial concessions from the Crown, Bâville described conditions in his region as considerably less bright. The truth probably is that business in Languedoc and its chief commercial city Nîmes experienced some ill effects from the emigration of Protestants, but it was not completely disrupted or permanently impaired.[54]

FRENCH TRADE WITH FOREIGN COUNTRIES

It has already been demonstrated that France's foreign trade did not expand greatly after Colbert's death. Her trade with England and Holland—two countries presumably enriched by the skill and knowledge of refugee Huguenots—deteriorated more than her trade with other nations. According to David MacPherson,[55] the English House of Commons estimated in 1675 that France each year sold merchandise to England valued at £1,500,000 (or 36,750,000 livres, with the pound estimated as equivalent to 24½ livres) and imported from her commodities

---

51 Archives Nationales, F12 1356.

52 Boislisle, *op. cit.*, II, 146.

53 Bibliothèque Nationale, *Fonds français*, MS 7045, fol. 85.

54 Writing in 1755, M. Ménard drew a contrary conclusion *(Histoire civile, ecclésiastique et littéraire de la ville de Nismes avec des notes et des preuves, VI [Paris, 1755], 291).* Several others have also thought that Languedoc languished for many decades.

55 *Annals of Commerce, Manufactures, Fisheries, and Navigation etc.* (London, 1805), II, 574.

worth only £170,000 (or 4,165,000 livres). Ambroise Arnould calculated that France's exports to the same country dropped from 23,300,000 livres in 1686 to 8,000,000 in 1716, whereas her imports from England fell only from 18,000,000 to 13,876,000 livres.[56] According to the same author, in the 1650's France had been selling goods to Holland valued each year at approximately 72,000,000 livres; by 1716, their estimated value had fallen to 30,700,000 livres.[57] These figures, the best yet available, should be treated as rough guesses and used only for ordinal comparisons.

It appears that before 1685 France's commodity trade with England was "favorable," despite the extremely high duties England levied on French goods from 1678 to the accession of James II. Arnould's estimates for 1686, after many legal restrictions on trade with the French had been lifted, showed that France's export surplus with England still amounted to 5 million livres. Bonrepaus wrote Seignelay on February 11, 1686, that this surplus, which he himself estimated at 2 million livres a year, was fast turning into a deficit. He thought this helped to explain why the English mint in 1685 had obtained about 500,000 gold pistoles from France.[58] Whether the balance turned against France before or after 1685 is impossible to determine at the present time. That it turned against her sometime after Colbert's death seems certain. The deputies of trade from Rouen and Languedoc in 1700 and 1701 and Anisson, whom the king sent to London to negotiate trade relations in 1713, have all confirmed this.[59] So did David MacPherson, in his summary of trade between the two countries in 1697:

---

[56] *De la Balance du commerce et des relations commerciales extérieures de la France* . . . (Paris, 1791), I, 168–171. Arnould's figures, calculated in terms of a livre of fixed silver content, include estimated values for smuggled goods. Exports and imports in 1686 were probably appreciably higher than in earlier or later years, for trade between the two countries was freer in that year than immediately before 1685 or in 1716.

[57] *Ibid.*, I, 185–194. See also Émile Levasseur, *Histoire du commerce de la France* (Paris, 1911), I, 411 and n. 2. The Dutch reëxported about 36 per cent of these imports in 1658. One reason for the decline in French exports to Holland between 1658 and 1716 was the severe tariff and military wars between the two countries in the interval. That France sold more goods in the Dutch market in 1716 than in England doubtlessly reflected in part that Dutch-French trade was freer than English-French trade in 1716.

[58] Archives du Ministère des Affaires Étrangères, *Ancien fonds,* "Angleterre," *registre* 157, fol. 61.

[59] Archives Nationales, F12 641; G7 1699; Boislisle, *op. cit.,* II, 477.

Notwithstanding the restitutions which France had obtained by the treaty of Ryswick, yet her foreign trade seemed still to languish. . . . [England] had been accustomed before the war to send great sums of money to France for wine, brandy, paper, stuffs, linen, hats, silks, and many other things, over and above the merchandize they carried thither from England, whereby the balance was always greatly in favor of France. But the French commissary, now sent over to England for a treaty of commerce between the two nations, found insurmountable difficulties in his commission, not only on account of the high duties laid by England on French goods, which duties were appropriated to sundry uses, but likewise because the English, during the late long war, had learned to be without the merchandize of France, by supplying themselves mostly with the wines of Italy, Spain, and Portugal, and with the linens of Holland and Silesia. The French refugees settled in England now also supplied them with paper, stuffs, silks, and hats, made at home.[60]

Not only did France's trade with England and Holland decline and become more "unfavorable"; its composition also underwent significant change. Arnould thought that manufactured goods accounted for about 50 per cent of France's estimated exports to England in 1686 and for only 15 per cent in 1716.[61] Both MacPherson[62] and Adam Anderson[63] reasoned that between 1683 and the beginning of the nineteenth century France irrevocably lost her markets in England for such manufactured goods as silks, linens, sailcloth, canvas, hats, glass, watches and clocks, paper, ironware, and special fabrics from Picardy and Champagne. The English, and the French refugees in England, they said, had begun to manufacture these products in large enough quantities to supply their own needs as well as to export, and the quality was high enough to enable them to compete with French producers.

The composition of French exports to Holland likewise changed. Arnould estimated that manufactured goods had accounted for about 72 per cent of these exports in 1658 and for only 7.5 per cent in 1716.[64] MacPherson[65] and Anderson,[66] after concluding that annual French sales in Dutch markets were much

---

60 *Op. cit.*, II, 693. MacPherson, as in most of his work, was here quoting almost verbatim Adam Anderson, *An Historical and Chronological Deduction of the Origin of Commerce, from the Earliest Accounts etc.* (London, 1801), II, 633.

61 *Op. cit.*, I, 168–171. 62 *Op. cit.*, II, 609–610.
63 *Op. cit.*, II, 562. 64 *Op. cit.*, I, 185–194.
65 *Op. cit.*, II, 610. 66 *Op. cit.*, II, 563.

smaller at the beginning of the nineteenth century than in 1683, attributed the decline mainly to reduced purchases by the Dutch of rich silks, velvets, linens, woolens, paper, hats, glass, clocks and watches, household furniture, fringes, gloves, canvas, and sailcloth. These were precisely the articles whose manufacture refugee Huguenots presumably had introduced into Holland, or at least had strengthened.

Insofar as Arnould's, MacPherson's, and Anderson's rough guesses are reliable indicators of relative magnitudes, they leave the impression that French refugees were partially responsible, in one way or another, for the decrease in total exports to England and Holland and especially for the decline in the amount and the kinds of manufactured goods exported. Arnould did not mention the revocation when he was explaining these changes; MacPherson and Anderson did. And most persons who have subsequently utilized their figures have followed MacPherson and Anderson.[67]

Any country's comparative advantage is always unstable. As England and Holland developed new and old industries, their imports from France naturally changed. And it is true that Huguenots helped them perfect their industries. But it would be a mistake to conclude that the revocation suddenly closed English and Dutch markets to French goods or that it so reduced the output of French industries that French manufacturers no longer had any goods to send abroad. MacPherson[68] and Anderson[69] agreed that "France . . . did not immediately feel the bad effects of driving out so many industrious merchants, manufacturers, and artificers." As a matter of fact, they said, French goods

---

[67] Charles Weiss, apparently misreading MacPherson, stated that the decline in French trade with England and Holland (£1,880,000 for England alone and £3,582,000 for the two countries) occurred between 1683 and 1733 instead of between 1683 and the beginning of the nineteenth century (*Histoire des réfugiés protestants de France depuis la révocation de l'Édit de Nantes jusqu'à nos jours* [Paris, 1853], I, 336; II, 151). Reginald Lane Poole also erred when he referred to one of MacPherson's figures. MacPherson had estimated that France's total foreign trade fell by £75,288,160 between 1683 and 1733; Poole stated that it declined this much between 1683 and 1703. (*A History of the Huguenots of the Dispersion at the Recall of the Edict of Nantes* [London, 1880], p. 173.) When MacPherson and Anderson calculated the "total loss per annum to France, by England's great improvement in manufactures, and turning her imports into more profitable channels," the figure given (£1,880,000) was larger than their estimate for France's total exports to England in 1683!

[68] *Op. cit.*, II, 617.

[69] *Op. cit.*, II, 569.

flooded the English market in 1685–1688, after James II removed the prohibitive duties on French imports, and "the nation would have been soon beggared, had it not been for the happy resolution in the year 1688, when all commerce with France was effectually barred."[70] It is doubtful that the new industrial enterprises begun or bolstered by Huguenots could have permanently captured part of the English and Dutch domestic markets had not almost continuous warfare (from 1689 until the Treaties of Utrecht in 1713) drastically reduced commercial intercourse with France. The revocation may have hurt France in an indirect way. Huguenots may have been partially responsible for the fact that foreign countries stiffened their barriers against French goods. Rébenac, Louis XIV's ambassador at Berlin, for example, wrote home on November 12, 1686, that although the manufactories established in Brandenburg by French refugees were capable of supplying no more than a hundredth of the market demand, yet the elector was so anxious to encourage them that "the entry of foreign cloths is severely forbidden, which causes a great disorder in trade."[71] In 1695 silk manufacturers at Lyon accused Huguenots in London not only of persuading the English Parliament to forbid the importation of French fabrics into England, but also of devising effective ways "to corrupt all smugglers and to establish such reliable guards along the coast that they have finally succeeded in making the country inaccessible to our taffetas."[72] After Anisson and Fénellon arrived in England in 1713 to negotiate terms of trade between the two countries in accordance with Articles VIII and IX of the Utrecht Treaty, they found most English merchants and manufacturers unsympathetic and even hostile to their objectives. The emissaries complained bitterly in their reports to Paris that French refugees in that country were mainly responsible for the English attitude and that they would stop at nothing to block a peaceful settlement favorable to France. "Since publication of the treaty,

---

[70] MacPherson, *op. cit.*, II, 620; Anderson, *op. cit.*, II, 571. P. de Ségur-Dupeyron, *Histoire des négociations commerciales et maritimes de la France aux XVIIᵉ et XVIIIᵉ siècles, considérées dans leurs rapports avec la politique générale* (Paris, 1872–1873), II, 427–428, used the data presented by these authors to support his contention that "it is nevertheless difficult to sustain that before the war of 1689 emigration had already paralyzed the sale of French products abroad."

[71] Archives du Ministère des Affaires Étrangères, *Ancien fonds*, "Prusse," *registre* 27, fols. 367–368.

[72] Archives Nationales, G7 1685.

the *Bourse* and cafés resound with the outcry of French Protestants against its provisions. . . . They are nearly all scoundrels, very much opposed to the peace and more hostile to the nation than all the king's enemies."[73] The Whigs used the refugees' sentiments to full advantage and finally defeated ratification of the trade articles of the Treaty of Utrecht by nine votes. "Thus the commerce between . . . [England] and France has ever since remained in a kind of state of prohibition on both sides, especially with respect to the principal points."[74]

RESTRAINTS ON PROTESTANT MERCHANTS

Judged by the concern they showed, many officials in France must have felt that religious persecution and the efforts to check emigration were seriously compromising both foreign and domestic trade. Seignelay as minister of the marine, for example, was constantly reminding his subordinates in French seaports that they must not unduly jeopardize trade by trying to win converts to Catholicism or to prevent a few Protestants from escaping to foreign countries. Although he was aggrieved to hear that many Huguenots were landing on the English channel isles, he did not think it would be feasible to stop all boats from sailing between the mainland and those islands. He so informed his agent at La Rochelle on February 20, 1686: "I confess that I am surprised that you ever thought this expedient would be good. The precautions we have absolutely been obliged to take to prevent the escape of Religionists have interrupted trade enough already without undertaking anything else—short of necessity—which might decrease it still more."[75]

At one time or another Seignelay rejected suggestions that ships be forbidden to leave port at night, that newly converted captains of boats at Nantes be restrained from sailing, that French vessels bound for Dutch ports be retained lest they aid fugitives to escape, that new converts wishing to settle on French islands in the New World be refused passports because they might later escape to English and Dutch territories, and that French sailors not be allowed to sign aboard foreign vessels. All such measures, he thought, would hurt trade too much. He counseled his agents to resort to delaying tactics and subterfuges

---

73 *Ibid.*, G7 1699, 1704.
74 MacPherson, *op. cit.*, III, 31.
75 Archives Nationales, B2 *registre* 57, fol. 123.

rather than to deny outright requests for passports from persons whom they might strongly suspect of planning to leave the country. Seignelay also suggested that officials not harass important merchants and manufacturers unless they engaged in "insolent discourses or distinctive obstinacy." "There is nothing more important than to give new converts the opportunity to carry on their business advantageously."[76] He also endorsed Bezons's suggestion not to deport English merchants residing at Bordeaux as enemy aliens after war broke out because such action, coming on the heels of the revocation, would leave no one there to carry on business.[77]

Even the implacable Louvois showed concern in 1685 and 1686 lest efforts to stamp out heresy and prevent emigration interfere with trade. On November 8, 1685, he wrote that the king "does not want to disrupt commerce under the pretext of preventing Religionists from transporting their wealth out of the realm; he wishes trade to remain free."[78] On numerous occasions he told his agents to "handle wealthy and influential Protestants who are bankers and merchants as tactfully as possible," and not to attempt to force all of them in any given area to abjure their faith.[79] On January 8, 1686, for example, he wrote: "His Majesty expects you to prevent their desertion by whatever prudent means you can devise which will not ruin trade, and he also expects you not to be guided in this matter by the opinion of impassioned individuals."[80] A few months earlier Louvois had told Marillac at Rouen that "His Majesty prefers that of the 20,000 Religionists still in your jurisdiction there remain 400 or 500 who fail to abjure at present, rather than that you resort to violence in order to convert every one."[81] When trouble erupted in Cévennes late in 1686, however, Louvois assumed a different at-

---

[76] *Ibid.*, B2 *registres* 55, fols. 312, 453, 539, 542, 551, 582, 604; 57, fols. 77, 115, 123, 378, 387, 453; 58, fols. 671, 687, 770, 931; 61, fols. 373–374; 66, fols. 146, 151–152; Bibliothèque Nationale, *Nouvelles acquisitions françaises*, MS 1206.

[77] Archives Nationales, G7 134; B2 *registre* 70, fol. 12; Boislisle, *op. cit.*, I, 187–188.

[78] Archives Nationales, A1 757.

[79] *Ibid.*, A1 756 (letters to the archbishop at Reims and to M. Charvel at Metz, dated Oct. 15, 30, 1685), 757 (letter to Marillac at Rouen, dated Nov. 1, 1685), 758 (letter to M. le Roy at Metz, dated Dec. 3, 1685), 773 (letter to M. de Bissey, dated Jan. 30, 1686), 774 (letters to MM. de Boufflers and Foucaut, dated March 4, 5, 1686); Bibliothèque Nationale, *Fonds français*, MS 7044, fol. 153 (letter to Bâville in Languedoc, dated Sept. 8, 1685).

[80] Archives Nationales, A1 773.

[81] Bibliothèque Nationale, *Fonds français*, MS 7044, fol. 173.

titude. At that time he advised the Duke of Noailles to select a few leaders and punish them severely in the hope of intimidating others; if this tactic failed to restore order, then "His Majesty would prefer to see commerce in the province diminish rather than leave those people at liberty who are capable of using their influence in trade to stir up more trouble there."[82]

Both Seignelay and Louvois refused to entertain a suggestion by several zealous officials in 1685–1686 that postal inspectors open all letters and packages from foreigners to Protestant merchants and new converts in France.[83] Seignelay told the Bishop of Saintes on February 14, 1686, that his proposal "to intercept letters . . . from abroad is not practicable; it would destroy commercial freedom which should be safeguarded." Much later, in 1698, 1713, and 1718, when the government was contemplating new religious legislation, other individuals in responsible positions urged the king not to be too harsh on stubborn Protestants and insincere converts lest recovery in foreign and domestic trade be further postponed.[84]

Despite such professed desires to protect trade, the revocation, by driving Frenchmen abroad, thinned the ranks of those actively engaged in commerce at home and helped foreign countries produce many commodities formerly imported from France. Religious persecution hurt business in other ways as well. Foreign Protestants visiting or residing in France for business reasons, for example, found life more difficult. Theoretically, they could leave any time they chose and take their possessions with them. Louis, however, hoped they would stay at least long enough to be persuaded to renounce their faith. At the same time he realized that trade might suffer if they left precipitously because overzealous priests and officials were pestering them. He accordingly ordered that alien merchants and financiers were not to be molested so long as they conducted family prayers in the privacy of their homes and did not participate in religious contro-

---

82 Archives Nationales, A1 775.

83 *Ibid.*, B2 *registre* 57, fols. 69, 103; A1 757; Bibliothèque Nationale, *Fonds français*, MS 7044, fols. 211, 229. Confidence in the postal system was already imperiled. The lieutenant general of police at Paris, De la Reynie, reported that Protestant merchants and bankers leaving their church at Charenton after the 1685 Easter services were overheard to say that their English correspondents no longer dared mail them any letters "of consequence" (Bibliothèque Nationale, *Fonds français*, MS 7050, fol. 42).

84 Archives Nationale, TT 430, doc. 128; Bibliothèque Nationale, *Fonds français*, MSS 7046, fol. 29; 20967, fols. 222–223.

versies or discussions.[85] If they nonetheless sought permission to return home, he told intendants to procrastinate as long as possible before finally issuing them passports.

Foreigners in France became increasingly apprehensive when the king, on the eve of the revocation, redoubled his efforts to convert all Protestants, and revealed his reluctance to issue them passports when they got ready to leave. The French ambassador at The Hague had tried to reassure Dutch merchants that they could freely enter and leave France and need not fear religious persecution while there. On October 4, 1685, in a coded message, he told his superior in Paris that his action had somewhat calmed the Dutch:

[Some such assurance] . . . was essential because there was so much alarm throughout Amsterdam that trade might suffer greatly. Almost no money is available on the market for transactions involving France. What has especially frightened merchants here is that their correspondents [in France] have affirmed that even Catholics have to declare before the authorities what properties they are holding for Dutch Protestants. Merchants in Holland consequently no longer dare entrust their assets to fellow Protestants whom they send to France on business, or even to French Catholics.[86]

After the revocation edict appeared, foreign merchants grew even more apprehensive. French officials accused them of selling black-market passports to Huguenots who were trying to leave the country, or of smuggling across the border considerable wealth belonging to French refugees. Once again excuses were found for refusing alien merchants passports; sometimes a foreigner who had secured permission to return home was stopped at the border and held in prison until his passport could be returned to Paris for verification.[87] When Louis was finally con-

---

[85] Archives Nationales, G⁷ 339, 355; O¹ *registres* 29, fols. 565–566; 30, fol. 85; A¹ *registre* 753, p. 906; *liasses* 756, 757, 773, 775; B² *registre* 55, fols. 482, 487, 639; Bibliothèque Nationale, *Fonds français*, MS 7044, fol. 173; Archives du Ministère des Affaires Étrangères, *Ancien fonds*, "Hollande," *registre* 143, fols. 83–85; Adolphe Michel, *Louvois et les protestants* (Paris, 1870), pp. 186, 249; Vaurigaud, *op. cit.*, III, 61–62.

[86] Archives du Ministère des Affaires Étrangères, *Ancien fonds*, "Hollande," *registre* 143, fol. 91. See also the ambassador's letter of October 18, written in similar vein (*ibid.*, fol. 116).

[87] *Ibid.*, "Hollande," *registres* 143, fols. 91–92, 116; 145, fols. 31, 38, 221; 146, fols. 18 ff.; "Angleterre," *registre* 160, fol. 79; Archives Nationales, O¹ *registre* 30, fol. 206; A¹ 757; Bibliothèque Nationale, *Fonds français*, MS 7044, fol. 258.

vinced that such procedures had a harmful effect upon trade, the royal council issued two *arrêts*: the one on January 11, 1686, reaffirmed that foreign residents could leave France any time they pleased, and the other, on June 28, made it unnecessary for them to obtain passports provided they had never offered aid and comfort to French Protestants.[88] Bonrepaus had the first *arrêt* translated into English and published throughout the land when he was in England.[89] Yet foreigners hesitated to reënter France, for they always risked inconvenience or delay when they sought to leave.[90] Many Dutch and English merchants who had long resided at Lyon, Rouen, and Nantes hurriedly returned to their native lands after the revocation and never again took up residence in France.[91]

Foreign Protestants who had become naturalized citizens of France were treated exactly like native-born Huguenots. They could not renounce their citizenship or leave the country; and many of them were hounded into accepting Catholicism. Both naturalized and native merchants who were suspected of insincere conversion or who refused to renounce Calvinism encountered difficulties when they tried to carry on their business. All newly converted merchants, for example, had to obtain passports before they could embark on vessels destined for foreign countries or other French ports, and they had to post a bond, frequently of 10,000 livres or more, to assure their return.[92] Per-

---

88 Archives Nationales, O1 *registre* 30, fols. 206, 232; B2 *registre* 58, fol. 529; Bibliothèque Nationale, *Fonds français*, MS 21617, fols. 246–247; Elie Benoît, *Histoire de l'Edit de Nantes, contenant les choses les plus remarquables qui se sont passées en France avant et après sa publication . . . jusques à l'Edit de Révocation en Octobre, 1685* (Delft, 1693–1695), V, 877; *Recueil des Édits, Declarations et Arrests concernans la Religion Prétendue Réformée, 1662–1751, Précédés de l'Édit de Nantes*, ed. Léon Pilatte (Paris, 1885), pp. 270–271, 290–291. Foreigners still had to obtain, without charge, a certificate from a local judge before they could leave.

89 Archives Nationales, B2 *registre* 57, fols. 189–190.

90 Archives du Ministère des Affaires Étrangères, *Ancien fonds*, "Angleterre," *registre* 157, fols. 55–56; Boislisle, *op. cit.*, I, 144–145.

91 Bibliothèque Nationale, *Fonds français*, MSS 4286, fol. 29; 4288, fol. 66; Vaurigaud, *op. cit.*, III, 229; René Durand, "Louis XIV et Jacques II à la veille de la Révolution de 1689: les trois missions de Bonrepaus en Angleterre (1686–1687–1688)," *Revue d'histoire moderne et contemporaine*, X (1908), 39–40.

92 Archives Nationales, TT 454, *dossier* 37, doc. 170; 463, doc. 6; Weiss, "Mémoire sur les protestants," *op. cit.*, XX, 123–124. Although Louvois exempted merchants at Metz from the necessity of posting bond when they visited fairs at Frankfort and Strasbourg, those traveling to England and Holland were required to do so as late as 1738.

haps more important in deterring them from undertaking commercial ventures was the uncertainty of their present and future status. They rarely understood how existing legislation affected them, and they had no way of anticipating how laws might be modified in the future. Enforcement waxed and waned as the Crown's chief interest shifted back and forth between the domestic and the international front. After the War of the League of Augsburg was over and Louis, in his special decree of December 13, 1698, reaffirmed the revocation edict and promised strict enforcement of all religious regulations, most newly converted merchants once more grew apprehensive about the future. Some began to wind up their affairs. To preclude this, d'Argenson assured some of the wealthiest ones in Paris that His Majesty had no intention of barring them from trade with Holland or of forbidding them to visit foreign markets provided they obtained passports and posted bond.[93]

Not only did newly converted merchants find restrictions on their travel irritating and humiliating; they sometimes found that the restrictions placed their businesses in jeopardy. A young merchant at Rouen, for example, complained bitterly on October 28, 1688, how he had been affected. He and his father, both new converts, engaged in foreign trade together. His father had secured permission to visit Holland on business but had been unable to return to Rouen within the stipulated time because of illness and inclement weather. Both father and son had applied for an extension of time, and the son had submitted numerous documents showing that he was in good standing with the Church and had an excellent reputation for honesty in business. The police, nevertheless, seized all the father's property at Rouen and threatened to confiscate the son's possessions as well. Fellow businessmen did not dare deal with the son after they realized that his wealth and reputation were jeopardized. It is true that the son secured legal relief four months after the initial seizure, but during all that time his business was at a standstill.[94] Thus could a cloud of suspicion hamper activities of a newly converted merchant, even though he performed his Catholic duties faithfully and never sought to escape from oppression.

Until the king exempted them from the general regulation that no Protestant or new convert could keep or carry firearms

---

93 Archives Nationales, TT 464, doc. 48.
94 *Ibid.*, TT 450, *dossier* 38.

or swords, merchants belonging to this class had no way of protecting themselves or their goods from highwaymen when they traveled overland. Unless they were allowed to arm themselves, the Duke of Noailles warned Louvois on November 25, 1688, trade would surely suffer "because they carry on all the trade in Cévennes."[95] Some provincial officials also interpreted the law as forbidding former Protestants to trade in powder and lead and to manufacture munitions; and as late as 1699 the government in Paris, anxious to encourage this line of activity, was having to countermand local orders restraining converts from dealing in ordnance.[96]

Although Louis had sought only to prevent desertions when he forbade Huguenots and new converts to send their sons abroad to be educated, his action had the effect of depriving these merchants of an opportunity to acquire new industrial and commercial techniques and to make valuable business contacts abroad.[97] The intendant in Guyenne suspiciously scrutinized traders when they gathered at Bordeaux's seasonal fairs,[98] and the intendant in Brittany made a practice of dispersing groups of individuals he did not recognize whenever they gathered around the docks at Nantes.[99] This continuous surveillance intimidated well-intentioned merchants into restricting their business activities lest they get into trouble with the authorities. Some officials were so anxious to check emigration that they favored drastic action regardless of its effect on trade; a few others[100] were astute enough to realize that the government could easily go too far and unintentionally destroy the credit and business standing of new converts who did not plan to leave the country.

From October, 1685, until the outbreak of the War of the League of Augsburg, Louis's patrols cruised along the Atlantic coast, hunting for possible stowaways and searching all vessels leaving France. In vain did the English ambassador at Versailles remonstrate.[101] The practice continued except for a few months

---

95 *Ibid.*, A¹ 837, doc. 89. Louvois hearkened to this warning and gave the merchants permission to carry arms while traveling.

96 *Ibid.*, O¹ *registre* 43, fol. 87.

97 Pierre Dez, *Histoire des protestants et de l'Église Réformée de l'île de Ré* (La Rochelle, 1926), pp. 102–103.

98 See, e.g., Archives Nationales, G⁷ 133, 134; Boislisle, *op. cit.*, I, 90–91.

99 Vaurigaud, *op. cit.*, III, 90.

100 Especially Le Bret when at Lyon (Bibliothèque de la Société Protestante, MS 444, fol. 222) and Bouchu in Dauphiné (Archives Nationales, TT 243, *dossier* 4, doc. 37).

101 Layard, *op. cit.*, pp. 138, 141.

in 1687, when Louis threw open his frontiers to see whether this would lessen emigration. The government also had port authorities inspect ships before they sailed, occasioning costly delays and considerable expense in opening and repacking crates. When Seignelay heard that searchers were taking advantage of their function to demand gratuities from ship captains, he angrily forbade such extortion. In May, 1686, with Seignelay's permission, the intendant at La Rochelle tried fumigating all vessels headed for Holland in the hope of driving from concealment any Protestants aboard. When the Dutch protested that the smoke contaminated the fruit in the cargo and that those who later ate the fruit became seriously ill, Seignelay withdrew his permission.[102]

The dragonnades and similar coercive methods employed to wring conversions from Religionists disrupted domestic trade. Soldiers billeted in their homes pillaged them without mercy; local Catholic judges and other officials arbitrarily levied on them excessive fines and prison sentences upon the slightest pretext;[103] and tax assessors and collectors frequently discriminated against them.[104] Consequently, many merchants who were reluctant to leave France fled their homes and went to Paris or other large cities where persecution was less intense and where they could hope to conceal their religious background.[105] This must have caused at least temporary disequilibrium in local markets.

According to royal declarations in 1686, 1698, 1712, and 1715, the state would confiscate property belonging to converts who reaffirmed their Protestant faith on their deathbeds or who died without benefit of clergy. Whenever this happened, other new converts or Catholics who had funds tied up in the deceased's estate suffered financial loss. Confusion and discontent always resulted. Amelot wrote the president of the Parliament at Rouen on March 16, 1701, regretting that several merchants had recently sustained loss when local judges had enforced the law against a merchant draper at Elbeuf who had died after repudiat-

---

[102] Archives Nationales, B2 *registres* 57, fols. 378, 453; 58, fols. 514, 821; Archives du Ministère des Affaires Étrangères, *Ancien fonds*, "Hollande," *registre* 146, fols. 296 ff.

[103] See, e.g., Archives Nationales, G7 339; TT 449II, *dossier* 24, doc. 115; Bibliothèque Nationale, *Fonds français*, MS 20967, fols. 222–223.

[104] In 1693, for example, the intendant at Montauban complained that a special levy against new converts (*taxes de milice*) doubled or tripled their property taxes and had caused commerce to suffer unduly (Boislisle, *op. cit.*, I, 309).

[105] Archives Nationales, G7 449; "Journal d'un marin protestant," p. 323; Dez, *op. cit.*, pp. 85–86; Rossier, *op. cit.*, p. 218.

ing his earlier conversion to Catholicism. Since the judges had acted within their right, and since the king was unwilling to change the law, the aggrieved individuals could not seek redress. Amelot asked the president at Rouen, however, to assure merchants that in future similar cases the courts would protect their interests.[106]

Verbal assurances alone, however, could not restore confidence among businessmen. An engineer at Dieppe wrote the controller general on October 15, 1700, that "Religionists are so terrified . . . that commerce suffers a great deal."[107] Residents of Bordeaux were grumbling as late as 1715 that the uncertainties and disorders in business transactions created by penalties against relapsers had stultified trade.[108] Particularly in the months immediately following the revocation, foreigners refrained from trading with France because of the excessive risks involved. They could never be certain that they would receive funds owed them or goods they had purchased. Dutch merchants complained bitterly of their losses when the French government confiscated money they had entrusted to French agents who ran afoul of the law by seeking religious asylum abroad or in Paris.[109] And an official at Boulogne, in January, 1686, seized eighteen packages of silk consigned to an English merchant merely upon the suspicion that the silk belonged to a Huguenot who was trying to get his wealth out of the country.[110]

Still another set of regulations adversely affected business. In November, 1680, as already indicated, Louis XIV promised Protestants throughout his realm a three-year moratorium on all personal debts if they converted. He had made the same promise much earlier (in 1666, 1668, and 1676) to Protestants living in Languedoc, Guyenne, Dauphiné, and Pignerol. His reason had been to encourage them to convert by protecting them from reprisals by fellow Religionists who happened to be their creditors. This moratorium was naturally susceptible to great abuse, and

---

106 Archives Nationales, F12 *registre* 115, fol. 36. Amelot specifically stated that the creditors of van Robais at Abbeville had no cause to worry because this particular Protestant family had been accorded special permission "to live in their religion without anyone's being able to molest them."

107 Boislisle, *op. cit.*, II, 58.

108 Bert, *op. cit.*, p. 77.

109 Archives du Ministère des Affaires Étrangères, *Ancien fonds*, "Hollande," *registres* 143, fols. 79–82; 144, fols. 137–138; James Westfall Thompson, "Some Economic Factors in the Revocation of the Edict of Nantes," *American Historical Review*, XIV (1909), 48.

110 Archives Nationales, B2 *registre* 57, fols. 55–56.

both Catholic and Huguenot creditors protested against it. Some Protestants incurred heavy obligations and then embraced Catholicism in order to defraud their creditors; others hid behind the moratorium and failed to honor legitimate bills of exchange drawn against them in the course of business. It is not strange, therefore, that foreign and domestic moneylenders refused to lend funds to Protestant merchants. The risk was too great. Many merchants who had no intention of defrauding complained that it was almost impossible for them to obtain funds and that they could not carry on their business.[111] The king eventually recognized the validity of such complaints and amended his original order (on November 5, 1685, and on January 12 and 18 and December 16, 1686) so as to exclude from the moratorium (1) such items as bills of exchange, (2) other credit instruments arising from legitimate commercial transactions between foreigners and Frenchmen, (3) debts contracted by new converts with other Frenchmen in the course of business, and (4) interest and principal on debts contracted by one new convert with another.[112]

According to other laws, the state would confiscate all possessions left behind by Protestants or new converts who escaped to foreign countries or would turn the property over to the nearest of kin who were Catholics in good standing. The king tried to expedite the process of locating and confiscating refugees' property by promising, on August 20, 1685, to give half of it to any informer who disclosed its whereabouts. Confiscation gave fugitives a strong incentive for taking as much as they could with them. Louis declared null and void any sales they might have made during the year (and, after 1699, during the three years) preceding departure. These orders in particular hampered trade. Anyone buying goods or property from Protestants ran the risk of losing what he had bought in good faith if the seller later left the country; anyone selling to a Protestant on credit had no way of obtaining payment if the buyer fled abroad and the state confiscated his property or awarded it to his next of kin. Some Protestants deliberately incurred debts with Catholics before es-

---

111 *Ibid.*, G⁷ 337; TT 430, doc. 110; O¹ *registre* 29, fols. 449–450; B² *registre* 55, fol. 641; Bibliothèque Nationale, *Fonds français*, MS 7045, fol. 33; Bibliothèque de la Société Protestante, MS 485ᴵᴵ, fol. 47.

112 Archives Nationales, O¹ *registre* 30, fol. 33; TT 264, *dossier* 14, doc. 63; A¹ 773; Bibliothèque Nationale, *Fonds français*, MSS 10623, fols. 71–72; 21623, fols. 40–41; Jacques Lefèvre, *Nouveau recueil de tout ce qui s'est fait pour et contre les protestans* . . . (Paris, 1690), Appendix, pp. 34–35.

caping;[113] others who continued in business in France found that they could not freely sell their goods, buy on credit, incur other obligations, or dispose of their real property.[114] The king attempted to modify his regulations so as to avoid these undesirable effects, and he cautioned officials who applied the law to distinguish between obligations incurred in good faith and those designed to defraud.

The king was unwilling to allow former subjects who had established themselves in foreign countries to recross his borders in order to frequent French markets.[115] When his representative in Brandenburg stated on January 14, 1687, that several refugees living in Berlin, Breslau, and Leipzig had requested special passports to revisit France for purposes of trade, Louis immediately replied that "as of the present moment, I do not wish to make any concession to the merchants of Leipzig, and I shall see after the passage of time what should be done [in such matters] for the good of commerce."[116] Bâville also sought special permission for six Protestant merchants who wanted to return temporarily from Geneva in order to buy woolens and silks at the Languedocian fairs. "Their commerce represents an annual value of 1,500,000 livres," he said, "and is very useful to the development of domestic manufactures." The controller general nonetheless denied the request in 1693 and again in 1696 and 1697.[117] Many refugees, however, managed to continue trading with France through the medium of brokers. In 1711 French Catholics stationed in Holland complained that this practice gave Huguenots in that country an unfair competitive advantage over them. The refugees supposedly had valuable commercial contacts with relatives and insincere converts in France, and even managed to receive inside information from the Council of Trade and various chambers of commerce which enabled them to profit from favorable business opportunities.[118] Even when trading through a broker, however, a refugee merchant ran the risk of losing his money or the goods bought in his name. One

113 See, especially, a letter addressed to the controller general by several merchants at Tours (Archives Nationales, G⁷ 519).

114 *Ibid.*, A¹ 773; Bibliothèque de la Société Protestante, MS 485ᵛ, fols. 146–147; Boislisle, *op. cit.*, II, 18; Weiss, *Histoire des réfugiés*, II, 152.

115 Archives Nationales, O¹ *registre* 30, fol. 248.

116 Archives du Ministère des Affaires Étrangères, *Ancien fonds*, "Prusse," *registre* 28, fols. 21, 25.

117 Boislisle, *op. cit.*, I, 324–325.

118 Archives Nationales, G⁷ 1696 (letters attached to Pontchartrain's letter to Desmaretz dated May 19, 1711).

such refugee, who had set up business in Switzerland, had 1,678 livres taken from his agent at Lyon by officials who claimed that all property belonging to fugitives was confiscable.[119]

A royal declaration of January 12, 1686, ruled that French Catholics could not employ Protestants as their agents in foreign countries. Almost immediately bankers at Paris protested that strict enforcement of this law would ruin them. Since they had to employ cashiers in the country with which they were dealing, they had no choice but to employ Protestants in predominantly Protestant countries. In view of this, Seignelay privately informed them that the king would allow each firm to hire one Protestant abroad, provided the man was a native-born foreigner.[120] Louvois similarly informed the Bishop of Lyon at about the same time that "in order to favor trade, His Majesty is perfectly willing for Huguenot merchants in France to employ foreign Protestants as their agents abroad."[121] Louis never intended these concessions to extend to French refugees. In February, 1687, for example, as soon as he learned that a French merchant was employing a refugee as his purchasing agent at Hamburg, he ordered the merchant to discharge the man and thenceforth to employ only French Catholics in this capacity.[122] Thus, neither Protestant nor Catholic businessmen in France could freely employ whomever they pleased to represent them in foreign markets. Whenever political or religious principles are superimposed upon purely economic criteria, rational maximization by entrepreneurs becomes more difficult. It is true that refugees in one way or another managed to maintain trade relations with France and that French merchants continued to employ Protestants as their foreign agents and factors. Still, the net effect of legal discriminations against refugees was to hamper trade rather than to encourage it.

SHIPPING

Protestantism had many adherents among France's seamen and shipmasters along the Atlantic coast from Bordeaux to La Rochelle and, to a lesser extent, from Nantes to Dieppe. Bonrepaus, while serving as intendant-general at Rochefort, for example, wrote Seignelay in 1685 that 40 of the 60 masters of merchant

---

119 *Ibid.*, G7 356.
120 *Ibid.*, O1 *registre* 30, fol. 31.
121 *Ibid.*, A1 773.
122 *Ibid.*, B2 *registre* 61, fol. 121.

ships at La Rochelle were Huguenots, as well as 318 of the 1,482 officers and seamen at La Rochelle, in the province of Aunis, and on the island of Ré. According to him, 1 of the 3 boats at the little harbor of Marennes and 15 of the 20 sloops at La Tremblade belonged to Huguenots; and Protestants or new converts owned all 28 boats of the 15- to 25-ton class which regularly sailed between Royan and Bordeaux, as well as all ships based at Bordeaux which traded with the American isles.[123] Many people, including Bonrepaus, were convinced that Protestants figured too prominently in French shipping and that the government should remedy the situation while at the same time preventing the defection of Huguenot shippers and seamen.

Louis had already decreed in December, 1680, that any French pilot, calker, gunner, sailor, or fisherman caught serving under a foreign flag without permission would be sent to the galleys for life. Thereafter, and until the revocation edict appeared, he and Seignelay tried to divert as many cargoes as possible into the hands of Catholic shippers in the hope of discouraging Huguenots and inducing them to sell their vessels to other Frenchmen. The government actually bought a few sloops and turned them over to Catholics. It also degraded Protestant naval officers and sometimes forbade shipowners to employ Protestant crews on vessels sailing between certain ports.[124]

The regulations were stiffened after October 18, 1685. At least two-thirds of the crew on each French vessel had to be Catholic; Protestant pilots could not guide ships into and out of harbors except under restrictions; and officials carefully searched each vessel for Huguenot passengers and crew members before it sailed. Also, severe penalties were imposed on seamen who helped Religionists to escape. The punishment was confiscation of all property and confinement in the galleys for life if the person aided had never renounced Protestantism. If the refugee happened to be a new convert, the seaman who helped him faced execution. It is not known how faithfully nor for how long the government enforced these and similar regulations. It never withdrew them, and officials at La Rochelle were still insisting

123 *Ibid.*, B3 *registre* 48, fols. 289–242, 314–317, 331. Bonrepaus may have been misinformed when he wrote about Bordeaux's American trade. After studying that trade prior to 1685, Professor Lane concluded that perhaps half of it was in Protestant hands.

124 Eugène Guitard, *Colbert et Seignelay contre la religion réformée* (2d ed.; Paris, 1912), p. 116.

as late as 1714 that new converts had to furnish written evidence that they were in good standing with the Catholic Church before they could serve as pilots, seamen, or ship captains.[125]

Seignelay was afraid that severe disciplining of Protestants engaged in shipping would drive able-bodied seamen out of the country and interfere with maritime activity. Like his father Colbert, he fostered the merchant marine in every possible way because it was an excellent school for training naval personnel and because it could take away business from Dutch and English carriers. As early as 1681 he had warned local and regional officials not to station troops in the homes of Protestant seamen and not to seek conversions in other ways.[126] After Louis outlawed Protestantism, Seignelay could do little to protect seamen except restrain overzealous persons from carrying coercion too far. He urged his own subordinates, for example, to refrain from violence so long as they could accomplish the same end by pestering Protestants with annoying red tape and contrived delays in gaining clearance for sailing. He forbade port authorities to invade the homes of seamen; and in 1687 he temporarily suspended the right to search departing vessels. He flouted the law by allowing ships to leave port when less than two-thirds of the crew was Catholic, provided the captain left his own family behind and posted sufficient bond to assure the ship's return. He refused to deprive Huguenots of employment in the French marine or to forbid new converts ever to work on foreign ships.[127]

The government succeeded neither in sincerely converting most Protestant seamen, as Louis and the clergy had wished, nor in preventing many of them from leaving the country, as Seignelay had hoped. According to reports Louis received in November, 1681, a large number from the area around La Rochelle and Rochefort had recently fled to England and Holland. More alarming were the reports reaching him in 1685–1688. Bonrepaus wrote on May 3, 1685, that 51 sailors had deserted the province of Saintonge and its adjacent islands since 1681; the intendant at Bordeaux reported in 1686 and 1687 that 100 sailors had left

---

125 Nazelle, *op. cit.*, pp. 88–89.

126 Archives Nationales, B² *registres* 44, fol. 417; 45, fols. 347–348; Émile Lesens, *Le Protestantisme dans le pays de Caux (ancien colloque de Caux, Havre et Dieppe excepté)*, ed. Victor Madelaine (Bolbec, [1906]), pp. 160–161.

127 Archives Nationales, B² *registres* 55, fols. 453, 542, 571–572, 573, 582; 57, fols. 18, 453; 58, fol. 931; 66, fols. 146, 151–152; B³ *registre* 55, fols. 500–506; Guitard, *op. cit.*, pp. 119–120, 130.

the region around La Tremblade and many others had fled Royan; and a marine official stationed at Nantes voiced concern in 1688 over the number from that port who were then sailing under the Dutch flag.[128] Disquieting news also arrived from outside the country. Bonrepaus, sent to England and Holland on a special mission for the king, wrote in 1686 that many French seamen were serving these two nations, but that their number probably did not yet surpass 800; a Huguenot spy told the French ambassador at The Hague on April 12, 1687, that 200 had arrived recently in Zeeland from La Tremblade; and Seignelay became disturbed over reports that William of Orange was successfully recruiting Frenchmen for his navy.[129]

Such information, of course, does not provide an adequate basis for estimating the number of seamen France lost to her enemies. Vauban's estimate of between 8,000 and 9,000 seems much too large,[130] and the Venetian ambassador at Paris was probably exaggerating when he wrote home in 1688 that the majority of sailors along the western coast of France had departed.[131] One thing is certain: at least enough of them left to worry Louis. He counseled Bonrepaus to be on the lookout for sailors during his secret mission to England and Holland and to offer them pardons, money for their passage home, and assurance of future employment if they would return to France.[132] Though the evidence is scanty, several persons have nonetheless concluded that religious persecution drove away so many seamen that it must be ranked as an important factor in the decline of France's merchant marine after 1683.[133]

Colbert had worked hard to strengthen the marine, and his

128 Archives Nationales, B2 *registres* 44, fol. 417; 58, fol. 770; B3 *registres* 48, fol. 260; 55, fols. 500–506; G7 133.

129 *Ibid.*, B2 *registre* 66, fols. 100, 191; Archives du Ministère des Affaires Étrangères, *Ancien fonds,* "Angleterre," *registre* 157, fol. 146; "Hollande," *registre* 153, fol. 64.

130 Bibliothèque Nationale, *Fonds français,* MS 7044, fols. 286 ff.; *BSHPF,* XXXVIII (1889), 195. Apparently, however, both Charles W. Cole (*French Mercantilism, 1683–1700* [New York, 1943], p. 106) and Boissonnade (*op. cit.,* p. 42) have accepted Vauban's estimate.

131 Layard, *op. cit.,* p. 149.

132 Archives du Ministère des Affaires Étrangères, *Ancien fonds,* "Angleterre," *registre* 157, fols. 42, 90.

133 See, e.g., Amphoux, *op. cit.,* pp. 436–439; Boissonnade, *op. cit.,* pp. 40, 44; Thomas Miller Maguire, "Frenchmen on the Seas," *PHSL,* VIII (1905–1908), 168; Nazelle, *op. cit.,* p. 186; Frank Puaux, "La Révocation à Marennes. Le temple et les écoles," *BSHPF,* XXXIII (1884), 13.

efforts had met with substantial success, although he seems never to have made his country self-sufficient in coastwise and foreign shipping. He had retained Fouquet's differential duty of 50 sous per ton on foreign vessels; he had subsidized French shippers; he had chartered several trading companies; and he had dredged and improved several harbors, protected them with new fortifications, and equipped them with new dock facilities. Even before his death in 1683, however, the English and the Dutch had begun to recapture part of the shipping he had taken away from them. Because their vessels were larger and could operate with proportionately smaller crews, they were able to underbid French carriers. Of the 935 foreign ships calling at Bordeaux in 1682, the great majority were of Dutch and English register. Although they constituted only about 29 per cent of all the ships that dropped anchor in that harbor, they handled somewhat more than 62 per cent of all the freight.[134] Scattered monthly data for the period 1686–1688 yield almost exactly the same percentage.[135] Foreigners had also regained control of shipping out of Nantes by the end of the seventeenth century, and anyone who visited the port in 1700 would have seen only ten or twelve French ships lying in the harbor alongside fifty or sixty flying foreign flags.[136]

Whether religious persecution made the French marine less capable of meeting the competition of foreigners is the crucial question. It would help if there were some way of ascertaining whether Bordeaux and Nantes were typical of other ports and whether the situation anywhere was appreciably different after the revocation from what it had been shortly before. The figures for Bordeaux covering twelve consecutive months in 1682 are admittedly not strictly comparable with those for twelve months scattered over 1686–1688; yet they suggest that the relative share of shipping handled by Frenchmen in that port had changed little in the interim. Even so, it is possible that conditions were entirely different elsewhere. At La Rochelle, for example, the merchant

---

134 Malvezin, *op. cit.,* II, 354. The intendant wrote in 1699 that most of the time there were 100 foreign ships in Bordeaux's harbor, and up to 400 or 500 at the time of the great seasonal fairs (Bibliothèque Nationale, *Fonds français,* MS 4287, fol. 36).

135 Archives Nationales, G7 134. The data cover the months of January, February, March, July, August, September, October, and December, 1686; January, 1687; and June, July, and September, 1688.

136 Gabory, *op. cit.,* p. 262.

marine increased from 32 vessels in May, 1664, to a peak of 105 in August, 1682; it then fell to 65 in January, 1687, to 53 in November, 1689, and to only 36 in December, 1690.[137] Since Protestants figured prominently in La Rochelle's shipping industry, religious persecution may have been a significant factor in the decline.

The shrinkage in France's foreign and domestic trade, the destruction or capture of her merchantmen by enemy privateers and warships in the War of the League of Augsburg and the War of the Spanish Succession, the conscription of seamen in the royal navy (which boosted the number on the reserve rolls from 52,000 to 90,000),[138] and the general depression which hung like a pall over the economy from 1684 to 1717, all help to explain why the merchant marine failed to maintain the prominence it had achieved under Colbert. The defection of Protestant seamen certainly did not help matters, but probably no port suffered from this as much as La Rochelle. There had never been large nuclei of Protestants at Marseille, Toulon, Bayonne, Brest, Saint-Malo, and Nantes; and no evidence has come to light to suggest that shipowners in these places were unable to assemble crews because Huguenots had fled. The 2,000 to 3,000 sailors and captains who might have left France because of religion represented only slightly more than 2 or 3 per cent of the total number registered on the reserve rolls of the king's navy. Stated somewhat differently, the flight of Protestant seamen must have deprived the merchant marine of only one-nineteenth or one-thirteenth the man power it lost through the conscription of 38,000 sailors during the Augsburg war. The chances are that from 2,000 to 5,000 men in the royal navy perished in combat or died of disease and thereby reduced the long-run supply of maritime labor by at least as much as the desertion of Huguenots. In the absence of convincing evidence to the contrary, therefore, it seems reasonable to conclude that religious persecution was not the paramount depressant of French shipping.

Whether the revocation seriously damaged France's trade and shipping by driving some of her most capable merchants and

---

137 Boissonnade, *op. cit.*, pp. 2, 14, 17, 44–45. For some inexplicable reason Boissonnade is inconsistent on the figure for 1682. On one page he says that there were 105 vessels; elsewhere in his article he adds 89 to 16 to arrive at 106; and in still another place he says there were 118.

138 Cole, *op. cit.*, p. 106.

seamen abroad or by embarrassing and shackling those who remained at home is not an easy question to answer. The quantitative data available on the volume of trade in the critical years are not sufficient to support the generalization that commercial activity declined more in seaports and areas where Protestants occupied key positions than in other commercial centers. Since government officials frequently reported that emigration was endangering trade in a certain city, or was undermining shipping in a certain port along the Atlantic, it is understandable that an impressionable individual might conclude that the revocation had been a grievous economic blunder. No economic historian in the twentieth century can afford to overlook such reports, but he should read them critically, remembering always that some officials were not above coloring the facts or choosing the data that would best suit their purposes, and that they often attributed economic difficulties to whatever was most unpopular at the time or happened to be uppermost in the public's or the king's mind. Some agents were not astute enough to recognize and rank causal factors according to relative importance, and their interpretations, however suggestive, cannot be accepted uncritically. The economic historian must also bear in mind the kind and the quantity of information he would need, under ideal conditions, to argue convincingly that the revocation had disastrous effects upon trade and shipping. He would then see the inadequacies and shortcomings of his actual data, and could better judge how to employ the information at hand.

There is little reason to doubt that French foreign and domestic trade declined after 1683, and that some 200,000 Huguenots, including many important merchants and perhaps 2,000 or 3,000 seamen, fled abroad and helped other countries develop their trade, their merchant marines, and certain "infant" industries. Severalfold this number remained at home and tried to continue in business. Whether or not they underwent the formality of accepting Catholicism, they had to cope with greater social, political, and economic discrimination than their immediate forebears had faced, and hence found it more difficult to carry on trade. The debt moratorium for new converts, the confiscation of property belonging to those who emigrated or who died after repudiating their conversion, the suspicious prying into Protestants' activities, the necessity of obtaining passports when business carried them out of the country, the restrictions on carrying arms when they traveled and on sending their children abroad to be educated, the attempts to ease them out of important positions in trade and shipping, and the patroling and inspecting of vessels and shipments in order to detect stowaways and illicit exports of wealth—in short, nearly all the regulations designed to prevent emigration and to encourage conversions interfered in one way or another with normal commercial activity. It is true that the government, especially while Seignelay was alive, tried to keep these regulations from unduly harming trade and modified them whenever it felt the need was great enough. It is equally significant, however, that the king never eliminated all the friction and embarrassment caused merchants. He refused to rescind any legislative act once he had adopted it. The task of evaluation is even more difficult because, after 1683, such factors as war, monetary and fiscal difficulties, tariffs, and economic regimentation could, singly or collectively, have caused all the commercial decline.

In view of the foregoing evidence, is it reasonable to conclude that the revocation seriously hurt French trade and shipping? Unquestionably, Louis's attempt to free his realm of heresy created difficulties which might otherwise have been avoided. Emigrant merchants probably carried away with them more tangible wealth than manufacturers and artisans; and their departure may have caused commercial crises in certain communities. Sometimes, however, other persons were able to step into the vacancies left by refugees, or the refugees themselves, while residing abroad, were able to continue their business in France through relatives or brokers. After all, French trade and shipping expanded with remarkable speed between 1717 and 1789. The increase in discrimination and penalization seems to have spurred Huguenots and new converts who remained in France to even greater endeavor and success. It would be rash to conclude that the revocation did not depress commerce in the latter half of Louis XIV's reign, but it would be equally rash to conclude that it destroyed trade and shipping or that it was primarily responsible for the secular stagnation that beset the economy after 1683.

IX

Effects of the Revocation on Finance and Agriculture

FINANCE

Not only did Huguenots occupy important positions in certain industries and figure prominently in both foreign and domestic trade, but many of them had also become influential in French financial circles before 1685. Foreign Protestants residing in such cities as Lyon, Paris, Bordeaux, and Nantes also had a hand in banking. Most historians have thought that religious persecution drove so many bankers and wealthy individuals abroad that the supply of loanable funds on the French market declined drastically, thereby pushing interest rates up and embarrassing businessmen who needed short- or long-term credit.

It is impossible to say whether most Protestant financiers of French or foreign nationality left the country or whether relatively more of them fled than manufacturers and merchants. Some financiers escaped abroad, like the brothers Marc and Jean-Henri Huguetan at Lyon;[1] many others bowed to the king's wishes and abjured, as did the wealthy Parisian banker Samuel Bernard. Most German financiers at Lyon hastily returned to their native land after the revocation edict appeared;[2] yet nearly all the Swiss bankers remained, and their number actually increased in the eighteenth century.[3] One might expect, a priori, that religious persecution uprooted financiers rather easily. Their assets were usually in the form of cash or credit instruments,

---

[1] André-E. Sayous, "Le Financier Jean-Henri Huguetan à Amsterdam et à Genève," *Société d'histoire et d'archéologie de Genève*, VI (1937), 255–274.

[2] Émile Levasseur, *Histoire du commerce de la France* (Paris, 1911), I, 421.

[3] Natalis Rondot, *Les Protestants à Lyon au dix-septième siècle* (Lyon, 1891), p. 33.

and they frequently had important investments abroad. Hence they could easily salvage most of their wealth when they emigrated, whereas manufacturers, whose assets were ordinarily in the form of real and tangible personal property, could liquidate only at a large discount and only with considerable risk of detection.

The large majority of people living at that time confused money with wealth, and they regarded the real or imaginary export of specie as one of the worst consequences of the revocation. Bouchu, as intendant in Dauphiné, warned the government in 1687 that emigration might drain the country of gold and silver.[4] The Venetian ambassador at Louis's court reported in 1688 that wealthy Huguenots were exporting or burying their hoards of precious metals in order to keep them from falling into the king's hands.[5] The deputy of trade from Bayonne in 1701, and another Frenchman in 1704, accused Huguenots of having smuggled "an infinite quantity of gold and silver" out of the country. And two individuals, one of whom was probably the Archbishop of Paris, stated in 1698 that the drainage of specie and the loss of many able-bodied men convincingly demonstrated that coercion had not been the most desirable way to win conversions.[6] Others bemoaned "the prodigious quantity of French money found in neighboring countries" and "the flight of an infinite number of Protestant families who carried abroad the most dependable part of our monetary riches."[7]

---

[4] Archives Nationales, G7 240; TT 243, *dossier* 4, doc. 37.

[5] Henry Austen Layard, "The Revocation of the Edict of Nantes. Illustrated from State Papers in the Archives of Venice," *Proceedings of the Huguenot Society of London* (hereinafter cited as *PHSL*), II (1887–1888), 150.

[6] Archives Nationales, G7 1687; Bibliothèque Nationale, *Fonds français*, MSS 7045, fols. 77, 205; 8038, fols. 434–435.

[7] [Charles Ancillon], *La France intéressée à rétablir l'Édit de Nantes* (Amsterdam, 1690), pp. 135 ff., 142–143; François Véron Duverger de Forbonnais, *Recherches et considérations sur les finances de France depuis 1595 jusqu'en 1721* (Liége, 1758), III, 305; *Testament politique du Marquis de Louvois, premier ministre d'Etat sous le Règne de Louis XIV, Roy de France, où l'on voit ce qui s'est passé de plus remarquable en France jusqu'à sa mort* (Cologne, 1695), p. 370. See also Adam Anderson, *An Historical and Chronological Deduction of the Origin of Commerce, from the Earliest Accounts etc.* (London, 1801), II, 568, 569; David C. A. Agnew, *Protestant Exiles from France in the Reign of Louis XIV; or, The Huguenot Refugees and their Descendants in Great Britain and Ireland* (2d ed.; London, 1871–1874), II, 240; *Bulletin de la société de l'histoire du protestantisme français* (hereinafter cited as *BSHPF*), XXIX (1880), 190; W. Cunningham, *Alien Immigrants to England* (London, 1897), p. 228; M. Ménard, *Histoire civile, ecclésiastique et littéraire de la ville de Nismes avec des notes et les preuves*, VI (Paris, 1755), 291; Johann-Caspar Moerikofer, *Histoire des réfugiés de la Réforme en Suisse*, trans. G. Roux (Paris, 1878), p. 240.

How much wealth and specie fugitives spirited out is not known. Contemporary and later observers have tried to estimate the number who fled and the amount they took with them, but their calculations vary widely. Antoine Court, preaching and writing in exile in the first half of the eighteenth century, thought that France had lost about 1 billion livres;[8] and Pierre Jurieu, the great theologian, expressed the opinion on June 1, 1688, that fellow Religionists had taken out about 150 million livres in specie and, in addition, had robbed France of approximately 400 million livres of real wealth which yielded 20 million livres in annual revenue.[9] At the other extreme, Abbé Novi de Caveirac estimated that the circulating media in France averaged only 25 livres per person, and hence that Protestants could have taken out no more than 5 million or 1.25 million livres, depending upon whether 200,000 or only 50,000 had emigrated. Even if the larger figure was the more realistic, he pointed out, it was unlikely that the economy had suffered serious damage. Much larger sums were lost in other ways. France sent 4 million livres abroad each year, he contended, to pay for imports, and warfare had forced Louis to "spread more gold and silver . . . [in Germany] than twenty revocation edicts could have done."[10] According to one methodical scholar, Huguenots withdrew approximately 14 million livres from Paris alone after 1681;[11] a less cautious historian estimated that altogether France lost about 360 million livres in specie.[12] Adam Anderson believed that Great Britain alone gained some £3 million.[13] Although admitting

8 *Le Patriote françois et impartial ou reponse à la lettre de M*ʳ *l'evêque d'Agen à M*ʳ *le controleur genéral contre la Tolerance des Huguenots, en datte du 1 mai 1751* (new ed.; Villefranche, 1753), I, 379.

9 *Lettres pastorales addressées aux fidèles de France, qui gemissent sous la captivité de Babylone* (4th ed.; Rotterdam, 1687–1688), II, 151. Jurieu thought that many of the 200,000 who fled took with them 50,000, 100,000, or 200,000 livres or even more; "certain families from Lyon have withdrawn 500,000 to 600,000 livres." Charles Weiss, in quoting Jurieu, for some inexplicable reason raised this last figure to 600,000 *écus* (or 1,800,000 livres) (*Histoire des réfugiés protestants de France depuis la révocation de l'Édit de Nantes jusqu'à nos jours* [Paris, 1853], I, 132).

10 *Apologie de Louis XIV et de son conseil, sur la révocation de l'Edit de Nantes, etc.* (n.p., 1758), pp. 90 ff., 96–97.

11 Emmanuel-Orentin Douen, *La Révocation de l'Édit de Nantes à Paris d'après des documents inédits* (Paris, 1894), II, 429.

12 Camille Rabaud, *Histoire du protestantisme dans l'Albigeois et le Lauragais depuis la révocation de l'édit de Nantes (1685) jusqu'à nos jours* (Paris, 1898), pp. 87–88.

13 *Op. cit.*, II, 569. See also David MacPherson, *Annals of Commerce, Manufactures, Fisheries, and Navigation etc.* (London, 1805), II, 617.

that the wealthiest refugees chose England and Holland as their asylum, Erman and Reclam pointed out that large quantities of "old louis" were still circulating in Prussia at the end of the eighteenth century, and cited one historian who had estimated in 1751 that refugees from Metz had brought 2 million *écus* into Brandenburg.[14]

Government records for the years immediately after the revocation contain a few references to the specie France lost. D'Avaux, the French ambassador at The Hague, wrote Louis on October 11, 1685, that he had just learned from an informant that Huguenots were planning to smuggle out about 20 million livres in property and money; [15] on October 23, 1687, he reported that refugee funds had so inundated the Dutch money market that financiers in Amsterdam could hardly find borrowers at 2 per cent interest. He confidently affirmed that the London mint had recently recoined 960,000 gold louis.[16] The intendant at Lyon told the controller general on May 30, 1688, that Huguenots had taken away from that city "more than" 2 million livres; four days later he wrote: "Had I been at Lyon at the time of the revocation, I could have prevented the removal of more than 4 million livres." [17] Louis's official representative in Switzerland reported on May 31, 1687, that three brothers at Geneva supposedly had withdrawn "more than" 1 million livres from Dauphiné and Lyonnais since the revocation.[18]

Both Forbonnais[19] and Ambroise Arnould[20] estimated that the amount of silver in France decreased appreciably between 1683 and 1697. The former attributed the decline primarily to a flight of specie caused by fear of debasement; the latter, esti-

14 *Mémoires pour servir à l'histoire de réfugiés françois dans les états du Roi* (Berlin, 1782–1799), I, 318–319; II, 31. Helmut Erbe, more recently, has affirmed that of all the refugees settling in Prussia only those from Metz had been able to bring much money with them (*Die Hugenotten in Deutschland* [Essen, 1937], p. 40).

15 Archives du Ministère des Affaires Étrangères, *Ancien fonds*, "Hollande," *registre* 146, fols. 110–111. A week later, however, d'Avaux wrote that he had since become convinced that his informant had been listening only to vague rumors.

16 *Ibid.*, *registre* 152, fols. 107–109. See also Weiss, *op. cit.*, II, 19; J. Arnal, "De l'Influence des réfugiés français aux Pays-Bas," *Bulletin de la commission pour l'histoire des églises wallonnes*, 4th series, 2d issue (1929), p. 4; Samuel Smiles, *The Huguenots, Their Settlements, Churches, and Industries in England and Ireland* (6th ed.; London, 1889), p. 263.

17 Archives Nationales, G7 356.

18 Archives du Ministère des Affaires Étrangères, *Ancien fonds*, "Suisse," *registre* 83, fol. 453.

19 *Op. cit.*, IV, 98, 137.

20 *De la Balance du commerce et des relations commerciales extérieures de la France* . . . (Paris, 1791), II, 195–198, 200 ff., 205.

mating the loss at 20 per cent of the total stock, held Louis's military expenditures abroad as well as the emigration of Huguenots responsible.

Even though it is impossible at the present time to determine whether any of these estimates are realistic, it appears probable that refugees helped to reduce France's stock of precious metals. Many Huguenots were rich; others were well-to-do. Many of the 200,000 who successfully eluded or bribed guards at the frontiers must have been resourceful enough to smuggle out all or part of their worldly possessions. In 1685–1688 Louis's representatives in Holland were constantly sending back reports of refugees who had arrived there with credit instruments or large sums of money concealed on their persons. The parents of two refugees from Bas-Poitou, they said, had already sent "more than" 50,000 livres to Holland by October, 1685; the wife of a wealthy Parisian banker had come to Amsterdam with a considerable quantity of gold and silver; a coach from Paris had arrived at Brussels with 17,000 livres in gold; a certain shipmaster from Rotterdam had been instrumental in getting "more than" 500,000 livres out of France; and a guide in the vicinity of Royan had supposedly led to safety some 112 persons who together brought out 36,000 or 37,000 *écus*. The French agents at The Hague reported that a Parisian had sent 30,000 livres to Holland before he himself arrived, and mentioned several other individuals who had salvaged up to 50,000, 100,000, or even 150,000 livres. The ambassador himself affirmed in a letter to His Majesty on March 15, 1686, that several Huguenot refugees had recently offered to lend the province of Friesland 1 million livres at current interest.[21]

Other sources shed light on how much wealth and specie certain refugees took with them. Authorities at Saint-Quentin, for example, complained on September 18, 1685, that in the past week three individuals had withdrawn 200,000 livres in money and other possessions;[22] a collector of the taille at Périgueux reportedly left in 1685 with 80,000 *écus;* and a wealthy merchant

21 Archives Nationales, B2 *registres* 58, fol. 529; 65, fol. 38; B3 *registre* 57, fols. 38–40; TT 430, doc. 100; Archives du Ministère des Affaires Étrangères, *Ancien fonds,* "Hollande," *registres* 143, fols. 183–184; 145, fols. 207, 240; 148, fols. 162, 220–221; 149, *passim.*

22 Archives Nationales, G7 85; A. M. de Boislisle, *Correspondance des contrôleurs généraux des finances avec les intendants des provinces,* I (Paris, 1874), 56; Alfred Daullé, *La Réforme à Saint-Quentin et aux environs, du XVIᵉ siècle à la fin du XVIIIᵉ siècle* (Le Cateau, 1901), p. 183.

at Rouen had sent his wife and "more than" 200,000 livres ahead of him to Holland before he himself died on the eve of departure. The intendant at Lyon wrote on February 24, 1689, that one Solomon Negret had recently smuggled 300,000 livres into Zurich, and in July he warned officials at Paris that Marc Huguetan had escaped from Lyon with 200,000 or 300,000 livres of his family's fortune, leaving his brother Jean-Henri behind to liquidate the remainder.[23] A certain young lady of Protestant background who had accepted Catholicism sought permission from the king's council to enter a particular convent because, she claimed, her father had fled with "more than" 500,000 livres and had left her penniless.[24] One of the police commissioners in Paris informed his superior on November 8, 1685, that he suspected several wealthy Protestants—some of whom he mentioned by name—of converting their wealth into cash. Although these men no longer engaged in trade, he said, they frequented the money market and conspired with one another as how best to get their money out of the country: "Some well-informed persons have assured me that these merchants have withdrawn 14 million livres from ordinary commercial channels."[25] A tax farmer at La Rochelle complained on October 20, 1699, that two wealthy merchants had escaped three days earlier with an undetermined but probably large sum of gold and silver. One of them had always paid at least 45,000 to 50,000 livres in excise taxes each year.[26] As late as 1742 and 1751 well-to-do Huguenots in the Montpellier area were still fleeing; one merchant draper supposedly left with 400,000 livres, another with 75,000 livres, and several others with 480,000 livres in silver among them.[27] When a French refugee was nominated in 1719 for a public office in Brandenburg, it is interesting to note in passing, his most telling campaign argument was that he had helped fellow Religionists at Metz bring "more than" 600,000 livres into his adopted country.[28]

Many who tried to smuggle out money were caught. In Sep-

---

23 Archives Nationales, G⁷ 133, 356; A¹ 903, doc. 46; TT 85, *dossier* 27, doc. 164.

24 *Ibid.,* TT 435, *dossier* 6.

25 Bibliothèque Nationale, *Fonds français,* MS 7051, fols. 149–150.

26 Archives Nationales, G⁷ 338.

27 Philippe Corbière, *Histoire de l'Église Réformée de Montpellier depuis son origine jusqu'à nos jours* (Montpellier, 1861), p. 296. Corbière got his information from the intendant's files.

28 Erman and Reclam, *op. cit.,* II, 32. One of the descendants of these refugees claimed in 1782 that a Protestant from Normandy had taken 40,000 *écus* into Germany (Bibliothèque Nationale, *Fonds français,* MS 6432, fol. 151).

tember, 1688, two Swiss bankers at Lyon lost 13,800 livres in silver which they had hidden in four parcels addressed to correspondents in Switzerland. The intendant seized the parcels because he suspected the bankers of aiding French Protestants.[29] A judge of the admiralty at La Rochelle was apprehended at Lyon in February, 1686, when he sought to gain Switzerland with 61,200 livres in letters of exchange concealed on his person.[30] And local authorities discovered in the same month that a widow at Nîmes whom they accused of having sent her children to Geneva had bills of exchange totaling 61,896 livres hidden in her strongbox.[31]

All such information is too fragmentary and unreliable for estimating the total amount of specie and wealth France lost as a result of the revocation. In the first place, the process whereby the data were selected and made available probably had an inherent bias. It is unlikely that individual cases that found their way into government records were typical. Unspectacular departures and those involving small sums of money would not elicit the attention of high-ranking officials or give rise to written reports. Most refugees were probably unable to salvage much of their property. In the second place, many sums cited in extant documents do not seem reliable. Figures so well rounded could have originated only in hearsay or guesswork. The scattered bits of information taken together, however, do indicate (1) that persons close to the king were wrong in predicting that material self-interest bound wealthy Protestants so tightly to France that she ran little danger of losing them, and (2) that the government's heroic efforts to prevent refugees from taking all or part of their wealth with them were not entirely successful.

Because Louis confiscated all property left behind by either new converts or Protestants who departed the realm without permission, Huguenots planning to flee tried feverishly to liquidate their possessions in the hope of smuggling them out of the country in the form of money or credit instruments. The first panicky wave of selling property at whatever price it would bring got under way in Poitou soon after the intendant there brought in royal dragoons in 1681.[32] Thereafter, Protestants throughout France who had any thought of leaving the country borrowed

29 Archives Nationales, G7 356.
30 Bibliothèque de la Société Protestante, MS 444, fol. 189.
31 Archives Nationales, TT 449I, *dossier* 25, docs. 119, 120.
32 *Ibid.,* G7 356.

as much as they could from members of their own sect or from unsuspecting or sympathetic Catholics, called for immediate payment of loans, and withdrew their funds as quickly as possible from the market.[33] Some persons, observing this sudden increase in the preference for liquidity, suggested that Protestants be prohibited from acquiring intangible property.[34] The government, however, could not adopt such a suggestion without ruining thousands of merchants and businessmen who had no intention of emigrating, and yet whose economic activities at times required them to keep a large part of their operating capital in the form of money or credit instruments. Many officials pointed out that they were powerless to check the outflow of wealth so long as merchants found it possible to escape.[35] Protestant merchants experienced little difficulty in buying exchange and letters of credit from Catholic bankers in all large cities, from government agents in Paris and elsewhere,[36] from Swiss financiers at Lyon,[37] and from foreign diplomatic representatives residing in France.[38]

Stagecoaches and both foreign and French vessels regularly carried disguised shipments of bullion and specie for Protestants.[39] Gold and silver were frequently concealed in casks of wine or brandy, in barrels of ashes, in crates of prunes, or in packages of other merchandise.[40] Immediately after 1685 merchants from Protestant countries calling at Bordeaux and other ports fictitiously purchased plate and jewelry which Huguenots

---

[33] *Ibid.*, TT 85, *dossier* 27, doc. 164; 430, doc. 97; 431, doc. 42; 449[I], *dossier* 25, docs. 119, 120; Bibliothèque Nationale, *Fonds français*, MSS 7050, fols. 256–257; 7051, fols. 149–150; Bibliothèque de la Société Protestante, MSS 444, fol. 189; 485[VI], fol. 93; Layard, *op. cit.*, p. 140.

[34] Archives Nationales, TT 243, *dossier* 4, doc. 37; Bibliothèque Nationale, *Fonds français*, MS 7050, fols. 256–257.

[35] Archives Nationales, G⁷ 133, 356; Bibliothèque de la Société Protestante, MS 444, fol. 222; Boislisle, *op. cit.*, I, 90–91; B. Vaurigaud, *Essai sur l'histoire des églises réformées de Bretagne, 1535–1808* (Paris, 1870), III, 61–62, 90.

[36] Archives Nationales, B³ *registre* 57, fol. 43; Archives du Ministère des Affaires Étrangères, *Ancien fonds*, "Hollande," *registre* 143, fols. 183–184.

[37] Archives Nationales, G⁷ 356; A¹ 903, doc. 46; Bibliothèque de la Société Protestante, MS 444, fol. 172.

[38] Bibliothèque Nationale, *Fonds français*, MS 7052, fol. 322; Archives du Ministère des Affaires Étrangères, *Ancien fonds*, "Hollande," *registre* 143, fol. 170.

[39] Archives Nationales, B² *registres* 45, fol. 349; 65, fol. 38; Archives du Ministère des Affaires Étrangères, *Ancien fonds*, "Hollande," *registre* 143, fol. 184.

[40] Archives Nationales, TT 430, doc. 100; A¹ 775; B² *registres* 53, fols. 209–210; 55, fol. 505; Archives du Ministère des Affaires Étrangères, *Ancien fonds*, "Hollande," *registre* 149, fol. 305; Boislisle, *op. cit.*, I, 144; Vaurigaud, *op. cit.*, III, 30–31.

were anxious to get out of the country;[41] and exports by French Protestants engaged in foreign trade suddenly increased. Officials noted, for example, that a particular wine merchant at Bordeaux was shipping unusually large quantities of wine abroad and suspected him of transferring his wealth out of the country in this manner.[42] According to a letter written from Holland in 1687, Huguenots had already robbed France of wealth valued at "more than" 8 million livres by shipping it out in the form of merchandise.[43]

Protestants devised many subterfuges for circumventing the laws forbidding them to sell their possessions before they left. They mortgaged their property, for example, with Catholics and other Protestants, or they simulated other debts. Then they declared bankruptcy before they left France, thereby allowing the lenders to gain legal possession of the property. If the borrowers fled before they went into bankruptcy, their creditors could still foreclose. Some Protestants first secretly sold their property outright to friends for cash, then signed promissory notes for the amount of the sale to make the transaction appear like a loan, and finally declared bankruptcy so their friends could legally gain possession of what they had actually bought. In this way they avoided the risk of subsequent confiscation by the state. That the government was able to do little to break up such procedures is attested by frequent complaints as late as 1723 that Protestants were obtaining royal permission to sell assets in order to pay fictitious debts. Some refugees, before leaving France, turned over their real property to friends in exchange for an annual income. On July 26, 1686, the king decreed severe penalties for anyone who helped Huguenots falsify their indebtedness; yet neither he nor his advisers were able to devise a feasible way of distinguishing between bona fide and simulated indebtedness.[44]

Many Protestants escaped abroad knowing full well that their

---

41 Archives Nationales, A1 773; B2 *registre* 58, fol. 613; Bibliothèque de la Société Protestante, MS 444, fol. 215.

42 Archives du Ministère des Affaires Étrangères, *Ancien fonds*, "Hollande," *registre* 148, fols. 164–165.

43 *BSHPF*, XLIII (1894), 190.

44 Archives Nationales, G7 134, 240; O1 *registres* 30, fols. 250–251; 42, fols. 68–69; TT 264, *dossier* 14, doc. 63, and *dossier* 15, doc. 67; 430, doc. 97; 436, "1723 Memorandum of the Bishop of Nantes";B2 *registre* 58, fol. 694; Bibliothèque de la Société Protestante, MSS 485II, fol. 48; 485VI, fol. 93.

property would be confiscated. Until September, 1699, the law stipulated that their nearest of kin, whether newly converted or regular Catholic, could then claim possession. The refugee believed that family ties would prove stronger than differences in religion and that his relative would manage the property for him and remit regularly all the revenues derived therefrom.[45] One scholar of the late eighteenth century thought that in this way refugees from the vicinity of Marennes and La Rochelle alone received approximately 2.5 million livres in annual income![46] Thus it was possible for some refugees to find liberty of conscience abroad without sacrificing the revenues from worldly possessions left in France.

If the revocation occasioned an appreciable decline in France's specie and in her supply of loanable funds, as many writers and much of the preceding evidence have suggested, there should have been repercussions on the capital and money markets both at home and abroad. Reliable information on this particular point is scant. But even if complete time series for short-term and long-term interest rates, for foreign exchange rates, and for specie exports were available, it would still be difficult to link the trends in these series to the activities of Huguenots. Other contemporary forces, such as frequent revaluations of French currency, wars and threats of war, tariffs, and more or less "normal" shifts in the balance of payments, affected the capital and money markets. How can one disentangle all the forces and attribute to each its net effect? In the absence of reliable figures for the purchasing power taken out by Huguenots, inferences must be drawn from qualitative data.

The wealthiest Protestants, it seems, sought refuge either in Holland or in England; relatively few of those who settled in Germany and Switzerland were well-to-do. Bonrepaus wrote from England on February 11, 1686, that as much as 500,000 pistoles

---

45 Archives Nationales, G⁷ 134, 356; TT 430, doc. 100; 435, *dossier* 3; 449ᴵᴵ, *dossier* 27, doc. 149; Archives du Ministère des Affaires Étrangères, *Ancien fonds,* "Hollande," *registre* 145, fol. 13; Bibliothèque Nationale, *Fonds français*, MS 21618, fols. 92 ff.; Bibliothèque de la Société Protestante, MS 444, fol. 229; François Baudry, *La Révocation de l'édit de Nantes et le protestantisme en Bas-Poitou au XVIIIᵉ siècle* (Trévoux, 1922), p. 273 and n. 4.

46 Claude-Carlomau de Rulhière, as quoted in Ernest Lavisse and others, *Histoire de France illustrée depuis les origines jusqu'à la révolution* (Paris, 1911), Vol. VIII, Part 1, p. 345.

had reached that country in 1685 and that the London exchange rate on the *écu* had fallen from 56s. or 57s. to 52s. or 53s. He attributed this both to the unfavorable trade balance and to the facility with which gold could be smuggled from France. He reported a week later that when he let it be known that thereafter it would be almost impossible to get gold from his country, the rate of exchange rose to 55s. and showed every indication of reaching 56s. On March 28 he jubilantly wrote that since his letter of February 18 no French specie had arrived in England.[47] Normally, the threat of an embargo on French specie exports would have depressed, rather than improved, the exchange rate of the *écu* in London, and an actual embargo would have caused it to fall below the specie import point in London. If Bonrepaus faithfully reported the facts, and if no exogenous influences suddenly pulled the exchange rate in the opposite direction, Englishmen and Huguenots who held balances in France must really have accepted Bonrepaus's propaganda and stopped trying to convert their money into English pounds. A decrease in the number of *écus* seeking English pounds would have stiffened the price of French money in London. When it became apparent, however, that the French government could not successfully prevent gold from leaving, the rate must have fallen again to the London gold import point (or risen to the French gold export point). Otherwise, the French ambassador in Holland could not have written in October, 1687, that 960,000 gold louis had recently been melted and recoined at the London mint. It is evident that not all Huguenots arrived penniless in England, for after 1690 many of them invested in the public debt, loaned money to the City of London, held stock in the Million Bank and the Bank of England, cashed winning tickets in government lotteries, and took shares in the South Sea and the East India companies.[48]

The evidence that Huguenots caused a drain of specie is more ample for Holland than for England. They purportedly took so large a supply of loanable funds to Amsterdam that the interest rate there fell and wealthy Dutchmen were irked because they could not lend at more than 2 per cent. A group of refugees

---

47 Archives du Ministère des Affaires Étrangères, *Ancien fonds*, "Angleterre," *registre* 157, fols. 61–62, 72, 100.

48 Alice C. Carter, "The Huguenot Contribution to the Early Years of the Funded Debt, 1694–1714," *PHSL*, XIX (1955), 21 ff.

TABLE 3

QUINQUENNIAL AVERAGES OF DEPOSITS AND METAL RESERVES
OF THE BANK OF AMSTERDAM, 1651–1750

(In millions of guilders)

Quinquennium	Deposits	Reserves	Quinquennium	Deposits	Reserves
1651–1655	7.99	7.18	1701–1705	12.94	10.61
1656–1660	7.01	6.33	1706–1710	10.06	8.69
1661–1665	8.32	7.27	1711–1715	11.18	9.08
1666–1670	6.84	5.68	1716–1720	17.04	16.33
1671–1675	6.92	6.22	1721–1725	25.82	23.44
1676–1680	5.95	4.50	1726–1730	17.47	13.90
1681–1685	7.55	6.64	1731–1735	20.95	18.91
1686–1690	11.21	9.77	1736–1740	20.03	15.35
1691–1695	12.75	11.68	1741–1745	18.51	12.08
1696–1700	13.75	11.44	1746–1750	15.50	12.33

SOURCE: J. G. Van Dillen, *Bronnen tot de Geshiedenis der Wisselbanken (Amsterdam, Middelburg, Delft, Rotterdam)* (2 vols.; 'S-Gravenhage, 1925), II, 963–965.

offered in 1686 to lend the government of Friesland 1 million livres at current interest. Table 3 demonstrates that both deposits and metal reserves in the Bank of Amsterdam increased significantly after 1685. The number of its depositors also rose by about one-third. It is reasonable to infer that religious persecution in France had at least something to do with these increases. Jean Meuvret has pointed out that the sudden increase in the bank's reserves and deposits occurred in the same year as the revocation of the Edict of Nantes "with all the exodus of capital which this implies."[49] According to a letter written on November 8, 1685, by a member of France's diplomatic staff at The Hague, William was trying to strengthen his argument that Louis XIV had revoked the Edict of Nantes for political reasons by claiming that Louis knew he would have to pay a great price, and yet was willing to pay it. The "price" that Louis had been willing to pay for the presumed political advantages in Europe was the loss of many subjects "as well as very considerable sums [of specie] which he knew to be passing into the banks of Amsterdam and Venice."[50]

---

[49] "Les Mouvements des prix de 1661 à 1715 et leurs répercussions" (communication to the Société de Statistique de Paris, May 17, 1944), p. 4.

[50] Archives du Ministère des Affaires Étrangères, *Ancien fonds,* "Hollande," *registre* 143, fols. 147–148.

Rébenac, Louis's representative at the court of Brandenburg, thought that the revocation had not driven much specie into Germany. On February 5, 1686, he wrote:

As to money, Sire, I have only one bit of evidence to cite. . . . As to the little that is necessary for me, I find a 3 per cent increase in the exchange rate in my favor since the revocation, and the rate rises daily instead of decreasing by 8 or 9 per cent as it did in the past four years. This indicates that much less money is leaving your realm these days than before the edict.[51]

Whether the increase in the exchange rate was only seasonal or temporary, or whether it persisted over a considerable period of time, is not known. Neither is it definitely known what caused the improvement. Other bits of information leave the impression that Huguenots did not take a great deal of money capital into Germany.

Since complaints about the scarcity of loanable funds and specie on various local markets in France were common throughout the reign of Louis XIV, it is difficult to judge when the real or imaginary shortages were greatest. Individuals, then as now, rarely had enough money to buy all they wanted, or to pay taxes. They were also prone, then as now, to attribute economic difficulties to the unavailability of funds. Nevertheless, it is significant for our purposes that some people held the Huguenots responsible for money shortages at one time or another. The intendant in Dauphiné, for example, after remarking on August 29, 1687, that "on my frequent trips through my province I have noticed that the supply of money has diminished considerably" and that "trade and even the king's revenue from taxes might suffer therefrom," attributed most of the scarcity to the export of specie by Protestants. A group of merchants at Tours complained earlier (April 13, 1685) that several Huguenot debtors had fled without first settling their accounts and that the resulting drainage of funds had hurt business.[52] The revocation presumably caused Alençon to lose a large number of its inhabitants as well as considerable wealth.[53] And an anonymous writer, addressing himself to the Duke of Orléans, claimed that the scarcity of money stemmed entirely from religious persecution

51 *Ibid.*, "Prusse," *registre* 26, fols. 75–76.
52 Archives Nationales, G7 240, 519.
53 Bibliothèque Nationale, *Fonds français*, MS 4286, fol. 102.

which had driven specie from the country and had forced Protestants remaining in France to withdraw from business. He went on to explain that no one had dared suggest such was the cause, for "each person, having particular causes in mind which he prefers to the general, follows his own interest."[54]

Perhaps others would have openly blamed the Huguenots had they not been afraid of displeasing their king. In any event, some thought that other factors were important. According to the intendant at Rouen in 1703, although "the retreat of Calvinists, long wars, and weakness in our trade have occasioned a loss of specie, . . . diverse monetary regulations during the past fifteen or sixteen years have occasioned an even larger loss and have prevented the reëntry of gold and silver into the realm."[55] The intendant at Bordeaux, commenting the same year upon the shortage of loanable funds, denied that Huguenots were responsible. "No one at all," he said, "has perceived for some time now that they are transporting their effects abroad."[56] Whereas the government itself had been able to borrow at 5 per cent in 1688, it had to pay 7.14 per cent in 1694 and 8.33 per cent in 1696.[57]

GOVERNMENT FINANCE

In an earlier chapter I have described the fiscal difficulties confronting the government after 1683. While two major wars were causing expenditures to skyrocket, net revenues from taxes shrank as the national income declined and the costs of collection mounted. Facing a rapidly increasing annual deficit, the government manipulated money, created and sold public offices, devised new taxes, and plunged deeper and decper into debt. Many writers have concluded that the revocation contributed to these difficulties.[58] According to them, it caused wealthy taxpayers to leave the country and reduced the taxable base by decreasing the national income and wealth; and the campaign to convert

---

54 Archives Nationales, TT 464, doc. 89.

55 Boislisle, *op. cit.*, II (1883), 157–158.

56 *Ibid.*, II, 154.

57 Forbonnais, *op. cit.*, IV, 38. In 1699 it refinanced at 5 per cent by forcing its creditors to take less.

58 See, e.g., Antoine Court's "Mémoires pour servir à l'histoire des églises réformées," in Bibliothèque de la Société Protestante, MS 628, pp. 362–363; Jurieu, *op. cit.*, II, 151; Lièvre, *op. cit.*, II, 181–182; Layard, *op. cit.*, pp. 140, 149; J.-A. Galland, *Essai sur l'histoire du Protestantisme à Caen et en Basse-Normandie de l'édit de Nantes à la Revolution (1598–1791)* (Paris, 1898), p. 258; Dom H. Leclercq, *Histoire de la Régence pendant la minorité de Louis XV* (Paris, 1921–1922), I, lxix.

all Protestants or to keep them from emigrating increased government expenditures. What is the evidence?

It was frequently said after 1685 that taxes were harder to collect and that their yields were smaller than before. A group of Protestants at Elbeuf in Normandy, for example, tried to tell friends in Holland how bad conditions in France were in the last months of 1686. Whereas their taille had formerly amounted to 1,800 livres, they wrote, they could no longer pay more than 50 livres.[59] The intendants at Bordeaux, Poitiers, and Soissons all petitioned the king in 1687 or 1688 to grant their jurisdictions tax relief because the departure of Religionists had caused trade to diminish greatly.[60] The intendant at Limoges was grateful for reductions obtained by the same argument for such villages as Saint-Jean-d'Angély, but he confessed that temporary tax relief could not effectively reëstablish prosperity. Only a general revival in economic activity, he said, could nullify the harm caused by emigration.[61] Another official wrote the controller general on March 19, 1696, that the depression was worsening in Auvergne and that residents in the parish of Job were selling the wood from their roofs for fuel in order to subsist. He pleaded for a substantial reduction in tax rates to alleviate the misery caused by the departure of wealthy Huguenots, the cessation of trade, and a high mortality rate.[62] Bouchu in Dauphiné was much more optimistic, even though his province was one of those hit hardest by emigration. He denied that tax officials were experiencing unusual difficulty in collecting the taille in 1686–1688, and assured the king that receipts from this tax in Dauphiné would not drop sharply. He admitted, however, that Protestant fugitives had been responsible for a drastic decline in trade, a marked increase in the scarcity of money, and a shrinkage in the taxable base resulting from the depreciation of their abandoned properties.[63]

Bouchu was not so optimistic about the yields from other taxes as he was about the taille. Although he thought the tax farmers

---

[59] Archives du Ministère des Affaires Étrangères, *Ancien fonds*, "Hollande," *registre* 149, fols. 368–370.

[60] Archives Nationales, G7 133, 450, 511; Boislisle, *op. cit.*, I, 97.

[61] Archives Nationales, G7 345.

[62] Boislisle, *op. cit.*, I, 419.

[63] Archives Nationales, G7 240, 241; TT 243, *dossier* 4, doc. 37. The taille in Dauphiné was real rather than personal, which means that it was assessed against property rather than against persons.

exaggerated their difficulties, he nonetheless predicted in 1687 that the customs and salt tax (gabelle) would provide less revenue than in the past because all commerce was slowing down and because less salt was being consumed by the reduced number of people and livestock in his province. Farmers of the gabelle in Upper Normandy complained in mid-1687 that they could not collect all the taxes due them because many new converts had fled and had depopulated twenty parishes around Dieppe. They asked permission to force new Catholics who still remained in their district to take the salt that had formerly been apportioned among those who had escaped. They also wanted to seize the property of anyone suspected of planning to leave the country in order to protect themselves against additional nonpayment of the gabelle. The controller general denied both requests on the ground that such action would drive more converts abroad and at the same time reduce the effectiveness of the king's efforts to repatriate those who had already left.[64]

The octroi also yielded less revenue in some places. At Caen, for example, it had been adjudicated at 156,000 livres in 1679; the figure fell to 147,500 livres in 1685, to 141,000 in 1686, and to 137,000 in 1694. The farmers to whom the octroi had been adjudicated in January, 1685, felt they had a legitimate claim for reimbursement the following year. According to them, no one had dared submit a bid in 1685 because religious troubles had made the economic outlook uncertain. Assurances that they would be reimbursed if they incurred any loss had finally led them to bid 147,500 livres. The departure of a great many Protestants, a poor fruit harvest, and the heavy garrison of troops in the winter, they claimed, had piled up their losses to "more than 20,000" livres.[65]

The farmer of the tax on raw wool in Metz lamented in 1688 that a great many Protestant drapers had fled the area and that those who remained had experienced a marked decline in their business. Consequently, his collections were less than a fourth of the amount he had expected. The controller general refused to return three-fourths of the purchase price as had been requested; but he must have been convinced that collections were down, for he remitted one-eighth of the farmer's payment. The

---

64 *Ibid.*, G7 3, 492; Boislisle, *op. cit.*, I, 105.

65 Archives Nationales, G7 214; Boislisle, *op. cit.*, I, 59; Galland, *op. cit.*, p. 256; Lavisse, *op. cit.*, Vol. VIII, Part 1, p. 343.

citizens and municipal authorities at Metz successfully petitioned the government to excuse them from paying the *taxe de subvention* for 1691, which amounted to 30,079 livres, because their city had a deficit of some 56,000 livres in 1692 and of 63,700 livres in 1693. These deficits arose, they said, because many wealthy Protestants had moved away. The king took cognizance of Metz's difficulties still a third time. When its citizens demonstrated that the city was much worse off in 1700 than in 1697, he reduced all taxes from 95,584 to 86,030 livres.[66]

The intendant in Champagne contended on January 29, 1691, that Châlons could not acquit the *ustensile*, amounting to 38,250 livres, because "most individuals on whom the tax rested have abandoned the city."[67] His colleague at Orléans informed the government on March 23, 1689, that of all the cities and towns in his *généralité* only Orléans could participate in raising money for the "gift" requested by the king. Other places like Gien, "ruined by the desertion of Religionists," could pay nothing.[68]

Not only did the revocation increase the difficulty of collecting taxes, but it also led to an expansion in public expenditures. Persuading Protestants to accept Catholicism by offering them bribes or by having missionaries visit them, policing the land and water frontiers to prevent emigration, punishing those who failed to observe the law, and seeking to repatriate those who escaped abroad all proved costly. Then, too, what the Protestant Church had formerly done in the way of looking after its own sick and needy and in educating its young people now created a financial burden for local communities. The directors and administrators of the general hospital in Rouen, for example, complained in 1686 that the city had had to increase its budget for public charity after the desertion of several rich Huguenot merchants who had formerly spent 20,000 livres a year on the poor and the sick of their religion.[69] The citizens of Vitry-le-François protested that they could not afford to construct and operate a new hospital which the king had instructed them to build to care for the indigent and to house Protestants who were

---

66 Maurice Thirion, *Étude sur l'histoire du protestantisme à Metz et dans le pays messin* (Nancy, 1884), pp. 395–397.

67 Boislisle, *op. cit.*, I, 232.

68 *Ibid.*, I, 177.

69 Archives Nationales, G7 492.

being instructed in the Catholic faith.[70] Charles Ancillon seized upon such discontent and grumbling to argue from exile in 1690 that French Catholics would benefit financially if Louis would repeal the revocation edict and allow Protestant *émigrés* to return home and live in peace. The tax burden on Catholics, Ancillon wrote, had increased appreciably from 1685 to 1689 and was mounting rapidly since war had broken out. He said that "Protestants are like trees which have been cut down at their roots and felled to the earth. There they lie like broken and sterile trunks which yield no fruit."[71]

Seventeenth- and eighteenth-century Frenchmen, like most people, were never happy about paying taxes. Even in prosperous years they moaned about their inability to pay. They seemed to delight in the competitive sport of seeking special concessions by painting conditions in their regions in as somber colors as possible. Experience had taught sensible men in government to discount heavily all such cries of distress and to disregard most of them.[72] It is quite possible, therefore, that contemporaries exaggerated local expenditures and the inability to pay or collect taxes because a great many Huguenots had left. Still, one cannot easily brush aside the fact that the king on several occasions reduced or forgave taxes. Louis was in desperate need of additional revenue. It is hard to believe that he would forego any tax revenue unless he thought conditions warranted it. The concessions he made probably did not make appreciable inroads into his net revenues. Still, if religious persecution adversely affected the taxable base by shrinking France's wealth and income after 1684, it must have contributed significantly to the Crown's fiscal difficulties. There is no convincing evidence that the revocation was primarily responsible for the shrinkage that unquestionably occurred. About the only reasonable inference is that the campaign against heresy led to reductions in tax receipts from certain areas and made it somewhat more difficult for the government to squeeze enough revenue from its highly regressive and inequitable tax structure to meet its rapidly mounting expenditures.

---

[70] G. Hérelle, *Documents inédits sur le protestantisme à Vitry-le-François, Épense, Heiltz-le-Maurupt, Nettancourt et Vassy depuis la fin des Guerres de Religion jusqu'à la Révolution française* (Paris, 1903–1908), I, 319–323.

[71] *Op. cit.*, p. 247.

[72] See chap. vi, p. 163, for the remark Nicolas Desmaretz made to this effect in 1686.

AGRICULTURE

Protestantism in France drew its strength mainly from the urban middle class; yet there were significant clusters of peasants who professed the faith in certain provinces like Dauphiné, Gex, Languedoc, and Poitou. The dragoons dispersed in these areas to win converts to Catholicism pillaged and robbed peasants without mercy. When troops approached a village, the inhabitants fled in terror, leaving their livestock unfed and untended and their fields unsown and uncultivated. The probability that crops and animals would be destroyed or confiscated by foraging bands caused peasants to forego planting and harvesting and to neglect or slaughter their livestock. Mere rumor that troops were on their way was sufficient to disrupt or suspend agricultural activities. Thousands of individuals deserted their fields near the northeastern and eastern frontiers and sought asylum in Switzerland and Germany. Much arable land lay uncultivated and rapidly reverted to wilderness; farm buildings deteriorated and property values shrank; and tax revenues dwindled as collectors found it almost impossible to perform their duties.

The standard of living of most Frenchmen, even in good years, lay precariously close to the subsistence level; and inadequate transport facilities and reluctance to share local supplies with neighboring regions interfered with the easy mobility of grain between provinces. The resulting regional or local food shortages frequently occasioned much suffering. In such a society any short-run disruption of normal agricultural routine was likely to occasion real distress. As previously indicated, France suffered two of its most severe and extensive famines in 1692–1694 and in 1709–1710. Unfavorable weather conditions were primarily responsible for these periods of dearth; yet the dislocations in agriculture occasioned by religious persecution probably made matters worse. What, then, is the evidence that the revocation of the Edict of Nantes intensified agricultural distress after 1685?

Pertinent data are even more fragmentary and less reliable than the evidence for industry, trade, and finance, because contemporary observers and government officials commented less precisely about agriculture. A possible reason for their comparative silence is that the harm was not easily discernible. Agriculture was geographically decentralized, and its ups and downs did not strike local observers as forcefully as did economic crises focalized in cities. The reason might be, of course, that agriculture did not actually suffer very much except in a few localities.

The intendants in Burgundy and Dauphiné, more so than elsewhere, showed concern over agriculture. The inhabitants of Gex, near Geneva, fled in a body in late 1685; those in the valley of Prajelas near the Italian frontier did the same in 1687, and their neighbors in the valley of Queyras and Perouse were growing more and more restless. There were times when literally thousands in these areas deserted their homes and land within a few days, taking all their movable possessions and livestock with them.[73] Many of them, it is true, returned within a few months after their hysteria had subsided, but enough of them remained out of the country to make the intendants worry over the rapid depreciation of deserted farms and the dwindling revenues from taxes. Bouchu, in particular, was alarmed. He wanted to repeople Dauphiné as soon as possible. In a long memorandum of September 27, 1687, he stated: "I cannot deny that the valley [of Prajelas] has suffered a great deal from the aforementioned desertion; yet I cannot assert that matters cannot grow even worse." He recommended that all fertile land and village properties confiscated by the king be disposed of quickly in order to prevent administrative expenses from eating up the revenue. Farms in mountainous and inaccessible places yielded just enough income to pay taxes, and they were so inhospitable that "only a blind love for one's native soil keeps anyone on them." If the Protestants who cultivated these farms left, the only solution would be to move destitute Catholics into the area and give them the land.[74] The governor of Pignerol, almost as concerned as the intendant in Dauphiné, promised in his letter of September 5, 1687, to visit the valley of Perouse in an effort to calm the inhabitants and persuade them to remain at home.[75]

The intendant in Burgundy admitted in a letter to the controller general on June 10, 1686, that religious emigration had so depopulated the area of Gex that the people who remained could not possibly consume all the grain they harvested. They

---

[73] Archives Nationales, G⁷ 240; Boislisle, *op. cit.*, I, 58, 120; Charles Charronnet, *Les Guerres de religion et la société protestante dans les Hautes-Alpes (1560–1789)* (Gap, 1861), p. 437; Edmond Chevrier, *Notice historique sur le protestantisme dans le département de l'Ain (Bresse, Bugey, Pays de Gex) et lieux circonvoisins (Savoie, Lyon, Mâcon)* (Paris, 1883), p. 236.

[74] Archives Nationales, G⁷ 240; see also TT 243, *dossier* 4, doc. 37.

[75] *Ibid.*, G⁷ 240.

needed to sell the surplus abroad, but the king had forbidden them to ship grain to Geneva, their usual market, because he wanted to punish the citizens of that city for opening their homes to religious refugees. The intendant warned that continued enforcement of the restrictions would hurt Gex more than Geneva and, by depressing farm incomes, might force additional persons to leave home.[76]

There is also some evidence that persecution hurt agriculture elsewhere. Bossuet, writing from Soissons on July 31, 1686, commented upon the damage to crops from fires, hail, storms, rodents, and "the desertions of a great many Protestants and new converts."[77] The intendant at Limoges had informed the controller general nine months earlier that dragonnades had left his district in such "great misery" that peasants were eating roots and chestnuts and were feeding their livestock brake instead of hay.[78] Many farms in Lower Poitou, which the government had confiscated after their owners emigrated, remained out of production for a long time. Their fields lay uncultivated; and, as their buildings fell into ruin, the officials charged with administering them refused to authorize repairs. One such farm at Saint-Gemme-des-Bruères remained abandoned from 1723 to 1730.[79] Vineyardists and gardeners around Metz fled, and many peasants in Saintonge and Languedoc also escaped abroad. A Swiss pastor who traveled through France in the first part of the eighteenth century could not help but notice that field after field was neglected and that whole sections of the countryside seemed deserted.[80] In 1695 an observer summarized the situation in the following manner: "France begins to need laborers especially to cultivate its land. . . . Every province suffers more from this than from any other shortage. Vineyards are abandoned [and] arable fields lie uncultivated [while] spades and sickles are being made into lances and swords."[81]

---

76 *Ibid.*, G⁷ 157; Boislisle, *op. cit.*, I, 72. The intendant in Franche-Comté was of the same opinion (Archives Nationales, G⁷ 276).

77 Archives Nationales, G⁷ 511.

78 Boislisle, *op. cit.*, I, 54.

79 Baudry, *op. cit.*, pp. 304–305. See also Auguste-François Lièvre, *Histoire des protestants et des églises réformées du Poitou* (Paris, 1856–1860), II, 130, 181–182.

80 *BSHPF*, XXIX, 190; Douen, *op. cit.*, I, 97; Frank Puaux, "La Révocation à Marennes. Le temple and les écoles," *BSHPF*, XXXIII (1884), 13; Charles Weiss, "Mémoire sur les protestants de France au XVIIᵉ siècle," *Séances et travaux de l'Académie des sciences morales et politiques*, XX (1851), 122.

81 *Testament politique du Marquis de Louvois*, p. 372.

Such laments should not be taken too literally or too seriously. Anyone seeking to interest the government in a pet project for reform, or to gain tax relief for his district, was apt to exaggerate conditions. This makes it difficult to interpret the evidence. Religious persecution apparently caused a substantial number of peasants to leave France, especially in strongly Protestant regions. Their departure may have caused an embarrassing shortage of agricultural labor and may have led to a poorer utilization of farm resources. At one time peasants in Dauphiné were accused of taking silkworm eggs, mulberry seeds, and young mulberry plants with them when they fled to Switzerland in order to raise raw silk there for the new silkworks already started by other Huguenot refugees.[82] But there is no evidence that the diffusion of farming methods and garden crops in less developed countries hurt French agriculture by shrinking its foreign markets or worsening its barter terms of trade. If reliable figures on the average yield per acre and on the amount of land under cultivation in France for several years before and after 1685 were available, it might be possible to estimate whether there was any appreciable withdrawal of resources from farming. Then, by comparing provinces where Protestant peasants were relatively numerous with areas where they were not, one might generalize with some degree of confidence about the extent to which farming suffered from the revocation. It is extremely unlikely that any such figures will ever come to light. We must therefore rely upon intuitive judgment.

The agricultural yield for France as a whole does not appear to have been any better or any worse in the decade beginning in 1682 than in ordinary times. Whenever a dearth seemed likely, the government usually forbade the export of grain. That it sanctioned exports and even suspended export duties on grain from 1686 to 1689[83] thus seems significant. The revocation may have retarded agricultural development in certain areas for a few years, and may have accentuated other depressants, but it seems to have had little effect throughout France as a whole even in the short run. It probably left no enduring scars anywhere.

---

[82] Archives Nationales, G7 241; Boislisle, *op. cit.*, I, 151. When Louis heard of this, he prohibited such exports on May 21, 1688.

[83] Charles W. Cole, *Colbert and a Century of French Mercantilism* (New York, 1939), II, 519.

INTERNATIONAL RELATIONS

According to many individuals, religious persecution worsened France's diplomatic and military relations with the rest of Europe. Specifically, it is sometimes said that anti-Protestantism helped to unify Louis's enemies and to occasion the outbreak of war with the League of Augsburg in 1688–89; that the defection of large numbers of Huguenots who were capable officers, soldiers, and seamen strengthened enemy forces and weakened the might of France; and that Protestants who remained at home supplied the enemy with useful information and, by stirring up internal trouble and discontent, interfered with France's war effort. Although these charges do not bear directly on the economic repercussions attributed to the revocation, they have an indirect bearing and hence should be examined briefly. Few would deny that Louis's military misfortunes after 1689 greatly hampered the growth of the French economy.

There is some evidence that religious policies in France were instrumental in uniting her enemies into the League of Augsburg and in bringing on the war. This is not to say that in the absence of such policies the other countries might not have joined together to oppose Louis's ambitions. Yet France's attitude toward Protestants made good propaganda in some countries and served to rally popular support. Consider William of Orange, himself a stanch Protestant. As Dutch stadholder and Louis's implacable enemy, he astutely realized that he could use the persecution of French Huguenots to consolidate his own position in Holland and to rally the seven Dutch provinces and the most influential burgomasters behind him.[84] Louis's representatives at The Hague began to warn their sovereign in October and November, 1685, that William was posing as Europe's champion of Protestantism and might succeed in forming an alliance of Protestant states against France with his claims that Louis was trying to unite all Catholic powers.[85] The appearance of *Les Plaintes des protestans, cruellement opprimez dans le Royaume de France,* which Jean Claude had written and published at Cologne under

---

84 Simonde de Sismondi, *Histoire des français* (Paris, 1821–1844), XXV, 527–528; James Westfall Thompson, "Some Economic Factors in the Revocation of the Edict of Nantes," *American Historical Review,* XIV (1909), 45–46, 47.

85 Archives du Ministère des Affaires Étrangères, *Ancien fonds,* "Hollande," *registres* 143, 145, *passim,* and especially fols. 90, 147–148, in *registre* 143.

William's patronage, alarmed the French ambassador, who considered the book "a manifesto to begin a religious war just as soon as the Calvinists are in a position to do so." The ambassador sent a copy of the book to Louis on April 18, 1686. The king sought to allay his representative's fears by replying that the book would probably do no more harm than "all the libel which those of this religion have already spread throughout Europe" and that one must "allow them to spew their venom without getting too upset."[86]

Although William capitalized on the persecution raging in France to strengthen his position at home and abroad, it cannot be said that the persecution was the chief reason for the success of his plans or for the creation of the League of Augsburg on July 9, 1686.[87] After all, Catholic rulers such as the king of Spain, an original signer of the pact, or the Duke of Savoy, who joined in 1687, would hardly be drawn into an alliance to protect Protestantism. They and others joined the league primarily to thwart Louis's political ambitions. They resented his preponderant influence in European affairs and his arrogant high-handedness. The Duke of Savoy is a good example. Immediately after signing the revocation edict, Louis tried first to persuade and then to intimidate the duke into proclaiming a similar edict for Savoy. Louis took scarcely any care to veil his threats when he sent instructions to his diplomatic representative at Turin:

You should, nevertheless, make the duke understand that so long as he allows Huguenots to live along that part of his frontier which borders my states, he will be unable to keep my Calvinist subjects from deserting to his territory. . . . Since he can well surmise that I will not tolerate this desertion and that the insolence of these heretics will cause me displeasure, he should realize that I will no longer entertain the same cordial sentiments I have shown him up to now. I feel certain that he will seriously reflect on this matter.[88]

Apparently the duke "seriously reflected" on this ultimatum, for he outlawed Protestantism in his realm on January 31, 1686. The

---

86 *Ibid., registre* 146, fols. 60–61, 69.

87 Some Protestant partisans, however, have affirmed that it was. See, e.g., Frank Puaux and A. Sabatier, *Études sur la révocation de l'Édit de Nantes* (Paris, 1886), pp. 5–6; and Guillaume-Adam de Félice, *Histoire des protestants de France* (8th ed.; Toulouse, 1895), p. 439, quoting another author.

88 Paul-M. Bondois, "Le Duc de Savoie Victor-Amédée II et la Révocation de l'Édict de Nantes," *Bulletin philologique et historique du Comité des travaux historiques et scientifiques*, years 1928–1929 (1930), 150, 154.

following year, however, he joined forces with the League of Augsburg and later entered the war against France.

In all probability England and Holland would have allied themselves with the league had they never differed with Louis over religion, and war would doubtless have erupted in any event. The persecution of Huguenots, however, outraged Protestants in these two countries and made them feel that they were fighting to protect their religion. The governments of both England and Holland mentioned Louis's persecution of Protestants when they listed the reasons for going to war. In his declaration of war dated May 7, 1689, William, then king of England, called attention to the

... unchristian persecution of many of our English Protestant subjects in France for matters of religion, contrary to the law of nations and express treaties; forcing them to abjure their religion by unusual cruelties; imprisoning some of the masters and seamen of our merchant ships, and condemning others to the galleys, on pretence of having onboard, either some of his own miserable subjects or their effects.

As far as the Dutch were concerned, Louis, "having begun a horrible persecution of his own Protestant subjects, . . . had therein involved the subjects of the states-general, though only living in France, on account of commerce; parting wives from their husbands, and children from their parents. . . ."[89] Both governments carefully refrained from using language suggesting that they were fighting to reëstablish Protestantism in France. When the time finally arrived for drawing up a treaty of peace, they and their allies did not insist that Louis rescind the revocation edict. They had diligently tried throughout the fighting never to give Louis legitimate cause for complaining that they were waging a religious war against him, and during the peace talks in 1697 they took the position that his campaign against Protestantism had never been one of their grievances.[90] The most they would do for French Huguenots was to beseech Louis, in a document entitled "Memorandum of the Ambassadors and Plenipotentiaries of Protestant Princes in Behalf of the Reformed Churches in France," to treat Huguenots less harshly, to recognize their rights and liberties, to reëstablish freedom of

---

[89] MacPherson, *op. cit.*, II, 636. MacPherson quotes directly from William's declaration of war and paraphrases Holland's.

[90] Bibliothèque de la Société Protestante, MS 648¹, pp. 160–161.

conscience, and to release all Protestants in prison and in the galleys.[91]

Not only has it been suggested that the revocation helped bring about the formation of the League of Augsburg and the Grand Alliance, as well as the outbreak of war, but it has also been contended that it helped to determine the outcome by driving Protestant soldiers, seamen, and officers into foreign armies. Vauban, for example, stated in 1689 that 500 or 600 army officers had already fled abroad, accompanied by 8,000 or 9,000 seamen and 10,000 or 12,000 soldiers. By simply reëstablishing liberty of conscience, he thought, the king could get most of these men to return and at the same time weaken an international alliance against France and deal William a vital blow.[92] Another Frenchman, writing in similar vein six years later, urged Louis to call off his campaign against Protestantism while the war was in progress and its outcome still uncertain. He predicted that the ensuing mass repatriation would deprive the enemy of its best officers and soldiers.[93]

There are no reliable figures on the number of Huguenots who served in the enemy's armed forces; inferences must therefore be drawn from contemporary statements. The lieutenant general of the Paris police learned from one of his officials early in 1685 that foreign countries were actively seeking to enlist men at Paris and that Protestants there maintained a regular recruiting service for members of their faith who wanted to fight against France.[94] In the first half of 1686, according to a Huguenot at Haarlem who sold the French ambassador information about other Huguenot refugees, William of Orange had seen a list of some 75,000 French refugees, 40,000 of whom were capable of bearing arms. The list was said to include 532 colonels, lieutenant colonels, majors, captains, lieutenants, and sergeants, as well as 868 volunteer soldiers and cadets.[95] Huguenots presumably made up three infantry regiments and one cavalry squad-

91 Bibliothèque Nationale, *Fonds français,* MS 7036, fols. 108–109.

92 *BSHPF,* XXXVIII (1889), 195. A doctor at the Sorbonne supported Vauban's views (Bibliothèque Nationale, *Fonds français,* MS 7044, fols. 298 ff.).

93 *Testament politique du Marquis de Louvois,* pp. 377 ff.

94 Bibliothèque Nationale, *Fonds français,* MS 7052, fols. 367 ff.

95 Archives du Ministère des Affaires Étrangères, *Ancien fonds,* "Hollande," *registre* 149, fols. 180–181. The ambassador at The Hague had written Louis in March, 1686, that William had recently pensioned forty-seven French captains, seventy-four lieutenants, and four sergeants (*ibid., registre* 145, fols. 200–203).

ron in the army of 15,000 men which accompanied William when he invaded England on November 5, 1688.[96] The Duke of Schomberg, one of France's ablest generals and a Protestant refugee after 1685, died at the Battle of the Boyne in Ireland while fighting alongside many other Huguenots who were helping William against James II. Rébenac, Louis's diplomat at Berlin, wrote home on December 22, 1685, that the Elector of Brandenburg was trying to attract as many refugee army officers as he could by offering them posts in his army or pensions. So far, he said, no more than 300 had arrived. Rébenac reported again on June 25, 1687, that Huguenots then made up one Prussian regiment of 800 men, a battalion of 200, and two companies of 50 cadets each. A few months later he wrote that the elector was forming two new companies of mounted musketeers of 100 refugees each.[97] A German scholar has concluded that about 3,000 Protestant army officers escaped France and that between 500 and 600 of them wound up in Brandenburg, where they constituted more than a third of its officers' corps.[98]

Even though Frenchmen may have increased the military strength of foreign countries by serving as officers and soldiers and by diffusing French military strategy and techniques, it does not necessarily follow that France's military power declined absolutely, as some writers have contended.[99] Other persons probably filled the gaps caused by Huguenots who deserted. It is more likely that France lost part of her relative superiority, just as certain of her industries lost part of their comparative advantage.[100] About the middle of the eighteenth century, however, Novi de Caveirac claimed that the revocation had deprived his country of very few potential servicemen and that those who had gone abroad were so widely scattered that they did not

---

[96] Albert Carré, *L'Influence des Huguenot français en Irlande aux XVIIe et XVIIIe siècles* (Paris, 1937), p. 17; William A. Shaw, "The English Government and the Relief of Protestant Refugees," *PHSL*, V (1894-1896), 348; Weiss, "Mémoire sur les protestants," *op. cit.*, XX, 263.

[97] Archives du Ministère des Affaires Étrangères, *Ancien fonds*, "Prusse," *registres* 25, fols. 426–428, 450; 26, fols. 43–44; 28, fols. 347–348; 29, fol. 232. See also G. Pagès, "Les Réfugiés à Berlin d'après la correspondance du comte de Rébenac (1681–1688)," *BSHPF*, LI (1902), 132.

[98] Erbe, *op. cit.*, pp. 60–61, 66.

[99] Notably N. Weiss (*BSHPF*, XXXVI [1887], 196).

[100] Bibliothèque Nationale, *Fonds français*, MS 7045, fol. 77; Bibliothèque de la Société Protestante, MSS 339, fol. 27; 6481, fol. 416; *Testament politique du Marquis de Louvois*, pp. 370–371.

appreciably affect the military strength of any one country.[101]

The third way in which religious difficulties presumably affected France's military fortunes was sabotage of the war effort by Huguenots and new converts. Joseph Dedieu, writing in 1925, has charged them with fomenting insurrection among the Vaudois in 1688–1689, raising armies of Camisards in open rebellion from 1702 to 1710, spying for the enemy during the War of the League of Augsburg and the War of the Spanish Succession, and doing everything in their power during both wars to embarrass their king.[102] How valid are these accusations? After the League of Augsburg was formed, certain Protestants attempted to persuade the Vaudois near the Swiss and Savoy borders to invade Dauphiné and Cévennes in the hope of rallying all the oppressed. Apprehension ran high at Paris from October, 1688, until the end of 1689.[103] Then, after war had broken out, rumors flew thick and fast that the English and the Dutch were ready to invade the French coast north of La Rochelle, where masses of Protestants supposedly were poised to join them. Some refugee zealots actually managed to sneak back with the financial aid proffered by William, and unsuccessfully tried to arouse the peasants to rebellion in Languedoc and in a few other provinces.[104] All this helps to explain why Louis felt it necessary on October 16, 1688, to order Huguenots and new converts to surrender their arms, and why he later diverted some of his troops from the battle front to police the spots where trouble was likely to appear.

The revolt of the Cevenoles, or the so-called War of the Camisards, coming in 1702–1710 when France was again fighting most of Europe, engaged a considerable number of troops before it was finally suppressed. Although foreign states had doubtless helped to provoke the rebellion, they offered no direct assistance

---

101 *Op. cit.*, p. 145; *Mémoire politico-critique, où l'on examine s'il est de l'intérêt de l'Église et de l'Etat d'établir pour les Calvinistes du Royaume une nouvelle forme de se marier* (n.p., 1756), pp. 83–91.

102 *Histoire politique des protestants français (1715–1794)* (Paris, 1925), I, xii–xiii. See also René Prigent, "Les Protestants à Brest après la Révocation," *Mémoires de la société d'histoire et d'archéologie de Bretagne,* 9th year (1928), 132 ff.

103 Archives Nationales, A1 902, 903, 904, 906, 907.

104 The Protestant preacher Vivens, for example, returned to Languedoc in 1689 with 1,000 livres supplied by William with which to buy powder and arms. He organized small bands which probably never numbered more than 400 followers and never did much damage. He was finally taken and killed in February, 1692. (Boislisle, *op. cit.,* I, 279; Lavisse, *op. cit.,* Vol. VIII, Part 1, p. 364.)

until 1710, when a small contingent of English soldiers disembarked at Sète for a few days. By then it was too late. The insurgents failed to join the enemy or to offer them aid. As for the Camisards themselves, they thought they were fighting tyrannous religious persecution at home and never considered the possibility of committing treason by aiding the enemy.

There is no conclusive evidence that many Huguenots engaged in espionage in either 1688–1697 or 1701–1713. Some certainly did, but the information they supplied the enemy seems to have had no appreciable effect upon the outcome of the two wars. It would be grossly misleading to conclude, as Dedieu has done,[105] that French Protestants "allowed themselves to be drawn en masse toward foreign powers and committed the error of entrusting their fate to leaders who exploited them in nefarious political adventures. . . ." They did not "become, in effect, the allies, accomplices, and soldiers of the League of Augsburg," nor did "the activity of a multitude of spies paralyze France's war effort and annul her defensive measures." They did not "consecrate all their forces from 1685 to 1715 to assuring the triumph of Louis XIV's enemies."

Religious persecution and the flight of Huguenots affected French agriculture in certain limited areas by disrupting normal activities and by reducing the available labor supply. Yet no nationwide shortages of farm products appeared before 1692; and the government not only allowed grain to be exported but also lifted the export duties on grain from 1686 to 1689—a thing it never did unless there appeared to be a generous supply on the domestic market. Disastrous weather seems to have been mainly responsible for the great famines in 1692–1694 and in 1709–1710. There is some basis for concluding that the revocation led to a poorer use of agricultural resources, but it is impossible to quantify this or make it meaningful in other ways.

The government's difficulties in raising revenues to meet its skyrocketing expenses apparently stemmed more from other sources than from the revocation. It is probably true that the yields of some taxes fell when Huguenot taxpayers left the country. Furthermore, their departure may have contributed to the decline in tax revenues by depressing the level of economic

---

105 *Op. cit.,* I, xii–xiii.

activity throughout the country. This again is a hypothesis hard to refute or to substantiate. It is unlikely, however, that the government could have avoided its fiscal problems or would have handled them more successfully if it had not sought to destroy Protestantism. Neither is it likely that Louis could have avoided the two great wars that plagued the last half of his reign.

It is regrettable that present information about specie movements and fluctuations in the loanable-funds markets is so scant for 1680–1715 that one can form only vague conjectures about the amount of specie France lost because of the revocation. There can be no serious doubt, however, that religious refugees withdrew funds from the market and occasioned the export of some specie which might otherwise have remained at home. On the other hand, wars and military expenditures abroad, shifts in foreign trade balances traceable to tariffs and wars, and flights of currency to escape devaluation and monetary uncertainties must also be held accountable for the drain. To rank these causes as to relative importance, without bias or prejudice, is well-nigh impossible in the light of the evidence now available. Even without knowing how much specie and liquid capital Huguenots took with them, one might still ask whether the loss hurt the French economy and in what ways. These questions are not so simple as they might seem at first glance. Most Frenchmen living at the time, for example, were confused about the significance of the loss.

Economists today usually emphasize the fact that specie or money is not synonymous with wealth. If a country suffers a net loss of real wealth in the form of goods and services, its standard of living will be lowered, and the real income available for employing productive factors to create capital goods (i.e., its "capital fund" supply) will usually shrink. In the short run, the loss of specie will tend to reduce the supply of loanable funds, drive up money rates, and strengthen deflationary tendencies. Seldom has deflation provided an atmosphere conducive to capital accumulation and economic expansion. The specie lost by France after 1684 created deflationary pressures. It was, in part, to counteract this that the government debased the coinage and emitted bills of credit. These measures served only to increase monetary uncertainty and hence to drive more specie abroad.

To the extent that Huguenots transported to foreign countries whatever capital goods they possessed, the availability of such goods in France was obviously reduced. To the extent that they shipped consumer goods abroad, the amount of goods that could have been used to sustain current resources while they were producing additional capital goods was reduced. Insofar as they took specie instead of either capital or consumer goods, a decrease in the supply of goods available for capital accumulation at home may also have resulted. In line with the now-familiar gold-flow mechanism, changes in the relative monetary stock of countries occasion shifts in their relative income and price levels (assuming all other things to remain unchanged), so that the country losing gold or silver tends to experience a commodity export balance with the rest of the world, and the countries receiving gold or silver tend to have a commodity import balance. To the extent that Huguenots bought sterling bills of exchange or letters of credit before leaving, the livre price of sterling may have been driven away from France's specie import point and toward France's specie export point. Whether or not it rose high enough to lead to specie exports, the higher price of sterling in France must in any event have tended to increase her exports and diminish her imports. There is one important complication in all this. No one can predict how much time is required for unilateral capital transfers, even under the best conditions, to change the relative income and price levels of the countries involved and to work themselves out as shifts in the barter terms of trade. The solution becomes quite indeterminate when exchange rates, specie flows, and movements of goods and services are subject to all kinds of capricious and arbitrary interference by government, and especially when other important exogenous variables such as major wars and internal inflation come into play. The situation in France was complicated in both these ways after 1689.

French exports relative to imports declined during the period Huguenots were transferring their purchasing power to England and Holland. This was the reverse of what one would normally expect of unilateral capital transfers. The explanation probably is to be sought in wars, tariffs, and monetary uncertainty which exercised a stronger pull upon France's balance of trade in the opposite direction than did the capital transfers attributable to Huguenots. The fact that most Huguenots accompanied their funds is also significant. If they had remained at home, the capital-fund transfer would have eventually worked itself out mainly by increasing France's export of capital and consumer goods. Since they did not do this, the capital transfer partially resolved itself, in a manner of speaking, into the export of labor instead of the export of goods. A good part of the funds went to meet the cost of getting Huguenots out of France and providing them with subsistence until they became fully productive once more. And their subsistence, in all probability, consisted chiefly of locally produced goods and services taken from the current output of host areas. Furthermore, since Huguenots had provided considerable man power and skill to some of France's chief export industries, and since the refugees helped England and Holland develop their own competitive manufactures, it was to be expected that the capital transfer would not lead to a short-run expansion of French exports to these two countries, as it would have done if all Hugenots had remained at home. Insofar as refugees took more capital funds with them than they needed to get established in their new homes or arrived with more per capita funds than their new neighbors had to spend, their action must have strengthened the tendency for England and Holland to import more (as well as to expand domestic production) and hence have cushioned to some extent French exports to these countries against the dampening impact of war and other depressants.

Aside from shortages of hand-to-hand currency in French areas where credit could not easily fill the void of hard money and where a drainage of silver or gold would thus embarrass market exchanges, the transfer of specie or loanable funds would represent a real loss to the French economy only if it resulted in the export of valuable goods unmatched by comparable imports. There is little empirical evidence that the capital transfers significantly increased the pressure behind such net exports. Ordinarily, Huguenots did not dismantle their factories and take manufacturing equipment with them; and they used a large part of their funds to tide them over the readjustment period in their adopted countries. The most reasonable conclusion seems to be that the transfer of funds did not deplete France's stock of circulating and fixed capital, nor did it suddenly swell the supply in other countries. Its greatest long-run significance probably was that the capital facilitated the transfer of labor and industrial skills, which in turn raised the manufacturing level in foreign countries and worsened France's barter terms of trade.

X

The Revocation and the Diffusion of Technology

By carrying abroad their special skills in industry and trade, Huguenots helped to close the technological gap separating certain European countries from France. The governments of most host areas warmly welcomed the refugees, gave them extensive privileges, and in other ways facilitated their efforts to transplant new processes. As a result, French manufacturers and merchants after 1685 confronted mounting competition and higher trade barriers when they tried to sell their goods in foreign markets. Although France did not permanently lose her European markets, her barter terms of trade apparently worsened and particular industries found themselves handicapped. In the present chapter I propose to bring together all the available evidence pertaining to this problem in order to determine whether, and to what extent, the refugees improved the industrial and technological levels in England, Ireland, Holland, Germany, and Switzerland.

THE HUGUENOTS IN ENGLAND

Professor E. Lipson has suggested that Englishmen were less hostile to immigrants after the Restoration of the Stuarts than they had been in the sixteenth century and the first part of the seventeenth century because of a growing belief that their country was underpopulated.[1] They occasionally complained that foreigners engaged in unfair competitive practices, but on the whole the populace joined with the Crown in extending immigrants a welcome. As early as February 9, 1666, Charles II de-

---

[1] E. Lipson, *The Economic History of England* (4th ed.; London: A. and C. Black, 1947), III, 57–59.

clared that he would protect the property and person of any Frenchman—especially one of the "Religion Reputedly Reformed"—who sought refuge in England.[2] In 1672 he invited any Dutchman who wished to migrate to come to England, and even introduced a bill into Parliament for naturalizing all Protestant immigrants.[3] On August 28, 1681, shortly after French dragoons began forcibly to convert Huguenots in the province of Poitou, Charles II issued another declaration.[4] He promised that all Protestant refugees would be welcomed and allowed to follow commerce, arts, and trades as permitted by the laws of the realm; that he would introduce at the next session of Parliament a bill to naturalize them; that they would be subject only to the duties and the taxes paid by other citizens; that they might send their children to English schools and colleges on the same footing as others; that they might import all their possessions duty free; that he would raise funds to aid the most needy; and that his officials at the ports of debarkation would issue refugees passports free of charge. Charles's brother James II, who had strong Catholic tendencies and close ties with Louis XIV, was not very sympathetic. Public sentiment, however, was so strong in favor of the refugees that even James acknowledged to representatives from the French court that he dared not display openly his true feelings.[5] He confirmed the privileges granted by Charles and in March, 1686, permitted another fund-raising drive. As soon as William and Mary ascended the throne after the Bloodless Revolution, the king, on April 25, 1689, declared that "all French Protestants that shall seek their refuge in our Kingdom shall not only have our Royal protection for them-

---

[2] M. Naert, "Les Huguenots du Calaisis au XVIIᵉ siècle," *Bulletin de la société de l'histoire du protestantisme français* (hereinafter cited as *BSHPF*), LXIII–LXIV (1914–1915), 332 n. 1.

[3] Lipson, *op. cit.*, III, 60.

[4] Bibliothèque Nationale, *Fonds français*, MS 21616, fols. 349–350. This was published in the *London Gazette* on September 12, 1681.

[5] Archives du Ministère des Affaires Étrangères, *Ancien fonds*, "Angleterre," especially *registres* 156, fol. 46; 157, fol. 28. James II ordered Jean Claude's indictment of Louis XIV (*Les Plaintes des protestans, cruellement opprimez dans le Royaume de France* [Cologne, 1686]) publicly burned, and issued a quo warranto against a French church in London ordering it closed unless its ritual was made to conform to that of the Anglican Church. Since it was generally thought that the Huguenots would refuse to change their ritual, it was suggested that James could employ the quo warranto to close all French churches and thereby drive the refugees, whom he considered his enemies, out of the realm (Domestic State Papers, William and Mary, Bundle 42, p. 340, as reprinted in the *Proceedings of the Huguenot Society of London* [hereinafter cited as *PHSL*], II [1887–1888], 449–450).

selves, families, and estates, but we will also do our endeavor in all reasonable ways and means so to support, aid and assist them in their several trades and ways of livelihood as that their living in this realm may be comfortable and easy to them."[6] The king was unable, however, to persuade Parliament to pass a bill granting them citizenship. This was accomplished under Queen Anne in 1709.[7]

The various fund-raising campaigns authorized by the Crown in 1681 and subsequently for the purpose of aiding needy refugees yielded approximately £90,000; and Parliament in 1696 voted toward relief a sum of £15,000 a year, but relief was rarely distributed.[8] The reports of refugees who eventually abjured Protestantism and returned to France, to the effect that 10,000 or more Huguenots had died in England from starvation, fatigue, and change of climate,[9] are not credible. After all, Louis XIV's agent Bonrepaus had to admit that he had succeeded in persuading and bribing only 507 of them to return home from January to May, 1686.[10] If conditions in England had really

---

[6] Bibliothèque Nationale, *Fonds français*, MS 7044, fol. 278; Grace Lawless Lee, *The Huguenot Settlements in Ireland* (London, 1936), p. 17.

[7] David MacPherson, *Annals of Commerce, Manufactures, Fisheries, and Navigation etc.* (London, 1805), III, 5–6; Charles Weiss, "Mémoire sur les protestants de France au XVIIᵉ siècle," *Séances et travaux de l'Académie des sciences morales et politiques,* XX (1851), 263. It is worth noting, also, that the English ambassadors at Paris aided many Huguenots to escape by taking them to England as their personal servants or by forging passports for them (Emmanuel-Orentin Douen, *La Révocation de l'Édit de Nantes à Paris d'après des documents inédits* [Paris, 1894], II, 430). A French intendant complained that the English circulated tracts in his province which promised great advantages to those who would flee to the English colonies in America, especially to the Carolinas (L.-J. Nazelle, *Le Protestantisme en Saintonge sous le régime de la Révocation, 1685–1789* [Paris, 1907], p. 39).

[8] George B. Beeman, "Notes on the City of London Records Dealing with the French Protestant Refugees, Especially with Reference to the Collections Made under Various Briefs," *PHSL,* VII (1901–1904), 109; William A. Shaw, "The English Government and the Relief of Protestant Refugees," *PHSL,* V (1894–1896), 343–348; César Pascal, "Les Collectes nationales anglaises en faveur des réfugiés protestants (1681–1699)," *BSHPF,* XLI (1892), 329; David C. A. Agnew, *Protestant Exiles from France in the Reign of Louis XIV* (2d ed.; London, 1871–1874), I, 62.

[9] See, for example, Bibliothèque Nationale, *Fonds français*, MS 7044, fol. 109. That there was much suffering and physical hardship is indisputable; and it may well have been true in the eighteenth century that "when an Englishman wished to insult a naturalized person of French origin, he called him a son-of-a-refugee" (Novi de Caveirac, *Mémoire politico-critique, où l'on examine s'il est de l'intérêt de l'Eglise et de l'Etat d'établir pour les Calvinistes du Royaume une nouvelle forme de se marier* [n.p., 1756], p. 131 n. 1).

[10] Archives du Ministère des Affaires Étrangères, *Ancien fonds,* "Angleterre," *registre* 157, fol. 139.

been intolerable, his efforts would doubtless have met with greater success.

It has been suggested that between 20,000 and 50,000—or, more likely, between 40,000 and 50,000—refugees settled in England. What effect did they have upon the economy? What branches of old industries and what new industries, if any, did they introduce? What technology did they diffuse? Did their immigration constitute, as Professor Lipson has suggested,[11] "the third great landmark in the industrial history of England"? A survey of the industries benefited by the Huguenot migration may shed light on these and similar questions.

France had long enjoyed a comparative advantage over northern European countries in the production of fine silk fabrics, particularly those of luxury quality; and England had been anxious to free herself from dependence upon manufacturers at Tours, Nîmes, and Lyon. Although she had made silk since about the beginning of the seventeenth century and had more than 40,000 members in the silk throwsters gild in 1661,[12] England imported large quantities of lustrous taffetas and other fine silks from France. For example, after James II persuaded Parliament to repeal its 1678 prohibition against French imports, English purchases of lustrings, alamodes, and other silk fabrics averaged more than £700,000 a year in 1686–1688.[13] All refugees skilled in preparing and manufacturing silk consequently received a cordial welcome when they settled at Blackfriars in Canterbury and at Spitalfields in London.

The Royal Lustring Company, chartered in 1692,[14] is said to have had 768 looms at work in Ipswich and London by 1695.[15] French refugees were among its founders and provided much of its skilled labor and management. Aided by the war which had cut off French imports after 1689, by an annual subsidy from

11 *Op. cit.*, III, 60.

12 W. H. Manchée, "Memories of Spitalfields," *PHSL*, X (1912–1914), 318.

13 Adam Anderson, *An Historical and Chronological Deduction of the Origin of Commerce, from the Earliest Accounts etc.* (London, 1801), II, 571. Before 1683 the average value each year was said to have been £600,000 (*ibid.*, II, 562; MacPherson, *op. cit.*, II, 609).

14 MacPherson, *op. cit.*, II, 651. A group of English and French promoters, who a few years earlier had obtained a patent to make alamodes and lustrings, made no use of their grant before they sold it to the new entrepreneurial group (Vincent B. Redstone, "The Dutch and Huguenot Settlements of Ipswich," *PHSL*, XII, [1917–1924], 201–202).

15 Redstone, *op. cit.*, pp. 201–202; W. H. Manchée, "Some Huguenot Smugglers. The Impeachment of London Silk Merchants, 1698," *PHSL*, XV (1934–1937), 423.

King William, by an increase in import duties which French silk manufacturers at Lyon said amounted to about 53 per cent of the value of taffetas, and by an act of Parliament in 1697 which prohibited all imports,[16] the company prospered. Its shares increased in value as long as the contemporary South Sea Bubble lasted; but after the bubble burst in 1720 the Royal Lustring Company failed. Of course, it had not been the only silk manufactory in England. As a matter of fact, thirty-eight mercers and manufacturers in the industry, including many Huguenots, combined to fight the company about 1693 and, with the connivance of Frenchmen at Lyon, tried to smuggle French silk into the English market.[17] They were brought to trial in 1698, and surveillance at the ports was increased so as to make smuggling difficult.

Two Huguenot workmen by the name of Mongeorge, father and son, had escaped to England with the secret of how to give a lustrous sheen to taffeta. Although the French ambassador persuaded them to return to France, the son, disguised as an Italian, regained England in 1688,[18] and the English presumably acquired the highly prized technique of the Lyon industry. Other refugees introduced new methods for throwing silk, new designs for damasks and other figured patterns, special knowledge of dyeing and finishing cloth, improvements in ribbon weaving and in knitting silk stockings, skill in working the looms and supervising all activities in the trade. All these techniques, chiefly of the handicraft variety, were closely guarded secrets of French manufacturers; and it would have been more difficult and taken longer for the English to have acquired and mastered them without the immigration of skilled artisans.

The English silk industry had been declining steadily for about two decades before 1680. With the advent of the Huguenots, it increased rapidly in importance, first at Canterbury and then in the Spitalfields district of London.[19] Contemporary Frenchmen

---

16 Bibliothèque Nationale, *Fonds français,* MS 4288, fols. 118–119; Manchée, "Some Huguenot Smugglers," p. 411; Anderson, *op. cit.,* II, 598; Redstone, *op. cit.,* pp. 201–202.

17 Manchée, "Some Huguenot Smugglers," pp. 412 ff.; Archives Nationales, G7 1685.

18 Manchée, "Some Huguenot Smugglers," p. 409.

19 Charles Weiss, *Histoire des réfugiés protestants de France depuis la révocation de l'Édit de Nantes jusqu'à nos jours* (Paris, 1853), I, 322 ff.; Anderson, *op. cit.,* II, 569; Agnew, *op. cit.,* II, 134–136; Reginald Lane Poole, *A History of the Huguenots of the Dispersion at the Recall of the Edict of Nantes* (London, 1880), p. 83; Samuel Smiles, *The Huguenots, Their Settlements, Churches, and Industries in England*

actually became alarmed lest they lose for all time the English market for their silks. Although admitting that the newly established works in and around London were not yet able to produce as lustrous black taffetas and as fine grades of brocades, satins, and ribbons as the industry around Lyon, they feared that consumers would eventually become accustomed to the "inferior" English product and forget all about the more stylish French models; that the cheaper foreign fabrics might even be imported into France and undermine French standards of quality; and that the English factories, once established, would acquire all the trade secrets and eventually produce just as good silk as the French.[20] The company of silk weavers at London stated in a petition to Parliament in 1713 that their industry was more than twentyfold its size in 1664, and that silks, brocades, and ribbons made in England were as good as those produced in France.[21]

The Huguenots also strengthened other branches of the English textile industry. In 1681 and 1685 two shops were opened at Ipswich so that refugees could make white linen fabrics for the East Indian trade and for sailcloth.[22] Since the French had formerly supplied these commodities, Louis XIV was much disturbed lest the new manufactories absorb a major part of the English market. He encouraged his agent, Bonrepaus, to do his utmost to persuade these particular refugee workers to return to Normandy and Brittany. Bonrepaus reported in 1686 and 1687 that he had succeeded in ruining the establishments by getting most of the refugees to return.[23] Nevertheless, sailcloth and white-linen works later reappeared at Ipswich and elsewhere, and English imports of these fabrics from France supplied a smaller

---

and Ireland (6th ed.; London, 1889), p. 271; Beeman, *op. cit.,* p. 147. According to Weiss, a European traveler maintained in 1730 that a merchant trying to sell silks in Naples usually said they were of English origin in order to attract customers. Anderson, writing in 1801, claimed that English broadsilk "outdid" the French, and for this he largely credited the Huguenots (*op. cit.,* II, 597).

20 Archives Nationales, G7 1685, 1692, 1701 (*registre,* fol. 136); Bibliothèque Nationale, *Fonds français,* MSS 4288, fols. 118–119; 7044, fols. 279–283. See also A. M. de Boislisle, *Correspondance des contrôleurs généraux des finances avec les intendants des provinces,* II (Paris, 1883), 488–489.

21 MacPherson, *op. cit.,* III, 34.

22 Weiss, *Histoire des réfugiés,* I, 328–329; Weiss, "Mémoire sur les protestants," *op. cit.,* XXI, 74–76; Beeman, *op. cit.,* pp. 145–147; W. Cunningham, *Alien Immigrants to England* (London, 1897), p. 240; Bodleian Library (Oxford), Rawlinson MSS, C. 984, fol. 59 (reproduced by N. Weiss in *BSHPF,* XXXIV [1885], 277).

23 Archives du Ministère des Affaires Étrangères, *Ancien fonds,* "Angleterre," *registres* 157, fols. 60–61, 99, 135; 163, fol. 100; Redstone, *op. cit.,* pp. 183 ff.

share of the domestic market than before 1680.[24] Refugees also taught Englishmen how to make the finest grades of woolens and velvets and how to weave such linens as batiste patterned after that produced at Cambrai.[25] At Edinburgh, Scotland, large numbers of refugees specializing in batiste settled in a section since called the Picardy Quarter.[26] They helped make Barnstaple famous in the woolen trade by introducing new processes of manufacturing and dyeing.[27] They were also among the first in England to print calicoes, and later they apparently had an important part in the rapidly expanding cotton industry.[28]

Frenchmen around Angoulême and in the old province of Auvergne had for a long time been proficient in the art of making fine white paper suitable for writing and printing. Although English mills had adequately supplied the domestic market for coarser grades, England had become accustomed to buying most of her white paper from Holland and from these French manufacturers.[29] In good mercantilist fashion, her government re-

24 MacPherson, writing in 1805, said that "with respect to the linen manufacture, more especially in the south parts of England, it is probable it will never prove very successful; neither, perhaps, is it for England's benefit that it should succeed there, since it might not a little interfere with our antient [sic] and noble woollen manufactures, and also with the silk and steel ones, by diverting our workmen therefrom" (*op. cit.*, II, 703).

25 Weiss, *Histoire des réfugiés*, I, 331; Weiss, "Mémoire sur les protestants," *op. cit.*, XXI, 77; [Antoine Court], *Le Patriote françois et impartial ou reponse à la lettre de Mr l'evêque d'Agen à Mr le controleur genéral contre la Tolerance des Huguenots, en datte du 1 mai 1751* (new ed.; Villefranche, 1753), I, 384–385; Anderson, *op. cit.*, II, 569; Agnew, *op. cit.*, II, 138.

26 Weiss, *Histoire des réfugiés*, I, 332; Florence Layard, "The Huguenots in North Britain," *PHSL*, III (1888–1891), 36; Edouard Fleury, "Notice sur l'histoire du protestantisme dans le département de l'Aisne," *Bulletin de la société académique de Laon*, XI (1861), 257.

27 Charles E. Lart, "The Huguenot Settlements and Churches in the West of England," *PHSL*, VII, 290. According to Weiss ("Mémoire sur les protestants," *op. cit.*, XXI, 78), members of Parliament in 1703 stated that, as a result of the new fabrics begun and old lines perfected by the Huguenots, the export of English woolens already exceeded the amount under Charles II by more than £1 million.

28 Cunningham, *op. cit.*, p. 239 n. 2; Agnew, *op. cit.*, II, 138; Weiss, *Histoire des réfugiés*, I, 331; Weiss, "Mémoire sur les protestants," *op. cit.*, XXI, 77. One of the French emissaries in London for the negotiation of the trade treaty after the War of the Spanish Succession wrote on March 28, 1713, that, although the English forbade the selling or wearing of Indian prints, they allowed imported white cottons to be stamped "by their own workers and especially by the French refugees" (Archives Nationales, G7 1699).

29 In 1668–1669 England imported paper valued at almost £88,000; from 1686 to 1688 her imports averaged roughly £50,000 yearly; and according to some authorities they amounted to about £100,000 in many years (Robert H. George, "A Mercantilist Episode," *Journal of Economic and Business History*, III [1930–1931], 265 n. 3; Anderson, *op. cit.*, II, 571, 594).

joiced, and the French government grieved, to see a number of skilled papermakers of the Protestant faith seek refuge in England shortly before and after the revocation.

Refugees did not introduce the manufacture of fine white paper into England. In the reign of Elizabeth and before 1685 Parliament had issued at least nine letters patent for inventions in this field, and several mills had begun work.[30] The Huguenots, however, fortified what had been a sickly industry by bringing improved paper molds and forms, by disclosing some of their most important and secret processes of manufacturing and bleaching, and by helping establish several new mills with their capital, managerial ability, and skilled man power.[31] France's ambassador Barrillon diligently tried to undermine the White Papermaker's Company, chartered in July, 1686, by bribing the manager of one of its mills and several of his workmen to return to France.[32] He succeeded, but his victory was short lived. After William III ascended the throne, the mills were reopened, new ones were built and staffed with other refugees, and England was well on the road to independence of French manufacturers.[33] Both Anderson[34] and MacPherson[35] confirmed this at the beginning of the eighteenth century:

Till about this time [i.e., 1690] there was scarce any other kind of paper made in England but the coarse brown sort. But the war with France occasioning high duties on foreign paper, the French protes-

---

30 George H. Overend, "Notes upon the Earlier History of the Manufacture of Paper in England," *PHSL*, VIII (1905–1908), 178, 181 ff., 196 ff. Overend, one of the best authorities on the subject, is of the opinion that Protestant refugees from the Spanish Netherlands and France in the sixteenth century should be credited with bringing the industry to England. He thinks, and I agree with him, that historians have often confused the Protestant immigrations of the sixteenth and seventeenth centuries as to their effect upon the English economy.

31 *Ibid.*; Anderson, *op. cit.*, II, 569; Agnew, *op. cit.*, II, 132–134; Boislisle, *op. cit.*, II, 488; Henry J. Cowell, *The Edict of Nantes and Afterwards. The Story of the Huguenots, 1685–1935* (3d ed.; London, [1936]), pp. 10–11; Cunningham, *op. cit.*, p. 242; Layard, *op. cit.*, p. 36; MacPherson, *op. cit.*, II, 647, 703; W. J. C. Moens, "The Walloon Settlement and the French Church at Southampton," *PHSL*, III, 70; Smiles, *op. cit.*, pp. 272–273n; Weiss, "Mémoire sur les protestants," *op. cit.*, XXI, 80; Archives Nationales, G7 345, 1692.

32 An extremely interesting account of his efforts is given by George, *op. cit.* Part of Barrillon's correspondence is in Archives Nationales, A1 795, doc. 183, and in Archives du Ministère des Affaires Étrangères, *Ancien fonds*, "Angleterre," *registres* 159, fol. 272; 161, fol. 147; 162, fols. 65–66, 319–320.

33 It is interesting to note that one refugee, Henry de Portals, finally got the exclusive right to supply the paper used by the Bank of England for its bank notes.

34 *Op. cit.*, II, 594.

35 *Op. cit.*, II, 647.

tant refugees settled in England, and also our own few paper-makers, now began to make white writing paper and printing paper: which, in length of time, has been brought to so great perfection, both for beauty and substance, that, in our own time [i.e., 1801–1805] we import only certain kinds of Genoa and Dutch paper; which, however, bears but a small proportion to all the paper used in the British dominions.

Charles Davenant, however, stated near the close of the seventeenth century that "as to ordinary paper . . . we are very much improved in that manufacture, though we are not come up to the French perfection";[36] and men on both sides of the channel thought as late as the mid-eighteenth century that French writing paper was still somewhat superior to the English.[37]

Although Protestant refugees from Flanders and France had introduced into England the art of making felt hats at least as early as 1543,[38] some of the Huguenots from Normandy who migrated there almost a century and a half later were also skilled in the trade.[39] According to a report to the controller general in 1708,[40] the English already had an advantage over the French in preparing beaver skins and fashioning from them hats "of great beauty and lightness"; it was in the cheaper felt lines that the English were backward. The Huguenots from Rouen and Caudebec helped to correct this by showing workmen in their adopted country how to mix rabbit fur with wool fibers so that the felt became rain-resistant. As a result, the hat manufactory established by Huguenots at Wandsworth prospered, and the industry whose products had long been known as "caudebecs" practically disappeared from the little Normandy village of that name.[41] Somewhat ironically, the Catholic Church thereafter had

---

36 Quoted by Lipson (*op. cit.*, III, 352–353n).

37 In a memorandum addressed to the controller general in 1708, David, the inspector of manufactures at Grenoble, confirmed that the paper made in England by Huguenot refugees was, by their own admission, inferior in quality to that produced in France and that the French mills could sell their output at 20 per cent less than the English and still make a reasonable profit (Archives Nationales, G7 1692).

38 Lipson, *op. cit.*, I, 492.

39 See, for example, a partial listing of refugees from the districts of Rouen and Caudebec compiled by the intendant Marillac in June, 1685 (Archives Nationales, TT 264, *dossier* XI, doc. 51).

40 Archives Nationales, G7 1692.

41 Anderson, *op. cit.*, II, 569, 597; Cunningham, *op. cit.*, p. 243; Douen, *op. cit.*, II, 481; MacPherson, *op. cit.*, II, 609, 618, 650; Archives Nationales, G7 1687 (a

to buy its cardinals' hats from Protestant England; and, curiously, a Huguenot who later returned to France with the trade secrets he had acquired by working in the hat shops around London helped to rehabilitate the industry in Normandy about forty years after it had practically disappeared.[42]

Numerous other trades benefited from the special skills, processes, and ideas brought to England by refugees. Protestant glassworkers from Normandy and Picardy, for example, helped the English gain proficiency in making crown glass for windows, cast plate glass, and mirrors.[43] Imports from the Low Countries and France had helped to supply the domestic demand for such glassware until the wars of 1689–1713 cut off the trade. France, even in the seventeenth century, had acquired fame for such high-quality, luxury goods as laces, gloves, fancy buttons, gold and silver galloons, tapestries, and jewelry. In all these crafts the Huguenots were instrumental in diffusing designs and technical processes.[44] An examination of the records of the wardens of the Goldsmiths' Company for the period from just before the revocation to 1710 has revealed that there were among the French refugees at least 146 goldsmiths, silversmiths, jewelers, and diamond cutters in London; 14 watchmakers in London; 7 goldsmiths in other English towns; and 43 goldsmiths, jewelers, and watchmakers at Cork and Dublin. Other Frenchmen skilled in these occupations had already fled to England in the sixteenth century, and between 1710 and 1780 their number in London and Dublin continued to increase.[45] Huguenots skilled in the metal trades also set up shops in England, where they fashioned needles and pins, fine-quality knives and scissors, surgical instruments, elaborately wrought locks, and kitchenware of iron and copper.[46]

1704 memorandum on commerce prepared by one De la Hestroy); Archives du Ministère des Affaires Étrangères, *Ancien fonds*, "Angleterre," *registre* 157, fol. 61.

42 Weiss, "Mémoire sur les protestants," *op. cit.*, XXI, 78–79.

43 Lipson, *op. cit.*, III, 369–370; Anderson, *op. cit.*, II, 597; MacPherson, *op. cit.*, II, 650.

44 Agnew, *op. cit.*, II, 138; Anderson, *op. cit.*, II, 597; Douen, *op. cit.*, II, 481; Weiss, *Histoire des réfugiés*, I, 322, 333; Bibliothèque Nationale, *Fonds français*, MSS 7044, fols. 279–283; 21622, fol. 82.

45 Joan Evans, "Huguenot Goldsmiths in England and Ireland," *PHSL*, XIV (1930–1933), 496 ff., 506, 512, 513; see also a review of this article in *BSHPF*, LXXXII (1933), 540. Miss Evans thinks that her list for the period ending in 1710 may be far from complete.

46 Court, *op. cit.*, I, 384–385; Cunningham, *op. cit.*, p. 263; J.-A. Galland, *Essai sur l'histoire du Protestantisme à Caen et en Basse-Normandie de l'édit de Nantes*

It is extremely difficult, if not altogether impossible, to evaluate the over-all effect of the Huguenots on the English economy. They apparently popularized certain products, and especially cloth patterns, and a contemporary stated in 1702 that "the English have now so great esteem for the workmanship of the French refugees, that hardly anything vends without a Gallic name."[47] Merchants sometimes complained that they could sell nothing unless they hired French salesmen.[48] And austere Scots around Edinburgh blamed the refugees for shifting the fashion in clothing among ordinary citizens to finer grades of cloth and frivolous personal adornment.[49] Before 1685 English imports had greatly exceeded the exports in the commodity trade with France. In the first part of the eighteenth century, if not earlier, the balance was reversed.[50] Bonrepaus wrote Seignelay on February 11, 1686, that an assembly of French and English merchants whom he had called together concluded that, whereas France had formerly exported goods to England worth 2 million livres more than the goods she had purchased there, now it was exactly the reverse and England had gained 500,000 pistoles of specie from France in 1685.[51] High tariffs, the Augsburg and Spanish Succession wars, and the normal development of the English economy were important factors in this shift in the balance of trade; but it is very likely that the Huguenot refugees also exercised some influence.

As suggested previously, at least part of the 500,000 pistoles mentioned by Bonrepaus was specie smuggled out of France by religious fugitives. The French ambassador at The Hague wrote Louis XIV on October 23, 1687, that the mint in London had

---

à la Revolution (1598–1791) (Paris, 1898), p. 258; P. de Ségur-Dupeyron, *Histoire des négociations commerciales et maritimes de la France aux XVIIᵉ et XVIIIᵉ siècles, considérées dans leurs rapports avec la politique générale* (Paris, 1872–1873), II, 462 ff.

47 Francis Brewster, *New Essays on Trade; Wherein the Present State of Our Trade . . . Is Considered . . .* (London, 1702), p. 177 (quoted by Weiss, "Mémoire sur les protestants," *op. cit.*, XXI, 81 n. 1).

48 Weiss, *Histoire des réfugiés*, I, 336–337.

49 Layard, *op. cit.*, pp. 37–39.

50 See chap. vii, pp. 265–267. For a scholarly and critical discussion of the evidence available on this point, see Lipson, *op. cit.*, III, 99 ff. The customhouse accounts, though unreliable, show that from 1700 through 1787 England had a so-called unfavorable balance of trade with the rest of the world in only 1781 and 1784 (Anderson, *op. cit.*, IV, 692–694).

51 Archives du Ministère des Affaires Étrangères, *Ancien fonds*, "Angleterre," *registre* 157, fol. 61.

recently received some 960,000 gold louis which the Huguenots had taken with them. "I should think myself shirking my duty, Sire, and failing in the fidelity I owe Your Majesty, if I did not render you a faithful account of what comes to my attention and regards the welfare of your service."[52] An unidentified church-man or government official in England addressed an interesting letter to a correspondent of high rank about James II's attempt to force a Huguenot church in London to conform to the Anglican ritual. The merchants who supported the church in-formed its ministers and elders that if the king's orders were obeyed they would withdraw their maintenance. The writer continued:

Upon which it's thought they will be forced to breake up and retire else where, which will not only force away abundance of those Hugonetts, many of which are substantiall merchants and have great stocks of money and merchandise, but many other of our merchant dissenters, who resorted to the said church, and discourage all the rest, who will take this for a forerunner of a great storme, and will thereupon discontinue their trade and withdraw their money, *which is thought to be att least 6 partes of tenn of the moveing cash that drives the trade of the whole nation;* which cannot but much deaden our traffick, and extremely diminish the King's customes.[53]

Although such a statement is probably a gross exaggeration, it is likely that it had some basis in fact. It is also noteworthy that in 1714 the legal rate of interest in England was reduced to 5 per cent, after having remained at 6 per cent since 1660.[54] This does not imply that the actual rate of interest conformed exactly to the legal, but one may presume that the market and the legal rates showed some correlation. The establishment of the Bank of England in 1694 and the concurrent development of other credit institutions helped to pull the rate down. It is impossible to assess the relative importance of the Huguenot influence in this respect, but it seems probable that with their industriousness, their low average propensity to consume, their commercial and financial contacts, and their imported specie, they may have in-creased the supply of liquid capital in England more than they increased the demand for it.

---

52 *Ibid.,* "Hollande," *registre* 152, fols. 107–109. The ambassador suggested that, if Protestants were tolerated throughout France as they were at Paris, Versailles, and Rouen, and were not persecuted, practically none of them would flee.

53 Domestic State Papers, William and Mary, Bundle 42, p. 340 (reprinted in part in the *PHSL,* II, 449–450). Italics are not mine.

54 Anderson, *op. cit.,* II, 415, 451; III, 59.

In a recent study, Alice C. Carter has shown that French refugees figured prominently as investors and dealers in the English public debt after 1690.[55] The City of London borrowed from them; they owned 106 of about 3,000 Million Bank annuities purchased in 1693–1694 which were not converted by subscribers into Million Bank stock; by 1697 they accounted for slightly less than 10 per cent of the Bank of England's original loan to the government; they participated in the 1693 Tontine Loan; and they later bought other government annuities and held various short-term loans. Approximately 10 per cent of the winners in government lotteries in 1711–1712 were refugees. They comprised about 16 per cent of the subscribers in the Million Bank and held altogether 14 per cent of its £200,000 stock. Some also invested in the South Sea and the East India companies. It is equally significant that many Huguenots domiciled in England acted as brokers and dealers in the public debt. As such they were instrumental in attracting funds from relatives and friends living in other countries and in getting the Sephardim interested. Those who argued in the House of Commons in favor of the 1709 bill to naturalize Protestant refugees claimed that the Huguenots had supplied "near £500,000" to the Bank of England and, "by a modest computation," more than £2,000,000 to the government. Those who argued against the bill claimed that "in process of time, aliens would be advanced in riches, and Her Majesty's subjects impoverished, for those beneficial trades, buying and selling by commissions, remittances, and exchanges of money, could, in a great measure, be engrossed by foreigners, by reason of their many friends and relatives abroad."

Although the evidence is not wholly conclusive, French refugees apparently did not add any major new industry to the English economy. Rather, they developed special branches along lines for which France had become famous. They raised the level of production qualitatively, and they diffused many of the skills and arts that had long been cherished secrets of French manufacturers:

During the last two wars with France the manufacturers of England did irreparable damage to the French, by imitating them in, and even out-doing them in, many of their best manufactures, wherewith they had before supplied almost all the rest of Europe. Necessity,

---

[55] "The Huguenot Contribution to the Early Years of the Funded Debt, 1694–1714," *PHSL,* XIX (1955), 21 ff.

indeed, first prompted our people thereunto, in which they were much assisted by the French refugees. . . .[56]

There can be little doubt that Huguenots acted as leaven. Their migration was one of three that have occurred since William the Conqueror's time;[57] and, as such, it figured importantly in lifting England's industrial and technological level and in pushing her into the role of industrial leader in the eighteenth and nineteenth centuries.

Since most of Louis XIV's officials sought never to offend him by mentioning the unfavorable economic consequences of the revocation, those who did speak up were not prone to exaggerate the evils. Anisson and Fénellon, sent to England to help negotiate a trade treaty after the Peace of Utrecht, apparently could not refrain from summarizing the effects as they saw them while in London:

It is principally since the time of the Prince of Orange's reign that our trade with the English has decayed. The privileges and favors he accorded our Protestants who withdrew to England in great number and who carried there our manufactories of silk, hats, hardware, paper, linen, and several other commodities, have broken the usage in England of all similar imported goods which they formerly obtained from us. And the refugees have carried the manufactories to such a degree of perfection that even we begin now to import some of their output. There is reason to fear that they may cause our manufactories to fail by offering their output at lower prices. The raw materials used in these manufactures pay no import duties and neither do the drugs used in dyeing. And all manufactured products that leave the realm are exempted from export levies. Labor which was formerly very expensive in England when employers hired only Englishmen has become as cheap as in France since our religious refugees have gone there in such large numbers.

. . . .

It is during the reign of this same prince that import duties on provisions and other merchandise from France were considerably raised and that the Dutch profited from the protection he gave them in order to increase their commerce at our expense.

Furthermore, since the two wars the English have established manufactories similar to ours for hats, paper, silk fabrics, linen cloth,

---

[56] Anderson, *op. cit.*, III, 56; MacPherson, *op. cit.*, III, 34.

[57] The other two were the Flemish weavers in Edward III's reign and the Walloons and the Huguenots in the sixteenth century.

fine hardware, gold and silver thread, window glass, glass tableware, soap, and several other products. This has diminished our exports to England and has changed the balance of trade to such an extent that the subdirector of the mint at London, a French refugee named Foucquier, confessed to us that in the four years of peace after the Treaty of Ryswick he had received a considerable quantity of our gold louis. This he regarded as certain proof that we were debtors of English merchants.[58]

THE HUGUENOTS IN IRELAND

The size of the population of Ireland in the last quarter of the seventeenth century is uncertain. Sir William Petty estimated the number in 1672 at 1,100,000,[59] and George O'Brien has cautiously concluded that the best one can say on the basis of present knowledge is that the actual figure for 1700 probably fell between 1 and 2 million.[60] Most writers agree that the island was sparsely populated, largely because of the devastation wrought by Cromwell and later by William III's sympathizers, and that this fact was one of the most important reasons that the government was anxious to encourage immigration.

Charles II in 1661 ordered his Lord Deputy, the Duke of Ormonde, to see that proper steps were taken to attract immigrants. A year later the Irish Parliament passed a law inviting all foreign Protestants to settle in Ireland and promised them free naturalization if they arrived within seven years and if they took the oath of allegiance.[61] A circular entitled "Mémoire pour encourager les Protestans de venir habiter en Hirlande," written at Ormonde's suggestion,[62] extolled the opportunities the underpopulated island offered to all thrifty and skilled immigrants; promised the Huguenots freedom to establish their own churches; stated that although ready-built houses would not be turned over to them, they could freely build their own from abundant mate-

---

[58] Archives Nationales, G⁷ 1704.

[59] Referred to by Alice E. Murray, *A History of the Commercial and Financial Relations between England and Ireland from the Period of the Restoration* (London, 1903), p. 19.

[60] *The Economic History of Ireland in the Eighteenth Century* (Dublin, 1918), p. 10. In *The Economic History of Ireland in the Seventeenth Century* (Dublin, 1919), O'Brien implies that the number was probably much closer to 1 million than to 2 million (pp. 122–123).

[61] O'Brien, *Ireland in the Seventeenth Century*, pp. 174–175; Murray, *op. cit.*, p. 44; Albert Carré, *L'Influence des Huguenots français en Irlande aux XVIIᵉ et XVIIIᵉ siècles* (Paris, 1937), pp. 3 ff.; Lee, *op. cit.*, p. 12.

[62] Bibliothèque Nationale, *Fonds français*, MS 21622, fols. 74–76.

rials at hand; guaranteed them freedom to bring in and later to take out all their property and money; stated that the Duke of Ormonde would borrow their idle funds (up to 15,000 *écus* per person) at 10 per cent interest until they found other investment opportunities; and even committed Ormonde to sending a boat to France to help them escape. After Louis XIV revoked the Edict of Nantes, Ireland made further overtures to the Huguenots. Its Parliament in 1692 and again in 1703 passed bills that naturalized them en masse, and many who first landed in England later transferred their persons and properties to Ireland at government expense. Moreover, some of the cities in Ireland went out of their way to attract the newcomers. In 1693, for example, Waterford provided homes for fifty families and granted them the freedom of the city without charge.[63] Between 5,000 and 10,000 individuals responded to these pleas. As to be expected, most of them settled in the northeastern counties where Protestantism was already well entrenched.[64]

In the Irish economy the Huguenots exercised their most profound influence upon the manufacture of linen and helped to make it the leading industry. By 1727 it was providing one-third of Ireland's total exports. The industry, however, was not new, for in the sixteenth century the natives were already growing flax and spinning and weaving linen fabrics rather extensively.[65] In the early years of the following century the industry was in a depressed state; and the efforts of the Earl of Strafford, Lord Deputy of Ireland under Charles I, to revive it about 1636 by investing large sums of his own money, by importing flaxseed from Holland, and by bringing over skilled workers from Flanders and France, were unavailing.[66] The Cromwellian civil wars practically destroyed its last vestiges. The Duke of Ormonde, Lord Deputy from 1662 to 1669, tried to resuscitate the industry by sending agents to Holland to observe the manufacture of linen there, by bringing over about 500 Brabantine families and skilled artisans from La Rochelle and the isles of Ré and Jersey, by appealing to other French Huguenots to settle on his estates, and by establishing linen workshops at Chapelizod near

---

63 Murray, *op. cit.*, pp. 44–45, 117; Carré, *op. cit.*, pp. 10–11.
64 Conrad Gill, *The Rise of the Irish Linen Industry* (Oxford, 1925), pp. 20–21.
65 See, e.g., O'Brien, *Ireland in the Seventeenth Century*, pp. 76–77.
66 Gill, *op. cit.*, pp. 8–9; Murray, *op. cit.*, pp. 113–114; John F. Burke, *Outlines of the Industrial History of Ireland* (rev. ed.; Dublin, 1946), p. 54.

Dublin and at Carrick-on-Suir.[67] When Ormonde left Ireland, the industry began to languish once again, and it was only after the Huguenots arrived at the time of the revocation of the Edict of Nantes that the manufacture was placed on enduring foundations.

In 1697 William III invited Louis Crommelin to Ireland to superintend the industry. Crommelin, a refugee in Holland, was of an old linen-making family in Picardy. He accepted the invitation in 1698 and located about ten miles southwest of Belfast at Lisburn, a small town which had been completely destroyed in the civil wars. The king appointed Crommelin "Overseer of the Royal Linen Manufactory of Ireland" and issued him a patent in 1700 guaranteeing him £800 a year interest on the £10,000 capital which he and his associates were to raise, and granting him an annuity of £200 as his salary and also £120 for the salaries of three assistants.[68]

Crommelin immediately brought over twenty-five families skilled in linen making from Holland and France. Others joined them later, and the Ulster colony was soon said to number about 500 families. He also imported about 1,000 linen looms and spinning wheels and offered a bonus of £5 for each Dutch or French loom that the Irish used. In 1705 Crommelin published his *Essay on the Improving of the Hempen and Flaxen Manufactures in the Kingdom of Ireland,* and set up schools to teach Irish women how to spin the finer grades of yarn. His assistants traveled around the country, offering advice and instruction on the growing and harvesting of flax, on the spinning and weaving of fine fibers, and on the proper methods of bleaching. In fact, Crommelin built a bleachhouse near Lisburn which he invited all to visit and where he demonstrated improved bleaching processes involving wood potash and buttermilk instead of varec soda and lime. He and other Huguenots drained swamps[69] and imported flaxseed from Holland, Germany, and Russia because Irish seed yielded sickly plants. He was instrumental in getting laws passed in 1705 and 1709 requiring seven

67 O'Brien, *Ireland in the Seventeenth Century,* p. 189; Carré, *op. cit.,* pp. 1–3, 56; Burke, *op. cit.,* p. 55; Murray, *op. cit.,* p. 114.

68 Murray, *op. cit.,* p. 116; Lee, *op. cit.,* p. 19; Carré, *op. cit.,* pp. 60–61; Gill, *op. cit.,* p. 17; O'Brien, *Ireland in the Eighteenth Century,* p. 200. Queen Anne renewed the contract in somewhat more general terms in 1701.

69 Boislisle, *op. cit.,* II, 489 (memorandum submitted to the Council of Trade by the deputy from Nantes on March 4, 1701).

years of apprenticeship and journeyman work before a native might set up a shop on his own.[70] Crommelin himself opened sailcloth works in Waterford and started the manufacture of linen in Kilkenny. The Linen Board (created in 1710–1711) recommended in 1712 that the government continue its contract with him and testified that "the said Crommelin and colony have been very serviceable and greatly instrumental in . . . improving and propagating the flaxen manufacture in the north part of this kingdom; and [that] . . . the perfection to which the same is brought in that part of the country is very much owing to the skill and industry of the said Crommelin."[71]

There is little doubt that Huguenots introduced advanced methods of growing and preparing flax and of spinning and weaving its fibers. They were also among the first to manufacture cambrics, damasks, and the finest broadcloths; they persuaded the industry to supply the widths and varieties of cloth which the export market demanded; by building and operating bleach-yards themselves they removed the necessity of sending brown linen abroad to be whitened; and they helped to organize the domestic wholesale market. A London merchant in 1737 stated that Irish linen at that time was of much better quality than when he began to import it twenty-five years earlier; and in 1741 German and Scottish manufacturers were counterfeiting Irish marks so they could get higher prices for their output.[72]

The inspector of manufactures at Grenoble stated in 1708, in a memorandum to the French controller general, that the Irish linen industry, according to Crommelin himself, still needed tariff protection if it was to survive and that the refugees in Ireland could never duplicate the fine linens made in France.[73] He spoke too soon. The value of linen cloth exported from Ireland rose from about £14,000 in 1701 to £105,537 in 1710, to £121,899 in 1720, and to £206,810 in 1730. For each year from 1751 to 1755 it averaged £753,151. Because of changes in the value of money and the price of cloth, the number of yards ex-

---

[70] Carré, *op. cit.*, 74. Gill believes these acts were mainly designed to promote the near-monopoly position of the refugees, for he claims that a seven-year apprenticeship was much longer than was needed to gain proficiency in the industry (*op. cit.*, p. 19).

[71] Gill, *op. cit.*, p. 19.

[72] *Ibid.*, pp. 16, 20; Carré, *op. cit.*, pp. 81–87; O'Brien, *Ireland in the Eighteenth Century*, p. 200.

[73] Archives Nationales, G7 1692.

ported annually constitutes a more reliable index of growth than the figures on value. In 1665 Ireland is said to have exported 11,800 ells of linen;[74] in 1705, her exports came to about 520,000 yards, and in 1710 to 1,688,574 yards. They probably quadrupled between 1700 and 1710.[75] They doubled again by 1720 and quintupled from 1720 to 1751. The total quantity of linen fabrics exported in 1751–1755 was almost 6.7 times the total for 1711–1715. Irish exports of linen yarn experienced a less phenomenal increase. In the year ending on March 26, 1641, and in 1665 Ireland exported 2,297 and 3,477 hundredweights, respectively.[76] In 1710, the comparable figure was 7,975. The amount of yarn exported in 1751–1755 was only slightly more than twice the total for 1711–1715.[77]

It would be a mistake to attribute all this remarkable growth to the Huguenots. Ireland's natural resources and system of landholding gave her a comparative advantage in this field; and both the Irish Parliament and, to a lesser extent, the English Parliament encouraged manufacture. In 1698 and 1699 England practically destroyed the Irish woolen industry by forbidding all exports to any English colony or foreign country and by placing prohibitive duties on all woolens exported to England and Wales. In partial recompense,[78] England allowed Irish linens to be imported into the kingdom duty free and to be carried directly to her colonies. In addition, she granted export bounties on Irish as well as on Scotch and English linens. The Irish Parliament did much more. Besides levying protective import duties, it gave bounties to manufacturers and exporters, subsidized the importation and distribution of flaxseed, established the Linen Board, and disbursed a total of £1,295,560 in 1700–1775 to aid the industry. Some of its efforts to regulate the cultivation, preparation, spinning, and weaving of flax, however, may have interfered with the industry's growth more than they aided it. Although it is difficult to assess the relative importance of the Huguenot influ-

---

[74] O'Brien, *Ireland in the Seventeenth Century*, p. 189.

[75] Gill, *op. cit.*, pp. 65, 101.

[76] O'Brien, *Ireland in the Seventeenth Century*, pp. 80, 189.

[77] The export data, unless otherwise noted, are based on figures found in Murray, *op. cit.*, pp. 129 ff.; O'Brien, *Ireland in the Eighteenth Century*, pp. 202–203; Carré, *op. cit.*, p. 138.

[78] See the excerpts from debates in both houses of Parliament and from the king's pronouncements in J. G. Swift MacNeill, *English Interference with Irish Industries* (2d ed.; London, 1886), pp. 28 ff.

ence and of the encouragement provided by the state, most
writers are of the opinion that the linen industry in Ireland was
indebted more to the former than to the latter.

The Huguenots were also responsible for considerable expansion in silk weaving. During the first half of the eighteenth century the silk industry at Dublin prospered, and in 1730 about
300 looms were said to be at work there.[79] A Huguenot named
Goyer introduced the industry at Lisburn, and others began elsewhere to make poplin. Whereas most branches of the silk industry declined after 1750, Irish poplin continued to enjoy a good
reputation in the world market.[80] Some of the Huguenots attracted by Ormonde in the 1660's, as well as those who settled
in Ireland in 1681–1698, raised the technological level of the
woolen industry and introduced new varieties of cloth. In 1698
it was stated that woolens engaged the energies of some 42,000
Protestant families in Dublin and other places.[81] As already
stated, however, this industry was destroyed by adverse English
legislation in 1698–1699. Some refugees also engaged in lacemaking and glovemaking, and the membership lists of Huguenot churches include artisans skilled in fashioning precious
metals, glassmaking, sugar refining, beermaking, tanning, hatmaking, and various other trades.[82] Finally, it should be noted
that in 1716 a Huguenot named La Touche formed one of the
strongest banks Ireland had in the eighteenth century.

THE HUGUENOTS IN HOLLAND

Holland, with scarcely 1,000,000 population at the time of the
revocation, had been experiencing for about a century an era of
extraordinary economic prosperity. After freeing themselves
from Spanish rule in the last quarter of the sixteenth century,
the seven United Provinces (of which Holland was unquestionably the most important) had rapidly become the chief maritime nation of Europe and were carrying a good share of
England's and France's trade. The Dutch had also become the
rivals of the French and the English in many branches of indus-

---

79 O'Brien, *Ireland in the Eighteenth Century*, pp. 208–209. Some writers have
claimed that there were about 800 looms in use (Carré, *op. cit.*, p. 89; Burke,
op. cit., pp. 104–105).

80 John Lord Sheffield, *Observations on the Manufactures, Trade, and Present
State of Ireland* (London, 1785), p. 193; O'Brien, *Ireland in the Eighteenth Century*,
p. 209.

81 Murray, *op. cit.*, p. 102; Burke, *op. cit.*, p. 51.

82 Carré, *op. cit.*, p. 94; Murray, *op. cit.*, pp. 44–45; Burke, *op. cit.*, p. 59.

try, and Amsterdam had displaced Antwerp as the international financial center of western Europe. The country, moreover, had developed a special kind of mercantilism which allowed almost complete freedom in foreign trade and in the import and the export of bullion. Although Calvinism had become the official religion, the republic had long served as a haven for persecuted minorities such as Spanish and Portuguese Jews and Protestants from the Spanish Low Countries. In view of this rather unique liberalism in commerce and religion, it is not surprising that Holland opened her doors to Huguenots trying to escape the persecution of Louis XIV; in view of her economic rivalry with France, it is not surprising that she actively encouraged them—provided they were self-sustaining[83]—to settle within her jurisdiction. She probably received between 50,000 and 75,000 immigrants.

In May, 1681, just after the French dragoons were set loose in Poitou, the state of Friesland resolved that all refugees settling in its territories would have all rights enjoyed by natives.[84] On July 13, 1709, the Estates-General of the United Provinces decreed that all Protestant refugees "shall be acknowledged and received for the future as our subjects; and they shall enjoy the right of Naturalization." The decree stated that the prosperity of most nations, and especially of Holland, had been greatly enhanced by immigrants seeking sanctuary from the wrath of the French king, and that they had contributed greatly to the increase of trade, manufactures, and the common good.[85] Even before this, according to the French ambassador d'Avaux at The Hague, the Estates-General had voted 150,000 livres to aid refugee army officers and in June, 1687, had agreed to appropriate 30,000 livres a year for their salaries.[86] The Dutch ambassador at Paris secretly distributed among Protestants in that city a small

---

[83] Bibliothèque Nationale, *Fonds français*, MS 7044, fol. 109. Professor James Westfall Thompson has argued that in this connection the Dutch were almost entirely motivated by their economic self-interest and that "religious sympathy was never more than niggardly given" ("Some Economic Factors in the Revocation of the Edict of Nantes," *American Historical Review*, XIV [1909], p. 45).

[84] Poole, *op. cit.*, p. 35. This was probably the first official act of any foreign power designed to aid the harassed Huguenots.

[85] F. P. de Labillière, "Incidents of Huguenot History in the Reign of Queen Anne," *PHSL*, IV (1891–1893), 70–71; J. Arnal, "De l'Influence des réfugiés français aux Pays-Bas," *Bulletin de la commission pour l'histoire des églises wallonnes* (hereinafter cited as *BCHEW*), 4th series, 2d issue (1929), p. 2.

[86] Archives du Ministère des Affaires Étrangères, *Ancien fonds*, "Hollande," *registre* 151, fol. 65.

brochure enumerating the advantages offered by the Low Countries, the proper roadways to follow to elude frontier guards, and
the best precautions to take to avoid detection.[87]

Dutch cities appear to have vied with one another in trying
to attract the largest number of Huguenots. Amsterdam is said
to have constructed a thousand dwellings to be let at minimal
rentals to immigrants,[88] and in September and October, 1681,
she declared that all refugees within her jurisdiction would enjoy bourgeois status, the right to exercise their crafts freely,
exemption for three years from import and other ordinary city
charges no matter how wealthy they were, access to interest-free
loans so they could acquire the tools of their trade, and an assured
market for their output so long as they needed public assistance.[89]
On October 7, 1681, the city magistrates voted to grant 10,000
guilders to skilled craftsmen who needed immediate financial
assistance, and on December 13, 1682, entered into an exceedingly liberal provisional contract with one Pierre Bayle.[90] The
city agreed to provide Bayle (or Baille) with a house suitable
for forty looms, to give him 300 florins to furnish his own living
quarters, to lend him forty beds, either to advance him 400
florins for one year without interest for the upkeep of his workmen or to lend him up to 3,000–4,000 florins without interest
but under suitable bond, and to expand his works later on if
need arose.[91] Bayle, on his part, was to make certain kinds of
silk cloth not previously produced in Holland and to hire only
Huguenot refugees unless he could prove there were not enough
of them to staff his manufactory. Probably no other immigrant
entrepreneur received so many privileges and subsidies as Bayle,
but many of them were favored in one way or another.[92]

Nearly all Dutch cities followed Amsterdam's example in
granting immigrants freedom to practice their arts and other
similar rights. Native Dutch artisans and workers, facing new
competition, soon began to resent the tax exemptions and other

---

87 Douen, *op. cit.*, II, 431.

88 Solomiac, "Le Réfuge dans le pays de Vaud (1685–1860)," *BSHPF,* IX (1860), 360.

89 Weiss, *Histoire des réfugiés,* II, 6–7.

90 Leonie van Nierop, "Stukken Betreffende de Nijverheid der Refugiés te
Amsterdam," *Economische-Historisch Jaarboek*, VII (1921), 155, 160–161.

91 A short time later the city advanced him 10,000 guilders more without
interest (*ibid.*, pp. 173–175).

92 *Ibid.*, VII and IX (1923), *passim.* The city council was informed in July, 1690,
that 1,708 refugees were receiving financial aid from the city and that the number
was still growing. The council then decided to rescind all tax exemptions except
for those who had just arrived. (*Ibid.*, IX, 193–195.)

privileges accorded the newcomers and complained that they themselves could not find work. Despite such friction, however, the magistrates were unwilling to see any of the Huguenots return to France. D'Avaux wrote Louis XIV on March 20, 1687, that although there were many Frenchmen in Holland who wanted to return, they dared not let their wishes be known lest they be arrested by the police. The Dutch were even threatening, he continued, to search all ships headed for France in their efforts to prevent repatriation.[93]

Holland, hoping to get revenge for Colbert's success in transplanting certain branches of the textile industry by importing Dutch workmen and copying their techniques, encouraged the Huguenots to initiate production along the lines for which France had become famous. And to a considerable extent she was successful. Many of the refugees—including Pierre Bayle— who arrived in Amsterdam before and after 1685 were subsidized to manufacture silk, especially black and lustrous taffetas.[94] Immigrants from Nîmes and Tours opened silk workshops in Haarlem and Utrecht, and it was soon reported that Haarlem had from 15,000 to 20,000 workers employed in the industry and that Utrecht had a famous manufactory employing 500 people.[95] One refugee developed an especially strong silk gauze,[96] and another introduced the cherished French secret of dyeing scarlet silks.[97] It is worth noting that in March, 1690, English customs officials acknowledged that they had mistaken Dutch silk exported to England for French silk.[98] A high French official complained that the Dutch were imitating the rich silk brocades for

[93] W. E. J. Berg, *De Réfugiés in de Nederlanden, na de Herroeping van het Edict van Nantes* (Amsterdam, 1845), pp. 33, 161 ff., 187, 193; Archives du Ministère des Affaires Étrangères, *Ancien fonds*, "Hollande," *registres* 143, fol. 180; 145, fol. 26; 146, fol. 158; 150, fols. 231–233.

[94] Berg, *op. cit.*, pp. 166–168; Nierop, "Stukken Betreffende de Nijverheid der Refugiés te Amsterdam," *op. cit.*, VII, 158, 162, 163–165; IX, 164–165, 167–168. Nierop concludes that the taffeta industry in Amsterdam kept 1,000 looms busy (*ibid.*, IX, 177–181).

[95] Léon Dutil, "L'Industrie de la soie à Nîmes jusqu'en 1789," *Revue d'histoire moderne et contemporaine*, X (1908), 321–322; Archives Nationales, G7 1701 (*registre*, fol. 136); Arnal, *op. cit.*, p. 18; C. Landré, "Souvenirs du Réfuge," *BCHEW*, 1st series, 2d issue (1887), p. 393.

[96] Landré, *op. cit.*, p. 393.

[97] Archives Nationales, B2 *registre* 61, fol. 219. Seignelay wrote d'Avaux that His Majesty was willing to bribe the worker into returning to France if d'Avaux established the fact that the man actually was using the secret process and that his manufactory would close down upon his departure.

[98] Nierop, "Stukken Betreffende de Nijverheid der Refugiés te Amsterdam," *op. cit.*, IX, 186.

which France was renowned, and the intendant at Lyon reported in 1699 that, whereas the Dutch had formerly imported large amounts of black taffetas from that city, now they bought just enough to serve as models and patterns for their own manufactories.[99] One last bit of evidence may suffice to demonstrate the success achieved in silkmaking in Holland. The Prussian ambassador at The Hague in 1686 reported to the Great Elector in Berlin that French shops in the United Provinces had achieved "a prodigious success" and were copying the lustrous black taffetas of Tours and Lyon. The price of silk fabrics on Dutch markets, consequently, had fallen by 28 per cent.[100] Despite its auspicious beginning and lusty early growth,[101] the silk industry apparently declined in the latter half of the eighteenth century, and French producers recaptured the Dutch market.[102]

Somewhat the same thing happened in velvetmaking. Refugees at Utrecht and Haarlem started the manufacture of rich velvets and flowered plushes, which gained a favorable reputation in Dutch and foreign markets. French manufacturers at Amiens even began to sell their output as "Utrecht velvets" in order to compete with the new shops. Before the end of the eighteenth century, however, the Dutch industry was declining.[103]

In his instructions on December 20, 1685, Louis XIV asked Bonrepaus to find out why the Dutch were buying less French linen than formerly for their East Indian trade, and to recommend corrective action.[104] Louis himself suggested improving the quality of French linen or persuading French refugees who had set up shop in the United Provinces to return home. There can be no doubt that many Huguenots carried the skill and the knowledge they had gained in linen and sailcloth establishments in Picardy and Normandy to a large number of Dutch cities. Louis Crommelin, who did so much for the Irish linen industry, had first taken refuge in Holland, where he and other members of

---

99 Bibliothèque Nationale, *Fonds français*, MSS 4288, fol. 117; 7044, fol. 279 ff.

100 Quoted by Weiss, *Histoire des réfugiés*, II, 136.

101 It is true that high protective tariffs aided their efforts, but the refugees certainly were instrumental in diffusing the technology of silkmaking and in initiating many Dutch enterprises. Natalis Rondot thinks otherwise (*Les Protestants à Lyon au dix-septième siècle* [Lyon, 1891], p. 64 n. 1).

102 Berg, *op. cit.*, p. 293.

103 Arnal, *op. cit.*, pp. 17–18; Berg, *op. cit.*, p. 208; L. Rossier, *Histoire des protestants de Picardie, particulièrement de ceux du département de la Somme* (Amiens, 1861), p. 251.

104 Archives du Ministère des Affaires Étrangères, *Ancien fonds*, "Angleterre," *registre* 157, fol. 16.

his family had built up thriving enterprises. More than twenty linen shops, producing the heaviest duck for sails or the finest fabrics for clothing, were opened by refugees in Haarlem. Along with others located elsewhere, they successfully exported their output as "French linens"; and, unlike the making of silk and velvet, the manufacture of linen continued to be an important part of the Dutch economy.[105]

On May 9, 1686, d'Avaux wrote Seignelay that Huguenots had recently opened a factory at Rotterdam to make coarse woolen cloth (*draps de meunier*), which France had formerly sold in large quantities throughout the world. Seignelay at once urged Bonrepaus to persuade the workers to return home, sparing no expense, for "this affair is close to His Majesty's heart." He reminded Bonrepaus that one of the principal purposes of his visit to Holland was to repatriate as many French workmen as possible, for "nothing is more capable of ruining the commerce of His Majesty's subjects than the establishment of our manufactures in Holland."[106] Amsterdam subsidized some Protestants who promised to make serge,[107] and a French inspector of manufactures in 1708 complained that serge manufacturers in Lower Normandy had lost their market in Holland after refugees there had set up their own looms.[108] There is some evidence that Huguenots also engaged in lacemaking, stocking knitting, calico printing, drawing gold and silver thread, and weaving rugs and tapestries.

In addition to textiles and allied products, Protestant immigrants from Normandy transplanted, to Rotterdam especially, their skill in making hats from beaver fur and other materials.[109] Louis XIV, Seignelay, and d'Avaux evidenced as much concern

---

105 Bibliothèque Nationale, *Fonds français*, MSS 7044, fols. 279 ff.; 20967, fol. 4; Arnal, *op. cit.*, pp. 17–18; Berg, *op. cit.*, p. 170; Weiss, *Histoire des réfugiés*, II, 140.

106 Archives Nationales, B2 *registre* 57, fol. 395; Archives du Ministère des Affaires Étrangères, *Ancien fonds*, "Angleterre," *registre* 160, fol. 270.

107 Nierop, "Stukken Betreffende de Nijverheid der Refugiés te Amsterdam," *op. cit.*, IX, 161–162.

108 Cited from records in the Archives Départementales du Calvados by J.-A. Galland, *op. cit.*, p. 257. In denying the validity of the statement of some authors that the serge and woolen industries at Leiden prospered after Huguenots from Sedan and elsewhere arrived, Ségur-Dupeyron quotes figures from the records of the "halls and markets" of Leiden to show that the number of pieces of serge made there declined drastically from 1668 to 1708, whereas the output of two other kinds of woolens (*draps* and *bayettes*) increased somewhat but not phenomenally (*op. cit.*, II, 440).

109 Arnal, *op. cit.*, p. 17; Nierop, "Stukken Betreffende de Nijverheid de Refugiés te Amsterdam," *op. cit.*, IX, 174–176.

over the loss of this manufacture as they did over linen, and the Prussian ambassador at The Hague stated that the price of beaver hats in Holland had fallen by 40 per cent since the new shops were started.[110] To encourage the enterprise the Dutch abolished all export duties on hats, raised import duties by 40 per cent, and rescinded an old rule restricting an entrepreneur to eight employees.[111]

Papermakers from Angoulême and Auvergne also found employment in Dutch mills, and the French ambassador was concerned lest Dutch printers use the output of refugees to the exclusion of French paper.[112] The French deputies of trade on two separate occasions in 1708 confirmed the belief that Huguenots had established several mills in Holland and were imitating "only too well" the better grades of paper suitable for playing cards, fine books, and reproductions of etchings and prints.[113] According to a student of the industry in Auvergne, the Dutch acquired superiority over the French in paper for the last use and enjoyed a virtual monopoly in its manufacture "for more than a century."[114]

Many printers fled Lyon and other centers of the book trade in France and set up their presses in Holland.[115] The Dutch also hoped to acquire the special techniques involved in making Norman crown glass and crystalware, but it is not clear how many of the Protestant glass blowers who planned to go to Holland were able to avoid detection at the border.[116] Some writers have claimed that the Dutch brewing and sugar refining industries were also strengthened by man power and skills provided by immigrants.[117]

Finally, the shipping and whaling industries deserve mention. The great concern of officers in the French marine and the exten-

---

110 Weiss, *Histoire des réfugiés,* II, 136, 137; Archives Nationales, B2 *registre* 57, fol. 395; Archives du Ministère des Affaires Étrangères, *Ancien fonds,* "Angleterre," *registre* 160, fol. 270.

111 Arnal, *op. cit.,* p. 17; Weiss, *Histoire des réfugiés,* II, 137 and n. 2.

112 Arnal, *op. cit.,* p. 19; Berg, *op. cit.,* p. 172; Weiss, *Histoire des réfugiés,* II, 145–146.

113 Archives Nationales, G7 1691, 1692.

114 Michel Cohendy, *Note sur la papeterie d'Auvergne antérieurement à 1790* (Clermont, 1862), p. 7.

115 Berg, *op. cit.,* pp. 175 ff.

116 Archives Nationales, G7 493; TT 430, doc. 100; B2 *registre* 62, fols. 126–127.

117 Arnal, *op. cit.,* p. 19; Berg, *op. cit.,* p. 209.

sive efforts to patrol all seaports and seafaring vessels leaving France suggest that many Protestant sailors and fishermen sought refuge in Holland after 1681. With the information at present available, it is impossible to ascertain just how much the Dutch navy, merchant marine, and fishing fleets profited from this migration. The figures for the number of Dutch whalers off the coast of Greenland each year, however, reveal that the average for 1681–1685 was some 50 per cent higher than the average for 1676–1680, and that the number did not decline markedly until 1690.[118] The lists of personnel and directors in the whaling companies suggest that the Huguenots participated in the expansion.[119]

It is thus apparent that French Protestants affected a great variety of Dutch industries. Holland's economy, however, was primarily commercial rather than industrial; and with the return of peace, especially after the Treaty of Utrecht, and the reopening of normal trade routes, many of the new manufactories and branches of industry introduced by immigrants either failed or ceased to expand when confronted with competition from France. Two Dutch historians have concluded that the long-run effects of Huguenot influence upon Holland's industries were not very pronounced.[120] Furthermore, it is generally recognized that Holland's development in the eighteenth century did not maintain its seventeenth-century tempo, and that relative to other European countries she lost ground. She still remained, however, the chief commercial and financial center; and in these spheres the Huguenots may have exercised their greatest and most lasting influence.

Many contemporaries agreed that the most prosperous merchants and the wealthiest Protestants fled to Holland. Ambassador d'Avaux wrote Louis XIV on October 23, 1685, that several rich merchants of La Rochelle, Dieppe, Rouen, and Lyon had already arrived in various Dutch cities or had made plans to come as soon as they could smuggle their wealth out of France.[121] "Yesterday I received information from Friesland," he wrote on

---

118 Anderson, *op. cit.*, IV, 693. Anderson's figures differ somewhat from those given by Weiss, *Histoire des réfugiés*, II, 143, and Arnal, *op. cit.*, p. 19, but all implant the same impression of growth.

119 Berg, *op. cit.*, p. 210.

120 *Ibid.*, pp. 260 ff.; Nierop, "Stukken Betreffende de Nijverheid der Refugiés te Amsterdam," *op. cit.*, VII, 150.

121 Archives Nationales, TT 430, doc. 100.

March 15, 1686, "that . . . several other refugees from France
have offered to lend the province 1 million livres at current
interest; this clearly demonstrates how much money they have
been able to take out of the country."[122] He complained again
on October 23, 1687, that from all appearances the richest
Huguenots still remaining in France were planning a mass emigration to Holland, and that capitalists in Amsterdam were already irked because they were finding it increasingly difficult to
lend their money at more than 2 per cent interest.[123] The city
itself found it could borrow at 3 per cent in 1684[124] instead
of at 4 per cent, as it had done before 1679; and the interest
it paid refugee creditors was said to be about 150,000 florins a
year.[125] The interest rate paid the Bank of Amsterdam by the
East India Company fell from 4 per cent before 1685 to 3½ per
cent in the period 1685–1723, and then to 2½ per cent.[126] Deposits in the bank rose from an average level of about 5,950,000
guilders in 1676–1680 to an average of 13,750,000 guilders in
1696–1700, and its specie reserves rose from an average level of
4,502,787 guilders to an average of 11,444,887 guilders. The number of depositors increased by about one-third between 1671 and
1701. Although it would be unwise to attribute all this to the
revocation of the Edict of Nantes, certainly the Huguenots arriving in Holland appreciably increased the supply of liquid
capital and helped lower interest rates.[127]

THE HUGUENOTS IN GERMANY

The technological gap separating Germany from France was
much larger than the difference between the Dutch and the Eng-

---

122 Archives du Ministère des Affaires Étrangères, *Ancien fonds,* "Hollande,"
registre 145, fols. 207, 240.

123 *Ibid., registre* 152, fols. 107–109. About 1700 someone wrote that only 3 per
cent could be had on money in Holland (Bibliothèque de la Société Protestante,
MS 617n, p. 73).

124 Eugène Bersier, *Quelques pages de l'histoire des Huguenots* (Paris, 1891), p.
183, has given the rate as 2 per cent. Poole, *op. cit.,* p. 170.

125 Arnal, *op. cit.,* p. 5. At 3 per cent, this would mean that Huguenots had
lent the municipal government 5 million florins.

126 J. G. van Dillen, "The Bank of Amsterdam," in *History of the Principal
Public Banks,* collected and edited by Dillen (The Hague, 1934), p. 95.

127 Professor Earl J. Hamilton has pointed out to me that such an inference
could be faulty. This might well be. The interest rate was declining at the same
time in Spain and even in France, where the drain of specie, other things being
equal, should have raised it. It might well have been, however, that the demand
for loanable funds in France was declining more rapidly than the supply because
of depressed conditions in its economy.

lish economies, on the one hand, and the French economy, on the other. Germany, like Ireland, had been depopulated by warfare in the sixteenth and seventeenth centuries, and by 1685 she was anxious to repeople her villages and farms. Certain areas were predominantly Lutheran; others were stanchly Catholic; and those with an admixture of the two were the most generous in their treatment of Calvinists. Since there was no true Germany but only a conglomeration of Germanic kingdoms, principalities, dukedoms, and free cities, each with its own largely autonomous government and differing public policies, it is difficult to generalize about the government's and the public's attitude to the Huguenots, the number of immigrants who settled there, or the effect they had upon the level of technological practice. With the exception of Austria, Prussia (or Brandenburg) had become the foremost German state by the second half of the seventeenth century. Certainly, viewed as a refuge for French Protestants, it was the most important. Most of what follows pertains chiefly to Prussia rather than to all Germany.

Twenty-one days after Louis XIV revoked the Edict of Nantes the Great Elector Frederick William issued his famous Potsdam decree written in both French and German.[128] Since this decree became something of a model for other German rulers,[129] it will be worth while to analyze its contents in some detail.[130] The elector ordered his agents at Amsterdam and Hamburg to provide sustenance and transportation to all Huguenots who traveled that route to Berlin or other Prussian cities. Those who chose to enter his realm via Frankfort-on-the-Main could get money, boat passage on the Rhine, and passports from his agent in that city. The immigrants could freely choose their places of residence, their occupations or trades, and the materials they would need to set up shop or build homes. The elector promised to give them free of charge any ruined dwellings and enough materials

---

128 The decree bore the date October 29, 1685, but the German Protestant states used the Julian calendar rather than the Gregorian. The Julian calendar was ten days behind the Gregorian.

129 Helmut Erbe, *Die Hugenotten in Deutschland* (Essen, 1937), p. 30; Gustav Aubin, *Der Einflusz der Reformation in der Geschichte der deutschen Wirtschaft* (Halle, 1929), p. 23; Herbert W. Ellinger, *Les Réfugiés Huguenots en Saxe-Weimar; leurs manufactures de bonneterie* (Gap, 1933), p. 33.

130 The decree may be found in the Bibliothèque Nationale, *Fonds français*, MS 7057, fols. 171 ff. It has also been reproduced in its entirety in several publications, e.g., Erbe, *op. cit.*, pp. 30 ff., and Eugène and Émile Haag, *La France protestante, ou Vies des protestants français qui se sont fait un nom dans l'histoire* (Paris, 1846–1859), X, 465–467.

to repair them, or to allow them several years' free occupancy of empty houses provided they set to work to construct their own. They might bring with them duty free all their furniture, personal effects, and properties useful in their trade; they were accorded all city and gild rights of natural-born citizens; and the elector promised to grant them privileges and tax exemptions to help them start new manufactories and even to advance them money, tools, and raw materials. French nobles were to enjoy noble status in their adopted country; all were to have complete freedom of worship, and the government offered to pay the salary of one minister for each town; and until they became acclimated to their new legal and social environment special judges and courts were to be established to handle all legal difficulties that might arise among them or between them and their German neighbors. Members of the French military as well as men of letters received a most cordial welcome at court and were pensioned by the government.[131]

The Landgrave of Hesse-Cassel appears to have been one of the first German princes openly to proclaim (April, 1685) that all Huguenots would find a haven in his jurisdiction;[132] and on December 12, 1685, he promulgated an edict of concessions and privileges similar in tone to the Potsdam decree, although somewhat less generous.[133] The Duke of Brunswick and Luneburg likewise accorded all such immigrants religious, civil, and economic freedom and promised to aid their new economic enterprises in every way possible.[134] Some rulers, like the Elector of the Palatinate, stood in fear of displeasing Louis XIV and were very cautious about overtly encouraging settlement in their areas.[135] Others whose provinces were strongly Lutheran or Roman Catholic took no action.

---

131 Archives du Ministère des Affaires Étrangères, *Ancien fonds,* "Prusse," *registre* 25, fols. 344–345, 426–428. The best contemporary account of the measures adopted in Prussia to aid and encourage the refugees is Charles Ancillon, *Histoire de l'établissement des françois dans les états de son altesse electorale de Brandebourg* (Berlin, 1690).

132 Erbe, *op. cit.,* p. 29.

133 Haag, *op. cit.,* X, 472–474; C. Couderc, "L'Abbé Raynal et son projet d'histoire de la Révocation de l'Édit de Nantes, documents sur le Réfuge," *BSHPF,* XXXVIII (1889), 601; Bibliothèque Nationale, *Fonds français,* MS 6432, pp. 123–124.

134 Erbe, *op. cit.,* p. 29; Bibliothèque Nationale, *Fonds français,* MS 21616, fols. 379–381. The king of Denmark did the same thing (Bibliothèque de la Société Protestante, MS 6171, p. 250).

135 André Paul, "Les Réfugiés huguenots et wallons dans le Palatinat du Rhin de XVI⁰ siècle à la Révolution," *Revue historique,* CLVII (1928), pp. 264 ff.; see also Bibliothèque de la Société Protestante, MS 6171, pp. 56–57.

In addition to the privileges granted by governments, Huguenots settling in Germany received relief aid from funds raised by public collections and also from more ample funds supplied by sympathizers in Holland, Switzerland, and England.[136] The Great Elector encouraged new enterprises by providing them with working quarters, some equipment, and loans without interest; by buying some of their output for himself and his court; and by clothing his troops in woolens produced by refugees. He and other rulers levied tariffs on foreign goods that would compete with the new domestic products and exempted raw materials from local excises.[137]

The native populations did not always wholeheartedly endorse the special treatment accorded to immigrants by their rulers. In Saxe-Weimar, for example, the jealousy of the populace, as well as the hostility of the Lutheran Church, has been cited as one reason that the French colony of manufacturers there lasted only fifteen months.[138] Even in Prussia considerable friction developed.[139] Rébenac, Louis XIV's representative at Berlin, wrote in 1686 and 1687 that the refugees were holding aloof from the natives; that many of them were becoming disgruntled and wished to return to France; and that the Germans had developed "a prodigious aversion" to the newcomers.[140] In Dresden, Leipzig, Frankfort-on-the-Main, and Halle the refugees faced outright discrimination by local craftsmen and the Lutheran Church; and most gilds in Brandenburg accepted Huguenots as members only because they were required by law to do so. Frederick William, however, was so anxious to attract and then to retain them that in 1688 he ordered that no Frenchman could leave the country without a passport issued by the elector himself.[141] This infuriated Louis XIV. He wrote Rébenac on February 12, 1688:

---

136 Erbe, *op. cit.*, pp. 40, 42; Bibliothèque de la Société Protestante, MS 617n, p. 71; Couderc, "L'Abbé Raynal," *BSHPF*, XXXVIII, 602.

137 Archives du Ministère des Affaires Étrangères, *Ancien fonds*, "Prusse," *registres* 27, fols. 367–368; 28, fol. 347.

138 Ellinger, *op. cit.*, p. 132.

139 Helmut Erbe, *op. cit.*, has attempted, among other things, to trace and to evaluate the attitude of the rulers and also of the natives to the newcomers. The Huguenots practically formed a "state within the state" until October 30, 1809, when the king abolished the last vestiges of autonomy at law, in education, in religion, and in local government.

140 Archives du Ministère des Affaires Étrangères, *Ancien fonds*, "Prusse," *registres* 26, fols. 75–76, 194–195; 28, fols. 347–348; 29, fols. 56–57; 30, fol. 94.

141 *Ibid., registre* 30, fol. 54.

I desire you to inform the Elector of Brandenburg that I would already have had sufficient reason to complain because of all his publications and declarations which have excited my subjects of the Reputedly Reformed Religion to desert and retire to his states, but that I will not suffer him to retain by force those who see the error of their ways and wish to return to my realm; and that, if this violence continues, it will indeed cause me to take certain measures which will not be agreeable to him.[142]

Approximately 30,000 Huguenots fled to Germany, and perhaps two-thirds of them settled in Brandenburg. About 70 per cent were between 20 and 50 years of age and represented a great diversity of occupations. A list prepared in 1700 of those in Prussia reveals that 88 were apothecaries, doctors, architects, or opticians; 164 were teachers, students, notaries, preachers, artists, or jewelers; 409 were tradespeople (bakers, distillers, brewers, confectioners, barbers, wigmakers, and merchants); 169 were civil or domestic servants; 213 were engaged in gardening, raising tobacco, or farming ("countrypeople"); 540 were craftsmen;[143] 46 were listed as workpeople and 34 as landlords; 11 made gauzes or printed cloth; 35 were engaged in hatmaking and 14 in button making; 93 were tailors; 739 were employed in the lace, silk, stocking, woolen, and tapestry industries; 710 were widows, maiden ladies, or wives of army officers; and 479 either did not give their occupations or were "persons of quality."[144] Because Germany had lagged behind most European countries in economic development, the refugees must have exercised a leavening influence in many branches of trade and industry. One of these was the manufacture of various kinds of woolen cloth in which France had developed a special proficiency.

The Elector Frederick William financed the construction of several fulling mills, presses, and dyeing shops; advanced operating capital; forbade the export of raw wool and taxed woolen imports; ordered his troops to be clothed in domestic fabrics; and promulgated rules and standards to guide the manufac-

---

[142] *Ibid., registre* 33, fol. 18.

[143] This number included blacksmiths, bookdealers and printers, brass founders, candlers, coopers, coppersmiths, cutlers, engravers, furriers, glassworkers, glaziers, joiners, locksmiths, masons, mirror makers, needle- and pinmakers, papermakers, perfumers, pewterers, potters, saddlers, soapmakers, shoemakers, sword cutlers, tanners, tinsmiths, tobacco workers, and watchmakers.

[144] Erbe, *op. cit.,* pp. 268–271.

turers.[145] Most of the woolen shops established by Huguenots in Berlin, Brandenburg, Cassel, Erlangen, Frankfort-on-the-Oder, Halle, Magdeburg, and elsewhere were built on a small scale; but a few apparently employed scores of workers.[146] One refugee from Rouen, formerly employed at Gobelins, carried with him the secret of dyeing fine woolen fabrics a bright red. Others established silk mills, introduced ribbon weaving in Konigsberg, carried with them the art of printing calicoes, and introduced the manufacture of gauze into Brandenburg from Soissons.[147] Some made the oils and liquid soaps so essential in washing the wools used in better fabrics. Frenchmen complained that Huguenot refugees had been so successful in their attempts to manufacture linen at Hamburg and other places in Germany that they were taking the English, Spanish, and Indian markets away from the French and imitating quite well the famous products of Saint-Quentin, Laval, and Morlaix, and that they were even likely to try to sell their output in France.[148]

There were about 260 stocking workers among the Huguenots in Prussia in 1700. Apparently they introduced into Prussia the knitting frame and made large quantities of wool stockings at Magdeburg.[149] Even though the French colony in Weimar lasted only a short time, it left distinct traces on the industry there.[150] One stocking manufacturer from Languedoc, who had settled in Magdeburg, wrote his brother at Zurich in 1687 that

145 Erman and Reclam, *Mémoires pour servir à l'histoire de réfugiés françois dans les états du Roi* (Berlin, 1782–1799), V, 10 ff.; Ancillon, *op. cit.*, pp. 218–219; Weiss, *Histoire des réfugiés*, I, 156; Archives du Ministère des Affaires Étrangères, *Ancien fonds*, "Prusse," *registre* 28, fol. 347.

146 Bibliothèque Nationale, *Fonds français*, MSS 6432, pp. 125–127; 7044, fols. 279–283; Erman and Reclam, *op. cit.*, IV, 323, 329 ff., 340–342; Couderc, "L'Abbé Raynal," *BSHPF*, XXXVIII, 602; Edouard Sayous, "La Colonie réformée d'Erlangen en Bavière," *BSHPF*, XXXVI (1887), 6–7.

147 Archives Nationales, G7 1701 (*registre*, fol. 136); Aubin, *op. cit.*, p. 19; Erman and Reclam, *op. cit.*, V, 120; VI, 11; Weiss, *Histoire des réfugiés*, I, 162–163; Edmond Chevrier, *Le Protestantisme dans le Mâconnais et la Bresse aux XVIᵉ et XVIIᵉ siècles* (Mâcon, 1868), p. 68; Fleury, *op. cit.*, p. 257.

148 Archives Nationales, G7 1700B (*registre*, p. 170); B7 *registre* 495, fol. 39; Boislisle, *op. cit.*, II, 489; John Southerden Burn, *The History of the French, Walloon, Dutch, and Other Foreign Protestant Refugees Settled in England etc.* (London, 1846), p. 19. Anderson (*op. cit.*, II, 597) stated that such linen goods as dowlas and lockram, formerly the pride of Normandy and Brittany, were being produced in Hamburg.

149 Erbe, *op. cit.*, pp. 268–271; Couderc, "L'Abbé Raynal," *BSHPF*, XXXVIII, 602; Erman and Reclam, *op. cit.*, IV, 330–331; V, 124; Bibliothèque Nationale, *Fonds français*, MS 6432, pp. 125–126, 157–158.

150 Ellinger, *op. cit.*, pp. 109, 112–113, 132–133.

he should join him without delay. "Wool is of good quality and cheap," he wrote. "The spinners are skillful and their wages low; the country is beautiful; food is cheap; and one easily becomes accustomed to beer."[151] Hat manufacturers from Burgundy and Normandy began to fashion beaver, rabbit, and fine felt hats in various places where only the coarsest variety had been made before.[152] Erman and Reclam, writing in the last two decades of the eighteenth century, stated that there had been only one tanner in Berlin at the time of the revocation, and that he had understood his trade imperfectly. The refugees established several tanneries and so increased the output of leather goods that King Frederick William in 1717 and 1726 forbade the wearing of wooden shoes in his cities, and the number of people who went barefoot also declined. Glove factories were started at Halle, Halberstadt, and Magdeburg; and in 1702 the glovemakers in Berlin, not organized along factory lines, received a charter for their Gild of French Refugee Glovers.[153]

The Great Elector sought to encourage the weaving of fine tapestries in the Aubusson tradition, and to this end he granted letters patent in November, 1686, to one Pierre Mercier. Other Protestant refugees working in the same art supplied the palaces at Berlin and Potsdam for several decades, and sent some of their panels to Russia, Sweden, and Denmark. Tapestry weaving was an industry Germany could ill afford; and it prospered only so long as the princes continued to subsidize it.[154] A Frenchman who had first started a plate-glass factory at Copenhagen shortly before 1690 went to a window- and bottle-glass shop at Neustadt and began to make blown plate glass. His son later introduced there the French method of casting large plates. The factory was successful and continued operations until at least the nineteenth century.[155] Other Huguenots helped to make Hanau famous

151 Ernest Lavisse and others, *Histoire de France illustrée depuis les origines jusqu'à la révolution* (Paris, 1911), Vol. VIII, Part 1, p. 207.

152 Bibliothèque Nationale, *Fonds français*, MS 6432, pp. 125–126, 157–158; Couderc, "L'Abbé Raynal," *BSHPF*, XXXVIII, 602; Erman and Reclam, *op. cit.*, IV, 330; V, 49, 54–57; Weiss, *Histoire des réfugiés*, I, 161; Court, *op. cit.*, I, 382–383.

153 *Op. cit.*, V, 57, 61, 66, 69.

154 *Ibid.*, IV, 330; V, 128, 134–135; Alfred Leroux, *Histoire de la réforme dans la Marche et le Limousin (Creuse, Haute-Vienne, Corrèze)* (Limoges, 1888), pp. 331–333; Fernand de Schickler, "Le Protestantisme dans la Marche et l'Église d'Aubusson," *BSHPF*, XXX (1881), 299–300.

155 Erman and Reclam, *op. cit.*, V, 194–195, 203–204. It was this enterprise that caused Louis XIV in 1700 to entertain the idea of asking the Royal Plate Glass

for its jewelry, and still others in 1686 founded a shop for gold and silver galloons which the king finally took over as a royal enterprise in 1737. The privilege of making playing cards, it may be noted, remained in the hands of a refugee family throughout the eighteenth century.[156]

With many of its fields laid waste by a century of almost constant warfare, and with ample lands that had never been cultivated, Germany offered special advantages to French peasants who were too poor to pay their passage to England, Ireland, or Holland or to acquire farms once they arrived, and yet were somehow able to make their way up the Rhine Valley from the southern and northeastern French provinces. The Great Elector gave them land, building materials, livestock, and seed in order to get the new agricultural colonies under way.[157] The French peasant, like the French craftsman, was more advanced than his German neighbor. Not only did he bring new land under cultivation and use intensive methods of gardening which caused his farms to sparkle like jewels along the countryside, but he also introduced new crops. He planted mulberry trees and attempted to raise silkworms; he introduced a variety of woad which was said to be especially good for various dyeing tints; he grew tobacco on a large scale; and he planted artichokes, asparagus, cauliflower, potatoes, and fine fruit trees.[158]

As pointed out previously, the wealthiest Huguenots fled to England or Holland. Some, however, escaped to Germany with their wealth more or less intact, and from 1686 to 1691, it was said, those in Berlin loaned the elector almost 90,000 thalers at 6 to 8 per cent interest.[159] A German historian writing in 1751 estimated that the refugees from Metz alone introduced about 2 million *écus* into Brandenburg. And in 1689 and 1692 Frenchmen occupied high positions in the administration of a loan bank

---

Company to open a branch factory in Alsace near Haguenau. He hoped that the resulting competition would force the works at Neustadt to close down. (Warren C. Scoville, *Capitalism and French Glassmaking, 1640–1789* [Berkeley and Los Angeles, 1950], p. 35 n. 29.)

156 Erman and Reclam, *op. cit.*, V, 78–79, 122–123, 272–273.

157 Ancillon, *op. cit.*, pp. 280–281.

158 Erman and Reclam, *op. cit.*, VI, 253 ff.; Ellinger, *op. cit.*, p. 114; Paul Beuzart, "Une Famille de réfugiés de la Thiérache," *BSHPF*, LXXXIX (1940), 266–267; Bibliothèque Nationale, *Fonds français*, MS 6432, pp. 157–158.

159 Erman and Reclam, *op. cit.*, I, 320–324. The interest rate in Germany was certainly higher than in Holland (Bibliothèque de la Société Protestante, MS 617n, p. 73).

set up by the elector.[160] Others founded important commercial houses in Berlin, Halle, and Magdeburg. Their contributions to the German economy in finance and large-scale commerce, however, fell far short of their contributions in agriculture and the crafts.

King Frederick I (or Elector Frederick III), in his edict issued at Cologne on December 14, 1709, acknowledged the benefits Huguenots had bestowed upon his country:

In general the welfare of countries consists of the multitude of their subjects, and in particular our realm and our provinces have experienced a considerable improvement by the large number of persons, who, having been chased from their homeland for religious reasons and various other oppressions, have come to seek a haven under our protection, [and] by establishing a number of manufactures have helped industry to increase and trade to flourish. In this process particularly the refugees from France who have withdrawn into our states have greatly participated.[161]

Ségur-Dupeyron, who has argued that the Huguenot influence in England and Holland was not very great, has admitted that it had "an incontestable success from the point of view of manufacturing" in Prussia, where in 1685 all industries except those associated with cloth were yet to be started.[162]

David MacPherson quoted a historian of Brandenburg as saying that " 'the most industrious part of . . . [the refugees] settled in Brandenburgh, where they introduced the manufactures of cloth, serges, stuffs, druggets, crapes, caps, stockings, hats, and also the dying of all sorts of colors . . . [and] Berlin now had goldsmiths, jewellers, watchmakers, and carvers: and such as were settled in the open country planted tobacco, and variety of fruits and pulse.' "[163] Some writers think that Huguenots initiated up to sixty-five trades in Germany, and Gustav Schmoller has acknowledged their "most durable and favorable influence on all the intellectual and economic development of the country."[164] As

---

160 Erman and Reclam, *op. cit.*, II, 31; V, 29 ff.

161 Mme Alexandre de Chambrier, "Naturalisation des Réfugiés français à Neuchâtel, de la Révocation de l'Édit de Nantes à la Révolution française, 1685–1794," *Musée neuchâtelois,* 37th year (1900), 201.

162 *Op. cit.*, II, 443.

163 *Op. cit.*, II, 616.

164 *Die Preuszische Kolonisation des 17. und 18. Jahrhunderts* (Leipzig, 1886), p. 15.

all economic historians are aware, Germany did not close the economic and technological gap that separated her from her western neighbors until well into the nineteenth century; but the Huguenots helped strengthen various crafts and helped people her cities with traders and artisans, thus probably facilitating the transition from a feudal agricultural economy to a highly industrialized one. Had the Huguenots identified themselves more completely with their new neighbors and been less clannish, German economic growth in the eighteenth century would surely have been more impressive than it actually was.

THE HUGUENOTS IN GENEVA AND SWITZERLAND

Approximately 60,000 religious refugees surged across the frontier into Geneva and various Swiss cantons between 1682 and 1720; about 25,000 settled there while the others moved on. Despite strong religious ties between the Swiss Protestant cantons and the Huguenots, the Swiss could not or at least did not proffer the refugees as warm a welcome as other nations. In four decades Geneva, Bern (including Vaud), and Zurich may have spent more than 10 million florins for food, clothing, and temporary shelter for refugees,[165] but they offered them very little inducement to settle there. Louis XIV so cowed Geneva with dire threats of economic and even military sanctions that before 1688 the city refused to accept any Huguenots as "inhabitants." From 1688 to 1729 it accorded this right to only 1,235, and refused to grant them full status as citizens (i.e., admit them to the *bourgeoisie*).[166] The natives complained in the economic crisis of 1693–1696 that the newcomers had doubled the cost of living, had artificially swollen the economy, and were so avid of gain that many undesirable business practices had sprung up. The City Council held eighteen public hearings "to remedy the disorder which foreign merchants introduced into the commerce of this city."[167]

---

165 J. Gaberel, "Les Suisses romands et les réfugiés de l'édit de Nantes," *Séances et travaux de l'Académie des sciences morales et politiques,* LIV (1860), 100; Johann-Caspar Moerikofer, *Histoire des Réfugiés de la Réforme en Suisse,* trans. G. Roux (Paris, 1878), pp. 230–232.

166 Pierre Bertrand, *Genève et la Révocation de l'Édit de Nantes* (Geneva, 1935), pp. 96, 98, 120, 124, 193. Because they were not citizens, Huguenots were restricted to selling their wares only on the two fair days each week and could not keep open booths.

167 *Ibid.,* pp. 109 ff.

Elsewhere the story was pretty much the same. At the outset towns advanced money for new enterprises or underwrote loans made by private individuals; some urged the gilds to open their doors to the newcomers; others received them as inhabitants or even as citizens. The Huguenots, however, proved to be almost as clannish in Switzerland as in Germany, and remained an easily identifiable minority. When the War of the League of Augsburg disrupted the Swiss economy, the natives blamed their hardships on their newly arrived competitors, many of whom seemed to be prospering while the profit margins of older establishments were shrinking. The gilds in Zurich, for example, manifested an increasing reluctance to accept the new artisans, who probably possessed more skill than the older members.[168] High French officials, both in Switzerland and in Paris, stated that the refugees were increasingly unhappy in their exile because of social and economic discrimination against them.[169]

The important question here is whether the refugees initiated new industries or diffused advanced techniques in old crafts. By and large, most of the immigrants appear to have been members of the *petite bourgeoisie* and to have engaged in such trades as baking, butchering, confectionary, glovemaking, lacemaking, printing, building, tailoring, and wigmaking, or in horticulture.[170] A few industries, however, profited from their skills and new techniques. Although it is doubtful whether the French introduced the printing of cotton cloth into Geneva and other Swiss cities because the revocation chased them from their homeland or because the French government on October 26, 1686, forbade the stamping of calicoes and the printing of all white cottons so as to protect its older textile industries, there is no doubt that Huguenots played an important part in perfecting and expand-

---

[168] Moerikofer, *op. cit.*, pp. 246–247.

[169] Archives Nationales, G⁷ 1685; Archives du Ministère des Affaires Étrangères, *Ancien fonds,* "Suisse," *registre* 83, fol. 281. For the generalizations as to the Swiss attitude toward the Huguenots, see Archives du Ministère des Affaires Étrangères, *Ancien fonds,* "Suisse," *registres* 80, fol. 399; 83, fol. 32; Moerikofer, *op. cit.*, pp. 233 ff., 250 ff.; Solomiac, *op. cit.*, pp. 145, 360; Weiss, *Histoire des réfugiés,* II, 214 ff.

[170] See, for example, Bertrand, *op. cit.*, p. 187, and the list of those who settled in Vevey in Jules Chavannes, *Les Réfugiés français dans le pays de Vaud et particulièrement à Vevey* (Lausanne, 1874), p. 139. Louis XIV's ambassador wrote on April 5, 1687, that Piedmontese refugees created a special problem in Switzerland because they knew only agriculture and the Swiss were not at all lacking in farmers (Archives du Ministère des Affaires Étrangères, *Ancien fonds,* "Suisse," *registre* 83, fol. 376).

ing the industry, especially after 1700.[171] The factory established by Huguenots at Geneva about 1702 employed from 600 to 800 persons in 1728 and as many as 2,000 in 1785.[172] Silkworkers fled Nîmes and manned a manufactory at Lausanne;[173] others from the same area and from Orange began to make silk sewing thread, stockings, ribbons, fabrics, and taffetas at Geneva;[174] a silk shop was opened at Vevey in 1682;[175] and two brothers set up two silk-stocking factories at Zurich in 1686 and 1689.[176] In Geneva, at least, the weaving of silk fabrics did not prove a financial success because of competition from Lyon, the war, economic blockades, and the dearness of materials; and by 1700 there was not a single silk mill at work in the city. But the ribbon, silk-stocking, and silk-thread branches continued there during a large part of the eighteenth century.[177] It is interesting to note, on the other hand, that the French statesman Daguesseau predicted in 1714, when France was negotiating a trade treaty with Switzerland, that the Swiss would undersell domestic silk manufacturers in the French market unless import duties were collected on their products. Because labor was cheap in Switzerland and because no excises were levied on raw silk and wool imports, as they were in France, Swiss manufactures would have low operating costs. Furthermore, he advised, "the French refugees have perfected their industry to such a point that the Swiss, who used to buy all necessary items from us, would like to send us their products without having further need of ours."[178] Daguesseau also referred to woolens in the same document. The Huguenots did set up a few looms for knitting stockings and for weaving serges and coarser woolens, as well as dyehouses and places where wool nap was clipped.[179]

---

171 Bertrand, *op. cit.*, pp. 138 ff.; Moerikofer, *op. cit.*, p. 235; Chavannes, *op. cit.*, p. 62; Guillebert, "Le Réfuge dans le pays de Neuchâtel (1685)," *BSHPF*, IV (1856), 154.

172 Bertrand, *op. cit.*, p. 144.

173 Dutil, *op. cit.*, p. 321.

174 Bertrand, *op. cit.*, p. 99.

175 Chavannes, *op. cit.*, pp. 63–64.

176 Moerikofer, *op. cit.*, p. 238.

177 Bertrand, *op. cit.*, p. 131.

178 Archives Nationales, G7 1700C (*registre*, pp. 217–218). The intendant at Lyon in his 1699 *Mémoire* wrote that the Swiss had learned so well to imitate French fabrics and "nearly all the different manufactures of France" that they threatened to compete with French manufacturers (Bibliothèque Nationale, *Fonds français*, MS 4288, fol. 125).

179 Bertrand, *op. cit.*, pp. 99, 125; Gaberel, *op. cit.*, p. 110; Chavannes, *op. cit.*,

Some writers have claimed that the French who arrived in Switzerland after 1685 were primarily responsible for the truly remarkable growth of the watch and clock industries.[180] This is somewhat misleading. As Bertrand points out,[181] there were two important waves of Protestant immigration from France: the first occurred in the fifty years preceding the Edict of Nantes (1598), and the second came a century later when the edict was revoked. The first wave profoundly affected the political, social, and economic life at Geneva and resulted in the establishment of many new trades, such as clockmaking. Those who sought refuge in the city at the end of the seventeenth century, instead of diffusing technology, apprenticed themselves to watch- and clockmakers who were on the average far more skilled than they.[182] They probably participated in the industry's growth during the eighteenth century,[183] but there is little concrete evidence that permits a quantitative or qualitative assessment of the importance of their participation. French jewelers, goldsmiths, and makers of passementerie expanded their trades in Geneva, but gilding steadily declined after the revocation.[184] One Frenchman advised his government at the time of the projected trade treaty with Switzerland that unless tariffs were levied on Swiss goods "it will become necessary to abandon a great many of our light manufactures which our refugees, who are much more industrious than the Swiss, have introduced into that country since they have withdrawn from the realm."[185]

---

pp. 63–64; Moerikofer, *op. cit.*, p. 238. Zurich denied Huguenots permission to set up laundries and dyehouses in order to protect the jobs of its own citizens. And Louis XIV rejoiced to hear that the manufacture of stockings at Bern was meeting with no success (Archives du Ministère des Affaires Étrangères, *Ancien fonds*, "Suisse," *registres* 83, fol. 399; 84, fol. 155).

180 Théodore Claparède, "Les Réfugiés protestants du pays de Gex," *BSHPF*, XXIV (1875), 69; Gaberel, *op. cit.*, p. 109; Weiss, *Histoire des réfugiés*, II, 219.

181 *Op. cit.*, p. 92.

182 *Ibid.*, pp. 145–146, 188. This position is supported by Pierre Dubois, *Histoire de l'horlogerie depuis son origine jusqu'à nos jours etc.* (Paris, 1849), p. 126.

183 In about 1685 Geneva had 100 master clockmakers and 300 workers and turned out almost 5,000 watches a year; a century later the city employed 6,000 people in the industry and made more than 50,000 watches a year (Weiss, *Histoire des réfugiés*, II, 219; Bertrand, *op. cit.*, p. 145).

184 Bertrand, *op. cit.*, pp. 136–138, 148; Ernest Combe, *Les Réfugiés de la Révocation en Suisse* (Lausanne, 1885), pp. 152–153.

185 Archives Nationales, G7 1700C (*registre*, pp. 206–207). Bertrand claims that the Huguenots "incontestably" introduced at Geneva the trades of making gloves, wigs, and lace, and perfected hatmaking and the branch of metalworking specializing in the construction of stocking-knitting looms (*op. cit.*, pp. 187–188).

Some wealthy Huguenots escaped to Switzerland with all or part of their liquid assets and invested their funds with other merchants or set up financial houses of their own. By 1710, according to one writer, Geneva was well on the way to becoming a center of finance for central Europe.[186] More immediately important than the development in finance was the expansion of commerce, especially with foreign countries. One refugee at Zurich made a fortune from his trade in silks, cloth, and wool with Italy and with such towns as Antwerp, Amsterdam, and Nuremberg.[187] Neuchâtel gradually developed an active commerce with many parts of the world, and the Huguenots helped to supplant colportage in Vaud with regular trade carried on in booths and stores. Aided by their connections with friends who had not emigrated, they built up a thriving business in smuggling all sorts of cloth and other wares from France.[188] The French ambassador wrote Louis XIV, on May 31, 1687, that the refugees in Switzerland were trying to establish all kinds of shops and industries but that the market for their products was so small and the initial cost so high that few of them were succeeding. In this connection he mentioned a rug shop begun at Bern by two families formerly employed at Gobelins. On the other hand, he complained, many were engaged in smuggling goods through Geneva from Lyon and had become so proficient in avoiding customs officials that they would guarantee delivery of a particular kind of French cloth or lace within a few weeks.[189] Still another Frenchman wrote from Geneva on June 20, 1708, that the Genevans, and especially the resident Huguenots, were waxing wealthy as middlemen in the trade among France, Germany, and Italy, and that some had even opened branch offices in Lyon to facilitate their illegal activities.[190] There is no doubt that much of this commerce received its impetus from the dislocations caused by war. Once the contacts were made and the channels cut, however, they persisted after the return of peace and help to account for the prosperity that developed in the second half of the eighteenth century.

---

186 Gaberel, *op. cit.*, p. 110. See also Moerikofer, *op. cit.*, p. 240.

187 Moerikofer, *op. cit.*, pp. 240–241.

188 Guillebert, *op. cit.*, p. 154; Combe, *op. cit.*, pp. 151, 153; Bertrand, *op. cit.*, pp. 126–127.

189 Archives du Ministère des Affaires Étrangères, *Ancien fonds,* "Suisse," *registre* 83, fols. 452–454.

190 Archives Nationales, G7 1691.

Of the 200,000 Protestants who probably fled France between 1680 and 1720, perhaps 40,000 or 50,000 settled in England, between 5,000 and 10,000 in Ireland, from 50,000 to 75,000 in the Dutch United Provinces, approximately 30,000 in German territory, and perhaps as many as 25,000 in Geneva and Switzerland. The rest migrated to other regions in Europe or to South Africa and the New World. All the countries studied in this chapter, except Switzerland, welcomed the refugees and extended them all kinds of financial aid and privileges in the hope that they would strengthen the economies of their adopted lands by introducing new industries and by imparting their skills and special techniques to native-born craftsmen. Most of the Huguenots hoped eventually to return to France, and expected the allies fighting Louis XIV in the War of the League of Augsburg to insist upon amnesty for them and reëstablishment of the Edict of Nantes as part of the terms of peace. When this did not occur, many of them still hoped that in one way or another the king or his successor could be persuaded to rescind the revocation of 1685. As a matter of fact, during a good part of the eighteenth century various schemes of persuasion and intrigue aimed at this goal were afoot. As long as the Huguenots thought of themselves as basically French, it is not surprising that they maintained their religious, social, and economic identity in no matter which adopted country they found themselves. This clannishness, together with their success in industry and trade and the special privileges and exemptions they enjoyed, helps to explain much of the popular displeasure over their presence. Save in some areas in Germany and Switzerland, the public's ill will never became strong enough to repel the refugees or completely to nullify their effect as diffusers of technology. But resentment among the natives and clannishness among the Huguenots must have interfered with the process of diffusion to some extent.

In 1685 England and Holland were not very far behind France industrially and commercially, if at all; whereas Ireland and Germany were. Switzerland, because of her limited resources and markets, lay somewhere in between. Hence the English and the Dutch had less to learn from the French than did the others, but the very fact that their technological gap was not very wide made diffusion easier and more rapid. The English silk industry acquired a new vitality after the immigrants introduced new patterns of cloth and new processes for making lustrous and figured fabrics. The sailcloth and fine-linen branches, the manufacture of white paper, hatmaking, and many crafts producing items of luxury quality increased in importance. In Holland the Huguenots developed various lines of the silk, velvet, linen, hat, paper, and glass industries and apparently participated in shipping, fishing, and whaling activities. There is also some evidence that they increased the supply of loanable funds. In Ireland they greatly improved the manufacture of linen and helped it become the foremost industry of the economy. In Germany they introduced several kinds of textiles; they made ribbons, gloves, laces, woolen and silk stockings, and fine felt hats; they began the manufacture of blown and cast plate glass; they improved tanning and the hardware trades; and they brought additional land under cultivation and extended the margin of intensive farming. In Switzerland they engaged in a large number of service and other minor trades, contributed to the growth of cotton weaving and cotton printing in the eighteenth century, and tried, though with little success, to develop the stocking, woolen, and silk industries. And, finally, they helped the little country become a financial and commercial center.

If it were possible to list all the direct and indirect costs and all the direct and indirect economic gains for which the Huguenots were conceivably responsible in each country, the balance would probably be large in their favor. It is true that most of the costs were felt in the short run and that most of the gains were realized in the long run; but, even if the gains could be discounted over time, the account would more than justify on strictly economic grounds—not to mention social and moral considerations—the efforts made by the various countries to attract and retain Huguenots. The Huguenot migration did not promote an immediate and marked acceleration of economic growth in England; it did not prolong for many decades that remarkable period of prosperity in Holland which ended about 1730; it did not close the technological and economic gap separating Germany from France, Holland, or England; and it did not change Ireland and Switzerland into lands of plenty. In the last half of Louis XIV's reign, all Europe evidenced less economic progress than either before or after this period. Tariff wars, naval and land warfare, monetary disorders, and increased statism were forces too powerful to be completely counteracted by the 200,000 Protestants who disseminated their individualism, their economic drive, their skills and techniques, and their labor and capital resources abroad. Any historian would be rash indeed if he claimed that the revocation of the Edict of Nantes was the chief cause for the acceleration of economic development in western Europe after 1720–1730. At the same time, however, he would be in error if he stated that the diffusion of technology resulting from the revocation was a wholly insignificant factor.

XI

Nonreligious Impediments to Economic Growth

Historical change is always complex. Because of the multiplicity and the interdependency of causes it is difficult to formulate meaningful hypotheses or to develop useful interpretations of even relatively simple historical phenomena, and problems involving economic growth and stagnation are never simple. Western Europe as a whole apparently slackened its pace of economic advance in the latter part of the seventeenth century and the first decades of the eighteenth; yet other competitive economies, such as the English and the Dutch, remained more prosperous than the French. Wars, tariffs, fiscal problems, and similar depressants, affecting all three economies, might help explain the over-all deceleration in growth, and it would seem that the persecution of Protestants, which was unique to France, might have been responsible for the relatively greater damage to her economy. In order to assess the importance of the revocation of the Edict of Nantes in causing economic stagnation in France, we must first examine what other factors were at work and whether their influence in France was somehow or other different from their influence in England or Holland.

THE IMPACT OF OTHER FACTORS UPON THE FRENCH ECONOMY

Some of the more thoughtful Frenchmen living in the latter half of Louis XIV's reign realized that their economy was stagnating and sought to ascertain what forces or events had arrested economic growth after Colbert's death. Many of them, recognizing religious persecution as a responsible factor, nevertheless stressed the importance of other causes. This was true of most intendants and deputies of trade who voiced their opinions on the subject.

These officials occupied positions that allowed them to observe and evaluate economic change at close range. The intendants were the Crown's administrative agents in the provinces. They implemented instructions and government policies which the controller general in Paris sent them, and they kept their superior informed on local and provincial matters. Their correspondence with him and the lengthy surveys they prepared at the king's request in 1698–1700 to enlighten the young Duke of Burgundy show that they were well aware of the decline in economic activity. These documents contain suggestions as to which factors were most responsible for the decline. The deputies of trade, usually selected by local businessmen from among successful wholesale merchants or financiers in leading commercial cities, served as advisers to the Council of Trade, which the king created in 1700. The deputies' first assignment after the council began to meet regularly was to study the economic state of the country and to suggest ways for increasing the national income and for reducing unemployment. This they did.[1] They also gave opinions in writing on hundreds of different petitions and projects coming before the council in its early years. Although individual intendants and deputies differed from one another in innate ability, economic acumen, and serious application to duty, their appraisals near the turn of the century nonetheless contain a hard core of unanimity.

Most of them agreed that the long and costly wars of the League of Augsburg and of the Spanish Succession had severely taxed the country's productive capacity, disrupted the normal channels of trade, and led the state and the economy as a whole to the brink of financial disaster. Government expenditures had skyrocketed, and the public debt had mounted at an alarming rate. In a frenzied effort to raise revenue the Crown had increased taxes on industry and trade, had frequently revalued and recoined the currency, had resorted to paper money and forced lending, and had created and sold innumerable public offices. Its maneuvering for advantage in world markets by jockeying tariff duties and restrictions had led other countries to retaliate, and

---

[1] The deputies' manuscript reports have been preserved in the Bibliothèque Nationale (*Fonds français*, MS 8038). In 1955–56, as a Guggenheim and Fulbright research scholar, I worked through these reports and other records pertaining to the activities of the Council of Trade from 1700 to 1791. I hope to publish the results of this study at a future date.

foreign trade understandably languished. Many deputies and intendants also pointed out that there had been no appreciable lessening of internal trade barriers. In many branches of the economy monopoly privileges and government favoritism still stifled individual initiative and freedom of entry. Some thought that state regimentation had gone too far. Also, epidemics had taken a heavy toll in human life, and poor harvests had created famine conditions in many places. The introduction of Indian cottons, they suggested, had threatened the woolen, silk, linen, and hemp industries; and the increasing popularity of loom-knit stockings had created considerable technological unemployment among hand knitters. Finally, most of the spokesmen agreed that society bestowed too little esteem and prestige on those engaged in business and that the more successful merchants and bankers consequently withdrew from the market as soon as they had amassed enough wealth.

Were the wars, the fiscal policies, and the economic statism of the latter half of Louis's reign sufficient in themselves to have caused economic stagnation? Perhaps no one will ever be able to formulate a definitive answer to this query. Even so, we must consider all the evidence before drawing even tentative conclusions.

THE IMPACT OF WAR

Forty-five of Louis XIV's seventy-three years on the throne were years of war. During the first half of his reign, his armies under such capable leaders as Turenne and Condé had gained decisive, quick victories over the enemy; and all Europe had come to fear and to distrust Louis as well as to think his forces well-nigh invincible. The latter half of his reign, when he was at war with his neighbors in all but twelve years, tarnished his earlier record. Although he briefly and successfully invaded the Netherlands (September, 1683, to August, 1684) while fighting Spain and the emperor, his subsequent victories became progressively rarer and less decisive. The War of the League of Augsburg (1688–1697) and the War of the Spanish Succession (1701–1713) were long drawn out and costly. Nearly all Europe was aligned against France. Fairly early in each war Louis XIV sent out peace feelers, but the allies were unwilling to negotiate at the time and under the terms he had suggested.

The latter half of the seventeenth century and most of the

eighteenth century have been characterized as an age of limited warfare.[2] As compared with the religious and civil conflicts of the preceding hundred years, or with the revolutionary and Napoleonic struggles after 1789, the Augsburg and Spanish Succession wars were fought with considerably less intensity and were relatively less destructive of life and property. They were primarily wars of position, of fortress against fortress, and of fortress against besiegers. But all war is destructive. Acting under Louvois's orders the French invaders of the Palatinate in 1688, for example, followed a scorched-earth policy. The battle at Malplaquet (1709), one of the bloodiest battles Europe had ever seen, left almost 40,000 dead or dying in an area of approximately 10 square miles.[3]

As had been his custom, Louis succeeded in confining most of the fighting to foreign soil and to the peripheral provinces he himself had annexed. His troops fought mainly in the Rhineland, the Netherlands, northern Italy and Savoy, and beyond the Pyrenees. Some of the most bitter fighting occurred in North America, and the theater of war at one time or another encompassed even Ireland and India. It is impossible at the present time to give an accurate estimate of the number of Frenchmen actually under arms. At their peak the French forces may have included between 400,000 and 500,000 men.[4] Although the large standing army of professional and mercenary soldiers was already becoming the mainstay of most west European powers, Louis XIV resorted to conscription for the first time in 1688. By ordering each village of any size to furnish an unmarried man between

---

[2] See especially John U. Nef, *War and Human Progress: An Essay in the Rise of Industrial Civilization* (Cambridge, Mass., 1950), and John B. Wolf, *The Emergence of the Great Powers, 1685–1715* (New York, 1951).

[3] Wolf, *op. cit.*, p. 85.

[4] Edouard de la Barre Duparcq ("Des Rapports entre la richesse et la puissance militaire des états," *Séances et travaux de l'Académie des sciences morales et politiques*, LXXXIV [1868], 304, 307) estimated the number at 446,000 in 1690–1691 as compared with 158,000 seven years earlier, scarcely 165,000 in 1726, and almost 1 million in 1793. Nef refers to this estimate of 446,000 (*op. cit.*, p. 202), and Wolf supposes that the French forces numbered about 400,000 men during the War of the Spanish Succession (*op. cit.*, p. 171). A. de Saint-Léger denies that the French army ever attained the size of 300,000 during the Augsburg War, and thinks that there probably were no more than 200,000 actually engaged in combat at any one time in either war (Ernest Lavisse and others, *Histoire de France illustrée depuis les origines jusqu'à la révolution* [Paris, 1911], Vol. VIII, Part 1, pp. 26, 90). The deputy of trade from Languedoc wrote in 1701 that there had been half a million men under arms during the preceding war (Archives Nationales, F12 641; Bibliothèque Nationale, *Fonds français*, MS 8038, fol. 456).

twenty and forty years of age,[5] he raised several thousand soldiers. The great bulk of his army, however, comprised professional soldiers and officers, recruits who shouldered arms in response to propaganda and promises of pay, and many unfortunate individuals whom unscrupulous agents rounded up on the streets and in taverns.

At the outbreak of the War of the League of Augsburg the might of the French navy was near its all-time peak. In 1690, according to Sismondi,[6] France had 110 vessels of the line with from 60 to 104 guns each and a large number of frigates, galleys, and fire ships. Altogether they carried 14,670 guns and 100,000 men.[7] In view of the fact that the French navy in 1661 had consisted of about 18 vessels, some of which were twenty years old and carried only 36 guns, this represented a monumental achievement of which Colbert and his son Seignelay could justly be proud. The royal arsenal at Rochefort had been established in 1665 expressly for outfitting and providing a base for the Atlantic fleet.[8] Before its defeat in the battle at La Hogue (May, 1692), the French navy surpassed the combined English and Dutch fleets in both size and quality. Thereafter, although her ships of the line increased in number, France lost her comparative advantage, and eventually had to abandon the high seas to her enemies.[9]

What effect did these wars have upon the French economy? Of a total population of about 19 million, the armed forces retained from 200,000 to 500,000 able-bodied men at any one time. This represented a significant diversion of potentially productive

---

[5] Lavisse, *op. cit.,* Vol. VII, Part 2, p. 235; Vol. VIII, Part 1, p. 26.

[6] Jean C. L. Simonde de Sismondi, *Histoire des français* (Paris, 1821–1844), XXVI, 55.

[7] Wolf, *op. cit.,* pp. 12, 172; Lavisse, *op. cit.,* Vol. VIII, Part 1, p. 26; Charles W. Cole, *French Mercantilism, 1683–1700* (New York, 1943), p. 107. The intendant in Provence wrote in 1699 that the Maréchal de Tourville had commanded 98 vessels equipped with 5,243 guns and manned by 33,855 persons in his fight with the English and Dutch navies in 1691 (Bibliothèque Nationale, *Fonds français,* MS 4289, fol. 183).

[8] The intendant at La Rochelle in his 1699 memorandum glowingly described this superb establishment, where 10,000 muskets were made in 1689 to send to Ireland in addition to those destined for the king's troops in France and whose foundries in 1690 cast 100 cannons for 36-pound balls, 33 for 24-pound balls, and "a prodigious number of other pieces" (Bibliothèque Nationale, *Fonds français,* MS 4287, fols. 21–22).

[9] Wolf, *op. cit.,* p. 45; Cole, *op. cit.,* p. 107; Lavisse, *op. cit.,* Vol. VIII, Part 1, p. 26.

man power and hence involved an enormous economic cost equal to the value of alternative goods and services they might otherwise have produced. Even recruitment from the vast army of unemployed would have entailed a cost by reducing the supply of labor available to agriculture, industry, and trade. Historians have frequently represented the emigration of Huguenots after 1680 as having seriously drained the country's labor supply. These fugitives, numbering about 200,000, however, included men, women, and children of all ages and in every state of health. The much larger number of individuals siphoned off into the armed forces included only men in their prime. Recruitment therefore must have reduced France's labor supply much more than religious emigration.[10] Furthermore, the wars themselves seem to have caused additional emigration. Many soldiers deserted their regiments while fighting in the Netherlands and never returned home for fear of retribution;[11] artisans divorced from their markets by the wars sometimes sought a new life on foreign soil; and several hundred townspeople and peasants alike fled abroad rather than face the harassment of incessant troop movements and the economic burdens of taxes and of soldiers billeted in their homes.[12]

The wars not only diverted men from productive to nonproductive channels in the short run, but they also reduced the labor supply in the long run. Even "limited warfare" takes human lives. It is impossible, however, to estimate accurately how many Frenchmen died on the battlefields or in army camps and how many noncombatants perished because of hardships directly or indirectly attributable to war. Whereas, according to Voltaire, no more than 8,000 Frenchmen were among the dead and dying after the bloody battle at Malplaquet, only about 20,000 of the approximately 50,000 French-Bavarian troops had not been

---

10 The Abbé Novi de Caveirac expressed a similar view in 1756 (*Mémoire politico-critique, où l'on examine s'il est de l'intérêt de l'Eglise et de l'Etat d'établir pour les Calvinistes du Royaume une nouvelle forme de se marier* [n.p., 1756], p. 64).

11 Ph. Sagnac, "L'Industrie et le commerce de la draperie en France à la fin du XVIIᵉ siècle et au commencement du XVIIIᵉ," *Revue d'histoire moderne et contemporaine,* IX (1907–1908), 30.

12 Archives Nationales, G⁷ 520; Bibliothèque Nationale, *Fonds français,* MSS 4284, fol. 26; 4285, fol. 139; 4286, fols. 28, 31, 123; 8038, fol. 346; Comte Louis de La Boutetière, "Note sur l'émigration protestante du Poitou à la suite de la révocation de l'Édit de Nantes," *Bulletins de la société des antiquaires de l'Ouest,* XIV (1877), 353.

killed, taken, or irretrievably scattered after the English victory at Blenheim (August 13, 1704).[13] The loss was so great at Blenheim that Madame de Maintenon was selected to break the news to the king. As to the civilian population there is even less evidence to go on. It is significant, however, that intendants and other government officials customarily held the wars responsible for much of the depopulation that beset the country after 1683.

Since most of the fighting occurred on foreign soil, the last two wars of Louis XIV did not severely damage the French economy by destroying its capital wealth. Dauphiné, Provence, and Flanders suffered some destruction;[14] and the English fleet in 1694 tried to attack Brest, Dieppe, Le Havre, Dunkirk, and Calais. Of these, only Dieppe suffered extensive damage; scarcely 300 houses there remained after the bombardment on July 18.[15] Certain sections of the country also suffered from the movement and quartering of troops. An official at Reims, for example, complained to the controller general in 1712 that he had seen French soldiers plunder village after village as they passed through.[16] Such ravages of war are difficult to quantify.

Maritime trade was greatly affected. Between October 1 and November 13, 1689, 41 vessels leaving La Rochelle fell into enemy hands.[17] As wartime expenditures mounted, and especially after the allied naval forces gained ascendancy over the French after 1692, Louis XIV made little effort to protect his merchantmen.[18] Barbary Coast pirates and English and Dutch

13 Voltaire, *Le Siècle de Louis XIV* ("Classiques Garnier," new ed.; Paris, n.d.), chaps. 19, 21. See also Lavisse, *op. cit.*, Vol. VIII, Part 1, p. 98.

14 Bibliothèque Nationale, *Fonds français*, MS 4284, fol. 77; A. M. de Boislisle, *Correspondance des contrôleurs généraux des finances avec les intendants des provinces* (Paris, 1874–1897), I, 295; II, 434, 450; III, 400, 482.

15 Lavisse, *op. cit.*, Vol. VIII, Part 1, p. 38; Samuel Hardy, *Histoire de l'Église protestante de Dieppe* (Paris, 1896), p. 389; Émile Levasseur, *Histoire de commerce de la France*, I (Paris, 1911), 338.

16 Boislisle, *op. cit.*, III, 441. For complaints from other sections of the country see, e.g., *ibid.*, I, 59; II, 450; III, 464; Archives Nationales, G7 135, 520; Bibliothèque Nationale, *Fonds français*, MSS 4284, fol. 22; 4285, fol. 139; 4286, fols. 13, 28, 31; 4289, fol. 121; 8038, fol. 346. The Venetian ambassador at Paris wrote home in his final report (1695) that the French population had been reduced by 2 million since the outbreak of war and that rural areas were heavily burdened by the winter quartering and levying of troops (Henry Austen Layard, "The Revocation of the Edict of Nantes. Illustrated from State Papers in the Archives of Venice," *Proceedings of the Huguenot Society of London* [hereinafter cited as *PHSL*], II [1887–1888], 151–152).

17 Archives Nationales, G7 337; Cole, *op. cit.*, p. 6.

18 Lavisse, *op. cit.*, Vol. VIII, Part 1, pp. 31, 203.

privateers preyed unmercifully upon French vessels in the Mediterranean, and the Atlantic sea lanes also became unsafe. Manufacturers in Languedoc in 1708 could no longer ship their woolens to the Levant;[19] the number of sugar refineries at Rouen had fallen from thirteen to three by the beginning of 1709 because enemy action had created a shortage of raw sugar;[20] trade with Spain was greatly diminished although not entirely interrupted;[21] and in 1711 Pontchartrain as secretary of the marine was begging for funds to outfit frigates to protect French shipping from enemy privateers "who have considerably increased in number because of the wealth they have obtained from the numerous seizures already made."[22] The English Admiralty may have exaggerated when it defended its position before Parliament by saying that between 1702 and 1707 it had captured or destroyed 70 French warships, 170 privateers, and 1,346 merchantmen.[23] Professor G. N. Clark has estimated that declared prize goods taken from French and neutral vessels and imported into England averaged less than £60,000 a year in the Augsburg War and more than £90,000 a year in the following war.[24] Dutch privateers probably did as much damage.

French vessels and seamen also turned to privateering, and they may have been more successful than either the English or the Dutch. Dunkirk alone is said to have had an annual take several times more valuable than the total figures for the English. Jean Bart, for example, in a cruise of three weeks captured or destroyed four warships, five frigates, and fifty merchantmen. Insurance rates in 1703 on Dutch vessels leaving Holland varied from 5 per cent on those crossing the Channel to England without escort to 20 per cent on ships destined for the Levant or Italy.[25]

On August 24, 1689, after his declaration of war on France, William III forbade all trade with the enemy.[26] The Dutch

19 Boislisle, *op. cit.*, III, 19, 78.

20 Archives Nationales, F12 662–670 (letter from the sugar refiners at Rouen addressed to the controller general on Jan. 4, 1709).

21 Lavisse, *op. cit.*, Vol. VIII, Part 1, p. 252.

22 Boislisle, *op. cit.*, III, 356.

23 Wolf, *op. cit.*, p. 202.

24 "War Trade and Trade War, 1701–1713," *Economic History Review*, I (1927–1928), 266. Cf. Cole, *op. cit.*, pp. 13–14.

25 Wolf, *op. cit.*, p. 202; Lavisse, *op. cit.*, Vol. VIII, Part 1, p. 41.

26 David MacPherson, *Annals of Commerce, Manufactures, Fisheries, and Navigation etc.* (London, 1805), II, 639.

were unwilling to follow his example. They listed certain goods as contraband and constantly expanded the list, but otherwise tried to carry on "business as usual." As the war progressed the English relaxed their restrictions and shifted more and more toward the Dutch position. The result was that neutral vessels could still trade with France in nonproscribed commodities. The naval policies of all belligerents toward neutral countries were more liberal in the War of the Spanish Succession than in the preceding war or at any subsequent time.[27]

Although available evidence is insufficient for measuring the damage done to French shipping or for appreciating fully the role played by privateers in provisioning home markets, there can be little doubt that warfare on the seas from 1688 to 1713 was directed at crippling the French economy, and that it succeeded to some extent. Adam Anderson thought that the new industries recently begun in England by Protestant refugees could scarcely have acquired so firm a footing so quickly if the wars had not severely restricted French imports.[28] Several French industries and trades which tapped foreign markets in selling their output or in buying their materials felt the impact of war acutely. Wines and brandies accumulated on the docks at Bordeaux; salt exports declined, and the farmers of the gabelle could not market all that was produced; the intendant at Alençon complained in his 1698 memorandum that the output of the leather industry at Argentan amounted to only two-thirds of its peacetime value and that the linen industry had declined by one-half at Vimoutiers, Domfront, and Lisieux; linen spinning and weaving in Brittany also suffered severely after hostilities closed the English market; and the number of master pinmakers at Limoges fell from twenty to three or four because of insufficient imports of brass wire. *Auvergnats* producing hardware, paper, playing cards, ribbons, laces, thread, and certain kinds of linen and woolen textiles experienced real hardship in 1688–1697 when customers from Savoy, Italy, Spain, and other enemy countries could no longer buy from them.[29]

The depression in the silk industry at Lyon, Tours, and Nîmes

---

27 Wolf, *op. cit.*, pp. 198 ff.; Nef, *op. cit.*, p. 164; Clark, *op. cit.*, p. 272.

28 *An Historical and Chronological Deduction of the Origin of Commerce, from the Earliest Accounts etc.* (London, 1801), II, 597.

29 Archives Nationales, G⁷ 103, 135, 136; Bibliothèque Nationale, *Fonds français*, MSS 4283, fols. 39, 62, 67, 68; 4286, fols. 94, 97, 123, 124; 4287, fol. 76; 4288, fols. 9, 11, 83, 84; 4289, fols. 14–15; Boislisle, *op. cit.*, I, 184, 185–186, 244; III, 529.

after 1685 stemmed in part from the wars which reduced the supply of raw silk drawn from Piedmont, closed down foreign markets, and diverted domestic consumption to less costly items.[30] Some of the unemployed Catholic workmen at Lyon became discouraged and sought work in other countries. The number of paper mills around Angoulême declined from fifty in 1688 to twelve in 1697; in the short interval of peace between the two wars twenty-three were reopened. Of the thirty-five at work in May, 1701, only ten were active at the conclusion of the War of the Spanish Succession.[31] These mills had formerly exported a large part of their paper to England and Holland.[32] The difficulty encountered in importing silk and raw wool from Spain and Germany supposedly led to a 50 per cent decline in the weaving of druggets and sagathies at Lille. Merchant drapers at Lyon complained that by 1699 their sales had dropped off by "more than one-half" because they could no longer attract foreign buyers without a complete stock of fine woolens drawn from England and Holland to supplement the coarser varieties made in France. Three-fourths of their annual sales, which they said had amounted to some 13 million livres, had formerly been sold "in Savoy, Piedmont, Milan, Rome, Venice, and other Italian cities and in Malta, Switzerland, Alsace, and Lorraine." War also played havoc with the export trade in laces made at Sedan.[33]

When an economy shifts from a peacetime to a wartime basis, the pattern of market demand changes suddenly. Certain industries experience a relative strengthening of demand for their products while others experience a contraction. The necessary

---

30 Archives Nationales, F12 registre 51, fol. 222; Bibliothèque Nationale, *Fonds français*, MS 4290, fol. 299; Boislisle, *op. cit.*, I, 296; Abbé L. Bosseboeuf, "Histoire de la fabrique de soieries de Tours, des origines au XIX⁰ siècle," *Bulletin et mémoires de la société archéologique de Touraine*, XLI (1900), 275; Léon Dutil, "L'Industrie de la soie à Nîmes jusqu'en 1789," *Revue d'histoire moderne et contemporaine*, X (1908), 323; E. Pariset, *Histoire de la fabrique lyonnaise. Étude sur le Régime social et économique de l'Industrie de la Soie à Lyon, depuis le XVI⁰ siècle* (Lyon, 1901), pp. 116, 120; Natalis Rondot, *Les Protestants à Lyon au dix-septième siècle* (Lyon, 1891), pp. 61–62.

31 Archives Nationales, F12 1475; Prosper Boissonnade, *L'Industrie du papier en Charente et son histoire* (Ligugé, 1899), p. 5; Auguste Lacroix, *Historique de la papeterie d'Angoulême suivi d'observations sur le commerce des chiffons en France* (Paris, 1863), pp. 8–9.

32 The paper mills at Vire in Lower Normandy also suffered when they were cut off from these markets (Bibliothèque Nationale, *Fonds français*, MS 4286, fol. 168).

33 *Ibid.*, MSS 4284, fol. 26; 4285, fol. 151; 4288, fols. 124–125.

reallocation of resources normally creates frictional unemployment which varies inversely with the occupational and geographic mobility of labor and other resources. Although the wars of the late seventeenth and early eighteenth centuries did not occasion so marked a shift in market demand as does modern warfare, resources then were probably much less mobile than they are today. Hence unemployment arose in several French industries when the domestic demand for their output fell off. Royal restrictions on the use of precious metals by jewelers led to a mass emigration of Parisian goldsmiths;[34] the Beauvais tapestry and rug manufactory in 1698 was employing only a fraction of its former staff of workers and was on the threshold of failure;[35] and lacemaking at Saint-Denis, Aurillac, and elsewhere was languishing or ruined.[36] The fishing industry declined as sailors and pilots were diverted to wartime use and as the risks of capture at sea mounted. Whereas Honfleur had sent out forty boats to the fishing grounds in 1688, only twenty left the harbor in 1699; the number leaving Le Havre dropped from eighty to seventeen in the same period.[37]

At the opening of the eighteenth century the deputy of trade from Languedoc blamed war for many of the difficulties confronting the region's woolen industry.[38] But these difficulties stemmed from an abnormally large demand rather than from an insufficient or declining demand. The necessity of providing some 300,000 soldiers with "long underwear, coats, pants, stockings, and hats and even overcoats for the cavalry and dragoons" several times in the fighting created an extraordinary consumption of wool and raised its price so high that manufacturers for civilian use could ill afford to compete with army suppliers. Throughout France, those who made coarse-grade woolens for army clothing prospered, while those who specialized in the finer

---

34 Joan Evans, "Huguenot Goldsmiths in England and Ireland," *PHSL*, XIV (1930–1933), 508.

35 Bibliothèque Nationale, *Fonds français*, MSS 4282, fols. 481–482; 21785, fol. 91; Lavisse, *op. cit.*, Vol. VIII, Part 1, p. 239n. The intendant in Bourbonnais wrote in 1699: "In regard to the trade resulting from the manufacture of tin, iron, tapestry, drapery, cutlery, [and] faïence one can only hope that peace, by reëstablishing order and abundance among families, will give to each industry the courage it has lost" (Bibliothèque Nationale, *Fonds français*, MS 4287, fol. 64).

36 Archives Nationales, G7 103; Boislisle, *op. cit.*, III, 487.

37 Bibliothèque Nationale, *Fonds français*, MS 4286, fol. 30. See also *ibid.*, fols. 20–21; Boislisle, *op. cit.*, I, 225.

38 Archives Nationales, F12 641.

fabrics for domestic and foreign consumers found themselves caught in a price squeeze.[39] As was to be expected, foundries and forges making all kinds of metal goods useful in battle on land and sea expanded in the last half of Louis's reign.[40]

One must conclude, therefore, that the Augsburg and Spanish Succession wars left their scars on the French economy. Although the destruction of life and property was not appalling, men and other resources were withdrawn from their normal occupations and shifted into the nonproductive channels of warfare. Shipping, fishing, and foreign trade were especially hurt. It is interesting to note a collective opinion sent by the deputies of trade to their council on May 25, 1716. They mentioned two of the many factors responsible for the great change in France's foreign trade since the 1660's: "The first is the flight of our Religionists who have transplanted our industry to foreign soil, and the second is the war of 1702, which we fought with the two leading maritime powers. These two events absolutely changed the entire complexion of our trade."[41] Professor Émile Levasseur saw in these wars a major cause of the failure of the overseas trading companies which the government had favored with extensive monopoly privileges.[42] Many peacetime industries suffered from dislocations in both foreign and domestic markets. Even Charles Weiss, who placed so much emphasis upon the revocation of the Edict of Nantes, admitted that "the calamitous wars of the second half of Louis XIV's reign were without doubt the most active cause for the decay of that monarchy which Richelieu and Mazarin had rendered so powerful and which Colbert [had made] so rich and prosperous."[43]

Moreover, the wars created a heavy drain upon the financial resources of the government. Daniel Defoe observed shrewdly

---

39 Bibliothèque Nationale, *Fonds français*, MSS 4289, fols. 20, 28–29; 4290, fol. 296; 8037, fols. 72, 297, 351–352, and *passim;* Boislisle, *op. cit.,* I, 196; Lavisse, *op. cit.,* Vol. VIII, Part 1, pp. 202–203, 234; Wolf, *op. cit.,* p. 180.

40 Cole, *op. cit.,* p. 142; Lavisse, *op. cit.,* Vol. VIII, Part 1, pp. 243–244; Wolf, *op. cit.,* p. 177.

41 Archives Nationales, F12 693.

42 *Op. cit.,* I, 383.

43 *Histoire des réfugiés protestants de France depuis la révocation de l'Édit de Nantes jusqu'à nos jours* (Paris, 1853), II, 150–151. Weiss added, however, that the manufactures carried abroad by Huguenot refugees "contributed equally to this fatal decline." P. de Ségur-Dupeyron (*Histoire des négociations commerciales et maritimes de la France aux XVII⁰ et XVIII⁰ siècles, considérées dans leur rapports avec la politique générale* [Paris, 1872–1873], II, 360 ff.) concluded that the wars had been vastly more important.

that Europe in his day (1661–1731) was spending less blood and more money in its military campaigns. He was doubtless right. To most Frenchmen—whether peasant or craftsman, rich or poor, merchant or banker—war primarily meant increased taxes and more frequent visits from the tax collector. They may not have understood, and hence not fully appreciated, the horrors of the battlefield, but they realized full well that war meant additional financial sacrifice and interference with their normal economic occupations. On April 26, 1701, Chamillart pleaded with his friend De Harlay to help him uncover new sources of revenue. "I have the misfortune of serving as controller general at the beginning of a new war [which follows on the heels] of another which has [already] exhausted all the resources necessary to sustain it."[44]

Military expenditures (*extraordinaire des guerres*) for each of the years 1689–1697 averaged 68.5 million livres and were almost twice their annual average for 1685–1687. They totaled somewhat more than 616 million livres and accounted for approximately 40 per cent of all payments made by the government during those years.[45] Total expenditures from 1684 to 1699 exceeded ordinary revenues by more than 1,200 million livres. Small wonder that Chamillart felt sorry for himself in 1701! The succeeding war—by far the costliest Louis waged—increased the "extraordinary expenses for war" to an annual average of 91.3 million livres for 1701–1713 and to as much as 130 million for 1705 and 132 million for 1707.[46] Altogether, they totaled 1,187.4 million livres, or about 44 per cent of all government disbursements in the war years. From 1700 to Louis's death in 1715 ordinary revenues of the treasury fell short of total expenditures by more than 2,200 million livres.

It would be unwise to accept these figures, based upon not wholly reliable data, as accurately measuring the direct financial costs of the two wars; they are nonetheless useful in suggesting the magnitudes involved. They also help explain the financial

44 Guillaume-B. Depping, *Correspondance administrative sous le règne de Louis XIV* (Paris, 1850–1855), III, 321.

45 Boislisle, *op. cit.*, I, 598–599; François Véron Duverger de Forbonnais, *Recherches et considérations sur les finances de France depuis 1595 jusqu'en 1721* (Liége, 1758), IV, 38, 145. And the financial account *extraordinaire des guerres* did not include all expenditures on the army, navy, and defense (see Ph. Sagnac in Lavisse, *op. cit.*, Vol. VIII, Part 1, pp. 166–167).

46 Forbonnais, *op. cit.*, IV, 291, 328, 351, 397, 411, 417; V, 17.

difficulties besetting the Crown after 1685 and the heroic efforts made by the controllers general to find sufficient funds.

FISCAL DIFFICULTIES

The state's financial and accounting practices were so oddly complicated, and existing records are so bewilderingly chaotic, that many years of patient, skillful research by competent economic historians will be required before one can present a faithful account of fiscal transactions in the latter half of Louis's reign. Since an earlier chapter has sketched the story in the light of available information, only a few of the more salient features need be recounted at this time.

From 1684 through 1714 total government expenditures, including interest payments and reimbursement of various short-term and long-term advances, amounted to more than 5 billion livres.[47] From a low of 92 million livres in 1687 they climbed to a high of 264 million in 1711. The public debt had been only about 157 million livres prior to the invasion of the Spanish Netherlands (1683–1684); in 1715 the funded and unfunded debt totaled something like 3 billion livres.[48] Each year there was a sizable deficit, and each year the controller general frantically sought new funds from extraordinary sources to replenish the treasury. Only a thoroughgoing revision of the tax system could have offered much hope of additional revenues, for the existing structure, in addition to other undesirable features, was inflexible as to yield and costly to administer. Because the government relied so heavily on tax farmers for advances, because the nobility and the clergy had a strong vested interest in maintaining a system that exempted them from taxes, and because the financial pressure on the government was unremitting and ever increasing, it is not surprising that the controllers general did not seriously consider the advisability of a complete overhaul. They followed the line of least resistance and simply increased taxes whenever they could and levied new ones. This procedure did not always increase net revenues, but it usually resulted in increased penalties on economic enterprise. The econ-

---

47 Forbonnais, *op. cit.*, III–V, *passim*. Since expenditures had steadily mounted with the passing years, Voltaire's estimate that Louis XIV spent 18 billion livres during his reign seems excessive (*op. cit.*, chap. 30, p. 84).

48 Earl J. Hamilton, "Origin and Growth of the National Debt in Western Europe," *American Economic Review, Proceedings*, XXXVII (1947), 121–122.

omist C. Ferrare Dutot, an important official in John Law's India Company, summarized the situation as follows: "We all know that public finance was in frightful disorder at the death of Louis XIV or at the beginning of the Regency, and that the way in which it had been administered since 1683 had perhaps done as much harm to the state as the immense expenditures occasioned by the last two wars."[49]

In the early part of 1695 the Crown introduced the capitation, a sort of income tax which varied from 2,000 livres on members of the royal family to 1 livre on persons in the poorest classes. Instead of an anticipated 30 million livres, the tax yielded only 22.5–23 million livres a year until it was revoked in 1698. The government revived it in 1701 and succeeded in wringing approximately 30 million livres yearly from it. In addition, the government in 1710 levied the *dixième,* which supposedly taxed each Frenchman 10 per cent of his annual gross revenue. Both the capitation and the *dixième* soon shed their distinctive features and came to rest regressively on the same shoulders that bore the burden of all other taxes. The capitation rapidly degenerated into a surtax on the taille. This was unfortunate, for the taille was a property tax which most often penalized peasants or artisans who attempted to improve their property or who invested in other tangible assets. The deputy from Languedoc wrote about 1701 that peasants in his province were uprooting mulberry trees in order to reduce their taille assessments; the recent dearth of silkworms had cut their revenues so much that the trees became a liability after payment of taxes.[50] Many intendants complained in their 1698–1700 memoranda and in letters to the controller general that the taille burdened the economically productive more and more severely as increasing numbers of individuals gained exemption from the tax, as depopulation reduced the number of taxpayers, and as the amounts to be collected rose.[51] People were reluctant to acquire ships, shops, or other physical assets lest their assessments be increased. The injustices committed by collectors and the arbitrariness with

49 *Réflexions politiques sur les finances et le commerce* (1738), in *Collection des principaux économistes,* Vol. I: *Économists financiers du XVIIIe siècle,* ed. E. Daire (2d ed.; Paris, 1851), p. 800.

50 Archives Nationales, F12 641.

51 See, e.g., Bibliothèque Nationale, *Fonds français,* MSS 4286, fols. 19–20, 51, 76; 21773, fol. 146; Boislisle, *op. cit.,* II, 6, 23, 304, 329–330; III, 57; Depping, *op. cit.,* I, 321–322.

which the taille was apportioned among taxpayers in any province or township were other undesirable features of the tax.[52] The economist Boisguillebert vainly insisted that the actual tax should be completely revised and applied to all property regardless of the owner's station in life.[53]

"To maintain that in the past forty years open war has not been declared on consumption and trade," Boisguillebert wrote in 1704, "would be the same as maintaining that the Seine does not pass through Paris."[54] All the excises and other internal duties levied on commodities, which yielded approximately twice as much revenue as the taille, restricted production and the flow of goods.[55] According to the intendant in Languedoc, total impositions in his jurisdiction had steadily increased through 1707 until they were four and a half times what they had been in 1653. To collect the rest of the capitation for 1708, he predicted, would surely destroy the region.[56] The deputy of trade from Marseille, while conceding in 1701 that emigrant Huguenots probably had hurt the economy by diffusing industrial skills and knowledge abroad, added: "But it is also true that the taxes that have often been levied on manufactures and their output without careful consideration of their effect have caused a good part of this misfortune."[57] Vauban pointed out in 1699 that a recent tax on coal mined in the north of France simply caused the owners to raise coal prices at the expense of domestic consumers, exporters, and even the king's treasury.[58]

Despite the warnings and the pleas for tax relief voiced by provincial officials, deputies of trade, and men like Vauban and Boisguillebert, the controller general felt he had no choice. Old duties were retained and new ones were levied. Sugar refining, leather tanning, saltmaking, and the production of wines and brandies were some of the industries that felt the depressive effect of excises.[59] Hatmaking especially suffered. First, import

52 Dom H. Leclercq, *Histoire de la Régence pendant la minorité de Louis XV* (Paris, 1921–1922), I, xlviii.

53 Boislisle, *op. cit.*, II, 552; Germain Martin, *La Grande industrie sous le règne de Louis XIV* (Paris, 1898), p. 251.

54 Boislisle, *op. cit.*, II, 536.

55 *Ibid.*, II, 530, 550; see also Boisguillebert's *Le Détail de la France* (1697) in Daire's *Collection des principaux économistes*, I, 172, 184, 196.

56 Boislisle, *op. cit.*, III, 18.

57 Bibliothèque Nationale, *Fonds français*, MS 8038, fol. 506.

58 Boislisle, *op. cit.*, I, 527.

59 Archives Nationales, F12 *registre* 51, fol. 227; G7 337, 345; Bibliothèque

duties were levied on beaver fur and other materials used in making hats; second, after the Crown renewed and strengthened its regulations of the industry in 1699 and 1700, manufacturers had to have each hat certified, marked, and taxed (*droit de marque*); and, third, all their exports were subject to an additional duty.[60] As a result, production declined and workers emigrated. As soon as the Council of Trade began to function in 1700, the deputies urged it to revoke the fee for marking hats and to remove all import duties on raw materials. Later on, whenever someone proposed taxing another industry, the deputies always violently objected and pointed out how the manufacture of fine felt hats had been destroyed earlier by similar action.[61]

Paper and playing cards also suffered from special excises. In 1656 the government had established *droits de contrôle et de marque* which varied from 6 sous per ream for finer grades of paper to 4 sous for coarser grades. In 1680 other duties were levied, at least in Auvergne. Paste and old linen rags used in production had to pay duties, and the finished product had to acquit customs (*droits de traite-foraine*) when it passed certain stations. Playing cards were subject to special levies. The intendants in every region where these items were manufactured claimed that taxes were destroying the industry and causing papermakers to migrate and set up mills in England, Holland, Spain, and Germany. The last two wars, by reducing export markets, accentuated the trouble. By 1715 the industry in Auvergne, Angoumois, and around Rouen was badly depressed, and the deputies of trade were urging the government to accord manufacturers some relief from burdensome duties and vexatious controls.[62]

Nationale, *Fonds français*, MS 4283, fol. 44; Boislisle, *op. cit.*, I, 37; III, 537; Émile Levasseur, *Histoire des classes ouvrières et de l'industrie en France avant 1789* (2d ed.; Paris, 1901), II, 349; Marcel Marion, *Histoire financière de la France depuis 1715* (Paris, 1927), I, 17. The intendant at Orléans pointed out on October 26, 1693, that the sales or transfer tax of 6.25 per cent on wheat (*droit de seterage*) sometimes, because of resales, amounted to as much as a fourth of the wheat's value (Boislisle, *op. cit.*, I, 343).

60 Forbonnais, *op. cit.*, IV, 62–63; Boisguillebert, *op. cit.*, p. 196.

61 Archives Nationales, F12 *registres* 51, fols. 39, 227, 285; 54, fol. 63; *liasses* 694 (opinion dated 8 août 1718, and one other for 1718); 697 (26 mai 1727); G7 1692; Bibliothèque Nationale, *Fonds français*, MS 8038, fols. 506–507.

62 See, e.g., Archives Nationales, F12 *registres* 51, fols. 227, 285; 54, fol. 63; *liasses* 694, 697, 1475; G7 1685; Bibliothèque Nationale, *Fonds français*, MSS 4287, fols. 28–29; 4288, fol. 83; Victor Bujeaud, *Chronique protestante de l'Angoumois, XVIᵉ, XVIIᵉ, XVIIIᵉ siècles* (Paris and Angoulême, 1860), pp. 304, 310–311; Henri Gazel,

When silk manufacturers at Nîmes complained in 1686 about
the heavy taxes they had to pay, the intendant Bâville supported
their position by saying that the industry "is in such a condition
that it will soon be entirely ruined if it does not receive some
relief."[63] Firms at Lyon also suffered when new taxes were
levied,[64] and the deputies of trade unanimously opposed the
creation of an inspectorate for silk in 1705 on the ground that
extra duties and regulations would only harass producers without yielding much revenue.[65]

In addition to excises on raw materials and finished products
there were innumerable tolls and charges levied on goods in
transit from one province to another. The Rhône and Loire
rivers in particular were so heavily burdened with private and
public tolls that shippers frequently sent their consignments overland rather than by water.[66] The deputy from Nantes in June,
1701, complained that recently increased duties on Loire traffic
were driving foreigners away from Nantes, where they formerly
had come to purchase French goods produced in Brittany or in
interior provinces.[67] All deputies recognized that internal barriers to trade hurt the economy and strongly urged the Council
of Trade to initiate far-reaching reforms. The deputy from
Languedoc, at the beginning of the eighteenth century, said that
the system was so complex and the duties so indefinite that collectors often modified the charges according to what they thought
the traffic would bear. He suggested (1) that the myriad duties
be reduced to three types—export, import, and interprovincial;
(2) that all taxes be specific rather than ad valorem so that collectors could not arbitrarily decide in each instance how much
had to be paid; and (3) that all tolls exacted by seigneurs be
suppressed and that local communities adequately compensate
the seigneurs for their loss in revenue.[68] Such pleas did not result
in material improvement. Those who had a vested interest in
maintaining the *status quo* were able to quash all programs for
reform until after 1789.

Les Anciens ouvriers papetiers d'Auvergne (Clermont-Ferrand, 1910), pp. 18 n. 5, 19,
106; Lacroix, *op. cit.*, pp. 8–9; Leclercq, *op. cit.*, I, lvi.

63 Archives Nationales, G7 297.

64 Rondot, *op. cit.*, p. 62.

65 Archives Nationales, F12 *registre* 51, fol. 316.

66 *Ibid.*, F12 693; Bibliothèque Nationale, *Fonds français*, MSS 4283, fols. 13–14;
4290, fol. 361; Boislisle, *op. cit.*, III, 463.

67 Archives Nationales, G7 1686.

68 *Ibid.*, F12 641.

Louis XIV was too financially dependent upon those who farmed his taxes to do very much to alleviate the burden on peasants and members of the middle class. Tax farmers had every incentive to increase their collections by any and all means available. They were consequently harsh, capricious, and arbitrary. Taxpayers were at their mercy. During his mission to La Rochelle about 1686 to help convert Protestants, Fénelon wrote:

I hear on every hand that the agents of the king's tax farmers hamper trade unduly. Each one who passes through here makes new rules. Merchants do not know from one day to the next what is expected of them. Booby traps are often set to ensnare them; and when their goods are confiscated, the merchants are thrown into despair, whereas a little leniency and accommodation in their behalf would keep them from emigrating.[69]

In 1706 the Duke of Chevreuse, governor of Guyenne, accused collectors of increasing the tax burden without any resulting benefit to the king.[70] Apparently he was right. Net revenues to the treasury steadily declined after 1683.[71] In that year, for example, the treasury received 97 million livres of 119 million collected; in 1703, 51.7 million of 104.8 million collected; and in 1714, only 32.2 million of 118.4 million collected. This decline in net tax yield was partially due to the previous hypothecation of revenues; but the rapidly growing cost of collecting taxes was also responsible. Tax farming was perhaps the most lucrative way any Frenchman could employ his time and capital.[72] It should not be surprising, therefore, that the Crown gained little additional revenue from increasing indirect taxes and that it had to resort to other expedients.

One such expedient was the creation and sale of offices. Although he was not responsible for originating the practice, Louis XIV made use of it much more frequently than his predecessors. During his last two wars he created and sold thousands of posts. It has been estimated that he obtained upward of 900 million livres in this way,[73] and about one-half billion of the public debt in 1715 represented what officeholders had paid for their posi-

---

[69] Bibliothèque Nationale, *Nouvelles acquisitions françaises*, MS 507, fol. 47.

[70] Boislisle, *op. cit.*, II, 358.

[71] See table 1, p. 201.

[72] Bibliothèque Nationale, *Fonds français*, MS 21773, fol. 144; Lavisse, *op. cit.*, Vol. VIII, Part 1, pp. 171 ff.; Henri Sée, *Histoire économique de la France*, ed. Robert Schnerb (Paris, 1939), I, 160.

[73] Wolf, *op. cit.*, p. 186.

tions. The offices ranged from directors of finance, secretaries to the king, and high judicial magistrates to municipal authorities, examiners of gilds, and inspectors of local markets. In Paris alone there were 2,461 such officeholders in 1715, and in 1700 the intendant at Orléans counted 7,747 royal, seigneurial, and judicial positions in his *généralité* as compared with 6,182 wholesale and retail merchants.[74]

"Every time your majesty creates an office, God creates a fool to buy it," Pontchartrain once jokingly remarked to the king.[75] The purchaser of an office received not only a good annuity from his investment, but also considerable social prestige. Many of the offices were hereditary; most of them carried exemption from taxes. Frenchmen of the seventeenth and eighteenth centuries who had made their fortunes in trade or industry were usually anxious to retire from active business as soon as possible and to buy their way into officialdom and hence into respectability. Furthermore, the king had numerous ways of "persuading" wealthy individuals to purchase the posts if they did not voluntarily step forward. The creation and sale of offices thus drained the economy of capable entrepreneurs and diverted men from productive to less productive channels; it also increased the financial burdens upon those who remained economically active and snarled them in bureaucratic red tape. The new officers received their salaries from fees collected from individuals who were obliged to use their services. Their functions usually served no useful purpose and only complicated business procedures.

The Crown found gilds a lucrative source of revenue. It created gild auditors, examiners, and inspectors upon the slightest pretext. Whenever possible, the gilds purchased the offices and then either suppressed them or perpetuated them on their own terms. The six major gilds in Paris paid the king 634,000 livres for the offices created by edict of March 14, 1691, and three years later they had to buy another post (auditor of records) for 400,000 livres.[76] Louis XIV formed new gilds primarily to serve as milch cows for his treasury. And both new and old gilds soon sank hopelessly into debt. To keep the milk flowing, they were allowed to increase their membership and initiation fees and to tighten their strangle hold on crafts.

---

74 Levasseur, *Histoire des classes ouvrières et de l'industrie*, II, 368.
75 Quoted by Wolf, *op. cit.*, p. 185.
76 Levasseur, *Histoire des classes ouvrières et de l'industrie*, II, 359–361.

Offices were also created for wholesale and retail markets throughout France. According to Levasseur, the number of market officials for Paris alone surpassed 2,000. Brokers rudely intruded between buyers and sellers in bills of exchange and other financial instruments and in wines, brandies, and other commodities sold abroad. Almost no conceivable position was overlooked. Although the creation and sale of offices proved a lucrative short-run expedient for raising additional revenue in a time of emergency, it cost the economy a great deal in the short run and did incalculable damage in the long run.[77]

Even more baneful were Louis's monetary manipulations. Between 1685 and 1715 he arbitrarily raised or lowered the livre equivalent of hard currency, or devalued by recoining specie, more than forty times! This brought into his treasury something like 146 or 164 million livres in "profit." In addition, in the War of the Spanish Succession he resorted to issuing paper money (*billets de monnaie*) and various kinds of short-term interest-bearing notes (*billets d'état*) which also circulated as money. In October, 1706, there were outstanding more than 180 million livres in depreciating *billets de monnaie;* by 1710 most of these had been suppressed[78] or converted into short-term claims on various sources of revenue. When Louis died in 1715, these and other badly depreciated *billets d'état* in circulation amounted to more than 600 million livres.

Whatever the treasury gained by frequently changing the tariff of specie and emitting paper money was more than offset by private losses and the harm done the economy as a whole. According to Sismondi, money or "the common measure of value was altered so many times that trade became a game of chance, and no one knew any longer exactly what he owned."[79] Once the government began to tinker with currency, those who held specie sought desperately to smuggle it out of the country in order to escape further losses. As the king and his ministers realized, unilateral devaluation ordinarily can stop specie exports and even reverse the flow. What they did not realize, apparently, is that

---

[77] Boislisle, *op. cit.,* II, 14, 234; III, 633; Cole, *op. cit.,* pp. 187 ff.; Lavisse, *op. cit.,* Vol. VIII, Part 1, pp. 181–185; Leclercq, *op. cit.,* I, l–li; Levasseur, *Histoire des classes ouvrières et de l'industrie,* II, 355 ff.; Marion, *op. cit.,* I, 44; Martin, *op. cit.,* pp. 342–343; Sée, *op. cit.,* I, 161.

[78] By royal declaration of October 7, 1710, their circulation in trade was forbidden (Boislisle, *op. cit.,* III, 357).

[79] *Op. cit.,* XXVII, 6–7.

the loss of confidence in a country's money, with anticipation of further devaluation, can intensify the flight of currency. This is what happened in France. Those who could transferred their funds abroad; those who could not hoarded specie. Consequently, the total monetary stock in France declined,[80] even though a few private individuals and the royal household obeyed an order of December, 1689, and delivered plate to the mint to be coined which yielded about 5 or 6 million livres. Also, the substantial quantities of gold and silver reaching France through her trade with Spain and South America[81] did not fill the gap. Huguenots also took specie out with them, and the provisioning of French armies on foreign soil constituted still another drain. It is impossible to estimate how much specie left because of monetary instability.

Intendants and other government officials frequently complained about the export of specie. Some of them, like the intendant at Lyon in 1700, bluntly told the controller general that uncertainty about its value was driving money out. A merchant at Saint-Malo had written him the same thing a year earlier.[82] Occasionally there were not enough fractional coins for business transactions because the coins were either hoarded or sent abroad when their intrinsic value became greater than their nominal value.[83]

Real or imaginary shortages of hard money evoked loud complaints.[84] When the mints were recoining, stringency developed; after tax collectors made their rounds and forwarded their collections to Paris, there was usually a temporary shortage of hard money in the provinces which interregional trade only gradually repaired; and whenever creditors became alarmed and insisted

---

[80] Ambroise Arnould has estimated that monetary specie fell from 18.5 million marks of silver in 1683 to 13.5 million in 1715. With the mark tariffed at 27 livres in 1683 and at 35 livres in 1715, this would mean that France had about 500 million livres in silver coins circulating in 1683 and 474 million in 1715. (*De la Balance du commerce et des relations commerciales extérieures de la France* [Paris, 1791], II, 195–198, 205.)

[81] It has been estimated that from 1700 to 1720 silver worth about 250 million livres came in from Peru, Chile, and the South Seas trade (Lavisse, *op. cit.*, Vol. VIII, Part 1, p. 186).

[82] See, e.g., Boislisle, *op. cit.*, II, 9–10, 64, 73–74, 77–78, 84–85, 184, 332; III, 334, 375, 529, 567, 582.

[83] Levasseur, *Histoire du commerce*, I, 326.

[84] See, e.g., Archives Nationales, G7 85, 240, 356, 1689; Boislisle, *op. cit.*, I, 217, 234, 245, 387, 470, 533–534; II, 10, 91, 144, 151, 154, 267, 268, 396–397, 444, 446, 608; III, 169, 348, 544, 603.

upon immediate payment or payment in cash, the money supply tightened. Several times provincial merchants claimed they could not get their hands on enough cash to pay their workers or those who supplied them with basic materials. Monetary uncertainty caused merchants to hold on to their goods rather than sell them, to accumulate unusually large stocks of imported products rather than run the risk of having their cash balances depreciate in value, and to hoard specie rather than deliver it to the mint for recoinage as the law required.

Raising the value of money rarely, if ever, counteracts the harm done by lowering its value. Any revaluation occasions new hardships and adds to uncertainty. The Crown apparently was unaware of this. After debasing the coinage by 30 per cent in 1709, for example, it restored its value in eleven successive stages from December 1, 1713, to September 1, 1715. This deflation, coming at the end of the war, was especially ill timed, and bankruptcies became rife.[85] In 1738 the economist Dutot summarized the situation that had existed earlier:

It is obvious that far from alleviating the ills, these operations only intensified the trouble. The daily decrease in the king's revenues and the progressive decline in trade, the arts, and industry offer incontrovertible proof. Only usury flourished. The best letters of exchange were discounted for silver at 20, 25, and 30 per cent.[86]

The paper money met with a great deal of resistance. It did not depreciate significantly immediately after the government first issued it in 1701 in exchange for specie delivered at the mint for recoinage. This initial success led to further issues, inadequate reserves precluded redemption, and by the end of 1706 depreciation had climbed to 54 per cent. Until then the circulation of paper money had been confined to Paris. On April 12, 1707, the king ordered everyone in the realm to accept paper money after May 20 for one-third of any payment due him. Merchants and manufacturers in leading commercial centers at once violently objected, pointing out that domestic bills of exchange had already risen in price by 28 or 30 per cent from fear that they would be paid in paper. Furthermore, they asked, how would Frenchmen be able to pay foreigners? Paper was unacceptable in inter-

---

[85] See, e.g., Earl J. Hamilton, "Prices and Wages at Paris under John Law's System," *Quarterly Journal of Economics,* LI (1936), 43 and n. 6.

[86] *Op. cit.,* pp. 807–808.

national transactions, and its forced circulation at home would drive specie into hiding and prevent merchants from acquiring enough specie to meet foreign obligations. Intendants, almost without exception, took the same position. They predicted that the law would cause a complete cessation of trade and force thousands of workers to emigrate.[87] In the face of such opposition the order was rescinded. Then, by royal declaration of October 18, the controller general attempted to force people in most French provinces to accept paper money up to one-fourth the amounts due them. Again, merchants and intendants in such cities as Rouen, Lyon, and Marseille raised a loud cry.[88] The government finally recognized that the only solution to depreciation was to retire most of the money. This it proceeded to do, and the part it allowed to circulate for two more years after 1707 was confined to Paris and to two-thirds payment of sums larger than 400 livres.

When Louis XIV, realizing his end was near, confessed on his deathbed that he had loved war too dearly, and advised his great-grandson to live in peace with France's neighbors, he should also have advised the five-year-old prince to benefit from the mistakes he himself had made in the realm of finance. The French monarchy was bankrupt. It had borrowed at 10 per cent interest in 1702, and thirteen years later it obtained only 8 million livres in exchange for promises to pay totaling 32 million livres. The interest on the funded debt was about equal to the annual net revenue; interest payments were two years in arrears, and most of the expected income for 1716 and 1717 was hypothecated. There is no way of estimating the amount of indebtedness forced upon provinces, municipalities, gilds, religious organizations, and other groups which had been required to make substantial "gifts" to the king or to buy up various offices. Wealthy individuals had been pressured several times into lending to the government; all who had acquired titles of nobility in the past ten years were forced in 1701 to subscribe to 1 million livres in *rentes;* naturalized foreign families also had to buy *rentes* in 1709; and officeholders were frequently tapped for substantial subscriptions.[89]

The Crown's fiscal policies must therefore bear a significant

---

87 See, e.g., Boislisle, *op. cit.*, II, 323, 352–353, 368, 396–398, 402–404, 411–412.
88 *Ibid.*, II, 446 ff.
89 Marion, *op. cit.*, I, 42.

share of the responsibility for the depression that developed after Colbert's ministry. The tax system, highly regressive in nature, unduly burdened those individuals who were economically most active. When new taxes like the capitation and the *dixième* were levied, the large and wealthy privileged classes sooner or later managed to escape them. The taille discouraged capital investments in agriculture, trade, and industry; new or higher excise duties restricted production. Methods of apportioning and collecting taxes, particularly the system of farming taxes, increased the burden on taxpayers and reduced the amount of revenue reaching the royal treasury. The creation and sale of public offices brought into existence a new tax-exempt officialdom which collected tribute from merchants and manufacturers and encumbered their activities with useless red tape. The forty-odd revaluations of the currency from 1685 to 1715 and the issuance of paper money created financial chaos and drove specie abroad or into domestic hoards. How could economic activity possibly remain vigorous in such circumstances? The amazing thing is that the economy did not collapse completely!

ECONOMIC STATISM

According to most students of the period, the state made the mistake of regimenting economic life too completely. Colbert had built up an elaborate system of government aid and controls whereby he had sought to establish new industries specializing in luxury goods and to broaden the markets for old industries by regulating the quality of their output and by rewarding entrepreneurs who coöperated most effectively in his over-all plan. He was instrumental in luring many skilled foreigners into the country to initiate production along certain lines or to familiarize native workmen with new techniques; he attempted to diffuse superior technical knowledge and practices in other ways as well, despite the resistance, passive or active, of French artisans and gilds; he fostered the growth of large-scale enterprises by granting direct and indirect subsidies to their founders; he rewarded those who successfully duplicated English, Dutch, and Italian fabrics; he persuaded or "gently coerced" wealthy individuals to venture their capital in overseas trading companies; he sought to encourage internal trade by removing such man-made hindrances as local tolls and heterogeneous weights and measures and by simplifying provincial customs barriers; he used the tariff to protect domestic producers from foreign competition; and he sought to lift the social status of merchants and industrialists.

Colbert's wish to aid the economy, however, was matched by his desire to regulate it. As a matter of fact, he thought the two were synonymous. To raise, and then maintain, a high level of workmanship required direct government regulation; otherwise artisans, seeking quicker and larger sales, would use cheaper materials and inferior methods, and the reputation of French goods would deteriorate on both foreign and domestic markets. For various kinds of cloth, for example, Colbert issued about 150 regulations and 4 detailed ordonnances which prescribed what materials, dyes, and methods weavers could use; how much the thread count must be; and exactly what length, width, and selvedge each piece must have.[90] He also established rules for dyers, papermakers, and knitters. To enforce these regulations and to supervise production required an army of officials. Some —like intendants, judges, municipal authorities, and gild wardens—were already at hand, but their specific functions and responsibilities had to be coördinated and their powers of enforcement increased. Others—like inspectors of manufactures—had to be appointed to fill newly created posts.

Upon Colbert's death in 1683, the various economic powers that had been centralized in his hands were divided among (1) Le Pelletier as controller general; (2) Seignelay as secretary of the marine with control over colonies, foreign trade, shipping, and chartered companies; and (3) Louvois as superintendent of buildings with control over manufactures and considerable influence in internal trade. Seignelay died in 1690 and Louvois in 1691. Pontchartrain, who had succeeded Le Pelletier as controller general in 1689, then gained control of the marine as well as of most of the important economic powers associated with the superintendency of buildings.[91] He soon (1693) divested himself of some of the duties incumbent upon the minister of the marine by securing the succession of this office to his son, Jerôme Phelypeaux, Comte de Maurepas.[92] Phelypeaux formally assumed all responsibility for the marine in 1699. Pontchartrain

---

[90] Levasseur, *Histoire des classes ouvrières et de l'industrie*, II, 214–215.

[91] Colbert de Villacerf, a cousin to both Seignelay and Louvois, inherited the office of superintendent of buildings, which thenceforth carried control only over such state enterprises as the Louvre, Gobelins, Savonnerie, and the art academies in Paris and Rome. Jules Hardouin Mansart succeeded him in 1699.

[92] Phelypeaux later was known simply as "Pontchartrain."

also turned over many of the functions associated with the post of controller general to his cousin Henri Daguesseau, for whom he created a sort of superintendency of commerce in 1695. Pontchartrain himself became chancellor in 1699, and Chamillart succeeded him as controller general.[93] Thus, after 1699, domestic and foreign economic matters were officially divided between Phelypeaux, as minister of the marine, and Chamillart, as controller general; but Daguesseau and his nephew Amelot de Gournay, especially after the Council of Trade was established in 1700,[94] perhaps interested themselves more directly in commercial and industrial matters than either Phelypeaux or Chamillart.

More significant than this fragmentation of economic power was the fact that none of these men—Seignelay, Louvois, Le Pelletier, Pontchartrain, Chamillart, Daguesseau, Phelypeaux, or Amelot—was Colbert's equal. None of them had his imagination, his great drive, or his intense desire to build up the country's economy. Even if this had been otherwise, they would not have had a very favorable opportunity to manifest their abilities. The Huguenot problem proved very distracting after 1681; and foreign affairs and war dominated the scene after 1688. Recurrent fiscal emergencies absorbed most of the attention of the controller general. Daguesseau, Amelot, and others on the Council of Trade, including the practical businessmen serving as deputies, found all their proposals for economic aid and reform stymied by the exigencies of war and the need for additional revenue. It was not mere chance that Colbert achieved his greatest economic successes from 1664 to 1672, when he had the king's complete confidence and support. This was also the period in Louis's reign when France enjoyed the greatest degree of internal and external peace.[95]

The vast majority of government officials in high station after 1683 limited themselves to enforcing and implementing the Colbertian system. Bâville, for example, wrote in his 1699 memorandum on Languedoc that it was not necessary to frame new regulations in order to increase trade and industry. "The late

---

[93] Desmaretz was controller general from 1708 to 1715.

[94] Daguesseau was president of the council; Amelot, who had succeeded his uncle as director or superintendent of commercial affairs in 1699, was one of its most active members.

[95] See Martin, *op. cit.,* pp. 352–353.

M. Colbert has already . . . exhausted this matter; it is a question only of enforcing his regulations."[96] And the intendant in Bourbonnais at the same time urged the government to apply Colbert's rules and regulations meticulously, for "his rare genius, completely dominated by considerations of public welfare and abundance, has missed nothing that might contribute to this end."[97] When Boisguillebert addressed letters to Paris suggesting that taxes be reformed and that more scope be allowed individual initiative, as he did time and time again, the chief assistant to the controller general, on August 24, 1710, politely but firmly informed him that it was useless for him to send any more suggestions. The controller general, after all, was fully cognizant of his responsibilities and was in a better position than Boisguillebert to know what should be done for the good of the country.[98] No matter how many times officials and other observers in the provinces blamed the decadence of industry and trade on continual warfare and the crushing burden of taxes, those at Paris and Versailles remained convinced that the source of all evil was the nonobservance of regulations.[99]

According to Charles W. Cole,[100] at least three major aspects of the government's industrial policy stand out after 1683. First, the government sought to coördinate and improve the regulatory machinery inherited from Colbert. Second, it made the regulations more numerous, detailed, and rigid, and allowed less room for exceptions and less opportunity for officials to exercise discretionary judgment. Third, it sanctioned the industrial *status quo* by obstructing change and by protecting old industries from new ones. The number of inspectors grew from twenty-four in 1683 to thirty-four in 1715; new procedures for visiting, for certifying cloth, and for judging and punishing recalcitrant offenders were established to improve enforcement and to expedite justice; numerous new bureaus were opened where rural weavers had to bring their cloth for inspection; gild wardens were exhorted to

---

96 Bibliothèque Nationale, *Fonds français*, MS 4290, fol. 357. Somewhat inconsistently he added that there were only three principal rules to follow if the government wished to see trade more flourishing than it had ever been: (1) to reduce import and export duties, (2) to protect merchants, and (3) "which is the most essential, to accord men complete liberty to carry on their trade in accordance with their taste, their ability, and their knowledge."

97 *Ibid.*, MS 4287, fol. 65.

98 Boislisle, *op. cit.*, III, 311.

99 Martin, *op. cit.*, p. 249.

100 *Op. cit.*, pp. 142–143.

tighten their functions; and provincial and municipal officials received innumerable directives concerning their responsibilities. The penalties for violating rules were stiffened; defective fabrics were confiscated and burned, fines were collected, and sometimes offenders were put in pillories. Although enforcement varied widely with time and place, it is probably true that officials tried to enforce the regulations more conscientiously (and more blindly and less imaginatively) after 1683 than before.

Colbert's successors usually did not attempt to draft new codes for industry; instead, they added meticulous details to the old codes and extended their coverage. The general instructions for dyers drafted in 1671, for example, had contained 317 articles; the revised code in 1688 was even longer.[101] The government sought continually to improve the quality of Languedoc cloth destined for the Levantine markets by adding to and amending the rules governing its manufacture. Other woolens, linens, silks, ribbons, laces, knitwear, hats, and printing received attention as well. With the passage of years, as Professor Levasseur has pointed out,[102] changes in consumer taste and progress in technology rendered the regulations more and more obsolete and irritating to producers. The multiplicity and complexity of rules made for confusion. Even intendants began to formulate special codes for certain crafts or areas in their jurisdictions. Whereas Colbert had frequently allowed manufacturers to deviate from established norms in making special kinds of coarse cloth for specific foreign or domestic markets, his successors attempted to enforce conformity. They did not consider consumer preference a sufficient reason for abrogating the rules. New styles and designs, new products, and new techniques received little encouragement.

The central government grew wary of change in trade and industry just as it became suspicious of new developments in political, social, and religious matters. When clothiers began to use cloth-covered buttons instead of embroidered, metal, or bone buttons, it forbade anyone in 1694 to make or wear the new variety under pain of confiscation and heavy fine. It also outlawed half-beaver hats, certain new-style laces, new types of metallic thread, and such beverages as rum and gin as well as brandy made from grape skins, pulp, and seed. It sought to limit the use

---

101 Levasseur, *Histoire des classes ouvrières et de l'industrie*, II, 217, 338.
102 *Ibid.*, II, 339.

of frames for knitting stockings and other wear by an order of March 30, 1700, which confined such looms to only eighteen cities.[103] More spectacular and persistent were its efforts to protect the linen, woolen, and silk industries from the competition of Indian-style cottons.[104]

Beside resistance to change, other aspects of government policy after 1683 were not conducive to economic growth. Mention has already been made of Colbert's success in borrowing and diffusing foreign technology by attracting skilled artisans and entrepreneurs from abroad. A decree of January, 1687, offering a bounty of 30 gold louis to any skilled craftsman who would come to France, evoked little response. One gets the impression that responsible officials were not seriously interested in attracting foreigners; they were chiefly concerned with luring emigrant Huguenots back home. It is true that Louvois tried to encourage new enterprises as Colbert had done, but too many things diverted his attention. His successors did even less. According to Levasseur,[105] from the death of Colbert to the end of Louis's reign the government issued only about twenty permissions for new establishments. This estimate is certainly too small; still, the number of new firms chartered declined after 1683. Direct financial subsidies, either as loans with or without interest or as outright gifts, were used less frequently and practically disappeared. In the ten years from 1664 through 1673, for example, the royal treasury had disbursed more than 1,500,000 livres in encouragement to industry; in the decennium 1681–1690 it paid out only a little more than 200,000 livres.[106] Once war began to drain the treasury, all such gratuities ceased. The privileged drapers in Languedoc continued to receive a bounty of 10 livres on each piece of fine cloth they made for the Levant, but they collected this subsidy from the provincial parliament rather than from the royal exchequer.[107] Most firms that had received subsidies earlier not only found it impossible to obtain renewed assistance, but they also found themselves subject to taxes from which their letters patent had originally exempted them.

---

103 *Ibid.*, II, 337.

104 See, e.g., Cole, *op. cit.*, pp. 164 ff.

105 *Histoire des classes ouvrières et de l'industrie*, II, 335 n. 2.

106 Martin, *op. cit.*, p. 414.

107 There was at least one other similar arrangement. In 1691 Pontchartrain granted a new manufacturer of gold and silver cloth at Marseille an annual subsidy of 8,000 livres for ten years, payable from the local excise (octroi) of that city (Cole, *op. cit.*, p. 116).

Colbert had also encouraged infant industries by granting individuals and companies either exclusive or nonexclusive privileges. The *manufactures du roi*—like Gobelins, Savonnerie, and certain armament works—were owned and operated by the king. The *manufactures royales* were private enterprises enjoying extensive privileges, subsidies, and the right to display the royal coat of arms over their portals. The *manufactures privilégiées,* also privately owned and operated, enjoyed less government favoritism than royal manufactories but they also had royal charters and such valuable concessions as tax exemptions and priorities in the acquisition of basic materials. A fourth category included unchartered, nonprivileged enterprises which usually operated on a small scale and produced goods that had long been available in French markets. Although Colbert frequently extolled the merits of competition, he had nonetheless employed government favoritism and privilege whenever he wanted to build up new industries or to expand and improve old ones. He may not have fully appreciated that vested interests, once created and buttressed with state sanction, are hard to destroy. He may also have ignored the fact that infant industries do not always mature. Two significant developments stemmed from his policy. First, currying favor with the controller general or with other important persons at court who might be able to influence government action rapidly became an essential entrepreneurial function. And, second, the business world—as had long been true of the social world—soon became inextricably enmeshed in a system of privilege and status. It is doubtful that Colbert would have modified his policies if he had lived longer or that he could have revivified competition if he had tried. Certainly his successors did neither.

Louvois and Pontchartrain did not establish any new state monopolies in manufacturing and apparently were less willing than Colbert had been to create private monopolies; nonetheless, they renewed old exclusive privileges when these expired and continued to shower new enterprisers with favors which gave them a competitive advantage over others.[108] The van Robais family at Abbeville, for example, experienced little difficulty in renewing its exclusive privileges for fine woolens; the Royal Plate Glass Company had its monopoly extended and strength-

108 *Ibid.,* pp. 115 ff.; Lavisse, *op. cit.,* Vol. VIII, Part 1, pp. 212–213, 232 ff.; Levasseur, *Histoire des classes ouvrières et de l'industrie,* pp. 335 ff.; Martin, *op. cit.,* pp. 232–233, 238 ff., 283 ff., 346 ff.; Sée, *op. cit.,* I, 265 ff.

ened; woolen manufacturers at Sedan retained all their special favors; the royal manufactories in Languedoc producing woolens for the Levantine market increased in number from two in 1683 to six in 1700; certain courtiers or other influential persons retained exclusive mining rights; in 1699 one de Launoy received the sole right to engrave crystal throughout the realm; and at the end of the seventeenth century there were still five major overseas trading companies enjoying monopoly privileges. Tobacco had long been a government monopoly which brought in considerable revenue from those who farmed it. An edict of January, 1692, tried to do the same thing for tea, coffee, chocolate, vanilla, and sherbet, but the effort did not succeed.[109] Lead, hunting powder, and the retail trade in brandy were also farmed out as state monopolies. These examples suggest that government favoritism remained a potent force in industry while Louvois and Pontchartrain served as controller general. And the situation did not improve after 1700. If anything, it worsened. Individuals found it easier to acquire exclusive privileges within limited markets, tax exemptions, titles of "royal manufactory," and similar concessions for their enterprises without having first to demonstrate that they followed a novel method in production or made a new kind of product.

The state discriminated among localities as well as among individuals. Merchants sometimes had legal priority in purchasing textiles or raw materials produced in neighboring rural areas. Marseille not only paid lower import and export duties than other ports throughout most of the period 1683–1715, but she also enjoyed a virtual monopoly in her trade with the Levant.[110] Rouen and Dunkirk were the only Atlantic ports that could buy and sell in the Levantine market, and even they had to pay a 20 per cent import duty which did not apply to Marseille. At one time Rouen, Nantes, La Rochelle, and Bordeaux were the only cities that could legally trade with the French West Indies.

The silk industry at Nîmes and Tours suffered acutely from the favoritism shown Lyon. Raw silk from Italy, Piedmont, and the Mediterranean basin could enter France only by way of

---

109 The monopoly was withdrawn on May 12, 1693, and the import of these items was heavily taxed instead.

110 Languedoc drapers, for example, could not import raw wool from the Barbary and Levantine coasts except via Marseille (Sagnac, *op. cit.,* p. 25).

Marseille and Pont-de-Beauvoisin in Dauphiné. Then it had to be carried to Lyon, where it was taxed and distributed through a clique of merchants. Manufacturers at Nîmes and Tours, unable to find enough domestic raw silk for their needs, had to buy supplies from Lyon and pay the added transport costs, taxes, and profits exacted by monopolistic middlemen. Even the raw silk produced in Provence and the Papal Comtat Venaissin had to pass through the same channels after 1687. The officials of the Lyon customs, not content with collecting duties on raw silk, had begun to insist about 1682 that all silken fabrics made in Languedoc and exported abroad or sold in the central part of France (the Five Great Farms) had first to go out of its way and pass through Lyon so that they could inspect and tax it. Producers in Languedoc and Touraine persistently and bitterly complained of this discrimination. Commercial interests in Nantes and most deputies of trade sided with them. Still the king continued to respect the privileges of Lyon. He did, however, allow manufacturers in Languedoc to draw fixed amounts of raw silk for a limited period of time directly from Marseille provided they paid all the transport duties along the Rhône and the customs at Lyon which would have been collected had the silk gone from Marseille to Languedoc via Lyon. It is difficult to justify such discrimination in favor of Lyon. Government policy was thus partially responsible for the decline in silk production around Nîmes and Tours after 1683.[111]

Still another aspect of France's economic statism which accentuated the depression and postponed recovery was the effort to revivify and extend the gild system. Following the policy enunciated under Colbert in 1673, the government attempted to force all craftsmen and retail merchants into gilds. It thought this would simplify the regulation of industry and of consumer markets and also assure the proper training of apprentices. After 1689 it viewed the creation of gilds primarily as a means of raising additional revenue. An edict issued in March, 1691, ordered that all gild statutes be submitted to appropriate authorities for reëxamination and revision and that elective wardens and syndics

111 See, e.g., Archives Nationales, G7 297, 1685, 1686; Bibliothèque Nationale, *Fonds français*, MSS 4283, fol. 23; 4288, fols. 27–29; 8038, fols. 444, 449; Bosseboeuf, *op. cit.*, p. 275; Abbé Jean Novi de Caveirac, *Apologie de Louis XIV et de son conseil, sur la révocation de l'Edit de Nantes, etc.* (n.p., 1758), p. 118; Dutil, *op. cit.*, pp. 320, 323–329; Lavisse, *op. cit.*, Vol. VIII, Part 1, pp. 212–213, 236–238.

be replaced by hereditary officials who would acquire their posts by purchase.[112] New gilds invaded trades that had formerly remained free and forced their way into cities that had quietly but stubbornly refused to incorporate their crafts.

Relentless financial demands from the government soon caused most new and old gilds to run heavily into debt. They had to raise their initiation fees and other assessments so high that some became exclusive corporations with unwarranted control over employment opportunities and market prices. Others that sought to expand their membership lists in order to reduce the per capita financial burden found that their high debts frightened away potential members. Meanwhile, the government was steadily increasing its regulation of their internal and external affairs, thereby sapping their autonomy and reducing them to the status of dependent agencies. There was, however, no concomitant reduction in the wasteful jurisdictional wrangling among the gilds or in their bickering with those who bought their products or supplied them with materials. Merchants, for example, found it increasingly difficult to employ unorganized artisans in rural areas to work up whatever raw materials they furnished. And endless litigation diverted the energies of gild members from more productive activities. Most gilds sought to protect their vested interests by resisting change. They often fought the introduction of new products and new technological processes.

At least one constructive action to revive trade and industry was taken after Colbert's death. By order dated June 29, 1700, Louis created the Council of Trade. It was to meet at least once a week and discuss all proposals and memoranda coming before the government which concerned foreign and domestic trade as well as crafts and industries. In addition to the controller general and the secretary of the marine—who, by mutual agreement, did not attend its sessions—the council's membership included Daguesseau, its first president, and Amelot de Gournay, a councilor of state; two other councilors and masters of petitions; a secretary; twelve deputies; and two men selected by the controller general to represent the tax farmers when their interests were at stake.[113] The deputies of trade, who had no vote but

---

112 Cole, *op. cit.*, pp. 187–188.

113 The composition of the council soon changed. The two directors of finance, appointed in 1701, served until their offices were suppressed in 1708; the lieutenant general of police in Paris began to attend in 1705; Amelot temporarily withdrew

were to advise the council on all matters, had to be practical businessmen "whose probity, capacity, and experience in trade are well known." Two were to represent Paris, and each of the remaining ten was to be freely elected by the municipal corps and leading wholesale merchants of Rouen, Bordeaux, Lyon, Marseille, La Rochelle, Nantes, Saint-Malo, Lille, Bayonne, and Dunkirk. A special *arrêt,* dated September 7, 1700, allowed the Parliament of Languedoc to select a thirteenth deputy.

To supplement the Council of Trade the king on August 30, 1701, asked Lyon, Rouen, Bordeaux, Toulouse, Montpellier, La Rochelle, Nantes, Saint-Malo, Lille, and Bayonne to create chambers of commerce like those already functioning at Dunkirk and Marseille.[114] Any merchant or other businessman who had a grievance to air or a suggestion to make for improving the economy was to submit his views to one of these chambers. After studying his proposal, the chamber of commerce was to formulate its own recommendations and then forward all the documents to the appropriate deputy at Paris, who was to submit the matter to the other deputies for consideration before the proposal went before the council.

The Council of Trade itself was neither a legislative nor an administrative body. It was advisory to the controller general and to the secretary of the marine on all matters brought before it by these two officials or submitted by the chambers of commerce. The king had hoped that the council might coördinate the policies of and reconcile differences between the controller general and the secretary of the marine, who shared the jurisdiction over economic matters after Colbert's death. All depended upon whether these two officials sincerely coöperated in the scheme. They did not always seek advice from the council before they acted; but when they did seek it, they usually followed it. And the commissioners on the council nearly always adopted the deputies' point of view on specific requests from individuals or on proposed legislation. When the deputies advanced their own suggestions for major policy changes or advocated far-reaching reforms, the council ordinarily listened politely and then, with-

in order to serve as ambassador at Madrid; the six intendants of trade, created in 1708, had seats on the council; and another commissioner was added in 1708 and still another in 1715.

114 Lyon complied in 1702, Rouen in 1703, Toulouse in 1703, Montpellier in 1704, Bordeaux in 1705, La Rochelle in 1710, Lille in 1714, and Bayonne in 1726. Nantes and Saint-Malo never did.

out further comment, promised to bring the proposals to the king's attention.

The creation of the Council of Trade did not mark a radical change in government economic policy. This was perhaps too much to expect. Economic statism feeds upon itself. Direct regulation of some industries necessarily creates inequities which the government then seeks to correct by broadening its sphere of regulation. In France, this process encouraged fraud and brought businessmen into constant argument with the administration.[115] Special privileges dulled individual initiative and caused too many enterprises to rely primarily upon royal favoritism. Then, when the exigencies of war and a depleted treasury forced the government to retract its direct or indirect subsidies, many firms failed.

The deputies of trade were united in their opposition to proposals to establish inspectorates in silk, paper, hats, and other fields. They also fought new excises, urged better trade relations with foreign countries, and exhorted the government to do all it could to improve the social position and public esteem accorded entrepreneurs. But they did not all agree that economic liberty was preferable to economic regulation. Some opposed the creation of exclusive overseas trading companies; others would restrict them to trade with unknown regions where the risks and capital needs were large; others gave their blessing to one or another specific company but spoke out against the rest; and a few endorsed them all. Upon occasion most of the deputies extolled the merits of competition and warned the government against further infringement of freedom of consumer's and producer's choice; at other times they paradoxically voted in favor of protecting established industries against new products. The trouble was that all of them had grown up in a mercantilist society under an absolute monarch, where the state was the ultimate arbiter in economic and other matters. As businessmen, their sympathy was with freedom and competition; as advisers to the government, their reason was trammeled by all the mercantilist principles and practices that had long guided public policy. Small wonder, then, that their views in the abstract were sometimes inconsistent with the concrete actions they endorsed!

The creation of the Council of Trade, nevertheless, was a

---

115 See, e.g., Levasseur, *Histoire des classes ouvrières et de l'industrie,* II, 341.

step in the right direction. With the advice of practical business-men, the government was less likely to act capriciously or arbitrarily on an individual request for special privileges or im-pulsively to levy a new excise or create a new inspectorate with-out first considering the consequences. The commissioners on the council, who were expected to become expert statesmen in eco-nomic matters, were in a position to influence public policy. Adam Anderson, writing in 1801, observed that "from the very first erection of this famous new council, or board of commerce, we have good ground to date the great and almost surprising increase of the commerce, woolen manufacture, mercantile ship-ping, and foreign colonies of France."[116]

RESTRAINTS ON FOREIGN AND DOMESTIC TRADE

According to Colbert, the fundamental rules of protectionism were simple: place heavy duties on imported manufactured goods and light or no duties on imported materials needed by domestic industry; encourage the sale of manufactured goods abroad with low export duties and severely tax the export of raw materials. These principles he had followed in his famous tariff of 1667.[117] From that date to 1786, when the Eden Treaty was signed, France was almost continuously engaged in a tariff war with her chief competitors, England and Holland. Those who succeeded Col-bert in office readily adopted his perfectionist principles, since they, too, were jealous of the same two nations. Between 1683 and 1700 they initiated several hundred changes in tariff duties.[118] The rates on imported manufactured goods were nearly always raised in order to provide greater protection for French industry. And the increases were usually quite stiff. Most of them ranged from 20 to 100 per cent; some were much higher. The 1664 duty on rock crystal, to mention an extreme example, was raised 1600 per cent on January 3, 1690.

Upon the close of the War of the League of Augsburg, France and England renewed the tariff fight they had begun before the outbreak of military action; the Dutch, however, in the Treaty

---

[116] *Op. cit.*, II, 646; MacPherson, *op. cit.*, II, 708.

[117] This tariff helped precipitate the Dutch War in 1672. The Treaty of Nimwegen (1678) reëstablished many of the lower 1664 duties on Dutch goods. The English had secured similar concessions for their products in 1672.

[118] Charles W. Cole's work on French mercantilism *(op. cit)*, with its compre-hensive and reliable account of French tariff and trade policies in this period, has proven invaluable in the summary given here.

of Ryswick (1697), insisted upon trade concessions and the promise of even greater relief from French duties. Dutch vessels no longer had to pay the 50 sous tonnage duty which all foreign ships visiting French ports had had to pay since 1659. The two nations signed a tariff agreement in 1699, to become effective on January 1, 1700. From the hundreds of Dutch products she was taxing, France selected thirty items on which she agreed to lower duties; Holland reciprocated by reducing her tariffs on nine types of French goods, only two of which—window glass and drinking glasses—were industrial products. According to Professor Cole, twenty-two of the thirty Dutch goods on which France lowered her duties in 1699 had appeared in the tariff schedules of both 1664 and 1667. If the duties on these twenty-two items in 1664 are represented as 100, then the index number of duties collected on the same items would be 471 for 1698 and 177 for 1700.[119] The tariff of 1699 hence did not reëstablish the 1664 rates on the twenty-two items. If all Dutch goods taxed by France are included, the index number for 1700 would show a much smaller reduction in the 1698 tariff wall.

The Treaty of Utrecht (1713), at the end of the War of the Spanish Succession, reaffirmed the tariff of 1699 for Holland. French emissaries meanwhile had been negotiating with England since 1711; and, in fact, two articles of the Utrecht Treaty stipulated that the reciprocal trade of England and France would be free and that each would consider the other the "most favored nation." At the behest of Huguenot sympathizers and English manufacturers who feared French competition, the House of Commons rejected these two provisions of the treaty. France then applied to English products the duties established for Holland in 1699; and England, in her turn, somewhat reduced her tariffs on certain French goods. Both countries, however, remained jealous of each other and subjected their mutual trade to all sorts of vexatious restrictions. According to MacPherson,[120] "the commerce between us and France has ever since remained in a kind of a state of prohibition on both sides, especially with respect to the principal points."

This dismal picture does not accurately portray all the ob-

---

119 *Ibid.*, p. 15. The duties collected in 1698 were either those that had not been changed since the tariff of 1667 or those that had been subsequently revised.

120 *Op. cit.*, III, 31.

stacles that French merchants trading with England or Holland
had to surmount in 1683–1715. The two major wars created additional barriers to trade. England tried at various times to persuade the Dutch to join her in prohibiting all trade with their
enemy, but the Dutch wished insofar as possible to continue
"business as usual." England usually followed Holland's example
of listing only certain contraband items which could not be sent
to or brought from France. Both countries lengthened this list
as the wars progressed. France, on her side, set out to stop all
commerce with her enemies. Neutral goods on enemy ships, as
well as enemy goods on neutral ships, were subject to seizure.
Eventually, however, she relaxed her stand and was soon issuing
passports to neutrals and even to Dutch vessels. The navies and
the privateers of all three powers preyed relentlessly on shipping.
Marine insurance rates mounted, and smuggling became much
more hazardous than in times of peace. Cargoes captured at sea
and sold as lawful prizes on the domestic market supplied consumers and manufacturers in all three countries with goods which
they otherwise could not have legally acquired. It would be a
mistake, however, to conclude that the Augsburg and Spanish
Succession wars disrupted trade between the belligerents to the
same extent as did later conflicts in the eighteenth and nineteenth centuries. Never again would neutrals be so free to carry
on their trade, and never again could citizens of warring nations
maintain their commercial contacts with each other so easily.
But the difficulties and the uncertainties of foreign commerce
were still much greater in wartime than in years of peace.

Toward the latter part of Louis's reign a few encouraging
signs gave promise of greater freedom in the field of trade. More
and more businessmen began to urge the king to seek reciprocal
trade agreements with his neighbors. Several deputies of trade
pointed out that high French duties on foreign goods or outright prohibitions always provoked retaliatory measures against
French products. Two deputies, representing Bayonne and
Nantes, listed tariff wars as a major cause for the depression.[121]
And the deputy from Nantes wrote: "If foreigners get by without
our wines, brandies, and salt, they can also get by without our
linens, paper, and lustrous taffetas. They have [already] established these manufactures at home with the aid of our fugitive

---

121 Bibliothèque Nationale, *Fonds français*, MS 8038, fols. 428 ff.; Boislisle, *op. cit.*,
II, 479–480.

Religionists."[122] The deputy from Bordeaux, in suggesting that God had distributed his gifts unequally over the earth's surface in order to force men to love one another by becoming mutually dependent through trade, implied that nations should not seek to become economically self-sufficient.[123] Similar views were also expressed by the deputy from Lyon: "One must forget about M. Colbert's maxim which pretended that France could get along without everyone and yet which sought to oblige foreigners to run to us."[124] The representative from Languedoc claimed that other countries had ceased to buy agricultural and manufactured goods from France because of the tariff. Refugee Huguenots, he said, were helping them start their own industries, and they might soon forget all about trading with France. He urged the government to remedy this by "allowing commercial liberty with all European nations."[125] In a unanimous opinion in 1704 the deputies held the high tariff of 1667 responsible for forcing England to manufacture products she had formerly imported. "We [now] find ourselves deprived of the most advantageous trade we can carry on," they said.[126]

The state on a few occasions seemed ready to heed their advice. Dunkirk recovered its status as a free port in 1700; Marseille once again became partially free in 1703; France negotiated and signed trade treaties with Russia and Persia in 1708, with Portugal and Prussia in 1713, and with the Austrian Low Countries in 1714; and the Treaty of Utrecht reëstablished the tariff of 1699 with Holland. Although the attempt proved abortive, it should be recalled that France tried to negotiate a reciprocal "most-favored-nation" trade treaty with England in 1711–1713. These concessions should not be interpreted, however, as a definite break with the past. It is doubtful that the deputies of trade or other businessmen would have welcomed complete freedom if the government had moved in that direction. Increased competition from imports in the domestic market would probably have led them to urge protection for first one industry and then another. What they wanted was greater freedom to sell abroad those manufactured goods in which France had a com-

---

122 Boislisle, *op. cit.*, II, 489.

123 Bibliothèque Nationale, *Fonds français*, MS 8038, fol. 405.

124 Boislisle, *op. cit.*, II, 480. Yet the deputy thought France should export more than she imported in order to attract specie. He denied only that she could expect to sell abroad without importing any goods whatever in exchange.

125 Bibliothèque Nationale, *Fonds français*, MS 8038, fol. 467.

126 Archives Nationales, F12 693.

parative advantage and to buy from foreigners those raw materials which were in short supply at home. Most of them did not favor exporting raw materials or importing manufactures that would compete with domestic products.

France's economy suffered from all these restrictions on trade. An earlier chapter has already summarized in aggregative terms what happened to her foreign trade from 1684 to 1715. It will suffice at this time to illustrate how the restrictions affected segments of the economy.

Because of tariffs the southern and southwestern provinces found it difficult to market their agricultural surpluses.[127] When France reiterated her prohibitions on the import of Dutch manufactures in 1688, Holland retaliated by forbidding French wines and brandies to enter her ports.[128] During the two wars, when Dutch and English merchants were seeking their supplies in Portugal and Spain, Bordeaux vintners had to disguise their wines in Spanish casks in order to sell them. With the return of peace they had to reëstablish old commercial contacts and win back former markets. Since wine and brandy exports were substantial, the regional economy was especially sensitive to changes in international trade. When other countries sought to cripple France, they raised their duties on French wines;[129] when Louis XIV needed additional revenue, he thought at once of taxing wine exports. On October 17, 1708, the deputies of trade predicted that additional duties on wine would surely decrease exports and probably cause vintners to leave the country. They pointed out that similar duties and regulations had had this effect in the hat, paper, and linen industries. Whenever a commodity was abundant, they concluded, nothing should be done to hinder its export.[130]

A citizen of Saint-Malo pleaded with Seignelay on January 18, 1688, to remove certain duties on English draperies. When Englishmen could not sell their cloth in France, he argued, they ceased coming to Brittany, where they usually spent three times as much for linen and hempen fabrics as they received for their own cloth.[131] There must have been substance in his complaint. The intendant in Brittany echoed it in 1699, when he wrote

---

[127] Lavisse, *op. cit.*, Vol. VIII, Part 1, p. 209; Martin, *op. cit.*, p. 253.

[128] Arnould, *op. cit.*, I, 188.

[129] England, for example, taxed a cask of French wine at 700 livres and a cask of brandy at 900 livres.

[130] Archives Nationales, G7 1692.

[131] *Ibid.*, B7 *registre* 495, fol. 39.

that few English merchants were now coming to Morlaix and other Breton ports to buy linens. He blamed the *arrêt* of November 8, 1687, which required foreign woolens to enter France via Calais and Saint-Valery-en-Caux. Why should English ships come to Brittany for linens if they could not there unload their own merchandise?[132] The 1687 *arrêt* had already led England to retaliate by taxing unbleached linen from France at 70 per cent and other kinds at 50 per cent. England had also forbidden the export of raw wool, hides, and other materials which French manufacturers customarily bought from her.[133]

Among the reasons for the decline in the fine-woolen industry in France at the beginning of the eighteenth century, Professor Sagnac has listed the increasing difficulty Frenchmen experienced in acquiring the finer grades of raw wool. England forbade anyone to export raw wool to France, and less Spanish wool went across the Pyrenees after English and Dutch buyers invaded the Spanish market and competed effectively with French merchants there. Sagnac also thought that France had accentuated the decline by levying export duties on her own draperies and high import duties on raw wool.[134]

Silk was another important export of the French textile industry. In 1684 the lieutenant general of police at Paris received a memorandum stating that "more than 4,000 families" of silk merchants and artisans in the capital were in dire need because England had recently restricted imports of their products and because war with Spain and Germany was closing other markets.[135] The intendant at Lyon complained in 1699 that England had raised her duties on taffetas[136] and more recently had even forbidden their importation in order to protect the taffeta factory that Huguenots had started there. Unless the prohibition was removed and the duties were reduced, he predicted, Lyon would permanently lose the English market. He also blamed the drastic decline in the output of fustians and *bazins* in his jurisdiction on a recent increase in the import tax on cotton yarn used in their production.[137] The deputy from Languedoc thought that the retaliatory duties levied on French silks by

---

[132] Bibliothèque Nationale, *Fonds français*, MS 4283, fol. 67.

[133] Lavisse, *op. cit.*, Vol. VIII, Part 1, p. 261.

[134] *Ibid.*, p. 235; Sagnac, *op. cit.*, pp. 37–38.

[135] Bibliothèque Nationale, *Fonds français*, MS 21773, fol. 142.

[136] Some merchants had told him that the duties and import expenses on taffeta amounted to 53 per cent of its value.

[137] Bibliothèque Nationale, *Fonds français*, MS 4288, fols. 118–119, 123–124.

Switzerland, Holland, England, and other countries, as well as the French import duties on raw silk, were partly responsible for the trouble besetting manufacturers in the vicinity of Nîmes.[138] A student of the industry at Lyon has denied that the revocation of the Edict of Nantes was primarily responsible for the introduction and early growth of silk manufacturing in Holland. Instead, he concluded from his examination of Dutch documents that the tariff wars between the two countries were the most important cause.[139]

Ironmasters in French Hainaut claimed that the export duty on iron was ruining them.[140] The intendant in the same region explained in 1699 that export duties were also responsible for the reduction in coal output. After the coal mines near Tournai, Mons, and Condé were annexed to France, he said, their sales in the Low Countries fell off because their coal now had to acquit heavy duties.[141] In other words, new boundary lines, sharply etched by tariff walls, separated the sources of supply from their former chief markets.

Domestic trade apparently made even less progress than foreign trade in the latter half of Louis's reign.[142] One reason for this was the inadequacy of overland transport facilities. Although Sully, Henry IV's able minister, had outlined an ambitious road-building program, and although Colbert had reconstituted the administration of roads and bridges, France did not have anything like an adequate network of roads by 1683. Thereafter, to judge from reports reaching Paris from the provinces, the roads she had were fast becoming less and less usable. The intendant in Hainaut, for example, wrote on September 1, 1685, that the roads in his jurisdiction were in such a deplorable state that they could not be repaired but would have to be rebuilt. "Communication has become impossible almost everywhere," he continued, "not only for carriages but even for horses."[143] His colleague at Limoges in 1687 claimed that roads were not "practicable" for hauling freight.[144] The controller general had advised him a year earlier that the best way to aid the poor was

---

138 *Ibid.,* MS 8038, fol. 476.
139 Rondot, *op. cit.,* p. 64 n. 1.
140 Boislisle, *op. cit.,* I, 39.
141 Bibliothèque Nationale, *Fonds français,* MS 4284, fols. 63–64.
142 See, e.g., Henri Sée, *L'Évolution commerciale et industrielle de la France sous l'ancien régime* (Paris, 1925), pp. 90 ff.
143 Boislisle, *op. cit.,* I, 53.
144 *Ibid.,* I, 106.

by a system of public works and that he should be careful to select projects that would "prove useful to trade, like building highways and making rivers navigable."[145] The intendants all asserted in their 1698–1700 memoranda that roads had deteriorated in the past several years. Central and provincial authorities did not have the necessary funds for repairs and certainly not enough for major construction.[146] Overland travel was both costly and time-consuming. It took two days for passengers to go from Paris to Orléans and ten or eleven days to go from Paris to Lyon. Goods took longer. Freight shipped from the capital, for example, ordinarily arrived at Orléans four days later.

In the seventeenth and eighteenth centuries transportation by water was everywhere preferable to transportation by land. Compared with England or Holland, France was at a distinct disadvantage in this respect, for she possessed far less navigable waterways per square mile of territory. The Briare Canal, connecting the Loire with the Seine, had been opened in 1640; the famous Languedoc Canal,[147] begun in 1665 and completed in 1681, joined the Atlantic to the Mediterranean by means of the Garonne River; another joined Calais with Saint-Omer; and a fourth—the canal of Orléans or of the Loing River (completed in 1692)—connected Orléans with the Briare Canal and hence with the Seine. These achievements, important though they were, did not appreciably widen markets or reduce transportation costs except in adjacent regions. Some rivers became less navigable after 1683, and only a few were improved by individuals or groups who received a monopoly of transport in return for doing so.[148]

---

145 *Ibid.*, I, 72.

146 For roads and bridges the central government appropriated 446,000 livres in 1683; 1,655,000 livres in 1687; 446,000 livres in 1690; and between 1,200,000 and 1,300,000 livres in 1715. Even when local and provincial expenditures were added, the total was wholly inadequate. Certain *généralités* had only 8,000 or 10,000 livres a year to spend on their roads. (Lavisse, *op. cit.*, Vol. VIII, Part 1, p. 250.)

147 This canal, 7 feet deep and 175 miles long, had 15 locks on its western side and 45 on its eastern side. It tunneled under mountains (the longest single tunnel was about 240 meters) and flowed over ravines and streams in 8 aqueducts. It was fed at the divide by an auxiliary basin and a large reservoir into which 45 kilometers of ditches channeled water from the surrounding hills. Its cost amounted to 13 million livres. (Bibliothèque Nationale, *Fonds français*, MS 4290, fols. 371 ff.)

148 For example, in 1702 for the Loire from Saint-Rambert to Roanne, in 1704 for the Eure from Chartres to Pont-de-l'Arche, and in 1708 for the Clain from Châtellerault to Vivonne through Poitiers (Lavisse, *op. cit.*, Vol. VIII, Part 1, p. 250).

Innumerable tolls on bridges, roads, canals, and rivers reduced their effectiveness in widening markets. Colbert had tried to effect substantial reforms in this area, but his efforts had met with little success. Furthermore, France itself was not a free market area. There was a customs wall around the Five Great Farms, which included Île-de-France, Orléanais, Picardy, Normandy, Champagne, Maine, Anjou, Poitou, Burgundy, Aunis, Berry, and Bourbonnais. The "provinces reputedly foreign"—Artois, Brittany, and the regions in the south—had to pay duties on goods shipped to and from the Five Great Farms. The "provinces effectively foreign"—Alsace, the Three Bishoprics, and Franche-Comté, which had been added to France later than most other provinces—were treated like foreign countries insofar as their trade with the rest of the country was concerned, but they could trade freely with foreign nations if they wished. In addition, there were special customs areas in the "provinces reputedly foreign," like the Customs of Lyon, the Customs of Valence, and the *Comptablie* of Bordeaux. Local tolls and provincial customs not only directly increased the cost of shipping goods, but they also consumed time and exasperated shippers with excessive red tape.

Fairs continued to play an important role in domestic trade. The fairs at Saint-Laurent and Saint-Germain at Paris, and those at Bordeaux, Lyon, and Beaucaire (in Languedoc) attracted large numbers of wholesale merchants from all over France as well as from abroad and acted as clearinghouses for financial transactions. Many other seasonal fairs served regional markets. In addition, most cities and towns of any consequence had their own local markets in which suppliers had to display their goods before retailers or domestic consumers could purchase them. In the latter half of the seventeenth century towns, provinces, and the central government tended to regulate these fairs and markets more closely.[149] New offices for inspecting and controlling transactions were created and sold in order to raise revenue. Some agents, such as brokers, acquired considerable power and soon came to dominate certain markets. Others were interested only in collecting their fees to assure themselves a return on the investment they had made when they acquired their offices.

The grain trade especially fell under government control.[150]

---

[149] See especially Levasseur, *Histoire des classes ouvrières et de l'industrie,* II, 369 ff.

[150] Cole, *op. cit.,* pp. 197 ff.

When harvests were poor, grain exports were forbidden; when crop yields ran high, export barriers were lifted and imports were discouraged. Dealers never knew from one year to the next what regulations they would encounter. Furthermore, each province or locality jealously guarded its supplies in short years and refused to share them with other parts of the country; in good years it would relax its marketing restrictions. When crops were plentiful and prices were low, farmers and dealers usually complained about the controls, and a few officials would cautiously extol the merits of freedom in the grain trade. Frequently, because of regulations and inadequacies in transport facilities, there was a glut of grain in some areas while acute shortages were causing suffering and famine elsewhere.[151] Bouchu, the intendant in Dauphiné, wrote the controller general on September 18, 1699, that "the prohibitions to ship wheat . . . from one province to another have always seemed to me to encourage individuals to hoard their supplies, hence to constitute one of the causes for the increase in price and scarcity on the market."[152] The intendant at Caen in 1707 favored permission to export grain even to enemy countries because he thought this would facilitate the sale of surpluses accumulated in the past three years. These surpluses had depressed prices to such an extent, he said, that farmers had been unable to pay the rent on their land.[153] Samuel Bernard, the Parisian banker and the purchaser of wheat for the government, dissuaded the controller general from fixing maximum prices in times of crisis. Instead, he wrote, "one should free the trade in order to bring in abundant supplies of grain and to force prices down."[154] The government was always more anxious to protect consumers in urban areas and to prevent bread riots than it was to help farmers get adequate prices. Vauban had in mind all the fiscal and regulatory hindrances to domestic trade when he wrote, at the end of the seventeenth century, that "peasants and proprietors prefer to let their crops rot in the fields rather than transport them at such great risk and with so little profit."[155]

There were other reasons that internal commerce did not grow

---

[151] See especially the correspondence between intendants and the controller general for 1697–1698 in Boislisle, *op. cit.*, I.

[152] *Ibid.*, II, 2.

[153] *Ibid.*, II, 384.

[154] Lavisse, *op. cit.*, Vol. VIII, Part 1, p. 228.

[155] Quoted by Henri Sée (*L'Évolution commerciale et industrielle de la France*, p. 96).

vigorously after 1683. At least three deserve mention. Monetary instability resulting from frequent revaluations created uncertainty, encouraged specie hoarding, and caused numerous bankruptcies. Carriers in certain areas formed exclusive groups and repelled shippers with their excessive rates. And, finally, the decline in population and the increasing misery of the masses which accompanied economic stagnation reduced consumer demand.

Depopulation and Famines

There is little doubt that France's population decreased from 1683 to 1715, but it is not at all certain how great was the decline. A conservative estimate would probably be about 2 million (or roughly 10 per cent); a liberal estimate would be about 4 million (or roughly 20 per cent). According to intendants, some provinces and several cities lost a third, a fourth, or a fifth of their inhabitants. This meant a sizable decrease in the demand for agricultural and industrial products, as well as in the potential labor supply. Under certain circumstances, such a decrease could have created a labor shortage and raised wage rates. This did not happen. Actually there were far more complaints about unemployment, particularly in the luxury fields, than about an insufficient supply of laborers to staff the workshops and till the soil. Because of the depression, the demand for labor decreased more rapidly and more drastically than the labor supply.

The level of economic activity and the size of a country's population are interdependent. Other things remaining equal, a sudden, prolonged fall in economic activity tends to depress population; and a decrease in population (or even a decrease in the rate of growth) tends to dampen economic activity. But were there any independent or quasi-independent causes for the drop in France's population? If so, they would justify considering depopulation after 1683 as a contributory factor in the decline of economic activity.

Contemporaries and subsequent commentators have placed most of the blame for the decrease in population upon war, general impoverishment, emigration, and famines.[156] Warfare took its

---

156 Bibliothèque Nationale, *Fonds français*, MSS 4282, fol. 334; 4283, fol. 20; 4284, fol. 26; 4285, fol. 139; 4286, fols. 13, 28, 30, 93–94; 4287, fol. 18; 4288, fol. 30; Boislisle, *op. cit.*, II, 210; La Boutetière, *op. cit.*, p. 353; Novi de Caveirac, *Mémoire politico-critique*, p. 64; Layard, *op. cit.*, pp. 151–152; Auguste-François Lièvre,

toll on the battlefields, and disease exacted its due in army camps. The billeting of soldiers impoverished families, and the continual passage of troops stripped the countryside of food and laid bare fields and vineyards. The tax collector struck the *coup de grâce* with his heavy exactions. Peasants and townspeople alike were impoverished and frequently reduced to starvation. Those in the towns sought to escape by moving to the country; those in the country sought asylum in the cities. Many living near the frontier emigrated to escape financial ruin. The revocation of the Edict of Nantes and religious persecution drove some 200,000 abroad. And two severe famines following poor harvests caused alarming increases in mortality.

In the latter half of the seventeenth century and the first decades of the eighteenth, French peasants, like farmers everywhere and at all times, were frequently victims of nature's inclemency. Windstorms, hail, early freezes, inundations, and droughts plagued them; fires burned their buildings, and epidemics such as the epizoötic of 1715 decimated their livestock. The intendant at Soissons, for example, after making a tour of the agricultural areas in his jurisdiction, wrote on July 31, 1686, that several places had suffered severely from hail, extraordinarily severe storms, and "a frightful quantity of small mice which eat up all the grain."[157] Regional distress due to crop failures and local weather conditions was not a new thing, and there is no reason to conclude that such distress was more frequent after 1683 than before. But the general crop failure in 1692–1694 and the extreme winter of 1708–09 were not common occurrences.

The harvest in Guyenne was below normal in the fall of 1691; a year later other provinces were beginning to experience a similar decline; and crops were disastrously poor throughout the country in 1693. Famine conditions prevailed everywhere, and people were reduced to eating grass and roots in the fields like cattle. Disease broke out and spread swiftly among the people, who were too weakened by starvation to resist its ravages. Several hundred thousand may have perished. Government officials long referred to this in their memoranda as the "great mortality," and modern historians believe it was the most severe famine France experienced in the seventeenth century. Then another

---

Histoire des protestants et des églises réformées du Poitou (Paris, 1856–1860), II, 251.
[157] Archives Nationales, G7 511.

natural catastrophe occurred in 1708–09. A prolonged siege of frigid weather killed fruit trees and vines, destroyed crops in the field and delayed spring planting, froze harvested grain which then rotted after the thaw, decimated livestock and wildlife, and even froze the ink on scriveners' desks.[158] Famine and high mortality again prevailed. Professor Jean Meuvret, after comparing the percentages of deaths-to-conceptions (at Dijon and the region of Gien) with the five-year moving median of price relatives for wheat at Rozay-en-Brie, has concluded that the index of deaths-over-conceptions increased every bit as much as the rise in wheat prices in 1693–1694 and 1709–1710.[159]

Perhaps no one would seriously quarrel with the statement that the combination of events in the latter half of Louis XIV's reign was not conducive to economic growth. The conjuncture had a singularly depressing effect. The two long wars waged against most of western Europe may have been less destructive of human life than the religious wars of the preceding century or than the revolutionary and Napoleonic wars of the late eighteenth and early nineteenth centuries, but they cost the lives of several tens of thousands of Frenchmen in their prime. They also destroyed large amounts of property in frontier areas where fighting occurred at one time or another. But, from an economic standpoint, these were not the most important costs. War always diverts productive resources from peacetime to wartime uses. While 200,000 to 500,000 Frenchmen were serving under arms, the economy lost the consumer goods and services and the capital equipment which they might otherwise have been producing. All the ships, munitions, and other military supplies required to prosecute the wars, and all the labor expended behind the lines of battle to maintain the troops and naval forces, meant

---

158 The 1708–09 winter was more severe than the one that held most of Europe in its grip during January–March, 1956. Having spent 1955–56 in Paris, I can easily imagine what hardships it must have occasioned. Despite modern heating, merchandising, and transport facilities, fruits and vegetables in 1956 froze in the Paris markets and in the kitchens of steam-heated apartments. Such foods were in very short supply in Paris for months, and most people turned to canned goods, dried beans, and to such pastes as noodles and macaroni.

159 "Les Crises de subsistance et la démographie de la France d'ancien régime" (typescript prepared for the Institut Nationale d'Études Démographiques). The number of conceptions was obtained by counting back nine months from the date of birth. I am indebted to Professor Meuvret for providing me with a copy of this paper.

a reduction in the output of other goods and services. The cost of war in terms of alternative products foregone may be impossible to quantify, but it is nonetheless real.

The War of the League of Augsburg and the War of the Spanish Succession disrupted France's foreign trade, made it difficult (but not impossible) to market exportable surpluses abroad, and reduced the supplies of raw materials which French industries had been accustomed to import. Foreign trade, when disturbed over long periods of time, rarely returns to its original channels after the disturbances have ceased. So Frenchmen after 1713 had to rebuild their former foreign markets and open new ones. War also necessitates a reallocation of a country's productive resources because the pattern of market demand is violently changed, and it is a commonplace among economists that sudden reallocations of factors of production entail considerable wastage in the form of frictional unemployment and of relative gluts and shortages of goods on the market. Because of interdependency, whenever any segment of an economy is forced to contract or expand its activities, there are repercussions upon other segments. Unemployment in one industry tends to generate unemployment elsewhere. Hence Louis's wars did not cause unemployment and distress only in industries producing such items as silk and fine woolens, which were directly and adversely affected by the shift in demand, but also in those that supplied complementary products or that usually sold their output to people who were now unemployed and unable to buy. Finally, the wars occasioned such financial strains upon the government's resources that it was forced to adopt fiscal policies that proved detrimental to economic activity.

Old taxes were retained and, whenever possible, raised; new taxes were devised; and the whole structure became more and more regressive. Most of the tax burden rested on the shoulders of peasants, artisans, merchants, and manufacturers. The public debt mounted dizzily while the government's credit steadily deteriorated. The king exacted loans from wealthy individuals and the clergy, as well as from cities and provinces. Whenever the slightest opportunity for gain arose, the controller general refinanced the loans, arbitrarily reducing the interest rate or even scaling down the principal. In order to raise additional revenue, the king created and sold offices by the hundred, thereby saddling industry and trade with a stultifying, yet costly, officialdom. He peddled titles of nobility to the highest bidder while at the same time he was ordering a sweeping investigation of existing titles. Finally, and most reprehensibly, he tinkered incessantly with his country's money. He revalued the currency more than forty times, crying it up or down or actually recoining specie; and after 1701 he resorted to issuing paper money which rapidly depreciated in spite of efforts to make it legal tender and keep it at par.

On the whole, the officials who succeeded Colbert blindly accepted his economic principles and religiously implemented his economic policies without displaying the resiliency and the imagination so desirable and so essential in administering economic affairs. On the one hand, private monopoly and other forms of legal favoritism became increasingly common; on the other hand, government control of industry and trade expanded. New gilds were formed and old ones were strengthened. More and more it seemed that the right to work, the right to form new enterprises, the right to engage in wholesale or retail trade, the right to buy and sell what one wished and where one wished, the right to adopt innovations, the right to develop new products—more and more it seemed that these and other rights depended upon government. And, whenever possible, the government sold these rights. Always it interpreted the rights as granting it authority to regulate. Consumer sovereignty and producers' freedom of choice were compromised to a greater extent after 1683 than before. Also, fewer efforts were made to diffuse technology by importing foreign industries, foreign craftsmen and entrepreneurs, and foreign methods of production.

Tariff walls were frequently and arbitrarily raised (and less often lowered), and outright prohibitions to import certain manufactured goods or to export raw materials became common. All these actions evoked retaliatory measures by other nations. France fought her enemies with tariffs as well as with guns. Her foreign trade consequently declined, and many of her industries found themselves deprived of foreign markets, where they could sell their output or where they could buy the basic materials they needed. Domestic trade also languished as consumer purchasing power dwindled and as the cost in shipping overland or by water mounted with the deterioration of transport facilities and the application of additional tolls and internal customs.

Depopulation became a problem after 1683. War, the revocation of the Edict of Nantes, emigration caused by unemployment

and financial reverses, and high mortality due to famine conditions were the principal causes. This decline in population—to
some extent itself the aftermath of economic stagnation—further
depressed the economy by reducing consumer demand and the
potential supply of laborers for agriculture and industry.

In addition to such general depressants as war, fiscal difficulties,
economic statism, tariffs and internal trade restrictions, depopulation, and famines, several specific developments help to explain
why certain industries got into trouble. Knitting stockings by
hand had provided full- or part-time work for many thousands of
women and girls throughout the country, who usually received
their yarn from a merchant capitalist to whom they later turned
over the finished product. Sometime during the second half of
the seventeenth century the knitting frame was perfected and
rapidly invaded the field. At first the government forbade its use;
then, in 1700, it unsuccessfully tried to restrict the looms to eighteen cities. Because loom-knit stockings were cheaper and finer
than those knit by hand, artisans built and operated looms everywhere to supply the increasing demand. As usually happens with
successful technological innovations and shifts in consumer pre-
ferences, widespread unemployment and distress developed among
hand knitters while the knitting of woolen and, especially, silk
stockings on looms boomed. Technological unemployment may
not create a serious problem in a vigorously expanding economy,
but it can—and did—become a canker in a stagnating or declining economy.

One source of trouble for the French silk industry was the
growing popularity of Chinese silk fabrics and of Indian printed
cottons.[160] Although the king, by decree of October 26, 1686, forbade anyone to import or sell Indian calicoes (after January 1,
1688) and to print imitations in France, the pressure of consumer
preference was too strong to be ignored. Calicoes were smuggled
in, and Frenchmen printed their own in "secret and hidden
places." In 1695 the East India Company was allowed to import
a limited quantity each year, thus making it almost impossible
to enforce earlier decrees against the use and the sale of such
materials.[161]

Lacemaking and the manufacture of gold and silver cloth were

---

160 Archives Nationales, F12 641; G7 1697; Bibliothèque Nationale, *Fonds
français*, MS 4283, fols. 24–25; Boislisle, *op. cit.*, III, 227.

161 See Cole, *op. cit.*, pp. 168 ff.

two other industries that suffered from a shift in consumer demand.[162] The deputies of trade, in an opinion dated March 27,
1730, recommended that the Council of Trade reject the request
of a certain individual that he be accorded exclusive production
privileges for Spanish-style laces and certain stuffs of gold and silver. Although denying that there was a shortage of skilled labor
capable of making such things in France, the deputies agreed
that the industry had declined primarily because of changes in
style and habits of dress.[163] The Abbé Novi de Caveirac, who refused to credit the expulsion of Huguenots with any of the
economic misfortunes of Louis's reign, wrote as follows:

I know that several [industries] have suffered a great decline and
that some have disappeared; but these changes should be attributed
either to luxury, which has proscribed an infinity of poor-quality
fabrics, or to fashion—that tyrant of Frenchmen—which had never so
completely subjugated men to its laws as it has done since women
have commenced to promulgate them. . . .[164]

One more example of this sort of thing deserves mention. The
Caudebec hat industry, which utilized fine vicuna wool and rabbit
fur, suffered from the increasing popularity of beaver and half-
beaver hats, and this was at least one of the factors responsible
for its decline.[165]

Shifts in consumer demand and trade patterns occur continually,
and they ordinarily necessitate the reallocation of resources. Such
adjustments create friction. Unemployment of labor and bankruptcies of firms usually result. There is no reason to presume
that French industries experienced more drastic or more numerous shifts in normal market demand patterns from 1683 to 1715
than they did previously or subsequently, or that they had more
adjustments to make than industries in other countries. The necessary adjustments doubtless proved more difficult in France from
1683 to 1715 because the economy as a whole was depressed, but
it may also have been true that businessmen were less enterprising
and labor and resources were less mobile in France than in such
countries as Holland and England. Regimentation dampens en-

---

162 Bibliothèque Nationale, *Fonds français,* MSS 4285, fol. 151; 4288, fol. 82;
Lavisse, *op. cit.,* Vol. VIII, Part 1, p. 239.
163 Archives Nationales, F12 698.
164 *Apologie de Louis XIV,* pp. 119–120.
165 Novi de Caveirac, *Apologie de Louis XIV,* pp. 110–113; Cole, *op. cit.,* p. 68.

trepreneurship and increases the immobility of resources. The deputies of trade and other contemporary observers frequently compared French entrepreneurs unfavorably with their competitors elsewhere. They thought that commerce and industry in France failed to attract and retain individuals endowed with unusual business abilities and substantial wealth.

In 1701 Des Casaux du Hallay, deputy from Nantes, voiced his resentment at the way society regarded trade and merchants. As soon as anyone accumulated enough wealth in the commercial world, the deputy wrote, he sought to buy a public office or an estate and then to settle down to a more agreeable and easier life. Like all men, he craved social prestige and esteem, and these he could not find in trade. As long as he remained a merchant, he was disdained and mistreated by hordes of government clerks and overwhelmed "by the multiplicity of bureaus and taxes. . . . Other nations render a great deal more justice to trade."[166] The deputy from Lille likewise wrote that "this commercial science is much better practiced in republican nations, and especially by the Dutch, than in monarchial states." [167]

Several intendants also deplored the attitude of Frenchmen toward business. The official in Auvergne claimed that leather tanning at Riom had been declining recently because "the richest families which sustained the trade have left the business in order to acquire for themselves or for their children official positions in the judiciary."[168] And his colleague at Nantes voiced regrets at the turn of the century that French merchants in that port did not devote themselves wholeheartedly to foreign commerce; instead, "not having all the understanding of it they should have, they leave the advantage of great undertakings to foreigners who live in Nantes."[169] The intendant in Hainaut stated in 1699 that peasants had already exhausted the outcropping coal seams and that deeper mine shafts would have to be sunk if production in that area was not to decline drastically. Only if wealthy Frenchmen could be persuaded to venture their capital could coal mining in his jurisdiction burrow as deeply and use as expensive machinery as neighboring mines did in the Spanish Low Countries.[170] And in the province of Berry, where hemp grew in

---

166 Boislisle, *op. cit.*, II, 484–485.
167 Bibliothèque Nationale, *Fonds français,* MS 8038, fol. 105.
168 *Ibid.*, MS 4288, fol. 10.
169 *Ibid.*, MS 4283, fol. 50.
170 *Ibid.*, MS 4284, fol. 62.

abundance, it was not worked up into cloth because no one there had the courage to venture his entrepreneurship and capital in the industry.[171] A student of the French *bourgeoisie* has recently suggested that the declining price level after 1683 may have been partially responsible for driving able men out of the field. As the opportunities for making profits decreased, except in industries producing luxury goods or possessing lucrative monopoly privileges, businessmen forsook trade and industry and sought to invest their capital in property and securities yielding more or less fixed incomes, such as *rentes*.[172] Be this as it may, all deputies of trade were vitally concerned about the failure of families to remain in business from one generation to the next. They thought this could be corrected if the king accorded certain honors and privileges to those who engaged in wholesale trade. All too often, they said, the public and especially the nobility confused all forms of merchandising with menial store-keeping.[173]

Colbert, by royal *arrêt* of December 5, 1664, and edict of August 3, 1669, had attempted to entice entrepreneurs and capital into overseas trade by allowing nobles to participate without derogation of their status.[174] The establishment of the Council of Trade in 1700, with its twelve deputies selected from the world of trade and finance, gave additional recognition to the utility and the dignity of commercial activities. One of the first pieces of constructive legislation for which the council was primarily responsible was a royal edict issued in December, 1701. It materialized from the recommendations of the deputies presented earlier in that year. Thenceforth any noble, except those actually invested with magistracy, could engage in foreign or domestic wholesale trade without derogation of status, and no noble selling at wholesale could be forced to join a merchant gild.[175] The edict did not go so far as the deputies would have liked, but they thought it was a step in the right direction. And the king more and more frequently allowed gentlemen to associate with mining

---

[171] *Ibid.*, MS 4289, fol. 21.

[172] Joseph Aynard, *La Bourgeoisie française* (Paris, 1934), p. 299.

[173] Archives Nationales, F12 641; Bibliothèque Nationale, *Fonds français*, MS 8038, *passim;* Boislisle, *op. cit.*, II, 477 ff.

[174] Prosper Boissonnade, "La Marine marchande, le port et les armateurs de la Rochelle à l'époque de Colbert (1662–1682)," in *Bulletin de la section de géographie: Comité des travaux historiques et scientifiques* (Paris, 1922), pp. 18–19; Bibliothèque Nationale, *Fonds français*, MS 21773, fols. 381–383.

[175] Archives Nationales, F12 847–854A; Bibliothèque Nationale, *Fonds français*, MS 21773, fols. 414 ff.

and large-scale manufacturing ventures without jeopardizing their privileges as members of the nobility.

It is not possible to ascertain how justified were the accusations that Frenchmen of the late seventeenth and early eighteenth centuries were poor entrepreneurs. There must have been some basis for the criticism because it was so frequently voiced by a number of different officials, including some whose personal interests and background aligned them with the class they were criticizing. It is also impossible to ascertain to what extent the royal concessions made in 1664 and subsequently improved French entrepreneurship. The consensus among economic historians is that they did not have much effect and that entrepreneurship in France remained relatively undeveloped, as compared with other countries, until rather late in the eighteenth century. Insofar as this is true, it helps to account for the trouble and delay the economy experienced in combating the depressants that beset it after Colbert's death.

CONTEMPORARY DEVELOPMENTS IN THE DUTCH AND ENGLISH ECONOMIES

If other competitive economies, such as the English and the Dutch, were no more prosperous than the French economy during the latter half of Louis XIV's reign, the argument that the revocation of the Edict of Nantes was primarily responsible for the depression in France would lose much of its cogency. If the English and the Dutch suffered much less than the French and yet faced the same vicissitudes of war, ill-advised fiscal and monetary policies, interference with domestic and foreign commerce, economic regulation, and depopulation, then the opposite would be true. Two questions thus remain to be considered at this point. Did economic stagnation plague other European countries in 1683–1717 as much as it did France? And, was the impact of war and other factors peculiar to France? The evidence adduced by other economic historians suggests that both England and Holland continued to expand commercially and industrially in 1680–1720, although at an appreciably lessened rate than in the late sixteenth and early seventeenth centuries. France, as compared with her two chief economic rivals, therefore followed a differentiated pattern; and this requires explanation. Whereas Louis unmercifully persecuted the Protestant minority in his kingdom, the other two countries followed what, for that day, passed as religious tolerance. The important questions are: Was this the only or the most important institutional difference between them? To what extent can this alone satisfactorily account for the differences in economic development? Might there not have been other factors more compelling than the religious one? I propose here to examine the evidence as briefly as possible and to show that the factors treated above were, in fact, more or less peculiar to France, and thus provide a more plausible explanation than the revocation of the Edict of Nantes for the stagnation of the French economy.

THE DUTCH ECONOMY

The Dutch had built their prosperity upon maritime foundations such as fishing, shipbuilding, shipping, trade, and an overseas empire; and their success in these areas had incurred the envy and enmity of both England and France. The herring fisheries, it has been said, yielded the Dutch more riches than the silver mines in the New World provided for the Spanish. Although these fisheries had declined in relative importance by 1700, they still constituted a valuable asset. Furthermore, between 200 and 250 boats left Dutch ports each year to hunt walrus and whale in northern waters.[176]

The Dutch were preëminent in building ships. Their shipyards, well organized and equipped with the best available machinery, were capable of launching one ship every day. The cost of constructing a flyboat in Holland was about a third or a half less than the cost in England.[177] Despite the Navigation Acts, designed to force Englishmen to buy and operate boats built in English yards, about a fourth of the English merchant marine in 1680 was of foreign (and predominantly Dutch) origin.[178]

The low cost of constructing boats and the relatively smaller number of sailors required to operate them allowed Dutch shippers to acquire a virtual monopoly of Europe's carrying trade.

---

[176] Petrus Johannes Blok, *History of the People of the Netherlands*, IV (New York and London: Putnam, 1907), 534; Charles A. Wilson, "The Economic Decline of the Netherlands," *Economic History Review*, IX (1939), 116.

[177] Violet Barbour, "Dutch and English Merchant Shipping in the Seventeenth Century," *Economic History Review*, II (1930), 275, 278; John Clapham, *A Concise Economic History of Britain from the Earliest Times to 1750* (Cambridge: Cambridge University Press, 1951), p. 234.

[178] Clapham, *op. cit.*, p. 235; Barbour, *op. cit.*, p. 289.

They dominated shipping in the Baltic and the North Sea, and as late as 1721 the bulk of English trade with France traveled in Dutch bottoms. The Dutch had learned to circumvent the Navigation Acts with ease. Even the maritime wars with England and France in the latter half of the seventeenth century did not destroy or permanently disrupt Dutch shipping. It seems to have reached an unprecedented volume in 1698–1699 and to have sustained this peak rather well until after 1715.[179] No other country in Europe offered so good or so cheap marine insurance as Holland, and middle-class Dutchmen were eager to invest their savings in the merchant marine.

Foreign commerce was extremely important to the Dutch economy. Holland had become the entrepôt of western Europe, and Amsterdam had replaced Antwerp in the sixteenth century as the international commodity and financial center. Goods imported from all corners of the world and then reëxported provided a handsome livelihood for hundreds of brokers, merchants, and speculators. The commodity and financial exchange at Amsterdam was a beehive of activity and served as the international clearinghouse for settling commercial accounts. In no other country of Europe was foreign trade so free from customs and government regulation, and nowhere else could bullion so freely enter and leave the country.

The Dutch had also created a rich colonial empire, especially in the Far East; their East India Company was perhaps the most powerful and most successful of any similar enterprise in Europe. In sharp contrast with the unusual freedom that characterized the domestic market, Dutch colonies were closed to all interlopers and were subjected to rigid controls by monopolistic companies.

Most Dutch industries relied primarily upon imported raw materials, and employed workmen equipped with special skills, as well as labor-saving devices. It has been suggested that the silk industry may have provided more employment than the East India Company. Whereas the woolen industry at Leiden seems to have declined after the 1680's, the manufacture of hats, gauze, silk, velvet, fine leather, and trimmings at Amsterdam, Haarlem,

---

179 Barbour, *op. cit.*, p. 290; Blok, *op. cit.*, IV, 514–515; Wilson, *op. cit.*, p. 112; Charles H. Wilson, *Anglo-Dutch Commerce and Finance in the Eighteenth Century* (Cambridge: Cambridge University Press, 1941), pp. 6, 20; E. Lipson, *The Economic History of England* (5th ed.; London: A. and C. Black, 1948), III, 9–10.

Utrecht, and other cities continued to prosper. The number of paper mills increased; and malting, brewing, tobacco cutting, sugar boiling, cotton printing, dyeing, and bleaching were still flourishing in 1730. Many brandy and gin distilleries sprang up during the wars with France. While many French manufacturing cities were languishing and trying to cope with mounting unemployment and hunger, Dutch cities appear to have been searching for additional hands with which to staff their enterprises.[180]

The Dutch were good farmers. They continued their agelong fight against the sea, reclaiming additional lands for cultivation and protecting those they had already drained. Since arable land was scarce, they lavished both labor and capital upon it. Contemporaries claimed that the small gardenlike farms in Holland followed the best and most advanced methods of soil care and cultivation.

Although the political and military prestige of the United Provinces lessened and the golden age of Dutch culture waned after 1680, the country continued to be economically prosperous. Many economic historians now think that the industrial and commercial decline did not set in until about 1730 and did not become serious until after 1750.[181] The wars of the League of Augsburg and of the Spanish Succession did not drain the economy of productive resources and dislocate trade to the same extent in Holland as in France. They left Dutch provinces and cities saddled with heavy debts, yet the government could still borrow on better terms than any other European power.[182] Holland's military strength stemmed chiefly from her powerful navy, which in 1695–1696 numbered between 100 and 115 fine ships, equipped with 4,000 or 5,000 cannons and manned by 20,000 or 24,000 sailors.[183] Because of this naval might and the government's wartime policy of "business as usual," the Dutch merchant marine was able to continue carrying goods for most of Europe. The wars, however, did have at least one important effect. They led Holland to relinquish her military and political ambitions in Europe after 1713 and to concentrate upon trade

180 Blok, *op. cit.*, IV, 531; Wilson, "Economic Decline of the Netherlands," p. 113.

181 Blok, *op. cit.*, IV, 513; Wilson, *Anglo-Dutch Commerce*, pp. 16–17, 88; "Economic Decline of the Netherlands," p. 111; Herbert Heaton, *Economic History of Europe* (rev. ed.; New York: Harper, 1948), p. 284.

182 James E. Thorold Rogers, *The Story of Holland* (New York, 1889), p. 337; Wolf, *op. cit.*, p. 121.

183 Blok, *op. cit.*, IV, 480.

and finance.[184] She remained neutral during the Anglo-French wars of the eighteenth century and contented herself with profits gained from foreign investments and shipping.

Capital had long been relatively abundant in Holland, and interest rates were the lowest anywhere. Most French and English writers of the time attributed Dutch prosperity to this ample supply of capital and to its low cost. Unlike France, Holland had a calm currency. For many decades after 1681 the silver guilder enjoyed stability, and the deposits of the Bank of Amsterdam served as an excellent currency in domestic and international transactions. The rich mercantile classes controlled not only the bank, the Bourse, and the East India Company, but also the government at civic and provincial levels and hence the Estates-General. These classes were more interested in following economic policies that would protect their commercial ventures than they were in adopting fiscal policies that might replenish the public treasuries. Consequently, few customs were collected on goods moving in domestic and foreign markets, there was no manipulation of the money to gain seigniorage, and public offices were not created and sold to raise revenue. Capital was so plentiful that the government experienced little difficulty in borrowing at 3½ and 4 per cent to meet wartime expenditures. Instead of resting primarily upon the commercial and productive classes, the burden of taxation fell heavily upon consumers. By 1713 practically every commodity in Holland was taxed, which appreciably reduced the real value of the nominally high wages paid craftsmen and laborers.[185] Though the fiscal policies followed in 1680–1720 cut into the standard of living of the average citizen, they did not unduly discourage trade and other economic activity as did the government's program in France.

Holland, of course, faced discriminatory duties levied against her goods and her ships by both England and France, but her commercial-minded diplomats worked unceasingly, and often successfully, to mitigate their effect. She herself imposed few restraints on either domestic or foreign commerce, and she interfered far less than France with the activities of manufacturers and workers.

Another point of comparison is worth noting. Unlike France, Holland experienced no general depopulation in the decades

---

184 Wolf, *op. cit.,* p. 120; Wilson, "Economic Decline of the Netherlands," p. 114.
185 Wolf, *op. cit.,* pp. 193–194.

after 1680, and her people continued to drift to the cities. This movement was not so marked as it had been at the end of the sixteenth century and in the first decades of the seventeenth, yet the country in 1700 was the most urban in Europe. Haarlem and Leiden were on the decline; The Hague and Rotterdam were increasing in size. Amsterdam continued to grow and had attained a population of between 150,000 and 200,000 by 1732.[186] Although the famines of 1692–1694 and of 1708–1710 affected all western Europe, they did not occasion so much suffering or so high a mortality in Holland as in France. The Dutch had long followed the practice of importing a major portion of their grain supplies and of keeping ample amounts in storage at Amsterdam.[187] They were therefore better able to cope with crop failures and severely cold winters than the French, who strangled their grain market with all sorts of regulations and regional restrictions.

In conclusion, it seems that the Dutch economy was spared the constriction that afflicted the French economy after 1683. Holland had an excellent network of internal waterways and a number of good harbors which lowered the cost and facilitated the handling of goods coming down her great rivers from a rich European hinterland, and of cargoes brought overseas from all corners of the world. The low cost of building and navigating her ships allowed Dutch carriers to underbid competitors for freight. Low customs duties and the small number of internal trade barriers helped the country become and remain Europe's chief entrepôt. The high rate of capital formation made for low interest rates; the stability of the currency and the extensive use of many forms of credit encouraged financial activity; and the Bank of Amsterdam and the Bourse attracted funds and businessmen from all over Europe. Experienced merchants formulated government policies in state councils, and mercantile lawsuits were handled expeditiously. The Dutch were tolerant of religious differences and avid for new labor-saving devices in industry. They educated their children, daughters as well as sons, and held in high esteem all forms of commercial and industrial activity. They managed to survive the trade wars with England

---

186 Blok, *op. cit.*, IV, 532; Gerald L. Burke, *The Making of Dutch Towns* (London: Cleaver, 1956), pp. 133, 152; Roger Mols, *Introduction à la démographie historique des villes d'Europe du XIVe au XVIIIe siècle*, II (Gembloux, 1955), 523.
187 Rogers, *op. cit.*, pp. 311–312.

and France in the seventeenth century, and after 1689–1713 they gave up their political and military ambitions in Europe and concentrated their energies upon commerce and finance.

THE ENGLISH ECONOMY

The English economy in 1680–1720 grew at perhaps an even faster rate than the Dutch; certainly there were no signs of general stagnation similar to those visible on every hand in France. The combined English and Welsh population at the turn of the century numbered approximately 5,500,000, which made the estimated density some 111 persons per square mile.[188] This represented no reduction in numbers and may have indicated a 10 per cent increase over 1640. The years 1692–1694 and 1708–1710 brought dearth and even famine; and, although the price of wheat doubled in London in the first period, there was less suffering than in France.[189]

Consider the different segments of England's economy. Her merchant marine continued to expand after 1650, at first at a varying pace and then rather steadily in the first half of the eighteenth century.[190] By 1700 at least 400 of her ships were engaged in the plantations trade; in 1688 two-thirds of her total exports left port in British bottoms. Underwriters were busy with marine insurance, and Lloyd's coffeehouse was already becoming their regular meeting place. The first fire insurance company made its appearance in 1680. It is true that England had not yet acquired a dominant position in European shipping, for she was still a poor second to Holland; but she was well on the way to becoming self-sufficient in this field by 1720.

England's foreign trade, estimated at about one-sixth of her domestic trade in 1700, had been steadily growing throughout the preceding century. The official export and import figures, which were based on customary valuations of merchandise and which, of course, did not include products smuggled into and out of the country, show that the totals for 1700 and 1715 were almost identical and that exports and imports combined (excluding specie) were only 5 per cent larger in 1720 than in 1700.[101]

---

[188] T. S. Ashton, *An Economic History of England: The 18th Century* (London: Methuen, 1955), p. 2; Abbott Payson Usher, *An Introduction to the Industrial History of England* (New York: Houghton-Mifflin, 1920), p. 89.

[189] Rogers, *op. cit.*, pp. 311–312; Ashton, *op. cit.*, p. 49.

[190] Lipson, *op. cit.*, III, 139; Clapham, *op. cit.*, p. 234.

[191] Ashton, *op. cit.*, p. 252; Arthur Birnie, *An Economic History of the British*

Although these figures suggest that England's foreign trade had not yet begun the rapid expansion that characterized the eighteenth century as a whole, they do indicate that trade with other countries was not declining. London was by far the nation's most important port, dispatching in 1700 roughly four-fifths of all English exports and owning two-fifths of her marine tonnage. A London directory for 1677 listed approximately 3,000 merchants, two-thirds of whom were engaged in foreign trade.[192]

England was also busy developing her industries. Both the domestic or putting-out system and the factory form of industrial organization were spreading rapidly. It has been said that a single woolen merchant might have provided employment for as many as 1,000 people, most of whom worked for piece-rate wages in their own homes but some of whom labored in dyeing and finishing shops owned by capitalists. The manufacture of woolens ranked first among England's industries; and the government sought to protect it by forbidding the American colonies and Ireland to export woolen fabrics, by requiring the dead to be buried in woolen shrouds, and by regulating the introduction and discouraging the use of Indian calicoes. Almost half her total exports in 1700 were woolens.[193]

Although domestic producers had not yet begun to weave all-cotton fabrics, they faced an expanding market for fustians made of linen and cotton. At the turn of the century England was importing about 2 million pounds of raw cotton each year which her manufacturers processed under truly capitalistic conditions. There were also several establishments that printed the white calicoes brought into the country by the East India Company. Silk-throwing mills engaged as many as 500 to 700 workers. Improvements in the knitting frame and the increasing popularity of loom-knit stockings and underwear led to the expansion of the knitting industry (as in France); and despite legal restrictions, Englishmen were already beginning to export industrial machinery. Between 1670 and 1695 they sold more than 400 knitting frames abroad.[194]

Laborers had also been drawn away from their homes into

Isles (7th ed.; London: Methuen, 1950), p. 166; W. Stanford Reid, *Economic History of Great Britain* (New York: Ronald, 1954), p. 162.

192 Heaton, *op. cit.*, pp. 319, 321; Lipson, *op. cit.*, II, 191.

193 Lipson, *op. cit.*, II, 7, 188; Clapham, *op. cit.*, p. 252.

194 Lipson, *op. cit.*, II, 7, 97, 103, 106; Reid, *op. cit.*, p. 165.

shops or factories owned by capitalist employers to make cambrics and lawns of linen, bar iron and ironware, all sorts of glassware, pottery, copper- and brassware, paper, soap, salt, sugar, beer, tapestries, ships, sails, rope, nets, and bricks. Professor E. Lipson has concluded that at the beginning of the eighteenth century the larger part of the English working population, including those employed in agriculture and the extractive industries, did not labor in their own homes.[195]

The coal industry ranked next to woolens in importance. In 1700 several coal mines each employed from 500 to 1,000 individuals, and about half of all miners worked in collieries employing 100 or more persons. In 1871 the Coal Commission estimated that the output had increased from 2,148,000 tons in 1660 to 2,612,000 tons in 1700.[196] According to Professor John U. Nef, although the industry expanded in 1680–1720, its rate of growth was considerably less than in 1580–1620 or after 1750.[197] English iron mines were not able to satisfy the requirements of England's foundries and forges, and thousands of tons of pig and bar iron were entering the country each year from Sweden. This suggests that the iron industry, though it may not have been expanding so rapidly as before and after 1680–1720, was not declining, for there is no evidence that domestic iron mines were decreasing their output. There was a rash of new copper mines and brassworks after 1689, when the government amalgamated the Mines Royal and the Mineral and Battery Works and withdrew the monopoly privileges they had long enjoyed.[198]

English agriculture also became more and more capitalistic. The enclosure of wastelands and the consolidation of arable strips, which royal authority had opposed under the Tudors and the first Stuarts, now had parliamentary sanction. Enterprisers were at work, draining the Fens and reclaiming other areas; the rapid growth of the metropolitan market of London and the expanding consumption of white bread and meat throughout the country encouraged landlords and independent farmers to produce things to sell; and the Commission for Trade and Planta-

[195] Lipson, *op. cit.*, II, xlvi–xlvii.

[196] *Ibid.*, II, 113, 115; S. B. Clough and C. W. Cole, *Economic History of Europe* (3d ed.; Boston: Heath, 1952), p. 304.

[197] *The Rise of the British Coal Industry* (London: G. Routledge and Sons, 1932), I, 19–22, 123–124; II, 357; "A Comparison of Industrial Growth in France and England from 1540 to 1640," *Journal of Political Economy*, XLIV (1936), 507 and nn.

[198] Clapham, *op. cit.*, p. 233; Reid, *op. cit.*, p. 166.

tions stated in 1702 that since 1670 there had been a noticeable improvement in the use of clover and other grass seeds.[199] The government had allowed farmers freely to export grain since 1670, and it even gave them export bounties in 1675–1680 and after 1689. It adopted a sliding scale of import duties, which varied inversely with the domestic price of grain, in order to protect farm incomes.[200] The gentry and mercantile classes, after acquiring control of Parliament in the Civil War and strengthening their position upon the accession of William and Mary, favored legislation compatible with their own interests. It might be said, then, that the government was no longer intent upon seeing that agriculture provided an ample supply of food at low prices but, rather, that it sought to assure farmers that they could market their output at profitable prices. The net effect was to bring agriculture and the use of land under the regulative influence of the profit motive.

At the end of the seventeenth century Charles Davenant suggested that the wealth of England, which he estimated at £88 million for 1688, was increasing at the rate of £2 million a year.[201] This wealth was far more widely diffused among social classes than was property in France. The English standard of living was relatively high but not luxurious. According to Davenant, there was "no Country in the World where the Inferior Rank of men were better . . . fed," and Professor Clapham thought that this might well have been true.[202] Whereas France specialized in luxury goods of fine craftsmanship and excellent taste which its very wealthy and limited upper class preferred, English manufacturers were concentrating on solid, durable, utilitarian items which found buyers among members of all its income classes. The English were also saving and investing a substantial portion of their incomes. Not only did the Bank of England (1694) readily find subscribers to its capital stock, but so did many other companies which offered investors less security. From 1692 to 1695 there occurred a rather unusual boom, and the amount of capital invested in joint-stock enterprises climbed

199 Birnie, *op. cit.*, p. 185; Lipson, *op. cit.*, II, 373; E. Lipson, *The Growth of English Society: A Short Economic History* (New York: Henry Holt, 1950), pp. 128–129.

200 Clapham, *op. cit.*, p. 248; Lipson, *Economic History of England*, II, 460; Lipson, *Growth of English Society*, p. 164.

201 Lipson, *Economic History of England*, III, 209; Reid, *op. cit.*, p. 157.

202 *Op. cit.*, p. 221.

to above £4 million. By 1720 this may have increased by more than twelvefold. During the final phase of the Bubble, which burst in that year, 175 joint-stock companies were organized.[203]

The Augsburg and the Spanish Succession wars do not seem to have interfered as much with economic expansion in England as in France. William and Mary and Queen Anne had fewer military ambitions than Louis XIV; they were chiefly interested in checking his power on the Continent. The enemy did not invade England, and she did not have to rob her farms and shops of man power to send large armies of men across the Channel. She did most of her fighting on the sea and in her colonies. The inflated demands for military goods in the first war caused certain industries like iron and shipbuilding to boom, whereas the military misfortunes of the early years deepened the depression in trade and led people to remark that the woolen industry was "much decayed" and "quite down."[204] After the Bank of England was founded and after the political situation noticeably improved, confidence was restored and trade soon began to revive. The short respite provided by the Treaty of Ryswick inevitably brought some curtailment because resources had to be reallocated and the industrial pattern readjusted to conform with peacetime demands. The War of the Spanish Succession created artificial prosperity, after which unemployment caused the public workhouse to reappear.[205] Because naval activity, privateering, and economic reprisals reduced the flow of imports and thus protected English manufactures from foreign (especially French) competition, many wartime enterprises emerged and several infant industries thrived.

It has been estimated that the two wars cost the English government more than £83 million, and caused the national debt to rise from £664,000 in 1688 to about £54 million in 1714.[206] Whereas the government had previously borrowed on short term, during and after the wars it was able to borrow on long term. By

203 Clapham, *op. cit.*, pp. 262, 270–271; Lipson, *Economic History of England*, III, 217; Lipson, *Growth of English Society*, p. 120; Clough and Cole, *op. cit.*, p. 294.

204 Lipson, *Economic History of England*, III, 297.

205 *Ibid.*; Wolf, *op. cit.*, p. 205.

206 Birnie, *op. cit.*, p. 203; Wolf, *op. cit.*, p. 171; Reid, *op. cit.*, p. 176; Hamilton, "Origin and Growth of the National Debt in Western Europe," p. 127; Charlotte M. Waters, *An Economic History of England, 1066–1874* (London: Oxford University Press, 1925), p. 305.

1717 less than a fourth of its debt was unfunded. Parliament had chartered the Bank of England primarily to obtain long-term credit, and thereafter the funded public debt relieved the government of the financial embarrassment usually entailed by a floating short-term debt. Not only did England have a sounder public debt structure than France, but she also had a more broadly based and more equitable tax system. Annual government revenues totaled almost £5.5 million by 1715. Of this, about 42 per cent came from excises levied on salt, candles, windows, spirits, soap, leather, and a host of other items; customs yielded about 31 per cent; and the land tax returned about 18 per cent. Nearly all the revenues collected reached the treasury, for after 1671 there was no farming of taxes. Government agents, who had gradually been building up an *esprit de corps* and a system that approached civil service, collected them.[207] Unlike France, England's tax structure did not penalize the economically active; even the land tax rested primarily upon the landed gentry who could best afford to pay, for the shortage of good farmers allowed tenants to shift the burden to their landlords. Time proved Davenant right when he predicted in 1698 that after the war England would probably reëstablish her industry and trade more quickly than France because she had a sounder fiscal system.

Neither Parliament nor the sovereign tried to make a profit by tampering with the country's money.[208] Debasement and crying currency up and down had long ceased. The embargo on the export of bullion was removed in 1663, and the mint began to mill the edges of coins to prevent clipping. In 1664 the government abolished seigniorage. The general recoinage of 1696, which caused some deflation because it substituted full-bodied coins for lightweight ones at the same tariff and overvalued gold at the mint, did not yield a single penny of profit. As a matter of fact, it cost the government an estimated £2.7 million.[209] In addition to being spared the risks accompanying an unstable monetary system, English businessmen benefited from the development of sound banking and credit. Perhaps in no other country in Europe was modern banking so fully devel-

---

207 Clapham, *op. cit.*, pp. 288, 289; Wolf, *op. cit.*, pp. 189, 193; Reid, *op. cit.*, p. 176.

208 Birnie, *op. cit.*, p. 197; Lipson, *Growth of English Society*, p. 155; Heaton, *op. cit.*, pp. 366 ff.

209 Birnie, *op. cit.*, pp. 197–198; Clapham, *op. cit.*, p. 293; Wolf, *op. cit.*, p. 192.

oped by 1720 as in England and Scotland. The Bank of England, after it was chartered in 1694, loaned to the state and private enterprise by issuing bank notes and discounting commercial paper. The Bank of Scotland, a similar institution, was organized in 1695.

One of the most important legacies of the Civil War in England was the general relaxation of all kinds of industrial restraints. The Bloodless Revolution of 1688 established once and for all the supremacy of parliamentary power. And Parliament was itself under the influence of an emerging capitalist class which now demanded its liberation from all legislative shackles. There was a distinct trend toward the decentralization of economic regulation; and craft gilds, although they were not explicitly shorn of their power, found it increasingly difficult to enforce strict observance of their rules.[210] Parliament had already lashed out against royal monopolies in 1624, when it passed the Monopolies Act and created the first inclusive patent law to encourage inventions.[211] Much later, employers were freed of the necessity of keeping their help employed during slack seasons, and the central government itself no longer attempted to control wages and apprenticeship. Then, after 1681, Parliament banned the importation of several luxuries, granted industrial charters freely to enterprisers who offered to start new manufactures, and embarked upon a thorough program of encouraging new industries.

The government also removed many restraints upon foreign and domestic commerce. Chartered monopolistic companies, for example, found themselves on the defensive.[212] Any Englishman had long been able to trade with France, Spain, and Portugal; and the markets of Sweden, Norway, and Denmark were opened to him in 1673, as were those of Russia and Newfoundland in 1699. The Merchant Adventurers lost their most important privilege in 1689, when the government ruled that anyone could export woolens. Nine years later the African Company lost its monopoly of the slave trade. After 1698 even the East India Company had to contend with a rival until the two companies

---

210 Lipson, *Economic History of England*, II, xlix–l, lxxv, cxvii, cxxv, cxxx–cxxxi; *Growth of English Society*, pp. 176–177.

211 Clapham, *op. cit.*, p. 265; Lipson, *Economic History of England*, II, cxxxviii.

212 Ashton, *op. cit.*, p. 130; Birnie, *op. cit.*, pp. 166, 170; Lipson, *Economic History of England*, II, 266.

were amalgamated in 1706. The Hudson's Bay Company and the Levant Company were the only other companies that still retained their original privileges. Parliament gradually lifted the export duties on most goods until, by 1721, practically none remained.[213] Not only could Englishmen freely export grain, but they actually received export bounties.

There were also few barriers to domestic trade. The gilds had lost much of their power, and the freedom established in the inland grain and cloth markets formed part of a larger movement to remove all restraints on internal commerce. The union of Scotland and England in 1707 created the largest free-trade area anywhere in Europe.[214]

Thus, in terms of fiscal and monetary policies, regulation of economic life, restrictions on internal and external trade, and the impact of the Augsburg and Spanish Succession wars, it seems that in 1680–1720 England was in a better position than France to sustain and to increase economic activity. By that time Englishmen held trade in high esteem. According to Professor Lipson, "it was the normal practice in England . . . for the younger sons of gentlemen and 'sometimes of the nobility' to be 'bred' to trade 'without prejudice to their gentility.' "[215] The modern historian, looking back over the period, can see that the economic man, that coldly calculating profit seeker of economic theory, was fast becoming a reality. The reign of law and the stability of political institutions after the Civil War made both persons and property secure and allowed England's business leaders to give full scope to their energies and their resourcefulness. Even had Louis XIV not persecuted his Protestant subjects, there still would be ample basis for explaining why the French economy stagnated in 1683–1717 while the English economy slowly expanded.

---

213 Reid, *op. cit.*, p. 161.
214 Birnie, *op. cit.*, pp. 209–210; Heaton, *op. cit.*, p. 320.
215 *Growth of English Society*, p. 114.

XII

Summary

In the seventeenth century the Huguenots in France constituted
an easily identifiable minority, never amounting to more than
10 per cent of the country's population. Their dress, their behavior, and their religious practices and beliefs set them apart
from others. Until Louis XIV began his personal reign in 1661,
the government was not openly hostile to Huguenots and actually tried to enforce the truce outlined in the Edict of Nantes
and reaffirmed in the Edict of Alais. The Catholics, however,
disliked and distrusted Protestants and discriminated against
them in any way and at any time they could.

After 1661, and especially after 1679, it became more and
more apparent that the king wanted to destroy Protestantism and
to unite all his subjects under one religion. He closed down or
demolished one temple after another upon the flimsiest pretext;
he allowed gilds to adopt a religious oath as a prerequisite to
membership; and he barred Protestants from most professions
and systematically harassed them by regulating their private and
religious activities and by interfering with their social and family life. He also endorsed an extensive campaign to convert them
to Catholicism. At the outset this campaign relied upon education
and propaganda, bribes, economic discrimination, and other more
or less "gentle" tactics, but in 1681 it took another turn. That
was the year when Poitou's intendant began to quarter idle
dragoons in the homes of hapless Huguenots. From then until
the outbreak of the War of the League of Augsburg, French
Protestants underwent a veritable "reign of terror."

Huguenots had already established themselves securely in industry, trade, and finance. As a penalized minority, subjected first
to unorganized spontaneous acts of discrimination and later to
systematic legal attacks upon their freedom, they had come to
realize that they could expect to find a haven from persecution

only in business. The free market ordinarily rewards individuals according to their comparative success in achieving economic efficiency, and not according to their conformity with religious, social, or cultural standards. The competitive market is inherently impersonal, and its operation is automatic. This helps to explain why penalized minorities throughout the history of man have so often devoted their energies to business and, in the words of Arnold J. Toynbee, have conjured "out of it, by a *tour de force* which fills the dominant race with astonishment and resentment, a harvest of wealth and power. . . ." [1] The Huguenots threw themselves wholeheartedly into economic activity, for the teachings of John Calvin seemed to approve, or at least to condone, such a reaction to the challenge of penalization. Calvinism taught that mundane achievement was one way of serving God and of demonstrating to others that a person was "elected to grace." Certainly, since it seemed to separate temporal and eternal goals into watertight compartments, it no longer subordinated economic achievement to moral attainment. When members of a penalized minority are bolstered by a spiritual faith that supports or approves the way they respond to the challenge confronting them, they are likely to approach their work with a zest that at times borders on religious fervor.

In the years immediately before and after the revocation of the Edict of Nantes, about 200,000 men, women, and children fled France and sought religious freedom in other parts of the world. Many were entrepreneurs, capitalists, and skilled workmen in some of France's most important industries; others were merchants, shippers, and seamen; still others were important financiers or members of various professions; some were peasants; a few were nobles; and others belonged to the military and naval forces. Extant records, incomplete as they are, create the impression that scarcely any occupation was unaffected by the emigration of Huguenots. The primary purpose of the present study has been to determine whether any occupation or segment of the French economy felt the impact of the revocation so keenly as to warrant listing the persecution of Protestants as the most significant factor, or even as a prime factor, in the prolonged stagnation that afflicted the French economy after 1683.

---

[1] *The Study of History* (London: Oxford University Press, 1934), II, 217. I wish to acknowledge my indebtedness to my colleague, Professor Armen A. Alchian, for several provocative suggestions on this particular point.

The Huguenots driven abroad by the revocation probably amounted to somewhat more than 10 per cent of all French Protestants and to no more than 1 per cent of France's total population. Some might suppose offhand that so small a decline in population, when spread over twenty or thirty years, would have little effect upon a country's development. Perhaps this explains why some historians who have believed that religious persecution was an important cause of the 1684–1717 stagnation have consciously or unconsciously exaggerated the numbers involved. As far as certain economic problems are concerned, however, incremental changes in basic data may prove as significant as absolute or relative changes in other situations. Economists, for example, have found that relatively small increments and decrements in the volume of savings and investments, in total employment, or in the volume of foreign trade may greatly affect the economy as a whole. The same may well be true of certain aspects of historical growth.

It is conceivable that a 1 per cent increase or decrease in a country's population, given certain key characteristics of that population, might initiate a set of chain reactions and thereby exert great influence upon that country's history. Hence it is possible that the emigration of French Huguenots may have ultimately led to so drastic a reduction in the volume of employment and in the level of national income that it should be listed as the single most important factor in bringing on the depression. Most of the emigrants came from the most industrious, the most economically active, or the wealthiest classes. Penalization had served as a selective process over the decades preceding 1685 by weeding out those with less stamina and spiritual resolve and driving the rest to concentrate upon business, and emigration had the same effect. It was the more daring and enterprising individuals and those with ample initiative and imagination who had enough courage to move into the strange environment offered by a foreign country. Emigration attracted Huguenots who possessed the same human qualities that usually make for good entrepreneurship and success in business.

All this is to say that historians cannot judge whether the revocation was or was not a serious economic blunder simply by looking at the absolute number of Huguenots who left France. They must examine the effects of the emigration upon particular segments of the economy. If certain geographic areas, industries, and trades in which Huguenots were known to have achieved unusual success declined more drastically than other segments of the economy, this could be accepted as evidence that religious persecution appreciably dampened French economic development. It might also provide a reasonable basis for ranking the persecution among such other causal factors as war, famine, monetary and fiscal chaos, spreading statism, and adverse foreign policies.

As is frequently true of historical problems of this nature, there are not enough reliable data either to "prove" or "disprove" any pertinent hypothesis. One can only "test" or examine different hypotheses in the light of existing data. Hence the conclusions must remain tentative. The present study has continually stressed the necessity of selecting between conflicting and oftentimes contradictory data and of relying heavily upon inferences in interpreting existing data and in bridging gaps where no data exist. The validity of the results or conclusions therefore depend upon whether the investigator has exercised due reason and caution in selecting his facts and in drawing his inferences.

I am not convinced that religious persecution was primarily responsible for the decline in the industries that scholars in the past have singled out as supporting their view that the revocation had disastrous effects upon the French economy. Consider first the manufacture of silk. The number of looms and of people at work in this industry at Tours and Lyon had begun to decline several years before religious persecution became intense. Furthermore, there were at most only a few hundred Protestants associated with the industry in those places. Although some of them left the country, there were more complaints about the inability to find employment for workers seeking jobs than about the shortage of skilled labor or of entrepreneurial talent. The industry at Nîmes was in Protestant hands; and except for the branch concerned with knitting silk stockings, it, too, suffered after 1680. Although it is true that many Huguenot workmen and entrepreneurs fled from all three cities and helped establish or improve various branches of silkmaking in foreign countries, there is little evidence that their departure seriously embarrassed production at home.

In the latter half of the seventeenth century silk manufacturers at both Tours and Nîmes were increasingly unable to compete effectively with producers at Lyon because the Crown favored the latter with special concessions and privileges. Since silk was a luxury good whose market demand showed a high price and a high income elasticity, the industry in all three places suffered acutely when France's national income began to fall after 1683 and when foreign countries clapped new and higher import duties on its output. The Augsburg and Spanish Succession wars also hurt domestic production by closing down foreign markets. The increasing popularity of Indian-style cottons both at home and abroad made further inroads into the market for French silks. Higher excises on raw materials and finished fabrics, the red tape accompanying greater government regimentation, and the king's unwise monetary and fiscal policies probably harmed silkmaking more than other industries because it relied heavily on foreign markets and because the domestic demand for silk was very sensitive to changes in price and consumer incomes.

Consider next the manufacture of woolens. In some places this industry prospered because of the unusual demand for woolens for clothing the king's troops. In other places it suffered from the shortage and the high price of raw wool and, as far as the finer draperies were concerned, from a reduction in the domestic demand caused by the shrinkage in national income and the shift in consumer preference to inferior substitutes. Manufacturers in Languedoc and Normandy fared relatively well, and those in Poitou did not begin to suffer until several years after 1685. The industry at Sedan, it is true, encountered difficulties after many Protestant manufacturers and workmen fled the area, and several writers have pointed to this experience as though it were typical of draperies everywhere. Even at Sedan, however, the revocation did not ruin the industry. In the first quarter of the eighteenth century, for example, about half of its manufacturers were newly converted Catholics who remained Protestant at heart, and the deputies of trade affirmed in 1724 that "the manufacture of draperies at Sedan is certainly one of the most considerable in all the realm."

It has sometimes been said or implied that the revocation dealt a cruel blow to woolen mills that operated on a large scale and produced the finest fabrics. Although persecution drove the entrepreneurs and skilled workmen in some such mills to emigrate, apparently not a single mill had to close down. The van Robais factory at Abbeville, the Montmirel works in Brie, the Mousnier mill at Elbeuf in Normandy, Massieu's manufactory at Caen, and the important shops in Sedan and Languedoc all managed to survive. Not one of them fared so badly during the depression as the Royal Plate Glass Company, which employed practically no Protestants.

Other writers have also singled out the manufacture of felt hats as demonstrating that the revocation hurt French industry. Many hatters fled to England, Holland, or Germany and carried with them the secret of making felt that was soft and at the same time impermeable to moisture. Beyond any question they helped these countries improve the quality of their own output and thus deprived French manufacturers of a portion of their foreign sales. Foreign-made hats even began to appear on the French market. The industry is generally represented as having suffered most at Caudebec in Normandy. Although it is true that hatmaking had practically disappeared at Caudebec before the middle of the eighteenth century, the decline extended over a period of some sixty years after 1685. And there were a number of developments other than the revocation of the Edict of Nantes which might have occasioned its difficulties. Frenchmen came to prefer beaver and half-beaver hats to fine felt ones; the government raised its taxes and broadened its regulation of the industry; manufacturers themselves lowered the quality of their output by using inferior animal fibers; and the general depression caused the domestic market to shrink, while tariffs and wars reduced foreign sales. Nowhere does it seem that the revocation deprived the French industry of essential man power and technical know-how.

Louis XIV's attempt to eradicate Protestantism did not prevent the number of sugar refineries in his realm from increasing. There were at least as many mills at work in 1697 as in 1683, and new ones began to appear in the first two decades in the eighteenth century. Protestants had been employed in several of them. Whether they converted or remained true to their faith, most Protestant refiners stayed in France and continued their work; and Catholic entrepreneurs, capitalists, and laborers quickly and easily replaced the few who fled abroad.

Various historians have erred in concluding that religious persecution destroyed the manufacture of tin plate and steel in France. The only two important mills making tin plate before 1685 continued to operate for many years thereafter and to employ several Protestants who never accepted Catholicism. Although the steel industry had never been very strong in France and had been relatively backward compared with that in other countries, several shops maintained their production in the latter half of Louis's reign.

The revocation hurt the manufacture of the better grades of paper in Angoumois, Auvergne, and Normandy perhaps more than any other single industry. Many papermakers at both the entrepreneurial and the laboring levels escaped to foreign countries and helped set up new mills or improve the output of old ones. Representatives of Louis XIV tried desperately to get the refugees to return home before the new enterprises had had time to become firmly established. Intendants and other officials were unanimous in attributing the distressing plight of the domestic industry, partially or entirely, to this diffusion of French technology by Huguenot refugees. Many of the same officials, however, pointed out that war, increased taxes, and regulation of production at home were also responsible factors. It is significant that, as a consequence of new excises on paste and rags and new charges for the marking of output, the number of mills around Angoulême and in Auvergne had begun to shrink well before 1680. Thereafter, high wartime duties on imports of French paper and the disruption of normal trade channels by warships and privateers provided effective protection for infant firms in England and Holland. The fact that the number of paper mills operating in France increased in the few years of peace after 1697 and expanded noticeably as soon as the War of the Spanish Succession ended in 1713 suggests that papermaking was particularly sensitive to international conditions.

Many writers have contended that Louis's religious policies adversely affected French commerce and shipping. A good many merchants who had made substantial fortunes in foreign and domestic trade did in fact flee, and thereby disturbed wholesale and retail trade in their communities. Bordeaux, for example, may have suffered in this way even though her foreign trade does not seem to have declined seriously from 1685 until the outbreak of war in 1689. Commercial activity at La Rochelle, a citadel of Protestantism, must have felt the impact of the revocation more than it did at Bordeaux. Foreign merchants residing at Nantes hurriedly departed when Louis put their religious freedom in jeopardy, and foreign and domestic trade in a few large cities in Upper and Lower Normandy experienced a recession after several French merchants had moved abroad. Government officials at one time or another reported that commercial activity had also lessened appreciably at Alençon, Blois, Gien, Job, Lyon, Metz, Nîmes, Orange, Saint-Quentin, and Sedan.

Not only did France's trade with England and Holland decline, but its composition underwent significant change. Manufactured goods figured less prominently in her exports to these countries after 1685 than before. This suggests that Protestant refugees had been instrumental in helping these countries become self-sufficient in certain goods formerly bought from French manufacturers.

The merchant marine continued to lose ground to English and Dutch shippers after Colbert's death in 1683. Many Protestants had owned, operated, or manned vessels engaged in French overseas and coastwise shipping, and they found their enterprises so suspected and regulated by the government after 1685 that they either had to circumscribe their activities drastically or else had to transfer their bases of operation and sail under foreign flags.

To evaluate the evidence that the revocation was a major factor in the decline of France's trade and shipping is difficult. War seems to have been a much more important cause. Both the War of the League of Augsburg and the War of the Spanish Succession, spread over twenty-three of the years between 1685 and 1715, were to a great extent wars on trade. They divorced French manufacturers from markets where they had been accustomed to buy their materials and to sell a large part of their output; they increased shipping and insurance rates; they effectively protected infant industries in foreign countries until they were able to stand on their own feet; they occasioned a rash of privateering which resulted in the destruction or capture of a large number of merchant vessels; and they drained funds and man power, which might otherwise have sustained trade and shipping, into the army and the navy.

By no means did all Protestant merchants and shippers leave France. As a matter of fact, most of them stayed at home and formally, though insincerely, accepted Catholicism. As new converts they faced more intensive discrimination than before and found it more difficult to carry on their businesses. In the hope of winning conversions and of preventing emigration the government did many things that embarrassed trade. Foreign Protestants were reluctant to come to France for commercial purposes lest they experience difficulty in leaving the country or in taking their goods and money out with them. Refugees were denied access to French markets, and new converts had to obtain passports and post bail whenever they needed to board vessels to visit foreign or other French ports. Outbound vessels were stopped and searched for possible refugees and contraband. Former Protestants had to obtain special permission to carry firearms to protect themselves while traveling overland. They also discovered that there was often someone ready to denounce them for having violated some religious regulation or for preparing to leave the country, even though they were doing nothing more than trying to carry on their regular business. French Catholics and foreigners were reluctant to entrust their funds to new converts or to transact business with them lest the government confiscate their possessions if the converts tried to flee or relapsed into their former faith on their deathbeds. The moratorium on debt offered to Protestants who converted, and all the restrictions on the right of former Huguenots to dispose of their property, frustrated newly converted merchants whenever they sought additional credit or tried to buy or sell property. It is impossible to estimate to what extent all this legislation discouraged economic activity. Earlier chapters have indicated that Seignelay and other responsible officials tried to lessen its effect upon trade, and frequently persuaded the king to modify his rulings. Louis, however, was never willing to rescind them entirely.

It has frequently been claimed that the revocation led to a serious drainage of wealth and specie from France and thus significantly contributed to the shortage of loanable funds on the domestic market and retarded the accumulation of capital. There is, in fact, substantial evidence that a number of wealthy bankers and capitalists emigrated and transferred their assets abroad. Most of them settled in either England or Holland, where they invested in public securities, offered to lend their funds to private enterprises, or increased the stock of circulating specie. On the other hand, there is not enough evidence to estimate, even roughly, how much wealth or purchasing power they took out. They apparently did not dismantle their factories and transfer the equipment abroad. The real wealth they carried with them was in the form of consumer and household goods. The purchasing power they had acquired in the form of specie and credit instruments out of past hoarding and by selling their tangible property before they left did not, it seems, cause a net increase in

French exports, as unilateral capital transfers ordinarily do. Hence it did not reduce the stock of goods and services in France which might otherwise have been used to employ productive services to produce capital goods. In other words, the drainage of purchasing power probably did not directly or immediately slow down the accumulation of capital in France. Insofar as this unilateral capital-fund transfer harmed France and benefited England and Holland, its effects were spread out over a considerable period of time and may have been offset or aggravated by other influences of greater weight which were operative at the same or at a later time. Perhaps the most important repercussion of the export of specie and credit was the long-run worsening of France's barter terms of trade. The unilateral transfer, to a great extent, went to finance the migration of Huguenots and to help them get established in foreign countries. Its "income and price effects" both in France and abroad were probably much less important in determining the future trade balance and prosperity of the countries directly involved than were its indirect effects in diffusing French technology and in changing the character of the real income and production levels of the different countries.

The evidence that Huguenots helped diffuse many of France's industrial secrets and processes in England, Ireland, Holland, Germany, and Switzerland is convincing. The refugees stimulated silkmaking in England by introducing certain new patterns and methods of finishing various fabrics; and they helped expand the sailcloth, linen, hat, white paper, and crown-glass industries there. They also helped the Dutch perfect the same manufactures and were instrumental in building up the linen industry in Ireland. Germany in particular learned a great deal from those who settled within her borders. Although they were unable to develop many large-scale enterprises in Germany, the refugees introduced several kinds of textiles; they taught the Germans how to make ribbons, laces, gloves, woolen and silk stockings, and fine felt hats; they improved tanning and the hardware trades; and they helped to bring new land under cultivation, to introduce new crops, and to improve farming techniques. The Huguenots who settled in Switzerland seem to have had more influence on the retail trades and minor crafts and on commerce and banking than on the major industries. All in all, the refugees seem to have narrowed everywhere the economic and technological gap separating France from other countries; by so doing, they were

directly or indirectly responsible for causing many French manufacturers to lose part of their foreign markets after 1685. Most
economists, however, recognize that any country stands to gain
in the long run from improvements in the productivity and national income of other countries with which she trades. Insofar
as the refugees accelerated economic development elsewhere,
they may have been responsible for lessening France's relative
gains from world trade; it does not follow that they must have
thereby reduced the absolute level of French economic activity.

Certain other factors seem to have been much more important
than religious persecution in the stagnation after 1683. The two
wars disrupted both foreign and domestic markets, diverted
resources from productive activities into military channels, depressed normal peacetime industries, and contributed to the emigration of Frenchmen. Above all else, these wars were costly and
helped drive the government to the brink of financial bankruptcy.
The heroic measures to obtain additional revenue penalized productive effort and rested upon the shoulders of the bourgeois
and working classes.

Crying money up or down and issuing paper money which rapidly depreciated in value made business a "game of chance" and
drove specie into hiding or abroad. By creating and selling innumerable public offices the government saddled economic activity with additional red tape and taxes; increased the number of
tax-exempt, nonproductive officials by recruiting them from the
entrepreneurial class; and extended beyond all reasonable
bounds the Colbertian system of economic statism and regimentation. The men who succeeded Colbert, and especially those who
took over after Seignelay's death, either were not primarily interested in strengthening France's economy or were devoid of the
imagination and the initiative that adequate statesmanship calls
for in such troubled times. Tariffs and other barriers interfered
with international trade, while little was done to widen domestic
markets. Even the unforseeable, uncontrollable vagaries of nature
worked against France. The famine in 1692–1694, the severe
winter of 1708–09, and the epizoötic in 1715 created food shortages of alarming proportions and increased human mortality.
Almost any one of these factors could have caused or deepened
the depression as much as the revocation of the Edict of Nantes;
taken together, they certainly exerted more influence.

Few of these factors, furthermore, affected the English and

Dutch economies in the same way or to the same extent they influenced French economic development. The Augsburg and Spanish Succession wars did not drain so many men away from industry, trade, and agriculture as they did in France, and they did not occasion so much property damage. After the English and the Dutch defeated the French fleet off the Cap de la Hogue (May, 1692), they were left in control of the seas, and their navies thereafter managed rather well to protect the trade and shipping of their nationals. The wars also created less financial strain upon the English and Dutch governments, and both countries emerged on a sounder financial and fiscal basis than did France. Both Holland and England managed to maintain monetary stability, and their tax and debt structure was much superior to that of the French. Instead of penalizing economic activity, the mercantile and landed classes who controlled the English Parliament and the Estates-General in Holland favored fiscal and monetary policies that would least conflict with their own interests. They also successfully opposed economic regimentation, public monopolies, and government interference in business. Both external and internal trade was much freer in Holland and England than in France, and transportation facilities were much more efficient and less costly. Instead of declining, the English population probably was slowly increasing, and the Dutch was at least holding its own and still drifting to urban areas. In both countries merchants and manufacturers, unlike their French competitors, enjoyed considerable social and political prestige and trained their children to carry on family businesses. It is not necessary to fall back upon differences in religious history to explain why England and Holland fared better than France in 1683–1717.

No more than 10 per cent of France's Protestant population left the country after 1680; the other 90 per cent remained at home. Those who stayed at home faced even more excessive penalization after 1685 than before. As a result, their religious convictions and courage were fortified and their devotion to business increased markedly. Throughout the eighteenth century Protestants strengthened rather than weakened their position in French economic life. The refugees and their descendants abroad remained in contact with fellow Religionists and relatives in France and rendered them valuable service as purchasing and selling agents. French Protestants thus had better contacts with foreign markets than their Catholic competitors. As early as 1711 Catholic merchants trading in Holland complained that Protestant refugees in that country had an unfair advantage over them because the refugees always managed to discover, through relatives and friends in France, what the Council of Trade and various chambers of commerce were planning to do.[2] One might even argue, with considerable justification, that the Huguenot dispersion in 1680–1720 and the increased penalization of Protestants in France in the first half of the eighteenth century aided, rather than hindered, the revival and expansion in French economic activity which got under way about 1717.[3]

In concluding that the revocation of the Edict of Nantes did much less harm to the French economy, both in the short run and in the long run, than most historians of the nineteenth and twentieth centuries have heretofore believed, I do not in the least intend to exonerate Louis XIV and his advisers. The revocation still stands condemned as a crime against man, for it violated individual freedom and human dignity. How can one estimate the harm wrought by distorting and perverting the moral decency and character of Frenchmen who actively participated in the persecution of their fellow men, or who passively witnessed the acts of cruelty? How can one quantify the loss occasioned to society by driving out thousands of persons who may have provided intellectual and cultural leadership?

Many eminent individuals, with demonstrated creative ability in spheres other than the economic, joined the ranks of refugee merchants and traders, manufacturers and laborers, capitalists and financiers, peasants and lords, seamen and captains, and soldiers and military officers. Although it is true that France, in the reign of Louis XIV, was blessed with a large number of intellectual and cultural leaders who helped to make that period a golden age, no country is ever so richly endowed with creative personalities that the loss of some one of them can be considered a trifling matter. A country may rapidly recover from temporary reductions in its trade and wealth, but it cannot easily overcome the loss of creative artists, scientists, and other intellectual leaders.

----

2 Archives Nationales, G7 1696 (letters attached to Pontchartrain's letter to Desmaretz dated May 19, 1711).

3 This seems to be the position taken by Professor Émile-G. Léonard at the Sorbonne (see especially his "Économie et religion, les protestants français au XVIIIᵉ siècle," *Annales d'histoire sociale*, II [1940]).

The revocation edict ordered all Protestant clergymen to leave the country immediately unless they accepted Catholicism and became pensioners of the Crown. Most of the vigorously intellectual left. Among them were Pierre Jurieu, Jacques Abbadie, Pierre Alix, Jacques Basnage, Jacques Saurin, Jean Claude, Pierre du Bosc, and Claude Brousson. These men, perhaps unfamiliar to many economic historians, are as well known to students of Protestantism as are Arnold Toynbee, Max Weber, or William J. Ashley to students of economic history. Some of these Protestant churchmen ranked with the Catholic prelate Bousset in erudition, general enlightenment, oratorical power, and persuasiveness. Some wrote valuable treatises on theological questions and on the moral issues involved in religious persecution. Their abrupt departure from France probably delayed the development of rational humanism.

Both Thomas Savary and Denis Papin, who made major contributions to the utilization of steam power, were driven abroad by Louis's religious intolerance. Abraham de Moivre, the celebrated mathematician who formulated important theories about imaginary numbers and probability and who is sometimes considered the father of human mortality tables, also fled. So did other mathematicians like William Loré and James Bernard. Pierre Lyonnet, the naturalist, and Pierre Latane, professor of medicine, also sought asylum in foreign countries. Perhaps French intellectual development experienced its greatest reverse when Pierre Bayle, the noted philosopher, left. In view of such losses as these and in view of its senseless violence and inhumanity, the revocation stands condemned even though it may not have had disastrous effects in either the short run or the long run upon the French economy.

BIBLIOGRAPHY

Bibliography

PRINTED SOURCES

Abord, Hippolyte. *Histoire de la Réforme et de la Ligue dans la ville d'Autun, précédée d'une introduction et suivie de pièces justificatives.* 3 vols. Paris and Autun, 1855–1886.

[Achard, Daniel]. *Chronique de la Colonie réformée française de Friedrichs-dorf suivie de documents et pièces explicatives.* Hombourg-es-Monts, 1887.

Agnew, David C. A. *Protestant Exiles from France in the Reign of Louis XIV; or, The Huguenot Refugees and Their Descendants in Great Britain and Ireland.* 3 vols. 2d ed. London, 1871–1874.

Aguesse, L. *Histoire du protestantisme en France contenant l'histoire politique et religieuse de la nation depuis François Ier jusqu'à l'Édit de Nantes.* 4 vols. Paris, 1882–1886.

Alibaux, Henri, E. Creveau, and others. *Contribution à l'histoire de la pape-terie en France.* Vol. I of *L'Industrie papetière.* Grenoble: Librairie de l'industrie papetière Creveau, 1933.

Amphoux, Henri. *Essai sur l'histoire du Protestantisme au Havre et dans ses environs.* Le Havre, 1894.

[Ancillon, Charles]. *La France intéressée à rétablir l'Édit de Nantes.* Amsterdam, 1690.

Ancillon, Charles. *Histoire de l'établissement des françois réfugiés dans les états de son altesse electorale de Brandebourg.* Berlin, 1690.

Anderson, Adam. *An Historical and Chronological Deduction of the Origin of Commerce, from the Earliest Accounts etc.* II–IV. London, 1801.

Andréadès, Andreas M. *History of the Bank of England, 1640 to 1903.* 2d ed. London: P. S. King and Son, 1924.

Anquez, Léonce. *De l'État civil des réformés de France.* Paris, 1868.

Arnal, J. "De l'Influence des réfugiés français aux Pays-Bas," *Bulletin de la commission pour l'histoire des églises wallonnes,* 4th series, 2d issue (1929).

Arnaud, Eugène. "Les Derniers jours de l'église d'Orange, 1703–1731," *Bulletin de la société de l'histoire du protestantisme français,* XXXII (1883).

———. *Histoire des protestants d'Annonay en Vivarais pendant les trois derniers siècles.* Paris, 1891.

———. *Histoire des protestants de Crest en Dauphiné pendant les trois derniers siècles.* Paris, 1893.

———. *Histoire des protestants du Dauphiné aux XVIe, XVIIe et XVIIIe siècles.* III. Paris, 1876.

———. *Histoire des protestants de Provence, du comtat Venaissin et de la Principauté d'Orange.* 2 vols. Paris, 1884.

———. *Histoire des protestants du Vivarais et du Velay, pays de Languedoc, de la Réforme à la Révolution.* 2 vols. Paris, 1888.

Arnould, Ambroise. *De la Balance du commerce et des relations commerciales extérieures de la France, dans toutes les parties du Globe, particulierement à la fin du règne de Louis XIV et au moment de la Révolution.* 2 vols. Paris, 1791.

Aubin, Gustav. *Der Einflusz der Reformation in der Geschichte der deutschen Wirtschaft.* Rede gehalten bei der Reformationsfeier der Vereinigten Friedrichs-Universitat Halle-Wittenberg am 31. October 1929. Halle (Saale), 1929.

Avril, Adolphe d'. "La Révocation de l'Édit de Nantes dans ses conséquences industrielles," *Revue des questions historiques,* 8th year, XV (1874).

Aynard, Joseph. *La Bourgeoisie française.* Paris: Perrin, 1934.

B. B. "Protestants Sedanais au XVIIIe siècle," *Bulletin de la société de l'histoire du protestantisme français,* LXXXIV (1935).

Babinet de Rencogne, G. *Recueil de documents pour servir à l'histoire du commerce et de l'industrie en Angoumois.* Part 3: *Recherches sur l'origine des moulins à papier de l'Angoumois.* Angoulême, 1879. Extracted from *Bulletin de la société archéologique et historique de la Charente,* 5th series, II (1878).

Bachelier. *Histoire du commerce à Bordeaux.* Bordeaux, 1862.

Baird, Charles Washington. *History of the Huguenot Emigration to America.* 2 vols. New York, 1885.

Baird, Henry M. *The Huguenots and the Revocation of the Edict of Nantes.* 2 vols. New York, 1895.

Bamford, Paul Walden. *Forests and French Sea Power, 1660–1789.* Toronto: University of Toronto Press, 1956.

Basnage, Jacques. *Histoire de la Religion des Eglises Réformées . . . pour servir de Réponse à l'Histoire des Variations des Eglises Protestantes, par M. Bossuet Eveque de Meaux, etc.* 2 vols. Rotterdam, 1690.

Baudry, François. *La Révocation de l'édit de Nantes et le protestantisme en Bas-Poitou au XVIIIe siècle.* Trévoux: J. Jeannin, 1922.

Beaujour, Sophronyme. *Essai sur l'histoire de l'Église Réformée de Caen.* Caen, 1877.

Beaumont, Chevalier de. *L'Accord parfait de la nature, de la Raison, de la Révélation et de la politique.* 2 vols. Cologne, 1753.

Beeman, George B. "Notes on the City of London Records Dealing with the French Protestant Refugees, Especially with Reference to the Collections Made under Various Briefs," *Proceedings of the Huguenot Society of London,* VII (1901–1904).

Belton, Louis. "Notes sur l'histoire des protestants dans le Blésois," *Mémoires de la société des sciences et lettres de Loir-et-Cher,* XI (1886–1887).

Benoist, Charles. *Condition juridique des protestants sous le régime de l'Édit de Nantes et après sa révocation.* Paris: A. Rousseau, 1900.

Benoît, Elie. *Histoire de l'Edit de Nantes, contenant les choses les plus remarquables qui se sont passées en France avant et après sa publication . . . jusques à l'Edit de Révocation en Octobre, 1685. . . .* 5 vols. Delft, 1693–1695.

Berg, W. E. J. *De Réfugiés in de Nederlanden, na de Herroeping van het Edict van Nantes.* Amsterdam, 1845.

Bernard, Pierre. *L'Explication de l'Edit de Nantes avec de nouvelles observations, et les Nouveaux Edits, Declarations et Arrests donnez jusqu'a present, touchant la Religion Pretenduë Reformée.* Soulier ed. Paris, 1683.

Bersier, Eugène. *Quelques pages de l'histoire des Huguenots.* Paris, 1891.

———. *Les Réfugiés français et leurs industries.* Paris, 1886.

Bert, Paul. *Histoire de la révocation de l'édit de Nantes à Bordeaux et dans le Bordelais (1653–1715).* Bordeaux: Mounastre-Picamilh, 1908. Extracted from *Revue historique de Bordeaux et du département de la Gironde.*

Bertrand, Pierre. *Genève et la Révocation de l'Édit de Nantes.* Geneva: Imprimerie Soullier, 1935.

Beuzart, Paul. "L'Édit de Nantes: Création ou aboutissement," *Bulletin de la société de l'histoire du protestantisme français,* XCI (1942).

———. "Une Famille de réfugiés de la Thiérache," *Bulletin de la société de l'histoire du protestantisme français,* LXXXIX (1940).

———. *Le Protestantisme en Thiérache (Haute Picardie) depuis les origines jusqu'à la Révolution.* Paris: Honoré Champion, 1931.

Bianquis, Jean. *La Révocation de l'édit de Nantes à Rouen, essai historique.* With an appendix by Émile Lesens. Rouen, 1885.

Biran, Élie de. "La Révocation de l'édit de Nantes à Bergerac," *Bulletin de la société historique et archéologique du Périgord,* XXII (1895).

Boegner, Charles-Frédéric. *Études historiques sur l'Église protestante de Strasbourg, considérée dans ses rapports avec l'Église catholique, 1681–1697.* Strasbourg, 1851.

Boisguillebert, Le Pesant de. *Le Détail de la France* (1697). In *Collection des principaux économistes.* Vol. I: *Économistes financiers du XVIIIᵉ siècle.* E. Daire, ed. 2d ed. Paris, 1851.

———. *Factum de la France* (1707). In *Collection des principaux économistes.* Vol. I. *Economistes financiers du XVIIIᵉ siècle.* E. Daire, ed. 2d ed. Paris, 1851.

Boislisle, A. M. de. *Correspondance des contrôleurs généraux des finances avec les intendants des provinces.* 3 vols. Paris, 1874, 1883, 1897.

———. "Liste des protestants de Nîmes émigrés à la suite de la révocation d'édit de Nantes," *Revue des sociétés savantes des départements,* 6th series, VIII (1878).

Boissonnade, Prosper. *L'Industrie du papier en Charente et son histoire.* Liguré, 1899.

———. "La Marine marchande, le port et les armateurs de la Rochelle à l'époque de Colbert (1662–1682)," in *Bulletin de la section de géographie: Comité des travaux historiques et scientifiques.* Paris, 1922.

Boissonnet, Ch. "Révocation de l'édit de Nantes. Un corps de ville au XVIIᵉ siècle—Niort (1677)," *Bulletin de la société d'agriculture, sciences et arts de Poligny* (Jura), XXIX (1888).

Bondois, Paul-M. "Colbert et le développement économique de la Basse-

Normandie (draperie, bonneterie et dentelles à Caen et Alençon, etc.)," *Bulletin de la société des antiquaires de Normandie,* XLI (1934).

―――. "Le Duc de Savoie Victor-Amédée II et la Révocation de l'Édit de Nantes," *Bulletin philologique et historique du Comité des travaux historiques et scientifiques,* years 1928–1929 (1930).

―――. *État de l'industrie textile en France d'après l'enquête du contrôleur général Desmarets (début du XVIIIᵉ siècle).* Paris, 1944. Extracted from *La Bibliothèque de l'école des chartes,* CIV.

―――. "L'Industrie sucrière française à la fin du XVIIᵉ siècle," *Revue d'histoire économique et sociale,* 22d and 23d years (1935).

Bonet-Maury, Gaston-Charles-Auguste. *Histoire de la liberté de conscience en France depuis l'Édit de Nantes jusqu'à juillet 1870.* 1st ed. Paris: F. Alcan, 1900.

Bonnet, Jules. "L'Église réformée de la Calmette: pages d'histoire locale," *Bulletin de la société de l'histoire du protestantisme français,* XXXIII (1884).

―――. "Fuite d'une famille huguenote, victime de la Révocation (Jacques Fontaine)," *Bulletin de la société de l'histoire du protestantisme français,* XXVI (1877).

Bonzon, A. "La Banque à Lyon aux XVIᵉ, XVIIᵉ et XVIIIᵉ siècles," *Revue d'histoire de Lyon,* I (1902); II (1903).

Bosseboeuf, Abbé L. "Histoire de la fabrique de soieries de Tours, des origines au XIXᵉ siècle," *Bulletin et mémoires de la société archéologique de Touraine,* XLI (1900).

"Bossuet et la révocation de l'Edit de Nantes, dépêches ministerielles et autres pièces inédits (1683–1699)," *Bulletin de la société de l'histoire du protestantisme français,* IV (1856); IX (1860); X (1861).

Bost, Charles. *Récits d'histoire protestante régionale: Normandie.* Le Havre, 1926.

Boulainvilliers, Comte de. *Etat de France . . . extrait des Mémoires dressés par les Intendans du Royaume.* 6 vols. London, 1737.

Boulenger, Jacques. *Les Protestants à Nîmes au temps de l'Édit de Nantes.* Paris: Fischbacher, 1903.

Bourde de la Rogerie, H. "Les Fugitifs protestants aux îles Chausey (1685–1701)," in *Le Pays de Granville: Bulletin trimestriel de la société d'études historiques et économiques.* 1939.

Bourrilly, V.-L. "Les Protestants à Marseille au XVIIIᵉ siècle, notes et documents," *Bulletin de la société de l'histoire du protestantisme français,* LV (1906).

―――. "Les Protestants de Provence au temps de Louis XV," *Annales de la faculté des lettres d'Aix,* XIV (1923–1928).

―――. "Les Protestants de Provence et d'Orange sous Louis XIV," *Bulletin de la société de l'histoire du protestantisme français,* LXXIV (1925); LXXV (1926); LXXVI (1927).

―――. "La Révocation de l'Édit de Nantes à Marseille," *Bulletin de la société de l'histoire du protestantisme français,* LIV (1905).

Boutetière. *See* La Boutetière.

Boysson, Richard de. *L'Invasion Calviniste en Bas-Limousin, Périgord et Haut-Quercy.* 2d ed. Paris: Picard et fils, 1924. Extracted from *Bulletin de la société scientifique, historique et archéologique de la Corrèze,* XXXVIII–XLII.

Briet, Elisée. *Le Protestantisme en Brie et Basse-Champagne du XVIe siècle à nos jours.* Paris, 1885.

[Brousson, Claude]. *Etat des réformés en France, où l'on fait voir que les Edits de Pacification sont irrévocables, que néanmoins on les renverse entièrement, et que par là on ôte aux Réformés tous les moyens de vivre et de subsister; Apologie du Projet des Réformés de France.* The Hague, 1685.

————. *Lettres aux catholiques romains.* Au Désert, 1687.

————. *Lettres et opuscules de feu Monsr. Brousson, ministre et martyr du St. Evangile; avec un abrégé de sa vie. . . .* Utrecht, 1701.

Brousson, Claude. *La Sortie de la France pour cause de religion de Daniel Brousson et de sa famille, 1685–1693.* Edited with notes and introduction by N. Weiss. Paris, 1885.

Bujeaud, Victor. *Chronique protestante de l'Angoumois, XVIe, XVIIe, XVIIIe siècles.* Paris and Angoulême, 1860.

Bulletin de la commission pour l'histoire des églises wallonnes. 1st-5th series. The Hague and Leiden, 1887–1945.

Bulletin de la société de l'histoire du protestantisme français. I-CI. Paris, 1853–1955.

Burke, John F. *Outlines of the Industrial History of Ireland.* Rev. ed. Dublin: Browne & Nolan, 1946.

Burn, John Southerden. *The History of the French, Walloon, Dutch, and Other Foreign Protestant Refugees Settled in England etc.* London, 1846.

Burnet, Gilbert. *Mémoires pour servir à l'histoire de la Grande-Bretagne sous les règnes de Charles II et de Jacques II avec une Introduction, depuis le Commencement du Règne de Jacques I, jusqu'au Rétablissement de la Famille Royale.* III. The Hague, 1725.

Cabrol, Camille. *Essai sur l'histoire de la Réforme à Clairac des origines à l'Édit de Tolérance (1530–1787).* Cahors: Imprimerie de A. Coueslant, 1900.

Cadier, A. "Les Églises réformées du Béarn de 1664 à 1685," *Bulletin de la société de l'histoire du protestantisme français,* XXX (1881).

Cambolive, Étienne. *Histoire de divers événemens, contenant en abrégé les persécutions éxercées en France, les moyens diaboliques dont on s'est servi pour détruire les Protestans, plusieurs Jugements de Dieu sur quelques-uns des Persécuteurs, des faits nouveaux fort curieux; les Moyens de Faux contre le Pape, les Jesuits, les Moines, les Religieuses, et l'Eglise Romaine, avec une ardente prière pour les Persécutez.* Amsterdam, 1698.

Campbell, Douglas. *The Puritan in Holland, England, and America.* 2 vols. 4th ed. New York, 1893.

Caneto, Abbé F., and Bernard Ducruc. "Recherches historiques sur l'influence du protestantisme dans la province d'Auch pendant la seconde moitié du XVIe siècle," *Bulletin du comité d'histoire et d'archéologie de la province ecclésiastique d'Auch,* I, II (1860).

Cantillon, Richard. *Essai sur la nature du commerce en générale.* Henry Higgs, ed. and trans. London: Macmillan, 1931.

Capefigue, Jean-Baptiste-Honoré-Raymond. *Louis XIV, son gouvernement et ses relations diplomatiques avec l'Europe.* 2 vols. New ed. Paris, 1844.

Carré, Albert. *L'Influence des Huguenots français en Irlande aux XVIIe et XVIIIe siècles.* Paris: Presses universitaires de France, 1937.

Carter, Alice C. "The Huguenot Contribution to the Early Years of the Funded Debt, 1694–1714," *Proceedings of the Huguenot Society of London,* XIX (1955).

Cavejrac, Abbé de. *See* Novi de Caveirac.

Chaillaud, Taré. *See* "Journal d'un marin protestante du XVIIe siècle."

Chambrier, Mme Alexandre de. *Henri de Mirmant et les réfugiés de la Révocation de l'Édit de Nantes, 1650–1721.* Neuchâtel: Fischbacher, 1910.

———. "Naturalisation des Réfugiés français à Neuchâtel, de la Révocation de l'Édit de Nantes à la Révolution française, 1685–1794," *Musée neuchâtelois,* 37th year (1900).

———. "Projet de Colonisation en Irlande, par les réfugiés français, 1692–1699," *Proceedings of the Huguenot Society of London,* VI (1898–1901).

———. "Les Réfugiés français en Suisse de 1593 à 1699 et la convention entre Berne et les cantons évangéliques," *Bulletin de la société de l'histoire du protestantisme français,* LVIII (1909).

Charronnet, Charles. "Evangélisation du diocèse de Gap en 1685, avec ou sans dragons, d'après Dangeau et un temoin gapençais," *Bulletin de la société de l'histoire du protestantisme français,* IV (1856).

———. *Les Guerres de religion et la société protestante dans les Hautes-Alpes (1560–1789).* Gap, 1861.

Chavannes, Jules. "Essai sur les abjurations parmi les réformés de France sous le règne de Louis XIV," *Bulletin de la société de l'histoire du protestantisme français,* XXI (1872).

———. *Les Réfugiés français dans le pays de Vaud et particulièrement à Vevey.* Lausanne, 1874.

———. "Les Réfugiés français dans le pays de Vaud et particulièrement à Vevey: La famille de Rochegude," *Bulletin de la société de l'histoire du protestantisme français,* XVII (1868).

Chevrier, Edmond. *Notice historique sur le protestantisme dans le département de l'Ain (Bresse, Bugey, Pays de Gex) et lieux circonvoisins (Savoie, Lyon, Mâcon).* Paris, 1883.

———. *Le Protestantisme dans le Mâconnais et la Bresse aux XVIe et XVIIe siècles.* Mâcon, 1868.

Chinard, Gilbert. *Les Réfugiés huguenots en Amérique.* Paris: Société d'édition "les Belles Lettres," 1925.

Claparède, Théodore. "Un Emigré de la Révocation," *Bulletin de la société de l'histoire du protestantisme français,* XXV (1876).

———. "Les Réfugiés protestants du pays de Gex," *Bulletin de la société de l'histoire du protestantisme français,* XXIV (1875).

Clark, G. N. "War Trade and Trade War, 1701–1713," *Economic History Review,* I (1927–1928).

Claude, Jean. *Les Plaintes des protestans, cruellement opprimez dans le Royaume de France.* Cologne, 1686.

———. *Les Plaintes des protestants, cruellement opprimez dans le Royaume de France. Nouvelle édition, augmentée d'une Préface, contenant des Réflexions sur la Durée de la Persécution, et sur l'Etat présent des Réformez en France.* Cologne, 1713.

Clément, Pierre. *Lettres, instructions et mémoires de Colbert.* 10 vols. Paris, 1861–1884.

Clément-Simon, Gustave. *Le Protestantisme et l'érudition dans le Pays basque au commencement du XVIIe siècle. Jacques de Bela: biographie, extraits de ses oeuvres inédites.* Paris, 1896. Extracted from *Bulletin de la société des sciences, lettres et arts de Pau,* 2d series, XXIV.

Clervaux, J. de. "Révocation de l'Édit de Nantes. Pièces relatives à Philippe Mesnard, Sr. d'Air, pasteur de Saintes, nommé par la reine de Danemark pasteur à Copenhague. Lettre d'un huguenot de Paris (1684–1686)," *Bulletin de la société de l'histoire du protestantisme français,* II (1854).

Cohendy, Michel. *Note sur la papeterie d'Auvergne antérieurement à 1790.* Clermont, 1862. Extracted from *Mémoires de l'Académie de Clermont.*

Cole, Charles W. *Colbert and a Century of French Mercantilism.* 2 vols. New York: Columbia University Press, 1939.

———. *French Mercantilism, 1683–1700.* New York: Columbia University Press, 1943.

Collisson. "Un Asile des huguenots, à l'Époque de la Révocation de l'Édit de Nantes: l'île d'Axholme, côte N.-E. d'Angleterre (1685)," *Bulletin de la société de l'histoire du protestantisme français,* VIII (1859).

Combe, Ernest. *Les Réfugiés de la Révocation en Suisse.* Lausanne, 1885.

Corbière, Philippe. *Histoire de l'Église Réformée de Montpellier depuis son origine jusqu'à nos jours.* Montpellier, 1861.

Coüard-Luys, E. "Les Religionnaires de Tracy avant la Révocation de l'Édit de Nantes," *Bulletin historique et philologique du comité des travaux historiques et scientifiques,* VI (1888).

Couderc, C. "L'Abbé Raynal et son projet d'histoire de la Révocation de l'Édit de Nantes, documents sur le Réfuge," *Bulletin de la société de l'histoire du protestantisme français,* XXXVIII (1889); XXXIX (1890).

Courpron, Paul. *Essai sur l'histoire du Protestantisme en Aunis et Saintonge depuis la Révocation de l'Édit de Nantes jusqu'à l'Édit de Tolérance (1685–1787).* Cahors: Imprimerie de A. Coueslant, 1902.

[Court, Antoine]. *Lettre d'un patriote sur la tolérance civile des protestans de France et sur les avantages qui en resulteroient pour le royaume.* N.p., 1756.

———. *Le Patriote françois et impartial ou reponse à la lettre de Mr l'evêque d'Agen à Mr le controleur genéral contre la Tolerance des Huguenots, en datte du 1 mai 1751.* 2 vols. New ed. Villefranche, 1753.

Courtecuisse, Maximilien. *La Manufacture de draps fins Vanrobais aux XVIIe et XVIIIe siècles.* Paris, 1920.

Couture, L. "Les Protestants et les 'nouveaux convertis' de Nérac après la révocation de l'Édit de Nantes (novembre 1685–mai 1686)," *Revue de Gascogne: Bulletin mensuel de la société historique de Gascogne,* XXXIX (1898).

Cowell, Henry J. *The Edict of Nantes and Afterwards. The Story of the Huguenots, 1685–1935.* 3d ed. London: Lutterworth Press, [1936].

Crottet, A. "Les Préludes de la révocation de l'édit de Nantes dans le pays de Gex," *Bulletin de la société de l'histoire du protestantisme français,* I (1853).

Cunningham, W. *Alien Immigrants to England.* London, 1897.

Cuvier, Orthon. *Les Réformés de la Lorraine et du pays messin.* Nancy, 1884. Extracted from *Mémoires de l'Académie de Stanislaus.*

Daire, E., ed. *Collection des principaux économistes.* Vol. I: *Économistes financiers du XVIIIe siècle.* 2d ed. Paris, 1851.

Dangibeaud, Charles. "Contribution à l'histoire du protestantisme à Cozes (1675–1699)," *Revue de Saintonge et d'Aunis,* XLI (1924).

Dannreuther, H. "Le Protestantisme dans la maison du Châtelet," *Journal de la société d'archéologie lorraine et du musée historique lorraine,* XXXV (1886).

Daullé, Alfred. *La Réforme à Saint-Quentin et aux environs, du XVIe siècle à la fin du XVIIIe siècle.* Le Cateau, 1901.

De Beer, E. S. "The Revocation of the Edict of Nantes and English Public Opinion," *Proceedings of the Huguenot Society of London,* XVIII (1950).

Dedieu, Joseph. *Histoire politique des protestants français (1715–1794).* 2 vols. Paris: Gabalda, 1925.

——. *Le Rôle politique des protestants français, 1685–1715.* Paris: Bloud et Gay, 1920.

Delacroix. "Notes pour servir à l'histoire des protestants en Dauphiné après la révocation de l'Édit de Nantes," *Bulletins de la société dauphinoise d'ethnologie et d'anthropologie,* VIII (1901).

Delaigue, Abbé Joseph. "Du Protestantisme en Bresse," *Revue de la société littéraire, historique et archéologique du département de l'Ain,* III (1874–1875).

——. "Le Protestantisme dans le pays de Gex," *Revue de la société littéraire, historique et archéologique du département de l'Ain,* V (1876–1877); VI (1877–1878); VII (1878–1879); VIII (1879–1880).

——. "Quelques notes sur l'organisation du protestantisme en Bresse, Bugey, Valromey et Gex," *Revue de la société littéraire, historique et archéologique du département de l'Ain,* IV (1875–1876).

Delmas, Léon. *L'Église réformée de la Rochelle: étude historique.* Toulouse, 1870.

Depping, Guillaume-B. "Un Banquier protestant en France au XVIIe siècle: Barthélemy Herwarth, contrôleur général des finances (1607–1676)," *Revue historique,* X–XI (1879).

——. *Correspondance administrative sous le règne de Louis XIV.* 4 vols. Paris, 1850–1855.

Desdevises du Dézert, G. *L'Église et l'état en France depuis l'Édit de Nantes jusqu'au Concordat (1598–1801).* Paris: Société français d'imprimerie et de librairie, 1907.

"Deux lettres écrites à l'abbé Raynal sur l'histoire de la révocation de l'Edit de Nantes, qu'il se proposait de publier (1782)," *Bulletin de la société de l'histoire du protestantisme français,* VIII (1859).

Dez, Pierre. *Histoire des protestants et de l'Église Réformée de l'île de Ré.* La Rochelle: F. Pijollet, 1926.

——. *Histoire des Protestants et des Églises réformées du Poitou.* I. New ed. La Rochelle: Imprimerie de l'Ouest, 1936.

Dillen, J. G. van. *Bronnen tot de Geschiedenis der Wisselbanken (Amsterdam, Middelburg, Delft, Rotterdam).* 2 vols. 'S-Gravenhage: M. Nijhoff, 1925.

Douen, Emmanuel-Orentin. *Essai historique sur les Églises Réformées du Département de l'Aisne d'après des documents pour la plupart inédits.* Quincy and Paris, 1860. Extracted from *Bulletin de la société de l'histoire du protestantisme français,* VIII (1859).

————. *La Révocation de l'Édit de Nantes à Paris d'après des documents inédits.* 3 vols. Paris, 1894.

————. "La Révocation de l'Édit de Nantes en Thiérache," *Bulletin de la société de l'histoire du protestantisme français,* XXVII (1878).

Dubois, G. "Les Protestants en Haute-Normandie à la fin du XVIIᵉ siècle. Statistiques et conditions sociales," *Bulletin de la société de l'histoire du protestantisme français,* LXXXIII (1934).

Dumons, Géraud [pseud. of Capt. Paul Rey-Lescure]. *Les Réfugiés du pays Castrais.* Albi: Imprimerie Julien, 1924.

Dupin de Saint-André, Armand. *Un Coup d'oeil sur l'histoire du protestantisme en Touraine.* Paris: Fischbacher, 1901.

————. *Histoire du protestantisme en Touraine.* Paris, 1885.

————. *La Révocation de l'Édit de Nantes.* Paris, 1885.

Durand, René. "Louis XIV et Jacques II à la veille de la Révolution de 1689: les trois missions de Bonrepaus en Angleterre (1686–1687–1688)," *Revue d'histoire moderne et contemporaine,* X (1908).

Durandard d'Aurelle, H. "Les Huguenots en Auvergne et les souches auvergnats du Jansenisme," *Revue de la Haute-Auvergne,* 35th year (1933).

Durengues, A. "Le Protestantisme en Agenais," *Revue des questions historiques,* 57th year (1929).

Durrleman, Freddy. *Éloge et condamnation de la Révocation de l'Édit de Nantes. Documents rassemblés.* Carrières-sous-Poissy, 1936.

Dutil, Léon. "L'Industrie de la soie à Nîmes jusqu'en 1789," *Revue d'histoire moderne et contemporaine,* X (1908).

Dutot, Charles Ferrare. *Réflexions politiques sur les finances et le commerce* (1738). In *Collection des principaux économistes.* Vol. I: *Économistes financiers du XVIIIᵉ siècle.* E. Daire, ed. 2d ed. Paris, 1851.

Ellinger, Herbert W. *Les Réfugiés Huguenots en Saxe-Weimar; leurs manufactures de bonneterie.* Gap: Imprimerie L. Jean, 1933.

Enschédé, A. J., trans. "Extraits de la *Gazette* de Haarlem sur les persécutions dirigées contre les protestants français (1679–1704)," *Bulletin de la société de l'histoire du protestantisme français,* XXVIII (1879); XXIX (1880); XXXII (1883); XXXIX (1890); XLI (1892); XLV (1896).

Enschédé, A. J., and N. Weiss. "Requêtes adressés aux États-Généraux des Pays-Bas," *Bulletin de la société de l'histoire du protestantisme français,* XXXVI (1887); XXXVII (1888); XXXIX (1890).

Erbe, Helmut. *Die Hugenotten in Deutschland.* Essen: Essener Verlagsanstalt, 1937.

Erman and Reclam. *Mémoires pour servir à l'histoire de réfugiés françois dans les états du Roi.* 9 vols. Berlin, 1782–1799.

Etat général des calvinistes et religionnaires de Champagne et Brie en 1685. Paris, 1878. Extracted from *Revue de Champagne et de Brie.*

Evans, Joan. "Huguenot Goldsmiths in England and Ireland," *Proceedings of the Huguenot Society of London,* XIV (1930–1933).

Fanfani, Amintore. *Catholicism, Protestantism, and Capitalism*. New York: Sheed & Ward, 1935.

Fargues, Paul. *De l'Édit de Nantes à la Révolution*. Vol. V of *Histoire du Christianisme*. Paris: Fischbacher, 1938.

Faurey, Joseph. *La Monarchie française et le protestantisme français*. Paris: De Boccard, 1923.

Félice, Guillaume-Adam de. *Histoire des protestants de France*. 8th ed. Toulouse, 1895.

Félice, Paul de. *La Réforme en Blaisois (documents inédits)*. Orléans, 1885.

Fleury, Edouard. "Notice sur l'histoire du protestantisme dans le département de l'Aisne," *Bulletin de la société académique de Laon*, XI (1861).

Foote, William Henry. *The Huguenots; or, Reformed Church*. Richmond, 1870.

Forbonnais, François Véron Duverger de. *Recherches et considérations sur les finances de France depuis 1595 jusqu'en 1721*. 6 vols. Liége, 1758.

Fraissinet, Justin. "Protestants fugitifs arrêtés et poursuivis devant le Parlement de Grenoble (1685–1687)," *Bulletin de la société de l'histoire du protestantisme français*, VII (1858); VIII (1859).

Francus [pseud. of Albin Mazon]. *Notes et documents historiques sur les Huguenots du Vivarais*. 4 vols. Privas: Imprimerie centrale de l'Ardèche, 1901–1904.

Fréville. *Mémoire sur le commerce de Rouen au XVIe siècle*. 2 vols. 1857.

Gaberel, J. "Les Suisses romands et les réfugiés de l'édit de Nantes," *Séances et travaux de l'Académie des sciences morales et politiques*, LIV (1860).

Gabory, Émile. "La Marine et le commerce de Nantes au XVIIe siècle et au commencement du XVIIIe (1661–1715)," *Annales de Bretagne*, XVII (1901–1902).

Gachon, Paul. *Le Conseil royal et les protestants en 1698. L'Enquête, la question de la Messe et le Rôle de Bâville*. Nogent-le-Rotrou: Imprimerie de Daupeley-Gouverneur, 1904. Extracted from *Revue historique*, LXXXV–LXXXVI.

———. *Quelques préliminaires de la Révocation de l'Édit de Nantes en Languedoc (1661–1685)*. Toulouse, 1899.

Gaitte. "L'Émigration des protestants de la principauté d'Orange sous Louis XIV (1703)," *Bulletin de la société de l'histoire du protestantisme français*, XIX–XX (1870–1871).

Galland, J.-A. "Les Deux procès du temple de Caen d'après des documents, pour la plupart, inédits (1661–1685)," *Bulletin de la société de l'histoire du protestantisme français*, XXXIX (1890).

———. *Essai sur l'histoire du Protestantisme à Caen et en Basse-Normandie de l'édit de Nantes à la Revolution (1598–1791)*. Paris, 1898.

———. "Le Protestantisme à Condé-sur-Noireau (Calvados) et dans le Bocage normand de la Révocation à Napoleon Ier (1685–1812)," *Bulletin de la société de l'histoire du protestantisme français*, LXI (1912).

Gariel, H. "Les Protestants de Grenoble, la veille et le lendemain de la Révocation de l'Édit de Nantes," *Petite revue des bibliophiles dauphinois*, I (1869).

Garnault, Émile. *Les Bourgeois rochelais des temps passés et les causes de la décadence du commerce rochelais*. Rogent-le-Rotrou, 1899. Extracted from *Revue historique*.

————. *Le Commerce rochelais au XVIIIe siècle.* 5 vols. La Rochelle, 1886–1898.

Garnier, J. "Tolérance de Colbert. Vingt-six lettres relatives à la religion pretendue réformée, écrites par les ministres Colbert, de Seignelay, Châteauneuf, de Louvois, en 1680, 1681, 1682, 1683, à M. de Breteuil, intendant de Picardie et d'Artois," *Bulletin de la société de l'histoire du protestantisme français*, XIV (1865).

Garrisson, Ch. "La Population protestante de la généralité de Montauban en 1685," *Bulletin de la société de l'histoire du protestantisme français*, XLVI (1897).

Garrisson, Robert. *Essai sur l'histoire du protestantisme dans la généralité de Montauban sous l'intendance de N.-J. Foucault (1674–1684).* Musée du Désert en Cevennes, 1935.

————. *Mémoires de Samuel de Pechels, 1685–1692, et Documents sur la Révocation à Montauban.* Musée du Désert en Cevennes, 1936.

Gaudilhon and others. *Contribution à l'histoire de la papeterie.* Lyon, 1935.

Gaudin, F. "Étude sur l'histoire du protestantisme," *Revue de la société littéraire, artistique et archéologique de la Vendée,* II (1883); III (1884); IV (1885); V (1886); VI (1887).

Gaullieur, E. *Histoire de la Réformation à Bordeaux et dans le ressort du Parlement de Guyenne.* Bordeaux, 1884.

Gaultier de Saint-Blancard. *Histoire apologétique, ou Défense des libertéz des Églises réformées de France.* 3 vols. Mayence, 1687–1688.

Gauthier, Gaston. "Le Protestantisme et la révocation de l'Édit de Nantes dans la paroisse de Beaumont-la-Ferrière (Nièvre)," *Bulletin de la société nivernaise des lettres, sciences et arts,* XVIII (1900).

Gauthier, Jules. "L'Industrie du papier dans les hautes vallées franc-comtoises . . . ," *Mémoire de la société d'émulation de Montbéliard,* XXVI (1897–1899).

Gazel, Henri. *Les Anciens ouvriers papetiers d'Auvergne.* Clermont-Ferrand: Imprimerie de A. Dumont, 1910.

Gelin, H. "Madame de Maintenon convertisseuse," *Bulletin de la société de l'histoire du protestantisme français,* XLIX (1900).

George, Robert H. "A Mercantilist Episode," *Journal of Economic and Business History,* III (1930–1931).

Gérin, Charles. *Le Pape Innocent XI et la révocation de l'Édit de Nantes.* Paris, 1878. Extracted from *Revue des questions historiques* (Oct., 1878).

Germain, Alexandre-C. *Histoire du commerce de Montpellier.* 2 vols. Montpellier, 1861.

Gill, Conrad. *The Rise of the Irish Linen Industry.* Oxford: Clarendon Press, 1925.

Godart, Justin. *L'Ouvrier en soie.* Lyon, 1899.

Godet, F. *Histoire de la Réformation et du Réfuge dans le pays de Neuchâtel.* Neuchâtel, 1859.

Gouron. "L'Industrie nîmoise aux XVIIe et XVIIIe siècles," *Ecole antique de Nîmes,* 17th session (1936).

Grant, A. J. *The Huguenots.* London: Home University of Modern Knowledge, 1934.

Grew, Marion E. *The House of Orange.* London: Methuen, 1947.

Guiffrey. *Histoire de la tapisserie.* Tours, 1886.

Guillebert. "Le Réfuge dans le pays de Neuchâtel (1685)," *Bulletin de la société de l'histoire du protestantisme français,* III (1855); IV (1856); IX (1860); X (1861).

Guitard, Eugène. *Colbert et Seignelay contre la religion réformée.* 2d ed. Paris: A. Picard, 1912.

Haag, Eugène. "Relevé général des persécutions exercées contre les protestants de France depuis la révocation de l'Édit de Nantes jusqu'à la Révolution française (1685–1789)," *Bulletin de la société de l'histoire du protestantisme français,* VI (1858).

Haag, Eugène and Émile. *La France protestante, ou Vies des protestants français qui se sont fait un nom dans l'histoire.* 10 vols. Paris, 1846–1859.

Hamilton, Earl J. "Origin and Growth of the National Debt in Western Europe," *American Economic Review, Proceedings,* XXXVII (1947).

――――. "Prices and Wages at Paris under John Law's System," *Quarterly Journal of Economics,* LI (1936).

――――. "Prices and Wages in Southern France under John Law's System," *Economic History (Supplement)* (1937).

Hardy, Samuel. *Histoire de l'Église protestante de Dieppe.* Paris, 1896.

Harsin, Paul. *Crédit public et Banque d'État en France du XVIe au XVIIIe siècle.* Paris: E. Droz, 1933.

Hauser, Henri. *Les Débuts du capitalisme.* New ed. Paris: F. Alcan, 1931.

――――. "L'Économie calvinienne," *Bulletin de la société de l'histoire du protestantisme français,* LXXXIV (1935).

――――. *Études sur la Réforme française.* Paris: A. Picard et fils, 1909.

――――. *Les Origines historiques des problèmes économiques actuels.* Paris: Vuibert, 1930.

――――. "La Réforme en Auvergne, notes et documents (1535–1671 [1568–1685])," *Bulletin de la société de l'histoire du protestantisme français,* XLVII (1898).

――――. *La Réforme et les classes populaires en France au XVIe siècle.* Paris, 1899. Extracted from *Revue d'histoire moderne et contemporaine,* I (1899).

――――. "La Révocation de l'Édit de Nantes et la papeterie en Angleterre," *Bulletin de la société de l'histoire du protestantisme français,* LXXX (1931).

Hérelle, G. *Documents inédits sur le protestantisme à Vitry-le-François, Épense, Heiltz-le-Maurupt, Nettancourt et Vassy depuis la fin des Guerres de Religion jusqu'à la Révolution française.* 3 vols. Paris: A. Picard, 1903–1908.

Heyer, Th. "Liste nominative des pasteurs, proposants et autres hommes sortis du Dauphiné, du Bas-Languedoc, des Cevennes et du Vivarais, et réfugiés à Genève en 1683," *Bulletin de la société de l'histoire du protestantisme français,* XIX–XX (1870–1871).

Holmes, Abiel. *A Memoire of the French Protestants, Who Settled at Oxford, in Massachusetts,* A.D. *MDCLXXXVI; with a Sketch of the Entire History of the Protestants of France.* Cambridge, Mass., 1826.

Hubert, Eugène-Ernest. *Le Protestantisme à Tournai pendant le XVIIIe siècle.* Brussels: J. Lebègue, 1903. Extracted from *Mémoires courronnés et autres mémoires publiés par l'Académie royale de Belgique,* LXII.

Huguenot Society of London. See *Proceedings of the Huguenot Society of London.*

Hugues, Edmond. "Liste de documents relatifs au protestantisme contenue dans la série TT des Archives nationales," *Bulletin de la société de l'histoire du protestantisme français,* XXVII (1878).

Jailliot, J. "Le Protestantisme dans le Rethelois et dans l'Argonne jusqu'à la révocation de l'Édit de Nantes," *Revue d'Ardenne et d'Argonne,* XI (1903–1904); XII (1904–1905); XIII (1905–1906).

Jal. "Préparatifs de la révocation de l'Édit de Nantes. Mesures prises pour la conversion des officiers de l'armée de mer et des matelots appartenant à la religion prétendue réformée (1680)," *Bulletin de la société de l'histoire du protestantisme français,* II (1854).

"Journal d'un marin protestant du XVIIe siècle (Taré Chaillaud)," *Bulletin de la société de l'histoire du protestantisme français,* XV (1866).

[Jurieu, Pierre]. *Lettres pastorales addressées aux fidèles de France, qui gemissent sous la captivité de Babylone.* 3 vols. in 1. 4th ed. Rotterdam, 1687–1688.

———. *Présages de la Décadence des Empires, où sont mêlées plusieurs Observations curieuses touchant la Religion et les Affaires du Temps.* Mekelbourg, 1688.

Jurieu, Pierre. *Réflexions sur la cruelle persécution que souffre l'église réformée de France. . . .* 2d ed. N.p., 1685.

Labillière, F. P. de. "Incidents of Huguenot History in the Reign of Queen Anne," *Proceedings of the Huguenot Society of London,* IV (1891–1893).

La Bouillerie, Baron Sébastien de. "Les Protestants dans le Maine. Le temple et le cimetière de l'église du Mans et l'église d'Ardenay," *Revue historique et archéologique du Maine,* XXIV (1888).

La Boutetière, Comte Louis de. "Note sur l'émigration protestante du Poitou à la suite de la révocation de l'Édit de Nantes," *Bulletins de la société des antiquaires de l'Ouest,* XIV (1877).

Lacoste, Roger. "Notes sur la bourgeoisie du Bergeracois à la veille de la Révolution," *Bulletin de la société de l'histoire du protestantisme français,* LXXXIII (1934).

Lacroix, Auguste. *Historique de la papeterie d'Angoulême suivi d'observations sur le commerce des chiffons en France.* Paris, 1863.

La Monneraye. *See* Monneraye, Jean de la.

Lamunière, Jacques. "Les Réformés bourguignons réfugiés en Suisse romande," *Mémoires de l'Académie des Sciences, Arts et Belles-lettres de Dijon,* CII (1933).

Lane, Frederic C. "Colbert et le commerce de Bordeaux," *Revue historique de Bordeaux et du département de la Gironde,* XVII (1924).

Lart, Charles E. "The Huguenot Settlements and Churches in the West of England," *Proceedings of the Huguenot Society of London,* VII (1901–1904).

Lasteyrie, Robert de, and d'Alexandre Vidier. *Bibliographie annuelle des travaux historiques et archéologiques publiés par les sociétés savantes de la France.* 3 vols. Paris: Imprimerie nationale, 1906–1910.

Lasteyrie, Robert de, and Eugène Lefèvre-Pontalis. *Bibliographie générale des travaux historiques et archéologiques publiés par les sociétés savantes de la France.* 4 vols. Paris: Imprimerie nationale, 1888–1904.

Lavisse, Ernest, and others, *Histoire de France illustrée depuis les origines jusqu'à la révolution.* Vol. VII, Parts 1 and 2; Vol. VIII, Part 1. Paris: Hachette, 1911.

Layard, Florence. "The Huguenots in North Britain," *Proceedings of the Huguenot Society of London,* III (1888–1891).

Layard, Henry Austen. "The Revocation of the Edict of Nantes. Illustrated from State Papers in the Archives of Venice," *Proceedings of the Huguenot Society of London,* II (1887–1888).

Leboitteux, A. *Les Huguenots des Isles: Histoire de l'Église Réformée de Condé-sur-Noireau depuis sa fondation jusqu'à la Révocation de l'Édit de Nantes (1555–1685).* Condé-sur-Noireau: G. L'Enfant, 1907.

Le Clerc, R. "Le Protestantisme à Saint-Lô," *Notices, mémoires et documents publiés par la société d'agriculture, d'archéologie et d'histoire naturelle du département de la Manche,* XXXVII (1925); XXXVIII (1926).

Leclercq, Dom H. *Histoire de la Régence pendant la minorité de Louis XV.* 3 vols. Paris: Librairie Honoré Champion, 1921–1922.

Lee, Grace Lawless. *The Huguenot Settlements in Ireland.* London: Longmans Green, 1936.

Lee, Hannah F. *The Huguenots in France and America.* 2 vols. Cambridge, Mass., 1843.

Lefèvre, Jacques. *Instructions pour confirmer les nouveaux convertis dans la foy de l'Église.* Paris, 1686.

———. *Nouveau recueil de tout ce qui s'est fait pour et contre les protestans, particulièrement en France où l'on voit l'establissement, le progrez, la Décadence et l'Extinction de la R.P.R. dans ce Royaume.* Paris, 1690.

———. *Recueil de ce qui s'est fait en France de plus considérable contre les protestants, depuis la Révocation de l'Edit de Nantes, avec un préface, pour justifier la conduite qu'on a tenue dans ce Royaume, pour porter les Pretendus Réformez à se réunir à l'Eglise.* Paris, 1686.

Le Gendre, Philippe. *Histoire de la persécution faite à l'église de Rouen sur la fin du dernier siècle.* Émile Lesens, ed. Rouen, 1874. First published at Rotterdam, 1704.

Lehr, Henry. *Les Protestants d'autrefois. Vie et institutions militaires.* 2 vols. Paris: Fischbacher, 1901, 1907.

Lelièvre, Matthieu. *De la Révocation à la Révolution. Étude sur l'histoire morale et religieuse du protestantisme français pendant un siècle. Première période (1685–1715).* Paris, 1911.

———. *Histoire du méthodisme dans les îles de la Manche, précédée de l'histoire de la réformation huguenote dans cet archipel.* Paris, 1885.

Lemoine, Jean. *Les Évêques de France et les protestants, 1698.* Paris, 1900. Extracted from *Revue de Paris* (Nov. 15, 1900).

Léonard, Émile-G. "Économie et religion, les protestants français au XVIIIe siècle," *Annales d'histoire sociale,* II (1940).

———. "Une Église protestante de notables (Caen) devant la persécution et la révolution." Unpublished manuscript. 1940.

———. *Histoire ecclésiastique des réformés français au XVIIIe siècle.* Paris: Fischbacher, 1940.

———. *Problèmes et expériences du protestantisme français.* Paris: Fischbacher, 1940.

———. *Le Protestant français.* Paris: Presses universitaires de France, 1953.

———. "Le Protestantisme français au XVIIe siècle," *Revue historique,* CC (1948).

————. *Un Village d' "opiniâtrés": les protestants d'Aubais de la destruction à la reconstruction de leur temple (1685–1838).* Musée du Désert en Cevennes, 1938.

Leroux, Alfred. *Histoire de la réforme dans la Marche et le Limousin (Creuse, Haute-Vienne, Corrèze).* Limoges, 1888.

————. *Les Religionnaires de Bordeaux de 1685 à 1802.* Bordeaux: Féret, 1920.

Leroy, G. "Le Protestantisme à Melun (1560–1787)," *Bulletin de la société de l'histoire du protestantisme français,* XXIV (1875).

Leroy, Stephen. "Les Protestants de Sedan au XVIIIe siècle," *Bulletin de la société de l'histoire du protestantisme français,* XLV (1896).

Lesens, Émile. *Le Protestantisme dans le pays de Caux (ancien colloque de Caux, Havre et Dieppe excepté).* Victor Madelaine, ed. Bolbec: Imprimerie de H. Yvon, [1906].

Lestrade, Abbé Jean. *Les Huguenots dans le diocèse de Rieux, documents inédits.* Auch and Paris: H. Champion, 1904.

————. "Les Huguenots en Comminges d'après les papiers des États conservés à Muret," *Revue de Comminges, Pyrénées centrales. Bulletin de la société des études du Comminges, du Nebouzan et des Quatre Vallées,* X (1895); XI (1896); XII (1897); XIII (1898); XIV (1899).

Lételié, André. "Fénelon en Saintonge et la révocation de l'édit de Nantes, 1685–1688," *Archives historiques de la Saintonge et de l'Aunis,* XIII (1885).

Lettres à M. l'abbé Raynal sur l'histoire de la Révocation de l'Edit de Nantes qu'il se propose de publier. N.p., 1782.

Levasseur, Émile. *Histoire des classes ouvrières en France depuis la conquête de Jules César jusqu'à la révolution.* 2 vols. Paris, 1859.

————. *Histoire des classes ouvrières et de l'industrie en France avant 1789.* II. 2d ed. Paris, 1901.

————. *Histoire du commerce de la France.* I. Paris, 1911.

————. *La Population française.* I. Paris, 1889.

[Le Vassor, Michel]. *Les Soupirs de la France esclave.* Amsterdam, 1689.

Lièvre, Auguste-François. "Correspondance inédite de l'évêque de Grenoble Le Camus, plus tard cardinal, avec M. de Barillon, évêque de Luçon, au sujet de leurs campagnes contre l'hérésie (1682–1696)," *Bulletin de la société de l'histoire du protestantisme français,* III (1855).

————. *Du Rôle que le clergé catholique de France a joué dans la révocation de l'Édit de Nantes.* Strasbourg, 1853.

————. *Histoire des protestants et des églises réformées du Poitou.* 3 vols. Paris, 1856–1860.

Louvois, François Michel Le Tellier. See *Testament politique du Marquis de Louvois.*

McCloy, Shelby T. *Government Assistance in Eighteenth-Century France.* Durham, N.C.: Duke University Press, 1946.

————. "Persecution of the Huguenots in the 18th Century," *Church History,* XX (1951).

MacPherson, David. *Annals of Commerce, Manufactures, Fisheries, and Navigation etc.* II, III. London, 1805.

MacPherson, James. *The History of Great Britain from the Restoration to the Accession of the House of Hannover.* 2 vols. London, 1775.

Maguire, Thomas Miller. "Frenchmen on the Seas," *Proceedings of the Huguenot Society of London,* VIII (1905–1908).

Malvezin, Théophile. *Histoire du commerce de Bordeaux depuis les origines jusqu'à nos jours.* 2 vols. Bordeaux, 1892.

Malzac, L. "La Révocation de l'Édit de Nantes à Marseille," *Provincia,* IX (1929).

Manchée, W. H. "Some Huguenot Smugglers. The Impeachment of London Silk Merchants, 1698," *Proceedings of the Huguenot Society of London,* XV (1934–1937).

Marcel, Louis. "La Révocation de l'Édit de Nantes à Langres," *Nouvelle revue de Champagne et de Brie,* III (1925).

Marchand, J. *Un Intendant sous Louis XIV: Étude sur l'administration de Le Bret en Provence (1687–1704).* Paris, 1889.

Marion, Marcel. *Histoire financière de la France depuis 1715.* I. Paris: A. Rousseau, 1927.

Marquand, Allen. "Huguenot Industries in America," *Proceedings of the Huguenot Society of America,* I (1884–1888).

Martin, Germain. *Bibliographie critique de l'histoire de l'industrie.* Paris, n.d.

———. *La Grande industrie sous le règne de Louis XIV.* Paris, 1898.

———. "La Monnaie et le crédit privé en France," *Revue de l'histoire des doctrines économiques,* II (1909).

———. *Les Papeteries d'Annonay.* Besançon, 1897.

Martin, Germain, and Marcel Bezançon. *L'Histoire du crédit en France sous le règne de Louis XIV.* I. Paris: L. Larose et L. Tenin, 1913.

Martin, Henri. *Histoire de France depuis les temps les plus reculés jusqu'en 1789.* 17 vols. 4th ed. Paris, 1855–1860.

Masson, Gustave. "L'Histoire du protestantisme français étudiée au Record Office," *Bulletin de la société de l'histoire du protestantisme français,* XVII (1868); XVIII (1869); XXIV (1875); XXV (1876).

———. *The Huguenots: A Sketch of Their History from the Beginning of the Reformation to the Death of Louis XIV.* London, 1881.

Masson, Paul. *Histoire du commerce français dans le Levant au XVIIᵉ siècle.* Paris, 1896.

Mazauric, R. "Le Parlement de Metz et les Protestants après la Révocation (1684–1724)," *Bulletin de la société de l'histoire du protestantisme français,* LXXXIV (1935).

Mellottée, Paul. *Histoire économique de l'imprimerie.* Paris: Hachette, 1905.

———. *Les Transformations économiques de l'imprimerie sous l'ancien régime.* Chateauroux: Imprimerie de Mellottée, 1905.

"Mémoire sur la population protestante du diocèse de Nîmes avant et après la révocation de l'Edit de Nantes," *Bulletin de la société de l'histoire du protestantisme français,* XXIX (1880).

Ménard, M. *Histoire civile, ecclésiastique et littéraire de la ville de Nismes avec des notes et les preuves.* VI. Paris, 1755.

Meuvret, Jean. "Les Crises de subsistance et la démographie de la France d'ancien régime." Typescript prepared for the Institut Nationale d'Études Démographique.

———. "Les Mouvements des prix de 1661 à 1715 et leurs répercussions." Communication to the Société de Statistique de Paris, May 17, 1944.

Meynier, Bernard. *De l'Exécution de l'Édit de Nantes.* Pézenas, 1662.

———. *De l'Exécution de l'Édit de Nantes dans les Provinces de Guyenne, Poitou, Angoumois, Xaintonge et Aunis Et dans les isles de Marennes, d'Oléron et de Ré.* 2d ed. Poitiers, 1665.

Michel, Adolphe. *Louvois et les protestants.* Paris, 1870.

———. "Louvois et la révocation de l'Édit de Nantes," *Bulletin de la société de l'histoire du protestantisme français,* XVII (1868).

Michel, Francisque. *Histoire du commerce et de la navigation à Bordeaux principalement sous l'administration anglaise.* II. Bordeaux, 1870.

Michelet, Jules. *Histoire de France.* Vol. XIII: *Louis XIV et la Révocation de l'Édit de Nantes.* 3d ed. Paris, 1863.

Minet, William. "Isaac Minet's Narrative," *Proceedings of the Huguenot Society of London,* II (1887–1888).

Missècle, Jacques de. *L'Édit de Nantes et sa révocation.* 2d ed. Colmar, 1931.

Moens, W. J. C. "The Walloon Settlement and the French Church at Southampton," *Proceedings of the Huguenot Society of London,* III (1888–1891).

Moerikofer, Johann-Caspar. *Histoire des Réfugiés de la Réforme en Suisse.* G. Roux, trans. Paris, 1878.

Mols, Roger. *Introduction à la démographie historique des villes de l'Europe du XIVᵉ au XVIIIᵉ siècle.* II. Gembloux: J. Duculot, 1955.

Monin, Louis-Henri. *Essai sur l'histoire administrative du Languedoc pendant l'intendance de Basville (1685–1719).* Paris, 1884.

Monneraye, Jean de la. "La Révocation de l'Édit de Nantes et le protestantisme en Bas-Poitou au dix-huitième siècle," *Revue du Bas-Poitou,* 36th year (1923).

Monod, Wilfred. *Du Protestantisme.* Paris: F. Alcan, 1928.

Montclar, Ripert, and Abbè Quesnel. *Mémoire théologique et politique au sujet des mariages clandestins des protestans de France.* 2d ed. N.p., 1756.

Moret, Ernest. "Fragment d'histoire sur les dernières persécutions sous Louis XIV (1711–1715)," *Séances et travaux de l'Académie des sciences morales et politiques,* XLIII (1858). Also published in *Bulletin de la société de l'histoire du protestantisme français,* VII, under a slightly different title.

Mours, Samuel. *Le Haut-Vivarais protestant.* Valence: Le Trait d'Union, 1935.

———. *Le Protestantisme en Vivarais et en Velay des origines à nos jours.* Valence: Imprimeries Réunies, 1949.

Mousseau, Maurice. "Protestants sedanais au XVIIIᵉ siècle," *Bulletin de la société de l'histoire du protestantisme français,* LXXXIII (1934).

Moutarde, Eugène. *La Réforme en Saintonge: Les Églises réformées de Saujon et de la Presqu'île d'Arvert.* Paris, 1892.

Moutier, A. *Recherches sur le commerce des toiles de lins.* Pont-Audemer, 1874.

Muret, Th. "Le Banquier protestant Samuel Bernard, dragonné nonobstant conversion en règle, épisode de la révocation de l'Édit de Nantes (1685)," *Bulletin de la société de l'histoire du protestantisme français,* V (1857).

Murray, Alice E. *A History of the Commercial and Financial Relations between England and Ireland from the Period of the Restoration.* London: P. S. King & Son, 1903.

Muzac, Amédée. "Notes pour servir à l'histoire de la R. P. R. à Argentat (1555–1757)," *Bulletin de la société scientifique, historique et archéologique de la Corrèze,* L (1928); LI (1929); LII (1930); LIII (1931).

Naert, M. "Les Huguenots du Calaisis au XVIIᵉ siècle," *Bulletin de la société de l'histoire du protestantisme français*, LXIII–LXIV (1914–1915).

Nazelle, L.-J. *Le Protestantisme en Saintonge sous le régime de la Révocation, 1685–1789.* Paris: Fischbacher, 1907.

Nef, John U. *War and Human Progress: An Essay in the Rise of Industrial Civilization.* Cambridge, Mass.: Harvard University Press, 1950.

Nicolai, A. *Histoire des moulins à papier du sud-ouest de la France (1300–1800).* Vol. II: *Dictionnaire des filigranes.* Bordeaux: Edition Delmas, 1936.

Nierop, Leonie van. "Stukken Betreffende de Nijverheid der Refugiés te Amsterdam," *Economische-Historisch Jaarboek*, VII (1921); IX (1923).

Noël de la Morinière. *Second essai sur le département de la Seine-Inférieure.* Rouen, 1795.

Norwood, Frederick A. *The Reformation Refugees as an Economic Force.* Chicago: The American Society of Church History, 1942.

Novi de Caveirac, Abbé Jean. *Apologie de Louis XIV et de son conseil, sur la révocation de l'Edit de Nantes, etc.* N.p., 1758.

———. *Mémoire politico-critique, où l'on examine s'il est de l'intérêt de l'Eglise et de l'Etat d'établir pour les Calvinistes du Royaume une nouvelle forme de se marier.* N.p., 1756.

O'Brien, George. *The Economic History of Ireland in the Eighteenth Century.* Dublin: Maunsel and Co., 1918.

———. *The Economic History of Ireland in the Seventeenth Century.* Dublin: Maunsel and Co., 1919.

O'Brien, Louis. *Innocent XI and the Revocation of the Edict of Nantes.* Berkeley, Calif., 1930.

Olry, Jean. *La Persécution de l'église de Metz.* Orthon Cuvier, ed. Paris, 1859. First published at Hanau, 1690.

Orcibal, Jean. *Louis XIV et les protestants.* Paris: J. Vrin, 1951.

Osmont de Courtisigny, C. "La Noblesse protestante de la Généralité de Caen, et le nombre des prétendus Réformés de France à l'époque de la Révocation," *Bulletin de la société de l'histoire du protestantisme français,* XXXVII (1888).

Overend, George Henry. "Notes upon the Earlier History of the Manufacture of Paper in England," *Proceedings of the Huguenot Society of London,* VIII (1905–1908).

Pagès, G. "Les Réfugiés à Berlin d'après la correspondance du comte de Rébenac (1681–1688)," *Bulletin de la société de l'histoire du protestantisme français,* LI (1902).

Pariset, E. *La Chambre de commerce de Lyon. Étude faite sur les registres de ses délibérations, 1702–1791.* 2 vols. Lyon, 1886–1889.

———. *Histoire de la fabrique lyonnaise. Étude sur le Régime social et économique de l'Industrie de la Soie à Lyon, depuis le XVIᵉ siècle.* Lyon: A. Rey, 1901.

Pascal, César. "Les Collectes nationales anglaises en faveur des réfugiés protestants (1681–1699)," *Bulletin de la société de l'histoire du protestantisme français,* XLI (1892).

———. "Louis XIV et les réfugiés huguenots en Angleterre à l'époque de la Révocation (1681–1688)," *Bulletin de la société de l'histoire du protestantisme français,* XL (1891).

Paul, André. "Les Réfugiés huguenots et wallons dans le Palatinat du Rhin du XVIᵉ siècle à la Révolution," *Revue historique*, CLVII (1928).

Pérathon, Cyprien. *Histoire d'Aubusson: la vicomté, la ville, les tapisseries, la maison d'Aubusson.* Limoges, 1886.

————. "Le Protestantisme à Aubusson," *Mémoires de la société des sciences naturelles et archéologiques de la Creuse*, XIX (1915).

Peringuey, L. "Les Réfugiés huguenots au Cap de Bonne-Espérance," *Bulletin de la société de géographie commerciale de Bordeaux*, III (1878).

Perrenet, Pierre. "Une Église réformée en Bourgogne au XVIIᵉ siècle: Is-sur-Tille," *Bulletin de la société de l'histoire du protestantisme français*, LXXXVI (1937).

————. "Les Protestants de la région dijonnaise durant la période de l'édit de Nantes," *Mémoires de l'Académie des Sciences, Arts et Belles-lettres de Dijon*, CII (1933).

————. "Les Protestants de la région dijonnaise et Langroise durant l'application de l'édit de Nantes," *Bulletin de la société historique et archéologique de Langres*, X (1931–1934).

Peyran, J. *Histoire de l'ancienne principauté de Sedan jusqu'à la fin du dix-huitième siècle.* 2 vols. Paris, 1826.

Peyrat, A. "Bossuet et la révocation de l'Édit de Nantes," *Bulletin de la société de l'histoire du protestantisme français*, IX (1860).

Philippoteaux, A. *Les Origines et débuts de la draperie sedanaise (1575–1594).* Sedan: Imprimerie de Suzaine, 1924.

————. *Origines et débuts de l'industrie sedanaise, 1577–1677.* Sedan: Imprimerie de Suzaine, 1927.

Pigeonneau, H. *Histoire du commerce de la France.* II. 2d ed. Paris, 1897.

Piguet, Émile. "Les Dénombrements généraux de Réfugiés au Pays de Vaud et à Berne, à la fin du XVIIᵉ siècle," *Bulletin de la société de l'histoire du protestantisme français*, LXXXII (1933).

Pin, Marcel. *Madame de Maintenon et les protestants: Contribution à l'Étude de la Révocation de l'Édit de Nantes.* Uzès: Peladan, 1944.

Poland, Burdette C. *French Protestantism and the French Revolution. A Study in Church and State, Thought and Religion, 1685–1815.* Princeton: Princeton University Press, 1957.

Poole, Reginald Lane. *A History of the Huguenots of the Dispersion at the Recall of the Edict of Nantes.* London, 1880.

Portal, Pierre Paul Frédérick de. *Les Descendants des Albigeois et des Huguenots, ou Mémoires de la Famille de Portal.* Paris, 1860.

Potter, Elisha R. *Memoir concerning the French Settlements in the Colony of Rhode Island.* Providence, 1879.

"Les Preliminaires de la revocation de l'Edit de Nantes. Mémoires politiques sur l'estat présent de la France," *Bulletin de la société de l'histoire du protestantisme français*, XIX–XX (1870–1871).

"Préparatifs de la révocation de l'Édit de Nantes. Interdiction aux dames de la Religion d'assister leurs coreligionnaires. Recherche déguisée du nombre des Réformés (1682). Deux lettres inédites de Colbert," *Bulletin de la société de l'histoire du protestantisme français*, II (1854).

Prigent, René. "Les Protestants à Brest après la Révocation," *Mémoires de la société d'histoire et d'archéologie de Bretagne*, 9th year (1928).

Proceedings of the Huguenot Society of London. I–XIX (1885–1954).

Les Protestantes refugiés ou Entretiens de Pauline et d'Agate dans léquels ceux qui souffrent persecution pour l'Evangile, pourront trouver des regles d'une bonne conduitte, dans les lieux ou la Providence de Dieu les appellera. N.p., 1689.

"Le Protestantisme à Bayonne (1677–1680)," *Bulletin de la société de l'histoire du protestantisme français,* XXV (1876).

Puaux, Frank. "Ephémérides de l'année de la révocation de l'édit de Nantes," *Bulletin de la société de l'histoire du protestantisme français,* XXXIV (1885).

———. "Essai sur les négociations des réfugiés pour obtenir le rétablissement de la Religion réformée au traité de Ryswick (octobre 1697)," *Bulletin de la société de l'histoire du protestantisme français,* XVI (1867).

———. *Histoire de l'établissement des protestants français en Suède.* Paris and Stockholm, 1892.

———. "La Révocation à Marennes. Le temple et les écoles," *Bulletin de la société de l'histoire du protestantisme français,* XXXIII (1884).

Puaux, Frank, and A. Sabatier. *Études sur la révocation de l'Édit de Nantes.* Paris, 1886.

Puaux, N.-A.-François. *Histoire de la réformation française.* 7 vols. Paris and Geneva, 1857–1863.

———. *Histoire populaire du protestantisme français.* Paris, 1894.

Purdon, C. D. *The Huguenots, a brief history of the Circumstances that obliged the Huguenots to leave France and Their Settlement in Ireland.* Belfast, 1869.

Quenot. "La Papeterie d'Angoulême au XVIIIᵉ siècle," *Études locales: Bulletin de la Charente,* 4th year (1923).

R. L. "Statistique protestante (XVIIᵉ siècle)," *Bulletin de la société de l'histoire du protestantisme français,* LVII (1908).

Rabaud, Camille. *Histoire du protestantisme dans l'Albigeois et le Lauragais depuis la révocation de l'édit de Nantes (1685) jusqu'à nos jours.* Paris, 1898.

Rameau, Abbé. "Les Huguenots dans le Mâconnais aux XVIᵉ et XVIIᵉ siècles," *Revue de la société littéraire, historique et archéologique du département de l'Ain,* VIII (1879–1880); IX (1880–1881).

Read, Charles. "Lettres inédites de plusieurs prélats relatives aux conversions de calvinistes sous Louis XIV," *Bulletin de la société de l'histoire du protestantisme français,* I (1853).

———. "L'Opinion du duc de Bourgogne sur la question protestante et le rappel des huguenots (1710)," *Bulletin de la société de l'histoire du protestantisme français,* XLI (1892).

———. "La Réponse de Madame de Maintenon consultée par Louis XIV, en 1697, sur un mémoire concernant les Huguenots, avec les Remarques de la Beaumelle (1755)," *Bulletin de la société de l'histoire du protestantisme français,* XXXIX (1890).

———. "Vauban, Fénelon et le duc de Chevreuse, sur la tolérance et le rappel des Huguenots (1689–1694–1710)," *Bulletin de la société de l'histoire du protestantisme français,* XXXIX (1890).

Recolin, Numa. *La Révocation de l'Édit de Nantes et ses conséquences.* Paris, 1885.

Recueil des Édits, Declarations et Arrests concernans la Religion Prétendue

Réformée, 1662–1751, précédés de l'Edit de Nantes. Léon Pilatte, ed. Paris, 1885.

Redstone, Vincent B. "The Dutch and Huguenot Settlements of Ipswich," *Proceedings of the Huguenot Society of London,* XII (1917–1924).

Reuss, Rodolphe. *Louis XIV et l'église protestante de Strasbourg au moment de la révocation de l'édit de Nantes (1685–1686).* Paris, 1887.

———. *Notes pour servir à l'histoire de l'Église française de Strasbourg (1538–1794).* Strasbourg, 1880.

"La Révocation de l'Edit de Nantes à Alais," *Bulletin de la société de l'histoire du protestantisme français,* XXVIII (1879).

La Révocation de l'Édit de Nantes. Discours prononcés à l'occasion du deuxième anniversaire séculaire de cet évènement. Montreal, 1885.

"Revocation de l'Edit de Nantes. Voies d'exécution à l'égard du duc de Caumont La Force et de divers membres de cette famille. Lettres inédites de Louis XIV et de Colbert de Seignelay, secrétaire d'Etat (1686–1687)," *Bulletin de la société de l'histoire du protestantisme français,* II (1854).

Richmond, L. de. "Après la révocation de l'Édit de Nantes. Voltaire et la liberté de conscience. Lettres inédites," *Académie de la Rochelle, Section de littérature, Annales,* XXIII (1885).

———. *Les Protestants rochelais depuis la Révocation de l'Édit de Nantes jusqu'au Concordat, 1685–1802.* Saintes, 1865.

Rivier, Théodore. *L'Église réformée française de Saint-Gall (1685 à nos jours).* Paris: Renouard, 1909.

Robert-Labarthe, Urbain de. *Histoire du protestantisme dans le Haut-Languedoc, le Bas-Quercy et le comté de Foix de 1685 à 1789.* 2 vols. Paris, 1892–1896.

Rondot, Natalis. *L'Industrie de la soie en France.* Lyon, 1894.

———. *Les Protestants à Lyon au dix-septième siècle.* Lyon, 1891.

Rossier, L. *Histoire des protestants de Picardie, particulièrement de ceux du département de la Somme.* Amiens, 1861.

Rouchon, Gilbert. "Les Fabriques de papier de l'Auvergne," *Mémoires de l'Académie des sciences, belles-lettres et arts de Clermont-Ferrand,* 2d series, LXXXVIII (1928).

Rouquette, Abbé J.-B. *Études sur la Révocation de l'Édit de Nantes en Languedoc.* 3 vols. Paris: Savaète, 1908.

Rousselet, Charles-Frédéric. "La Colonie huguenotte de Friedrichsdorf," *Proceedings of the Huguenot Society of London,* V (1894–1896).

Rouvière, François. *Les Religionnaires des diocèses de Nîmes, Alais et Uzès et la Révolution française.* Paris, 1889.

Rulhière, Claude-Carlomau de. *Eclaircissements historiques sur les causes de la révocation de l'Édit de Nantes, et sur l'état des protestants en France, depuis le commencement du Règne de Louis XIV, jusqu'à nos jours.* 2 vols. New ed. Geneva, 1788.

Sagnac, Ph. "Le Crédit de l'État et les banquiers à la fin du XVIIe et au commencement du XVIIIe siècle," *Revue d'histoire moderne et contemporaine,* X (1908).

———. *La Formation de la société française moderne.* Vol. I: *La Société et la monarchie absolue, 1661–1715.* Paris: Presses universitaires de France, 1945.

———. "L'Histoire économique de la France de 1683 à 1714, essai de bibliographie critique," *Revue d'histoire moderne et contemporaine*, IV (1902–1903).

———. "L'Industrie et le commerce de la draperie en France à la fin du XVIIe siècle et au commencement du XVIIIe," *Revue d'histoire moderne et contemporaine*, IX (1907–1908).

Sagnier, Charles. "Une Liste de réfugiés Nîmois en 1686," *Bulletin de la société de l'histoire du protestantisme français*, XXVIII (1879).

Saint-Blancard. *See* Gaultier de Saint-Blancard.

Savory, D.-L. "Industriels picards réfugiés en Irlande," *Bulletin de la société de l'histoire du protestantisme français*, LXXXVI (1937).

Sayous, André-E. "Le Financier Jean-Henri Huguetan à Amsterdam et à Genève," *Société d'histoire et d'archéologie de Genève*, VI (1937).

Schaff, Philip. "History of the Edict of Nantes," *Proceedings of the Huguenot Society of America*, II (1888–1891).

Schickler, Fernand de. *Les Églises du Réfuge*. Paris, 1882.

———. "Le Protestantisme dans la Marche et l'Église d'Aubusson," *Bulletin de la société de l'histoire du protestantisme français*, XXX (1881).

Scoville, Warren C. *Capitalism and French Glassmaking, 1640–1789*. Berkeley and Los Angeles: University of California Press, 1950.

———. "The Huguenots and the Diffusion of Technology," *Journal of Political Economy*, LX (1952).

———. "The Huguenots in the French Economy, 1650–1750," *Quarterly Journal of Economics*, LXVII (1953).

———. "Minority Migrations and the Diffusion of Technology," *Journal of Economic History*, XI (1951).

Sée, Henri. "Dans quelle mesure puritains et juifs ont-ils contribué aux progrès du capitalisme moderne," *Revue historique*, CLV (1927).

———. *Esquisse d'une histoire économique et sociale de la France depuis les origines jusqu'à la guerre mondiale*. Paris: F. Alcan, 1929.

———. *L'Évolution commerciale et industrielle de la France sous l'ancien régime*. Paris: F. Alcan, 1925.

———. "Hat Manufacture in Rennes, 1676–1789," *Journal of Economic and Business History*, I–II (1929).

———. *Histoire économique de la France*. I. Robert Schnerb, ed. Paris: Armand Colin, 1939.

Ségur-Dupeyron, P. de. *Histoire des négociations commerciales et maritimes de la France aux XVIIe et XVIIIe siècles, considérées dans leurs rapports avec la politique générale*. 3 vols. Paris, 1872–1873.

Shaw, William A. "The English Government and the Relief of Protestant Refugees," *Proceedings of the Huguenot Society of London*, V (1894–1896).

Sheffield, John Lord. *Observations on the Manufactures, Trade, and Present State of Ireland*. London, 1785.

Sismondi, Jean C. L. Simonde de. *Histoire des français*. 30 vols. Paris, 1821–1844.

Smiles, Samuel. *The Huguenots, Their Settlements, Churches, and Industries in England and Ireland*. 6th ed. London, 1889.

Solomiac. "Le Réfuge dans le pays de Vaud (1685–1860)," *Bulletin de la société de l'histoire du protestantisme français*, IX (1860).

Soulice, L. "Documents pour l'histoire du protestantisme en Béarn," *Bulletin de la société des sciences, lettres et arts de Pau,* 2d series, XVII (1888).

————. *L'Intendant Foucault et la Révocation en Béarn.* Pau, 1885. Extracted from *Bulletin de la société des sciences, lettres et arts de Pau,* 2d series, XIV.

Tessereau, Abraham. *Histoire des réformés de la Rochelle et du pais d'Aunis depuis l'année 1660 jusqu'à l'année 1685 en laquelle l'Édit de Nantes a été révoqué.* Amsterdam, 1709.

Tessier du Cros, Charles and Henri. "Une Activité cevenole à la fin du XVIIᵉ siècle," *Bulletin de la société de l'histoire du protestantisme français,* LXXXI (1932).

Testament politique du Marquis de Louvois, premier ministre d'Etat sous le Règne de Louis XIV, Roy de France, où l'on voit ce qui s'est passé de plus remarquable en France jusqu'à sa mort. Cologne, 1695.

Thirion, Maurice. *Étude sur l'histoire du protestantisme à Metz et dans le pays messin.* Nancy, 1884.

Thompson, James Westfall. "Some Economic Factors in the Revocation of the Edict of Nantes," *American Historical Review,* XIV (1909).

Tournier, Gaston. *Les Galères de France et les Galériens protestants des XVIIᵉ et XVIIIᵉ siècles.* 3 vols. Musée du Désert en Cevennes, 1943, 1944, 1949.

Touzaud, Daniel. "Histoire de la Réforme en Angoumois," *Bulletins et mémoires de la société archéologique et historique de la Charente,* 8th series, VII (1917).

Vaillant, V.-J. *La Révocation de l'Édit de Nantes dans le Boulonnais, le Calaisis et les pays conquis et reconquis.* Boulogne-sur-Mer, 1885.

Valmont, Gustave. *Esquisse de l'histoire de Caudebec-en-Caux et de sa région.* Caen, 1913. Extracted from *Annuaire des cinq départements de la Normandie,* LXXIX.

Vauban, Maréchal de. *La Dîme royale* (1708). In *Collection des principaux économistes.* Vol. I: *Économistes financiers du XVIIIᵉ siècle.* E. Daire, ed. 2d ed. Paris, 1851.

————. "Le Mémoire presenté en 1689 par le maréchal de Vauban, et ses efforts réitérés en faveur des huguenots" (edited with comments by Charles Read), *Bulletin de la société de l'histoire du protestantisme français,* XXXVIII (1889).

Vaurigaud, B. *Essai sur l'histoire des églises réformées de Bretagne, 1535–1808.* 3 vols. Paris, 1870.

Viénot, John. *Histoire de la Réforme française, de l'Édit de Nantes à sa révocation (1598–1685).* Paris: Fischbacher, 1934.

Villepelet, Ferdinand. "L'Exécution de la révocation de l'édit de Nantes dans une petite paroisse du Périgord," *Bulletin de la société historique et archéologique du Périgord,* XXIX (1902).

Viviens. "De l'Influence de la révocation de l'édit de Nantes sur l'industrie et le commerce de la France," *Journal des économistes,* XXXVI (1853).

Voltaire. *Age of Louis XIV.* Vols. XXII and XXIII of *Works of Voltaire. La Vérité* ed. New York and Paris: E. R. DuMont, 1901.

Vulliet, Adam. *Scènes de la révocation de l'édit de Nantes, 1685.* Lausanne, 1885.

Waddington, Francis. "Les Assemblées du Désert. Les Suites d'une assemblée des environs de Nîmes. Affaire dite 'des Prisonniers de la Rochelle,' (1720)," *Bulletin de la société de l'histoire du protestantisme français,* IV (1856).

————. "Les Colonies de réfugiés protestants français," *Bulletin de la société de l'histoire du protestantisme français,* VIII (1859).

————. "Influence de l'ambassade de Hollande à Paris sur les affaires des protestants de France au XVIIIe siècle (1715–1728). Établissement d'un cimetière pour les protestants étrangers en 1720," *Bulletin de la société de l'histoire du protestantisme français,* III (1855).

————. "La Noblesse protestante en Basse-Normandie après la révocation de l'Édit de Nantes (1685–1700)," *Bulletin de la société de l'histoire du protestantisme français,* VII (1858).

————. "Les Persécutions dans le Poitou après la révocation de l'Édit de Nantes et jusque sous la Régence (1688 à 1720)," *Bulletin de la société de l'histoire du protestantisme français,* IV (1856).

————. *Le Protestantisme en Normandie depuis la révocation de l'édit de Nantes jusqu'à la fin du dix-huitième siècle (1685–1797).* Paris, 1862.

Weber, Max. *The Protestant Ethic and the Spirit of Capitalism.* Talcott Parsons, trans. New York and London: Allen and Unwin, 1930.

Weekley, C. M. "The Spitalfields Silkweavers," *Proceedings of the Huguenot Society of London,* XVIII (1950).

Weiss, Charles. "Appréciation générale de l'influence des réfugiés protestants dans les pays étrangers et des conséquences de la révocation de l'édit de Nantes pour la France. Conclusion des mémoires sur l'histoire des réfugiés protestants," *Séances et travaux de l'Académie des sciences morales et politiques,* XXVI (1853).

————. "Appréciation générale des conséquences de la révocation de l'édit de Nantes à l'étranger et en France," *Bulletin de la société de l'histoire du protestantisme français,* I (1853.)

————. "De la Conversion de la noblesse protestante au XVIIe siècle," *Bulletin de la société de l'histoire du protestantisme français,* I (1853).

————. "De l'Influence politique des réfugiés protestants en Amérique," *Séances et travaux de l'Académie des sciences morales et politiques,* XXIV (1853).

————. *Histoire des réfugiés protestants de France depuis la révocation de l'Édit de Nantes jusqu'à nos jours.* 2 vols. Paris, 1853.

————. "Mémoire sur les protestants de France au XVIIe siècle," *Séances et travaux de l'Académie des sciences morales et politiques,* XX, XXI (1851).

————. "Mémoire sur l'influence littéraire des réfugiés protestants de France en Hollande," *Séances et travaux de l'Académie des sciences morales et politiques,* XXV, XXVI (1853).

Weiss, N. "Aperçu de la Révocation de l'Édit de Nantes en Poitou (1660–1686)," *Bulletin de la société de l'histoire du protestantisme français,* LIV (1905).

————. "Les Conséquences de la Révocation pour l'industrie de la draperie, du fer etc., à Sedan," *Bulletin de la société de l'histoire du protestantisme français,* L (1901).

————. "Le Nombre des prétendus Réformés six ans avant la Révocation, lettre de N. de La Mare (6 août 1680)," *Bulletin de la société de l'histoire du protestantisme français,* XXXVII (1888).

————. "Les Privilèges des protestants en Basse-Normandie en 1686, leur nombre, leurs enfants, etc," *Bulletin de la société de l'histoire du protestantisme français,* XLV (1896).

———. "Le Sort des réfugiés en Hollande, Angleterre et ailleurs en 1687, d'après une lettre originale et inédite (de G. Baux)," *Bulletin de la société de l'histoire du protestantisme français*, XLIII (1894).

———. "Statistique du protestantisme français en 1598, le bilan de la Révocation pour la généralité de Paris en 1700," *Bulletin de la société de l'histoire du protestantisme français*, XXXVIII (1889).

———. "Statistique protestante et catholique du Languedoc en 1698," *Bulletin de la société de l'histoire du protestantisme français*, LI (1902).

Weiss, N., and Henri Clouzot. *Journal de Jean Migault, maître d'école (1681–1688)*. Paris: Fischbacher, 1910.

Wilkinson, Maurice. "Survey of Languedoc in 1698 by Lamoignon de Bâville, Intendant of the two generalites of Toulouse and Montpellier," *Proceedings of the Huguenot Society of London*, XII (1917–1924).

Wolf, John B. *The Emergence of the Great Powers, 1685–1715*. New York: Harper, 1951.

Zoff, Otto. *The Huguenots, Fighters for God and Human Freedom*. E. B. Ashton and Jo Mayo, trans. New York: L. B. Fischer, 1942.

MANUSCRIPT SOURCES

Archives Nationales
Series A[1] (Archives de la Guerre): *liasses* 753, 755–758, 773–776, 795, 797–798, 835–837, 902–907.
Series B[2] (Archives de la Marine): *registres* 42–47, 49, 51–53, 55–62, 65–66, 69–70, 73.
Series B[3] (Archives de la Marine): *registres* 48, 51, 53, 55, 57.
Series B[7] (Archives de la Marine): *registres* 58, 495.
Series E: *registres* 704C, 739B, 776B, 885B.
Series F[12]: *registres* 42–44, 51, 54–55, 58, 72–73, 77, 114–115; *liasses* 641, 662–670, 673, 693–698, 709, 822A, 854B, 1349, 1353, 1356, 1359, 1423, 1475, 1834A.
Series G[7]: *liasses* 1–3, 71–73, 84–85, 103, 105, 113, 132–139, 157, 214, 239–241, 276, 296–298, 337–339, 345–346, 355–356, 390–391, 449–451, 491–493, 511, 519–520, 1685–1689, 1691–1692, 1696–1699, 1701, 1702, 1704; *registres* 1700A–C.
Series O[1]: *registres* 23–24, 26–32, 36–38, 41–44.
Series TT: *liasses* 85, 230–232, 235–237, 239–240, 243, 247, 251, 255, 258, 260, 263B, 264–266, 271–272, 274, 276B, 287, 430–431, 435–436, 446–448, 449[I–II], 450, 452, 454, 461, 463–464.
Archives du Ministère des Affaires Étrangères
Ancien fonds: "Angleterre": *registres* 156–164; "Hollande": *registres* 143–154; "Prusse": *registres* 25–33; "Suisse": *registres* 80–86.
Bibliothèque Nationale
Fonds français: MSS 4282 (intendant's memorandum on *généralité* of Paris); 4283 (intendants' memoranda on *généralités* of Orléans, Tours, Anjou, Maine, Bretagne); 4284 (intendants' memoranda on *généralités* of Amiens, Artois, Flandre Gallicane, Flandre Flamingante, Hainault); 4285 (intendants' memoranda on *généralités* of Soissons, Champagne, Trois Évêchés, Alsace, Franche-Comté); 4286 (intendants' memoranda on *généralités* of Rouen, Caen, Alençon, Perche); 4287 (intendants' memoranda on *généralités* of Bourbonnais, Limoges, Poitou, La Rochelle,

Bordeaux, Béarn and Basse-Navarre); 4288 (intendants' memoranda on *généralités* of Auvergne, Lyon, Dauphiné); 4289 (intendants' memoranda on *généralités* of Bourgogne, Bourges, Provence); 4290 (intendants' memoranda on *généralités* of Montauban, Languedoc); 6432; 7036; 7044–7047 ("Calvinistes de France, 1669–1788"—documents collected by Claude-Carlomau de Rulhière); 7048–7049; 7050–7055 ("Révocation de l'Édit de Nantes"—papers from the collection of M. de la Reynie, lieutenant general of police at Paris); 7057 ("Affaires des protestants"); 8037; 8038 (memoranda prepared by various deputies of trade in 1700–1701); 8248 ("Affaires de la religion en Béarn"); 10621 ("Mémoire sur les protestants," by M. Gilbert de Voisins); 10623 ("Loix concernants les protestants en France"); 10628 ("Recueil sur les protestants"); 10638; 11419; 17315; 20966–20967 ("Religionnaires et nouveaux convertis"); 21616–21623 ("Hérétiques"—papers from the collection of Nicolas de la Mare); 21773 and 21775 ("Commerce"—papers from the collection of Nicolas de la Mare); 21785–21787 ("Manufactures"—papers from the collection of Nicolas de la Mare); 26439 and 26482 (laws, declarations, and edicts concerning Protestants).

Nouvelles acquisitions françaises: MSS 507 (letters of M. de Fénelon); 944; 1206; 1555; 3517.

Bibliothèque de la Société de l'Histoire du Protestantisme Français

MSS 194, 194[3], 301, 339, 382, 444, 485[I–VI], 617l, 617n, 617o, 628, 648[1–2], 796, 816[I], 868[8], 874[7], 953, 1049, 1170, 1203[I], 1215.

INDEX

Index